Nellie Lyle Pattinson's

CANADIAN COOK BOOK
SI METRIC EDITION

Nellie Lyle Pattinson's

CANADIAN
COOK BOOK

REVISED BY HELEN WATTIE AND ELINOR DONALDSON WHYTE

SI METRIC EDITION

McGraw-Hill Ryerson Limited

Toronto Montreal New York St. Louis San Francisco Auckland Bogotá
Düsseldorf Johannesburg London Madrid Mexico New Delhi Panama
Paris São Paulo Singapore Sydney Tokyo

Design/Peter Maher

Drawings/Beverly Atkinson

Canadian Cataloguing in Publication Data

Pattinson, Nellie Lyle, d. 1953.
   Nellie Lyle Pattinson's Canadian cook book

Includes index.
ISBN 0-07-082612-9

1. Cookery, Canadian.   I. Wattie, Helen P., 1911-
II. Whyte, Elinor Donaldson, 1926-   III. Title.
IV. Title: Canadian cook book.

TX715.P3234 1978   641.5   C77-001764-9

ACKNOWLEDGEMENTS

Colour photographs were supplied through the courtesy of:
Beef Information Centre—opposite pages 168, 169 (foot)
Borden Company Limited—opposite page 313
Canadian Dairy Food Service Bureau—opposite page 344
Consumer Services, Catelli Ltd/Ltée—opposite page 137 (foot)
Graphics Division, Environment Canada—opposite page 137 (top)
H. J. Heinz Co. Canada Ltd.—opposite pages 73, 217 (foot)
Holland Cheese Exporters Association—opposite pages 88, 264
Lawry's Foods of Canada Ltd.—opposite pages 40, 72, 89, 121
Ontario Ministry of Agriculture and Food—opposite pages 24, 25, 41,
120, 136, 169 (top), 185, 216, 217 (top), 232, 233, 265, 280, 281,
312, 328, 329, 345

3456789 D 765432109

Printed and bound in Canada

Contents

Preface

The *Canadian Cook Book* has been the basic cook book of homemakers and students since 1923. New trends in cooking have been incorporated over the years but the old, time-tested favourites will still be found among the recipes in this book. Readers may select from a great variety of recipes, including gourmet dishes as well as convenient time-savers.

The first metric edition of the *Canadian Cook Book* now brings you a scientific system of measurement that simplifies and makes more efficient the preparation of food. Chapter 2 gives extensive information on how to measure using metric units.

Nutrition and economy determined the selection of recipes in this edition. Practical alternatives are given for foods likely to contribute to such problems as obesity; basic nutritional needs may be met, for instance, by using powdered skim milk instead of fresh whole milk wherever feasible as a way to cut down on cost while maintaining optimal food value. Subjects such as home canning and freezing are extensively covered, as is the preparation of mixes for making bread using whole grains for added nutrition. Salt quantities have been reduced in many recipes as personal tastes and diets vary. While the book contains recipes for cakes, candies and cookies, as well as for certain foods that may be expensive, there are many more recipes for economical dishes that contribute to a balanced and nutritious diet. Also, as befits the general and comprehensive nature of a basic cook book, there are detailed descriptions of cooking methods and techniques.

The authors wish to thank their friends, families and Elizabeth Hemsworth of McGraw-Hill Ryerson Limited for unfailing help and inspiration.

HELEN WATTIE
ELINOR DONALDSON WHYTE

1 Nutrition

Nowadays everyone is conscious of the relationship of good health to sound nutrition. The Nutrition Canada Survey carried out during 1970-1972, based on 19 000 Canadians from all walks of life,[1] confirms that the diets, and hence the health, of Canadians are far from ideal. CANADA'S FOOD GUIDE emphasizes the daily need for a variety of foods from four basic groups essential to good health.

Canada's Food Guide

Eat a variety of foods from each food group every day.

MILK AND MILK PRODUCTS

Children up to 11 years	2-3 servings
Adolescents	3-4 servings
Pregnant and nursing women	3-4 servings
Adults	2 servings

Skim, 2%, whole, buttermilk, reconstituted dry or evaporated milk may be used as a beverage or as the main ingredient in other foods. Cheese may also be chosen.

Examples of one serving:
250 ml	milk, yogurt, or cottage cheese
45 g	Cheddar or processed cheese

FRUITS AND VEGETABLES

4-5 servings—include at least two vegetables.

Choose a variety of both vegetables and fruits—

[1] Nutrition Canada, National Survey, Queen's Printer, 1973.

cooked or raw or their juices. Include yellow or green or green leafy vegetables.

Examples of one serving:
125 ml	vegetables, fruits (raw or cooked)
125 ml	juice
	1 medium potato, carrot, tomato, peach, orange, or banana

MEAT AND ALTERNATES

2 servings

Examples of one serving:
60-90 g	cooked, lean meat, poultry, liver, or fish
60 ml	peanut butter
250 ml	cooked dried peas, beans, or lentils
80-250 ml	nuts or seeds
60 g	Cheddar, processed, or cottage cheese
	2 eggs

BREAD AND CEREALS

3-5 servings, whole grain or enriched. Whole grain products are recommended.

Examples of one serving:
	1 slice bread
125-250 ml	cooked or ready-to-eat cereal
	1 roll or muffin
125-200 ml	cooked rice, macaroni, or spaghetti

In addition, a vitamin D supplement is recommended for those consuming milk to which this vitamin has not been added.

1

The Basic Components of Food

Foods contain at least one of these basic components: proteins, fats and carbohydrates.

Proteins are the building blocks of all body tissues; they are essential for growth and repair. Proteins play a role in the regulation of tissue fluids, in the formation of enzymes and hormones, and in the production of antibodies to fight specific diseases.

Proteins are composed of 22 different amino acids. Certain amino acids (approximately 8) are essential; they cannot be synthesized by the body and must be obtained from food. Other amino acids can be synthesized or made by converting one into another. Proteins can be compared to a series of beads on a string with the arrangement of the beads characteristic to the protein. Rearrangement or substitution of any amino acid for another results in a different protein.

Proteins which contain all the essential amino acids are called *complete proteins;* they are found in eggs, milk, meat and fish. Incomplete proteins, which lack one or more of the essential amino acids, are found in cereals and vegetables. Such foods as these may be teamed with each other to provide complete proteins. For example, legumes (dried peas, beans, lentils) combined or served with twice their volume of cereal or cereal products (rice, macaroni, bread, etc.) complement each other. The addition of small amounts of eggs, cheese, meat, or fish to incomplete protein foods is another way of improving overall protein quality. Soybeans are a source of all the essential amino acids, although one is present in only very small amounts; it can be supplied by bread or other cereal.

Meat is one of the most expensive sources of protein. The production of animal protein requires an average of ten times the amount of protein in the form of cereal animal feed.[2] North Americans comprise only 5% of the world population but consume 30% of the world's supplies of food of animal origin. Excess protein in the diet—that is, protein which is not used for energy—is eventually stored as fat. One serving of meat (or poultry or fish) per day is adequate with a balanced diet which contains legumes, cheese, or eggs—less costly sources of protein—to provide equivalent nutrients at less expense. The use of processed vegetable protein as a meat extender (or alternative) is gaining popularity; it will probably play a greater role in the future to relieve world protein shortages.

[2] *Diet for a Small Planet,* Frances Moore Lappe.

Steaks and roasts contain not only protein but also large amounts of fat, much of it within the meat muscle and not obvious. Poultry (with the skin removed after cooking) and fish contain much less fat than most red meats (see table SOME SOURCES OF PROTEIN).

Vegetarian diets can be nutritionally adequate with special planning. A wide variety of vegetables and whole grain cereals must be eaten daily to provide maximum complementation of proteins and the quantity must be sufficient to allow for their relatively low content of protein. If dairy products and eggs are used regularly, a balanced diet can be achieved fairly easily. Without dairy products and eggs only *very* careful planning, including reference to tables of food values, will yield a diet adequate not only in protein but in many other nutrients as well, including iron and calcium (see RECOMMENDED DAILY NUTRIENT INTAKE table). A supplement of vitamin B12 is essential for vegetarians who do not eat eggs or dairy products. Without it, body stores of this vitamin become depleted and pernicious anemia can develop.

The addition of skim milk powder as a supplement to breads, sauces, and desserts provides high quality protein (plus calcium and riboflavin) in the least expensive form, and permits the use of less of the expensive varieties of protein elsewhere in the menu. Used double strength, or added to fresh milk in milk shakes, skim milk powder is beneficial in the diets of convalescing and underweight people.

Fat is the most concentrated form of food energy, producing more than twice the energy produced by an equivalent amount of carbohydrate or protein. We need a certain amount of fat for energy, warmth, protection of organs and for the essential fatty acids it contains. However, when more than 1/3 of our total food energy is habitually supplied by fat, we risk overweight and the danger of overburdening the systems involved in the metabolism of our food.

Saturated fats are those which contain a high proportion of saturated fatty acids; they are solid, either naturally or by the addition of hydrogen during processing. Most animal fats are more saturated than vegetable fats; fish oils and chicken fat are less saturated than fat from beef, pork and lamb. Safflower oil is the least saturated of the vegetable oils, followed by sunflower, corn, soy, cottonseed, sesame, and peanut oils. Unlike other vegetable oils, coconut oil contains a high percentage of saturated fatty acids; it is often used as a basting material for deep-basted turkeys and as a basic ingredient of coffee creamer because it does not readily become rancid.

Saturated fats can be converted to *cholesterol,* a fatty substance which is present in all foods of animal origin. Our bodies have the ability to make cholesterol;

Some Sources of Protein

	Quantity	Protein g	Fat g		Quantity	Protein g	Fat g
Roast beef							
lean & fat	85 g	17	34	Peanut butter	15 ml	4	8
lean only	85 g	23	12				
				Yogurt, partly skimmed			
Steak, broiled				plain	180 ml	9	3
lean & fat	85 g	20	27	with fruit	180 ml	8	3
lean only	85 g	27	6				
				Skim milk powder	30 ml	3	0
Hamburger, broiled				Skim milk	250 ml	9	0
regular	85 g	21	17				
lean	85 g	23	10	Partly skim milk			
				(2% butterfat)	250 ml	9	5
Pork, cooked							
lean & fat	85 g	20	26				
lean only	85 g	25	8	Whole milk	250 ml	9	9
Chicken, roasted	85 g	20	3	Cheddar cheese	28 g	7	8
Fish, broiled				Cottage cheese,			
(average)	85 g	25	6	creamed	250 ml	31	9
				not creamed	250 ml	34	1
Beans, cooked							
navy	250 ml	14	1	Processed Cheddar			
soy	250 ml	22	6	cheese	28 g	7	9
Egg (1)		6	6				

Values for all foods except soybeans are from "Nutrient Value of Some Common Foods," Health & Welfare, Canada.

it is a necessary component of brain and nerve tissue. Excess cholesterol in the diet has been associated with arteriosclerosis and heart disease. Arteriosclerosis is the hardening of the arteries resulting when substances deposited on their inner surfaces reduce their capacity. With time, the accumulation of material in an artery can so constrict the flow of blood to a particular area that tissues are starved and fail to function; when a blood vessel of the heart is affected, heart attacks occur. Restriction of dietary cholesterol (plentiful in saturated fats, egg yolk, and organ meats) is prescribed for people with heart disease associated with high levels of cholesterol in the blood and for those, including children, whose family history shows this pattern. Although there is much controversy concerning the role of dietary cholesterol in the population as a whole, restriction of egg yolks, the most concentrated source of cholesterol, to 3 per week would seem to be a reasonable precaution for all of us since statistics show that many Canadians die from diseases of the heart and blood vessels.

Carbohydrate is our chief source and least expensive form of food energy. There has been a shift during the last few decades from the consumption of carbohydrate in the form of cereals and starches to the consumption of carbohydrate in the form of sugars; the yearly consumption per person of sugar averages over 45 kg

Whole grain and enriched cereals provide energy *plus* nutrients. Sugar, which is refined carbohydrate, provides energy and little else. "Empty calories" abound in candies and in soft drinks. The excessive use of refined carbohydrates coupled with a sedentary life style promotes overweight, diabetes, and possibly heart disease. Concentrated sugars in the form of sticky candies promote tooth decay.

Carbohydrates are a necessary part of the diet; the amount and form we eat (preferably in the form of less-refined starches such as cereals, macaroni, bread, potatoes) should be in keeping with our activity and hence, our energy requirements.

Fibre is the non-digestible part of cereals, fruits, and vegetables. It absorbs water and swells, thus providing bulk in the digestive tract. Meals low in fibre content have a slow transit time through the intestinal tract. Medical researchers[3] working in the developing regions of Africa noted that diseases of the intestinal tract—appendicitis, diverticulitis, colon cancer—are almost non-existant there, and they attribute this to the high intake of dietary fibre in the local diet.

Along with its bulk-forming properties, dietary fibre has the ability to bind other substances to it. Less cholesterol is absorbed into the blood when the diet contains some fibre; instead it is bound to the fibre and excreted with it. Potatoes, squash, peas and many other vegetables, fruits, and whole grain cereals supply fibre. Five slices of whole wheat bread per day has been recommended[4] to provide sufficient dietary fibre for the average adult; an alternative is a serving of whole grain cereal, about 250 ml

Natural bran is the most concentrated source of dietary fibre; a small amount will provide our daily need. Large quantities consumed on a regular basis may result in excessive excretion of nutrients. A recommended daily intake[5] is 30 ml

Vitamins and Minerals Vitamins and minerals help in the regulation of body processes including the breakdown and metabolism of carbohydrates, fats, and proteins; they are not sources of energy. Some minerals help form the framework of the body, and many vitamins play a role in maintaining healthy skin and other tissues. Tables later in this chapter provide details of vitamins and minerals known to be needed for good nutrition.

Water Although water is not a nutrient in the usual sense, it is essential for life. Needs increase whenever there is great loss through perspiration or during illnesses such as diarrhoea or polyuria.

[3] Burkitt, D. P., "Some diseases characteristic of Modern Western Civilisation," *British Medical Journal,* 1:274, 1973.

[4] *Ibid.*

[5] *Ibid.*

[6] Nutrition Canada, National Survey, Queen's Printer, 1973.

Special Dietary Needs of Canadians

The need for many nutrients exists throughout life although the amount required may vary according to age and physiological state. The Nutrition Canada Survey[6] studied different groups in our society to determine their nutritional states. Studies of the kinds and amounts of food eaten, biochemical tests to determine the presence or absence of nutrients, and medical and dental examinations provided the answers.

Calcium is needed by all age groups, but the greatest need occurs during the growth spurt between 13 and 15 years, and during pregnancy and lactation. (See RECOMMENDED DAILY NUTRIENT INTAKE.) Low calcium intakes occur in large portions of the population, according to the recent survey, with a high percentage of children and adolescents having insufficient intakes. Teen-age girls were the worst offenders. Their desire to remain slim should be respected by making available skim milk or a mixture of skim milk with 2% milk. Serving milk in soups, puddings and sauces, and substituting cheese and occasionally ice cream or ice milk are alternative methods to serving milk as a beverage.

Iron is deficient in large numbers of Canadians of all ages. Not only is iron deficiency a problem of infants and women as was previously assumed, it is also a problem of many older children, adolescents, and men. When planning meals it is wise to check menus frequently to determine if the iron needs of all members of the family are being met. A book of tables of food values entitled *Nutrient Value of Some Common Foods,* available free of charge from Health and Welfare, Canada, is useful for this purpose. Today many meals are eaten away from home. Adolescents may or may not choose nutritious lunches—or have access to them. The regular inclusion of iron-rich foods in meals served at home helps to compensate for inadequacies elsewhere.

Many other minerals and vitamins are needed for health: they are listed in the chart, ESSENTIAL MINERALS AND VITAMINS. Certain segments of the population show deficiencies in one or more of these. Folic acid is the vitamin most often deficient in Canadians' diet. The significance of widespread low levels of this vitamin in the blood will not be established without further research. It is possible, however, that our heavy reliance on instant and highly processed foods may be depriving us of some of this vitamin, which is easily destroyed by heat.

Not only adolescents may ignore the need for good nutrition. Many elderly persons may not realize that they still require balanced meals of nutritious foods

Recommended Iron Intakes

Age(a)	Sex	mg/d
0.0-.05	Both	7
0.5-1.0	Both	7
1-3	Both	8
4-6	Both	9
7-9	M	10
	F	10
10-12	M	11
	F	11
13-15	M	13
	F	14
16-18	M	14
	F	14
19-35	M	10
	F	14
36-50	M	10
	F	14
Over 50	M	10
	F	9
Pregnancy (second half) and lactation		15

From *Dietary Standard for Canada,* Health and Welfare, Canada, 1975.

even though their food energy needs are less. This age group was found to be among the most poorly nourished of all Canadians, having a high incidence of obesity, elevated levels of cholesterol in the blood, marginal intakes of protein, and low intakes of all the vitamins and iron.

The value of good nutrition is especially apparent during pregnancy. Women who maintain an optimum state of nutrition before and during pregnancy have a higher percentage of babies which are healthy, mentally and physically, and which have birth weights within the normal range, than women who are nutritionally deprived before or during pregnancy. During the latter half of pregnancy, increases are required in the intake of many nutrients, especially protein, minerals, and vitamins. See RECOMMENDED DAILY NUTRIENT INTAKE for those nutrients which should be increased. These standards cannot be met if dieting is undertaken. If weight must be lost, dieting should be postponed until pregnancy is terminated and lactation has been established. The recommended total weight gain during pregnancy is approximately 11 kg

A widespread malady of the adult Canadian population is obesity. Of the adults tested in the Nutrition Canada Survey, 40% of the young adults (20-39 years of age) were overweight, and 60% of the adults 40-64

Some Sources of Iron

	Size of Portion	Iron mg
Beef, lean, cooked	85 g	3.0
Chicken, cooked	85 g	1.4
Fish, most varieties, cooked	85 g	1
Ham, lean, cooked	85 g	2.2
Pork, lean, cooked	85 g	3.1
Legumes		
beans, cooked	250 ml	4.9
soybeans, cooked	250 ml	5.4
lentils, cooked	250 ml	3.2
lima beans, cooked	250 ml	5.9
Oysters, shucked	250 ml	13.2
Egg, whole, large	1 egg	1.1
Egg, yolk	1 yolk	1.1
Beef liver, cooked	57 g	5
Pork liver, cooked	57 g	12
Chicken livers, cooked	60 g	6
Broccoli, cooked	250 ml	1.2
Brussels sprouts, cooked	250 ml	1.7
Green lima beans, cooked	250 ml	4.3
Peas, cooked or canned	250 ml	2.9
Rice, short-grained, uncooked	125 ml	0.4
Brown rice, uncooked	125 ml	0.9
Converted rice, uncooked	125 ml	1.4
Tomato juice	250 ml	2.2
Potato, peeled after baking	1 medium	0.7
Potato, peeled after boiling	1 medium	0.8
Potato, peeled before boiling	1 medium	0.6
Spinach	250 ml	4.0
Bread, whole wheat 60%	1 slice	0.7
Bread, enriched white	1 slice	0.5
Rolled oats, cooked	250 ml	1.4
Corn flakes, enriched	250 ml	3
Corn flakes, plain	250 ml	0.2
Cream of Wheat, enriched	250 ml	15.5
Cream of Wheat, plain	250 ml	1.3
Flour, whole wheat	250 ml	3.6
Flour, enriched all-purpose	250 ml	3.2
Molasses, light	15 ml	0.9
Molasses, blackstrap	15 ml	3.2
Apricots, dried, cooked, unsweetened fruit & liquid	250 ml	5

Values for all foods except soybeans are from *Nutrient Value of Some Common Foods,* Health and Welfare, Canada

years of age were overweight. In the age group 65 years and over, more than 65% of the men and almost 80% of the women were overweight. Truly, obesity is a serious problem, and no doubt lack of exercise is a major factor in causing it.

Coupled with inactivity is our heavy reliance on foods which are high in food energy, often in the form of prepared or take-out foods and snacks that have a high content of sugar and fat. To put the problem briefly, too much food is consumed for the amount of activity undertaken.

The tendency to overeat may begin in childhood when anxious mothers overestimate the food needs of their babies and children, inadvertently training them to overeat. By introducing solid food in the diet of babies during the first few weeks of their lives, we are encouraging them to become prematurely accustomed to concentrated food in their mouths, even though little or no absorption may take place at this early stage. Good behaviour may be rewarded with food: a rich dessert may be the reward for eating all the carrots. Food attitudes and patterns developed in childhood can set patterns, good or bad, that carry through life. Recent evidence[7] suggests that many overfed children develop a greater number of fat cells; since fat cells remain during life, such people are constantly threatened by the possibility of becoming or remaining obese.

Along with its inherent social and psychological disadvantages, obesity increases the incidence of diabetes, cancer, and diseases of the heart and blood vessels; the obese are accident-prone and are poor surgical risks.

Reducing diets come and go, but only diets composed of a balance of nourishing foods and which lead to a modification of life style promote lasting results. Crash diets do not deal with the cause of the problem; their results are short-lived and sometimes harmful. For example, the practice of having only one meal a day may be appealing as a means of losing weight, but it raises cholesterol levels and reduces our ability to use glucose (blood sugar). The body is very efficient in storing excess nourishment as fat; when we eat a whole day's food at one time, we may be favouring fat storage. Many small meals providing the same amount of food energy are more beneficial, more satisfying, and less inducive to fat storage.

Severe dietary restriction should never be undertaken without medical supervision. It is almost impossible to obtain the necessary nutrients in sufficient amounts when caloric intakes are severely limited.

[7] Leveille & Romsos, "Meal Eating and Obesity", *Nutrition Today*, 9:6, 1974.

Dieting Suggestions

1. Eat a balanced diet; set reasonable goals to lose weight over a few weeks, or months if necessary.
2. Eat only when seated at the table; record kinds and amounts of food eaten and the time of eating, for reference.
3. Have at least 3 meals a day; calculate snacks in total food intake.
4. Eat slowly, chew thoroughly.
5. Use only lean meats; cut off visible fat. Broil or use non-stick pans that do not require the addition of fat.
6. Omit sauces and gravies; season cooked and raw vegetables with lemon juice and herbs.
7. Use skim milk; restrict the use of fats and oils.
8. Foods high in fibre content are usually low in food energy.
9. For dessert, eat fresh fruit or fruit that has been preserved or frozen without sugar.
10. Read food labels for a listing of ingredients, and for statements concerning nutritive value or special dietary use.

Special foods for use in weight reduction may add interest to the diet. However, they are usually expensive and are not necessary nor recommended for regular use.

Recommended Daily Nutrient Intake

Condensed from *Dietary Standard for Canada, 1975* Health and Welfare Canada

A *dietary standard* is a statement based on amounts of energy and essential nutrients which, when eaten daily, are considered adequate to meet the physiological needs of practically all healthy persons in a population. The standard does not provide for individual differences or therapeutic needs. It is only a guide and should be interpreted as such.

Recommended energy intakes are based on estimates of the requirement of an average active person within each age-sex group. Energy intakes in excess of actual needs are stored as fat.

Age (a)	Sex	Mass (kg)	Energy (kJ)	Protein (g)	Thiamine (mg)	Niacin[1] (mg)	Riboflavin (mg)	Folacin (µg)	Vitamin C (mg)	Vitamin A (R.E.[2])	Vitamin A (I.U.[2])	Vitamin D (I.U.[3])	Vitamin E (mg) Alpha-tocopherol	Calcium (mg)	Magnesium (mg)	Iron (mg)	Zinc (mg)
0-6	both	2.7-18	1500-7500	7-27	0.3-0.9	5-12	0.4-1.1	40-100	20	400-500	2200-2700	400	3-5	500	50-100	7-9	4-6
7-12	both	18-35	8400-10 500	33-41	1.0-1.2	13-17	1.2-1.5	100	30	800	4400	100	6-7	700-1000	150-200	10-11	7-9
13-18	male	—	—	54	1.4-1.6	19-21	1.7-2.0	200	30	1000	5500	100	9-10	1200-1000	300	14	10
13-18	female	—	—	43	1.1	14-15	1.3	200	30	800	4400	100	7-6	800-700	250	14	9
19-50	male	70	12 500-11 300	56	1.4	18	1.7	200	30	1000	5500	100	9	800	300	10	10
19-50	female	56	8800-8000	41	1.0	13	1.2	200	30	800	4400	100	6	700	250	14	9
50-65	male	70	9600	56	1.4	18	1.7	200	30	1000	5500	100	8	800	300	10	10
50-65	female	56	7500	41	1.0	13	1.2	200	30	800	4400	100	6	700	250	9	9
65 plus	male	70	8400	56	1.0	13	1.2	200	30	1000	5500	100	8	800	300	10	10
65 plus	female	56	6300	41	0.8	10	0.9	200	30	800	4400	100	6	700	250	9	9
Pregnancy	—	—	1300	61	1.3	16	1.6	250	50	900	5000	200	7	1200	275	15	12

[1] Approximately 1 mg niacin is derived from 60 mg dietary tryptophan.

[2] Vitamin A—1 Retinol Equivalent equals 1 mg retinol (3.33 I.U.) and/or 6 mg B-carotene (10 I.U.). Assumes 68% from vitamin A sources and 32% from B-carotene sources.

[3] A measure of 1 µg of cholecalciferol is equivalent to 40 I.U. vitamin D activity.

[4] Whenever a range of figures is given, the values correspond to the order of the ages given for that category.

Adapted from *Selected Nutrition Teaching Aids*, Health and Welfare Canada, 1976.

Food Energy Content Table

Food	Quantity	kJ
Beverages		
Carbonated beverages	250 ml	467
Cocoa, whole milk	250 ml	1100
Coffee, clear	250 ml	0
+ cream		125
+ 1 lump sugar		105
Juice, canned apple	125 ml	233
canned grapefruit	125 ml	233
orange (fresh)	125 ml	233
(frozen)	125 ml	164
tomato	125 ml	233
Tea, clear	250 ml	0
with milk	250 ml	84
with lemon	250 ml	0
Breads		
White	1 slice	310
Whole wheat	1 slice	350
Cinnamon toast	1 slice	520
Hamburger roll		630
Melba toast	1 piece	85
Muffin, bran	large	520
Sandwich, meat or cheese		840–1250
Wiener bun		650
Cereals		
Corn flakes	250 ml	467
Shredded wheat	1 biscuit	315
Oatmeal, cooked	250 ml	700
Biscuits (1 biscuit)		
Chocolate chip		210
Chocolate marshmallow		250
Crème sandwich		210
Ginger snap		60
Graham cracker		125
Macaroon		85
Ritz cracker		65
Soda cracker		125
Triangle thin		38
Eggs		
Boiled or poached	1 egg	315
French toast	1 slice	837
Fried	1 egg	460
Scrambled	1 egg	460

Food	Quantity	kJ
Meat, Fish and Poultry		
Bacon, side	3 slices	840
back	1 slice	250
Beef, stew	250 ml	934
sirloin steak	113 g	1289
Chicken, fried	leg	523
broiled	½ medium	523
stew and		
dumpling	250 ml	887
Ham, smoked	115 g	1409
Hamburger on a bun		1550
Hot dog on a bun		1550
Fish, white	85 g	423
salmon, canned	125 ml	794
Lamb, stew	250 ml	1168
chop, broiled	1 small	420
roast, leg	1 thin slice	420
Liver	100 g	597
Oyster stew	170 g	847
Milk and Milk Products		
Butter or margarine	pat	210
	15 ml	419
Cheese, cheddar	25 g	373
cottage, skim milk	25 g	93
processed	25 g	373
Cream, top milk	15 ml	126
sour	15 ml	126
whipping cream	15 ml	210
Milk, buttermilk	250 ml	397
skim	250 ml	397
whole	250 ml	770
Milkshake	350 ml	2200
chocolate malted	with ice	
	cream	2616
Salad Dressings		
Salad dressing	15 ml	315
Mayonnaise	15 ml	420
French dressing	15 ml	315
Salads		
Salad, cabbage,	250 ml	93
+ dressing	10 ml	300
Waldorf	125 ml	467

Food	Quantity	kJ	Food	Quantity	kJ
Soup (Condensed)			**Fruit, Canned**		
Bean or bacon	250 ml	1400	Apple sauce	250 ml	934
Vegetable and beef	250 ml	761	Grapefruit	125 ml	210
Consommé	250 ml	298	Peaches in syrup	2 halves	418
Cream of chicken	250 ml	934	Pears in syrup	2 halves	418
mushroom	250 ml	1270	Pineapple in syrup	1 slice	418
Pea, green	250 ml	1261	Rhubarb, stewed	250 ml	1775
Tomato	250 ml	840			
Vegetable	250 ml	747	**Fruit, Fresh**		
			Apple	1 medium	315
Vegetables			Avocado	1 half	790
Asparagus	125 ml	70	Banana	1 small	335
Beans, green	125 ml	70	Blueberries	185 ml	276
Cabbage, cooked	250 ml	186	Cantaloupe	1 half	167
raw	250 ml	116	Grapefruit	½ medium	315
Carrots, cooked	125 ml	140	Orange	1 medium	315
raw	1	84	Peach	1 medium	210
Celery	1 stalk	25	Pear	1 medium	418
Corn	1 ear	420	Raspberries	185 ml	373
Lettuce, leaf	1 large	13	Strawberries	250 ml	256
Peas, cooked	125 ml	256	Watermelon,	small wedge	500
Potatoes, baked	1 large	628			
French fries	10	418	**Fruit, Frozen**		
mashed with			Blueberries	¼ pkg	167
butter	125 ml	378–565	Raspberries	¼ pkg	315
gravy	125 ml	700	Strawberries	¼ pkg	335
sweet	1	795			
Rice, boiled	250 ml	934	**Desserts**		
Spinach, cooked	125 ml	116	Cake, angel,		
Tomatoes, raw	1 medium	84	unfrosted	1 serving	523
cooked	250 ml	186	butter, frosted	square	1050
Turnips, mashed	250 ml	186	cupcake, iced	1 cake	712
			fruit	small slice	940
Other Foods			jelly roll	slice	1050
Gravy	15 ml	210	strawberry shortcake	1 serving	1256
Macaroni and cheese	250 ml	980	Chocolate éclair	1 small	1050
Spaghetti and tomato sauce			Ice Cream, rich	125 ml	768
with meat	250 ml	1537	less expensive	125 ml	607
with cheese	250 ml	1215	sherbet	125 ml	584
Chocolate	1 square	586	Pie, wedge		
Jam or Jelly	15 ml	210	fruit	10 cm arc	1400
Nuts	60 ml	896	Puddings,		
Peanut butter	15 ml	419	cornstarch	125 ml	934
Syrup	15 ml	312	cottage	125 ml	467
Peanuts, salted	25 g	620	custard	125 ml	467
Fudge	25 g	422	tapioca	125 ml	934

Essential Minerals and Vitamins

	Functions	*Sources*
Calcium	Forming strong bones and teeth and maintaining and repairing the skeleton. Maintaining muscle tone, normal heart beat and healthy nerve function. Aiding normal blood clotting.	Milk (any type), ice cream, cheese (any type), yogurt, canned salmon and sardines (with bones), broccoli, navy beans (dried), string beans, turnips, carrots, dried apricots, cantaloupe.
Phosphorus	Forming strong bones and teeth and maintaining and repairing the skeleton. Aiding absorption and transportation of nutrients. Regulating the release of energy.	Meat, fish, poultry, eggs, nuts, milk, cheese.
Iron	Building hemoglobin in red blood cells, to transport oxygen and carbon dioxide. Preventing nutritional anemia.	Liver, red meats, egg yolks, dried beans, peas and lentils, green leafy vegetables; whole grain and enriched cereals, pre-cooked infant cereals, flours, bread, and pastas.
Iodine	Ensuring proper functioning of the thyroid gland.	Iodized salt.
Sodium	Essential for normal functioning of cells.	Salt, pickled foods, processed cereals, milk, cheese, bread, salted butter, baking powder, cakes, cookies, bacon, ham, frozen fish.
Potassium	Involved in cellular metabolism.	Meat, fish, potatoes, oranges, bananas, milk, legumes, most fruits and vegetables.
Fluoride	Preventing and controlling dental caries. Preventing osteoporosis.	Drinking water (natural or fluoridated water supplies) sea fish, tea.
Magnesium	Forming bone. Necessary in metabolism of calcium and phosphorus. Aiding normal growth and development.	Cocoa, nuts, whole grains, spinach, liver, clams, oysters, crabs.
Zinc, copper, cobalt, manganese, chromium, molybdenum, selenium	Known to be important, although functions in human nutrition are not fully understood.	The average Canadian diet should provide the required amount.
Vitamin A	Promoting normal growth and formation of skeleton and teeth. Maintaining normal vision. Resisting infection by keeping skin and lining layer of body healthy. Ensuring normal reproduction and lactation.	Dark green and yellow vegetables, yellow fruits, egg yolks, liver, butter, cream, whole milk, cheese, skim or 2% milk with added Vitamin A; margarine with added Vitamin A.
Vitamin D	Utilizing calcium and phosphorus in the development and maintenance of sound bones and teeth.	Vitamin D enriched milks (fluid, evaporated, and powdered); Vitamin D enriched infant formula preparations; Vitamin D enriched margarines; vitamin supplements or fish liver oils.

	Functions	Sources
Vitamin E	Protecting body's supplies of Vitamins A and C. Maintaining health of cell membranes by being an antioxidant. Participating in blood cell formation.	Vegetable oils, e.g., corn and soybean; wheat germ, margarine, whole grains, eggs, liver, fruits and vegetables.
Vitamin K	Ensuring normal clotting of blood.	Green and yellow vegetables.
Thiamine Vitamin B1	Releasing food energy from carbohydrates. Promoting growth. Maintaining food appetite. Promoting normal function of the nervous system.	Pork and pork products, liver, kidney, dried legumes (peas, beans, lentils), wheat germ, bran, whole grain or enriched cereals, flours, bread, potatoes, and pastas.
Riboflavin Vitamin B2	Aiding normal growth and development. Maintaining good appetite and normal digestion. Helping to maintain healthy skin and eyes. Helping to maintain a normal nervous system. Releasing energy to body cells during metabolism.	Milk and milk products (except butter), cheese, eggs, meats (particularly organ meats), salmon, leafy green vegetables, enriched cereals, flours, breads, and pastas.
Niacin	Aiding normal growth and development. Maintaining normal functions of the gastro-intestinal tract. Protecting normal function of the nervous system.	Lean meats, liver, fish, poultry, enriched cereals, flours, breads and pastas, tomatoes, peas, potatoes, peanuts and peanut butter, milk, cheese, and eggs.
Pyridoxine Vitamin B6	Contributing to protein and energy metabolism.	Meat, liver, vegetables, whole grain cereals, eggs.
Folic Acid	Maintaining healthy blood.	Liver, kidney, mushrooms, asparagus, broccoli, lima beans, spinach, lemons, bananas, strawberries, cantaloupe.
Pantothenic Acid	Needed for energy metabolism.	Liver, kidney, egg yolks, nuts, legumes.
Ascorbic Acid Vitamin C	Maintaining healthy teeth and gums. Maintaining strong blood vessel walls. Helping to form and strengthen the cementing substance which holds body cells together.	Oranges, lemons, grapefruit, limes, tangerines, and their juices; vitaminized apple juice, vitaminized fruit drinks, tomatoes and their juice; cantaloupe, strawberries, broccoli, cauliflower, brussel sprouts, cabbage (green), white potatoes, turnips.

Economy in Meal Preparation

Economy in the purchase and preparation of food is of constant concern to today's consumer. Throughout this book help is given on how to purchase foods, how to store them, and how to prepare them so that every dollar you spend on food delivers its full value in enjoyable, nutritious meals. Note especially MENUS FOR ALL OCCASIONS: ECONOMY MEALS, and the introductions to Chapters 10, 11, 12 and 15.

ECONOMY TIPS

1. Read newspaper advertisements to compare food prices; foods are usually advertised just before the weekend in daily papers.
2. Shop when stores are less crowded, for better selection and service.
3. A shopping list helps if it is well planned yet sufficiently flexible to allow for substitution of worthwhile specials.
4. Avoid shopping when you are hungry so as to avoid the temptation to buy on impulse.
5. Read container labels for the description of the product inside, the net contents, indications of enrichment, and directions for storing or cooking. On labels, ingredients in mixtures are listed in descending order on the basis of their proportion. Foods that are labelled as an "excellent" or "good" dietary source of protein, iron or vitamins must meet criteria defined by Food and Drug regulations.

   Look for the durable life date on foods that have a life of less than 90 d; store such foods as recommended, and use before the suggested date.
6. Choose the variety or grade of food to suit the purpose. Often Choice or Standard grade is quite suitable and less expensive than Fancy. Less expensive varieties of canned fish are acceptable for use in fish loaf or other mixtures; flaked tuna is cheaper than solid tuna and ideal for sandwich fillings. Buy broken nuts rather than halves, if you intend to chop them.
7. Substitute skim milk powder for fresh milk, reconstituted for use as a beverage (see TO RECONSTITUTE SKIM MILK POWDER). Add skim milk powder to dry ingredients when making cakes, muffins, etc., and substitute water for the liquid milk.
8. Bake several foods in the oven at the same time; thoughtfully plan oven-cooked meals.
9. Breakfast cereals that must be cooked are less expensive per serving than processed cereals, and many are more nutritious.
10. Weigh convenience against the additional cost when considering convenience foods; foods prepared at home are usually less expensive. They may also be more nutritious because they require less processing and do not need the addition of preservatives for long shelf life.
11. Since convenience foods are helpful when time is short, prepare your own convenience foods ahead of time. Freeze leftover bread to make crumbs for coating or extending meats. Save dry ends of cheese for grating. Freeze leftover whipped cream in rosettes or dollops for use on desserts. (Freeze first on a wax paper-lined cookie sheet; then transfer to a plastic bag or covered container). Crush finely and refrigerate cookie crumbs for stirring into softened ice cream for parfaits or for making crumb crusts for pies. Freeze rounds of pastry for use in tart or pie shells (separate them between sheets of waxed paper). Freeze cookie dough in cleaned empty cans of frozen juice or tomato paste; slice and bake dough when the oven is in use. Double the recipe for casseroles and baked foods; freeze the extra part to use later. Prepare TV dinners from leftovers or prepare dinners in advance, using a planned menu. For casseroles, freeze ingredients when they are plentiful, very fresh, and less expensive; green peppers, sweet red peppers, mushrooms can be done this way. See FREEZING.
12. Prepare homemade mixes. Specific recipes are given in this book for WHITE SAUCE MIX (ROUX), QUICK-BREAD BASIC MIX, cake mixes—see CAKE in index, COOKIE MIX, BABY FOODS, and other basic mixes, many of which can be frozen. See index under names of foods and also under FREEZING.

Menu Planning

Advance planning of meals is helpful in many ways. It provides for nutritional adequacy on a daily and weekly basis, for budgeting, and for marketing with a minimum of trips to the store. Post the planned menu on the door of a kitchen cupboard for all to see, and anyone can begin meal preparations if the "cook" is delayed.

Menus should be sufficiently flexible to allow for substitution when some foods are unavailable or when some foods are offered at bargain prices.

Menus should be in keeping with the food budget and the time and equipment available for preparing food.

Menus should reflect special occasions. Often just varying a basic recipe or adding an extra course is all that is needed to turn an everyday meal into a "special occasion" meal, but decorations also help: special colour schemes and traditional motifs add to the festivity.

Variations of colour, flavour, texture, size and shape should always be considered in meal planning. Avoid serving the same food more than once during a meal; e.g. tomato juice followed by tomato salad. Avoid serving two mashed vegetables at once, or two creamed mixtures. Serve *either* cabbage *or* turnip, to avoid clashing of strong flavours.

Foods should harmonize or contrast in colour. Separate colours that are similar with food of contrasting colour to heighten interest. Picture mashed potato, cauliflower, and creamed chicken served on a white plate—and imagine the improvement when the potato is baked in its skin and broccoli substituted for the cauliflower.

A weekly routine of roast beef on Sundays, cold roast beef on Mondays, and beef stew on Tuesdays shows lack of imagination. Vary the days for serving roasts, or break sequences with a completely different protein food.

A spirit of adventure is created at mealtime when a new food or a new recipe is introduced.

BASIC MEAL PATTERNS

Plan the main meal for each day of the week around a protein food—meat, fish, legumes, etc. Choose vegetables, raw and cooked, to complement it, taking advantage of foods in season which are more flavoursome, usually more nutritious, and less expensive than those which have travelled a long distance.

Plan lunches or suppers next. Usually they are simpler meals, often using leftovers from previous days.

Breakfasts should reflect energy requirements; one that includes potatoes and pie is not unreasonable for a farmer who has done several hours of chores before breakfast.

The day's meals and snacks should include food from all the four main groups in kinds and amounts recommended in CANADA'S FOOD GUIDE.

Recipes, tables, etc. that appear in small capital letters, e.g., PARSLEY BUTTER, CANADA'S FOOD GUIDE, are listed in the index. Consult the index for the number of the page on which the item appears.

Traditionally, the three meals follow these basic patterns:

BREAKFAST

①   **Fruit or Fruit Juice**

② {   **Whole Grain or Enriched Cereal**
          (hot or cold) with milk

③ {   **Egg   Bacon   Ham   Sausages**
       Cheese   Peanut Butter

④ {   **Waffles   Pancakes   French Toast**
      Hash Brown Potatoes
        Toast   Muffins

⑤   **Cocoa   Milk   Coffee   Tea**

The size of the breakfast will usually be determined by a person's activity and appetite, and the time available. Because breakfast follows a period of fasting and provides our launching fuel for the day's activities, it is an important meal of the day. The inclusion of a small amount of protein in breakfast (from ② or ③) prevents mid-morning fatigue.

For normal activity, most of us will fare nicely on a breakfast of: ① ② ④ and ⑤ *or* ① ③ ④ and ⑤.

A very active person might require a breakfast containing foods from all groups: ① ② ③ ④ and ⑤.

The late riser who expects an early lunch may require foods only from ① ④ and ⑤.

Brunch may replace both breakfast and lunch for late risers. It is usually served on a weekend or holiday when time is not limited. This hearty meal may include fruit, one or two items from ③, breads, and beverage. Cereal is usually omitted and may be replaced by dessert.

BREAKFAST-ON-THE-RUN, though not recommended on a daily basis, is surely better than no breakfast at all.

When the main meal is in the evening:

LUNCH
Soup or Juice
Salad Plate, Casserole, Sandwiches,
Cheese or Eggs
Vegetable Sticks
Bread, Enriched or Whole Grain
Fruit or Pudding
Milk

DINNER
Appetizer or Clear Soup
Meat, Fish or Fowl
Potatoes
Yellow, Green or Raw Vegetable
Another Vegetable
Fruit, Pudding, Pie or Cake
Beverage

When the main meal is in the middle of the day:

DINNER
Appetizer or Clear Soup
Meat, Fish or Fowl
Potatoes
Yellow, Green or Raw Vegetable
Another Vegetable
Fruit, Pudding, Pie or Cake
Beverage

SUPPER
Appetizer
Supper Dish or Omelet with Salad Greens
or
Salad Plate
Bread, Enriched or Whole Grain
Fruit or Pudding
Cookies
Beverage

Menus for All Occasions

ECONOMY MEALS
be enjoyed by family and friends

PARSLEY POTATO SOUP
SWEET & SOUR CHICKEN
Boiled Rice
Green Beens
CARROT STRAWS
FRUIT TAPIOCA CREAM

Pineapple Juice
SHEPHERD'S PIE
or RICE & BEAN CASSEROLE
COLE SLAW
GINGERBREAD

CHICKEN SOUP
CASSEROLE OF FISH & RICE
Spinach
Sliced Tomatoes in season
or Canned Tomatoes
PINEAPPLE SPANISH CREAM

Consommé
MACARONI WITH CHEESE SAUCE
GREEN SALAD
TOMATO ASPIC
DEEP APPLE PIE
or Fresh Apple

Tomato Juice
"BOILED" TONGUE
Creamed Onions
Green Beans
FOAMY LEMON PUDDING with CUSTARD SAUCE

TOMATO COCKTAIL
FISH LOAF
HOT POTATO SALAD
Broccoli
LEMON SPONGE PIE

ECONOMY OVEN-COOKED MEALS

When starred items of the menu are cooked at the same time in the oven, there is a saving of fuel; if the oven has an automatic timer, the cook can enjoy extra time off!

Half Grapefruit
PRAIRIE CASSEROLE*
GREEN SALAD
GINGERBREAD*

Tomato Juice
BAKED SAUSAGES*
SCALLOPED POTATOES*
Green Peas
APPLE CRISP*

POTATO ONION SOUP
BAKED FISH FILLETS IN SAUCE*
Green Peppers stuffed with canned kernel corn*
FUDGE JIFFY PUDDING*

Apple Juice
BAKED BEANS MARITIME STYLE*
Carrot Sticks and Celery
FOAMY LEMON PUDDING*

Pineapple Juice
HAM LOAF*
Broccoli with CHEESE SAUCE
DUTCH APPLE CAKE*

CHILLED CUCUMBER SOUP
NOODLE RING with **Creamed Tuna***
Baked Carrots*
Celery and Green Pepper Sticks
BAKED APPLES*

Recipes, tables, etc. that appear in small capital letters, e.g., PARSLEY BUTTER, CANADA'S FOOD GUIDE, are listed in the index. Consult the index for the number of the page on which the item appears.

TOMATO-VEGETABLE JUICE
Baked Haddock or Cod*
BAKED POTATOES*
Buttered or HARVARD BEETS
UPSIDE-DOWN CAKE*

TOMATO COCKTAIL
BRAISED BEEF*
BAKED POTATOES*
Wax Beans
Green Onions and Radishes
APPLE BETTY*

Tomato Juice
SWEET AND SOUR CHICKEN
or Foil-baked Turkey Legs
GREEN BEANS NISI
CAESAR SALAD
SHERBET **in** MERINGUES

Apple Juice
STIR-FRIED CHICKEN AND ALMONDS
PARSLEY RICE
Lettuce wedge with MAYONNAISE
Fruit SHORTCAKE

MEALS FOR ONE OR TWO

Although the following menus lend themselves to individual preparation, they are equally suitable for any number of servings. Many can be prepared without an oven.

Half Grapefruit
BRAISED FLANK STEAK
FRENCH FRIED POTATOES **(frozen)**
PARTY ONIONS
TOSSED SALAD
Ice Cream with CARAMEL SAUCE

SEAFOOD COCKTAIL
STUFFED PEPPERS
or STUFFED PORK CHOPS
SCALLOPED POTATOES
Carrots
BAKED APPLES

JELLIED CONSOMMÉ
CURRIED CHICKEN LIVERS
or Salmon Steak
HOT POTATO SALAD
Zucchini or Pepper Squash
Sliced Tomatoes
Fruit

TOMATO-VEGETABLE JUICE
Baked Ham Slice
FRUITY SWEET POTATOES
Spinach
CABBAGE SALAD
BAKED PEARS

Pineapple Juice
SWEDISH MEAT BALLS
MASHED POTATOES
Green Beans or Brussels Sprouts
Raw Vegetable Relishes
Assorted Cheeses and Fruits

MEALS IN A HURRY

The starred foods are invaluable when time is short and stocks of fresh foods are low.

Cook or heat	in	Serve with or on
wieners	*BARBECUE SAUCE	toasted buns
sausages		*noodles and grated cheese
chicken liver		*rice
leftover roast cut in strips		
*corned beef, luncheon meat, canned ham		toasted buns
*frozen meat balls		noodles, grated cheese
leftover roast pork	*SWEET AND SOUR SAUCE	rice or noodles
cooked or *canned cold meat		
frozen chicken wings		
canned *seafood,		
*tuna		
frozen meat balls		

Cook or heat	in	Serve with or on
cheese, grated	WHITE SAUCE	toast, tea biscuits (hot), noodles or rice
canned or cooked tuna	*cream celery, *mushroom, *chicken or vegetable soups	
frozen meat balls	Curry Sauce made by adding curry to WHITE SAUCE	
*fish fillets	TOMATO SAUCE	rice
fish patties		
hamburger patties, fresh or frozen	SPAGHETTI SAUCE	*instant scalloped potatoes, noodles or spaghetti, buns or tacos
meat balls, fresh or frozen	leftover gravy	noodles or spaghetti

Desserts such as instant puddings and mixes for cakes and toppings, frozen or canned fruits, ice cream, sherbet, cheeses are other useful additions to the emergency shelf.

SAMPLE EMERGENCY MENUS

Tomato Juice
Ham Slice (canned or fresh)
with SWEET AND SOUR MUSTARD RELISH
Canned Sweet Potato slices
Frozen Green Vegetable
Fresh Fruit
Cheese
Coffee

Stuffed Celery
SPEEDY BEEF STROGANOFF
Noodles or Instant Mashed Potatoes
Frozen Green Vegetable
Sliced Tomatoes
SEVEN-MINUTE PRUNE WHIP
Tea or Coffee

TOMATO-VEGETABLE JUICE
FISH PATTIES **with** TARTAR SAUCE
Pressure-cooked Scalloped Potatoes
Green Vegetable
Celery
SHERBET
Tea or Coffee

QUICK SOUP
SCRAMBLED EGGS **and Back Bacon**
BROILED TOMATOES **with grated Cheddar**
Assorted Fruits
Tea or Coffee

(Dehydrated) French Onion Soup with grated Cheddar
SWEET AND SOUR PORK
Frozen Green Vegetables
or STIR-FRIED VEGETABLES
Instant Rice
Side Salad of greens or fruit
Instant Pudding
Coffee

Half Grapefruit
HURRY CURRY *or* CURRIED LAMB
or SEAFOOD SCALLOP
Sliced Tomatoes and Cucumbers
Potato Chips
Ice Cream
Coffee

MENUS FOR ENTERTAINING

AFTER THE THEATRE
TOASTED SANDWICHES
Pickles
Fruit
Coffee

SUNDAY SUPPER
Juice
CHICKEN TETRAZZINI
TOSSED SALAD
ICE CREAM CAKE
or Fruit
Tea   Coffee

LUNCH BEFORE THE GAME
Baked Ham and SCRAMBLED EGGS **on buns**
or Sandwich buffet
Ice Cream Sundaes
Cookies
Coffee

BEFORE-THE-DANCE BUFFET
Fruit Juice
Onion Dip
Biscuits
Potato Chips
SEAFOOD IN SHELLS
FRENCH BREAD
ROLLS
GREEN SALAD
CHOCOLATE CHARLOTTE
Coffee

AT HOME AT CHRISTMAS
CHEESE DREAMS
Celery and Pickles
CHICKEN LIVER PATÉ
Biscuits
FRUIT CAKE
SHORTBREAD
EGGNOG

FAMILY BARBECUE
Vegetable Juice
SHISH KABOBS **(self assembled)**
CABBAGE SALAD
Buttered Bread
Watermelon
RHUBARB PUNCH
or Coffee

A "LITTLE" DINNER (for 6)
Iced Seafood
BEEF FONDUE **with sauces**
BAKED POTATOES
GREEN SALAD
FRENCH BREAD
Ice Cream in MERINGUES **with frozen**
or fresh raspberries
Coffee
Mints

DINNER FOR ALL OCCASIONS
Celery
Liver Sausage spread on MELBA TOAST
Baked Ham
BAKED SWEET POTATOES
Broccoli
Baked Cherry Tomatoes
GREEN SALAD
Rolls, Butter
Fruit in season
Tea
Coffee

A POT LUCK SUPPER
Cold Meats
SCALLOPED POTATOES
JELLIED SALAD
MUFFINS
Hot rolls
Biscuits
Ice Cream with FRUIT SAUCE
Coffee

A FONDUE FOURSOME
CHICKEN FONDUE
FRENCH BREAD
TOSSED SALAD
Fresh Fruit
Coffee

A SHOWER FOR THE BRIDE
FRUIT SALAD
Hot Rolls
MERINGUE TORTE
Tea
Coffee

A COFFEE PARTY
COFFEE CAKE
BUTTERSCOTCH MUFFINS
APPLESAUCE MUFFINS
RAISIN BREAD
Coffee

AFTERNOON TEA
Fancy Sandwiches
BOUCHÉES **filled with** CHICKEN SALAD
Raw Vegetable with GOLDEN DIP
Small CUP CAKES
MERINGUES
Fancy Cookies
Tea

BREAKFAST MEETING
Berries
Melon
BROILED GRAPEFRUIT
COFFEE CAKE
MELBA TOAST
BLACK CURRANT JAM
APPLE JELLY
Coffee

Recipes, tables, etc. that appear in small capital letters, e.g., PARSLEY BUTTER, CANADA'S FOOD GUIDE, are listed in the index. Consult the index for the number of the page on which the item appears.

LUNCH ON THE PATIO
VICHYSSOISE
RIBBON SANDWICHES
Platter of Assorted Fruits
Tea
Coffee

LUNCHEON FOR THE VISITING SPEAKER
Fruit Salad
CHEESE MUFFINS
CRÈME BRÛLÉE
Coffee

EASY AND INFORMAL MENUS

Varieties of breads—rye, French, homemade and foreign—all make wonderful sandwiches; so do rolls that have been heated for about 15 min. For those do-it-yourself sandwich fans, put the breads on a tray, serve rows of assorted cold meats, cheese slices, and slices of Spanish onions and tomatoes, along with a variety of substantial pickles such as garlic dills, mustard pickles, or homemade relishes.

Here are a few favourite combinations:

CABBAGE ROLLS or PIZZA
Potato Chips
Celery
Coffee

Assorted Cold Meats (tongue, ham, salami)
Spanish Onions
GREEN SALAD
Rye and FRENCH BREADS
Apples
Cheese
Coffee

LASAGNA
TOSSED SALAD
Garlic Bread
Fruit
Coffee

Assorted Cheeses
FRENCH BREAD
Biscuits
Pickles
Fruit
Coffee

Sandwiches or buns filled with Ham with
HOT MUSTARD SAUCE
Sliced Chicken
Relishes
Coffee

PIGS IN BLANKETS
BARBECUE SAUCE
Pickles
Olives
Coffee

PYJAMA PARTY
Sandwich buffet
or Toast variations
Ice Cream Sundae
or Fruit
Cocoa

AFTER THE DANCE
PIZZA or BREAKFAST BUNS
PEPPERMINT STICK ICE CREAM
CRANBERRY PUNCH

RECORD PARTY
COCKTAIL TIDBITS
PLATTER PATTERS
BROWN COW

WINTER PICNIC
DEVILLED STEAK BUNS
or HAMBURGERS
or BUNS DE LUXE
or BREAKFAST BUNS
DOUGHNUTS or BROWNIES
Fruit
Thermos of Hot COCOA
or Coffee

BIRTHDAY PARTY FOR A FIVE-YEAR-OLD
Sandwiches: RAISIN BREAD **and jam; peanut butter**
and banana
Ice Cream
Birthday Cake
Apple Juice

HALLOWE'EN PARTY FOR BROWNIES AND CUBS
Assorted Sandwiches
Hot COCOA **with marshmallow**
Fruit

TRADITIONAL MENUS

BRITISH
Roast Beef
YORKSHIRE PUDDING
HORSERADISH SAUCE
MASHED POTATOES
Brussels Sprouts
Stewed Fruit with CUSTARD SAUCE

CANADIEN

FRENCH ONION SOUP
HORS D'OEUVRES
TOURTIÈRE
Peas
GREEN SALAD
Fresh Berries with grated Maple Sugar

FRENCH

VICHYSSOISE
VEAL STEW
GREEN SALAD
CRÊPES SUZETTE

GERMAN

Barbecued Pig Tails
HOT POTATO SALAD
Green Beans
SOUR CREAM PIE

CHINESE

EGG ROLLS
STIR-FRIED CHICKEN
Shrimps with SWEET AND SOUR SAUCE
BOILED RICE
Ginger Fruit Compôte
Sesame Cookies
China Tea

JAPANESE

JAPANESE ROLL UPS
SUKIYAKI
Canned Lychée Fruit
or Kumquats

INDIAN

CURRIED LAMB or CURRIED CHICKEN
Rice
Cauliflower and Peas
Fruit

SWEDISH SMÖRGÅSBORD

PICKLED HERRING
Smoked Salmon
TOSSED SALAD
Cold Cuts
Pickles
FISH BALLS with Parsley Sauce
CABBAGE ROLLS
Assorted Cheeses

Recipes, tables, etc. that appear in small capital letters, e.g., PARSLEY BUTTER, CANADA'S FOOD GUIDE, are listed in the index. Consult the index for the number of the page on which the item appears.

OUTDOOR MEALS

Some of these menus require a barbecue; others need only be prepared indoors and kept warm outdoors.

BARBECUED SPARE RIBS
POTATO MACARONI SALAD
Sliced Tomatoes and Cucumbers
Fresh Peach or Berry SHORTCAKE

Hot CHOWDER **in mugs**
HEARTY CHEF'S SALAD
Potato Chips
Carrot Sticks and Celery
CHERRY PIE

Raw Vegetable Relishes
Foil-cooked Lima Beans
FRENCH FRIED POTATOES
FAN TANS
Sliced Tomatoes
Assorted Melons

HAMBURGERS or BARBECUED WIENERS
KETCHUP
Mustard
COLE SLAW
Pickles
Sliced Tomatoes
Watermelon

Consommé in mugs
SHISH KABOBS
Foil-baked Potatoes
CAESAR SALAD
LEMON SHERBET **and** ANGEL CAKE

FOOD FOR THE SICK

Every effort should be made to make meal time a pleasant time for a patient. Rapid recovery depends upon adequate nourishment. As far as possible, the meals served should be similar to those normally eaten.

The patient who is convalescing from surgery, or who has had a high fever or a stomach upset is often fed light foods before being given full meals. In some cases, when the mouth or teeth are affected, it may be necessary to sieve vegetables and mince meat. Infant foods may be used for convenience. The following diet sequence is frequently used for convalescents.

Convalescent Diets

1 Clear Fluids, No Milk	2 Add Milk	3 Proceed to Soft Diet	4 Continue with Light Diet
Breakfast:			
Strained Orange Juice Clear Tea or Coffee	Fruit Juice Milk Tea or Coffee	Fruit Juice Refined Cereal Milk Poached Egg Beverage Toast made from white bread	Soft Diet plus any foods that are neither highly seasoned nor very rich or sweet
10:00			
Strained Lemonade	Tomato Juice or Milk		
Dinner:			
Fruit Juice Clear Gelatine Dessert	Strained Soup Junket or Yogurt Ice cream Milk	Chicken or Fish (without skin or bones) Mashed Potatoes Green Beans and Carrots APPLESAUCE	
15:00			
Canned Fruit Juice	MILKSHAKE	Milk and Wafers	
Supper:			
Hot Consommé Clear Gelatine Dessert Clear Tea		Cream Soup Gelatine Dessert (without fruit) Custard Tea	Cream Soup FOAMY OMELET Asparagus Tips ORANGE CHARLOTTE Beverage
21:00			
Broth		Cocoa	Cocoa Enriched Bread, Butter

Snacks

Snacks have become part of our lifestyle and are here to stay. When well chosen from a wide variety of nutritious foods, and eaten to provide part of our total energy needs, snacks can be beneficial and refreshing. Snacks are often recommended in reducing diets to take the edge off the dieter's appetite for meals. They are also often a part of special diets for those with digestive problems. Snacks, therefore, can be an important part of the family's diet. Considerable thought should be given to the foods used for them.

Too often snacks have been synonymous with soft drinks, pastries, and candy—foods lacking in nutrients and rich in tooth-damaging sugar. Far preferable are "detergent foods" such as apples, raw vegetables, and nuts. Raw vegetables contain negligible amounts of food energy and can be eaten as desired. Other snacks should be considered as part of the day's intake of food. Whereas a hamburger might be considered a high-energy snack if eaten in addition to meals, it might be quite acceptable when included as part of the daily allotment of energy. Strong reliance on fruit, unsweetened fruit juice, and skim milk or buttermilk is recommended. Clear tea and coffee, and diet soft drinks may be included as thirst quenchers, although they provide no nourishment.

Snack Suggestions

Juicy Snacks	Crunchy Snacks	Thirst-quenching Snacks	Hearty Snacks
fresh fruits: 　apples 　pears 　oranges 　grapefruit 　tangerines 　melons 　pineapple 　berries	apples	water	yogurt
	carrots	tomato juice	processed or Cheddar cheese
	celery	skim milk	
	radishes	2% milk	cottage cheese
	green onions	whole milk	whole wheat or enriched bread
canned or frozen fruits without sugar	cucumbers	buttermilk	sandwiches
	lettuce wedges	unsweetened 　pineapple juice	ice cream
SHERBET made from unsweetened fruit juices	cabbage wedges	apple juice grapefruit juice	milk shakes
TOMATO FRAPPÉ	popcorn	orange juice	digestive biscuits
YOGURT DRESSING as a dip for fresh fruits	GRANOLA	JELLIED CONSOMMÉ with lemon juice and chives	hot dogs
	nuts		hamburgers
	curried nuts		pizza
	sunflower seeds		lean meat: salami; liver sausage
	dry enriched cereal or bite-size shredded wheat		
	NUTS AND BOLTS		

The School Lunch Box

From the humble lunch box can emerge a good-looking meal that is appetizing, nutritious, and enjoyable—one that provides 1/3 of the daily nutrients needed for energy.

If soup and milk are available at school, a paper bag will probably hold the other items carried from home. When a complete lunch must be carried, a lunch box with thermos is recommended. Small plastic containers or insulated jars can hold puddings or salad. Individual containers of juices and fruits can be purchased but it is usually less expensive to buy such foods in large containers and pour an individual portion into a leakproof container. Glass jars should not be used unless well protected against breakage.

A wide assortment of wrappings—waxed paper, plastic wraps, and foil—make it easy to wrap each food properly; there is no reason for box lunches to get dried-out or messy.

It is wise to chill foods before packing if the lunch must be kept at room temperature before eating. The inclusion of frozen yogurt or juice helps to keep the lunch cool; in a paper bag they will thaw by noon. It may be convenient to prepare and freeze many meat sandwiches for use as needed. They too can be packed frozen to keep the lunch cool.

LUNCHBOX MENUS

MONDAY
CHICKEN SOUP
**Ham sandwich with mustard
on whole wheat bread
Pickles, Celery
Banana
Milk**, ROLLED OATMEAL COOKIE

TUESDAY
Grapefruit Juice
BAKED BEANS **or** BEEF STEW **in a thermos**
CARROT STRAWS, **Celery**
Bread or MUFFIN
Frozen yogurt
GINGER COOKIE

WEDNESDAY
Vegetable Cocktail
DEVILLED EGG
POTATO SALAD, **Cucumber slices**
Rye Bread
Apple or Pear, BUTTER TART
Cheese

THURSDAY
VEGETABLE SOUP
STUFFED CELERY, **Radishes**
BARBER POLE FRANKS
CARROT AND RAISIN SALAD
APPLESAUCE
CUP CAKE
Milk

FRIDAY
VEGETABLE CHOWDER
HEARTY CHEF'S SALAD **with salami strips**
Green pepper strips, Pickles
FRUIT CUP
DATE SQUARES
Milk

Special Diets

People requiring special diets will receive instructions for these from their doctor or from a dietitian.

Hostesses preparing foods for guests requiring special diets (diabetic, low-fat, low-cholesterol, etc.) usually have no problem meeting the needs of their guests if a choice of food is offered, preferably buffet style, and if the choice includes lean meat, vegetables, and fruits, prepared and served without sauces, dressings, gravy, butter, or sugar. These latter accompaniments can be available separately and added by those who wish them.

The same principle applies to low-salt diets but for these foods should be cooked and served without salt as well. The ban on salt includes seasoned salt, garlic salt, celery salt, and monosodium glutamate. People following strict low-salt diets must avoid baked foods containing baking soda as well as baking powder; they will use salt-free bread and salt-free butter or margarine. Provide an alternative to ham, cold cuts, smoked meat, weiners, canned or frozen fish, or other food containing added salt. It is possible to buy some foods especially prepared for low-sodium (low-salt) diets; canned soup and tomato juice are examples. The labelling of these and other foods is governed by Food and Drug regulations.

Followers of low-residue diets will select foods with a minimum of fibre. They will avoid whole grains, bran, seeds, coarse raw vegetables, and most raw fruits. Applesauce or gelatine containing cooked fruit without skin or seeds would be suitable desserts for such people.

For people who must restrict their food intake in order to reduce, the considerate cook will voluntarily include in the menu dishes that contain little fat and carbohydrate.

Table Settings

Table settings should reflect harmony of appointments. Fine china is used with flatware and glassware of delicate pattern and lines; pottery and earthenware looks best with heavy glasses and plain, simple cutlery.

Place settings include what is necessary for eating a meal. The plates, silverware, and napkin are placed one inch from the edge of the table. Silverware is placed in the order of use, with the last piece to be used placed closest to the plate. The knife is placed to the right of the plate with the cutting edge toward the plate. The spoon is placed to the right of the knife. The fork is placed to the left of the plate. The napkin is placed to the left of the fork. The beverage glass is placed at the tip of the knife.

Setting for a formal dinner provides for additional courses (fish course, salad course) with additional glasses for each beverage served. This type of service requires assistance in serving.

Basic Table Setting

Setting for an informal 3-course dinner includes a fork and spoon above the plate for use with dessert. Any utensils not needed for the meal to be served should be omitted.

Table Service

Formality, or the lack of it, is a matter of choice. What is considered informal to one family might seem very formal to another. The style of service which follows combines some of the features of the traditional forms of table service; it can be modified to meet the needs of the individual family.

1. The cold appetizer is on the table when the meal begins or a hot appetizer or soup is brought from the kitchen when the guests have been seated.
2. The warm plates are brought in and placed in front of the host. If the meat is covered, the cover is removed, inverted, and set to one side. The meat is carved, served onto the plates, and passed to the hostess who serves the vegetables and then indicates to whom the plate is to be passed.

Today's hostess or host usually serves as waiter also; children in the household may be expected to assist. If there is a waitress or waiter, plates are carried between host and hostess as the meat and vegetables are served.

3. At the end of the first course the meat platter, then the vegetable dishes are removed. Beginning with the person who was served first, the dinner plate, then the side plate, are next removed before going on to the next guest.

Although serving from the left (except beverages) and removing from the right, has long been the practice, whatever pattern is most practicable should be followed, to eliminate accidents.

Salts and peppers and any silverware not needed for the dessert course are removed before the dessert course is served.

4. The dessert may be served and brought in from the kitchen or served at the table by the hostess. Coffee is served at the table by the hostess and passed to the guests; or it may be served from a coffee table in the living room or on the garden terrace.

5. All members of the group should leave the table together on the suggestion of the hostess.

That extra ingredient: Just as seasonings add zest to a dish, so does a pinch of drama add to its presentation. Often a menu will be planned around a particularly attractive serving dish. Cold appetizers, served in iced dishes surrounded by ice or snow, introduce the meal with a flourish as do hot fish appetizers in little scallop shells. Soup bowls with lids are perfect for onion soup, and a large tureen creates a focal point for a chowder party. Individual bowls for such things as salads and rice add interest—so do baskets big and little. A handsome chafing dish might call for MEAT BALLS ROMANOFF for the main course or CHERRIES JUBILEE for dessert. The family meat loaf becomes more festive when cooked in a ring mould and served on a platter surrounded by colourful vegetables.

The use of long-stemmed comportes adds a touch of elegance to the lowliest of puddings, while desserts such as charlottes, ices or instant puddings gain prestige when served in graceful parfait glasses. Melons cut in zig-zag fashion and topped with a scoop of sherbet are natural scene-stealers—as are platters of fruit and cheeses. Orange halves, scooped out, serrated, filled with orange charlotte and topped with mint, add much to eye appeal and little to the budget. The list is as endless as the imagination, but the wise hostess will choose only a few novelty appointments or creations for each occasion!

Tray Service

Tray setting is similar to informal table setting.

Buffet Service

Buffet meals are gaining popularity in this age of diminishing dining rooms and kitchen help, to feed four people or forty. This informal style of meal can be arranged on a dining table, a buffet, a tea wagon, or a kitchen counter—each having its own possibilities and limitations.

Foods are set out in a logical sequence, preceded by plates. Cutlery and napkins are picked up at the end of the sequence unless tables have been set elsewhere.

Each person serves himself or herself, then finds a chair in another part of the room or in an adjoining room. Small tables reduce the need for knee-juggling—and mishaps, too. Card tables covered with attractive table cloths can be set up to accommodate guests. Often such tables are set for four, with silverware, napkins and salt and pepper being provided here instead of at the buffet table. If space permits, one large table which allows all to sit down together is ideal for maintaining the unity of the group.

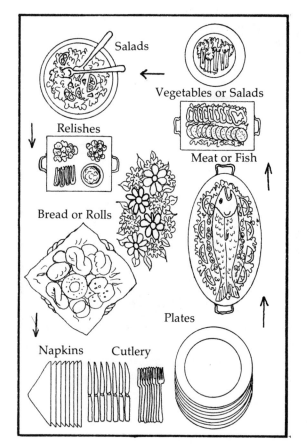

A Buffet Arrangement

Combine baked beans with whole grain bread for complete proteins.

A breakfast table setting.

A dinner may be cooked entirely in the oven by broiling or baking.

Outdoor Meals

Good food tastes even better when eaten outdoors—whether it is cooked indoors and transported to the patio, or barbecued in the garden with everybody helping. Outdoor meals can be the solution to entertaining when indoor space is limited or uncomfortably warm.

As with most meals, pre-planning of menu and equipment can do much to ensure success. Keep the menu simple, in keeping with the atmosphere of informality. Fresh air is the best appetizer, so the wise hostess will order her supplies with a generous hand.

HELPFUL EQUIPMENT FOR GARDEN MEALS

Serving table to hold plates, cold foods, condiments, etc., for self-service; a card table, or two or more card tables grouped together, will serve the purpose. The table should be located on level ground, out of the wind.

Chairs and benches should be grouped informally in twos and threes; upright chairs make for easier eating.

Little tables to be shared by two or three guests for holding beverages and extras are very useful.

Barbecue and/or electrical appliances and extensions to enable food to be prepared on the spot or kept hot will save trips to the kitchen. Electric percolators, frying pans, hot plates, and warmers are all useful.

Candle warmers or sterno (canned heat) keep hot foods hot.

Use trays and baskets for serving foods.

Provide plenty of paper serviettes. Individual vacuum-sealed paper towels which have been impregnated with skin freshener are very helpful for cleaning greasy hands at the end of a barbecue meal; these are sold at most drugstores.

2 Cooking Methods

Metric Measures

Metric cooking requires only that we replace our measuring spoons and cups with metric measuring equipment, and follow recipes that give quantities in metric units. Metric measures are marked in millilitres, and metric recipes give amounts in millilitres (ml or mL) or litres (ℓ or L). There is no change in cooking technique required and we will continue to place dry or liquid ingredients in a container to measure their volume.

The standard metric measures for domestic cooking are:
    small: 1 ml (millilitre), 2 ml, 5 ml, 15 ml, 25 ml
    larger: 50 ml, 125 ml, 250 ml
    largest: 500 ml and ℓ

A large cup of coffee contains about 250 ml of liquid. A small brick of ice cream contains one litre. A litre (1 ℓ) equals one thousand millilitres (1000 ml).

Where quantities are measured using scales in the way that foods such as macaroni, cereal, butter and cheese are usually marketed, the most common measure is the gram (g) and kilogram (kg). A kilogram equals one thousand grams.

Small Liquid/dry

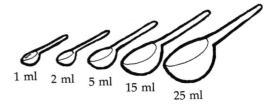

1 ml   2 ml   5 ml   15 ml   25 ml

Dry

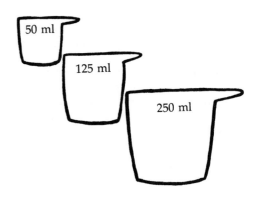

50 ml   125 ml   250 ml

Liquid

COOKING EQUIPMENT
CAKE PANS

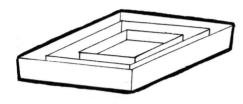

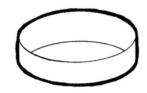

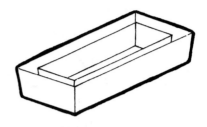

SQUARE

	cm	ℓ
Small	18 × 5	1.25
Medium	20 × 5	1.4
Large	22 × 5	1.5
Extra large	25 × 5	2.5

LAYER

	cm	ℓ
Small	20 × 4	1.25
Large	22 × 4	1.5

LOAF

	cm	ℓ
Small	20 × 10 × 7	1
Large	22 × 12 × 7	1.5

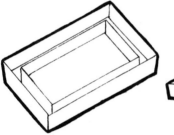

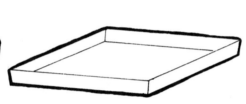

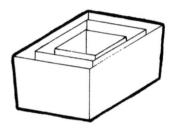

RECTANGULAR

	cm	ℓ
Small	15 × 25 × 4	1.5
Medium	17 × 28 × 4	2
Large	20 × 30 × 5	3

JELLY ROLL

cm	ℓ
40 × 25 × 2	3

FRUIT CAKE PANS

	cm	ℓ
Small	14 × 8	0.75
Medium	20 × 8	2
Large	25 × 8	2.5

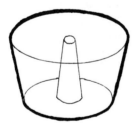

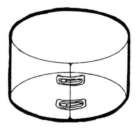

TUBE

	cm	ℓ
Small	17 × 6	1
Medium	20 × 10	1.5
Large	22 × 10	2.5
Extra large	25 × 10	3

SPRINGFORM

	cm	ℓ
Small	23 × 6	2.5
Large	25 × 8	3

BUNDT PAN

cm	ℓ
25 × 8	3

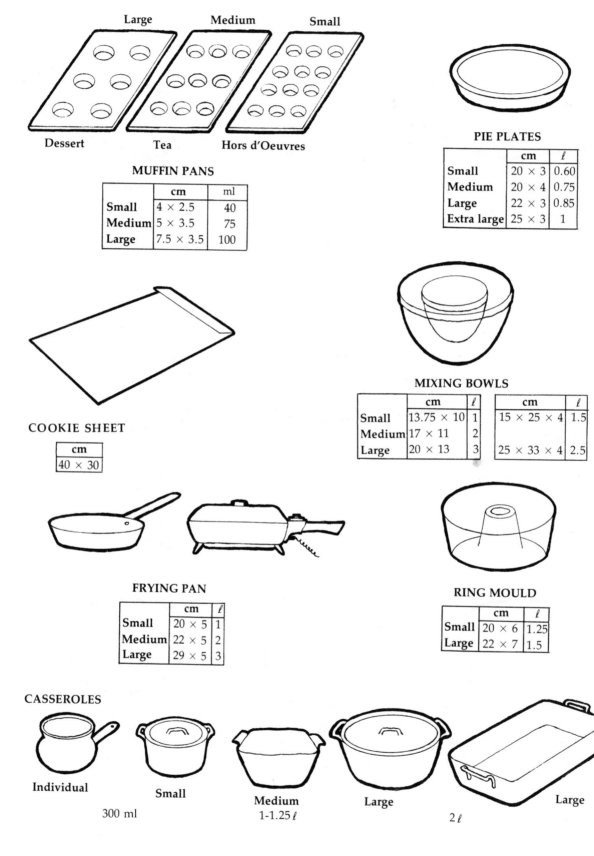

Large   Medium   Small

Dessert   Tea   Hors d'Oeuvres

MUFFIN PANS

	cm	ml
Small	4 × 2.5	40
Medium	5 × 3.5	75
Large	7.5 × 3.5	100

PIE PLATES

	cm	ℓ
Small	20 × 3	0.60
Medium	20 × 4	0.75
Large	22 × 3	0.85
Extra large	25 × 3	1

COOKIE SHEET

cm
40 × 30

MIXING BOWLS

	cm	ℓ	cm	ℓ
Small	13.75 × 10	1	15 × 25 × 4	1.5
Medium	17 × 11	2		
Large	20 × 13	3	25 × 33 × 4	2.5

FRYING PAN

	cm	ℓ
Small	20 × 5	1
Medium	22 × 5	2
Large	29 × 5	3

RING MOULD

	cm	ℓ
Small	20 × 6	1.25
Large	22 × 7	1.5

CASSEROLES

Individual   Small   Medium   Large   Large

300 ml   1-1.25 ℓ   2 ℓ

Table of Measures and Yields

Mass Measure	Food	Capacity Measure or Yield
	Cereals, Pasta, and other Starches:	
500 g	cornmeal or Cream of Wheat	750 ml
	250 ml cornmeal or Cream of Wheat after cooking yield	1 ℓ
500 g	rolled oats	1.42 ℓ
	250 ml rolled oats after cooking yield	450 ml
500 g	macaroni, noodles, spaghetti, after cooking yield	2.5 ℓ
	250 ml rice, after cooking yield	0.75-1 ℓ
	Crackers:	
500 g	soda crackers, crumbled, yield	500 ml
500 g	graham wafers, crushed, yield	1.5 ℓ
	Bread:	
500 g	bread yield	12-16 slices
680 g	bread yield	24 slices
28 g	1 slice bread yields	200 ml soft crumbs
28 g	1 slice bread yields	50 ml dry crumbs
	Flour:	
500 g	all-purpose flour	1 ℓ
500 g	pastry flour	1.125 ℓ
500 g	bread flour	1 ℓ
500 g	whole wheat flour	950 ml
500 g	cornstarch	900 ml
500 g	Cocoa	1 ℓ
200 g	Coconut, shredded	500-600 ml
200 g	Coconut, flaked	500 ml
200 g	Coconut, dessicated	400-500 ml
	Dairy Products:	
500 g	butter	500 ml
	cheese:	
500 g	Cheddar, shredded	1 ℓ
500 g	Parmesan, grated	1 ℓ
500 g	cottage	500 ml
85 g	cream	100 ml

Mass Measure	Food	Capacity Measure or Yield
	250 ml whipping cream yield	500 ml whipped cream
	Eggs:	
	8-10 egg whites yield	250 ml
	12-13 egg yolks yield	250 ml
	5 whole eggs yield	250 ml
	Fats:	
227 g	margarine or lard	250 ml
470 g	shortening	625 ml
450 g	suet, chopped	940 ml
	Fish and Seafood:	
	(see also AMOUNT OF FISH TO PURCHASE)	
500 g	oysters in the shell yield	500 ml oysters shucked
220 g	salmon, canned	250 ml
100 g	sardines	125 ml
500 g	scallops, fresh or frozen	500 ml
500 g	raw shrimp, when cooked and cleaned yield	450 ml
220 g	tuna	250 ml
500 g	1 medium lobster, cooked and shelled, yields	125 ml meat
	Fruit, Dried:	
500 g	apricots, cooked yield	1.125 ℓ
	60 dates, pitted and cut yield	400 ml
500 g	prunes, cooked yield	1 ℓ
500 g	raisins (seedless)	700 ml
500 g	raisins, plumped	1 ℓ
500 g	raisins, chopped	500 ml
	Fruit, Fresh:	
500 g	apples, chopped or sliced	750 ml
500 g	apples, cooked as applesauce	300 ml
500 g	apricots	500 ml
500 g	avocado, sliced or diced	650-750 ml
500 g	bananas, sliced	750 ml-1 ℓ
500 g	bananas, mashed	300 ml
500 g	blueberries, fresh	600 ml
250 g	blueberries, frozen	300 ml
500 g	cherries, sour red, unpitted	1 ℓ
500 g	cherries, large sweet, pitted, chopped	125-150 ml
550 g	cherries, frozen	600 ml
500 g	cranberries, fresh, cooked as sauce, yield	750-800 ml
500 g	1 medium grapefruit, sectioned	500 ml
500 g	grapes, Tokay, cut and seeded	700 ml
500 g	grapes, seedless	600 ml
	juice of 1 lemon yields	25-50 ml
	rind of 1 lemon yields	5-10 ml
500 g	3-4 oranges, sectioned	250 ml
	juice of 1 orange yields	100-125 ml
	rind of 1 orange yields	15-25 ml

Mass Measure	Food	Capacity Measure or Yield
500 g	3-4 peaches, sliced	500-750 ml
500 g	pears, diced	750 ml
1 kg	1 pineapple, cubed	1-1.5ℓ
500 g	20 plums, prune, stoned and halved	1ℓ
500 g	10 stalks rhubarb	1ℓ
	1 small box raspberries	750 ml
700 g	1 large box strawberries, sliced	1ℓ
700 g	1 large box strawberries, crushed	750 ml
	Meat:	
500 g	fresh or frozen, boneless, cubed	600 ml
500 g	ground, raw	500 ml
500 g	ground, cooked	750 ml
500 g	sliced, yield	16 slices
500 g	breakfast bacon, cooked, crumbled yield	650 ml
	Nuts:	
500 g	shelled almonds, blanched	750 ml
500 g	filberts, whole	800 ml
500 g	pecan halves	1ℓ
500 g	pecans, chopped	950 ml
500 g	walnut halves	1.125ℓ
500 g	walnuts, chopped	950 ml
500 g	unshelled nuts yield	250 g nuts, shelled
	Poultry (see AMOUNT OF POULTRY TO PURCHASE)	
	Sugar:	
500 g	granulated sugar	500 ml
500 g	brown sugar, firmly packed	700 ml
500 g	icing sugar	900 ml
	Vegetables:	
500 g	asparagus	16-18 spears
500 g	green beans, chopped	750 ml
	500 ml dried beans, cooked, yield	1.25ℓ
500 g	4 medium beets, cooked	500 ml
500 g	3-4 stalks broccoli, cooked	1.5ℓ
500 g	brussel sprouts	1.25ℓ
500 g	1 small cabbage, shredded	1-1.5ℓ
500 g	carrots, shredded or diced	1ℓ
500 g	1 small cauliflower, sectioned	350 ml
500 g	1 large bunch celery, diced	1ℓ
	6-8 cobs corn, kerneled, yield	750 ml
500 g	1 average cucumber, diced	300 ml
500 g	4-5 onions, chopped	750 ml
500 g	4-5 onions, sliced	1ℓ
500 g	7 medium peppers, ground	500 ml
500 g	7 medium peppers, chopped	800 ml
500 g	4 medium potatoes, raw, diced	1ℓ
500 g	4 medium potatoes, cooked, diced	750 ml

Mass Measure	Food	Capacity Measure or Yield
500 g	potatoes, cooked, mashed	500 ml
500 g	3 medium sweet potatoes, cooked, mashed	750 ml
285 g	spinach, raw	2 ℓ
285 g	spinach, cooked	500 ml
500 g	4 small tomatoes, raw, yield	25 slices
500 g	tomato pulp	300 ml
500 g	turnip, raw, diced	1 ℓ
500 g	turnip, cooked, mashed	750 ml

Quantities to Serve 50

Food	Quantity	Food	Quantity
Punch	10 ℓ	Fish Fillets	7 kg
Coffee	500 g	Vegetables	
Tea	125 g	potatoes (to mash)	7 kg
Cocoa	250 g	cauliflower	7 kg
Cream		carrots	6 kg
whipping	1.25 ℓ	beets	7 kg
for coffee	1.75 ℓ	peas (frozen)	5 kg
for tea	1 ℓ	asparagus	7 kg
Sugar Cubes	0.5-1 kg	celery, raw	3-4 bunches
Milk	7.5 ℓ	carrot strips	1 kg
Ice Cream (7-8 bricks)	10 ℓ	olives	1 ℓ
Cakes	3-4, 20 × 20 cm	cabbage	5 kg
Cookies	2 kg	lettuce	
Crackers	500 g	for salad plates	8-10 heads
Butter		for tossed salads	6 heads
for bread	750 g	tomatoes	5-6 kg
for vegetables	500 g	Salad Dressings	
Pickles	2.5 ℓ	mayonnaise	1-1.5 ℓ
Fruit or Tomato Juice	1.5 ℓ	French	1.25 ℓ
Macaroni	1.5 kg	Salads	
Rice, raw	2 kg	green salad	8-10 ℓ
Meat		potato, chicken or fruit	7-8 ℓ
boneless, cooked	3 kg	Fruit	
turkey	18 kg	bananas	8 kg
chicken	23 kg	raspberries or strawberries	8 ℓ
roast (depending on		peaches	5 kg
amount of bone)	9-10 kg	Jam	1 kg
ham, bone in	5-6 kg	Maple Syrup	2.5 ℓ

Table of Replacements

Replace
250 ml   butter
with
250 ml   margarine
or
200 ml   chicken fat
or
225 ml   oil
or
250 ml   shortening

Replace
250 ml   all-purpose flour
with
300 ml   pastry flour

Replace
15 ml   cornstarch
with
30 ml   flour
or
10 ml   minute tapioca
or
15 ml   uncooked rice

Replace
250 ml   white sugar
with
250 ml   brown sugar, firmly packed
or
125 ml   syrup, reducing liquid
    in recipe by 50 ml

Replace
1 square chocolate
with   same amount of carob powder
or
50 ml   cocoa
and
15 ml   fat

Replace
5 ml   baking powder
with
5 ml   baking soda

Replace
250 ml   sweet milk
with
250 ml   sour milk or buttermilk
and use baking soda , 2 ml
to replace equal amount of baking powder.

TO SOUR FRESH MILK

Measure
15 ml   lemon juice *or* vinegar
into a
250 ml   container
Add milk to fill container.

Protection Against Food-borne Illness

Food poisoning, which can cause extreme distress to its victims, and embarrassment and loss of reputation to those involved in food service, can be avoided by observing these precautions:

AT THE FOOD MARKET

1. Look for branded meat with government-approved stamp.
2. Keep vacuum-packaged meat refrigerated.
3. Buy barbecued meat hot, right off the spit, or completely reheat it at home.
4. Select frozen and perishable food last, especially in hot weather.

STORAGE

1. Follow storage directions on the labels of perishable or frozen foods.
2. Promptly refrigerate leftovers from prepared dishes. Do not give bacteria a chance to grow.
3. For safe storage, keep cold food cold, below 4°C
   Keep hot food hot, at least 60°C
4. Refrigerate all dairy and whipped vegetable oil products, e.g. toppings.
5. On a picnic or a trip, use insulated containers for foods which spoil easily when warm.

PREPARATION

1. Good hygiene is always necessary when handling food. Contamination may result from
     a dirty kitchen,
     food handlers with unwashed hands, bad coughs, infected cuts,
     flies, insects and rodents which may carry contamination to the food.
2. Serve prepared food containing eggs, milk or gravy within 2 h or refrigerate.

3. Refrigerate dishes like potato salad, chicken pies, or chicken salad as soon as they are made, to avoid bacteria growth.

4. Always follow the time and temperatures given on the labels for cooking frozen foods like TV dinners and meat pies.

5. Thoroughly cook all poultry and promptly refrigerate leftovers.

6. Thoroughly clean cutting boards after every use. Cracked or scarred boards are a health hazard.

7. The temperature of a slow-cooking pot should reach at least 60°C

Courtesy of Health and Welfare, Canada

Cooking Techniques

MIXING

Ingredients are mixed by

Creaming

Beating

Folding

Stirring

MEASURING

Measures designed for dry ingredients are divided so that the full measure is level with the top edge. Liquid measures leave a space to avoid spilling.

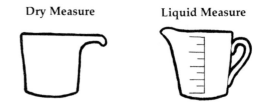

Dry Measure   Liquid Measure

To Measure Dry Ingredients
Spoon lightly into a measure without tapping; wipe level with a straight-edged knife.
Brown sugar: pack gently into the measure.
Icing sugar: sift before piling into the measure.

To Measure Fat
Soft fat: press firmly into the measure; level off.
Hard fat: place water in a measure to make the difference between the fat required and 250 ml
Add the fat until the water reaches the required level, making sure that all fat is covered by water. Empty the water.
Packaged fat: some packages or wrappers have printed measurements that enable you to slice off the required amount of fat.

To Measure Liquids
Set the measure on a flat surface; read at eye level.

TO SEPARATE AN EGG

Use two bowls and a saucer. Crack the shell; keep the yolk intact in the shell; let the white run into a saucer to be sure that the egg is fresh and the yolk unbroken. Place yolks in one bowl and whites in the other.

Yolk in the white prevents the formation of foam. If a small amount does get into the white, tip the bowl to bring yolk close to the edge and scoop it out with a spoon.

TO BEAT EGG WHITE

Have egg white at room temperature. Choose a deep bowl with a small base. Bowl and beater must be free of any trace of fat or yolk. If hand-beating, set the bowl on a damp cloth in the sink or in an open drawer to bring it to a comfortable height.

A recipe may require that the egg white be beaten until "foamy," which means that it is full of air bubbles, has become whiter in colour, and has increased in volume. "Stiff but not dry," means that the whites form large peaks that curve over when the beater is lifted up; the white looks wet and glossy. "Stiff and dry" is the stage beyond; the peaks are small and sharp, the bubbles smaller; the egg white looks dry and begins to fleck off. This stage is difficult to fold.

As the volume increases, the bubble of beaten egg becomes fragile; overbeating causes loss of volume. Use as soon as possible because the bubbles collapse when the egg white stands. This causes it to lose volume and become watery.

To Fold Egg White, incorporate the beaten white with other ingredients using a spatula, rubber scraper or large metal spoon. Cut down through the egg white to the bottom of the bowl, lift up a large spoonful of the mixture to be combined and turn it over the egg white. Rotate the bowl so that the spoon cuts down in a different place each time. Continue to cut down, lift up, turn over, rotating the bowl until there are no large amounts of unmixed egg white. Each unnecessary stroke will decrease the lightness of the mixture.

TO ROLL DOUGH

Roll pastry to a thin sheet, 2 mm
Roll cookie dough to medium thickness,
  5 mm
Roll shortbread dough to a thick sheet, 1 cm
Pat tea biscuit dough to a thickness of 2 cm

Roll chilled dough on a lightly floured board, between two pieces of waxed paper or on a pastry cloth. A clean, heavy linen tea towel makes a good substitute for a pastry cloth. Let one end hang over the front end of the work surface so that it may be held in position. Rub a little flour into the cloth. A rolling-pin stocking holds flour and keeps the pin from sticking. More important than any piece of equipment is lightness of touch.

Roll the dough from the centre out to the edge in each direction if a circle of dough is desired; roll it all in the same direction for a rectangle. Pinch together any cracks that form at the edge.

At the end of each stroke the pin should be lifted to be sure the dough is not sticking. After each 3 or 4 strokes, slide the pastry on the board to pick up a little more flour, and run a floured hand over the pin. If the dough will not move freely, loosen it carefully with the side of a knife and sprinkle a little more flour on the board.

DOUBLE-BOILER COOKING

A double-boiler is a saucepan or bowl placed over (not in) boiling water. The heat penetrates the contents of the saucepan or bowl slowly and remains constant at a temperature no higher than that of boiling water.

Double-boiler cooking prevents sticking or lumping of milk or starch mixtures and curdling of egg or cheese. Milk will not boil over in a double-boiler.

As a substitute for a double-boiler, a heavy saucepan may be placed on very low heat, or an ordinary saucepan may be raised above the heat source by means of a rack.

Double-boiler Cooking

OVEN-POACHING

An oven recipe that has a high egg or cheese content should be baked in a pan of water. The heat then penetrates slowly so the protein does not curdle before the dish is cooked in the centre. The water should come up to the level of the mixture. It should be prevented from boiling; add cold water if necessary.

Oven-poaching

STEAMING

Steaming is cooking on a rack over boiling water so that steam surrounds the food. Set the food on a small plate which will not cover the holes in the rack, or place on cheesecloth, so it may be lifted out. Racks which adjust to fit any size saucepan are available. Cover steamer or cover food with a sheet of foil so that the condensed water runs back into the boiler. Although cooking time is about twice that of boiling, steaming causes less loss of water-soluble nutrients.

Steamer

PRESSURE COOKING

A pressure cooker is a heavy pan with a screw-down lid. Pressure is created when heat creates steam which cannot escape. As pressure builds, the temperature increases beyond that of boiling water, thus greatly shortening cooking time. The pressure cooker's advantages are speed and the preservation of nutrients.

BLANCHING

Blanching is dipping food in and out of boiling water and rinsing in cold, to loosen the skins of tomatoes, peaches or almonds, or to destroy the enzymes that cause discolouration and softening in foods to be frozen.

PARBOILING

Parboiling is cooking briefly in water to prepare food for further cooking.

MICROWAVE COOKING

This is a new kind of oven cooking in which there is no temperature change in the oven. Heat is created inside the food by microwaves which penetrate the moisture in the food and cause the food molecules to vibrate. The friction caused by this motion creates heat throughout the food very quickly. Thus, a microwave oven cooks food in minutes without browning. To allow the microwaves to penetrate the food, non-metal containers must be used. The shorter cooking time, the lower overall fuel consumption and a cool kitchen are among the advantages of microwave cooking. The microwave oven is particularly suitable for the reheating of foods and the cooking of vegetables to maintain colour and texture. Complete

instructions are included with each microwave oven. Always follow the manufacturer's instructions carefully.

BARBECUING

There are two matters of prime importance for successful barbecuing. The first concerns the fire. Food must be cooked over a deep bed of coals with *no flame*. The second requisite is that foods must not dry out; therefore, meats and fish require marinating and/or basting.

Marinade
For recipes see MARINADES. Prepare marinade without salt or oil; soak 4-8 h; drain, add oil (1 part oil to 2 parts liquid). Baste with this mixture sparingly, using a wide brush, so that as little as possible will drip onto the fire. A drip pan will help to prevent flaring.

The Fire
Start the fire 0.5-1 h before cooking time. Use enough wood, briquets or charcoal pieces to produce, after the fire has died down, a bed of coals deep enough to retain a high heat for the necessary length of time. Having to add extra fuel or poke at the fire during cooking gives uneven results. Charcoal should be covered with a white ash before cooking is begun.

By raking some coals to the front or one side, an area of high heat and one of low heat can be arranged. Another way of changing the heat, if there is not an adjustable rack, is to use a bottle of water with a sprinkler to cool the fire.

A little dampened hickory wood added to the fire gives the smoked flavour popular with beef. Smoke powder can be substituted. A few fennel stalks thrown on the fire will add a pungent odour when fish is being barbecued.

The Food
Any food that can be broiled or roasted may be barbecued. Those that are usually braised may be wrapped in foil (see COOKING IN FOIL) and cooked over the coals.

Kabobs, shish kabobs, shaslik are terms for the simplified version of the flaming-sword cooking method of the Middle East. Small pieces of meat and vegetables are cooked on long metal skewers, easily cooked on a barbecue. Brush the skewer with oil, thread marinated cubes of meat alternated with vegetable. For menu suggestions see SHISH KABOBS.

Cooking in Foil
Foil-wrapped foods may be cooked in a hot oven or

on a barbecue by a combination of steaming and baking.

Prepare foil packets by tearing a length of heavy aluminum foil 2½-3 times as wide as the food to be wrapped. Fold in half, and triple fold the edges at the top and sides, making all the folds flat and firm. With the open end up, put in fresh or frozen vegetables, fish or meat, with a little water or liquid. Triple fold the remaining end and check all sides.

Foil Pouch

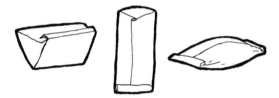

Cook according to the type of food, size of pieces, and intensity of the heat. Carrots and squash are particularly good cooked by this method.

The Menu
Plan the menu bearing in mind the capacity of the grill and the number of guests. Use the kitchen to prepare hot SCALLOPED POTATOES, broiled frozen french fries, or herb-flavoured rice.

If the barbecue has a hood with a flat top, it makes a good warming place; other useful equipment is a hot tray, a bun warmer, an electric frying pan, candle warmers for casseroles.

Exercise caution when using electric extension cords. If the grass is wet, a makeshift connection could cause severe shock.

CHAFING DISH COOKING (TABLE-TOP COOKING)

In the top part of the chafing dish, known as the blazer-pan, food can be prepared by sautéeing or boiling. Over the hot water in the lower section the food is kept warm by a candle or sterno flame. Too much water in the pan may boil out to spoil the table or put out the flame. A strong draft may blow out the flame.

Scrambled eggs, sautéed mushrooms, breaded oysters, CHICKEN À LA KING, clam chowder, hot appe-tizers, CHERRIES JUBILEE, CRÊPES SUZETTE are popular recipes for which the chafing dish is used.

Chafing Dish

SAUTÉEING

Sautéeing is cooking in a small amount of fat.

PURÉE

Purée of a vegetable or other food is made by forcing the food through a sieve or mixing it in a blender to a fine pulp.

STIR-FRYING

Stir-frying is a method of cooking tender meat and vegetables quickly over high heat, while stirring. Meat may first be marinated. All foods are sliced, diced, or shredded into pieces of equal size. The Chinese wok is an ideal cooking utensil for stir-frying, or a wide saucepan with sloping sides can be used. A small amount of cooking oil is heated in the pan and the previously prepared foods are added in sequence, beginning with those that require the longest cooking. The cooking, which combines the principles of sautéeing and steaming, is continuous, rapid and accompanied by constant stirring. By cooking each food until just done, maximum colour and flavour will be maintained, and vegetables will be slightly crisp. See index for recipes under STIR-FRIED.

Wok

The wok is a basin-shaped pan with a lid. A ring to hold the pan firm and keep it from touching the heating element is usually provided. Add a small amount of prepared food to the hot fat and stir-fry. Draw cooked food up the sides of the wok to make room for other foods to be added to the fat. When all the food has been fried, a small amount of chicken, meat or fish stock may be added and the pan covered to complete the cooking. Precut vegetables—green beans, sliced broccoli stalks, carrots, thinly sliced celery, cauliflower, mushrooms—slivered chicken breast, pork tenderloin, beef, scallops or fish fillets may be combined for endless variety. A thin paste of cornstarch and water may be added to thicken the stock. For recipes see STIR-FRIED VEGETABLES and SUKIYAKI.

DEEP FAT FRYING

French fried food brings to mind crisp, golden brown delicacies. With the right equipment, fat and temperature, this tempting vision is easy to obtain. Fried foods are not indigestible, as we used to believe, nor, with proper care of the fat, need they be expensive. Fats do, however, supply more food energy than the same amount of protein or carbohydrate.

Fat
Choice: Fat with a high smoking temperature is necessary; otherwise there will be decomposition of the fat with fumes, offensive flavour and odour. The smoking point is the temperature at which smoke comes from the kettle of fat. Use oil, high quality lard, or vegetable shortening for best results.
Quantity: A small amount of fat will make it difficult to get good results because an even temperature cannot be obtained. Space must be left between the top of the kettle and the surface of the fat to prevent fat boiling over.
Temperature: The longer the food cooks, the greater the absorption of fat. Food should therefore be cooked rapidly, but must be cooked through. Heat the fat to 185°C

If a fat thermometer is not available, the temperature may be checked by using the bread test: at the correct temperature a small cube of bread will brown in 50 s.
Preservation: Heat the fat slowly to the temperature required. Be sure the fat is not allowed to overheat; each time the fat smokes there is more decomposition. After using, cool the fat a little; strain through cheesecloth or towel. Cover and refrigerate.

Small particles left in the fat lower its smoking temperature, and so should be removed. Slicing a raw potato into the fat and heating it, then straining, will help to collect and remove such small bits.

Equipment
Use a heavy kettle large enough to contain the amount of fat necessary for the quantity of food to be cooked. The kettle should not be more than half full. Since the greater the surface the lower the smoking temperature, it is advisable to use a deep, narrow kettle.

A frying basket is best for potatoes and food that is crumb-coated. For batter-coated food a basket should *not* be used, as the batter cooks onto the wires; instead use an egg lifter or kitchen tongs.

Cover a baking sheet with paper towels or unglazed brown paper, to put fried foods on for draining.

Preparation of Food
Food to be fried should be cut into even-sized pieces and should be at room temperature when it is put into the fat.

In order to prevent food soaking up fat, it is often coated with crumbs or batter. The coating cooks quickly and forms an outside protection.

CRUMB COATING (BREADING)

250 ml	crumbs *or* cornmeal
10 ml	salt
	1 egg
30 ml	milk *or* water

1. Fill 2 plates with sifted crumbs; stir in salt.
2. Prepare egg by beating slightly with liquid in a shallow dish.
3. Dip the food in crumbs, then in egg and then in the second dish of crumbs; coat thoroughly (any uncovered spot will allow the fat to get in and push the crust off).
4. Let food stand 20 min on a rack at room temperature, so the crust will dry and remain on during frying; shake off any loose crumbs.

Dry pieces of bread until crisp. Put them through a meat chopper or in a blender, or roll in a paper bag with a rolling pin until fine. Sift; store until needed. Do not save buttered bread or dark toast for crumbs. Packaged crumbs are available and save time, but add cost.

BAKE-ON CRUMB COATING MIX

1 *l*	fine dry crumbs
15 ml	salt
15 ml	paprika
5 ml	pepper
125 ml	oil

1. Combine all ingredients; mix with a pastry blender or fork. Divide into suitable quantities for the amount of food usually prepared.
2. To use: Add seasoning:
   savory or poultry seasoning for fowl
   thyme or fennel for fish
   caraway, ground allspice for pork
   basil or rosemary for veal
   Dip the food into water or milk; shake one piece at a time in a bag with the mix.
   Arrange on a shallow baking pan; see TIMETABLES FOR ROASTING and BAKED FISH for oven temperatures and times.

BATTER COATING

250 ml	flour
2 ml	salt
5 ml	baking powder
15 ml	oil
250 ml	milk *or* water

1. Mix and sift dry ingredients; stir in oil and liquid.
2. Beat with rotary beater to a smooth, creamy consistency; do not overbeat.

For fish, add vinegar: **15 ml**
For fruit, reduce salt;
   add sugar: **30 ml**
For quick batter, use pancake mix and 1 package Italian Salad Dressing Mix. Add liquid as directed.

TO PASTEURIZE FRESH MILK

1. Sterilize bottles, drain, fill with milk; cork or cover.
2. Place on rack in a deep kettle; surround with cold water to the level of the milk.
3. Heat gradually and maintain temperature 30 minutes at 63°C
4. Cool quickly; keep in a cold place.

TO RECONSTITUTE SKIM MILK POWDER

1. Measure the milk powder in these proportions:

350 ml	skim milk powder
to	
1 *l*	water

2. Measure part of the cold water into a clean bottle or plastic container which has a lid.
3. Add the milk powder and shake gently or stir with a long-handled spoon until the milk is dissolved; avoid beating or the use of a blender, which creates foam. Add the remaining water.

4. Cover and refrigerate overnight. *Yield in skim milk: 1 l*

Increasing the quantity of milk powder slightly will give a better flavour; a richer product is obtained by adding 2% or whole milk. Equal quantities of reconstituted skim milk and whole milk will give a product approximately equal to 2% milk.

Recipes, tables, etc. that appear in small capital letters, e.g., PARSLEY BUTTER, CANADA'S FOOD GUIDE, are listed in the index. Consult the index for the number of the page on which the item appears.

TO WHIP SKIM MILK POWDER

125 ml	ice cold water
15 ml	lemon juice
200 ml	skim milk powder
50 ml	sugar
1 ml	vanilla

Combine water, lemon and milk powder in a clean, non-plastic bowl; beat well until mixture stands in firm peaks (5 min). Gradually beat in sugar and vanilla; chill. *Yield:* 750 ml

The addition of 1 envelope of gelatine soaked in a small amount of water dissolved over hot water, and beaten into the foam will stabilize it.

TO WHIP CREAM

Chill a deep bowl, the cream, and the beater. Cream must be 30% butterfat. Beat cream quickly until it thickens and holds its shape; overbeating will break the foam and cause butter to form. To flavour, vanilla and fine sugar may be added when the cream begins to thicken.

TO WHIP EVAPORATED MILK

Pour the milk into a freezer tray and chill until crystals of ice appear at the edges; whip rapidly in a chilled bowl with a chilled beater until the liquid triples in volume; add grated lemon rind for flavour.

TO MELT CHOCOLATE

Melt in a saucepan over *very* low heat. High temperatures spoil the flavour; steam from boiling water causes greyness. The addition of liquid in any form causes the starch in the chocolate to thicken.

Melted chocolate, either semi-sweet or bitter, may be swirled or dribbled over icing or cream filling. When spread thinly on wax paper and allowed to harden in the refrigerator, chocolate may be cut with tiny truffle cutters and lifted onto cake, pie filling or desserts. Spread onto small maple leaves, it may be peeled off when chilled and the chocolate "leaves" used as decoration.

TO MAKE CHOCOLATE CURLS

Let a square of chocolate stand where it will soften slightly. With a sharp vegetable peeler, cut off thin shavings.

EGG WASH

Egg wash is a glaze to brush on pastry or fruit breads. Beat an egg with a little milk or water to thin it; spread thinly over the pastry; sprinkle with salt or sugar.

Egg white beaten with a little water is often used to hold chopped nuts or other cake decorations in place.

TO MAKE BRAZIL NUT CURLS

Drop shelled Brazil nuts into boiling water; let stand 15 minutes. With a sharp vegetable peeler shave thin curls from the length of the nut.

TO TOAST COCONUT

Spread on a pie plate. Stir over low heat or brown under the broiler.

TO TINT COCONUT

Add 2-3 drops food colour to a little water; add coconut, cover and shake.

TO FLAVOUR COCONUT

Add undiluted frozen fruit concentrate; shake.

TO PLUMP RAISINS

Place raisins in a sieve over boiling water and allow the steam to rise through the raisins until they become fat and soft.

TO CARAMELIZE SUGAR

Stir sugar in a heavy pan over high heat until it becomes lumpy and begins to melt to a clear syrup. Reduce heat and push the larger lumps to the centre until lumps melt and syrup is reddish brown.

CARAMEL SYRUP

250 ml	sugar
250 ml	boiling water

In a heavy frying pan stir sugar until it first lumps, then begins to melt into a clear syrup and then into red-brown caramel. Immediately add boiling water, adding it slowly and without stirring. Simmer until

Green peppers, steamed for 5 minutes, then baked with tomato sauce and cooked rice make a flavourful and nourishing dish.

Pickles and condiments are made with fresh vegetables, fruit, herbs and spices, among other ingredients.

clear and the consistency of maple syrup; cool, bottle and refrigerate.

Use this syrup for CARAMEL CUSTARD, CARAMEL SAUCE, CROQUEMBOUCHE.

Seasoning: Spices, Herbs, Condiments, Flavourings

"The proof of the pudding is in the eating." A dish may win honour for its texture, shape, colour and nutritional value, but if it lacks a pleasant flavour, it will be eaten without enjoyment—or perhaps it will not be eaten at all.

Skill in the art of seasoning not only establishes a cook's reputation but enables him or her to serve simple, inexpensive foods with style and unlimited variation.

Spices include the dried buds, seeds, stems and roots of plants, whole or ground. Ground spices should be bought in small quantities, as the volatile oils which provide the flavour begin to disappear when the spice is ground. To retain the flavour they should be kept in a cool, dry place, in containers that are tightly covered after each use.

Used with care, spices enhance flavour; they should never smother it. With foods that require long cooking it is better to add the spices during the last half-hour, as overheating causes many spices to develop a bitter taste.

Add spices to cold foods well in advance of serving, for maximum flavour.

Herbs are derived from the leaves and stems of various plants. They may be used either fresh or dried. Buy or package dried herbs in small containers; once the fragrance has gone, they should be discarded.

One should never be conscious of the presence of specific herbs in a mixture—merely aware of a delightful blend of flavours.

Condiments are sauces of pronounced flavour used as a relish or to stimulate the appetite. KETCHUP and Worcestershire sauce are examples.

Flavourings are usually used in sweet dishes. They include vanilla, maple, peppermint, almond, and lemon.

Although a blend gives a subtler flavour than any one spice or herb used alone, the purchase of several spices or herbs is expensive and if they are not used frequently it will be wasteful. There are several solutions of which the simplest is to buy already blended seasoning: Spaghetti Sauce Mix, Seasoning Salt, A Pinch of Herbs, or similar products. Or you can prepare blends of seasonings that you use often, to save time when you are cooking. Even a mix of salt and pepper in a shaker means one operation instead of two every time food is seasoned at the stove. For the creative cook who likes to experiment, who has an herb garden, or who wishes to restrict the sodium content in the diet by reducing salt and monosodium glutamate, some recipes for spice and herb mixes are given below.

Team up with a group of friends to prepare several mixes. Bottle them in small jars and label with suggestions for use, or package individual quantities in plastic wrap to give away with a special recipe.

HERB BAGS

Prepare squares of cheesecloth, 10 ml
In each place

	5 peppercorns
	1 bay leaf crumbled
2 ml	**thyme**
1 ml	**each of basil and marjoram**

Tie the bags with string; store in an airtight container to use for soups, casseroles or stews.

MEXICAN SPICE MIX

50 ml	**salt**
25 ml	**cumin seed**
5 ml	**pepper**
25 ml	**celery seed**
25 ml	**onion flakes**
	1 bay leaf
10 ml	**oregano**
10 ml	**garlic powder**
25-50 ml	**chili powder to taste**

Crush in a mortar or blender. Use in Mexican recipes, with ground beef, beans or chicken.

CHINESE FIVE-SPICE MIX

25 ml	**peppercorns**
25 ml	**cloves**
25 ml	**fennel seed**
25 ml	**star anise**
25 ml	**stick cinnamon**

Crush in a mortar or blender.

Use sparingly in marinades, in Chinese recipes; in stews; in applesauce for pork or fowl.

INDIAN SPICE MIX

	3 cinnamon sticks
50 ml	cardamom pods
10 ml	cloves
10 ml	cumin seed
10 ml	peppercorns
15 ml	coriander seed

Heat 15 minutes in oven at 100°C

Remove the coating from the cardamom and return the seeds to the mixture; grind or blend.

Add to meat or chicken recipes which contain curry powder.

SEASONED SALT

250 ml	salt
5 ml	dried parsley
5 ml	onion flakes
5 ml	celery seed
2 ml	garlic powder
5 ml	savory
	3-4 dried mushrooms

Crush in a mortar or blender; sift; store in tight containers.

Use to replace salt in meat recipes.

ONION RICE MIX

50 ml	onion flakes
25 ml	beef concentrate
2 ml	garlic salt
1 ml	celery seed
2 ml	salt
5 ml	dried parsley

Combine the ingredients; divide into four plastic packages and store in a glass jar. Label with instructions:

Add 1 package to the cooking water or stock for raw (not instant) rice, per 250 ml

Serve with POT ROAST OF BEEF, MEAT BALLS, stewed tomatoes, MEAT LOAF.

BEEF RICE MIX

50 ml	beef concentrate
5 ml	salt
10 ml	thyme
1 ml	cracked black pepper

Combine the ingredients; divide into four packages; store in airtight jar; label with instructions:

Add 1 package to the water in which to bake or boil raw rice, per 250 ml

Serve with BRAISED BEEF.

CHICKEN RICE MIX

50 ml	chicken concentrate
5 ml	salt
10 ml	dried tarragon
10 ml	chopped chives
1 ml	white pepper
10 ml	dried parsley
2 ml	cracked black pepper
15 ml	grated lemon rind
	4 threads saffron (optional)

Combine the ingredients; divide into four plastic packages; store in a glass jar; label with instructions:

Add 1 package to the cooking water or stock for raw (not instant) rice, per 250 ml

Serve with chicken, VEAL STEW.

SPANISH RICE MIX

10 ml	dried parsley flakes
10 ml	salt
125 ml	dried sweet red pepper flakes
15 ml	onion flakes
7 ml	cracked black pepper
2 ml	saffron (if available)

Combine the ingredients; divide into four plastic packages; store in a glass jar; label with instructions:

Add 1 package to cooking water (or stock) for raw (not instant) rice, per 250 ml

Serve with BEEF STEW or pork chops.

GINGERBREAD SPICE MIX

50 ml	ground cinnamon
30 ml	nutmeg
50 ml	ginger
30 ml	allspice
15 ml	cloves

Combine and stir well; bottle in airtight containers; label with the following information:

To every **500 ml flour**

Add for GINGERBREAD: 10 ml

Add for GINGER COOKIES: 5 ml

Sprinkle Gingerbread Spice on baked squash, applesauce.

CAKE SPICE MIX

50 ml	**ground cinnamon**
20 ml	**cloves**
30 ml	**allspice**
30 ml	**nutmeg** *or* **mace**
5 ml	**cardamom**

Combine and stir well; bottle in airtight containers; label with the following information:

To every **500 ml flour**
Add for SPICE CAKE,
    OATMEAL CAKE: 10-15 ml
Add for HERMITS: 5-10 ml
Add for FRUIT CAKE,
    PLUM PUDDING: 30 ml
Variation: Replace cardamom
    with coriander seed, crushed, 10 ml
    or with anise seed, 30 ml

Herbs

These subtle enhancers of foods impart their characteristic flavour to soups, meats, vegetables, breads and sauces. To the salt-free diet, they are the saving grace. Wash and shake dry fresh herbs and refrigerate in plastic bags. They will keep about 3 weeks. For longer storage, fresh herbs should be frozen or dried.

Freezing Herbs

Wash, drain and chop herbs. Spread on tray and freeze; pack in freezer containers and store in freezer. They will keep 1 year.

Drying Herbs

Use tops and perfect leaves. Wash, drain and spread on cheesecloth on a rack. Cover with cheesecloth and leave for 2 to 3 d in a dry, warm place where there is good air circulation.

A little herb goes a long way. Even when following a specific recipe, start with a small amount and taste to determine if more is needed. Rosemary, oregano, sage and thyme have dominant flavours and are not pleasing to everyone.

Like spices, herbs should be added to roasts and stews during the last half-hour of cooking. Sprinkle

chops and steaks with herbs during broiling, or marinate in salad oil with herbs for several hours before cooking. When using herbs in cold dishes, such as tomato juice, salad dressing, cheese dips, etc., add herbs several hours before serving.

To season a dish for six, use
    fresh herb 5 ml
    dried herb 1 ml

COMMONLY USED HERBS

Anise The seeds of this Mediterranean plant have a delicate licorice flavour. They are sold as "aniseed."

Basil The "tomato herb" is equally good with fish. Chop and mix with cream cheese to stuff celery. Serve with tomato juice. Chop finely to replace lettuce in tomato sandwich. Add to mayonnaise for potato salad. Top tomato slice with butter, Parmesan cheese and chopped basil; broil. Add to omelet or macaroni and cheese.

Bay Leaf The leaf of a Mediterranean laurel, this herb has a strong flavour. Use sparingly in chowder, pickles, stews, boiled beef.

Chervil Similar in flavour to parsley. Chop fresh for fish, combine with cream cheese or cottage cheese, add to cheese soufflé; sprinkle over egg dishes.

Chives The most delicate of the onion family, the tender green spears may be minced and frozen or the plant may be grown indoors. Use to replace onion in many recipes; add minced to cottage cheese, sliced tomato, potato salad, or French dressing. Combine with scrambled egg, creamed or devilled egg; sprinkle over buttered new potatoes.

Cumin The aromatic seeds of a plant that was prized in Biblical times. Its pleasant lemon flavour contributes to the characteristic taste of Mexican cooking. Add to tomato recipes or refried beans; to sour cream or yogurt for cucumber dressing.

Dill does not dry or freeze well. Sprinkle shredded leaves in new potatoes or salads, in sour cream or yogurt for cucumber dressing. The flower head gives the flavour to dill pickles. Add dill seed to fish sauce, to cottage or cream cheese.

Recipes, tables, etc. that appear in small capital letters, e.g., PARSLEY BUTTER, CANADA'S FOOD GUIDE, are listed in the index. Consult the index for the number of the page on which the item appears.

Fennel The "fish herb," fennel resembles celery. All parts are edible. Use fresh leaves in salad, slice the stalk to replace celery or boil as a vegetable. Heat seeds in sauerkraut, add to crumb topping for fish casserole; stir into applesauce to accompany sausage or pork chops.

Marjoram, "the herb of a thousand uses," is the seasoning of bologna, liverwurst, Polish sausage. Add it to recipes for dried beans; add to meat, fish and eggs; add a pinch to the cooking water for vegetables. Grow it with sage, tarragon and English thyme for a kitchen garden.

Mint See Spearmint.

Oregano, the "pizza spice," also called Mexican sage, is similar in flavour to marjoram. Use sparingly in tomato sauce, for Mexican dishes, spaghetti, or pizza. Basil and oregano are a good combination.

Parsley Too often used only as a garnish, this herb is a worthwhile source of vitamins C and A, iron and iodine. Mince in egg dishes, add to butter for vegetables, to bread for dressing, to fish cakes, to dumplings for chicken stew, to tea biscuit crust for meat pies, to mashed potatoes.

Rosemary Sprinkle over hot coals when barbecuing meat. Use sparingly with lamb, add a few crushed needles to orange slices or to biscuits. Grows well in a pot if kept moist.

Saffron The world's most expensive spice comes from the 3 stigma of a crocus flower which grows near the Mediterranean. To make 1 kg of saffron, 175 000 blossoms are needed. After the Crusades, saffron was grown in England in Saffron Walden; the saffron bread, cakes and buns of Cornwall became famous. It is packaged in threads in small glass vials. Crush between sheets of plastic film. Braise with food in Spanish-style chicken dishes; add a pinch to flour for bread or cookies; add to butter for spreading on French bread.

Savory Summer savory is sweet and delicate; winter savory grows well indoors. Savory is known as the "bean herb." Add to bean or pea soup, to butter for green beens. Substitute for sage in dressing for poultry.

Sesame Seed Substitute toasted sesame seeds in any recipe that calls for chopped nuts. Add to flour for dumplings or pastry, to bread crumbs for poultry dressing; prepare HERB TOAST. To toast: shake in a pie plate over low heat until golden.

Mixed Pickling Spice contains ginger root, hot chili pepper, bay leaf and coriander. Available during the pickling season, it is a convenient source of spices infrequently used.

Spearmint is the "lamb" mint. It is easy to grow in a pot. Heat a few sprigs in lamb stew, pea soup, or green peas just before serving. Float a few sprigs in FRUIT CUP or fruit drinks. Chop finely and add to butter for green peas or to orange and onion salad.

Tarragon is one of the few kitchen herbs that do not dry well. It is easily grown in a kitchen garden and may be preserved in vinegar. Use the vinegar or the chopped leaves for BÉARNAISE or HOLLANDAISE SAUCE, add to marinades, tomato juice or aspic. Chop fresh leaves into salads, sour cream or fruit salad dressing. Use sparingly.

Thyme grows well in rock gardens. It is better dried than frozen. Use sparingly as an ingredient in Creole recipes—gumbos and JAMBALAYA—and in the ragouts of France. Add to tomato sauce, fish loaf, clam chowder, dressing for roast pork, creamed onions.

Turmeric A root from Jamaica which, when ground, is used for both colouring and flavour. It is a major ingredient in prepared mustard and curry. Sprinkle on noodles, rice, white sauce, and salad dressing, to add rich colour.

FINES HERBES

To make fines herbes (pronounced feen zerb) chop together equal quantities of chervil, tarragon, chives and parsley. Add to soups, sauces, egg dishes and cheese dishes just before serving.

BOUQUET GARNI

Tie together with string, leaving an end of string long enough to hang out of the saucepan:

> **3 sprigs parsley**
> **3 sprigs chervil**
> **10-12 spears chives**
> **1 piece tarragon *or* marjoram**

or

place inside overlapping celery stalks and tie:

> **3-4 sprigs parsley *or* chervil**
> **1 small bay leaf**
> **2 sprigs thyme (lemon thyme if available)**
> **1 leek (white portion) *or* 2-3 green onions.**

Simmer this classic seasoner in soups, stews, gravies, meat stocks and casseroles. Remove when the flavour is strong enough.

Flavoured Vinegars

Flavoured vinegars are easily prepared. Use in FRENCH DRESSING, GREEN BEANS VINAIGRETTE: add to the cooking water for fish; substitute for plain vinegar in aspics, marinades and appetizers.

SPICED VINEGAR

250 ml	white vinegar
15 ml	Mixed Pickling Spice
	2 blades mace
	1 stick cinnamon
	1 piece ginger root

Combine in a stainless steel or Pyrex saucepan; cover and bring to a boil; let stand 2 h; strain into sterilized bottles; cover.

Use Spiced Vinegar to prepare DARK MUSTARD SAUCE. Bottle in small jars for attractive gifts.

Variation
Sweet Spiced Vinegar—Use the vinegar from sweet mixed pickles
or dissolve sugar 50 ml
in an equal amount of water.
Add to Spiced Vinegar.

GARLIC VINEGAR

250 ml	wine vinegar
	1 small clove garlic
	1 bay leaf
2 ml	cracked black pepper

1. Peel garlic; mash in a glass jar; add pepper and bay leaf.
2. Add boiling vinegar; seal the jar, let stand 2 d.
3. Shake well; let stand another 2 d; strain into sterilized bottles; cover.

HERB VINEGAR

250 ml	wine vinegar
250 ml	chopped, fresh tarragon *or* basil
or	
50 ml	dried crushed tarragon or basil

1. Place herbs in a clean, hot container; add boiling vinegar; seal and let stand 2 weeks.
2. Strain, bring to a boil, pour into sterilized bottles; cover.

SWEET VINEGAR

500 ml	white vinegar
125 ml	water
350 ml	sugar

1. Combine sugar, vinegar and water; heat until sugar dissolves.
2. Pour into hot sterilized bottle; cover.

Salt in Cooking

To reduce dietary intake of salt, exact quantities are not always specified in recipes so that one may adjust the quantity to the lowest level possible for good taste and good health. The following proportions serve as a guide:

Amount of Salt	Type of Food	Quantity of Food
5 ml	water in rice, vegetables, pasta	1 ℓ
1 ml	meat	500 g
1 ml	cream sauce	500 ml
1 ml-2 ml	flour in cakes	250 ml
1 ml or less	flour in cookies	250 ml
1 ml or less	milk in tapioca, custard, or cornstarch dessert	500 ml

Flavourings

Vanilla, maple, peppermint, almond and lemon flavourings are available as true essences and as artificial extracts. True essences are usually alcoholic extracts and pure oils; artificial extracts are often synthetic, but are sometimes diluted versions of the original flavourings. Because true flavourings are stronger than artificial flavourings, less of them is required; 2 or 3 drops of oil of peppermint equals many drops of peppermint flavouring.

FLAVOURED SUGARS

Prepare Flavoured Sugars and keep on hand for instant use.

ANISE SUGAR

250 ml	sugar
15 ml	aniseed, crushed

Mix. Serve with melons, berries; sprinkle on unbaked cookies; add to applesauce.

CINNAMON SUGAR

250 ml	sugar
25 ml	cinnamon

Mix. Sprinkle on toast or coffee cake.

MEXICAN SUGAR

250 ml	sugar
15 ml	cinnamon
15 ml	cocoa

Mix. Sprinkle on warm custard or rice pudding.

SPICE SUGAR

250 ml	sugar
10 ml	cinnamon
2 ml	nutmeg
2 ml	cloves and allspice

Mix. Sprinkle on unbaked cookies, icings, apple pie or peach desserts.

ORANGE SUGAR

250 ml	sugar
50 ml	orange juice and rind

Mix. Spread thinly on hot buttered toast, warm cake; add to tea or eggnog.

VANILLA SUGAR

250 ml	icing or granulated sugar
	2 vanilla beans, split lengthwise

Mix; cover tightly and leave 1 month; remove beans. Sprinkle on berries; use in sponge or pound cake; shake with warm shortbread cookies in a paper bag. The beans may be cut up and soaked in the milk to be used for a pudding.

If, in preparing a recipe, too much flavouring is added, make a second recipe with no flavouring and combine the two quantities.

3 Appetizers

Appetizers are meant to stimulate, not satisfy, the appetite and should be chosen to complement other items on the menu. Use them to compensate for nutritional weak spots in the meal. Appetizers may be passed around before a meal or served at the table as a first course preceding or replacing soup.

Set in a bowl of crushed ice, the simplest cocktail becomes special.

Vegetable Cocktails

TOMATO COCKTAIL

	6 medium tomatoes *or*
796 ml	1 can tomatoes
60 ml	chopped green pepper
125 ml	chopped celery, green onions *or*
	chives and parsley
5 ml	prepared horseradish
	salt and pepper

1. Wash, peel, and dice the tomatoes; if using canned tomatoes, make sure they are firm and drained. Add the other ingredients.
2. Chill several hours to blend the flavours; serve over small chunks of lettuce in sherbet glasses or small tumblers. *Serves 6.*

   This cocktail provides an economical base for expensive ingredients such as shrimp.

TOMATO VEGETABLE JUICE

Season tomato juice with lemon juice, Worcestershire sauce, and fresh herbs; chill.
Tomato Madrilene: Combine seasoned juice with an equal amount of consommé.
Tomato Frappé: Freeze seasoned tomato juice to a mush or freeze in the ice cube tray; empty the frozen cubes into a plastic bag and crush with a hammer; serve in juice glasses with a little chilled juice added. Garnish with sour cream and a sprinkle of chopped fresh herbs. Serve with a spoon.

Fruit Cocktails

Cranberry, orange, apple, or any combination of juices may be served spiced and hot on cold days or cold or frappéd in hot weather; frozen unsweetened juice cubes may be added to carbonated beverages.

APRICOT ORANGE COCKTAIL

500 ml	ORANGE SHERBET
284 ml	1 can apricot nectar

In each sherbet glass place a scoop of sherbet; pour over it the refrigerated nectar; serve at once. *Serves 6.*
   Bottled green grape juice over lemon sherbet, pineapple juice over lime sherbet are other pleasing combinations.

AVOCADO COCKTAILS

Serve avocado halves brushed with lemon juice or FRENCH DRESSING.
Fill the centre with orange or grapefruit sections; add FRENCH DRESSING and drape cooked cleaned shrimp around it. Serve with a fork.
Mix cubed avocado with FRENCH DRESSING and a combination of celery, green pepper, chopped fresh tomato, seafood, or chicken or lobster salad; serve in the avocado shell or on lettuce in sherbet or cocktail glasses.

MELON COCKTAIL

Scoop balls from canteloupe, honeydew melon, Persian melon, or watermelon. Pile in sherbet glasses; garnish with a sprig of mint. Serve plain or with grapefruit juice, green grape juice, or lemon sherbet. Serve melon quarters with a lemon wedge; sprinkle with fine sugar and ginger, and drape paper-thin slices of cooked ham across the wedge.

Seafood

SEAFOOD COCKTAIL

Combine any of: shrimp, crab, lobster, salmon, tuna, cooked white fish.
1. Drain and flake the seafood. For quantities see TABLE OF MEASURES; for information on choosing and preparing, see PREPARATION OF FISH. Spoon over small pieces of lettuce in cocktail glasses.
2. Top with sauce; refrigerate until serving time. Serve with cocktail or salad forks.

COCKTAIL SAUCE

50 ml	CHILI SAUCE
200 ml	KETCHUP
30 ml	prepared horseradish
2 ml	Worcestershire sauce
30 ml	lemon juice
2 ml	salt

Combine the ingredients; spoon over the seafood.

This sauce keeps well; it may be added to MAYONNAISE for a milder sauce or for a quick Russian salad dressing.

For a less expensive Seafood Cocktail see TOMATO COCKTAIL.

SEAFOOD SCALLOP

LOBSTER THERMIDOR and COQUILLE ST. JACQUES may be served in scallop shells or individual ramekins as an appetizer. Most casserole dishes also, if served in small amounts and highly seasoned, may be used as appetizers. This is a good way to use small quantities of leftover creamed dishes. Extra amounts may be prepared and frozen for this purpose. Transfer the cooked mixture to shells, ramekins, or individual tart tins. Wrap in foil or plastic film, and freeze. To free containers for other uses, remove mixtures from the containers when frozen, and rewrap; package in a carton. To serve, replace in the original container, sprinkle with buttered crumbs; heat in oven at 200°C

CEVICHE

500 g	scallops
	8-10 limes *or* bottled unsweetened juice sufficient to cover scallops
2 ml	1 clove garlic, minced
5 ml	dried chili flakes
	2 minced green peppers
	salt; pepper; a sprinkle of sugar;
	fresh basil *or* cilantro, chopped
	1 small onion *or* bunch of green onions, chopped
30 ml	salad oil

1. Cut the scallops to the size of the smallest. (See PREPARATION OF FISH.). Put into a small, deep bowl; add salt.
2. Reserve 2 limes to slice for garnish. Grate the rind from one of the remainder before squeezing them; pour juice over scallops; cover and refrigerate at least 6 h or overnight, turning occasionally.
3. Combine the remaining ingredients; taste for seasoning.
4. Lift the scallops from the lime juice into the seasoned mixture; toss lightly and refrigerate until serving time.
5. Serve in scallop shells, saki cups, or demitasse cups with a wedge of lime. Use forks. *Serves 10-12.*

Since the acid in the lime juice "cooks" the protein of the scallops, they must be covered by the juice.

Fillets of any firm whitefish may be used to replace or extend the scallops. Haddock is a good choice. In Mexico the dolphin is used.

As an hors d'oeuvre at a cocktail party, Ceviche is served with cocktail picks. The above recipe will serve 12-15.

"Ceviche" is possibly derived from the Spanish term for pickling or "caveaching" fish in spices, oil and vinegar in the days before refrigeration.

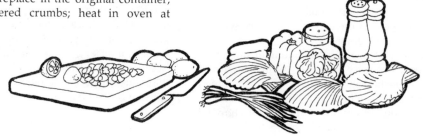

Antipasto

This Italian appetizer plate, literally "before the pasta" is well suited to today's life style, as it can be prepared well ahead of serving time, covered with plastic film, and refrigerated. Select an assortment from at least four of the groups below, balancing the simple and the elaborate, the expensive and the economical.

Cold Meats: salami, mortadella, ham, prosciutto, tongue

Seafood: sardines, anchovies, tuna, scampi

Digby Chicks from the Maritimes may replace anchovies. Cut these pungent, very salty strips of smoked herring into small pieces.

Scampi are large prawns found in the Adriatic. Jumbo shrimps are often served under this name except in Britain, where the term is restricted to Dublin Bay prawns.

Vegetables: cherry tomatoes, celery, fennel root, cilantro, marinated green pepper, mushrooms, zucchini, eggplant, pickled cauliflower, cucumber

Salad: green bean, macaroni, chick pea, cabbage

Cheese: Ricotta, Mozzarella, Bel Paese

Eggs: stuffed, devilled, pickled

Arrange small quantities of the foods attractively on salad plates; serve with FRENCH DRESSING; garnish with sour pickles.

Antipasto makes it easy to cope with a dietary problem. Avoid spiced meats for low-salt diets; choose skim milk cheese and vegetables for low-fat diets; substitute this course for dessert to restrict energy; include devilled egg and liver paste to increase the iron content.

Sweetbreads

Prepare Sweetbreads (see TO PARBOIL SWEETBREADS). Serve small bits from a chafing dish with picks, larger pieces on thin slices of French bread or threaded onto skewers before broiling; sprinkle lightly with freshly ground black pepper.

Recipes, tables, etc. that appear in small capital letters, e.g., PARSLEY BUTTER, CANADA'S FOOD GUIDE, are listed in the index. Consult the index for the number of the page on which the item appears.

Hors d'Oeuvres

Hors d'oeuvres, highly flavoured, colourful foods designed to be eaten with the fingers, are served as a prelude to refreshments at a cocktail party, with beverages before dinner in the living room or to replace more elaborate food in the evening.

The term, pronounced "or derv" means literally "outside the work" which is how the chef regarded these small extras.

FRUIT HORS D'OEUVRES

On a deep platter of crushed ice, serve, speared on toothpicks, pineapple chunks, balls of watermelon, cantaloupe, honeydew melon sprinkled with lime or lemon juice; fresh strawberries, avocado pieces, cherries, mandarin orange sections. Spear separately or combine 2 different fruits on one toothpick.

APPLE WEDGES

Choose red apples; cut into quarters; remove only the core, slice into thin wedges. Drop into lemon, orange or grapefruit juice to prevent discolouring; drain.

VEGETABLE HORS D'OEUVRES

Fill a large glass bowl or platter with small lettuce leaves, cherry tomatoes, small radishes, sprigs of watercress and parsley, sticks of carrot, celery, turnip, slices of cucumber, zucchini, small flowerets of cauliflower, green onions, stalks of Belgian endive, straws cut from the core of green cabbage.

Cover the bowl with a damp tea towel and refrigerate until serving time. Serve with FRENCH DRESSING or GOLDEN DIP.

GOLDEN DIP FOR VEGETABLES

250 ml	MAYONNAISE
20 ml	curry powder
5 ml	lemon juice
5 ml	Worcestershire sauce
2 ml	celery salt
	few grains cayenne

Stir all ingredients together. Serve in a bowl, surrounded by raw vegetables for dipping.

Serve raw vegetables with a sour cream dip, for a nutritious appetizer. The Borden Company.

MARINATED RAW VEGETABLES

Combine paper-thin slices (use a vegetable peeler) of potato, large carrots, and onions (rings), strips of red and green sweet peppers and enough oil-vinegar MARINADE to cover; marinate in the refrigerator, overnight or for several hours. Drain and serve as an appetizer or with cold meats.

CARROT STRAWS

Cut tender, cleaned carrots into lengthwise slices, cut each slice again into narrow strips; sprinkle with minced parsley, cover with a damp towel and chill. (Turnip, cucumber, kohlrabi, fennel or the midrib of Chinese lettuce may be used in the same way.)

STUFFED CELERY

1. Separate a bunch of celery by cutting the root end with a sharp knife. Save the coarse outside stalks and leaves for soup stock. Clean with a brush.
2. Soak in ice water until crisp; cut into short pieces; towel dry.
3. Cream yellow, white or blue cheese with a little mayonnaise and fill the celery pieces using a small flexible knife or pastry tube.
4. Wipe off surplus cheese with a damp cloth; cover with a damp towel and refrigerate until serving time.

CAULIFLOWER BUDS

Separate raw cauliflower into small flowerets; chill.

CELERY PINWHEELS

1. Choose a small celery heart. Remove each stalk and place in order in a shallow pan of ice water until crisp; dry on a towel, retaining the correct order.
2. Cream yellow cheese; beginning with the inside piece, stuff the celery. As each piece is filled, press it firmly onto the one before and so build up the heart again. Fasten if necessary with elastic bands; chill; slice into pinwheels.

MUSHROOMS

Marinated: Shake any well flavoured French dressing to blend; pour over mushrooms which have been washed, dried and quartered; chill several hours, tossing gently occasionally; drain, sprinkle with minced fresh herbs.

Stuffed: Choose small white mushrooms; wash and dry; remove stems; fill the cap with any cheese spread. Drop the stems into a plastic bag; freeze for later use in soups, or supper dishes, or chop and sauté before freezing.

Meat Hors d'Oeuvres

Arrange a tray of Polish sausage, ham, bologna, tongue or spiced beef. Slice, cube, or roll the meat. Slices may be stacked with a cheese spread in the layers. Cut into wedges to serve.

It is more economical to buy sausage in the piece. Slit the casing and peel it off; then slice thinly.

Alternate meat, cubed, with small pickled onions, pineapple cubes, marinated green peppers, on short skewers.

Hot Hors d'Oeuvres

ROLL UPS

Curried Banana Bacon Roll Ups—Cut bananas in pieces the width of a strip of bacon; roll in curry powder; sprinkle with lemon juice. Wrap a slice of bacon around the banana; cut off the excess with scissors and fasten the ends with a wooden toothpick. Bake on oven rack over a pan to catch the fat, at 160°C
When the bacon is almost cooked, dip the banana in chutney and return it to the oven for a few minutes.
Water Chestnut Roll Ups—Drain off the liquid from canned water chestnuts and slice them into two or three pieces. Sauté chicken livers and cut into bite-size pieces. Cut bacon strips in half. Place a piece of liver on a piece of water chestnut; wrap the bacon around and fasten with a toothpick or string on a skewer; broil until the bacon is crisp.
Japanese Roll Ups—Cut uncooked chicken livers in half and marinate for several hours in CHINESE MARINADE. Follow the directions for Water Chestnut Roll Ups.

Pitted olives, stuffed or plain; pitted prunes stuffed with broiled chicken livers make good roll ups. Serve dry or with CHINESE PLUM SAUCE.

PIGS IN BLANKETS

	1 recipe PASTRY
375 g	sausage

1. Preheat oven to 220°C
2. Cook cocktail sausage or small pork sausage; larger ones may be cut in three. Drain; cool.
3. Cut rolled pastry into squares and wrap each sausage; pinch edges together; bake until beginning to brown (10 min).
4. Serve hot with heated prepared mustard. *Makes 30.*

Variation
Simmer cocktail weiners 5 minutes in water to cover; drain. Split halfway through lengthwise, insert a piece of cheese; finish as above beginning at step 3.

EGG ROLLS

1. Prepare Filling:

250 g	cooked lean pork
	1 large onion
250 g	fresh mushrooms
250 g	cooked shrimp
500 ml	bean sprouts
10 ml	salad oil
10 ml	sesame seeds

Grind or chop finely pork, onion and mushroom; chop shrimp into little chunks; chop bean sprouts (drained if canned).

Heat oil in a saucepan, pour in sesame seeds and cook until brown and toasted; add other ingredients.

2. Prepare Wrappers:

375 ml	all-purpose flour
	6 eggs
7 ml	salt
550 ml	water
	salad oil for deep frying

Beat eggs until light; add flour and salt and beat until smooth; stir in water to make a thin batter.

Heat oil to just cover the bottom of a small frying pan; spoon in batter, enough to cover entire bottom when pan is tilted.

Fry over low heat until the edges begin to curl away from skillet. Fry one side only, then lift from pan and store on a tray until all the batter is used.
3. On the fried side of the wrapper put a large spoonful of the filling; fold in 2 ends of wrapper. Brush edges with remaining batter to seal, then roll up other 2 edges to form a package.
4. Heat oil until a cube of bread turns brown in one minute and fry egg rolls until golden brown; reheat in oven before serving. Serve with HOT MUSTARD SAUCE. *Yield:* 30 rolls.

Recipes, tables, etc. that appear in small capital letters, e.g., PARSLEY BUTTER, CANADA'S FOOD GUIDE, are listed in the index. Consult the index for the number of the page on which the item appears.

TARTS

Arrange tiny tart shells around a chafing dish of creamed food (chicken, seafood, sweetbreads). Or fill unbaked tiny tart shells with either of the fillings which follow. Cover with a circle of pastry. Bake or freeze until needed.

TURNOVERS

Roll pastry; cut into circles; cover half of each circle with cheese spread, chutney or one of the fillings which follow. Fold the unspread half over the filling; press the edges together with a fork, cut a slit to allow the steam to escape. Bake or freeze until needed.

Frozen patty shells thawed and cut into halves may be rolled or patted thin to make circles for turnovers or to line small tart tins.

CHICKEN LIVER FILLING

125 g	bacon
50 ml	chopped onions
500 g	chicken livers
50 ml	fat
	seasoning
	KETCHUP

1. Fry the bacon; drain; sauté the onions in the fat; lift out.
2. Sauté the livers; chop finely; season; combine with onions and bacon; moisten with liquid. Fills 48 small tarts or turnovers.

MUSHROOM FILLING

50 ml	fat
30 ml	minced onion
500 g	chopped mushrooms
	seasoning
15 ml	CHILI SAUCE, wine vinegar, lemon juice

1. Sauté onions in hot fat; lift out; sauté mushrooms; return onions.
2. Season; add liquid; simmer until the juice is absorbed. Fills 48 small tarts or turnovers.

BOUCHÉES

Prepare CREAM PUFF PASTRY dough. Sharpen the flavour by adding meat or chicken concentrate to the water or add to the dough a small quantity of minced chicken, chopped nuts or grated hard cheese (Parmesan). Bake.

Fill the puffs with hot creamed chicken or seafood; chicken or shrimp salad; paté or cheese spread.

TEA BISCUITS

Tiny baked tea biscuits, split, make easy appetizers; serve with FLAVOURED BUTTER.

Bambinos: Roll TEA BISCUIT dough thinly; cut into small circles and cover with PIZZA filling; bake.

FRITTERS

CROQUETTES and FRITTERS make good appetizers if the mixture is shaped into bite-size pieces. For small groups a fondue pot allows guests to fry their own.

MEAT BALLS

When MEAT BALLS or FISH BALLS are being made, if a few small balls are cooked and frozen a popular appetizer is ready for easy entertaining. To serve, reheat balls dry in a chafing dish, shaking gently, or heat in sauce using just enough to glaze the balls. Provide cocktail picks.

Turkey Meat Balls—replace the meat in SWEDISH MEAT BALLS with ground turkey; for flavour, add a little of the stuffing and well-drained CRANBERRY RELISH.

Salmon Balls—prepare the mixture as for FISH LOAF; shape into small balls, roll in dry crumbs; fry in deep fat or finish as FISH PATTIES.

Seafood Balls—Cooked shrimp, lobster, crabmeat, alone or combined with cooked fish fillets for economy, mixed with finely chopped green pepper and mayonnaise for flavour, may be prepared as FISH BALLS.

Recipes, tables, etc. that appear in small capital letters, e.g., PARSLEY BUTTER, CANADA'S FOOD GUIDE, are listed in the index. Consult the index for the number of the page on which the item appears.

CHINESE MEAT BALLS

540 ml	1 can water chestnuts
	1 bunch green onions
1 kg	lean ground pork
	1 egg
15 ml	soy sauce
	seasoning (salt, pepper, dry ginger)
250 ml	dry crumbs
	cornstarch
	oil

1. Drain and chop water chestnuts; chop onions; combine with the meat.
2. Beat the egg; add soy sauce and seasoning; add to meat.
3. Add crumbs; mix well using the hands; shape into small balls; drop into thé cornstarch spread on a shallow pan; roll to coat well.
4. Fry in deep fat (see DEEP FAT FRYING). Freeze until needed or heat in CHINESE PLUM SAUCE using just enough to glaze the balls.

BROILED MEAT CUBES

500 g	30 meat cubes
	MARINADE
	salt, pepper

1. Cut meat into cubes, 2 cm
2. Marinate cubes for 2 h; drain and dry on paper towels; sprinkle with seasoning.
3. Broil in a single layer in a shallow pan, turning once and draining off the fat if necessary. The surface should be brown and crisp and the inside pink for beef, just cooked for lamb, well done for pork and chicken.
4. Serve dry with cocktail picks.

Suitable meat would be flank, top round or sirloin beef; leg slices of lamb; tenderloin, steak or lean shoulder pork; breast of chicken.

Variations

If the meat is tender, the marinade may be omitted. Brush the cubes with oil. Finish according to the basic recipe.

Fondue—Cook cubes in deep fat as BEEF, LAMB, or CHICKEN FONDUE.

Kabobs—On short skewers alternate marinated seasoned cubes with squares of green pepper, cubes of pineapple; brush with oil; sprinkle with seasoning; broil.

A cookie cutter makes interesting bread shapes. Spread with cheese and garnish with slices of pickle or olives or sprigs of parsley. Holland Cheese Exporters Association.

Canapés

Canapés consist of a base, a spread, and a garnish. They are served as an accompaniment to cocktails or as an appetizer.

Base Although fried bread was the original base, today we choose from rye or pumpernickel bread, sliced crusty rolls, baked pastry circles, split tea biscuits, refrigerated CRESCENT ROLL dough flattened and shaped, thin slices of crisp raw vegetables, slices of apples cored but unpared and dipped in a little ice water to which lemon juice has been added, commercial biscuits or canapé bases.

Spreads Consult the index under FLAVOURED BUTTERS, SANDWICHES and PIZZA, to find spreads and filling recipes which may all be used for canapé spreads. In this chapter are recipes for patés, mushroom spreads and cheese spreads.

Garnishes Slivers of lemon, orange or lime peel, of red or green sweet peppers, of unpeeled red apples; wafers of radish, cherry tomatoes, stuffed olives, celery; slices of cucumber, hard-cooked egg; rings of green onions; minced parsley, chives, celery leaves, fresh herbs; tiny cleaned shrimp, bits of lobster; flakes of salmon, crabmeat, drained sardine, smoked oyster, anchovy, Digby Chick; strips of chicken; circles of cooked sausage, pepperoni; sieved hard-cooked egg yolk; pickles cut in circles or fans; tiny wedges of pineapple; snips of dried apricot, prunes, preserved ginger; sliced or chopped nuts.

Canapés can also be glazed (see SMØRREBRØD GLAZE.)

Dips

Dips, which may be made from recipes for spreads or sandwich fillings, should be thinner than spreads, thin enough to be scooped out of the serving dish with a biscuit, a piece of melba toast, a short piece of bread stick or a piece of vegetable.

CHEESE DIP

Increase the sour cream in CHEESE SPREAD (BASIC RECIPE) until the mixture is soft enough to scoop out but will not drip off the "dipper".

HOT CHEESE DIP

250 g	sharp Cheddar cheese, grated
25 ml	water
75 ml	TOMMY'S RELISH

Melt the cheese in a chafing dish, or in a serving bowl over hot water; add the remaining ingredients. Serve with short bread sticks. *Serves 6.*

PARTY GOUDA DIP

	1 baby Gouda cheese
125 ml	sour cream
125 ml	CHILI SAUCE
250 g	butter *or* margarine
30 ml	chopped chives

1. Cut a circle from the top of the cheese; scoop out the cheese with a sharp spoon, leaving a thin shell.
2. Combine all ingredients except chives; blend or beat until smooth; stir in chives.
3. Refill the shell; serve with raw vegetables or biscuits. *Serves 6.*

BEAN DIP

398 ml	1 can beans in tomato sauce
	crumbled, crisp bacon
	seasoning (garlic, Tabasco, CHILI SAUCE)

1. Drain beans, saving the liquid for soup.
2. Mash or blend beans to a smooth mixture; season.
3. Add enough of the reserved sauce to give the desired consistency; sprinkle with bacon.

Peanut butter, either crunchy or plain, or toasted sesame seeds or pumpkin seeds add flavour and texture interest. The complementary effect makes this an excellent high protein food (see PROTEINS).

CHICK PEA DIP

540 ml	1 can chick peas
	2 cloves garlic, crushed
50 ml	lemon juice
50 ml	sesame seed paste
125 ml	SALAD DRESSING
	seasoning

Purée drained peas with garlic and lemon juice; add drained sesame seed paste and salad dressing to give a creamy consistency; season to taste.

Sesame seed paste, also known as sesame butter, tahina, or tachina, may be found in oriental shops or health food stores.

Pâté

True pâté de foie gras is a paste of liver from specially fatted geese. Mock pâté is quickly made from liver sausage. Slit and remove the casing. Cream the sausage to spreading consistency with soft butter, chicken fat, sour cream or mayonnaise. Flavour to taste with salt and pepper.

Chicken Liver Pâté is almost as easy. Use chicken livers, cooked with other giblets in preparing chicken soup or sauté uncooked livers in butter or chicken fat. Mash or blend; remove any coarse fibre. Cream to a spreading consistency with soft butter. Add onion juice, garlic or herbs as desired, but do not obscure the delicate flavour of the chicken liver. The liver from one fowl will make one or two servings.

PÂTÉ SLICES

Cut the ends off narrow French rolls; with a fork carefully remove the crumbs. Fill the roll tightly with pâté; chill; cut in thin slices with a sharp knife.

MUSHROOM SPREAD

Wash, dry and slice large mushrooms into a heavy frying pan; add seasoning and cream to cover.

Heat over high heat until cream bubbles; reduce the heat and simmer until the mixture thickens and browns. Serve hot from a chafing dish.

SPANISH MUSHROOMS

500 g	mushrooms
30 ml	oil
15 ml	lemon juice
	1 garlic clove, minced
	1 small onion, sliced
250 ml	canned tomatoes
75 ml	wine vinegar
	1 or 2 drops Tabasco
	salt
	chopped parsley

1. Wash, dry and slice mushrooms; in a heavy saucepan heat the oil; sauté the mushrooms a few at a time until golden; remove to a bowl and toss with the lemon juice.
2. Sauté the onions and garlic, adding a little more oil if necessary; add tomatoes, vinegar and seasoning.
3. Simmer until thick (20 min); pour over the mushrooms; cover and chill several hours or overnight.
4. Drain in a sieve; lift the mushrooms into a serving bowl; sprinkle with parsley; serve on buttered dark rye triangles. *Serves 8-10.*

The liquid, blended with cucumber and green pepper, will form the base for GAZPACHO or, added to tomato juice, may be set with gelatine for an appetizing aspic.

Recipes, tables, etc. that appear in small capital letters, e.g., PARSLEY BUTTER, CANADA'S FOOD GUIDE, are listed in the index. Consult the index for the number of the page on which the item appears.

CHEESE SPREAD
(CHEESE BALLS, CHEESE LOG)

250 g	white cream cheese
250 g	blue cheese
125 g	sour cream
30 ml	minced chives
	minced parsley

1. Have the cheese at room temperature; cream with sour cream until light and fluffy; mix in the chives.
2. Pile the mixture into a serving bowl; sprinkle with parsley. Or shape the mixture into a log, a ball, or tiny balls; refrigerate. Or pack into paper cups, smooth the surface and chill several hours; cut the edge and peel off the cup, inverting the mould onto the serving plate. Remove from the refrigerator half an hour before serving and roll in parsley.

Variations

For a low-fat, low-cholesterol base, beat dry cottage cheese, skim milk cheese and buttermilk together.

For normal diet, vary the flavour by substituting ingredients suggested below, alone or in combination.

Replace blue cheese with:

nippy Cheddar,
grated Gouda
Camembert
cottage cheese
Gruyère
nippy processed
  cheese
Imperial cheese

Replace parsley with:

fresh herbs
watercress
chopped nuts
salted peanuts
walnuts
toasted almonds
pumpkin seeds
toasted sesame seeds
flaked coconut
  moistened with
  undiluted frozen
  orange juice
paprika

Replace sour cream with:

mayonnaise
chili sauce
yogurt

Replace chives with:

onion juice
fresh herbs
mashed garlic
lemon juice
Worcestershire sauce
curry powder
prepared mustard
chopped pickles
cranberry sauce
chopped celery
crumbled bacon
shredded ham
mashed shrimp
lobster
drained tuna
sardine

Cheese Pastries

Basic Recipe
CHEESE SHORTBREAD

125 ml	butter *or* margarine
500 ml	Parmesan cheese, grated
1 ml	salt
2 ml	baking powder
250 ml	all-purpose whole wheat flour

1. Cream fat and cheese; add dry ingredients; mix together; chill.
2. Turn onto a floured board; knead a few times to form a smooth ball.
3. Roll into a thin sheet; cut with a cookie cutter; bake until beginning to brown (15 min) at 180°C
Yield: 36.

Processed cheese, sharp Cheddar, blue cheese or a combination of cheeses may be used to replace the Parmesan. This is one way to use up ends of cheese.

Variations
Bars—Shape the dough into two bars; wrap and refrigerate; slice thin and bake.
Pistachio Stars—Cut dough with a star-shaped cutter; brush with egg white beaten with a little cold water; sprinkle with chopped pistachio nuts; bake.
Cheese Dainties—Put two rounds together with a little RED PEPPER JELLY, ORANGE MARMALADE, or GREEN TOMATO MARMALADE between. Press the edges together with the tines of a fork. Bake.
Cheese Olives—Drain and dry large stuffed olives; flatten a little ball of dough to fit around each olive, covering it completely. Bake.
Pâté Pinwheels—Spread a thin sheet of dough with a canned pâté (liver, ham, chicken); sprinkle with crushed salted peanuts; roll up in a jelly-roll fashion; chill; slice; bake.
Onion Cheese Squares—Replace the salt in the recipe with twice the amount of crushed onion soup mix; roll into balls; press flat on a baking sheet with a fork; bake.
Cereal Crisps—Reduce the flour, replacing it with twice the amount of crushed crisp cereal or GRANOLA; shape into balls on an ungreased sheet; press flat with a fork; bake.

This shortbread-type pastry is easy to make and uses few ingredients. The many variations keep well either refrigerated or frozen. Serve these shortbreads to replace canapés.

CHEESE STRAWS

Roll frozen puff pastry into a thin sheet; spread one half thickly with grated sharp Cheddar cheese. Fold the second half over the cheese and press together. Brush the surface with milk or EGG WASH; sprinkle thinly with cheese. Cut into strips 2 × 15 cm Place on a greased baking sheet allowing room between each strip. Bake until golden brown at 220°C

COCKTAIL TIDBITS
(NUTS AND BOLTS)

500 ml	oil
30 ml	Worcestershire *or* soy sauce
10 ml	seasoned salt, celery salt
	1 clove garlic
	or
5 ml	garlic powder
2.5 ℓ	cereal mix
500 ml	nut mix
500 ml	thin pretzel sticks
250 ml	sunflower *or* pumpkin seeds

1. Heat oil and seasonings with garlic clove cut into quarters, over low heat; remove the garlic.
2. Add the cereal (Cheerios, bite-size Shreddies, or Chex), and nuts (peanuts, almonds, cashews, mixed nuts), salted or unsalted.
3. Stir over low heat 10-12 min or bake in a shallow pan, stirring frequently, 30-45 min until golden brown, 150°C
4. Cool and store in tightly covered cans. *Yield: 3 ℓ*

Variation: for hot nibblers add:

chili powder	5 ml
dry mustard	2 ml

Recipes, tables, etc. that appear in small capital letters, e.g., PARSLEY BUTTER, CANADA'S FOOD GUIDE, are listed in the index. Consult the index for the number of the page on which the item appears.

4 Beverages

Beverages are useful as a pick-me-up in the middle of the day, a bed-time relaxer, or the finishing touch to a perfect meal. They are a focal point for hospitality—morning coffee, afternoon tea, or a cool drink on a hot day can provide the setting for friendly get-togethers. And beverages fill a wide range of needs: for example, a fortified milkshake gives the equivalent of a full meal's food energy, whereas clear tea or coffee gives no food energy at all—only the mild stimulation provided by the caffein it contains.

Instant coffee is natural coffee essence with the water removed. Freeze-dried instant coffee retains more of the characteristic coffee flavour and aroma. All varieties taste better when several servings are prepared at one time in a carafe, rather than separately in individual cups.

Coffee

At a meal, coffee may be served with the dessert course or following it. When there is no limit on time, serve coffee in the living room in demitasses.

Coffee may be purchased as beans for home grinding; it may be ground at the time of purchase; or it may be bought already ground or powdered. Since ground coffee loses flavour quickly, home grinding just before making ensures the most flavourful drink.

However, ready-to-prepare coffees are so convenient to use that they are very popular. For best results from these, buy the smallest available container and keep it tightly covered after first opening it.

Facts to Consider when Making Coffee
1. Use freshly ground coffee. Buy it in small amounts and keep tightly covered and cool. Flavours vary: choose the blend you find most pleasing.
2. Use the grind of coffee best suited to your coffee-maker; coarse for steeped coffee; medium for percolator; fine for vacuum and drip types.
3. Be sure the coffee-maker is washed and rinsed after each use; never use it for tea. The size should be suitable for the amount of coffee being made; do not try to make a single serving in a pot designed for eight.
4. Use a measured amount of coffee and water depending upon the strength desired. Strong coffee should be obtained by increasing the amount of coffee, not by longer heating.
5. Use boiling water, because the faster the coffee is made the better it will be. (However, there are some types of automatic percolators which must start with cold water to complete their cycle.) *Do not allow the coffee to boil,* nor to stand too long before serving.

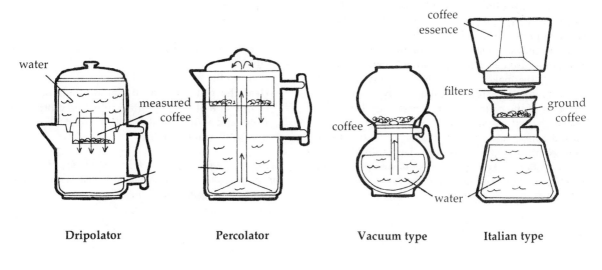

| Dripolator | Percolator | Vacuum type | Italian type |

DRIPOLATOR COFFEE

15-50 ml	coffee, dripolator grind
	per
250 ml	boiling water

1. Place the measured coffee in the middle section.
2. Pour the boiling water in the top section.
3. As soon as a little coffee has dripped through into the lower section, place the pot over low heat.
4. When all the water has dripped through the coffee into the lower section, remove the top two sections and serve.

PERCOLATOR COFFEE

15-50 ml	coffee, percolator grind
	per
250 ml	water

1. Pour the measured water into the percolator.
2. Measure coffee of medium grind into the basket; place the perforated cover on the basket. Put the lid on the pot.
3. Set the percolator on high heat; as soon as the water begins to bubble up through the tube, lower the heat to keep it bubbling slowly.
4. Percolate 7 min; remove the basket and tube; serve.

FILTERED COFFEE

15-50 ml	finely ground coffee
	per
250 ml	boiling water

There are many different methods for making filtered coffee, each requiring its own special pot. Some are based on principles used in standard coffee-makers.
Espresso coffee is made in an apparatus which uses steam pressure for extraction; simple versions of this Italian coffee-maker are made in many different styles. Water is heated to boiling in the lower compartment of the coffee-maker; it passes up through a funnel-shaped compartment which contains the ground coffee, and through a series of filters, and is collected in an upper chamber. Depending on the style of coffee-maker used, coffee may be poured out directly, or the whole unit may be inverted and the coffee chamber disengaged for pouring.

VACUUM COFFEE

15-50 ml	coffee, vacuum grind
	per
250 ml	water

1. Pour measured boiling water into the lower bowl of the coffee-maker; set on high heat. (Use medium heat for a glass coffee-maker or set it on a protective wire grid.)
2. If a cloth filter is used, rinse it in cold water and hook it into position; if a glass rod is used, place it in position.
3. Remove lower bowl from heat; place upper bowl in the lower after dampening the rubber gasket; twist it gently to make a tight seal. Place on heat.
4. Measure coffee into the upper bowl.
5. When the water is forced by the steam into the upper bowl, leave it for 3 min on low heat, stirring it carefully once.
6. Remove the coffee-maker from the heat. The pressure of the air will force the coffee extract back into the lower bowl, leaving the grounds on top. If the coffee will not go back down, it means that a tight seal was not formed between the upper and lower bowl, or that a grain of coffee got under the filter. In this case, place the coffee-maker back on the heat to allow the heat to send up again whatever coffee has dripped down. This may dislodge the grain of coffee if that was the trouble; tighten the seal and proceed as before. If this happens frequently, the rubber gasket may need replacing.
7. Remove the upper bowl.

STEEPED COFFEE

15-50 ml	coarsely ground coffee
	per
250 ml	boiling water

1. Put the measured coffee into any covered pan of suitable size.
2. Pour on the freshly boiled water.
3. Heat the water to just under the boiling point; keep it at that temperature 8 min; add a little cold water and allow it to stand off the heat a few minutes until grounds settle.

To prepare steeped coffee which is clear and free of tiny particles, crush 1 egg and shell and combine with an equal quantity of cold water; add coffee. Tie loosely in the bag; steep.

STEEPED COFFEE FOR 100

1 kg	**coarsely ground coffee**
25 *l*	**boiling water**

1. Prepare a bag from colourless porous cloth, twice the size of the bulk of coffee. Stitch double seams, and soak bag in cold water before using.
2. Tie coffee loosely in the bag, letting long strings hang out for easy removal of the bag later.
3. Drop bag into boiling water; cover pot and simmer (below boiling) 15-20 min, dunking bag down occasionally with a wooden spoon; remove bag.

CAFÉ AU LAIT

Combine equal parts of strong coffee and scalded milk.

ICED COFFEE

1. Make double-strength coffee by any method.
2. Fill a tall glass with ice cubes; pour in coffee slowly.
3. Serve with cream and simple syrup (see SYRUP, BASIC RECIPE).

Double-strength coffee may be made in advance and poured into the ice-cube tray. These cubes may be used with coffee of regular strength.

COFFEE IMPERIAL

	4 sticks cinnamon
1.5 *l*	**strong hot coffee**
75 ml	**sugar**
200 ml	**whipping cream**
	vanilla
	ice cubes

1. Add cinnamon sticks to hot coffee and let stand for 1 h
2. Remove cinnamon sticks; add sugar to taste and half the cream. Chill.
3. Pour liquid over ice cubes in 6 tall glasses.
4. Whip remaining cream; add a little sugar and vanilla if desired; top each serving with a spoonful of cream. *Serves 6.*

Tea

Tea is a popular beverage with meals. It stars as mid-afternoon refreshment at home or social gatherings. The best tea is made in an earthenware teapot.

HOT TEA

5 ml	**tea**
250 ml	**boiling water**
or	
	1 tea bag
375 ml	**boiling water**

1. Pour hot water into teapot; let stand until thoroughly heated; empty it.
2. Measure in the tea.
3. Add freshly boiled, boiling water. Cover.
4. Let stand in a hot place to infuse for 5 to 6 min. Do not let it boil; to alter the strength use more or less tea, do not alter the time.
5. Pour tea from leaves or remove tea bag. Serve clear or with milk or thin slices of lemon or orange and sugar.

ICED TEA

1. Make hot tea; when infused, strain from leaves or remove tea bags.
2. To tall glasses 1/3 full of crushed ice add tea; sweeten if desired with simple syrup (see SYRUP, BASIC RECIPE).
3. Serve with a thin slice of lemon or orange.

HOT MULLED CIDER

125 ml	**brown sugar**
2.5 *l*	**cider**
5 ml	**whole allspice**
5 ml	**whole cloves**
	1 stick cinnamon
	thin shaving of orange rind
	sprinkle of nutmeg
	sprinkle of salt

1. In a large saucepan combine sugar and cider.
2. Add spices to cider and heat slowly to boiling point. Cover and simmer 20 min
3. Strain to remove spices. Taste, and add a sprinkle of salt, if desired.
4. Serve hot in heated mugs with a floater of orange slice and a cinnamon stick for a muddler. *Serves 10.*

COCOA

Serve at breakfast or bedtime, or as a warming refreshment after outdoor winter activities.

30-50 ml	**cocoa**
30 ml	**sugar**
250 ml	**water**
750 ml	**milk**
2 ml	**vanilla**
	topping (optional)

1. Mix cocoa and sugar in the top of a double boiler.
2. Add water; bring to a boil over direct heat. Boil 1 min
3. Add the milk; set over hot water and leave until hot.
4. Just before serving add vanilla and beat with an egg beater until a thick froth forms, to break up any skin. (Skin is composed of fat and protein and so should not be skimmed off.)
5. A marshmallow may be placed in each cup or a topping of whipped cream or ice cream added. *Serves 4-6.*

For variety, add a little instant coffee and a sprinkle of cinnamon.

If cocoa is served frequently, time is saved by making up syrup which can be stored and used as needed. The recipe that follows makes a thin syrup that is easy to dilute later.

CHOCOLATE SYRUP

200 ml	**cocoa**
400 ml	**sugar**
400 ml	**water**
50 ml	**butter *or* margarine**

1. Combine cocoa, sugar and salt; add boiling water slowly.
2. Boil mixture 5 min, with occasional stirring; add fat. For extra nourishment, stir in 2 thoroughly beaten egg yolks, after first beating a little of the hot syrup into the beaten yolks.
3. Cool, pour into a jar, cover and refrigerate. *Yield:* 625 ml

To make cocoa or chocolate milk, dilute as follows:

15 ml	**syrup**
	per
250 ml	**milk**

Cold Drinks

LEMONADE

250 ml	**water**
25-50 ml	SYRUP (BASIC RECIPE) *or* **sugar**
30 ml	**lemon juice**

1. Combine water and syrup; if sugar is used, stir to dissolve.
2. Add juice; pour over ice cubes. Garnish glass with thin slice of lemon rind and a maraschino cherry. *Serves 1-2.*

LIMEADE

Follow directions for Lemonade; substitute limes for lemons and reduce the sugar to taste.

Decorative Ice Cubes for Use in Fruit Drinks
Fill an ice cube tray with water, coloured if desired, or substitute lemonade, orangeade, or other diluted fruit juice.

Place in each section any one of: a red or green maraschino cherry, slice of lemon or orange, piece of pineapple, a sprig of mint. When frozen, serve cubes in iced tea, lemonade, or other cold drinks.

LEMONADE SYRUP

400 ml	sugar
250 ml	water
	thin shavings of rind of 1 lemon
400 ml	lemon juice

1. Combine sugar, water and lemon rind; bring to boiling and simmer 5 min
2. Cool, add lemon juice; strain. *Yield*: enough syrup for 20 servings of lemonade.

To make lemonade, dilute as follows:

15 ml	LEMONADE SYRUP
	per
250 ml	ice water

LEMONADE CONCENTRATE FOR 100

1 kg	sugar
1.25 *l*	water
15 ml	grated lemon rind
5 ml	grated orange rind
125 ml	lemon juice
75 ml	orange juice
15 g	citric acid
15 g	tartaric acid

Acid crystals are obtainable at a drugstore.
1. Bring sugar and water to boiling; add grated rind; boil 3 min
2. Add fruit juice; stir in acids. Strain, bottle and refrigerate syrup until needed.

To make lemonade, dilute as follows:

15 ml	LEMONADE CONCENTRATE
	per
250 ml	water and ice cubes

Serve cold beverages frosty cold. Nestlé (Canada) Limited.

PINEAPPLE MINT PUNCH

	fresh mint sprigs
30 ml	sugar
125 ml	lime or lemon juice
1 *l*	1 can pineapple juice
750 ml	lemon-lime carbonated soft drink
	pineapple spears

1. Crush mint with sugar; add juices and chill for 1 h. Strain.
2. Just before serving, add carbonated soft drink and pour over ice in a punch bowl.
3. Serve in punch cups or glasses garnished with pineapple spears and sprigs of mint. *Yield:* approximately 20 servings: 2.5 *l*

Recipes, tables, etc. that appear in small capital letters, e.g., PARSLEY BUTTER, CANADA'S FOOD GUIDE, are listed in the index. Consult the index for the number of the page on which the item appears.

RHUBARB PUNCH

2 kg (4 *l*)	rosy rhubarb
2.5 *l*	water
750 ml	sugar
750 ml	boiling water
200 ml	lemon juice
354 ml	1 can frozen orange juice concentrate
3 *l*	4 bottles soda water
	mint sprigs

1. Chop rhubarb, cook in water until tender; strain through a jelly bag without squeezing.
2. Dissolve sugar in boiling water; add to rhubarb juice and chill. Add remaining juices.
3. To serve, combine with soda water, crushed ice, and sprigs of mint. *Yield:* approximately 50 servings: 8 *l*

CRANBERRY PUNCH

75 ml	sugar
500 ml	orange juice
50 ml	lemon juice
1.5 *l*	cranberry juice cocktail
400 ml	pineapple juice
750 ml	1 bottle lemon-lime carbonated beverage
	slices of lemon and orange

1. Dissolve sugar in orange juice. Add remaining juices and chill.
2. At serving time add lemon-lime beverage and pour over ice in a punch bowl; garnish with fruit slices. *Yield:* approximately 25 servings: 3 *l*

BUTTERMILK FRUIT DRINK

250 ml	fresh or frozen orange *or* pineapple juice
250 ml	buttermilk, chilled
15 ml	lemon juice
	sugar to taste

Combine all ingredients. Serve very cold. *Serves 1-2.*

FRUIT PUNCH FOR 100

8 *l*	tea (*or* cranberry juice)
8 *l*	fruit juice (Do not combine pineapple juice with grape juice; the mixture gives an unpleasant colour.)
1 *l*	small cans frozen orange concentrate
6 *l*	carbonated beverage: lemon-flavoured, Collins mix, bitter lemon, tonic water, *or* club soda
8 trays	ice cubes

1. Make tea; remove bags and cool.
2. Going down the list, pour one unit at a time of each ingredient to fill punch bowl or large pitcher. Each round yields approximately 30-35 servings. *Total yield:* approximately 23 *l*

Fruit Ice Block to Float in a Punch Bowl
Use a round pan or ring mould smaller than rim of punch bowl. Place pineapple rings in bottom, filling centres with maraschino cherries. Mix canned pineapple juice with water, about half and half, and fill pan. Freeze. Remove block from mould when ready to serve; place in a punch bowl; add punch.

STRAWBERRY SODA

250 ml	fresh strawberries
or	
100 ml	frozen strawberries
25 ml	sugar
300 ml	1 bottle soda water
250 ml	vanilla ice cream

1. Wash and stem berries. Set aside 2 whole berries; press remainder through a sieve and add sugar. If using sweetened frozen berries, omit sugar.
2. Divide mixture between 2 tall glasses; add a scoop of ice cream and a little soda water to each, and stir well.
3. Fill glass with soda water; top with a scoop of ice cream and garnish with a whole strawberry. *Serves 2.*

Recipes, tables, etc. that appear in small capital letters, e.g., PARSLEY BUTTER, CANADA'S FOOD GUIDE, are listed in the index. Consult the index for the number of the page on which the item appears.

Flavoured Milk Drinks

Prepare the following drinks either in a blender, or by first making a purée of the fruit, then beating ingredients together with an egg beater. Use fresh or reconstituted milk; drinks can be enriched by the addition of skim milk powder, about 15-30 ml

250 ml	milk

Combine the milk with any of the following:

125 ml	apricot nectar *or* one-half banana
	sprinkle of cinnamon
or	
250 ml	ginger ale
or	
10 ml	honey
	sprinkle of cinnamon *or* nutmeg
or	
30 ml	maple syrup

MILKSHAKES AND FLOATS

Use blender or egg beater as in the preceding recipe. If desired, reserve a little ice cream to float on top.

Brown Cow

	1 large banana
25-50 ml	chocolate syrup
	vanilla to taste
250 ml	milk
	1 scoop ice cream

Mocha Float

5 ml	instant coffee
25 ml	chocolate syrup
250 ml	milk
	1 scoop ice cream

Strawberry Milk Shake

250 ml	strawberries
25 ml	sugar
250 ml	milk
	1 scoop ice cream

LASSI

The ingredients for this refreshing Indian beverage are similar to those in Buttermilk Fruit Drink, but the texture is like snow. A blender that shaves ice is required.

350 ml	crushed ice
150 ml	buttermilk *or* yogurt
150 ml	fruit (strawberries, banana, and/or
	pineapple)
or	
25 ml	lemon juice
	sugar to taste

Combine at low speed; increase to high speed and continue until the mixture is like snow. Serve in a tall glass with a long-handled spoon. *Serves 1.*

Powdered Skim Milk

Powdered skim milk is a convenient and inexpensive form of milk. Enriched with vitamins A and D, it contains all the important nutrients of whole milk, except fat which we usually obtain in sufficient amounts from other foods. Skim milk is not recommended for babies' formulas (except where specifically prescribed) because on a baby's limited diet milk is the only source of fat.

To Use Reconstituted Skim Milk as a Beverage
Families who are accustomed to drinking only fresh milk can often be conditioned to drink a blend of fresh and reconstituted milk. Using skim milk powder results in a substantial saving on the food budget without compromising nutritional needs.

To introduce reconstituted skim milk, begin by adding a small amount (which has been prepared and chilled as directed (see TO RECONSTITUTE SKIM MILK POWDER) to fresh 2% milk; start with 1 part of reconstituted to 4 parts of fresh milk, changing the proportions gradually, until an acceptable level is reached. Results are usually more successful with younger children than with adolescents, and better if members of the family are unaware that an experiment is taking place!

Cooling milk shakes are popular for summer refreshment and children's parties. Supplemented with skim milk powder, they provide extra nourishment for convalescents.

Eggnogs

Nourishing drinks for breakfast-on-the-run, or for entertaining, eggnogs are easily prepared with a blender or beater. Add extra nourishment in the form of skim milk powder, about 15-25 ml

---

Basic Recipe
EGGNOG

	1 egg
5 ml	sugar
2 ml	vanilla
250 ml	milk
	sprinkle of nutmeg

1. Combine all ingredients except nutmeg in a blender, or beat egg with an egg beater; beat in sugar, vanilla, and milk.
2. Pour into a chilled glass and sprinkle lightly with nutmeg. *Serves 1.*

Variations
Beat egg and combine with the ingredients for any of the FLAVOURED MILK DRINKS.
Breakfast-on-the-run: Reduce milk by ½; omit vanilla. Add orange juice and skim milk powder, each 50 ml

EGGNOG TO SERVE 50

	12 eggs, separated
	salt
375 ml	sugar
1.25 *l*	whipping cream, chilled
1.25 *l*	milk
750 ml	1 bottle ginger ale
	nutmeg

1. Add a dash of salt to egg whites and beat until stiff, but not dry; gradually beat in one-third of the sugar.
2. Beat the chilled whipping cream until stiff.
3. In a large mixing bowl, beat egg yolks until thick and light; gradually beat in remaining sugar. Add the milk.
4. Stir chilled ginger ale into egg yolk mixture; fold in whipped cream and beaten egg whites.
5. Pour mixture into a chilled punch bowl and sprinkle with grated nutmeg. *Yield:* approximately 6 *l*

Treat your guests to nutritious eggnog. Keep refrigerated and serve immediately. Canadian Dairy Foods Service Bureau.

5 Sandwiches

Sandwiches come in all styles and sizes, from hearty to formal, from "open-face" to "make-your-own", from "knife-and-fork" to tiny "afternoon tea" varieties. Carefully chosen, sandwiches can make a substantial contribution to our daily nutrition. All breads provide food energy. Some have been enriched to compensate for loss of nutrients during milling by adding B vitamins, iron, and milk solids. Whole grain breads contain all the vitamins and minerals of the grain, plus important fibre.

The four essential parts of sandwiches of any type are the base, the spread, the filling, and the garnish.
Base—Bread is the most common base. For variety and nutrition use cracked wheat, whole wheat, rye, pumpernickel, oatmeal, cheese, or raisin bread. Once in a while, substitute English muffins or DATE AND NUT LOAF. Weiner, hamburger, or submarine buns are also good bases. Lebanese bread or pita, when torn across, opens like an envelope to hold fillings.

Bread is easier to slice if it is refrigerated or placed in a freezer for 30 minutes. Use a saw-edge knife. To avoid cutting a loaf on a slant, stand so that the knife and loaf are at a right angle to your body, and look along the back of the knife while slicing. Pile slices in order, and cover with plastic or waxed paper and a damp tea towel if they are not to be used immediately.

If crusts are to be removed, trim crusts from all but one side of loaf before slicing. The one crust left on will keep the loaf in shape. Crusts should always be removed before the bread is spread, so that butter and filling are not wasted. Save crusts to make crumbs or to dice for croutons. (Buttered crumbs will not keep.)
Spread—The spread prevents the filling from soaking into the bread and adds flavour; butter or margarine, alone or creamed with salad dressing or sour cream are most often used. Prepare the spread by removing ingredients from the refrigerator in advance. To hasten the softening process, place spread in a bowl in a pan of warm water or invert a hot bowl over a slice of butter or margarine; do not melt. Beat or cream the spread until it can be applied easily without tearing the bread. For a large quantity, save time by beating in salad dressing, to thin the spread.

Filling—Prepare all ingredients for fillings before bread is uncovered; tomatoes should be sliced, sprinkled with salt and pepper, and drained; cucumbers peeled, sliced, seasoned, and drained; lettuce washed and shaken in a towel to dry; mixtures made and tasted for seasoning on a piece of bread.

Fillings must be moist enough to stick together but not so moist that they soak the bread or drip out of the sandwich. Use plenty of filling, and spread it to the edges of the sandwich base. A thick layer of thinly sliced meat is preferable to one thick slice. Sometimes a thin slice of bread to separate two kinds of filling in a sandwich makes it easier to handle.
Garnish—Garnishes for sandwiches should be edible, colourful, and chosen to provide a flavour contrast and nutritive value. Watercress, parsley, pickles, decorative pieces of raw vegetables, small amounts of salad, and tomato are popular.

Making Sandwiches

The most efficient way to make sandwiches is the assembly-line method.
1. Lay out bread slices in matched pairs, all "tops" in one row, all "bottoms" in another.
2. Butter all slices with a flexible knife, using broad strokes; cover completely to the edge.
3. On all "top" slices spread a layer of salad dressing.
4. Allot the filling to the "bottom" slices to ensure an equal amount for each sandwich. If many sandwiches are being prepared, divide the filling equally into bowls beforehand, to make even allotment easier.
5. Spread the filling to the edge of each slice; place the "top" slice on the filling; press firmly.
6. To keep for a short time, pile four sandwiches together; wrap in precut wax paper or place in sandwich bags; cover with damp towels on a baking pan; refrigerate in the vegetable crisper. Package each kind of sandwich separately, to avoid mingling of flavours.

Some ways of cutting made-up sandwiches.

7. At serving time, open packages as needed and slice with a sharp knife. (A saw-edge knife tears the filling.) Wash the knife after each variety of sandwich is cut, to avoid transferring flavours.
8. Arrange attractively, add garnish, and serve.

Freezing

To prepare sandwiches that are to be frozen, omit lettuce, tomatoes, and cucumber; mash hard-cooked eggs thoroughly to prevent their becoming rubbery; use sour cream or salad dressing instead of mayonnaise, which often separates. Sliced or ground meat, seafood and peanut butter freeze well. Cheese tends to crumble. Jelly does not freeze well.

Wrap sandwiches before freezing, in individual sandwich bags if sandwiches are to be used one at a time for lunch boxes, or in convenient lots to be served at one time.

Freeze open-faced sandwiches on trays, covered with a sheet of heavy-duty wax paper or foil; freeze quickly; transfer to rigid, air-tight containers. Sandwiches may be kept frozen up to 6 weeks.

Thawing

Thaw open-faced sandwiches on serving trays, covered with a clean tea towel. Thaw other sandwiches in original wrappings, opened to let excess moisture escape. Allow 30-60 min at room temperature.

Sandwich Ingredient Quantities

SANDWICHES FOR 100

Bread	10 loaves, each	675 g
Butter or margarine		1 kg
Egg Filling	90 hard-cooked eggs	
	MAYONNAISE	1.25 ℓ
	salt	30 ml
	pepper	5 ml
	Worcestershire	5 ml
	grated onion	150 ml
	chives	150 ml
Meat Filling		
Slices	boneless roast, machine sliced	5 kg
	mustard, horseradish, *or* pickle relish	100-200 ml
Chopped	cooked meat, chopped	4 kg
	celery, sliced	2 ℓ
	SOUR CREAM DRESSING	1 ℓ
	lemon juice	100 ml
	parsley, minced	100 ml
Fowl Filling	one cooked turkey, sliced	5 kg
	or two cooked boiling fowl, sliced	5 kg
	or two cooked boiling fowl, chopped	4 kg
	or cooked fowl, diced	6 ℓ
	celery, sliced finely	2 ℓ
	MAYONNAISE	1 ℓ
	salt	30 ml
	pepper	5 ml
Lettuce	4 large heads	

QUANTITIES FOR 12 FULL-SIZE SANDWICHES

Bread, 1 loaf	680 g
Butter or margarine	125 g
Cheese, cream or processed	375 g
Meat, chopped	375 g
thinly sliced	375-750 g
Chicken: chopped (1 large fowl spreads 3 loaves)	600 ml
Seafood: 4 cans	
salmon	each 220 g
shrimp	each 115 g
sardines	each 100 g
tuna	each 200 g
Peanut butter	180-360 g

10 Eggs: hard-cooked, chopped

Recipes, tables, etc. that appear in small capital letters, e.g., PARSLEY BUTTER, CANADA'S FOOD GUIDE, are listed in the index. Consult the index for the number of the page on which the item appears.

Arrange sandwiches attractively.

BASIC SANDWICH FILLINGS FOR 4-5 FULL-SIZE SANDWICHES

CHICKEN FILLING

250 ml	finely chopped cooked chicken
50 ml	salad dressing
	seasoning

(To use canned chicken, first remove jelly, which will melt and make a sandwich soggy but can be used in tomato juice or consommé.)

Suggested additions: fresh rosemary; chopped olives; chopped almonds; pineapple, drained and crushed; chopped green pepper; thinly sliced celery; cranberry relish.

CHEESE

250 ml	shredded Cheddar, cottage *or* cream cheese
30 ml	MAYONNAISE
	seasoning

Add any of the following, drained if necessary, and chopped: 30-45 ml
sweet pickle, *or* CHUTNEY, *or* pineapple, *or* ground peanuts; *or* raisins or dates moistened with orange juice and mixed with grated rind. Cream ingredients together.

BASIC SANDWICH FILLINGS FOR 4-5 FULL-SIZE SANDWICHES

EGG FILLING

	3 hard-cooked eggs, chopped
30 ml	salad dressing
	seasoning (salt, pepper, dry mustard)

Chop the peeled eggs in a bowl, using a pastry blender or fork. Combine with dressing.

Add any of: watercress, minced chives or parsley; crumbled crisp bacon or 2-3 anchovy fillets, finely chopped. Season.

A little onion juice or grated onion may be used, but avoid coarsely chopped onion.

SALMON FILLING

220 g	1 can Coho salmon
5 ml	lemon juice
15 ml	MAYONNAISE
	pepper, freshly ground

Drain off and reserve liquid; remove from the salmon any black skin; flake the salmon; mash the bones. Add other ingredients, using a fork.

Suggested additions: chopped chives or green onions; chopped green pepper; chopped celery; ketchup.

Mix one can of red salmon and one of pink salmon or chicken haddies for a filling more economical than all-red salmon but with better colour and flavour than all-pink. Coho is midway between red and pink in colour, texture, and price.

Any unused salmon and its liquid may be used in supper dishes or salmon patties.

Other Seafood Fillings

Using the recipe for SALMON FILLING, substitute for salmon:

Sardines: drain off oil; drain sardines on paper towels; mash with a fork; add a little chili sauce or ketchup.

Tuna: if packed in oil, drain and rinse with boiling water; drain; flake.

Shrimp: drain; remove black line, rinse with cold water, drain; mash coarsely with a fork.

Lobster: drain and mash.

Crabmeat: flake.

To extend expensive ingredients such as shrimp, lobster, and crab, blend them into cream cheese.

HAM

250 g	sliced cooked ham
30-45 ml	HOT MUSTARD SAUCE, DARK MUSTARD SAUCE, *or* QUICK MUSTARD RELISH

Spread sauce or relish on buttered bread.

BEEF

250 g	sliced roasted or boiled beef
30-45 ml	HORSERADISH SAUCE *or* CHUTNEY

LAMB

250 g	sliced roasted lamb
30-45 ml	chopped mint

PORK

250 g	sliced roasted pork (A butt roast of pork stuffed with BREAD DRESSING makes an excellent filling.)
30-45 ml	APPLESAUCE
or	thin slices of raw apple

PASTRAMI

250 g	very thin slices of hot pastrami
30-45 ml	drained SAUERKRAUT (Heat sliced meat in its plastic package in boiling water; or wrap slices in foil and heat in double boiler, about 15 minutes.)

CORNED BEEF

250 g	thin slices corned beef, hot or cold
30-45 ml	HOT MUSTARD SAUCE *or* DARK MUSTARD SAUCE

TONGUE OR SAUSAGE

250 ml	sliced tongue, fresh or smoked, *or* smoked sausage
30-45 ml	HOT MUSTARD SAUCE *or* DARK MUSTARD SAUCE

BASIC SANDWICH FILLINGS FOR 4-5 FULL-SIZE SANDWICHES

MEAT, CHOPPED OR GROUND

250 ml	chopped or ground cooked ham, *or* cooked beef, *or* luncheon meat
30 ml	MAYONNAISE
	seasoning: salt, pepper, Worcestershire sauce, and curry powder
30-45 ml	chopped sweet pickle *or* QUICK MUSTARD RELISH

LIVER

250 ml	sautéed liver, sliced or chopped, *or* liver sausage
30-45 ml	prepared mustard or KETCHUP *or* CHILI SAUCE
15 ml	grated onion
50 ml	salad dressing
	salt, pepper
30 ml	crisp crumbled bacon

Serve cold or hot.

BAKED BEANS

250 ml	BAKED BEANS, drained and mashed
30-45 ml	KETCHUP or CHILI SAUCE
30 ml	crisp crumbled bacon
	salt
	dry mustard, to taste

Spread on buttered Boston brown bread or crusty brown rolls.

PEANUT BUTTER

175 ml	peanut butter
30-45 ml	crumbled bacon; *or* chopped raisins with grated orange rind and orange juice; *or* honey; *or* marmalade; *or* jelly; *or* KETCHUP or CHILI SAUCE or relish

Top with sliced banana.

Recipes, tables, etc. that appear in small capital letters, e.g., PARSLEY BUTTER, CANADA'S FOOD GUIDE, are listed in the index. Consult the index for the number of the page on which the item appears.

SALAD

250 ml	well-drained COLE SLAW *or* CARROT AND RAISIN SALAD *or* TOSSED SALAD

Spread bread with FLAVOURED BUTTER *or* cream cheese.

CUCUMBER

250 ml	thin slices of peeled cucumber
125 ml	FRENCH DRESSING *or* sour cream

Marinate cucumber in dressing for 1 h; drain; sprinkle with salt and black pepper. Arrange several layers of cucumber slices on buttered bread. Add thinly sliced red onions *or* shallots *or* leeks.

TOMATO

4 or 5 firm, ripe tomatoes, peeled and sliced
Sprinkle with salt; drain.
Arrange on buttered bread spread with MAYONNAISE *or* sour cream; *or* use HERB BUTTER. Add lettuce; cucumbers; thinly sliced onions *or* leeks. Sprinkle with fresh chopped basil *or* chives *or* dill.

ONION

	2 or 3 Spanish or red Italian onions, peeled and sliced paper-thin
200 ml	FRENCH DRESSING

Marinate slices for 1 h in FRENCH DRESSING; drain. Arrange on slices of French, oatmeal, *or* cheese bread spread with butter *or* softened cheese.
Serve with radishes, tomatoes, *or* carrot fingers.

GREEN PEPPER

1 green pepper, peeled, seeded, and coarsely ground
1 peeled, seeded cucumber, finely chopped
Combine pepper and cucumber; drain in a sieve with a weighted saucer on top. Mix with MAYONNAISE or cream cheese. Spread thinly on rye or whole wheat bread.
Serve with cherry tomatoes.

Lawry's Foods, Inc.

SUBMARINE SANDWICHES
(HERO OR POOR BOY)

Split French or Italian loaves; spread a mixture of prepared mustard and butter on both sides of the cut surface. Slice long loaves diagonally; cut round loaves in wedges. Select combinations of fillings for colour and flavour.

Fillings

Sliced olives; Mortadella sausage; salami; thinly sliced onion; Gruyère cheese; brick cheese; hard-cooked egg; sliced tomato.

Wafer-thin lemon slices; lemon juice; anchovy fillets; sour pickles or capers; thinly sliced onion; sardines; shredded green pepper; tarragon or parsley; tomatoes.

Chopped Italian parsley; drained COLE SLAW; thinly sliced pepperoni; processed cheese slice; thin ham slices; pressed chicken; Swiss cheese; bologna.

REUBEN SANDWICHES

Two or three slices of bread, often rye, or a combination of white and brown bread, are put together with filling between each layer; the centre slice of bread is spread on both sides, the top and bottom slices on one side only. FLAVOURED BUTTER or margarine is used, and lettuce may be added. The fillings suggested for SUBMARINE SANDWICHES may be used as well.

MAKE-YOUR-OWN SANDWICHES

Set out makings for sandwiches, grouping the ingredients that go well together. For quantity guide, see SANDWICH INGREDIENT QUANTITIES.

Provide a variety of breads—homemade, rye, crusty rolls
> FLAVOURED BUTTERS
> SALAD DRESSINGS

Arrange trays of sliced meats, cheeses, and relishes, with a bowl of VEGETABLE HORS D'OEUVRES. A hot or cold roast may replace the sliced meats.

RIBBON SANDWICHES

Choose white and brown loaves of the same size, or trim to match. Crosswise or lengthwise slices may be cut, depending on the number desired. Remove crusts and arrange slices in groups of three or five alternating brown and white.

Spread the inside slices on both sides with FLAVOURED BUTTER. Spread the fillings (see below); press together, wrap and refrigerate. Cut in thin slices or in thick slices; cut again into bars.

Filling Combinations

Sliced turkey *or* CHICKEN SALAD with CRANBERRY RELISH in cream cheese.

Sliced or ground tongue, corned beef *or* ham, with chopped MUSTARD PICKLES.

EGG FILLING with SEAFOOD FILLING.

Peanut butter and crumbled bacon with orange marmalade in cream cheese.

Tomatoes or lettuce may be used for colour; drain tomatoes and press the sandwich firmly.

Variations

Sandwich Loaf Cut one sandwich loaf into 6 horizontal slices; spread with different fillings and put together to form a loaf.

Sandwich Torte Cut the loaf in half and place the two pieces together to form a block.

Iced Sandwich Loaf Soften 3 packages cream cheese with a little mayonnaise to make it of spreading consistency; frost the sides and top of SANDWICH LOAF or TORTE; decorate with sliced olives *or* radishes *or*

A Sandwich Torte. Dept. of the Environment, Ottawa.

chopped nuts. Chill an hour; serve on a plate garnished with watercress *or* parsley. Cut slices; lift with a cake knife onto individual plates; serve with a fork.

Individual loaves may be made, using bread cut in small rounds.

OPEN-FACE SANDWICHES
(KNIFE AND FORK, DANISH)

From the Koldt Bord of Denmark and the Smörgåsbord of Sweden comes this delicious kind of sandwich. The base of each open-faced sandwich is one slice of bread (white, rye, or pumpernickel) spread with FLAVOURED BUTTER. The completed sandwich may be finished with a delicate glaze.

SMØRREBRØD GLAZE

325 ml	water
	2 peppercorns
2 ml	dill seed
	1 bay leaf
50 ml	vinegar
85 g	1 package lemon jelly powder

1. Simmer water and spices for 10 min; strain.
2. Add vinegar; measure; add water if necessary to make up the original quantity.
3. Dissolve jelly powder in liquid; chill until syrupy.
4. Arrange sandwiches on a rack and carefully spoon on the glaze.

Covers 6-8 sandwiches, allowing for each 30-50 ml

Variations
Substitute basil, thyme *or* fennel for peppercorns, dill and bay leaf; lemon juice for the vinegar; seasoned, cleared stock *or* canned consommé *or* tomato juice, set with gelatine, for lemon jelly powder and liquid.

TOASTED SANDWICHES

Hot buttered toast may be substituted for bread in any of the basic sandwiches. Ham and fried egg, mushroom and scrambled egg are popular fillings with toast as a base.

Club Sandwich is a two-layer sandwich on toast filled with sliced white chicken, crisp bacon, and sliced tomato and lettuce with mayonnaise. It may be made into a triple-decker with cheese slices in the third layer.

WESTERN SANDWICH

4 slices bacon
½ small green pepper
½ small onion
4 eggs
seasoning

1. Cut bacon into small pieces with scissors; sauté until cooked but not crisp; add finely chopped onion and green pepper and sauté until tender but not brown.
2. Beat the eggs; season with salt and pepper; pour into the pan with the vegetables; cook until egg is set; cut into pieces.
3. Turn and brown; place between slices of buttered toast. *Yield:* 4 full-size sandwiches.

GRILLED SANDWICHES

Spread two slices of bread with butter or margarine. Make the sandwich putting the buttered sides of the bread on the outside instead of the inside. Brown on a grill, in a heavy frying pan, or under a broiler, turning if necessary. Cut diagonally; serve hot, garnished with parsley, pickles or tomatoes.

Cheese is the most popular filling; thin slices of mild onions, cooked Canadian or breakfast bacon are good additions.

Recipes, tables, etc. that appear in small capital letters, e.g., PARSLEY BUTTER, CANADA'S FOOD GUIDE, are listed in the index. Consult the index for the number of the page on which the item appears.

A grilled ham and cheese sandwich.

FRENCH TOAST SANDWICHES

Prepare sandwiches on white bread, using one of these fillings:

Cheese: sliced Cheddar, Brick, Colby, Edam, Gouda, *or* Havarti.

Thin onion slices spread with a slice of Mozzarella *or* processed Cheese.

Corned beef spread with mustard and a slice of cheese.

Cooked ham with mustard and a slice of Swiss cheese.

Salami with Mozzarella cheese.

Finish as FRENCH TOAST.

SUPPER ON A BUN

Hot dog buns, salad buns, hamburger buns, and English muffins lend themselves to this informal dish for lunch, supper or late-evening snack.

Improvise a bun warmer with a rack in a pot placed on a top element, or use a covered roaster, a paper bag or foil wrap in the oven.

DEVILLED STEAK BUNS

1. Rub very thin minute steaks with a little dry mustard and a dash of Worcestershire sauce; broil; turn to broil other side. Do not overcook.
2. Sprinkle with salt and spread with grated cheese (try blue cheese crumbled); broil again to melt cheese.
3. Serve in split, toasted, buttered buns.

BUNS DE LUXE

1. Partly hollow out the top and bottom half of a bun (save the crumbs to dry or freeze for bread crumbs); brush hollow with soft butter.
2. Fill with prepared sandwich filling—egg, chicken, seafood.
3. Close the two halves; serve cold or wrap in foil and heat.

BREAKFAST BUNS

	2 eggs scrambled
	3 hamburger buns
75 ml	**devilled ham**
50 ml	**grated cheese**

1. Prepare SCRAMBLED EGGS: Do not overcook; season.
2. Split the buns; toast both sides under the broiler.
3. Spread with ham, then with egg to cover the bun completely; sprinkle with cheese.
4. Broil until the cheese melts. *Serves 6.*

Variation

Omit cheese and instead serve bowls of grated cheese and crumbled bacon to be added as desired. Omit devilled ham; cover the bun with hot weiners, sliced thinly.

HOT ROAST BEEF DIPPERS

500 g	**thinly sliced roast beef**
350 ml	**beef juice**
30 ml	**butter, margarine *or* beef dripping**
	seasoning
	French bread slices

1. Season juice with horseradish or Worcestershire sauce. Extend the quantity if necessary with vegetable stock.
2. Spread the bread with fat; sauté in a hot pan to brown.
3. Dip the beef, thinly sliced, either hot or cold, in the hot sauce; pile on the browned side of the bread.
4. Serve the dipping sauce in a small dish on the plate with the sandwich; garnish; serve with salad.

Chinese tea cups are attractive containers for the dipping sauce.

AFTERNOON TEA OR PARTY SANDWICHES

To add interest and variety, prepare several different sandwiches. Cut them into pieces smaller than for lunch sandwiches. Wrap and refrigerate prepared sandwiches until needed (see MAKING SANDWICHES).

Recipes, tables, etc. that appear in small capital letters, e.g., PARSLEY BUTTER, CANADA'S FOOD GUIDE, are listed in the index. Consult the index for the number of the page on which the item appears.

Many thin slices of cooked meat make a delicious filling for a submarine sandwich.

A sandwich made with whole wheat bread, garnished with pickles and fresh vegetables, makes a good after-school snack.

OPEN-FACE SANDWICHES

Cut lengthwise slices. Spread with filling and garnish (see SMØRREBRØD GLAZE); cut into small pieces.
or
Cut the bread into fancy shapes with cookie cutters; spread with filling and garnish.

PINWHEEL SANDWICHES

Remove crusts; cut lengthwise slices; spread with CHEESE SPREAD; arrange stuffed olives along one end; at intervals along the slice arrange crosswise strips of green (chopped chives, parsley, green pepper) and red (drained pimento strips, minced radish), alternating the colours.

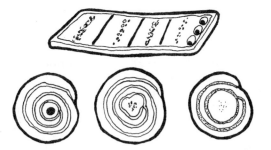

Holding the olives in place, roll; store cut side down until set; slice into wheels.

Make pinwheels with egg filling, with a row of gherkins along the end of the bread slice where you begin rolling it.

Make pinwheels using peanut butter as spread, rolling bread slice around a banana.

ROLLS

Cut thin crosswise slices; spread with FLAVOURED BUTTER, devilled ham or sandwich spread, or cover a buttered slice with cooked ham.

Across one end of each slice, extending beyond the edge, place one of: a spear of cooked asparagus; a few stalks of watercress; a spear of pineapple. Roll the bread around the filling; store cut side down to seal the edge.

PIES

Cut a round loaf horizontally into thin circles; spread with FLAVOURED BUTTER. With a pastry tube or bag, pipe on fillings to make concentric rings of contrasting colour and flavour (meat or fish; egg; creamed cheese).

Garnish the edge and centre with slices of stuffed olives *or* radish *or* pickle. Cut each slice in small wedges to serve.

TOAST SPREADS

Spreads on toast make good accompaniments for salads. They are popular for afternoon tea or as evening refreshments.

Cut ready-sliced bread into fingers or triangles; hamburger buns into circles; dinner rolls or weiner buns into fingers; a long French roll into circles or diagonally into ovals; split an English muffin. Toast, butter, and spread with FLAVOURED SUGAR.

CINNAMON TOAST

30 ml	butter *or* margarine
50 ml	brown sugar
5-10 ml	cinnamon

Cream the ingredients; spread on 6 slices of hot toast; broil until mixture bubbles.

HAM FINGERS

250 ml	ground ham
250 ml	grated cheese
125 ml	condensed tomato soup
2 ml	prepared mustard
2 ml	horseradish

Combine; spread on buttered toast; broil.

SAUSAGE TOAST

Cook sausage meat; drain; spread on buttered toast; place a triangle of cheese on the sausage meat; broil.

GLAZED SEAFOOD TOAST

Spread SEAFOOD FILLING on toast; top with a mixture of MAYONNAISE and grated cheese; broil until mixture melts and glazes the filling.

PARSLEY TEA STRIPS

50 ml	butter *or* margarine
30 ml	grated cheese
15 ml	cream
15 ml	minced parsley
5 ml	prepared mustard

Cream together; spread on bread; broil; cut in fingers.

HERB TOAST

	1 egg, beaten
125 ml	butter *or* margarine
15 ml	flour
30 ml	sesame seeds
5 ml	dried marjoram, basil, rosemary, alone or combined
	(If fresh herbs are available, use twice the quantity, finely chopped)

Cream ingredients together; spread on bread fingers; bake until lightly brown in oven at 180°C

SESAME STICKS

Spread bread sticks on three sides with HONEY BUTTER; roll in sesame seeds; bake until seeds are golden, at 180°C

BROILED SANDWICHES

1. Toast bread on one side under the broiler.
2. Spread the untoasted side with one of the following:
   Undiluted tomato soup with Parmesan cheese topping.
   Undiluted mushroom soup with cooked, drained, cut bacon on top (extra cooked mushrooms or chicken may be added).
   Undiluted cream of chicken soup with slivered almonds.
   Bean-bacon soup with a strip of partly cooked bacon.
   Commercial sandwich spread.
   Peanut butter and orange marmalade on raisin bread.
3. Return to the oven until bubbly. 1 can of soup spreads 12 slices.

Basic Recipe
CHEESE PUFF

50 ml	butter *or* margarine
250 ml	shredded Cheddar cheese
	1 egg, separated
2 ml	dry mustard
1 ml	Worcestershire sauce
	pepper, paprika *or* cayenne

1. Preheat oven to 200°C
2. Cream together butter, cheese and egg yolk; add seasoning.
3. Beat egg white stiff but not dry; fold into the first mixture.
4. Spread generously on bread slices; bake in oven until puffed, 15 min. Spreads 12 slices.

Variations
Cheese Cubes Remove all the crusts from an unsliced sandwich loaf; divide into four lengthwise pieces. Cut crosswise to make cubes 5 cm
Coat all but one side with the cheese mixture; bake until puffed.

Substitute a mixture of cream cheese and blue cheese for the Cheddar; whole wheat bread for white.

Fry bacon until cooked but not crisp; drain; cut into pieces; place on top of partly cooked Cheese Puffs or Cubes; continue to cook until the cheese is golden brown and the bacon crisp.
Cheese Dreams (Pinwheels) Cut thin slices of fresh bread, lengthwise for a large pinwheel, crosswise for a small one. Spread generously with the mixture; roll; refrigerate cut side down. At serving time, slice onto a baking sheet; bake or broil until golden. One loaf cuts 8 lengthwise slices, makes 40 pinwheels.

TOASTED ROLLS

Preheat oven to 200°C
Trim the crusts from fresh bread; slice very thin; spread with softened butter or margarine. Spread generously with fillings for BROILED SANDWICHES; roll; refrigerate cut side down until set, or fasten with wooden picks. Brush the roll lightly with butter; bake until brown (10 min) or broil, turning once.

HERB LOAF (GARLIC LOAF)

1. Preheat oven to 180°C
2. Cut a loaf of bread—French, Italian or round rye—in thick slices almost to the bottom of the loaf, or if the bread is already sliced place on foil.
3. Spread each slice with HERB BUTTER *or* GARLIC BUTTER. To spread one loaf use approximately 125 ml
4. Wrap in foil; heat in oven 15 min; open the foil and allow loaf to heat another 15 min
5. Turn down the foil to a basket-shape or use a bread basket. *Serves 6-8.*

Variations
Cheese Loaf Sprinkle grated hard cheese on slices that have been buttered with butter or FLAVOURED BUTTER
or
spread unbuttered bread with CHEESE SPREAD.
Cinnamon Loaf Sprinkle CINNAMON SUGAR on buttered bread; wrap and heat.

BREAD CASES OR CROUSTADES

1. Cut dry bread into thick slices: 5 cm
2. Remove crusts; cut into rounds or squares.
3. Remove part of bread from centre, leaving a shell about 8 mm
4. Brush over lightly with butter and brown in oven.
5. Fill with hot creamed fish, meat or vegetables.

BREAD CUPS

1. Preheat oven to 200°C
2. Cut crusts from thin fresh bread slices; flatten slices with rolling pin.
3. Brush both sides with melted butter to which minced parsley has been added.
4. Press into muffin pans; toast in hot oven about 10 min
5. Fill with any creamed mixture.

BREAD CRUMBS

Soft Bread Crumbs are prepared by crumbling day-old bread. This may be done by scraping the bread with a fork, by rubbing two thick slices together, or by grinding in an electric blender. Soft crumbs may be frozen in a plastic bag.
Dry Bread Crumbs are made by rolling or grinding dry bread. Keep in a closed container.

A Cheese Loaf. Lawry's Foods, Inc.

BUTTERED CRUMBS

30 ml	butter *or* margarine
250 ml	crumbs

Melt the fat; stir in the crumbs with a fork.
Buttered crumbs will in time become rancid; prepare as needed.

SPICED CRUMBS

250 ml	dried crumbs
125 ml	brown sugar
5 ml	cinnamon
2 ml	nutmeg
1 ml	allspice
1 ml	cloves
1 ml	ginger
50 ml	butter *or* margarine

Combine the crumbs and spices; stir into the melted fat with a fork, tossing gently until brown.

Line the sides and bottom of an ice-cube tray with spiced crumbs for refrigerator desserts. Fill with CHARLOTTE, CHIFFON PIE or CREAM FILLING.

Recipes, tables, etc. that appear in small capital letters, e.g., PARSLEY BUTTER, CANADA'S FOOD GUIDE, are listed in the index. Consult the index for the number of the page on which the item appears.

SPICED CRUMB TOPPING

50 ml	butter or margarine
125 ml	brown sugar
10 ml	spice (cinnamon, cloves, nutmeg, allspice and ginger)
200 ml	dry crumbs

Melt the fat; combine sugar, spice and crumbs; stir into fat, tossing gently until brown.

Sprinkle on CREAM FILLING; *or line the sides and bottom of an ice cube tray and fill with* CHARLOTTE, CHIFFON PIE *or* CREAM FILLING *for refrigerator dessert.*

STREUSEL TOPPING

150 ml	brown sugar
125 ml	flour
5 ml	cinnamon
100 ml	firm butter or margarine

Combine the dry ingredients; cut in the fat.

Use on FRUIT CRISP, OPEN-FACE PEACH PIE *or* GRAPE PIE, *or on* BREADS *and* QUICK BREADS.

Variations
Danish Streusel Topping Replace sugar and flour with dry cake or cookie crumbs.
Oat Streusel Topping Reduce flour to 50 ml
Add quick-cooking rolled oats 125 ml
Nut Streusel Topping Add finely chopped nuts or flaked coconut.

CRUMB TOPPING

30 ml	butter or margarine
250 ml	dry crumbs
	salt, pepper

Melt fat; stir in crumbs, salt and pepper with a fork; stir until the crumbs are brown.
Use on casseroles or vegetables.
Almond Crumbs Add to the crumbs finely chopped almonds 100 ml
Seasoned Crumbs Substitute GARLIC BUTTER or other FLAVOURED BUTTER; add grated cheese.

Leftover Bread Uses
Desserts: FRUIT BETTY, BREAD PUDDING, CARROT PUDDING.

Topping for casseroles or stuffing for fowl, fish and roasts.

CROUTONS, MELBA TOAST

FRENCH TOAST; GRILLED, BROILED or TOASTED SANDWICHES

Crumbs. Soft or dry, BUTTERED or SPICED CRUMBS.

6 Sauces

A good sauce, rich in flavour and smooth in texture, can convert the simplest food into gourmet fare. Because sauces form the base of so many recipes, it is important to become skillful in their preparation.

Sauces Thickened with Starch

Basic Ingredients

Starch is the ingredient that thickens; cornstarch, wheat flour, potato, rice, arrowroot, and tapioca all contain starch granules. In moist heat these granules swell and thicken a liquid. Flour, or wheat starch, is most often used because it is inexpensive and readily available. It has a definite flavour which changes as the starch cooks, so recipes sometimes say "cook until there is no taste of raw starch." Cornstarch is used when a translucent sauce is wanted. The other starches are generally used when an allergy to wheat or corn exists. To substitute one for another consult TABLE OF REPLACEMENTS.

Starch is broken down to sugar by prolonged heating with acid, which explains why such sauces as tomato or lemon may become thin after having thickened.

Fat is used to separate the starch granules and prevent their lumping together. Cold liquid and sugar have the same function and are used to replace fat in the COLD LIQUID METHOD and in desserts.

Butter, chicken fat, beef dripping and bacon fat each contribute a characteristic flavour, making each suitable for certain recipes and not for others. Vegetable oil or margarine may be used in any sauce that calls for fat, thus making "cream" sauces usable even in low-fat diets.

Liquid may be cream, milk, stock, or a combination of these. Avoid adding so much stock that the sauce looks watery. Skim milk powder may be combined with the flour, substituting water for the liquid milk; or milk may be used as the liquid as well as being added as powder to increase the nutritional value of the sauce.

Seasonings are vital in sauce-making. Skill in their use adds to the flavour without adding to the rich-ness. Each sauce should possess its own special flavour from the combination of all ingredients, and not taste too strongly of any one seasoning. See SEASONING: SPICES, HERBS, CONDIMENTS AND FLAVOURINGS.

PROPORTIONS FOR STARCH-THICKENED SAUCES
Recipes make approximately 250 ml

THIN SAUCE
(like milk; used for soups)

250 ml	liquid
15 ml	fat
15 ml	flour

MEDIUM SAUCE
(like rich cream; used for vegetable sauces, scallops, casseroles and pudding sauces)

250 ml	liquid
30 ml	fat
30 ml	flour

THICK SAUCE
(a spoonful dropped back into the sauce makes a well, but sauce still pours; used for croquettes and soufflés)

250 ml	liquid
50 ml	fat
50 ml	flour

It is easier to produce a smooth sauce when there is as much fat as flour. (Skim milk or vegetable stock as part of the liquid will compensate for the high proportion of fat.)

Basic Recipe
WHITE SAUCE, MEDIUM

40 ml	flour
40 ml	fat
250 ml	milk
	seasoning

Yields approximately 250 ml

Combine the ingredients using one of the methods that follow.

Melted Fat Method—particularly suitable when fat is hard or when there is fat in the roasting pan.

1. Heat the fat; as it melts, stir in dry ingredients. Let mixture bubble.
2. Remove the pan from the heat. Stir in cold liquid until smooth.
3. Return to low heat. Stir until thick; cook until there is no taste of raw starch; season.

Creamed Fat Method—a simple method to use when fat is soft.

1. Heat liquid until bubbles form.
2. In a small bowl, cream fat and dry ingredients.
3. Gather the mixture onto a spoon and stir into hot liquid; stir until thick; cook until no taste of raw starch remains.

Cold Liquid Method—a small jar with a tight-fitting top is required.

1. Estimate the amount of liquid to be thickened. For each measure of flour required, use twice the quantity of water or milk. Put flour and water or milk into jar. (Instantized flour is granular in texture and does not lump readily; it is particularly suitable for the Cold Liquid Method.)
2. Cover jar and shake vigorously.
3. Stir mixture into hot liquid until thick and smooth. Cook until there is no taste of raw starch.

Pan gravy, pot roast liquid, and stew are thickened this way when it is desirable to thicken liquid without adding fat.

Variations of White Sauce

Quantities given below are correct for adding to WHITE SAUCE, MEDIUM (BASIC RECIPE).

Caper Sauce
(for fish)

50 ml	chopped capers
15 ml	commercial sandwich spread

Celery Sauce
(for fish)

125 ml	thinly sliced celery
125 ml	water

Boil until just tender; use the cooking liquid as part of the total; add celery to thickened sauce.

Aurora Sauce
(for egg dishes, fish, or vegetables)

Add tomato paste, a little at a time, to the hot cooked sauce until the colour and flavour are pleasing.

Cheese (Mornay) Sauce
(for vegetables, pasta, fish, or hot hors d'oeuvres)

75-125 ml grated cheese

Add to the hot cooked sauce just before serving; stir; season with mustard, paprika.

Egg Sauce
(for fish, toast, or asparagus)

Add chopped hard-cooked egg to the sauce just before serving. To use left over egg yolks, slide them carefully into hot sauce. Cook until firm; break up with a fork or beater. (Overheating toughens the egg protein; resulting in a rubbery consistency.)

Onion Sauce
(for fish, meat, or eggs)

Sauté a thinly sliced small onion in the fat for the sauce until straw coloured; stir in the flour; finish by MELTED FAT METHOD.

Curry Sauce
(for fish, fowl, eggs, or vegetables)

15 ml curry powder

Prepare as ONION SAUCE, stirring curry powder into cooked onions. Cook slowly for a minute before adding the flour.

Béchamel Sauce is WHITE SAUCE in which the milk is infused with spices—a slice of onion, a bit of bay leaf, a blade of mace, 5-6 peppercorns—to give a delicate flavour.

Basic Recipe
VELOUTÉ SAUCE

30 ml	**fat**
30 ml	**flour**
250 ml	**white stock (stock prepared from chicken, fish or veal)**
	seasoning

Make sauce using MELTED FAT METHOD. *Yield:* approximately 250 ml

Cream to replace some stock gives a richer sauce called Sauce Suprème.

Variations of Velouté Sauce

Allemande Sauce
(for fowl or lamb)
1 beaten egg yolk
lemon juice
Beat the yolk; heat by adding a little hot cooked sauce; add mixture to sauce; squeeze in lemon to taste.

Horseradish Sauce
(for boiled beef brisket, corned beef, or pot roast)

30 ml	**prepared horseradish**

Stir into cooked sauce.

Normandy Sauce
(for fish)

Prepare the sauce using fish stock for part of liquid. Add lemon juice to taste: about 15 ml

Any variations of WHITE SAUCE may be prepared with a Velouté Sauce as base.

Herb Sauce
(for fish, fowl, eggs, or vegetables)

15-30 ml	**minced fresh chives, parsley, green onion, chervil, basil, rosemary**

Add one or a combination of above to well-seasoned WHITE or VELOUTÉ SAUCE.

Seafood Sauce
(for fish soufflé)
To the prepared sauce add chopped, cooked shrimp, lobster, or oysters.
Cook grated lemon rind with the sauce; add a few drops of lemon juice just before serving.

To Reheat Sauce
Place cold sauce in the top of a double boiler over hot water. Heat without stirring. When sauce is hot, stir until smooth and thin with a little liquid if necessary.

Sauce containing starch should not be kept longer than a week unfrozen in the refrigerator.

Freezing Sauces
Sauces, except those with a mayonnaise base, freeze well. Package in small cartons or freeze in ice-cube trays and package in plastic bags.

Frozen white sauce may be used as instant sauce for a small amount of vegetable. Remove one or two cubes from the freezer and allow them to thaw on a saucer; drop into hot drained vegetable; cover and leave on low heat a few minutes. Use a fork to stir sauce carefully into the vegetable.

To Add Egg Yolk to Sauce
Sauce may be enriched with egg yolk for added colour and flavour. The beaten yolk must be heated by adding a little hot cooked sauce to it before it is stirred into the sauce. Stir until the sauce thickens, and serve.

WHITE SAUCE MIX, OR ROUX

A large amount of fat and flour may be cooked together and refrigerated for later use as an instant thickener. Use equal parts flour and fat, approximately 250 ml

1. Melt fat over low heat; blend in the flour.
2. Stir until the mixture bubbles; cool, stirring occasionally to keep the mixture homogeneous.
3. Shape into a bar in a double thickness of foil, cool, and mark the bar into convenient portions; or distribute the roux evenly in small muffin pans. (See PROPORTIONS FOR STARCH-THICKENED SAUCES for the amount of fat/flour required for each type of sauce.) Refrigerate in a plastic bag.

To use the roux, measure the liquid, heat and season; stir in the required amount of roux, continuing to stir until the mixture thickens; cook until no taste of raw starch remains.

Basic Recipe
BROWN SAUCE

30 ml	fat
30 ml	flour
250 ml	brown MEAT STOCK
	seasoning

Follow the method for WHITE SAUCE, MEDIUM (BASIC RECIPE).

Variations

Mushroom Sauce
(for beef or lamb HAMBURGER PATTIES)

Wash and dry 4 or 5 mushrooms; slice; sauté for a few minutes in the fat for the sauce. Add the flour; finish by MELTED FAT METHOD.

Hunter's Sauce
(for beef, venison, or rabbit)

| 15 ml | tomato paste |

Add to Mushroom Sauce, above.

Orange Sauce
(for duck)

| 15 ml | grated orange rind |
| 65 ml | orange juice |

Add to Brown Sauce (Basic Recipe). Simmer uncovered to blend the flavours and to evaporate some of the liquid.

Sauces Made with Cornstarch

Cornstarch gives a translucent appearance.

CHINESE SAUCE
(for pork or chicken)

1. Replace the flour in BROWN SAUCE (BASIC RECIPE) with half the amount of cornstarch, mixing it to a thin paste with soy sauce.
2. Stir the mixture into the hot stock.
3. Stir and cook until clear. Simmer to blend the flavours.

A dried mushroom, crushed and simmered in the stock, or a few drops of mushroom or oyster sauce (available in oriental food shops) add to the flavour.

SWEET AND SOUR SAUCE
(for chicken wings, chicken, or pork)

	1 green onion, chopped
	½ green pepper cut into squares
30 ml	oil
125 ml	vinegar
15 ml	soy sauce
200 ml	ketchup
540 ml	pineapple tidbits
50 ml	cornstarch
75 ml	brown sugar

1. Sauté green onion and pepper in oil until almost tender but still bright green. Drain. Remove from pan.
2. Combine vinegar, soy sauce, ketchup and juice drained from the pineapple; bring to a boil.
3. Combine sugar, cornstarch; blend into the liquid, stirring until the sauce becomes clear.
4. Add vegetables and pineapple cubes.

RAISIN SAUCE
(for ham or pork chops)

200 ml	brown MEAT STOCK
15 ml	red wine vinegar
15 ml	red currant jelly
5 ml	dry mustard
15 ml	cornstarch
125 ml	raisins

1. Plump the raisins by heating in a sieve over boiling water.

2. Add the vinegar and jelly to the stock; heat.
3. Combine cornstarch and mustard; mix with enough cold water to make a thin paste. Stir into the hot mixture; stir until clear; add the raisins; simmer to blend the flavours.

Cherry Sauce
(for ham or MEAT LOAF)

Replace the jelly in Raisin Sauce with juice from canned red cherries; add a dash of cinnamon or ginger to the mustard; replace the raisins with coarsely-chopped, drained, pitted red cherries.

Sauce for chicken can be made with pineapple juice. Lawry's Foods, Inc.

Basic Recipe
TOMATO SAUCE

30 ml	flour
30 ml	fat
250 ml	tomato juice

Follow any of the methods for WHITE SAUCE, MEDIUM (BASIC RECIPE).
Add a sprinkle of sugar, pepper and salt, to taste, to the finished sauce.
Or add onion juice, grated onion or dried onion flakes to the thickened sauce.
Or sauté chopped onion in the fat before making the sauce.
Or simmer in the tomato juice for 10-15 min cumin seed and basil, oregano or thyme, a piece of stick cinnamon, and two or three cloves; strain, measure, and make up to original quantity with water or stock.
Or add a few drops of lemon juice to the finished sauce.
A little tomato paste may be added to reinforce colour and flavour.
Yield: approximately 250 ml

Variations

Fresh Tomato Sauce
(for veal, fish, or omelet)

Replace the juice with peeled, chopped, bright red tomatoes. Save out a quarter of the tomatoes to add to the thickened sauce, to give the fresh flavour.

Creole Sauce

125 ml	vegetables: chopped onion, celery, green pepper, sliced mushrooms, olives, minced garlic

Sauté vegetables in fat until limp. Omit flour. Replace juice with whole canned tomatoes. Simmer to desired thickness.

Spanish Sauce
Season Creole Sauce with Tabasco; purée.

Basic Recipe
SPAGHETTI SAUCE

	1 onion, chopped
	2 stalks celery, chopped
	1 clove garlic, minced
	1 green pepper, chopped
125 ml	oil or bacon fat
397 g	1 can tomatoes
155 g	1 can tomato paste
215 g	1 can tomato sauce
350 ml	water
	seasoning*

* For seasoning this sauce, the spices suggested for TOMATO SAUCE (BASIC RECIPE) are suitable. Oregano is always used, but sparingly. The addition of a packaged spaghetti sauce mix provides a good blend of seasoning but adds to the cost.

1. Sauté vegetables a few at a time in hot fat until limp but not brown (5 min); add seasoning and liquids; simmer until the sauce is very thick (1 h), stirring frequently.
2. Purée; season to taste. *Yield:* 6 to 12 servings; 1.5-2 *l*

Variations

Mushroom Spaghetti Sauce Wash, dry, slice and sauté mushrooms in a small amount of oil; add to the puréed sauce.

Meat Spaghetti Sauce To the basic recipe for Spaghetti Sauce add:

250-500 g   ground beef

After the vegetables are sautéed in the fat, lift them out of the pan; increase the heat and brown the meat a small amount at a time; add to the vegetables; finish according to the basic recipe but do not purée.

Spaghetti Sauce may be prepared in large quantities and frozen for future use. Cool and freeze in containers or plastic bags, in quantities suitable for one meal.

Recipes, tables, etc. that appear in small capital letters, e.g., PARSLEY BUTTER, CANADA'S FOOD GUIDE, are listed in the index. Consult the index for the number of the page on which the item appears.

Marinades

A marinade is a mixture of acid, oil and spice in which meat is steeped for several hours to become tender. The marinade also adds flavour, and it is important to remember that if meat is marinated for a long time it may become too highly flavoured; soy sauce and salt should be omitted from marinades in which meat is to remain overnight.

Marinade may also be brushed on meat during cooking, to provide a crisp, flavoursome outer crust and a moist interior. It then is called a Barbecue Sauce.

Basic Recipe
MARINADE

125 ml	oil
50 ml	wine vinegar
	1 clove garlic, minced
	seasoning:
	for beef: a sprinkle of tarragon
	for lamb: a sprinkle of marjoram, rosemary, or mint; a dash of lemon juice; *or* replace garlic with chopped onions; add a few grains of ground cloves, a sprinkle of oregano
	for pork: a few caraway seeds or a sprinkle of tarragon

Combine the marinade in a shallow dish which will hold the meat; baste meat with the marinade, cover, and refrigerate several hours or overnight, depending upon thickness and tenderness of the meat; turn the meat several times during the marinating period. Drain. *Yield:* approximately 180 ml

---

Variation

Chinese Marinade Combine 1 part oil; 1 part fruit syrup from canned pineapple, peaches, or fruit cocktail; 1 part lemon juice; 1 part soy sauce. Season with ginger. Use for pork or chicken.

Basic Recipe
BARBECUE SAUCE

125 ml	KETCHUP
125 ml	water
60 ml	vinegar
25-125 ml	oil
60 ml	chopped onion and green pepper
	1 clove garlic, minced
2 ml	sugar
2 ml	salt
2 ml	celery seed
10 ml	paprika
15 ml	Worcestershire sauce
	few drops of Tabasco

1. Combine all the ingredients; heat to boiling and simmer 15 min. Use the smaller amount of fat if the sauce is to baste fat meats such as ribs or pork; use the larger quantity for chicken and lean meats.
2. Brush over baked spare ribs or meats on the barbecue; marinate chicken pieces in the sauce before baking; pour over sausages or beef patties to cook. *Yield:* 375-500 ml

Variations
Replace vinegar with lime juice.
Add oregano, basil or cumin to the seasonings.
Add minced parsley to the cooked sauce.

Chinese Barbecue Sauces
Mix dry mustard with water to make a thick paste; thin with soy sauce. Use to baste chicken pieces.
Combine equal amounts of CHINESE PLUM SAUCE and soy sauce.

The chicken provides the fat for these two Chinese barbecue sauces.

Flavoured Butters

Serve Flavoured Butters on steaks, hamburgers, fish, vegetables, or fried or poached eggs. Add to cream sauce just before serving. Spread on bread or toast when making sandwiches or canapés.

Basic Recipe
MAÎTRE D'HÔTEL SAUCE
(PARSLEY BUTTER)

50 ml	butter
	sprinkle of black pepper and cayenne
15 ml	minced parsley
5 ml	lemon juice

1. Cream the butter; add seasonings and parsley.
2. Beat in the lemon juice, continuing to beat until light and fluffy. *Yield:* approximately   80 ml

For a last-minute substitute place the butter in a glass or earthenware custard cup, add the fresh or dried herbs and salt and pepper to taste, set in boiling water, and let stand 10-15 min while the hot butter absorbs the flavours.

Variations
Replace parsley with the flavouring materials that follow, alone or in combination; use 1/3 the quantity of dried herbs.
Anchovy Butter: drained and finely chopped anchovies 15 ml
Blue Cheese or Roquefort Butter: crumbled blue cheese 30 ml
Garlic Butter Drop 1 or 2 cloves of garlic into boiling water; leave 1 min; drain, peel and mash in a small wooden bowl with a sprinkling of salt. Shake out the loose garlic and cream the butter in the bowl to pick up the flavour.
Seafood Butter Add sardines drained and mixed with a little curry or ketchup; shrimp, lobster, smoked salmon; tuna drained and rinsed with boiling water.
Almond Butter Blanch and sliver a few almonds; sauté in butter until golden brown; cool; use to replace parsley. This sauce, usually served with fish (e.g., sole amandine) is also a delicious addition to cauliflower and beans.
Herb Butter Replace the parsley with minced fresh herbs: chives, dill, basil, peppercorns or watercress, celery leaves, rosemary. Combine a fresh herb with one or two dried ones, if possible, or simmer the herbs in water until the liquid is almost evaporated; strain into the butter to replace the lemon juice.

WHIPPED BUTTER

Beat butter (unsalted or sweet) at room temperature until smooth; increase the speed to high and continue to beat until light, fluffy and white in colour; refrigerate until needed. Soften at room temperature before serving on hot breads. A small butter crock is an attractive serving dish.

PEPPER SAUCE

This hot sauce is good with any fish.

	1 soft roll or peeled small potato
100 ml	fish stock
	2 cloves garlic
	2 canned pimentos
	salt , pepper
	basil or savory
	Tabasco or chili powder
30 ml	oil

1. Soak the bread in the stock; squeeze it dry. (If a potato is used, boil it in the stock.)
2. Mash or blend the garlic, pimentos, and bread or potato with seasonings.
3. Beat the oil in a few drops at a time to give the consistency of soft butter.
4. Before serving, beat in enough stock, a little at a time, to thin to a pouring consistency. *Yield:* 125-250 ml

Sauces with an Egg Base

HOLLANDAISE SAUCE

This sauce is surprisingly easy, and elevates a vegetable or fish to gourmet fare.

30 ml	boiling water
15 ml	lemon juice
	salt, pepper
50 ml	soft butter
	2 egg yolks

1. In a small heavy saucepan combine the water, lemon juice and seasoning; beat the egg yolks into the liquid with a fork or whisk.
2. Over low heat add the butter bit by bit, beating with a wooden spoon or whisk constantly until the egg thickens and a creamy emulsion forms (4-5 min). Pour immediately into a warm serving dish. *Serves 4-6.*

If Hollandaise becomes overheated it will curdle. To restore, immediately chill the pan in cold water, then slowly stir into the sauce hot water,   15 ml

Variation
Béarnaise Sauce

5 ml	dried tarragon
10 ml	chopped parsley
10 ml	chopped green onion
45 ml	wine vinegar
15 ml	water
	salt, pepper

1. Simmer together all the ingredients until only a little liquid remains (5 min). Strain, reserving the liquid.
2. Prepare Hollandaise Sauce according to the preceding recipe, using this liquid to replace the lemon juice.
3. Continue to beat over hot water until the sauce is thick.

Serve on broiled meat or fish.

MOCK HOLLANDAISE

125 ml	MAYONNAISE
15 ml	lemon juice
	water

1. Heat the mayonnaise in a double boiler over hot, not boiling, water.
2. Stir in the lemon juice and enough water to thin the sauce to the desired consistency. *Yield:* 125 ml

TARTAR SAUCE

250 ml	MAYONNAISE
60 ml	finely chopped olives, pickles, capers, parsley, onion; few drops of lemon juice

Combine all the ingredients. If the sauce is to be served hot, substitute cooked salad dressing for mayonnaise.

For an even quicker Tartar Sauce use commercial sandwich spread.

Recipes, tables, etc. that appear in small capital letters, e.g., PARSLEY BUTTER, CANADA'S FOOD GUIDE, are listed in the index. Consult the index for the number of the page on which the item appears.

QUICK MUSTARD RELISH

Stir HOT or DARK MUSTARD SAUCE into commercial sandwich spread; use for ham sandwiches or hot dogs; serve with cold meats.

SWEET AND SOUR MUSTARD RELISH

250 ml	orange marmalade
75 ml	prepared horseradish
75 ml	prepared mustard

Combine the ingredients. Serve with fried ham or baked back bacon.

HOT MUSTARD SAUCE

	1 egg
15 ml	sugar
5 ml	dry mustard
125 ml	vinegar
30 ml	salad oil

1. Beat the egg in the top of a double boiler; add remaining ingredients except the oil.
2. Place over hot water and stir until mixture thickens. Remove from heat; beat in the oil.

Serve hot or cold with ham, roast beef or weiners. *Yield:* 200 ml

DARK MUSTARD SAUCE

45 ml	dry mustard
30 ml	SPICED VINEGAR
5 ml	sugar
	salt
15 ml	oil

Combine dry ingredients in a cup or small mustard pot; smooth out lumps; stir in vinegar; beat in the oil with a spoon. Keep covered. *Yield:* 60 ml

MINT SAUCE

60 ml	mint leaves, finely chopped
60 ml	hot water
60 ml	vinegar
30 ml	sugar

1. Mix water, vinegar, sugar, stir until sugar is dissolved.
2. Pour over mint; let stand in a warm place 30 min

Serve with roast lamb. *Yield:* approximately 125 ml

Variations

Add finely chopped mint to currant jelly *or* to chutney; *or* replace vinegar and sugar with orange juice and grated orange rind.

CRANBERRY RELISH

250 g	cranberries
	1 large orange
	1 large red apple (optional)
175 ml	sugar

1. Pick over and wash cranberries; grind, using a medium setting. A large red apple, cored but unpeeled, may be ground with the cranberries.
2. Squeeze juice from orange; remove seeds and white membrane; grind the pulp.
3. Combine cranberries, sugar, and orange juice and pulp; refrigerate in a covered container. *Yield:* 500 ml

This relish has many uses:

Serve with poultry or ham.

Set with gelatine.

Fold into sour cream for fruit salad dressing.

WHOLE CRANBERRY SAUCE

500 g	cranberries
500 ml	sugar
500 ml	boiling water

1. Pick over and wash cranberries.
2. Make syrup of sugar and water; boil 2 min
3. Add the cranberries; simmer until berries are transparent.
4. Pour into a sterilized jar or individual moulds. *Yield:* 1 *l*

Cranberry Jelly Follow the recipe for Whole Cranberry Sauce omitting the sugar; purée the berries; return purée to the liquid with the sugar; simmer until sauce jells (5 min). *Yield:* 350 ml

SOUR CREAM SAUCE

250 ml	sour cream
	seasoning (salt, pepper, onion)
30 ml	MAYONNAISE (optional)
	One of the following flavouring ingredients:
30 ml	prepared horseradish, well drained
or	
75 ml	blue cheese or Roquefort, crumbled
or	
15 ml	HOT MUSTARD SAUCE
or	
15 ml	fresh herbs, minced: chives, parsley, dill, rosemary
or	half a medium cucumber, seeded, chopped finely or sliced thinly; sprinkle with salt and let stand; press out the juice; drain well.

Combine the ingredients; season to taste; refrigerate 30 min to blend flavours.

COTTAGE CHEESE SAUCE

250 ml	cottage cheese (plain)
15 ml	lemon juice
30 ml	skim milk powder *or* buttermilk

Combine in a blender or beat smooth. *Yield:* 250 ml
This substitute for sour cream sauce may be varied in the same way. It contains less saturated fat while providing calcium and protein.

Sauces for Desserts

Basic Recipe
SIMPLE SYRUP

Thickness	*Sugar*	*Water*
Thin	1 part	2 parts
Medium	1 part	1 part
Thick	2 parts	1 part

1. Combine sugar and water; stir until sugar is dissolved.
2. Bring to a boil; simmer 3 min
3. Pour into sterilized bottle; seal; refrigerate once the bottle has been opened.

A small amount of syrup poured over cornstarch, rice or custard pudding is an attractive garnish and permits the reduction of sugar in the pudding. Add SPICED SYRUP to fruit drinks for colour and flavour. Use SPICED SYRUP to sweeten fresh fruit or to poach pears, peaches or apple slices. Use SIMPLE or SPICED SYRUP to preserve fruit.

Spiced Syrup

500 ml	sugar
500 ml	water
	1 strip lemon or orange peel
	1 small piece ginger root
	3-4 allspice berries
	crushed seeds of 2 cardamom pods
	or 1 star anise crushed

Combine sugar and water; add spices tied loosely in cheese cloth; simmer 10 min or to taste; lift out spices; pour into sterilized bottle; seal.
Fruit Syrup Prepare a thick syrup (see SIMPLE SYRUP) substituting fruit juice for the water; flavour with lemon or orange rind if desired; pour into sterilized bottle and cover; refrigerate. The fruit juice may be the second or third extraction juice from jelly making (see JELLY PREPARATION) *or* juice left from canned fruit.

PANCAKE SYRUP

250 ml	corn syrup
50 ml	butter *or* margarine

Heat together until butter melts; stir and serve. *Yield:* 250 ml

Variations
Before adding butter, add one of the following and heat:

75 ml	strawberry jam
or	
312 ml	1 pkg. frozen blueberries
or	
375 ml	fresh cleaned berries
or	
250 ml	maple syrup

Recipes, tables, etc. that appear in small capital letters, e.g., PARSLEY BUTTER, CANADA'S FOOD GUIDE, are listed in the index. Consult the index for the number of the page on which the item appears.

HONEY BUTTER

125 ml	butter *or* margarine
175 ml	honey
15 ml	orange juice
5 ml	orange rind

Combine and beat to blend. This Honey Butter is delicious with pancakes

Variations
Cinnamon Honey Butter Add cinnamon, 15 ml
Peanut Butter Sauce Add peanut butter, 125 ml

MOCK MAPLE SYRUP

250 ml	brown sugar
250 ml	boiling water
125 ml	white sugar
5 ml	butter
2 ml	maple flavour

1. Combine the brown sugar and water and bring to a boil.
2. Caramelize the white sugar (see TO CARAMELIZE SUGAR); add the syrup from step 1.
3. Simmer until smooth and the thickness of maple syrup; pour into a pitcher containing the butter and maple flavouring. Stir before serving. *Yield:* 250-375 ml

BUTTERSCOTCH SYRUP

200 ml	brown sugar
125 ml	corn syrup
60 ml	water
30 ml	butter *or* margarine
125 ml	evaporated milk *or* thin cream

1. Combine all ingredients except the milk; stir over medium heat until sugar is dissolved; boil without stirring until a soft ball forms, about 5 min (See COLD WATER TEST FOR SYRUP).
2. Cool slightly; stir in the milk. *Yield:* approximately 250 ml

THICK CHOCOLATE SYRUP (CHOCOLATE FUDGE SAUCE)

250 ml	sugar
100 ml	cocoa
125 ml	boiling water
30 ml	corn syrup
5 ml	vanilla
30 ml	butter *or* margarine

Combine sugar and cocoa; add water; stir over low heat until sugar is dissolved; add corn syrup; bring to a boil and simmer without stirring over moderate heat until of syrup consistency (5-8 min); remove from heat; add butter. When cool add the vanilla. *Yield:* approximately 250 ml

Variations
For a richer, more expensive, sauce substitute 2 squares of unsweetened chocolate for the cocoa.
Chocolate Mint Syrup Substitute one or two drops of peppermint flavour for the vanilla

Serve any of the preceding syrups over ice cream or plain yogurt, or combine with milk for milk shakes. Store syrups in a covered jar in the refrigerator. Syrups which have been thickened with flour, cornstarch, or cocoa will keep for one week; unthickened syrups will keep longer.

HARD SAUCE

125 ml	butter
500 ml	brown sugar, fruit sugar, *or* icing sugar
10 ml	boiling water
	flavouring

Flavouring: vanilla is a popular flavouring with a few grains of nutmeg or cinnamon added.

Fruit juices such as cherry, pineapple or lemon juice may replace the water.

1. Cream the butter; add sugar and water; beat until light and fluffy; add the flavouring.
2. Shape into rosettes with a pastry tube; *or* shape into a bar, chill, and cut into squares. Serve on hot plum pudding, mincemeat pie, gingerbread, or spice cake. *Yield:* 250 ml

---

Basic Sauce
VANILLA SAUCE

75-100 ml	sugar
30 ml	cornstarch
50 ml	cold water
125 ml	boiling water
15 ml	butter *or* margarine
5 ml	vanilla

1. Combine the sugar and cornstarch in a small saucepan; add cold water, stirring until smooth.
2. Add the boiling water; stir over low heat until the mixture begins to boil. Taste to be sure there is no flavour of raw starch, allowing the sauce to simmer a few minutes more if necessary.
3. Remove from heat; add butter, cool and add vanilla. *Yield:* 250 ml

---

Variations
Butter Sauce Use the smaller amount of sugar; substitute milk for water.
Lemon Sauce Use the larger amount of sugar; add the grated rind and juice of half a lemon to the sugar to replace vanilla.
Chocolate Sauce Use the larger amount of sugar and half the quantity of cornstarch; to the sugar-starch mixture add cocoa: 50 ml
Caramel Sauce Use the larger amount of sugar; caramelize the sugar (see TO CARAMELIZE SUGAR), add the boiling water and simmer until smooth; measure and add water to bring up to 200 ml
Combine the cornstarch with the cold water; stir into the caramel syrup; finish as VANILLA SAUCE (BASIC RECIPE).
Fruit Sauce Replace the boiling water with fruit juice, and replace the vanilla with almond flavouring *or* lemon juice. If the fruit juice is already sweetened, omit or reduce the quantity of sugar; additional sugar may be needed for unsweetened juice. Chopped, drained fruit may be added to the finished sauce.

Fruit Sauce adds sparkle to cornstarch pudding, batter puddings or crisps; it makes a glaze for fruit tarts or fresh fruit sections. When cold, the sauce sets to a gel which can provide a quick dessert. Fold into the gel sour cream, ice cream, or stiffly beaten egg white. Garnish with sliced fruit, or sandwich between chocolate or ginger wafers and refrigerate.

SHORT CUT VANILLA SAUCE

To vanilla pudding mix add 1½ times the quantity of liquid required for the pudding. Other flavours may be used in the same way.

BLUEBERRY SAUCE

375 ml	blueberries, fresh
250 ml	orange juice
375 ml	water
125 ml	sugar
50 ml	cornstarch
	sprinkle of cinnamon
	few drops of almond flavour

1. Combine the cleaned berries and orange juice; bring to boiling point.
2. Blend cornstarch, sugar and water; stir into the berries and cook until there is no flavour of raw starch; remove from heat; add flavouring. *Yield:* 750 ml
Serve over pancakes, ice cream or milk puddings.

MARSHMALLOW SAUCE

125 ml	granulated sugar
60 ml	boiling water
	16 large marshmallows
	1 egg white

1. Boil sugar and water 2 min
2. Press marshmallows into syrup until melted; do not stir mixture.
3. Beat white of egg until stiff; add marshmallow mixture, slowly beating until smooth.
4. Add flavouring. *Yield:* 500 ml

Recipes, tables, etc. that appear in small capital letters, e.g., PARSLEY BUTTER, CANADA'S FOOD GUIDE, are listed in the index. Consult the index for the number of the page on which the item appears.

A steaming chowder is a hearty first course for a cold-weather supper.

Thick vegetable soup is almost a meal in itself.

7 Soup

In medieval days, the word "soupe" referred to a piece of bread boiled in meat stock or porridge (our word "sop" comes from this); the name eventually came to be used for the boiled meat and later, in our time, for the liquid.

Cream Soups

When planning menus, remember that cream soups are filling. Build a meal around cream soup by adding an interesting bread and a salad or fruit dessert. In this way the protein, calcium and riboflavin from the milk will be supplemented by vitamins and minerals from the other foods to make a nutritious meal. Here are a few suggestions:

OLD-FASHIONED CREAM OF TOMATO SOUP
Peanut Butter and Bacon Sandwich
ORANGE AMBROSIA

Cream of Pea Soup (see CREAM SOUP BASIC RECIPE**)**
CHEESE CARAWAY FRENCH BREAD
FRUIT CUP

POTATO ONION SOUP
Bread Sticks
STEWED RHUBARB

Cream of Spinach Soup
(see CREAM SOUP BASIC RECIPE**)**
Grilled Cheese Sandwich
(see GRILLED SANDWICHES**)**
COLE SLAW

Cream soup should be the consistency of rich cream, not porridge; if necessary, thin it with additional stock or milk.

Increase the nutritional quality of cream soup by adding a little skim milk powder to the flour and shaking with water.

Basic Recipe
CREAM SOUP

500 ml	THIN WHITE SAUCE
250 ml	**cooked vegetable pulp**
250 ml	**vegetable stock**
	seasoning

1. Prepare THIN WHITE SAUCE.
2. Prepare the cooked vegetable pulp and stock by boiling raw cubed, sliced or grated vegetables in water. Water quantity should be two times the quantity of chopped vegetable or one and a half times that of grated vegetable. Celery and mushrooms are best sliced, carrots grated.
   Purée cooked spinach and peas. Mashed potatoes, cream-style corn, or leftover cooked vegetables may be used by adding the stock saved from their cooking or extra milk or water and a chicken concentrate.
3. Combine the vegetable (pulp and stock) and the sauce; reheat to blend flavours but do not boil.
4. Taste and season.
5. Serve in heated bowls, mugs, or a tureen.
6. Garnish: possible garnishes include sour cream or lightly salted whipped cream (both at room temperature); shredded, toasted almonds; chopped parsley, watercress, chives or green onions; croutons, cheese popcorn; grated cheese; paprika.
   Serves 4-6.

Salt may be reduced or replaced by spices or herbs. (See SEASONING: SPICES, HERBS, CONDIMENTS AND FLAVOURINGS.) Float a slice of onion in the milk while it is heating; scrape a little onion juice into a soup that needs more flavour. Fresh or dry celery leaves, rings of green onion, leeks, or chives add flavour and also serve as a garnish.

You may save time by adding the milk to the cooked vegetable and water; thicken with prepared ROUX. Milk supplies protein, calcium and riboflavin. Serve milk this way to those who do not like to drink it.

POTATO CHEESE SOUP

Prepare Cream of Potato Soup from CREAM SOUP BASIC RECIPE, using mashed potatoes for the vegetable. Just before serving, stir in grated Cheddar cheese to taste. Allow cheese to melt on low heat and beat until smooth. Garnish with paprika.

CHEESE AND ONION SOUP

	2 medium size onions, thinly sliced
30 ml	melted butter
15 ml	flour
5 ml	dry mustard
500 ml	milk
250 ml	old Cheddar cheese, grated
	salt, pepper, celery seed, cumin
	4 slices French bread, buttered

1. Stir onions into melted butter in a saucepan; cover and cook over low heat until tender, about 10 min
2. Mix together flour and mustard in a small, covered glass jar; add enough milk to make a thin paste.
3. Add remaining milk to onions. Heat; stir in the paste as a thickener.
4. Cook mixture over medium heat for about 5 min, stirring constantly.
5. Sprinkle a little cheese over the bread; broil until brown.
6. Add the remaining cheese to the soup, remove from direct heat and allow cheese to melt. Do not overheat the soup or the cheese will curdle.
7. Stir; season; serve at once with the toasted bread. *Serves 3-4.*

OLD-FASHIONED CREAM OF TOMATO SOUP

500 ml	THIN WHITE SAUCE, seasoned and hot
450 ml	canned tomatoes, heated
	4-6 soda biscuits, crushed

1. Prepare THIN WHITE SAUCE in a large saucepan or double boiler.
2. Combine the tomatoes and sauce only when ready to serve, by slowly adding the tomatoes to the sauce. Stir; season.
3. Serve immediately, topped with biscuit crumbs. *Serves 4-6.*

To prevent the acid in the tomatoes from curdling the milk, follow the directions carefully.

Chowders

The term "chowder" comes from *chaudière,* the heavy iron pot in which soup simmered as it hung from the fireplace hook. Fish chowder sustained the earliest settlers through the long winters; corn chowder sustained farmers through days of harvesting.

ATLANTIC CHOWDER

125 g	salt pork *or* bacon
	3 onions, sliced
	6 small potatoes, sliced
	salt, pepper
250 ml	boiling water *or* vegetable stock
500 g	cod *or* haddock fillets
750 ml	milk
	salt, pepper
15 ml	butter (optional)
30 ml	chopped parsley
	6 soda biscuits *or* pilot biscuits, crushed

1. Dice the pork, fry it slowly to a crisp golden brown in a heavy pan; lift out the bits of pork and set them aside.
2. Add the onions to the fat and fry slowly until yellow and clear.
3. Add the potatoes, the seasoning and the water; heat.
4. Cut the fish into squares; drop onto the potatoes; cover and simmer until the potatoes are tender and the fish flaky (20 min).
5. Add the milk and heat; taste and season.
6. Just before serving, drop butter, the bits of fried pork, parsley, and biscuits into the chowder. Do not stir. *Serves 4-6.*

This filling soup supplies all the important nutrients inexpensively. Best of all, it tastes good.

Variations
1. Replace the fish with any of:

220 g	1 can salmon and liquid
500 g	diced and browned scallops
400 g	3 cans baby clams and liquid
398 ml	1 can corn kernels

Add scallops with the potatoes; add other ingredients after the potatoes are cooked.
2. Replace part of the milk with canned celery or mushroom soup.

VEGETABLE CHOWDER

	1 potato, diced
	3 coarsely grated carrots
	1 onion, diced
	1 stalk celery, diced
30 ml	bacon fat, butter, *or* chicken fat
30 ml	rolled oats
250 ml	vegetable stock *or* water (approximately)
500 ml	milk (approximately)
250 ml	canned tomatoes *or* tomato juice
	salt, pepper, basil

1. Lightly brown raw vegetables in the fat, in a large saucepan.
2. Add rolled oats and enough water or vegetable stock to cover.
3. Cover and simmer until vegetables are tender (20 min).
4. Measure liquid and add milk to make 750 ml
5. Slowly add the tomatoes; taste, season; reheat but do not boil. Serve immediately. *Serves 6.*

Replace expensive oyster stew with chowder served from a handsome tureen. To complete the meal, this hearty soup needs only corn sticks or garlic bread and a dessert. Lawry's Foods, Inc.

POTATO ONION SOUP

	3-4 onions
	2-3 potatoes
2 ℓ	water
5 ml	salt

1. Simmer the ingredients together until soft (30 min); purée, reheat; taste, season.
2. Serve garnished with minced parsley or chives. *Serves 6.*

Variations
Substitute: chicken stock for the water
   leeks for the onions
   whole milk for part of the water, adding it after the soup is puréed.

Potato Cheese Soup Add grated Cheddar cheese just before serving.

Watercress Soup Chop stems of the watercress and cook with the vegetables.
or
Wash, dry, and coarsely chop the watercress; add to the soup 5 min before puréeing.

Parsley Potato Soup Substitute parsley for the watercress.

Asparagus Potato Soup Cut off the tips of a bunch of fresh asparagus; simmer them in a little salted water until tender. Peel the remaining stems; chop and cook with potatoes. Before serving, stir in the tips and juice. Carrots, celery, or broccoli may be added in small quantities to add flavour without changing the basic potato quality.

Country Soup Do not purée; break the potatoes up with a masher. This is a versatile soup that may be varied to suit the mood and the pantry shelf and to supplement the nutrients supplied by the rest of the menu.

To Keep Leftover Cream Soup or Vegetable Stock
Freeze chilled vegetable stock or soup in small cartons or in ice-cube trays. Store in plastic bags, in the freezer. Use stock in soup or sauce. Reheat cream soup over hot water, without stirring; when hot, beat to blend and season as needed.

Recipes, tables, etc. that appear in small capital letters, e.g., PARSLEY BUTTER, CANADA'S FOOD GUIDE, are listed in the index. Consult the index for the number of the page on which the item appears.

Stock Soups

Veal or chicken provides the basis for white soup stock, while beef or lamb is used to make brown stock. Cracked shin or marrow bones and neck of beef are good for flavour; chuck beef will provide a main course when served hot or cold with HORSE-RADISH SAUCE.

Basic Recipe
MEAT STOCK

2 kg	meat and bones
1 *l*	cold water
	1 small onion
	1 carrot
	2 stalks celery
2 ml	salt
	1 bayleaf
5 ml	mixed herbs (thyme, marjoram, savory)
	4-5 black peppercorns
	1 sprig parsley

1. Cover meat with cold water; bring to a boil; skim off the froth.
2. Add vegetables; simmer for 2 h; add spice; add boiling water if necessary at the end of the first hour.
3. Strain. (The meat may be served separately or may be cubed and returned to the soup.)
4. Taste and season; cool; remove all fat. *Yield*: 1 *l*

The combination of herbs and spices in this recipe is *bouquet garni.* Tied in a small cheesecloth bundle, the bouquet can be lifted from the soup when the desired flavour is obtained. Mixed pickling spice may be substituted for the herbs.

For a darker stock, the meat may be browned by sautéeing in fat or browned in a very hot oven, before adding water.

Meat concentrates have a high salt and monosodium glutamate content. Use with discrimination, and experiment to find the brand best suited to your needs and taste.

Variations
Chicken Stock Chicken necks, wings, and backs; or a boiling fowl may be used for the meat. Season with herbs rather than the stronger spices. The giblets and bones from a roasted chicken may be used to prepare approximately half the quantity of stock.
Turkey Stock The broken-up carcass of a roasted turkey, washed to remove the dressing, may replace the meat. Omit the spices.
Fish Stock The bones, head, and trimmings of filleted fish may replace the meat. Omit the spices and herbs; add mushroom stems and one or two thin slices of lemon. Bottled clam juice may be used to reinforce the flavour (it is very salty).

To Clear Soup Stock

1 *l*	flavoured soup stock
1	egg white and shell
50 ml	cold water

1. Let stock become cold; remove fat.
2. Beat white of egg slightly, add it to the shell, crushed.
3. Add to stock; mix thoroughly.
4. Heat slowly without stirring to just simmering; continue simmering 15 min. Let rest undisturbed up to 1 h. Strain through a hot, damp cloth suspended over a bowl. Float unglazed paper on the surface to remove any fat.

Storage Stock may be frozen in the way suggested on page 91. Unfrozen stock soups may be refrigerated but must be used in a few days or brought to a full rolling boil, cooled, and returned to the refrigerator. Small quantities of warm stock should not be added to chilled stock, as dangerous bacteria may grow in lukewarm stock.
Bouillon is cleared beef stock
Consommé is a combination of meat and chicken stock, more highly seasoned than bouillon. It will jell if left several hours in the refrigerator.

Soups Made with Meat Stock

VEGETABLE SOUP

1 *l*	well-seasoned de-fatted meat stock, with or without diced meat
500 ml	diced or shredded vegetables
30 ml	washed rice

1. Heat the stock to boiling; add the other ingredients; return to boiling, stirring occasionally; simmer until the rice is cooked and vegetables tender (30 min).
2. Taste and season. *Serves 4-6.*

Variations

Barley Broth Replace rice with barley previously soaked in water overnight. Or, to soften barley in a shorter time, cover with cold salted water, bring to a boil, boil 3 min, leave 0.5 h

Bean and Barley Soup Include in the vegetable combination frozen lima beans. Replace rice with barley.

Minestrone Include in the vegetable combination shredded green cabbage, shredded spinach, minced garlic, canned tomatoes and canned kidney beans. The soup should be very thick. Serve with grated Parmesan cheese.

SAUERKRAUT SOUP

1 *l*	well-seasoned de-fatted meat stock
30 ml	barley
5 ml	paprika
	1 onion, chopped
	1 garlic clove, minced
100 ml	mushrooms quartered
150 g	Kielbasa sausage
390 g	1 can sauerkraut
250 ml	vegetable

A smoked ham bone and a piece of fresh shoulder pork are used to prepare the stock for this traditional Slovak dish. It is served for midnight supper on New Year's Eve so that the sauerkraut will bring good luck in the coming year.

Kielbasa, kielbasy, however it is spelled, is a delicious Polish sausage. Split the thin casing and peel it off before cutting the sausage.

Use any combination of vegetables; carrots and celery are excellent; cabbage and turnip should be used sparingly, as their flavours are strong. Potatoes must be added later or cut into large pieces.

1. Soak barley in cold water to cover for several hours; add to stock with onions, garlic, and paprika; bring to a boil; simmer.
2. Dice the meat removed from the bones and the sausage; add to soup.
3. Add vegetable; simmer until tender.
4. Rinse sauerkraut under running cold water; add to soup and simmer 20-30 min to blend the flavours; taste and season. *Serves 6.*

FRENCH CANADIAN PEA SOUP

250 ml	split peas
	smoked ham bone
3 *l*	water
125 ml	finely chopped celery with leaves
	1 onion, chopped
	1 bay leaf
	6 peppercorns
	thyme or savory
	2 carrots, shredded

1. Soak dried peas in cold water overnight. Use 3 parts water to 1 part peas.
2. Combine peas, ham bone, and water; add celery, onions, bay leaf and peppercorns.
3. Bring to a boil; skim off froth; cover and reduce heat; simmer for 2 h, stirring often to prevent peas sticking; uncover and reduce liquid almost to half original quantity by boiling.
4. Remove bone. Shred off the meat and return meat to soup; skim out spices. Chill; remove fat.
5. Add carrots; reheat; taste and season; simmer until carrots are soft. *Serves 6.*

Yellow or green peas may be used. The traditional soup used a combination of whole and split yellow.

Packaged peas have been processed so that overnight soaking is not necessary. To save fuel, leave them in cold water or stock while the other ingredients are being prepared.

The ham will add salt so none should be added until the soup is thick.

Variations

Basque Bean Soup Substitute white beans or small limas for peas in French Canadian Pea Soup. With the carrots, add a small head of cabbage, shredded, and 4 potatoes, peeled and cubed. Serve in earthenware casseroles. Sprinkle with grated cheese; brown under the broiler or serve with cheese in a bowl to be added as desired.

Lentil Soup Replace the peas with lentils. When all vegetables are soft, purée the soup. Taste, season, reheat; serve garnished with crumbled crisp bacon or sliced knackwurst sausage.

A bacon square or sliced ends of bacon will make a good substitute for the ham flavour if leftover vegetable stock is used instead of water.

Recipes, tables, etc. that appear in small capital letters, e.g., PARSLEY BUTTER, CANADA'S FOOD GUIDE, are listed in the index. Consult the index for the number of the page on which the item appears.

MULLIGATAWNY SOUP

250 ml	diced raw chicken
45 ml	fat
75 ml each	carrot, celery, onion, tart apple, chopped
10 ml	curry powder
1 *l*	chicken stock
	salt, pepper, bay leaf
75 ml	tomato juice
60 ml	flour

1. Sauté chicken in fat until lightly browned; remove chicken; add chopped vegetables and apple.
2. Stir in curry powder.
3. Combine stock, seasoning, tomato juice with the sautéed ingredients; simmer until tender (30 min).
4. Thicken with flour shaken with cold water (see COLD LIQUID METHOD).
5. Purée, taste and season. Garnish with a thin sliver of unpeeled apple and a little green mint, watercress *or* parsley; *or* with onion rings.

Variation
Senegalese Soup Substitute light cream for tomato juice.
These soups are delicious iced.

GROUNDNUT SOUP (STEW)

1 *l*	de-fatted seasoned chicken stock *or* brown beef stock
125 ml	tomato paste
250 ml	peanut butter

1. Combine tomato paste, peanut butter and a small amount of stock in a small bowl; beat until smooth; add to the stock.
2. Heat; taste and season. *Serve 4-6.*
In West Africa this soup, highly seasoned with ginger and red pepper, is served with meat or chicken over cooked rice.
   Tomato juice may replace some of the paste for a less sharp flavour.

Peas, beans, lentils, and peanuts—these legumes furnish high quality protein more cheaply than meat.

Recipes, tables, etc. that appear in small capital letters, e.g., PARSLEY BUTTER, CANADA'S FOOD GUIDE, are listed in the index. Consult the index for the number of the page on which the item appears.

Soups Made With Chicken Stock

CHICKEN SOUP

1 *l*	well-seasoned de-fatted chicken stock
250 ml	sliced celery
	1 onion, chopped
30 ml	washed rice

1. Add vegetables and rice to boiling stock; simmer until rice is soft and vegetables tender.
2. Taste; season. *Serves 4-6.*

CREAM OF CHICKEN SOUP

1 *l*	well-seasoned, de-fatted chicken stock
500 ml	cream *or* top milk
100 ml	chicken fat *or* butter
100 ml	flour

1. Combine stock and cream; thicken with fat and flour (see THIN WHITE SAUCE).
2. Taste, season; garnish with slivered toasted almonds. *Serves 6.*

AVGOLEMONO (LEMON SOUP)

1 *l*	well-seasoned, de-fatted chicken stock
50 ml	washed rice
	2 eggs
	1 small lemon
	salt, pepper
	minced parsley

1. Cook rice in stock until tender.
2. Beat eggs until frothy; add juice of the lemon; beat in a little stock.
3. Return to the hot stock slowly, stirring over low heat until soup is creamy. Do not boil; overheating will cause curdling.
4. Season; stir well and serve at once, garnished with parsley. *Serves 6.*
This Greek soup may be served iced.
   Shredded cooked chicken may be added after step 1.

Soups Made with Cleared Stock

MANDARIN SOUP

	4 dried mushrooms
250 ml	cold water
125 g	lean pork (1 chop)
1 *l*	cleared chicken stock
	1 piece fresh bean curd
125 ml	bamboo shoots
30 ml	cornstarch
50 ml	cold water
15 ml	soy sauce
	sliced green onion *or* dried salad onion

1. Clean, then soak mushrooms in water 20 min; drain the liquid into the stock; slice the mushrooms.
2. Cut pork into slivers; simmer in the stock until the meat is tender (15 min).
3. Cut bamboo shoots and curd into thin strips; add with mushrooms to the hot liquid; reheat.
4. Combine cornstarch, water, and soy sauce to a thin paste; add to the hot liquid, stirring until clear.
5. Taste and season. Garnish with onion rings. *Serves 4-6.*

BEET SOUP (BORSCHT)

125 ml	shredded beets
75 ml	shredded carrots
	water
125 ml	finely chopped onion
250 ml	cleared stock
75 ml	finely shredded cabbage
125 ml	tomato juice
75 ml	shredded beet tops
	dillweed
	seasoning
125 ml	thin cream

1. Pare the washed beets; grate or shred; chop the stems and shred the leaves. Boil shredded beets and stems barely covered in water until tender (about 30 min).
2. Chop the onions; add with carrots and stock to cooked beets.
3. Simmer until tender (15 min); add cabbage and beet tops; continue to simmer until tender.
4. Add tomato juice, dillweed, and seasoning as needed.

5. Add cream; heat but do not boil; serve immediately. *Serves 5-6.*

Sour cream at room temperature may replace thin cream.

Four fresh mushrooms, sliced, may also be added at step 3. This recipe, common to all European countries, has many variations. It may be made without stock, with added lemon juice, or with a whole, hot boiled potato in the serving bowl.

FRENCH ONION SOUP

	1 garlic clove, minced
	6 onions, thinly sliced
30 ml	fat
1 *l*	cleared brown stock, seasoned
5 ml	Worcestershire sauce
	6 slices French bread
200 ml	grated cheese (Swiss Gruyere and a sprinkle of Parmesan is recommended; Mozzarella may be used.)

1. Cook onion and garlic in fat until brown. Add stock; simmer until tender; add Worcestershire sauce; season.
2. Slice the bread; toast until golden.
3. Pour the soup into oven-proof individual casseroles arranged on a baking pan.
4. Float one or two slices of bread in each dish, sprinkle with cheese; heat in oven until cheese is melted and golden brown, 180°C

Ontario Ministry of Agriculture and Food

Soups Made with Fish Stock

SEAFOOD SOUP (BOUILLABAISSE)

1 *l*	well-seasoned fish stock
75 ml	fat
50 ml	thinly sliced onion
	1 garlic clove, minced
250 ml	tomato juice
500 g	cod fillets
500 g	scallops
113 g	1 can tiny shrimps
	seasoning: thyme, basil, cumin

1. Sauté onion and garlic in fat until soft.
2. Add stock, tomato juice; bring to a boil.
3. Cut fish and scallops into small cubes; add to liquid, simmer 15 min; add shrimp.
4. Taste and season. *Serves 6.*

A true Bouillabaisse contains at least six varieties of fresh seafood. The delicate fish break up, adding body to the soup. The shellfish and firm pieces are lifted out onto a platter to be eaten after the soup; the liquid is poured over garlic croutons and served with PEPPER SAUCE.

Oyster Soup See OYSTER STEW.

Chilled Soups

Refreshing additions to summer meals, chilled soups become glamorous winter appetizers when surrounded by a dish of crushed ice or fresh snow!

JELLIED CONSOMMÉ

375 ml	cleared meat stock or bouillon, well-seasoned
15 ml	1 envelope gelatin
75 ml	cleared meat stock or bouillon
	garnish

1. Heat the larger quantity of meat stock or bouillon.
2. Soften gelatin in remaining stock for 5 min. (If stock was jellied originally, the amount of gelatin can be reduced by 1/3).
3. Add the softened gelatin to the hot stock; heat to dissolve. Chill in a large pan, to set in a shallow layer.
4. Break up jelly using a wide-tined fork, or cut into small cubes and pile into chilled dishes.
5. Garnish with sour cream and a sprinkling of chopped chives. *Serves 3-4.*

Variation
Jellied Consommé Madrilene Substitute tomato juice for the liquid in which the gelatin is softened.

EASY JELLIED CONSOMMÉ

284 ml	1 can consommé
30 ml	sour cream
or	
15 ml	MAYONNAISE
	chives *or* green onion

Chill canned consommé at least 4 h in the refrigerator. Serve as Jellied Consommé, garnish. *Serves 2-3.*

Keep tins of consommé in the refrigerator ever ready for this easy appetizer!

CHILLED CUCUMBER SOUP

1 *l*	buttermilk
250 ml	sour cream
250 ml	diced cucumber
15 ml	finely chopped green onion
15 ml	chopped fresh dill
5 ml	salt
	few grains of pepper

1. Beat buttermilk and sour cream until smooth; add vegetables and season.
2. Chill several hours. *Serves 6-8.*

GAZPACHO

	1 large green pepper
	1 cucumber
	1 small onion
250 ml	chopped celery
284 ml	1 can bouillon
750 ml	tomato juice
30 ml	lemon juice *or* wine vinegar
	salt, pepper
60 ml	oil
	1 tomato

1. Set aside ¼ of green pepper and cucumber for later use. Finely chop or blend the remaining pepper and cucumber with the onion and celery; add bouillon, juices and oil; season and chill several hours.
2. Strain and discard chopped vegetables.
3. Serve chilled with separate side dishes of finely diced tomato and the remaining green pepper and cucumber, chopped. *Serves 4-6.*

Variations
Add ¼ bunch of watercress and 3 sprigs of parsley to the soup while it is chilling *or* add 1 clove garlic; remove before serving.

Replace ripe tomato with green tomato.

Provide a bowl of GARLIC CROUTONS to accompany Gazpacho.

VICHYSSOISE
(COLD POTATO LEEK SOUP)

	3 leeks
	1 onion
15 ml	butter
	4 potatoes, medium
750 ml	chicken broth
5 ml	salt
1 *l*	whole milk
	chives

1. Slice leeks and onion; sauté in butter until soft.
2. Slice potatoes thinly; simmer in broth with salt and the onions and leeks until potatoes are soft (35-40 min).
3. Purée; add milk and chill several hours.
4. Taste and season. Garnish with chives. *Serves 6-8.*
   The leeks give a mild, sweet flavour to Vichyssoise. Freeze leeks during the winter when they appear on the market, for use in this hot-weather soup. Prepare them by removing the root end and upper half of the green end; split the remainder and rinse out all sand. Slice; sauté in butter until soft and straw coloured. Pour into a small container and freeze. Or chop, blanch in boiling water for a few minutes, and freeze into cubes.

Variations
Replace the milk with cream, sour cream, or plain yogurt.
Chilled Watercress Soup Add 1 bunch of washed and coarsely chopped watercress before removing the cooked soup from the heat. Cook 5 min; finish as Vichyssoise.

AVOCADO SOUP

	2 ripe avocados
500 ml	sour cream
750 ml	chicken stock
	salt, pepper
	paprika

1. Peel and chop avocado and blend into sour cream.
2. Add stock; season and chill several hours.
3. Adjust seasoning if necessary; sprinkle with paprika. *Serves 6-8.*

Variations
Avocado Grapefruit Replace 2/3 of the chicken stock with grapefruit juice; season with salt and chopped fresh cilantro, or simmer a few coriander seeds in the stock.
   Cilantro is to be found in Chinese grocery stores. It resembles parsley; use sparingly and do not freeze.

CHILLED CARROT SOUP

500 g	carrots
	1 onion
50 ml	fat
1 ml	curry powder
5 ml	grated lemon rind
1 *l*	chicken stock
	salt, pepper
250 ml	10% cream

1. Peel and slice carrots, chop onion and sauté vegetables in fat until onion is soft; add curry and lemon rind.
2. Simmer in stock until carrots are tender.
3. Purée; add salt and pepper to taste, and the cream; chill for several hours.
4. Taste and adjust seasoning if necessary. Garnish with parsley, watercress, sliced green onion or chives. *Serves 4-6.*

Recipes, tables, etc. that appear in small capital letters, e.g., PARSLEY BUTTER, CANADA'S FOOD GUIDE, are listed in the index. Consult the index for the number of the page on which the item appears.

Quick Soups

No meat to simmer—no vegetables to chop—good soup can be made quickly from commercial soups but the price will be higher. Begin with a canned soup and experiment with combinations such as these.

Add	Method	Serve with	Name
The base is 1 can of consommé or bouillon. Add:			
1 can tomato juice	Combine; heat or chill.	Thin slice of lemon	Consommé Madrilene
1 can tomato juice 1 can minestrone shredded spinach leaves	Heat together.	grated cheese, crusty rolls	Peasant Soup
1 can tomato juice 1 can shredded beets and juice shredded spinach or beet leaves	Heat together.	sour cream	Borscht
1 can peeled, seeded cucumber 4 cans peeled chopped tomatoes ¼ green pepper, peeled 1 small garlic clove	Combine in a blender; add ⅛ canful of cooking oil; season with finely chopped chives, salt and pepper.	Pour over an ice cube; garnish with garlic croutons.	Gazpacho
1 can condensed pea soup 2 cans water ½ can shredded ham	Combine and heat; season with onion.		Canadian Pea Soup
1 can cream of celery soup 1 can milk ½ can shredded Cheddar cheese	Heat the soups; season with onion, Worcestershire sauce; add cheese and heat until it melts.	chopped chives *or* parsley	Cheese Soup
The base is 1 can of cream of chicken soup. Add:			
2 cans milk 1 can mashed potato	Heat together; season with onion, celery salt; beat or blend smooth.	Serve hot or cold; sprinkle with chopped chives *or* green onion rings.	Easy Vichysoisse
1 can cream style corn 3 cans milk	Heat and season.	crumbled crisp bacon, chopped parsley	Corn Bisque
2 cans bouillon 1 can peeled, diced cucumber ¼ can crabmeat	In bouillon, heat cucumber until translucent (15 minutes); add cream soup and heat; add crabmeat; reheat	chopped cress *or* parsley	Crabmeat Bisque

The base is 1 can of condensed cream of tomato soup. Add:

1 can condensed green pea soup 2 cans milk and vegetable stock	Heat together.	Cheese croutons	Purée Mongole
To Purée Mongole add 1 small can lobster	Season with Worcestershire; heat without boiling.		Lobster Bisque
1 can clam chowder 1 can vegetable stock	Heat together.	crumbled crisp bacon	Manhattan Chowder

Accompaniments for Soup

Accompaniments add interest as well as nutrients. Breads add thiamin (the quantity will be increased if whole grain breads are used); cheese adds protein, calcium and riboflavin.

MELBA TOAST

Cut bread in very thin slices and then into pieces of the size desired. Dry slowly in oven until crisp and golden brown, about 1 hour at 100°C

CROUTONS

Preheat oven to 200°C
Spread bread thinly with butter or margarine on both sides; cut into cubes; spread on a baking sheet and toast in oven.

Serve in SCALLOPED TOMATOES, in CAESAR SALAD, and as a garnish for soup. Cooled croutons will keep fresh in a covered container for several days; reheat before serving.

Garlic Croutons Omit the butter; sprinkle hot toasted croutons with seasoned salt; dribble melted GARLIC BUTTER over the cubes, tossing lightly.

BREAD STICKS

Slice crusty, day-old bread or buns. Rub slices with a split clove of garlic, slice again into sticks, brush with cooking oil. Bake until golden brown at 230°C
Cool; store in an airtight tin.

CHEESE CARAWAY FRENCH BREAD

500 ml	**grated cheddar cheese**
50 ml	**fat**
15 ml	**caraway seeds**

1. Split a long loaf of French bread lengthwise; spread with the grated cheese creamed with fat.
2. Sprinkle on the seeds; cut into servings; broil.

Cumin, sesame or celery seeds may be used to replace the caraway.
See index for CHEESE PUFF, CHEESE PASTRY, TEA BISCUITS, MUFFINS, and CHEESE STRAWS.

Recipes, tables, etc. that appear in small capital letters, e.g., PARSLEY BUTTER, CANADA'S FOOD GUIDE, are listed in the index. Consult the index for the number of the page on which the item appears.

8 Salads and Dressings

Salads offer colour, crispness and flavour along with a good measure of vitamins and minerals. By serving fruits and vegetables *raw* their content of vitamin C and folic acid are maintained at optimum levels. Greens supply vitamin A.

Salads served as a main course should include some form of protein: cheese or cooked meat, fish, eggs, or legumes. Side salads served as an accompaniment to a main course are usually served individually or in a large bowl for passing. As with salads served as a dessert, these usually contain little or no protein. Appetizer salads should be small in size and sharp in flavour in order to tempt the appetite—not satisfy it.

Salad Greens

Salad greens usually refer to the leafy green vegetables which include head and leaf lettuce, romaine, escarole, watercress, garden cress, Belgian endive, curly endive (chicory), spinach, dandelion greens and the many varieties of cabbage.

Wash greens carefully in plenty of cold water to remove sand and insects; discard discoloured portions of leaves. Dry by patting gently with a clean tea towel or by draining through a rack or colander. Devices in which to spin-dry greens are useful but not essential.

Store greens in a refrigerator up to a week, in a tightly closed plastic bag or container with paper towel to absorb excess water.

Head Lettuce—Cut out heart end of washed head lettuce. Hold the head under running, cold water with the cut end upward so that water forces the leaves open. Use hearts and loose leaves in tossed salads; reserve cup-shaped leaves for use in salad plates.

One medium head will provide lettuce cups for 5-6 salad plates, or tossed greens for 8 servings.

Leaf Lettuce (also romaine, escarole, curly endive, etc.)—Cut off root. Separate leaves, wash and drain. Very coarse stems should be removed. Serve large leaves such as leaf lettuce or romaine separately, as in CAESAR SALAD, or serve a mixture of greens, torn into pieces large enough that their identity is maintained. Curly endive has a somewhat bitter flavour but its

curliness is an attractive addition to a tossed salad; it is often served with citrus fruit in side salads.

Cabbage—Cut into quarters; remove the heart. Using a large, sharp chef's knife, shred cabbage thinly. The many varieties include red (purple) cabbage, the large, rough-textured savoy cabbage and the long Chinese cabbage.

Belgian Endive—Formerly produced only in Europe, this vegetable is now cultivated in small quantities under carefully-controlled conditions in Quebec. It has smooth, cream-coloured, buttery leaves compressed into a pointed head. Much more expensive than other greens, it is usually split into quarters and served with FRENCH DRESSING. Store unwashed and tightly wrapped in plastic wrap in the refrigerator.

Parsley—Wash, drain and store parsley in a tightly-closed jar or plastic bag with a piece of paper towel to absorb excess water. This flavoursome herb can be kept for several weeks as an ever-ready garnish.

Watercress—Washed, trimmed and drained, this dark-green, round-leafed plant should be tightly wrapped before refrigeration with a piece of paper

Wash, dry and wrap leafy green vegetables before storing them in the refrigerator. Ontario Ministry of Agriculture and Food.

Leafy salad greens. Ontario Ministry of Agriculture and Food.

towel added to absorb excess moisture. This way it will keep for a week. Serve combined with other salad greens in mixtures, with cream cheese in sandwiches, or use with fruit salads or as a garnish. If the stems are very long, use scissors to cut the excess into fine pieces to combine with mixtures of greens.

Celery—Use a vegetable brush to wash celery and a vegetable peeler to remove discoloured areas from the stalks and heart. If celery is to be diced, cut upper and outside coarse stalks into small lengthwise sections. Lay several sections together on a board and slice crosswise, finely.

For club celery, cut lengthwise through stalks and heart so that each section has a piece of the heart. Cut across each to form 2 parts so that the length of the heart section is about 8-13 cm

Serve club celery chilled in a relish dish, with or without crushed ice, on an appetizer tray with other foods, or as one item on a salad plate.

Upper sections may be served with the club celery or cut into shorter lengths. Prepare short lengths by making lengthwise gashes in each end, almost but not quite through to the centre. Chill in cold water until the ends curl. Serve as a garnish on a salad plate, or serve as an appetizer.

These curled or plain pieces can be stuffed with cream cheese or served with an assortment of raw vegetables and a dip.

Other Basic Salad Ingredients

Tomatoes—Wash tomatoes. If they are to be peeled, cover with boiling water for 15 s to loosen skins; plunge into cold water. Cut out the stem end and remove the skin.

Stuffed, as a tomato cup, do not scald or peel, but cut a slice from the stem end, scoop out the pulp and use for other purposes. Sprinkle the inside lightly with salt; invert to drain.

Stuffing—Fill hollowed tomato or cover tomato slices with diced celery, cucumber, cubes of chicken, veal or ham, fish, cottage cheese and olives (separately or in combinations), with salad dressing.

Serve cherry tomatoes unpeeled and whole or cut diagonally into slices or halves.

Cucumbers—Choose slim cucumbers which are dark green in colour or the English variety which is long, thin-skinned and less seedy. Wash; peel or score the unpeeled cucumber lengthwise using the tines of a fork. Slice.

Radishes—Cut off most of the stem end of the radish, leaving a short "handle." Cut off root end. Brush to remove all sand. Left in cold water for 15 min, they become deliciously crisp.

For garnishes, radishes can be cut into various shapes with a small paring knife, then chilled in cold water until the designs open. (Chilled radishes are too brittle to carve.)

Green Onions and Shallots—Cut off hairy root; trim any discoloured parts. Save excess green tops to slice for mixed green salad or to chop finely to add flavour and colour to cooked vegetables, soups and sauces. Trim length of the onion and stalk to about 10 cm

Carrots—Carrot sticks—carrots cut into fingers—are colourful and crunchy additions to vegetable salad plates, sandwich plates and appetizer trays.

Carrot curls, used for garnishing salads and sandwiches, are prepared by removing broad, thin slices of peeled carrot with a vegetable peeler. Shape into tight rolls around the forefinger; remove, holding shape with a toothpick; chill in ice water until needed; drain and remove toothpick before serving.

Fresh-Vegetable Salads

TOSSED SALAD

Ease of preparation and the wide choice of ingredients make tossed salads popular. Known by many names—"tossed greens," "green salad," or "chef's salad"—the salads range from the simplest mixture of torn lettuce with FRENCH DRESSING to an assortment of greens plus tomato wedges; usually this latter is known as CHEF'S SALAD.

One medium head of lettuce will produce approximately 8 servings of tossed salad.

1. Wash, dry and chill salad ingredients.
2. Rub the inside of a salad bowl with an onion slice or a cut clove of garlic.
3. Choose one or more leafy greens. Tear large leaves into pieces small enough to be eaten with a fork but large enough to retain identities. Chop, slice, or prepare other ingredients as required.

Suggested Additions

Dandelion, nasturtium leaves, sorrel.
Watercress, parsley, garden cress.
Tomato wedges.
Cabbage, bean sprouts.
Celery, green pepper, cucumber, green onions, carrots, turnip, cauliflower, radishes.
Cooked vegetables, cut or sectioned and marinated green beans, carrots, broccoli, cauliflower.
Cheddar, Parmesan or blue cheese, grated or finely diced.
Crumbled crisp bacon; sliced olives or pickles.

4. Just before serving, add FRENCH DRESSING and toss mixture lightly with two forks until ingredients are lightly coated, or do not add dressing to the salad but offer one or more dressings at the time of serving.

HEARTY CHEF'S SALAD

100 g	sliced Swiss cheese *or* crumbled blue cheese
200 g	cooked, sliced tongue, ham, fish *or* whole shrimps
	4 hard-cooked eggs
	½ bunch of green onions
	1 bunch radishes
	½ cucumber
	2-3 tomatoes
1 *l*	salad greens
25 ml	FRENCH DRESSING

1. Cut cheese and meat into thin strips; slice onions and radishes.
2. Peel and chop cucumber finely; cut tomatoes into wedges.
3. Line a salad bowl with crisp greens; arrange prepared foods on the greens and chill.
4. Toss lightly with garlic-flavoured FRENCH DRESSING just before serving; slice eggs and gently toss into the mixture. *Serves 6-8.*

NICOISE SALAD

225-300 g	fresh or frozen green beans
	1 head of lettuce *or* other greens
	1 large green pepper
	4 tomatoes
	½ Spanish or Bermuda onion
198 g	1 small tin solid white tuna
	1 tin anchovy fillets
150 ml	FRENCH DRESSING
500-750 ml	FRENCH POTATO SALAD
	3 hard-cooked eggs, quartered or sliced
125 ml	pitted ripe olives

1. Prepare beans; cut whole beans in half. Cook until just tender but slightly crunchy. Drain and spread on a towel to cool quickly. Chill.
2. Separate lettuce leaves; rinse, drain and dry.
3. Slice green peppers into thin rings; peel and cut tomatoes into thin wedges. Slice onion into thin rings.
4. Drain tuna and break into chunks; drain anchovies.

5. Just before serving, sprinkle the beans, pepper and tomatoes with a little FRENCH DRESSING. Toss the prepared lettuce leaves in a salad bowl with ¼ of the remaining dressing and arrange leaves around the edge of the bowl.
6. Place potato salad in the bowl and decorate with clusters of the remaining ingredients. Pour remaining dressing over all. *Serves 6-8.*

CAESAR SALAD

2 *l*	leaf or romaine lettuce
	1 garlic clove, crushed
or	
1 ml	garlic powder
100 ml	oil
	pepper, salt
	2 eggs, boiled 1 minute
50 ml	lemon juice
125 ml	grated Parmesan cheese
400 ml	GARLIC CROUTONS

1. Prepare greens, drain and chill; add garlic to oil and leave at room temperature for at least 15 min
2. To the chilled greens, add seasonings and oil; toss lightly.
3. Add eggs and lemon juice; toss well. Sprinkle with cheese and toss again. Toss in croutons until just mixed. *Serves 6-8.*

ENDIVE AND BACON SALAD

	1 head of curly endive
	6 slices of bacon
25 ml	fat
50 ml	vinegar
15 ml	sugar
	salt, pepper

1. Separate and prepare leaves and rinse thoroughly; pat dry on a tea towel.
2. Fry bacon until crisp. Remove from pan, drain and crumble; sprinkle over the endive.
3. Combine bacon, fat, vinegar, sugar, and seasonings; mix thoroughly.
4. Pour this vinaigrette over the endive and toss. *Serves 4.*

A slice of onion cooked with the bacon adds flavour. Chunks of lettuce, romaine or escarole can be substituted for endive.

CABBAGE SALAD (COLE SLAW)

Nearly all the countries of northern Europe have their own versions of cabbage salad with names that sound much like our "cole slaw". The general directions given here provide scope for many versions. Use green, Savoy, or red cabbage.
1. Cut cabbage into sections; slice very finely with a sharp chef's knife or slicer, discarding heart section.
2. Add salad dressing, using approximately ¼ as much dressing as cabbage. Chill, preferably for several hours.

Optional Additions—green pepper; pimento; carrot, grated or slivered; sliced radishes; sliced olives; chopped apple and raisins; diced pineapple, grapefruit sections; slivers of browned almonds; peanuts; toasted sesame seeds.
Yield:
1 kg cabbage = 2 *l* shredded cabbage = 12-15 servings

REFRIGERATOR COLE SLAW

This recipe makes a large quantity of salad which may be stored for a week or more in the refrigerator and used as needed. It carries well for school lunches and picnics. Dressing left over when all the salad has been used can be saved and reused; reduce sugar.

	1 large cabbage, shredded
	3 large onions, finely sliced
100 ml	sugar
200 ml	oil
200 ml	cider vinegar
10 ml	salt
5 ml	dry mustard
5 ml	celery seed

1. Quarter and remove heart sections from cabbage; slice remaining cabbage thinly with a sharp knife.
2. In a large, non-metallic bowl or container, layer cabbage and onions with sugar.
3. In a saucepan, combine remaining ingredients and heat to boiling.
4. Pour hot liquid over the cabbage, and cover. Refrigerate for several hours, then use as needed. *Yield:* approximately 20 servings.

Recipes, tables, etc. that appear in small capital letters, e.g., PARSLEY BUTTER, CANADA'S FOOD GUIDE, are listed in the index. Consult the index for the number of the page on which the item appears.

CARROT AND RAISIN SALAD

100 ml	raisins
300 ml	shredded raw carrots
50 ml	mayonnaise *or* salad dressing
15 ml	lemon juice
15 ml	sugar
	salt

1. Plump raisins in a sieve over boiling water; cool and combine with carrots.
2. Combine mayonnaise, lemon juice, sugar and salt; add carrot mixture and toss. *Yield:* about 4 servings.

The crunchy texture of this salad makes it a popular addition to the carried lunch; turnips can be substituted for carrots.

Chopped orange sections can be added.

For a good sandwich filling, spread bread with cream cheese, then carrot filling. Serve immediately.

FENNEL SALAD

	2 fennel bulbs
150 ml	sliced radishes
	3 green onions, chopped
150 ml	FRENCH DRESSING
	1 medium cucumber
	finely chopped parsley
	1 medium tomato, cut into wedges

1. Trim and slice fennel thinly.
2. Combine with radishes, onions and French Dressing; chill for about 1 h
3. To serve: add peeled and chopped cucumber; sprinkle with chopped parsley and garnish with tomato wedges. *Serves 4-6.*

This salad is especially suitable with cold fish and seafood.

A lettuce cup. Lawry's Foods, Inc.

Cooked-Vegetable Salads

Cooked-vegetable salads are make-ahead salads; sometimes non-leafy varieties of raw vegetables, such as chopped celery, are added. Such cooked vegetables as asparagus stalks or green beans are marinated for several hours, chilled and drained. Marinate each separately to retain its own flavour. Cooked vegetables served in mixtures (like potato salad) are combined with dressing and chilled for several hours so that the flavour of the dressing penetrates the vegetable.

CHICK PEA SALAD

540 ml	1 can chick peas, green *or* lima beans
100 ml	FRENCH DRESSING *or* SOUR CREAM DRESSING
	1 Spanish onion, thinly sliced

1. Drain peas or beans; cook and drain frozen lima beans. (Reserve stock for soup.)
2. Combine with dressing and chill for at least 1 hour.
3. Drain off but keep French Dressing.
4. Toss peas or beans with onion; chill; serve in lettuce cups. *Serves 2-3.*

FOUR-BEAN SALAD

540 ml	1 can kidney beans
540 ml	1 can lima beans
540 ml	1 can yellow (wax) beans
540 ml	1 can green beans
	2 medium onions, sliced
250 ml	diced celery
50 ml	sugar
1 ml	ginger
	or
	1 garlic clove, crushed
250 ml	FRENCH DRESSING

1. Drain liquid from beans (reserve for soup).
2. Combine all ingredients, using only enough French Dressing to coat vegetables; toss and chill several hours, preferably overnight.
3. Toss again, drain; season with salt and pepper to taste.

Serve in a lettuce-lined bowl or in lettuce cups.

Variation—Substitute twice the quantity of uncooked bean sprouts for the celery.

Basic Recipe
POTATO SALAD

750 ml	cooked potatoes
125 ml	chopped green onions
250 ml	mayonnaise, *or* salad dressing, *or*
	sour cream *or* YOGURT MAYONNAISE
	salt, pepper
	dillweed, basil *or* chopped parsley
	garnish

1. Combine potatoes and onions with any of these optional additions: chopped celery, green pepper or pimento; innermost leaves of head lettuce; chopped, thinly-sliced radishes; olives, cooked green peas, carrots, corn.
2. Mix with one of the dressings. Taste and season as desired with salt, pepper and herbs.
3. Chill for at least 1 h, preferably several hours.
4. Top with any of these garnishes: hard-cooked egg slices, radish slices, crisp bacon, onion rings, chopped green onions, chives or chopped fresh dill. *Serves 5-6.*

Variations
French Potato Salad—Make with FRENCH DRESSING, using 1/3 the quantity of dressing in the basic recipe. Potatoes are diced and marinated while hot, then cooled and mixed with other ingredients.
Potato Macaroni Salad—To basic recipe, add:

500 ml	cooked macaroni
250 ml	chopped celery
50 ml	chopped green pepper

(Use approximately half the amount of uncooked macaroni to produce the required cooked quantity. If desired, substitute double the quantity of cooked macaroni for all the potatoes.)

Combine and add to the potato salad with any of the other suggested additions desired, increasing the amount of dressing and seasonings used.

For an easy and appetizing side salad, serve a wedge of head lettuce, one wedge per serving, topped with dressing. Garnish, if desired, with any of: parsley or cress; sliced olives or pickles; sieved hard-cooked eggs.

Recipes, tables, etc. that appear in small capital letters, e.g., PARSLEY BUTTER, CANADA'S FOOD GUIDE, are listed in the index. Consult the index for the number of the page on which the item appears.

HOT POTATO SALAD

	6 slices bacon
125 ml	chopped onion
25 ml	sugar
25 ml	flour
	salt, pepper
5 ml	dry mustard
1 ml	celery seed
200 ml	water
50 ml	vinegar
1 *l*	sliced, cooked potatoes
150 ml	chopped celery
	2 hard-boiled eggs, quartered
250 ml	cherry tomatoes *or* tomato wedges
250 ml	small spinach leaves

1. Fry bacon until crisp; remove from pan. Pour off fat except for 50 ml
2. Add onions and cook until golden. Combine sugar, flour and seasonings and stir into the pan.
3. Add water and vinegar and cook stirring constantly until the mixture is thick; cook 1 min longer.
4. Add potatoes and celery; stir gently to combine while heating.
5. When potatoes are hot, add eggs, tomatoes, spinach and crumbled bacon; leave over low heat until the additions are warmed. *Serves 4-6.*

Meat and Fish Salad Mixtures

See also recipes for CHICKEN MOUSSE, HAM MOUSSE and SALMON MOUSSE. Serve as a main course at luncheon or supper.

VEAL, CHICKEN, TURKEY OR PORK TENDERLOIN SALAD

1. Remove skin and bone from cooked meat; cube; season and marinate with FRENCH DRESSING.
2. Add up to an equal quantity of diced celery; blend with dressing and chill.
3. Serve in salad bowl on a bed of lettuce or endive, or arrange on individual plates.

FRUIT CHICKEN SALAD

750 ml	**diced cooked chicken**
250 ml	**diced celery**
250 ml	**orange sections, diced**
250 ml	**pineapple tidbits, drained**
250 ml	**seedless grapes**
	6 ripe, pitted olives
125 ml	**toasted almonds, sliced**
30 ml	**salad oil**
30 ml	**orange juice**
30 ml	**vinegar**
2 ml	**salt**
125 ml	MAYONNAISE

1. Lightly toss diced chicken, celery, fruits and almonds.
2. Shake together salad oil, orange juice, vinegar and
   salt and pour over chicken mixture; let stand
   1 h
3. Drain off the liquid from the chicken; toss salad
   lightly with mayonnaise.
4. Serve in lettuce cups or as filling for BOUCHÉES.

CURRIED CHICKEN SALAD

250 ml	**diced cooked chicken**
125 ml	**diced unpeeled apple**
125 ml	**seedless raisins**
250 ml	**finely diced celery**
75 ml	**finely diced green pepper**
	6 pitted, slivered, ripe olives
2 ml	**curry powder**
125 ml	MAYONNAISE

Combine chicken, fruits and vegetables. Add curry
powder to mayonnaise, and toss salad lightly. Serve
in lettuce-lined salad bowls or in avocado halves, allowing ½ per person. (Sprinkle avocado halves with
lemon juice after cutting, to prevent darkening). In
place of curry powder, prepared horseradish may be
substituted.

FISH SALAD

1. Use one of the following, either freshly cooked or
   canned:
   Salmon—Drain; remove and discard skin if desired; mash bones and add to salmon which is broken into pieces.
   Mackerel—Prepare as salmon; sprinkle with
   lemon juice.
   Tuna—Drain, break into chunks.
   Chicken haddie or other white fish—Flake.

Shrimp—Drain, remove intestinal vein, leave in
salted water for a few minutes, rinse and dry.
2. Add to an equal quantity of diced celery. To give
   additional flavour and colour, add any of: pimento
   strips, red sweet pepper or green pepper, peas,
   chopped cucumbers, sliced olives or gherkins.
3. Blend with MAYONNAISE; season to taste.
4. Serve in lettuce cups or lettuce-lined bowl. Fish
   mixtures can be packed into a large mould or individual moulds, chilled and turned out onto a
   plate. Avoid packing shrimp mixtures down; the
   shrimps will break.

LOBSTER SALAD

1. Cube cooked lobster meat, reserving claw meat for
   garnishing; marinate with FRENCH DRESSING.
2. Add an equal quantity of diced celery; season with
   salt, cayenne; blend with MAYONNAISE.
3. Serve on lettuce or in lobster shell; garnish with
   claw meat, and any of: celery tips, cress, olives,
   capers, slices of cucumber, hard-cooked egg.

Fruit Salads

Colourful and refreshing fruits served on a platter or
in individual dishes make attractive side salads or
desserts. The addition of a protein-rich food converts
them into a main course for lunch or supper.

Chapter 15 gives details for preparing individual
fruits. For other fruit salad recipes, see SUGGESTIONS
FOR FRUIT SALAD PLATES, fruit variations of COLE SLAW,
MOULDED AND FROZEN SALADS, FRUIT CHICKEN SALAD,
and CURRIED CHICKEN SALAD.

WALDORF SALAD

400 ml	**cored and diced red apple**
250 ml	**finely diced celery**
150 ml	MAYONNAISE
50 ml	**coarsely chopped walnuts**

1. Prepare apples, leaving on red skins.
2. Combine immediately with mayonnaise or other
   dressing; add celery; chill.
3. At serving time, stir in walnuts and transfer mixture to lettuce cups. Garnish with leafy tips of celery, parsley, or watercress. *Serves 4-6.*

Slivered dates may be added. Cabbage, finely shredded, may replace celery. Fresh pears may be substituted for apples, or try a mixture of pears and
apples.

Jellied Salads

Meats, fish, cheese, vegetables and fruits can be jellied to produce decorative and delicious salads. Set the mixture in a rectangular pan; cut jelly into squares, *or* use a jelly mould, one large or many individual moulds. Details for preparing jellied foods are in Chapter 16 on Desserts.

Basic Recipe
ASPIC MOULD

15 ml	1 envelope gelatine
100 ml	stock *or* water
250 ml	boiling stock *or* water
50 ml	sugar
50 ml	vinegar *or* lemon juice
	salt, pepper
250-400 ml	raw or cooked vegetables *or* cooked meat *or* fish
	garnish

1. Sprinkle gelatine over cold stock or water to soften.
2. Combine boiling liquid and sugar; bring to boiling and add gelatine.
3. Remove from heat, stir until dissolved. Add vinegar or lemon juice.
4. Taste and season liquid. Chill.
5. When slightly thickened, add seasoned vegetables and/or meat or fish; transfer to a prepared mould. To produce a pattern or to set mixture in layers, see GELATINE MOULDS—GENERAL DIRECTIONS. If desired, include a garnish, remembering that the design will be reversed when unmoulded.
6. Unmould onto a platter. Serve with mayonnaise.

Garnish aspic with any of: slices of radish, cucumber, olives, pickles, hard-cooked egg, strips of pimento, or gherkins.

Vegetables and/or meat or fish can be moulded separately as, for example, asparagus tips, or as mixtures. Decoration may be simple or elaborate. Jellied consommé or bouillon can also be used. *Serves 4-6.*

The ring mould may be filled in the centre with vegetables or fruits; a dish of cottage cheese or salad dressing may be set in. To retain mould's shape, follow carefully instructions under GELATINE MOULDS—GENERAL DIRECTIONS in unmoulding jelly in fluted and ring moulds. Custard cups, paper cups, muffin pans and plastic dairy-food containers make excellent moulds.

TOMATO ASPIC

30 ml	2 envelopes of gelatine
100 ml	tomato juice
750 ml	heated tomato juice
10 ml	sugar
5 ml	Worcestershire sauce
30 ml	lemon juice
	celery salt and/or onion salt

1. Soften gelatine in the smaller amount of juice; heat part of remaining juice.
2. Dissolve gelatine in hot juice; stir in remaining ingredients, adding celery salt, onion salt, or other seasoning to taste.
3. Cool and pour into prepared moulds; chill. *Serves 6.*

Variations
When mixture is partly set, stir in any of: chopped parsley, hard-cooked egg slices, diced celery, well-drained cooked peas, stuffed olives, pickles, or peeled chopped tomato. Mayonnaise may be beaten in. Use 150-200 ml

Substitute onion slices and celery leaves for the seasoned salts, heating them in the hot juice for 5 min; remove. Season.

Substitute canned vegetable juice cocktail, or seasoned, puréed tomatoes for the tomato juice.

Substitute in place of the gelatine and sugar, 1 package of commercial jelly powder, lemon or lime flavoured: 85 g

A moulded salad. Borden, Inc.

Basic Recipe
FRUIT MOULD

15 ml	1 envelope of gelatine
50 ml	grapefruit juice
350 ml	grapefruit juice
50 ml	sugar
15 ml	lemon juice
150 ml	grapefruit sections
250 ml	other fruits*, celery, nuts

*Other fruits and ingredients to add with the grapefruit or to replace it: cooked or canned pineapple, grapes, nuts; cooked or canned pineapple and cherries (pitted); orange sections, prunes, marshmallows; melon cubes or balls; avocado slices; shrimp, celery, pimento and grapefruit; chopped apple, chopped celery.

1. Sprinkle gelatine into the smaller portion of juice to soften; heat half of the larger portion and stir in softened gelatine to dissolve.
2. Stir in sugar, reducing the amount as desired if juice was presweetened. Add remaining juice; chill.
3. When the mixture is beginning to set, stir in well-drained fruit sections and other suggested ingredients. *Serves 6.*

Variations
For gelatine and sugar, substitute a fruit jelly powder, 85 g

Golden Salad—Substitute cooked pineapple juice for grapefruit juice; and substitute equal quantities of drained, crushed pineapple and shredded carrots for the grapefruit and other fruit.

If fresh pineapple is used, it must be cooked before adding to a gelatine mixture, as an enzyme in the raw fruit will break down the protein of the gelatine and prevent jelling.

JELLIED LIME LAYERS

85 g	1 package lime jelly powder
250 ml	boiling water
200 ml	unsweetened pineapple juice
30 ml	prepared horseradish
100 ml	MAYONNAISE

1. Dissolve jelly powder in boiling water; add juice.
2. Pour 1/3 of the mixture into a prepared mould (see GELATINE MOULDS—GENERAL DIRECTIONS) and chill until firm.
3. Chill the remainder separately until it is slightly thick.

4. Beat until fluffy and stir in horseradish and mayonnaise; spread over the layer of set jelly; chill.
5. When set, unmould on greens; garnish with pineapple slices or other fruit. *Serves 4.*

Variations
Jellied Cucumber Cream—Use the ingredients from the preceding recipe, substituting an equal quantity of sour cream for the pineapple juice and omitting the horseradish. Add finely grated onion, 5 ml When the mixture begins to thicken, blend in the mayonnaise and the juice of half a lemon with 2 cucumbers, peeled, seeded and diced. Pour into prepared moulds and chill. *Serves 6.*
To seed cucumbers for dicing: peel; cut into lengthwise strips and remove seeds from centre with the point of a fine knife. Dice and drain.

MOULDED CRANBERRY SALAD

500 g	cranberries
	2 apples, cored
200 ml	sugar
85 g	1 pkg. strawberry jelly
250 ml	boiling water

1. Grind the fruit or chop finely.
2. Dissolve jelly powder in boiling water; add sugar and stir to dissolve; chill until thick and syrupy.
3. Fold in fruit; mould. *Serves 6-8.*

CHICKEN MOUSSE

30 ml	2 envelopes of gelatine
100 ml	chicken stock
200 ml	pineapple juice *or* chicken stock
200 ml	MAYONNAISE *or* sour cream
100 ml	drained, crushed pineapple and/or finely chopped celery
25 ml	finely chopped green onion *or* chives
500 ml	diced, cooked chicken
250 ml	whipping cream
	salt
	pepper

1. Sprinkle gelatine in chicken stock to soften; place dish over hot water until gelatine dissolves.
2. Stir in the liquid. Chill until mixture begins to thicken.
3. Blend in mayonnaise or sour cream; add pineapple, celery, onion and chicken.

4. Whip the cream and fold into the gelatine mixture; taste and season.
5. Pour into a prepared mould with a capacity of about 2 ℓ
6. Chill until firm, unmould and garnish with watercress or curly endive, black olives and carrot curls. *Serves 8-10.*

To reduce expense, and fat, substitute skim milk powder, whipped, for the whipping cream. Follow directions TO WHIP SKIM MILK POWDER, beating in about 1/3 of the dissolved gelatine from step 1; chill but do not allow to jell.

Variation

Ham Mousse—Substitute lean, cooked ham for the chicken and pineapple juice for the chicken stock. Into the mayonnaise or sour cream, stir equal quantities of tomato paste and prepared mustard: 10 ml
Salmon Mousse—Substitute canned salmon for the chicken. Drain off and use liquid; flake fish, mash bones and add to fish. Blend into the mayonnaise or sour cream:

5 ml	Worcestershire sauce
10 ml	prepared mustard
5 ml	fresh dill
or	
2 ml	dry dill weed

If desired, seeded and diced cucumber can be substituted for celery and pineapple. (See TO SEED CUCUMBERS.)

MOULDED CHEESE SALAD

15 ml	1 envelope of gelatine
50 ml	water
200 ml	hot milk *or* fruit juice
227 g	1 pkg. cream cheese, softened
100 ml	sour cream
1 ml	salt

1. Sprinkle gelatine in cold water to soften; dissolve in hot milk; cool.
2. Add remaining ingredients and beat until smooth.
3. Pour into a prepared mould or moulds with a total capacity of about 600 ml
4. Chill until set; unmould onto salad greens. *Serves 4-6.*

Recipes, tables, etc. that appear in small capital letters, e.g., PARSLEY BUTTER, CANADA'S FOOD GUIDE, are listed in the index. Consult the index for the number of the page on which the item appears.

Variations

Add any of chopped celery, green or red pepper, pimento, sliced olives, or well-drained pickle relish.

Add drained, crushed or diced pineapple (cooked or canned). Use other fruits, or chopped, candied ginger.

Fill larger moulds or additional moulds half full of TOMATO ASPIC or any flavour of fruit jelly; chill. When nearly set, add the mixture to the mould and chill until set.

FROZEN CHEESE AND FRUIT SALAD

15 ml	lemon juice
100 ml	mayonnaise *or* salad dressing
227 g	1 pkg. cream cheese, softened
2 ml	salt
100 ml	crushed pineapple, drained
100 ml	chopped pitted dates
50 ml	coarsely chopped maraschino cherries
100 ml	toasted almond slivers *or* shredded coconut
100 ml	miniature marshmallows (optional)
	2 bananas, sliced
250 ml	whipping cream

1. Gradually blend lemon juice and mayonnaise with cream cheese that has been softened at room temperature.
2. Add remaining ingredients except the cream.
3. Whip cream and fold into the mixture; freeze until firm. *Serves 6-8.*

FROZEN TROPICAL SALAD

15 ml	1 envelope of gelatine
50 ml	cold water
100 ml	MAYONNAISE *or* SALAD DRESSING
250 ml	whipping cream
250 ml	cooked pineapple, diced and drained
250 ml	orange sections
250 ml	grapefruit sections
	1 banana, sliced (optional)

1. Sprinkle gelatine in cold water to soften; dissolve over hot water, and stir slowly into the mayonnaise.
2. Whip cream and fold into mayonnaise mixture; fold in the fruits.
3. Freeze until firm. *Serves 6-8.*

Salad Plates

A Salad Plate is an assortment of salads, arranged on a plate and constituting a complete course for one person. Use 1 or 2 varieties of salad, some extra fruit or vegetable and a protein-rich food, if intended as a main course. Choose foods to complement each other in flavour and colour, while providing a contrast of textures, sizes, and shapes.

VEGETABLE SALAD PLATES

To make an attractive and nourishing Vegetable Salad Plate, choose one item from each of Categories 1, 2 and 3 below, and add two items from Category 4. Serve with MAYONNAISE.

Category 1
Cold, sliced meat or fish; meat or fish salads from recipes on preceding pages; DEVILLED EGGS; egg slices; cheese slices or balls; cottage cheese.

Category 2
TOMATO ASPIC; sliced tomatoes; carrot sticks; CARROT AND RAISIN SALAD; COLE SLAW; any light and colourful salad which does not repeat the ingredients already chosen.

Category 3
POTATO SALAD; FOUR-BEAN SALAD; WALDORF SALAD; serve in a lettuce cup.

Category 4
Club celery; celery sticks or curls; carrot sticks or curls; green onions; tomato slices; black olives; pickles; radishes; sprigs of parsley, watercress, or curly endive.

FRUIT SALAD PLATES

For a Fruit Salad Plate as a main course, choose one item from Category 1, below, and add any of the items in Category 2. Garnish with sprig of mint, watercress, or parsley. Serve with sour cream or a sweetened variation of MAYONNAISE, COOKED SALAD DRESSING, or FRENCH DRESSING.

Category 1
FRUIT CHICKEN SALAD; CURRIED CHICKEN SALAD; cottage cheese; cheese slices or cheese balls, a JELLIED or FROZEN SALAD which contains cheese.

Category 2
Apple; grapefruit or orange sections; melon balls; avocado wedges; grapes in small clusters; pineapple; pears; peaches; apricots; ripe olives; cherries with stems; dates or stuffed prunes; WALDORF SALAD; pineapple or grapefruit COLE SLAW; a jellied fruit salad, frozen fruit salad, or sherbet if not already included.

Salad Dressings

Basic salad dressings are few in number but their variations are unlimited.

Choose a dressing suited to the texture and flavour of the salad ingredients. It is convenient to have 2 or 3 different kinds on hand in the refrigerator; these, too, can be blended together to form new variations. The kinds of vinegar used may also be varied; see FLAVOURED VINEGARS.

Basic Recipe
FRENCH DRESSING

This liquid dressing is the most easily prepared and most versatile of dressings. It can be used on all salads with the exception of jellied and frozen salads. It is usually used on tossed green salads and serves as a marinade for cooked vegetable salads. It can vary in flavour from tart to sweet, and highly-seasoned to mild.

50 ml	mild vinegar *or* lemon juice
150 ml	oil
3 ml	salt
	pepper and/or additional seasoning*

*Season with any of garlic, celery seed, Worcestershire sauce, celery salt, onion salt, or other seasoned salt. (Reduce salt in the basic recipe when using a seasoned salt.)

In a bottle with a tight-fitting top, shake vinegar or lemon juice with oil and seasonings. *Yield:* 200 ml

---

Because it separates into two layers, French dressing must be thoroughly shaken before use.

Add to leafy salad mixtures just before serving; add to salads of cooked vegetables (potatoes, rice, beans) several hours before serving.

A bottle with a tight-fitting lid for measuring the ingredients can be marked on the outside, using a thin line of nail polish, to show the level to pour vinegar; add oil and mark again.

Variations
Herb French Dressing—Add to the basic recipe:

15 ml   fresh, minced tarragon, chervil,
         chives, *or* basil

or

 5 ml   dried tarragon, chervil, chives, *or*
         basil

If fresh herbs are used, add shortly before putting the dressing on salad.

Tomato French Dressing—Add to the basic recipe:

25 ml   finely chopped onion
25 ml   ketchup
15 ml   sugar
15 ml   Worcestershire sauce

Yield: 300 ml

Fruit French Dressing—Prepare according to the basic recipe:

25 ml   lemon juice
75 ml   oil
50 ml   pineapple juice
25 ml   orange juice
         sugar to taste

Yield: 175 ml

Vinaigrette Dressing (Hot French Dressing)

250 ml   FRENCH DRESSING
         2 hard-cooked eggs, chopped
15 ml   green onions *or* chives, chopped
15 ml   parsley, chopped
15 ml   celery leaves, chopped
 2 ml   dry mustard
 2 ml   Worcestershire sauce

Heat French dressing to boiling; add other ingredients and mix well.
Serve hot over hot green beans, asparagus, broccoli, hot sliced potatoes and boiled beef or tongue.

Recipes, tables, etc. that appear in small capital letters, e.g., PARSLEY BUTTER, CANADA'S FOOD GUIDE, are listed in the index. Consult the index for the number of the page on which the item appears.

Basic Recipe
MAYONNAISE

This thick dressing is an emulsion of oil, vinegar, egg and spices. Care must be taken in its preparation to develop the emulsion by the slow addition of the oil while the mixture is beaten constantly. Otherwise the emulsion will not form and the dressing will be liquid with separating layers of oil and vinegar. Egg, particularly the yolk, is an emulsifying ingredient which binds the oil and vinegar together.

Mayonnaise is used in heavy salad mixtures such as potato, chicken, or Waldorf salad, in sandwiches or in sandwich mixtures, or as a base for TARTAR SAUCE. It may be served as an accompaniment to salads in a separate dish, or in a tiny lettuce cup on the salad plate.

  5 ml   dry mustard
  5 ml   salt
  2 ml   paprika
          1 large egg *or* 2 yolks
250 ml   salad oil
 30 ml   vinegar

1. In a small but deep bowl, mix spices, egg and half of the vinegar.
2. Add oil one drop at a time, beating constantly; when about 1/3 of the oil has been added, the mixture will begin to thicken indicating that an emulsion has formed.
3. Beat in remaining vinegar and oil in larger portions.
4. Keep in a covered jar in the refrigerator. Do not freeze. *Yield:* 300 ml

Suggested Additions—chopped chives, olives, gherkins; capers, relish, horseradish; poppy seeds, celery seeds; onion juice or finely chopped onion; CHILI SAUCE and horseradish; whipped cream, honey and enough maraschino cherry juice to tint the dressing a delicate pink (WHIPPED CREAM DRESSING); FRENCH DRESSING.

Variations

Curry Mayonnaise

250 ml   MAYONNAISE
 10 ml   lemon juice
 15 ml   curry powder
 10 ml   soy sauce
 75 ml   cream *or* sour cream

Thousand Island Dressing

250 ml	MAYONNAISE
50 ml	CHILI SAUCE
	2 hard-cooked eggs, chopped
30 ml	chopped green pepper
30 ml	chopped celery
25 ml	finely chopped onion

Herb Mayonnaise—Substitute sour cream for half of the mayonnaise. Add:

5 ml	lemon juice
125 ml	watercress or garden cress and finely chopped parsley
	½ garlic clove, crushed
2 ml	tarragon
2 ml	basil
	salt, pepper

Roquefort Mayonnaise

100 ml	MAYONNAISE
50 ml	FRENCH DRESSING
50 ml	Roquefort cheese, crumbled

Blue Cheese Dressing

75 ml	MAYONNAISE
50 ml	lemon juice
5 ml	Worcestershire sauce
	1 crushed garlic clove
200 ml	crumbled blue cheese

One medium cucumber, chopped and peeled, may be added. If young and tender, leave peel on for colour.

COOKED SALAD DRESSING

15 ml	flour
15 ml	sugar
2 ml	salt
5 ml	dry mustard
50 ml	vinegar
125 ml	hot water
	1 egg or 2 yolks
30 ml	butter or margarine

1. In the top section of a double boiler, combine the dry ingredients; stir in vinegar.
2. Stir in hot water; cook stirring constantly until thick.
3. Combine egg and butter, and stir in a little of the hot mixture blending thoroughly. Now add this to the hot mixture.
4. Cook 1 min longer. Cover, cool, and refrigerate in a covered container. *Yield:* 200 ml

If dressing is too thick, thin with milk. For extra flavour and richness, stir sour cream into the chilled dressing.

Use any of the additions for MAYONNAISE.

MODIFIED MAYONNAISE

This dressing is a cross between mayonnaise and cooked salad dressing. Less creamy than mayonnaise, it has a lower percentage of oil; the emulsion, once formed, is less apt to break with extremes of temperature. Although cooked dressing is less expensive than mayonnaise, its relative cost will vary with the amount and type of oil used.

50 ml	flour
50 ml	sugar
5-10 ml	dry mustard
5 ml	salt
1 ml	paprika
25 ml	oil
200 ml	hot water
100 ml	vinegar
	2 eggs or 3 yolks, beaten
200-400 ml oil	

1. Thoroughly combine all the dry ingredients in the top of a double boiler with the small amount of oil.
2. Add the vinegar and hot water, stir and cook until thick.
3. Add a little of the hot mixture to the beaten egg and combine thoroughly. Beat into the hot mixture.
4. Cook until thick; cool.
5. When mixture is completely cool, beat at high speed in an electric blender or with an electric mixer or rotary beater using a small, deep container. Begin beating the mixture on high speed; add oil one drop at a time until mixture has doubled in quantity and has formed a thick emulsion. Add remaining oil in larger quantities, beating well after each addition. Refrigerate in a covered jar. Do not freeze. *Yield:* 400-600 ml

---

Recipes, tables, etc. that appear in small capital letters, e.g., PARSLEY BUTTER, CANADA'S FOOD GUIDE, are listed in the index. Consult the index for the number of the page on which the item appears.

SOUR CREAM DRESSINGS

The cultured variety of sour cream prepared by dairies, which contains 14%-18% butterfat, makes a delicious dressing for all varieties of salads.

Sour Cream Dressing

250-300 ml	sour cream
30 ml	lemon juice
15 ml	finely chopped green onion
2 ml	salt

Piquant Sour Cream Dressing

250-300 ml	sour cream
10 ml	celery seed
5 ml	dry mustard
	1 crushed garlic clove

Herb Sour Cream Dressing

250-300 ml	sour cream
5 ml	chopped fresh dill
5 ml	chopped parsley
30 ml	tarragon vinegar
	garlic powder

CREAM CHEESE DRESSING

85 g	cream cheese, softened
50 ml	red currant *or* grape jelly
5 ml	lemon juice
1 ml	salt
100 ml	whipping cream

Beat cheese with jelly, lemon juice and salt until smooth. Whip the cream and fold into the cheese mixture. *Yield:* 350 ml

PICNIC DRESSING

This dressing can be made very quickly and it thickens on standing. Serve the mustard variation with meat, fish and cabbage; the blue cheese variation complements fruit salads and tossed greens.

150 ml	evaporated milk, undiluted
150 ml	oil
50 ml	lemon juice
2 ml	salt
5 ml	Worcestershire sauce
50 ml	prepared mustard *or* blue cheese, crumbled

Shake all the ingredients together in a tightly covered jar. *Yield:* 400 ml

YOGURT DRESSINGS

Lower in fat and food energy than sour cream, but equally sharp in flavour, plain yogurt can be served alone or substituted for sour cream in the previous recipes. If desired, a few spoonfuls of mayonnaise can be added.

Although there is variation between flavours and brands, fruit-flavoured yogurt may contain up to twice the food energy of natural (plain) yogurt. It makes a delicious topping for fruits, alone or combined with half its quantity of any type of salad dressing.

Combine ingredients; chill.

Yogurt Mayonnaise

250 ml	yogurt
200 ml	MAYONNAISE
50 ml	lemon juice
10 ml	finely chopped onion
	salt, pepper

Yogurt Dressing

250 ml	yogurt
30 ml	chopped pickles
30 ml	chopped green onion
1 ml	celery salt
5 ml	sugar
5 ml	lemon juice

Dill Dressing

250 ml	yogurt
125 ml	MAYONNAISE
50 ml	finely chopped green onion
30 ml	chopped parsley
5 ml	prepared horseradish
5 ml	dill weed
	salt, pepper

Yogurt Dressing for Fruit

250 ml	yogurt
10 ml	chopped maraschino cherries *or* chopped preserved ginger syrup from cherries or ginger, *or* honey, to taste

9 Cereals, Pasta and Legumes

Cereal grains provide most of the world's food energy in the form of rice, corn, rye and wheat and their products.

Whole grain cereals contain bran layers and at least part of the germ, as well as the inner starchy portion of the grain. They supply not only carbohydrates for energy, but B vitamins and a small amount of incomplete protein and iron. Whole grain cereals are our best source of dietary fibre.

The quality of cereal protein is improved when it is eaten with other protein-containing foods including legumes.

Refined or starchy cereals have had the bran layers and germ removed. Many refined cereals have been fortified with some of the minerals and vitamins lost during refinement; these cereals are labelled *enriched*.

Cereals are available precooked, as ready-to-serve breakfast cereals; partially cooked, including quick-cooking varieties of breakfast cereals and rice; and uncooked cereals which require long, slow cooking.

General Directions for Cooking Cereals

1. Have the water boiling in the top section of a double boiler or in a saucepan; add salt.
2. Add cereal slowly, stirring with a fork until the water boils again and the cereal thickens.
3. Place top section of double boiler over bottom section containing boiling water, or if using a saucepan, turn heat to lowest possible level. Cover and finish cooking; cereal in saucepan may require occasional stirring.

Cereals requiring a long cooking period can be cooked at night and reheated at breakfast time; a double boiler is recommended. To reheat cereal, add a little milk, cover and heat over boiling water without stirring. When hot, stir and serve. Serve with milk, a few raisins, nuts, or GRANOLA. Popular but less nutritious additions are brown sugar, maple sugar, or syrup.

Proportions for Cooking Breakfast Cereals (Porridge)

The amount of cooked porridge will equal approximately the amount of liquid used.

Type	Example	Amount of Cereal per 250 ml of water	Cooking Time
Fine cereals	Cornmeal Farina Cream of Wheat	50-75 ml	30 min
Rolled or flaked cereals	Rolled Oats or Wheat	100-125 ml	5-15 min
Coarse cereals	Cracked Wheat (Bulgur Wheat)	75-100 ml	1 h
Quick-cooking cereals	Vita B Cream of Wheat Kasha	60-100 ml	3-8 min

Rice

Rice is sold in its natural state as brown rice (whole grain) or as polished (refined) rice. The many varieties may be short or long grained, the latter being popular for its attractive appearance.

Polished rice is available raw (regular rice), partially cooked as converted rice, or precooked in the form of quick-cooking rice. For the increase in convenience of quick-cooking rice, there is a sizable increase in the price—and a decrease in flavour.

Polishing results in a loss of nutrients—particularly thiamin. The process of "converting" rice, treating with steam before polishing, forces many of the nutrients which normally are found in the outer layers of the grain to pass into the centre where they are unaffected by polishing. Like brown rice, converted rice rates high nutritionally; but it is lower in dietary fibre.

Wild rice is not a true rice but the product of a water-grass which is cultivated by Indians in specific areas of the country.

Rice Quantities
500 g rice = 575-625 ml
Regular, converted and brown rice expand 3 to 4 times their volume when cooked. Quick-cooking rice expands to twice its volume. Follow package directions when cooking quick-cooking rice.

BOILED RICE

250 ml	rice
1 *l*	water
2 ml	salt

1. Remove excess starch from the rice by rubbing it in a sieve while cold water runs through; continue until the water draining off is clear.
2. Have water boiling rapidly in a large kettle; add salt.
3. Add rice, slowly stirring with a fork until the water returns to the boil.
4. Reduce heat and continue cooking until the rice is tender, about 12 min; test by tasting or rubbing a kernel between thumb and forefinger. There should be no "bone" in the centre.
5. Drain rice in a sieve; if any liquid remains, save for stock; rinse with boiling water and transfer to serving dish.
6. Toss rice lightly with a fork and leave in a warm place to dry slightly. *Yield:* approximately 875 ml

Unless otherwise stated in recipes, rice refers to uncooked regular or converted rice. In mixtures, if quick-cooking rice is substituted, adjustments must be made in procedure and in cooking time. It is neither practical nor economical to cook quick-cooking rice for long periods.

Thorough rinsing of regular rice before cooking and the avoidance of overcooking are essential if rice is to emerge as whole, separate tender grains.

STEAMED RICE

250 ml	rice
500 ml	boiling water *or* chicken stock

1. Rinse starch from rice as in step 1 of preceding recipe.
2. Combine rice with boiling water or stock in a saucepan; cover and bring to boiling point.
3. Reduce heat and continue cooking until all the water is absorbed and the rice is tender, about 15 min for white rice, 35-40 min for brown (unpolished) rice.
4. Let rice "rest" in a warm place for 15-20 min to dry; toss lightly with a fork. *Serves 4-6.*

Flavoured Rice
Each of the following is prepared from hot cooked rice (any variety), 500 ml
To keep the rice fluffy, the food being added should be sprinkled over the surface of the hot rice and then tossed in lightly with a fork.
Cheese Rice—Add grated Cheddar or Parmesan cheese, 175 ml
Serve with bacon, sausages, sliced tomatoes.
Coconut Rice—Add moist flaked coconut, 125 ml
Serve with chicken, curried mixtures.
Lemon or Orange Rice—Add the finely grated rind of lemon or orange, 5 ml
Slivered almonds and raisins may be added. Serve with seafood or curried mixtures.
Parsley or Chive Rice (Green Rice)—Add finely chopped parsley, or chives (or shallots), or a mixture of the two, 30 ml
Pineapple Rice—Add thoroughly drained crushed pineapple, 125 ml
Serve with ham, veal, or chicken.
Saffron Rice—Add a pinch of saffron to the cooking water. (Turmeric is less costly than saffron and can be substituted for it; the colour is not quite as bright.) Serve with seafood, curries, or chicken.

Serve boiled or steamed rice plain or flavoured as an accompaniment to meats, fish and fowl; or serve with curries, or in hot or cold mixtures for main course, salad or dessert.

RISOTTO

This Italian dish, known also as Pilaf or Pilau, is fail-proof. It requires no last-minute preparation and results in flavoursome, attractive rice that is the perfect accompaniment to most meat dishes including Chinese food.

100 ml	chopped onions
100 ml	chopped celery
30 ml	butter
350 ml	rice
700 ml	chicken stock

1. Sauté the onions and celery in the fat until the onions are golden.
2. Stir in rice; continue stirring until rice grains turn pale gold.
3. Add stock to mixture; taste and season.
4. Cover and bake for 45 min at 180°C

Or simmer on top of the stove for about 25 min until liquid is absorbed and rice is tender. If brown (unpolished) rice is used, cooking time will be 1 h or more.

Serve directly from the casserole or fluff up rice with a fork, adding a little chopped parsley or chives; serve in a bowl. *Serves 6.*

Variations

For the chicken stock substitute brown stock, beef bouillon, white wine and/or water depending on the food being served with the Risotto. Chicken or beef concentrate can be used to prepare stock.

Cook a fresh, seeded, chopped tomato in the rice mixture; stir in cooked peas when rice is cooked.

Sprinkle Risotto with grated Parmesan cheese.

Rice Ring—Prepare Risotto and press into a buttered small ring mould or small angel-cake pan. Keep in a warm place for 10 min. Unmould and serve filled with SMOTHERED CHICKEN, creamed mixtures, or curries.

Chinese Rice and Meat—Cut cooked pork, ham, or chicken into strips; sprinkle with soy sauce. Add thin strips of green pepper and the meat to the Risotto during the last 10 min of cooking. Garnish with sliced green onions. *Serves 4.*

BAKED RICE AND CHOPS

A Dutch oven is particularly useful for this recipe; browning and baking can take place in the same pan.

	4 lean pork chops *or* lean lamb shoulder chops
	fat
	salt, pepper
	2 chopped onions
	½ chopped green pepper *or*
125 ml	chopped celery
250 ml	rice
540 ml	1 can tomatoes
250 ml	stock *or* water
2 ml	oregano *or* thyme

1. Brown chops in a little fat cut from the meat; season and remove from pan.
2. To the fat in the pan add onion, green pepper or celery, and the rice; stir and cook until the rice is golden.
3. Add remaining ingredients; heat to boiling and transfer to a casserole.
4. Place browned chops on top of the rice, cover and bake until rice is tender, at 180°C

Remove cover during the last 5 min

SEVEN-LAYER CASSEROLE

250 ml	rice
250 ml	canned kernel corn, drained
	salt, pepper
540 ml	1 can tomato juice
5 ml	Worcestershire sauce
100 ml	finely chopped onion
100 ml	finely chopped green pepper
375 g	lean ground beef
	4 strips of bacon

1. In a large casserole, arrange foods in layers in the following sequence: rice, corn, a sprinkle of salt and pepper, half of the tomato juice which is combined with the Worcestershire sauce, the chopped onion, green pepper, beef, another sprinkling of salt and pepper and the remaining tomato juice.
2. Top with bacon strips which have been cut in half and partially cooked.
3. Cover and bake for 1 h; uncover and bake for 30 min more, at 180°C

Serves 6-8.

RICE AND BEAN CASSEROLE

400 ml	brown or white rice
150 ml	pinto or kidney beans *or*
	black-eyed peas
	1 large green pepper
250 ml	chopped onions
	2 crushed garlic cloves
30 ml	cooking oil
350 g	shredded brick or Cheddar cheese
250 ml	cottage cheese
	salt, pepper
250 ml	milk

1. Cook rice and beans according to directions. See BOILED RICE and GENERAL DIRECTIONS FOR COOKING DRIED LEGUMES.
2. Cut green pepper into strips and sauté in oil with onions and garlic; combine with rice and beans.
3. Place half the mixture in a greased, large, shallow baking dish.
4. Set aside a little of the shredded cheese for topping and combine the remainder with the cottage cheese; season and spread evenly over the rice mixture.
5. Cover with remaining rice mixture and pour milk evenly over all.
6. Bake for 30 min at 180°C

Sprinkle the remaining grated cheese over the mixture during the last 5 min. *Serves 6.*

The protein quality of rice and beans is improved when they are served together; cheese adds more protein.

CHINESE FRIED RICE

60 ml	cooking oil
30 ml	finely chopped onion
	2 eggs, beaten
	salt
1 ℓ	cooked rice
75 ml	sliced canned mushrooms
125 ml	frozen peas, thawed
125 ml	diced cooked ham, chicken, *or* pork

1. Heat oil in a frying pan over medium heat; add onion, eggs and salt.
2. Stir with a fork until egg forms small pieces; add remaining ingredients and continue heating and stirring until all is hot and well mixed. *Serves 4.*

PAELLA

Pronounced pie-ay-a, this spectacular Spanish dish has many versions, some taking their inspiration from the fruits of the sea, others tracing their origin to land and the good foods it provides. This version combines the best of two worlds!

Special paella pans are available for cooking and serving paella, but a dutch oven, or a combination of skillet and casserole will serve the purpose nicely.

	3-4 chicken breasts
	cooking oil
	2 cloves of garlic
150 ml	chopped onion
	1 green pepper, cut in strips
50 ml	pimento, cut in strips
2 ml	oregano
2 ml	pepper
500 ml	rice
250 ml	frozen or fresh peas
250.ml	canned tomatoes drained *or* 3
	peeled tomatoes, chopped
1 ℓ	chicken stock
1 ml	saffron or turmeric
500 g	raw shrimp, shelled and cleaned
	12 clams in the shell
	lemon wedges

1. Cut chicken breasts into halves, and each half into 3 or 4 pieces, to include bones. Brown each piece in oil.
2. Add garlic, onion and green pepper; sauté until just soft.
3. Add pimento, seasonings, rice, peas and coarsely chopped tomatoes.
4. Add chicken stock and heat to boiling; add saffron. Cook gently, uncovered, for about 10 min, with minimum stirring.
5. Add shrimp, pushing them down into the liquid. Cover and cook gently for about 15 min until all foods are cooked.
6. Stir through mixture gently to distribute the liquid and continue cooking uncovered over low heat until mixture is almost dry, about 15 min. Stir frequently to prevent sticking. (If oven is in use, transfer pan to oven.)
7. While mixture is cooking, scrub clam shells with a brush. Steam in a covered container over boiling water. (A metal sieve in a covered saucepan can be used for this.) Shells should open after about 10 min of steaming. Arrange opened shells on top of paella with wedges of lemon. *Serves 8.*

CABBAGE ROLLS

Each central European country has a different version of this recipe. The names given to it include Koldomar, Holupchi and Holubsti, each of which means "little pigeons."

	1 large green cabbage
125 ml	rice
500 g	minced lamb *or* beef
45 ml	fat
	1 onion, chopped
	garlic powder
	salt, pepper
250-375 ml tomato juice *or* tomato sauce	

1. Leave the cabbage whole; pull off any discoloured leaves; remove all the core; pour boiling water into the core to cover the cabbage; let stand over low heat until the leaves are pliable and will not break when folded.
2. Rinse rice under cold water, add to an equal quantity of boiling water and boil for 1 min; cover tightly, turn off the heat and leave until the water is absorbed.
3. Fry onion in fat until golden brown and combine with the meat and the rice which will still be firm.
4. Remove the cabbage; cool under cold water. Separate leaves carefully.
5. On the long side of each leaf, place meat mixture: approximately 30 ml
   Roll up, tucking in the ends to make a tight roll. Fasten with a toothpick if necessary.
6. If rolls are to be cooked on top of the stove, place a shallow rack in the pot, arranging the rolls on it in layers. Season.
7. Add juice or sauce; cover tightly and simmer about 1 h. If the pot is thin, check from time to time to be sure that it is not boiling dry or that the rolls are not scorching.
8. Rolls may be cooked in the oven in a casserole; add juice, cover tightly and bake in oven for 1-1.5 h at 160°C
   Another method is to pressure cook for 10 min
9. If desired, rolls can be browned slightly under the broiler; serve with crisp crumbled bacon and sour cream. *Serves 4-6.*

Variation
Substitute a mixture of pork and beef for the meat; season generously with paprika.

DOLMAS

Somewhat similar to Cabbage Rolls, Dolmas are of Turkish origin and are prepared by stuffing grape leaves, first blanched (3-5 min in boiling water) and thoroughly drained. Grape leaves (vine leaves) packed in brine can be purchased in specialty stores. To use, rinse in warm water, drain thoroughly on a rack and remove stem. Leaves are stuffed with a mixture of minced lamb and cooked rice.

1. Prepare lamb filling as in CABBAGE ROLLS (preceding recipe) but completely cook the rice in twice the quantity of boiling water (see STEAMED RICE).
2. Place filling near the stem end of the veined underside of the prepared leaf. Fold the sides over the filling and roll up from the stem end. Amount of filling per leaf is 15 ml
3. Heat a little butter or cooking oil in a heavy saucepan. Cover bottom of pan with a few grape leaves and place rolls tightly together on leaves. Sprinkle with lemon juice and pour stock or tomato juice over them. Cover and cook 30 min. Makes approximately 40-50 Dolmas. *Serves 6-8.*

To freeze fresh grape leaves for use later in Dolmas, blanch, drain and pat dry with a towel. Pile in bundles of 10; separate each bundle from the next with foil. Package and freeze.

SPANISH RICE

250 ml	chopped onions
	1 clove garlic
125 ml	chopped celery
125 ml	chopped green pepper
30 ml	fat
796 ml	1 can tomatoes
5 ml	sugar
	salt
	2 whole cloves
750 ml	cooked rice

1. Sauté the fresh vegetables in the fat; remove the garlic.
2. Add the tomatoes, sugar and seasonings; bring to a boil and simmer 10 min. Remove cloves.
3. Stir in the rice; pour into a greased casserole and bake for 30 min at 180°C
   Serves 4

Variations
Speedy Spanish Rice—Prepare ingredients to the end of step 2. Stir in half the quantity of quick-cooking rice. Simmer for 5-10 min and serve.

Jambalaya—Prepare Spanish Rice by either method. When the rice is tender and much of the liquid has been absorbed, stir in cooked ham, shrimp or chicken, browned minced beef, or cubed left-over roast beef or lamb.

WILD RICE

Long and greenish-black in colour, wild rice is much prized as an accompaniment to game and all poultry. It is very delicious—and very expensive.

Preparation
Thoroughly rinse rice under cold running water. Soak in water to cover, overnight, or until grains are just tender, not mushy.

Or stir rice into 3 times its volume of boiling water; boil gently for 5 min; let stand in same water for 1 h

Complete the cooking using water left from soaking plus additional water to cover generously. Boil over direct heat or bake in the oven for about 40 min at 180°C

WILD RICE AND MUSHROOMS

250 ml	wild rice
750 ml	chicken stock
2 ml	seasoned salt
2 ml	basil
50 ml	butter
500 ml	chopped mushrooms
50 ml	chopped onions

1. Soak rice for 30 min; drain and combine with stock, salt and basil in the top of a double boiler. Chicken or beef concentrate can be used to prepare stock; cover and cook over boiling water for 45 min
2. Melt butter in a frying pan and sauté mushrooms and onions gently for approximately 3 min, adding more butter if needed.
3. Combine rice, mushrooms, onions, remaining stock in a casserole; taste and season.
4. Bake for 30-45 min at 180°C
   Serves 4.

Recipes, tables, etc. that appear in small capital letters, e.g., PARSLEY BUTTER, CANADA'S FOOD GUIDE, are listed in the index. Consult the index for the number of the page on which the item appears.

BARLEY CASSEROLE

Better known as an ingredient for soup, barley can replace potatoes as a delicious accompaniment to meats, especially those that produce gravy.

As with other cereals, the whole hulled grain is most nutritious and requires the longest cooking time. It can be purchased in specialty food stores. Pot barley and pearl barley have undergone some degree of abrasion to remove bran layers. Pearl barley, the more refined of the two, is whiter and slightly smaller than pot barley; both are readily available.

	1 large onion, chopped
100 g	mushrooms, sliced
50 ml	cooking oil
250 ml	pearl barley
500 ml	chicken stock

1. Sauté onion and mushroom slices in oil until soft; lift out. Add barley and brown it lightly.
2. Taste stock and season if necessary; pour half of it over the barley.
3. Cover and bake barley for 30 min at 180°C
4. Add remaining stock and vegetables; continue cooking until the liquid is absorbed and the barley is tender. *Serves 4.*

For a nutritious economical dish, combine cooked legumes with cooked barley or bulgur.

The staple grain-dish of the Middle East is bulgur, cracked whole-grain wheat. Serve as a substitute for rice or potatoes or in stuffing for poultry.

KASHA

The triangular-shaped seeds of buckwheat, known as buckwheat groats or kasha, are a potassium-rich grain which is used extensively in eastern Mediterranean countries. This dish is served with meat and vegetables.

250 ml	whole buckwheat groats
	1 egg, beaten
	salt
500 ml	water or chicken stock
50 ml	butter or margarine

1. Warm a heavy frying pan which has a tight-fitting lid.
2. Combine buckwheat and beaten egg in a bowl and mix until all grains are coated.

3. Add to hot frying pan and stir mixture briskly until each grain is dry and separate.
4. Add water or stock and salt to taste; cook, covered over low heat, until groats are cooked and liquid absorbed, about 30 min
5. Mix with butter and serve. *Serves 2-3.*

Variation

Pasta and Groats—While groats are cooking, cook an equal quantity of small pasta (bows, rings, or wagon wheels) following package directions or see DIRECTIONS FOR COOKING PASTA. Sauté a finely chopped large onion and sliced mushrooms, if desired, in a little butter or margarine. Combine with cooked groats and cooked pasta; season.

A quick-cooking variety of milled Kasha is also available. It can be used uncooked to thicken soups and stews, or cooked to serve as a hot cereal or an accompaniment to meat.

Pasta

Macaroni, spaghetti and noodles are the best-known members of the pasta family. All pasta is made from a special type of hard wheat with a high protein content. Some brands are enriched with B vitamins and iron to compensate for the loss of some of the nutrients during the milling of the wheat.

Served with small quantities of meat, fish, or cheese—and imagination—pasta is not only an extender of protein but a versatile ingredient of many sumptuous dishes.

DIRECTIONS FOR COOKING PASTA

125 ml or 60 g/serving	pasta
	boiling water
	salt
15 ml	oil (optional)

Pasta expands on cooking to approximately twice its original volume.

1. Have a large quantity of water rapidly boiling in a pot; add a little salt. (For extra flavour, a few celery leaves or onion slices may be added to the cooking water; fine noodles can be cooked in chicken stock.) The addition of oil will reduce the tendency for pasta to stick together.
2. Boil uncovered with occasional stirring, handling large noodles very carefully to prevent tearing. Any protruding ends should be pushed down into the pot as the submerged ends soften.
3. Cook until *just* tender—the stage which the Italians call "al dente." Test large pasta (manicotti, lasagna) with the point of a sharp knife to determine doneness. Drain off water; small pasta can be drained in a sieve.
4. If not to be used immediately, pasta should be rinsed with cold water.

The simplest of sauces convert pasta into delicious accompaniments to braised meats, meat balls, scallopines, sausages and goulash, or into a side dish with a HEARTY CHEF'S SALAD.

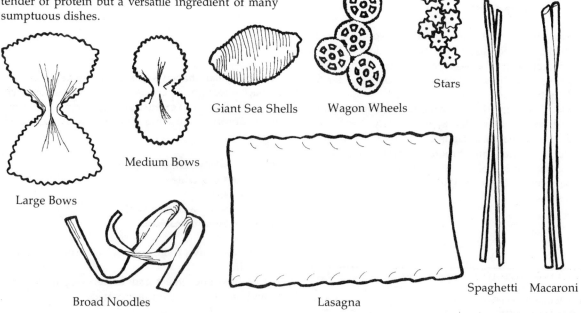

Giant Sea Shells   Wagon Wheels   Stars

Large Bows

Medium Bows

Broad Noodles

Lasagna

Spaghetti   Macaroni

Some popular pasta shapes.

Fresh vegetables make nutritious salads. Keep crisp by careful storage.

Crisp greens combine well with an oil and vinegar dressing.

Spicy tomato sauce with chunks of cooked meat, served hot on noodles.

Elegant Beef Stroganoff on buttered noodles.

Basic Recipe
DRESSING FOR PASTA

175 ml	vegetable oil *or* melted butter
	2-3 cloves garlic, crushed
	salt, pepper
125 ml	finely chopped parsley
125 ml	grated Parmesan cheese (optional)

1. Heat oil and add crushed garlic, pressing down on garlic with a fork to remove all juices. If any pieces of garlic remain, remove.
2. Cooked pasta should be thoroughly drained; pour oil over it, season, and lightly toss. Toss in chopped parsley.
3. If desired, grated Parmesan cheese can be sprinkled over the top or tossed through the pasta. *Yield:* dressing for 500 g of pasta

Variations

Substitute melted butter for oil and omit garlic and parsley. Into the buttered noodles toss any of toasted sesame seeds, poppy seeds, caraway seeds, or celery seeds; or flavour with chopped chives, green onions or a little fresh or dried basil, savory, or dill weed.

Green Dressing for Pasta—In an electric blender, combine a mixture of oil and soft butter, (substitute butter for 1/3-½ of the oil in the basic recipe), 1 garlic clove, 4 times the quantity of chopped parsley, and the Parmesan cheese; season with salt, pepper and basil, preferably fresh, to taste. Blend at high speed until smooth; toss with noodles, small shells, or other small varieties of pasta.

If pasta dishes are served often or are prepared in quantity, it may be convenient to prepare a large quantity of sauce to be kept on hand in the refrigerator or freezer. When freezing, package in several containers or plastic bags in quantities required for specific recipes.

Tomato Sauce and its derivatives, Spaghetti Sauce and Meat Sauce are used in a wide variety of pasta dishes. For this reason the basic recipe is given here for use in specified recipes. Canned, bottled and packaged spaghetti sauces can be substituted for these sauces; packaged spaghetti spices can be used to season home-made sauces. The convenience is accompanied by higher costs.

Basic Recipe
TOMATO SAUCE FOR PASTA

	2 large onions, chopped
	2 garlic cloves, crushed
	1 green pepper, chopped
	4 stalks celery, chopped (optional)
50 ml	oil
796 ml	1 can tomatoes
156 ml	1 can tomato paste
156 ml	water *or* stock
5 ml	basil
5 ml	oregano
1 ml	rosemary
	salt, pepper
10 ml	sugar

1. Sauté raw vegetables in oil until soft; add canned tomatoes, tomato paste, and liquid. (Use liquid to rinse the tomato paste can.)
2. Add remaining ingredients and heat mixture to boiling point; reduce heat and simmer uncovered with frequent stirring for 45 min, or until sauce thickens. *Yield:* approximately 1.125 *ℓ*

Variations

Spaghetti Sauce—Purée the Tomato Sauce in a food mill, coarse sieve, or blender. The blender gives a product greater volume and thicker texture—somewhat different from the usual spaghetti sauce. (Celery should be finely chopped to avoid stringiness when blended.) Sliced mushrooms, canned or sautéed, may be added to the sauce after puréeing. *Yield:* 4 servings, approximately 750 ml

Meat Sauce—To the basic recipe add: minced beef or chopped chicken livers, 250-500 g
After the vegetables have been sautéed in the fat, lift them out of the pan; increase the heat and brown the meat a small amount at a time. Add to the vegetables; finish according to the basic recipe. *Yield:* 6 servings, approximately 1500 ml

SPAGHETTI AND MEAT BALLS

Prepare MEAT BALLS and brown; cook in SPAGHETTI SAUCE. Pour sauce and meat balls over cooked spaghetti. Serve with grated Parmesan or grated strong Cheddar cheese. See DIRECTIONS FOR COOKING PASTA.

SPAGHETTI AND MEAT SAUCE

Pour MEAT SAUCE over cooked spaghetti. Serve with grated Parmesan cheese or grated strong Cheddar.

SPAGHETTI WITH EGGPLANT SAUCE

	1 medium-size eggplant cut into cubes of 2 cm
30 ml	flour
100 ml	oil
250 ml	sliced onions
500 ml	tomato juice
500 ml	TOMATO SAUCE FOR PASTA *or* SPAGHETTI SAUCE
5 ml	sugar
	salt, pepper
1 ml	basil
1 ml	oregano *or* rosemary

1. Sprinkle eggplant cubes with flour and toss to coat on all sides.
2. Heat oil in a large frying pan and brown cubes over medium high heat, stirring frequently. Remove with a slotted spoon.
3. Sauté onions in the fat over reduced heat, adding more fat if necessary; add remaining ingredients, except eggplant, and simmer, uncovered, for 20 min
4. Add eggplant, cover and simmer for 20 min or until eggplant is tender. Serve over cooked spaghetti, 315 g
   Sprinkle with Parmesan Cheese. *Serves 4-6.*

Spaghetti and meat sauce, with a salad, makes a wholesome meal. Lawry's Foods, Inc.

WHITE SAUCE, VELOUTÉ SAUCE and cream-soup variations of these sauces provide the base for an unlimited number of pasta dishes. Here are 3 examples. Macaroni and cheese can also be prepared using the recipe for CHEESE BOWS WITH GARLIC CROUTONS.

MACARONI WITH CHEESE SAUCE

	macaroni
225 g	macaroni
500 ml	WHITE SAUCE, MEDIUM
500 ml (250g)	grated Cheddar cheese
2 ml	minced onion (optional)
	salt, pepper
175 ml	soft, buttered crumbs

1. Cook macaroni according to directions on package or DIRECTIONS FOR COOKING PASTA.
2. Prepare seasoned WHITE SAUCE in the top section of a double boiler; add grated cheese and stir over low heat until melted.
3. Taste sauce and season with minced onion, salt and pepper as desired; combine with cooked macaroni.
4. Mixture may be heated on top of the stove or baked in a casserole in a moderate oven, topped with BUTTERED CRUMBS at 180°C
   Bake until crumbs are browned, about 35 min. *Serves 4-6.*

Variations
Add any of chopped green pepper, cucumber or PEPPER RELISH, Worcestershire sauce, or partly cooked bacon.

Beef or chicken concentrate may be dissolved in the hot sauce; sauce may be prepared from condensed cream of mushroom, celery, or cheese soup.

Grate only half the cheese and add to the sauce; leave remaining cheese in very thin flat pieces and carefully stir into the combined mixture.

Blender Macaroni and Cheese—in the blender combine the ingredients for WHITE SAUCE, the ungrated cheese and seasonings; blend until smooth. Combine with cooked macaroni and bake for approximately 35 min at 180°C

Recipes, tables, etc. that appear in small capital letters, e.g., PARSLEY BUTTER, CANADA'S FOOD GUIDE, are listed in the index. Consult the index for the number of the page on which the item appears.

CHICKEN TETRAZZINI

200 g	mushrooms
30 ml	butter *or* cooking oil
30 ml	flour
500 ml	chicken stock and cream
750 ml	diced cooked chicken
50 ml	toasted almonds (optional)
	salt, pepper
250 g	cooked spaghetti *or* noodles
125 ml	grated Parmesan or Cheddar cheese
125 ml	cream
	paprika

1. Sauté mushrooms in fat about 5 min; add flour; stir until well blended.
2. Add chicken stock and cream mixture; stir until it bubbles; add the chicken and almonds. Taste and season.
3. Combine the cooked spaghetti, half the cheese and the cream; heat.
4. Arrange the spaghetti around the outside of a platter.
5. Pour creamed mixture into the centre of the spaghetti; sprinkle with the rest of the cheese and with paprika. *Serves 6.*

Casserole Cookery

Family meals and party meals benefit from the use of casseroles. Ingredients range from the simplest to the most expensive; often leftovers can be used to advantage. These versatile dishes can be prepared hours or days before needed, reducing last-minute pressures. When serving a crowd, food will always be hot if many containers are used, some keeping hot in the oven while others are in use.

HOW TO FREEZE CASSEROLES

Most casserole mixtures of cooked or partially cooked ingredients freeze well. Those containing potatoes or hard-cooked eggs do not. Onions lose strength on freezing; herbs and sour cream are best added when food is being reheated. Mixtures containing uncooked, beaten egg should be completely thawed before cooking to permit even cooking. It is best to undercook mixtures slightly if they are to be frozen, so that the processes of freezing, thawing and reheating will not result in dry or over-processed food.

To freeze casseroles, line casserole dishes with foil, using a large piece which will extend up and beyond the sides of the dish. Fill with mixture and freeze. Remove the frozen mass and fold over the extended foil to enclose the mixture, making it airtight. Label and return package to freezer; the dish is available for other uses until the casserole is to be used. Then the foil is peeled off the frozen food and the mixture returned to the dish for thawing and reheating.

Thaw casseroles overnight in the refrigerator before heating. If necessary to thaw at room temperature, 1/3 to ½ time will be sufficient. If time does not permit complete thawing, place casserole dish in a pan of water and bake, allowing up to 1½ times the normal time required for reheating.

BUFFET CHICKEN CASSEROLE

This attractive and delicious casserole can be prepared the day before a party, or earlier if frozen. Begin by stewing a fowl. Save chicken stock and meat for casserole.

125 ml	chopped onion
	½ green pepper, chopped
250 ml	mushrooms, sliced
30 ml	fat
1.5 ℓ	liquid
350 g	thin, flat noodles
750-1000 ml	cooked chicken *or* turkey, diced
284 ml	1 can cream of mushroom soup
250 ml	pitted ripe olives
50 ml	pimento, cut in strips
285 g	1 small package frozen peas
	celery salt, salt, pepper
375 ml	grated Cheddar cheese

1. Sauté onion, green pepper and mushrooms in fat.
2. Combine chicken stock, liquid from canned olives and water to make the required amount of liquid; heat to boiling and add noodles. Cook until tender. Do not drain.
3. Stir in chicken, soup, pimento and olives, sautéed vegetables and thawed peas. Season to taste.
4. Pour half the mixture into a large casserole dish. Sprinkle over it half of the grated cheese.
5. Pour in remaining mixture and top with remaining cheese.
6. Cover and bake for about 45 min at 170°C Uncover and bake for 15 min more until top is browned. Garnish with parsley. *Serves 8-10.*

Basic Recipe
PASTA AND VEGETABLE CASSEROLE

500 ml	macaroni *or* noodles *or* spaghetti
125 ml	chopped onion
	½ green pepper, chopped
125 ml	chopped celery
50 ml	fat
500 ml	canned tomatoes
	salt, pepper
10 ml	brown sugar
250 ml	grated cheese

1. Cook pasta according to directions on package or DIRECTIONS FOR COOKING PASTA; drain.
2. Sauté the onion, green pepper and celery in fat until soft.
3. Combine with the cooked pasta and the remaining ingredients, saving the cheese to sprinkle on top of the casserole during the last 10 min of cooking.
4. Bake uncovered for 30 min at 180°C
Serves 4-6.

Variations

Substitute TOMATO SAUCE FOR PASTA in place of the onion, green pepper, celery and canned tomatoes in the basic recipe.

Add any of the following to the basic recipe:

250-500 ml cooked kernel corn *or* lima beans
or

250 ml	sautéed eggplant cubes
	or
	4 sautéed eggplant slices
	or
	1 chopped, peeled cucumber
	or
	1 sliced, unpeeled zucchini squash

and/or

250-500 g	minced beef, browned
	or
	8-10 sausages, parboiled for 5 minutes

Prairie Casserole—Add to the basic recipe:

500-750 g	minced beef, browned
341 ml	1 can kernel corn
15 ml	Worcestershire sauce
250 g	processed cheese, grated

Double the quantity of onions and omit the grated cheese topping. *Serves 8-10.*

LASAGNA

500-750 g	minced beef
50 ml	cooking oil
250 ml	chopped onions
	1 green pepper, chopped
540 ml	1 can tomato juice
156 ml	1 can tomato paste
175-225 g	lasagna noodles
454 g	creamed cottage cheese
	salt, pepper, seasonings
250 g	Mozzarella cheese, sliced
200 ml	Parmesan cheese, grated
150 g	½ package spinach, cooked (optional)

Choose a deep, square or rectangular casserole or baking dish for the most attractive arrangement of noodles. Determine the number of noodles required for 2 (or 3) complete layers of single noodles, allowing for expansion during cooking.

1. Sauté onions and green pepper in oil until soft; remove from the pan, increase the heat and brown meat a little at a time, adding more oil if necessary.
2. Pour off any accumulated fat; add tomato juice and paste, heat to boiling and then simmer for 15 min
3. Cook lasagna noodles according to directions, being very careful not to tear them; transfer with a slotted spoon to a dish of cold water, remove as needed and drain.
4. Assemble casserole, beginning with a layer of meat in sauce, a single layer of noodles to cover the meat, and a layer of cottage cheese. Sprinkle with half the Parmesan cheese. Season with salt and pepper and a sprinkle of oregano and basil. Top with slices of Mozzarella cheese.
5. If desired, a layer of well-drained, chopped, cooked spinach can be added; use all of the spinach.
6. Repeat layers of meat, noodles and cheeses—twice if possible, finishing with meat and sauce.
7. Top with Mozzarella slices arranged in triangles or a lattice pattern.
8. Bake in a moderate oven until the casserole is bubbly and the cheese is lightly brown; remove from the oven and let lasagna set for 5-10 min. Before serving cut into squares. *Serves 6-8.*

Recipes, tables, etc. that appear in small capital letters, e.g., PARSLEY BUTTER, CANADA'S FOOD GUIDE, are listed in the index. Consult the index for the number of the page on which the item appears.

Variations of Lasagna

Use SPAGHETTI MEAT SAUCE, 1.5ℓ   6 cups
in place of the first 6 ingredients of the Lasagna recipe

Use TOMATO SAUCE FOR PASTA, 875 ml
and combine with the browned meat in the Lasagna recipe, omitting the 5 ingredients which follow the meat.

Meatless Lasagna—Use TOMATO SAUCE FOR PASTA, 1.125 ℓ
Omit first 6 ingredients.

NOODLES ALFREDO

500 g	cooked broad noodles
175 ml	soft butter
500 ml	grated parmesan *or* strong Cheddar cheese
125 ml	warm cream

1. Thoroughly drain cooked noodles; place in hot casserole with butter; toss gently with fork until noodles are all buttered.
2. Add cheese and toss again; pour in cream and toss again.
3. Season with salt and pepper or seasoned salt. *Serves 8.*

PASTA SUPREME

250 g	pasta
60 ml	cooking oil *or* melted butter
5 ml	basil
75 ml	chopped parsley
	salt, pepper
500 ml	cottage cheese
250 ml	sour cream
125 ml	broken olives *or* sweet relish
175 ml	milk
250 ml	soft bread crumbs
125 ml	grated Cheddar *or* Parmesan cheese

1. Cook macaroni, medium shells, or large bows according to directions on package or DIRECTIONS FOR COOKING PASTA. Drain.
2. Combine pasta with oil, herbs and seasonings, tossing mixture lightly to coat pasta. Transfer to a greased, large, shallow casserole.
3. Combine cottage cheese, sour cream, olives or relish and milk; pour over pasta.
4. Top with buttered crumbs and grated Cheddar cheese; bake in oven for 30 min at 180°C
Garnish with grated parsley. *Serves 6-8.*

CHEESE BOWS WITH GARLIC CROUTONS

Combine cooked bows or other varieties of small pasta with an equal quantity of grated cheese (a mixture of Cheddar with a semi-hard cheese like Gruyère is best) and ¼ of the quantity of milk. Season with salt, pepper and basil. Sprinkle more grated Cheddar over top, and scatter GARLIC CROUTONS over cheese. Bake until cheese melts at 180°C
Serve with a green salad with or without meat.

Stuffed Pasta

Manicotti and giant shells are designed for stuffing with savory mixtures like the following. Recipes for attractive side and main dishes using stuffed pasta follow.

Basic Recipe
FILLING FOR STUFFED PASTA

500 g	finely ground, lean minced beef *or* creamed cottage cheese fat
280 g	1 package fresh or frozen spinach
	1 egg, beaten
	salt, pepper
	garlic powder *or* nutmeg

1. Brown beef in a little fat in a frying pan; remove from pan and cool. Drain excess fat from pan. If cottage cheese is used instead of beef, omit this step.
2. Chop spinach finely (if frozen, thaw it first and drain thoroughly.) Sauté in a minimum amount of fat in frying pan for 3 or 4 min
3. Combine meat or cheese with the spinach, beaten egg and seasonings, adding a little nutmeg to the cheese mixture and a little garlic to the meat mixture.
4. Use a blender to blend mixture to a coarse paste; otherwise, use a fork. Fill pasta; proceed with 1 of the 4 recipes that follow. *Approximate yield:* 500 ml
Enough to fill: 8 manicotti noodles, using in each 60 ml
or 16 cannelloni, 30 ml
or 16 giant shells, 20 ml
or 10 lasagna (for rolls), 45 ml

Stuffing is less likely to spill out of pasta while the casserole is being baked if the assembled casserole is chilled for a few hours before baking. Also, careful handling of the pasta is necessary to prevent tearing and leakage. Pasta should be completely dry (inside) before stuffing.

Variations
To filling prepared from cottage cheese:
Add 1 small tin of salmon or tuna, flaked, and the following vegetables chopped and sautéed: 2 stalks of celery, ¼ green pepper and ½ small onion
or replace spinach with a mixture of grated mozzarella and grated Parmesan cheese, 250 ml
or replace ¼ to ½ the quantity of cottage cheese with fine, herb-flavoured bread crumbs.

To filling prepared from meat:
Replace all or part of the meat with chopped cooked chicken livers, diced ham, or any other varieties of cooked meat, finely chopped or ground.

MANICOTTI CASSEROLE

In this dish, large pasta tubes are filled and baked in tomato sauce. This casserole requires considerable time for preparation; it should be assembled in advance and refrigerated or frozen until baked.

113 g	8 manicotti noodles
500 ml	FILLING FOR STUFFED PASTA
500 ml	tomato sauce
5 ml	oregano
60 ml	grated Parmesan cheese
	chopped parsley

1. Cook pasta, being very careful to prevent breaking. Transfer noodles with a slotted spoon to a container of cold water; remove as needed to a sieve so that they will be thoroughly drained.
2. Prepare filling from preceding recipe and fill pasta tubes using a fork or small spoon.
3. Spread half of the tomato sauce (purchased, or prepared from recipe for TOMATO SAUCE) in a shallow casserole; place filled noodles in rows in the sauce.
4. If oregano was not used in the sauce, sprinkle it over the noodles and cover with remaining sauce.
5. Cover and bake for approximately 30 min at 180°C
Sprinkle with grated Parmesan cheese and bake uncovered for 10 min more. Sprinkle with chopped parsley. *Serves 3-4.*

Variation
Manicotti Party Casserole—Cook double the quantity of noodles; prepare one lot of filling using meat and another using cheese (or double the amount of either). Fill noodles. Spread all of the tomato sauce in the casserole (2 casseroles may be required if they are small); cover with rows of filled noodles. Cover noodles with seasoned medium WHITE SAUCE, and bake covered for 30-40 min. Remove from oven and top mixture with overlapping triangles of sliced mozzarella cheese or sprinkle with grated Parmesan. Bake uncovered for 10 min until cheese melts. Garnish with parsley. *Serves 6-8.*

LASAGNA ROLLS

Cook 10-12 lasagna; handle very carefully to prevent breaking. Remove from water one at a time and place on a dish towel; pat dry. Prepare meat or cheese FILLING FOR STUFFED PASTA; allowing for each lasagna approximately 45 ml
Coat one side of the entire length of each noodle; sprinkle with grated Parmesan cheese. Roll up and place each roll on its end (with the spiral showing) in a flat-bottomed, lightly greased casserole, small enough in diameter to hold rolls upright. Add tomato sauce or TOMATO SAUCE FOR PASTA to a depth about ¾ that of the rolls. If the sauce was unseasoned, additional seasoning may be required (any of garlic salt, savory, basil, or oregano). Bake for 25 min at 180°C
Serves 5.

STUFFED GIANT SHELLS

115 g	16 giant shells

Cook giant shells and drain thoroughly. Prepare FILLING FOR STUFFED PASTA using cottage cheese; do *not* cream ingredients or use blender. Toss in 1 tin of drained and rinsed deveined shrimp. Sauté an equivalent amount of chopped celery with ½ small chopped onion until just tender; add to mixture. Fill shells with the mixture, allowing for each shell 30-40 ml
Prepare CHEESE SAUCE using chicken stock for part of the liquid, *or* add chicken concentrate to the milk. Spread sauce in a shallow casserole and place shells in the sauce, in 2 layers if necessary. Sprinkle shells with melted butter and bake, covered, for 25 min at 180°C
Remove cover for the last 10 min. *Serves 4-5.*

CANNELLONI

Cook lasagna; cut in half. Drain; pat dry with a dish towel. Prepare as MANICOTTI CASSEROLE or MANICOTTI PARTY CASSEROLE, preparing rolls by placing filling on one end of pasta and rolling it up. Filling for each roll: 30 ml
One recipe for filling will fill 16 cannelloni (8 lasagna cut in half).

NOODLE RING

175 g	½ pkg. broad noodles
325 ml	milk
	3 eggs
15 ml	butter
	seasoning

1. Cook noodles and drain; distribute evenly in a greased small ring mould.
2. Combine the milk, beaten eggs and melted butter; add to noodles.
3. Season with onion or celery salt and a little Worcestershire sauce.
4. Pour over pasta in mould; oven-poach for 1 h or until set at 180°C
5. Unmould; fill centre with creamed or curried mixtures, meatballs or braised meat with gravy, or place a small bowl of chili sauce in the centre and ring the noodles with cooked link or farmer's sausage. *Serves 4-5.*

MEXICAN SKILLET

500 g	pork sausage
500 ml	macaroni
250 ml	chopped green pepper
250 ml	chopped onion
796 ml	1 can tomatoes
5 ml	chili powder
	salt
30 ml	sugar
250-500 ml sour cream	

1. Brown sausages thoroughly on all sides; they should be almost cooked. Drain off fat.
2. Add remaining ingredients except sour cream; bring to boil.
3. Reduce heat, cover and cook with occasional stirring until vegetables and macaroni are cooked, about 30 min. If more liquid is needed before the mixture is cooked, add a little tomato juice or diluted tomato paste.
4. Stir in the sour cream and serve. *Serves 4-6.*

Legumes

Legumes, the pod-bearing vegetables which include peas, beans and lentils, have been used since prehistoric times for their sustaining value and ease of storage.

In Latin-American countries, where beans are a staple of the diet, they grow in many varieties and colours—white, black, pink, red, brown, green and spotted combinations. Although not all varieties grow in Canada, a greater appreciation of the bean has brought many foreign varieties to our shops. The terms peas and beans are sometimes interchangeable; chick peas are known also as garbanzo beans, and navy beans as pea beans.

The protein quality of legumes, particularly soybeans, is high. They need to be eaten with a small amount of cereal to contribute complete protein to the diet. Such dishes as the Maritime favourite, baked beans and brown bread, and combinations of beans and rice, which are common in Latin-American cooking benefit nutritionally from the combination of rice and cereal. A small amount of animal protein, meat, egg, cheese, or milk will also upgrade the quality of bean protein. Iron also is present in legumes in significant amounts.

The varieties of beans specified in the majority of recipes can be interchanged; cooking times may have to be adjusted. Main dishes containing legumes should be served with bread and a crisp salad or raw vegetables.

Preparation of Dried Legumes
Pick over legumes and wash. Split peas, lentils and beans marked "quick-cooking" need no presoaking. All other dried beans, peas and lentils must be soaked prior to cooking by either of the following methods.
Overnight Method—Combine legumes with 3 times their volume of water and leave overnight, preferably in the refrigerator. Cook the legumes in the same water.
Quick Method—Combine legumes with 3 times their volume of water, bring to boiling and boil 2 min. Turn off heat; cover and let stand for 1 h. Proceed with cooking, using the same water.

General Directions for Cooking Dried Legumes
1. Heat quick-cooking legumes in an amount of water equal to 3 times their volume; heat presoaked legumes in the water in which they were soaked. Bring to boiling.
2. A chopped onion, seasonings and/or herbs may be added if desired.

3. Reduce heat, cover and simmer until tender, stirring occasionally. Additional liquid may be required to prevent legumes from boiling dry.

Cooking time will depend on the type and age of the legumes: the older the legumes, the longer the cooking time. Soybeans may require many hours of cooking if very dry; if the cooking period becomes extended, the addition of a spoonful of vinegar or some tomatoes to the water will speed up the process. Ordinarily, do not add tomatoes or other acid foods until the legumes are almost soft; otherwise they may become mushy. The addition of a minute amount of fat reduces foam formation.

Quantities of Dried Legumes

500 g dried beans equals approx. 575 ml

250 ml uncooked dried beans yield approx. 625 ml cooked beans

Storing Dried Legumes

Legumes should be stored in a covered container in a cool, dry place. Since they are available the year round, it is wise not to buy large quantities at a time as prolonged storage causes them to become very dry. Cooked legumes freeze well.

BAKED BEANS MARITIME STYLE

450 g	navy beans (white beans)
1.5 ℓ	water
	1 onion sliced
100 g	salt pork, cubed
	salt, pepper
5 ml	dry mustard
125 ml	molasses
600 ml	liquid

1. Prepare beans and soak in water overnight or use the quick method (see PREPARATION OF DRIED LEGUMES); save liquid.
2. Simmer beans in liquid, covered, for 1 h; pour off liquid and save.
3. Place beans in a bean pot or deep casserole with a cover; add onion, salt pork, seasonings, molasses and the measured amount of reserved liquid (or part water, if insufficient).
4. Bake covered, for 6 h at 150°C
   Add more liquid or water if needed. Uncover during the last 30 min. *Serves 4-5.*

Baked beans, with oatmeal bread, make an economical source of protein. Ontario Ministry of Agriculture and Food.

Variations

Oil or butter can be substituted for the salt pork.

A ham bone from which most of the meat has been removed can be added to the beans during baking; it provides flavour, a little fat and a little meat. When beans have been baked, remove bone; pick off any remaining meat and add to the beans.

Maple syrup can be substituted for molasses, or served over the cooked beans in the French Canadian tradition.

Since approximately the same amount of oven heat is required to bake two pots of beans as one, it may be convenient to prepare two pots of beans of the same or a different variety at one time and to freeze the second pot.

LIMA BEAN AND SAUSAGE CASSEROLE

450 g	dried lima beans
250-500 g	pork sausage
	1 clove garlic, crushed
	1 large onion, chopped
	1 green pepper, chopped
5 ml	chili powder
2 ml	dry mustard
2 ml	thyme
10 ml	Worcestershire sauce
	salt and pepper
284 ml	1 can condensed tomato soup
250 ml	stock from beans
	grated Parmesan *or* Cheddar cheese

1. Prepare limas; soak overnight or use the quick method of soaking (see PREPARATION OF DRIED LEGUMES).

2. Cook beans and liquid, covered in a large pot until tender, about 1 h. Drain and reserve stock.

3. Brown sausage in a frying pan; when all sides are browned, slice half the sausage into thin slices. Set aside remaining sausages.

4. Discard all but a little of the fat from the sausages; in the remaining fat sauté the garlic, onion and green pepper.

5. Combine beans, sausage slices, garlic, onion and green pepper; add tomato soup and stock.

6. Bake uncovered in a greased casserole for about 35 min; remove from oven and cut remaining sausage lengthwise and place cut-side down on top of the casserole.

7. Bake for 10-15 min more or until sausages are thoroughly cooked; serve with grated cheese. *Serves 6-8.*

Variations

Substitute for tomato soup:

1 small can of tomato paste or tomato sauce plus additional stock or water to make up the required volume. Fewer seasonings may be required.

or TOMATO SAUCE FOR PASTA, approximately 750 ml

and omit garlic, onion, green pepper and stock from the recipe.

BAKED FAVA BEANS

Fava beans (also spelled fave) are dried broad beans—a variety of bean popular in Europe. Available here in many specialty food shops, they are large, with a distinct, strong flavour. Other varieties of beans can be substituted if cooking times are adjusted and the amount of seasonings reduced.

450 g	fava beans
1.5 *ℓ*	water
500 ml	beef stock
700 ml	water
350 ml	chopped onions
50 ml	fat
540 ml	1 can tomatoes
30 ml	tomato paste
5 ml	crushed red pepper
or	
2 ml	Tabasco sauce
	2 garlic cloves crushed
2 ml	sage
5 ml	savory
	1 bay leaf, crushed

1. Soak beans overnight in the first lot of water, or soak by the quick method (see PREPARATION OF DRIED LEGUMES). The soaking liquid from fava beans is strong flavoured; drain off and discard.

2. Combine beans with beef stock and water; cover and simmer for 2.5 h or until beans are tender. Drain and reserve the liquid.

3. In a large saucepan, sauté onions in fat until soft; add tomatoes, tomato paste, seasonings and herbs, and cook for 5 min

4. Combine liquid with beans and bring to boiling.

5. Transfer mixture to oven and bake, covered, for about 30 min until tender, at 180°C
Remove cover, stir and bake for 15 min to reduce liquid if necessary. Adjust seasoning. *Serves 6.*

The French cassoulet *is a combination of beans baked with meat, varying in definition and ingredients according to the region of France in which it is made. The meat might be goose, pork, lamb, or sausage. Traditionally, the dish is hearty country fare—long in preparation. Add meat to this or other bean casseroles which are cooked slowly in savoury sauces and we have a cassoulet.*

LENTILS AND BACON

200 ml	lentils
1 *ℓ*	water
100 ml	diced bacon
100 ml	diced onion
100 ml	diced green pepper (optional)
	salt, pepper
25 ml	chopped parsley

1. Cook quick-cooking lentils in water until tender. Regular lentils should first be soaked overnight or by the quick method (see PREPARATION OF DRIED LEGUMES). Cook in water left from soaking plus additional water if needed.

2. Drain lentils in a sieve.

3. In a large frying pan lightly fry bacon, add onion and green pepper; cook until bacon is crisp.

4. Stir in the drained lentils, season with salt and pepper and heat through, 3-5 min. Sprinkle with chopped parsley. *Serves 4.*

Recipes, tables, etc. that appear in small capital letters, e.g., PARSLEY BUTTER, CANADA'S FOOD GUIDE, are listed in the index. Consult the index for the number of the page on which the item appears.

LENTIL STEW

250 ml	lentils
50 ml	oil
125 ml	thinly sliced onion
	1 green pepper
125 ml	sliced celery
250 ml	thinly sliced carrots
500 g-1 kg	boneless pork *or* lamb
250 ml	canned tomatoes
750 ml	stock or water
125 ml	macaroni (optional)
	salt, pepper
	1 bay leaf
	ground cloves

1. Pick over and rinse lentils; if lentils are not marked "quick-cooking," presoak (see PREPARATION OF DRIED LEGUMES).
2. In a large saucepan or Dutch oven, heat oil, add all the raw vegetables and cook until onion is golden; remove to a bowl with a slotted spoon.
3. Brown cubes of meat in the pan, adding more oil if necessary; drain off any remaining fat.
4. Add cooked vegetables, lentils and remaining ingredients, including a sprinkle of cloves; bring to boiling.
5. Cover and simmer with occasional stirring until the meat is very tender, about 1 h. If more liquid is required, add a little more liquid from canned tomatoes. *Serves 6.*

LENTIL LOAF

250 ml	dried lentils
750 ml	water
30 ml	butter *or* margarine
225 g	Cheddar cheese, grated
	1 small onion, minced
	salt, pepper
1 ml	thyme *or* savory
	1 egg beaten
125 ml	soft bread crumbs
125 ml	coarsely grated carrots

1. Pick over lentils and rinse in cold water; if they are not quick-cooking, soak in water overnight or use the quick method (see PREPARATION OF DRIED LEGUMES).
2. Heat lentils and water left from soaking to boiling; cover and simmer until tender, about 1.5 h. Drain and reserve liquid for stock or other purposes.

3. Mash hot lentils and combine with butter, cheese, minced onion and seasonings.
4. Combine beaten egg, crumbs and carrots and mix thoroughly with the bean mixture.
5. Grease a medium loaf pan and pack the mixture evenly in the pan; bake until centre is not wet when tested with a toothpick, about 45 min, at 180°C
   Serves 5.

Serve this loaf with TOMATO SAUCE, MUSHROOM SAUCE, or a little sour cream.

The following recipes using legumes are in other chapters of this book: SPLIT PEA SOUP, CHICK PEA SALAD FOUR BEAN SALAD.

SAVOURY BAKED BEANS

In a casserole, combine canned or home-cooked beans in tomato sauce with sautéed chopped onions, chili sauce, a little brown sugar and a sprinkle of dry mustard. Fry a few slices of bacon until crisp; drain, crumble and sprinkle over beans. Cover and bake until bubbly at 180°C

Variations
Add any of canned kernel corn, cooked green lima beans; sautéed chopped green pepper and celery; diced cooked ham and other cooked meats; cooked noodles. Add or substitute other varieties of cooked dried beans. Stir in a little grated cheese or sour cream before serving.

HAWAIIAN BEAN POT

796 ml	1 can pork and beans
227 ml	1 can pineapple tidbits
15 ml	soy sauce
30 ml	minced onions
1 ml	celery salt
	4-5 slices bacon

Combine all ingredients except bacon in a casserole. Lightly fry bacon; drain and place on beans. Bake until bubbly, about 30 min at 180°C
Serves 4-5.

Try Chili Con Carne on toasted hamburger buns or in halves of pita bread as a sandwich.

Recipes, tables, etc. that appear in small capital letters, e.g., PARSLEY BUTTER, CANADA'S FOOD GUIDE, are listed in the index. Consult the index for the number of the page on which the item appears.

BEAN CAKES

125 ml	navy beans (white beans)
500 ml	water
125 ml	cornmeal
125 ml	flour
3 ml	baking powder
	salt, pepper
	1 egg
125 ml	milk
	1 clove garlic, crushed
30 ml	oil

1. Soak beans overnight or by the quick method (see PREPARATION OF DRIED LEGUMES), and cook until tender, about 1 h. Drain and save any liquid for stock. Cool beans.
2. Combine cornmeal, flour, baking powder and seasonings in a bowl; beat egg with milk and stir into the blended dry ingredients.
3. Stir in the beans and the crushed garlic clove.
4. Heat oil in a frying pan and drop bean mixture by spoonfuls to form small cakes; sauté cakes on each side until golden.
5. Drain cakes on paper towels; keep hot while cooking the remaining mixture.
6. Serve cakes hot with any of bacon, sausage, sliced tomatoes or green salad. *Yield:* 18 cakes (6 servings).

CHILI CON CARNE

125 ml	thinly sliced onions
30 ml	fat or oil
250 g	minced beef
5 ml	Worcestershire sauce
5 ml	chili powder
5 ml	cumin
796 ml	1 can tomatoes
398 ml	1 can kidney beans

1. Cook the onion in the fat until clear and yellow. Lift out.
2. Brown the meat; add the seasonings and the onions.
3. Add the tomatoes and simmer slowly, covered, for 1 h.
4. Uncover; add the beans and simmer until thick and tender.
5. Taste and season with salt, pepper and more chili if desired.

Quick Chili Con Carne—To a can of kidney beans add an equal quantity of commercially prepared Meat Sauce. Season with chili powder; heat.

MASHED OR REFRIED BEANS

Mexicans eat their beans, (frijoles) more often mashed than whole, as *frijoles refritos,* meaning refried beans. The term is somewhat misleading as the cooked beans are merely mashed with oil and reheated. Dried pinto or pink beans are used for this ubiquitous side dish to eggs and meat dishes.

Spread on tortillas which have been lightly fried until crisp, covered with chopped tomatoes, avocado and shredded lettuce, they are a customary ingredient of Mexican open-faced sandwiches known as *tostadas.* Folded over as a turnover, these are known north of the border as tacos.

250 ml	dried beans (pinto, kidney, soybeans *or* chick peas)
1 *l*	water
15 ml	fat *or* oil
	1 small onion, finely chopped
	1 garlic clove, crushed
2-5 ml	cumin
125 ml	tomato sauce
	salt and pepper

1. Soak beans in water overnight or use the quick method (see PREPARATION OF DRIED LEGUMES). Cook beans in their liquid until tender.
2. Mash beans (do not use an electric blender or mixer), beating in liquid left from cooking.
3. In a frying pan, heat fat; add onion, garlic, cumin and tomato sauce and bring to boiling. Simmer 5 min.
4. Combine thoroughly with mashed beans. Taste and season with salt and pepper as desired. *Yield:* about 4 servings, 625 ml

Variations

Blend grated cheese into hot, mashed beans after step 2. of basic recipe.

Shape into patties or balls and heat.

Serve as a stuffing: mix with equal quantities of chopped, canned tomatoes and stuff green peppers; top with grated cheese.

Serve as a spread: combine with an equal quantity of chopped spinach or watercress; add a little crumbled, crisp bacon and relish or chili sauce, and sufficient mayonnaise to give a spreading consistency. Spread on bread or crackers, or on toasted halves of hamburger buns topped with grated cheese and broiled.

10 Eggs and Cheese

Eggs

Eggs have many qualities that make them valuable in cooking. They hold ingredients together in meat loaves; form a coating which prevents fat soaking into food to be fried; entrap air which expands to cause soufflés, cakes and cream puffs to rise; thicken custards and sauces such as Hollandaise; emulsify fat in mayonnaise and cakes.

Grades—Eggs are graded according to cleanliness, shape and quality as Grade A1, A, B, C. Cold-storage eggs may not be graded A1. Within the A1 and A grades the size must be shown. Grade B and C eggs are reserved for such commercial users as bakeries.

Sizes are determined by weight. Choose the size best suited to the purpose. Recipes in this book, unless indicated, use medium size.

Extra large	63.8 g
Large	56.7 g
Medium	49.6 g
Small	42.5 g
Peewee, below	42.5 g

Eggs have a better flavour and are more efficient in baking when they are fresh. A new-laid egg has a "bloom" or dull finish; although this coating rubs off when the egg is handled, it does remain in the pores of the eggshell, forming a barrier to odours and germs. For this reason eggs are not washed before being stored. When an egg is opened onto a saucer, signs of freshness are prominent cords; a thick, jelly-like white; a ball-like yolk with a glossy, smooth surface. Blood spots or protein spots, which should not be found in Grade A eggs, are not harmful but are unattractive; lift out.

Yolk colour may range from pale yellow to deep orange, depending on the diet of the hen; shell colour is determined by the breed of the hen. Neither affects the quality of the egg.

Storage of Eggs

Since a few hours in a warm room are as harmful to eggs as weeks of storage at a temperature slightly above freezing, unrefrigerated eggs are a poor buy. Refrigerate eggs with the round end up, away from strongly flavoured foods.

Sodium silicate (water glass), which may be purchased in a drug store, will preserve eggs for 8-9 months. Follow the directions on the can and store in a cool place.

Yolks keep best unbroken in a small bowl covered with cold water; if broken, store in a covered jar and use promptly. There will be some darkening of colour which is not harmful. Refrigerate whites in a covered jar.

To Freeze Eggs—remove from the shells; prepare and package in quantities for a specific use; heat seal and store in cartons.

Whole eggs: mix well without beating.
  To 6 eggs add sugar, 10 ml
  or salt, 2 ml
Yolks: mix well without beating.
  To 6 yolks add sugar, 15 ml
  or salt, 2 ml
  or syrup, 15 ml
Whites: package without beating; when thawed, whites may be beaten.

Thawed Eggs

6 whole eggs when thawed will yield 250 ml
6 egg yolks when thawed will yield 100 ml
6 egg whites when thawed will yield 125 ml

The whites of eggs are an excellent source of high quality protein; the yolks are high in iron and contain all the vitamins except C, being especially high in A and B2. Eggs are an excellent food for young and old, able to replace more expensive meat protein. To what extent the cholesterol and saturated fatty acid content of the yolk calls for its restriction in some diseases of the blood vessels is a matter of debate.

A new product, "Egg Beaters," in which the yolk has been replaced by corn oil and skim milk powder provides less food value at a greater expense but does permit a wider menu for dieters who must avoid egg yolk.

For methods of handling raw eggs, see TO SEPARATE AN EGG, TO BEAT EGG WHITE, TO FOLD EGG WHITE, and MERINGUE.

For egg cooking techniques, see the following pages. High temperatures toughen protein. For this reason, dishes rich in eggs are cooked at low temperatures—by oven poaching, over hot water, or briefly sautéed in a frying pan.

SOFT- AND HARD-COOKED EGGS

Cold Water Method
1. Place eggs in cool water, enough to cover eggs completely.
2. Heat rapidly to boiling; turn down heat and cook:

soft-cooked	1 min
medium-cooked	3-5 min
hard-cooked	20-30 min

Hot Water Method
1. Leave eggs out of refrigerator until they reach room temperature.
2. Boil water; put in the eggs; add boiling water if necessary to cover them completely; reduce heat so the water ceases to boil, and cook:

soft-cooked	2-3 min
medium-cooked	4-6 min
hard-cooked	15-20 min

When many eggs are being cooked together, they will require a longer time; test one egg for hardness before removing all, by making a small crack at one end and pushing a toothpick into the yolk to see that the yolk is firm.

To keep the yolk in the centre of the white, turn eggs in the water three or four times. To prevent a dark ring forming around the yolk of a hard-cooked egg (which is caused by iron in the yolk reacting with the sulphur of the white), chill eggs immediately the yolk is firm by pouring off the hot water and pouring on cold water until the water remains cold.

Hard-cooked Eggs—Shells should be removed from hard-cooked eggs as soon as they are cooked, when they will come off easily; package shelled eggs in plastic bags until ready to use.

Hard-cooked eggs are used creamed, stuffed, sliced or chopped in sandwiches or salads, added whole to meat loaf mixtures, or pickled.

Soft- and Medium-cooked Eggs—serve in the shell in an egg cup, or remove from the shell into a cup or small dish and add butter, salt and pepper, and diced bread.

PICKLED EGGS

	12 hard-cooked eggs, shelled
500 ml	SPICED VINEGAR
	2 medium onions
	3 garlic cloves
2 ml	**dried dill weed**

1. Place the eggs in a jar; cover with boiling vinegar; add onion, garlic and dill.
2. Cover the jar but do not seal; refrigerate at least 4 days.

Serve quartered, sprinkled with freshly ground black pepper and salt, as an appetizer, on a salad plate; sliced in a sandwich filling; or whole in a lunch box.

CREAMED EGGS

1. Prepare a medium WHITE SAUCE seasoned with chopped herbs and a little MAYONNAISE.
2. Cut hard-cooked eggs in half or quarters and stir gently into the hot sauce.

Serve on toast, on cooked rice, on split TEA BISCUITS, on Chow Mein noodles, in patty shells, in pastry tart shells, or over cooked asparagus, broccoli, or baked potato.

STUFFED EGGS

1. Cut hard-cooked eggs in half lengthwise.
2. Carefully remove the yolks into a bowl; season; beat or mash with a fork; add MAYONNAISE or sour cream a little at a time to make a smooth mixture; add salt, pepper, celery salt, and a few drops of onion juice; mix to blend.
3. Restuff the whites, using a spoon or a pastry bag; garnish with paprika, chives, parsley, or other fresh herbs.

Variations
Devilled Eggs—When dry or prepared mustard or a few drops of Worcestershire sauce is added to the Stuffed Eggs mixture, they are called Devilled Eggs.

To vary Stuffed or Devilled Eggs, add any of the following. (These mixtures will not go through a pastry tube.) Curry powder and a spoonful of chutney; sautéed and chopped chicken livers; shredded cooked ham, tongue, or anchovies; sautéed and chopped mushrooms; cooked green peas; minced pimento; anchovy fillets; cooked and chopped shrimps.

Serve Stuffed Eggs in the same way as CREAMED EGGS.

Recipes, tables, etc. that appear in small capital letters, e.g., PARSLEY BUTTER, CANADA'S FOOD GUIDE, are listed in the index. Consult the index for the number of the page on which the item appears.

Arrange Stuffed Eggs in rows in a casserole; cover with cheese sauce; sprinkle grated cheese on top; bake until the cheese begins to brown (overheating will toughen the egg) at 180°C

Press Stuffed Eggs into a bed of cooked rice; cover with tomato sauce; heat at 180°C
Garnish with grated cheese, chopped parsley, chives, or green onion rings.

Serve Stuffed Eggs cold on salad plates or as ANTIPASTO.

Press Stuffed Eggs into almost-set TOMATO ASPIC in individual moulds or in a shallow pan. Pipe on a cream cheese border.

FRIED EGG

1. Add fat (butter, margarine, bacon fat, *or* oil) to just cover the bottom of a heavy frying pan.
2. Heat the fat until a drop of water sizzles in it; crack the egg and slide carefully into the pan.
3. Cook over low heat until the white is set.
4. For "sunnyside up," spoon fat over the top until a thin film cooks on the yolk; or put a cover on the pan for a few minutes to get the same effect.
   For "once over lightly," slide an egg lifter under and turn the egg over; then lift the egg onto a heated plate immediately.
   For "turned over," turn the egg and leave in pan until the yolk is firm.
Serve on a heated plate garnished with parsley, chopped chives, or fine green onion rings. Ketchup with fried egg is an American tradition.

Tough, greasy eggs are the result of too much fat and too much heat.

EGGS RANCH STYLE

	4 eggs
	4 MEXICAN PANCAKES
250 ml	REFRIED BEANS
50 ml	chili sauce
	cayenne pepper (optional)
125 g	mild cheese
	1 avocado

Fry the eggs, sunnyside up; serve on hot or reheated Mexican pancakes with a spoonful of REFRIED BEANS. Top with heated CHILI SAUCE, seasoned if desired with a sprinkle of cayenne. Garnish with slices of cheese and avocado.

SHIRRED EGG

This is a useful dish when many breakfasts are to be served.
1. Butter an individual muffin tin, ramekin, or custard cup; break an egg into it; season lightly.
2. Place in a shallow pan of hot water; bake until the white is set at 180°C
   Serve in the dish or on toast.
   or
   Pour a spoonful of cream or tomato juice and a little grated cheese over each egg and cook under the broiler until the white is set.

COUNTRY EGGS

1. Boil one potato for each serving, with salt, a little onion and a few celery leaves; mash; spread in a greased, shallow baking dish.
2. With the back of a spoon evenly space a depression for each serving. Break an egg into each depression; sprinkle with grated cheese and cooked crumbled bacon; bake until the eggs are set at 150°C
3. Cut in squares and serve with sliced tomatoes.

POACHED EGG

1. Fill a shallow pan with water deep enough to cover the egg completely, or use an egg poacher; bring the water to a boil; lift the pan off the heat.
2. Stir water briskly and slip the egg into water; return the pan to low heat.
3. Cook until the white is firm and a film has formed over the yolk, about 3 min
4. Lift the egg with a slotted spoon, tipping it against the pan to drain; serve on buttered toast, sprinkled with salt and pepper and garnished with parsley.

Variations
Eggs Benedict—Broil, grill, or toast split hamburger buns or English muffins. On each half place a slice of boiled or sautéed ham. On the ham place a poached egg. Top with HOLLANDAISE SAUCE.
Eggs Florentine—In an individual casserole place a layer of cooked, seasoned spinach; add a poached egg. Cover with CHEESE SAUCE; sprinkle with grated cheese and brown under the broiler. 1 bag of spinach or 1 package, frozen, serves 6.

Eggs may be poached in tomato juice, CREOLE SAUCE, or CONSOMMÉ MADRILENE instead of water. Lift the cooked eggs onto buttered toast or English muffins; thicken the liquid (see COLD LIQUID METHOD) and pour over the egg.

BASIC EGG MIXTURE

	1-2 eggs (per person)
15 ml	**milk *or* water per egg**
	seasoning (salt and pepper)
	butter *or* margarine

In a bowl combine the eggs, seasoning and liquid, beating with a fork.

SCRAMBLED EGGS

1. Choose a heavy pan of suitable size for the number of eggs; add enough fat to coat the surface and sides of the pan; heat until a drop of water sizzles in the fat.
2. Pour in BASIC EGG MIXTURE; cook over low heat, stirring the mixture toward the centre with the edge of a fork until the egg is set but still moist.
3. Remove pan from heat, stir the egg quickly, and serve immediately on buttered toast points. Sprinkle with parsley or chives; garnish with sliced tomatoes or bacon strips. Too much liquid will prevent the egg from setting; too much heat or too long a cooking time will result in a watery product.

Toast points

Variations

Cheese Scrambled Eggs—Just before the eggs are cooked add grated or shredded cheese, allowing for each serving, 15-30 ml

Kentucky Scrambled Eggs—Sauté chopped green pepper, sweet red pepper and minced onion in bacon fat until tender (5 min); add kernel corn (fresh, defrosted frozen, or drained canned), sauté until the corn is hot and tender; pour in the egg mixture. Follow the basic method beginning at step 2.

Creamy Egg—Cook the basic mixture over hot water, folding the egg with a large metal spoon as it cooks. This is a useful recipe when serving a number of people who will not all arrive for breakfast at the same time, as the egg will keep warm without drying out or curdling.

French Toast—In a deep pie plate or soup dish, prepare the basic mixture, allowing 1 egg for 2 slices of bread. Dip the bread into the egg mixture, lift out with an egg lifter, drain; sauté in the pan until brown; turn and brown; add fat as needed.

Serve with syrup, honey, jam, ketchup, or sour cream. Or sprinkle with icing sugar and pass a bowl of fresh fruit—blueberries, strawberries, sliced peaches.

Banana French Toast—Add a sprinkle of nutmeg or cinnamon and a little sugar to the egg mixture. Prepare FRENCH TOAST from raisin bread or split hamburger buns. Put together with a layer of bananas; serve with syrup.

FRENCH OMELET

1. Prepare BASIC EGG MIXTURE.
2. Choose a heavy frying pan or omelet pan of suitable size. (Too large a pan spreads the egg too thinly for a good result.)
   For a 2 egg omelet to serve 1-2, use a pan: 15 cm
   For a 4 egg omelet to serve 3-5, use a pan: 25 cm
3. Add fat; heat, tipping the pan so that the bottom and sides are evenly coated; pour out any excess fat.
4. Pour the mixture into the hot pan; shake the pan as the omelet cooks; with the tines of a fork lift the cooked portion and tilting the pan allow the liquid to run under, but do not stir; lift up an edge to check the colour of the underside; adjust the heat so that it will be a golden brown colour by the time the egg is cooked.
5. Fold and tip out onto a heated serving dish as follows:
   Tip the pan, pushing the egg to fold the half nearer the handle over the opposite half.
   Holding the handle in the right hand with the thumb on top and the heated plate in the left hand, tilt the pan and plate together.
   Quickly turn the pan upside down so the omelet slides out onto the plate.

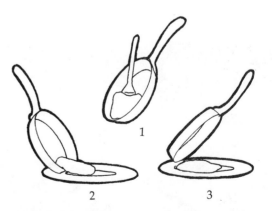

Garnish with sliced tomato, watercress, chopped parsley or chives.

Variations of French Omelet

Before folding the omelet cover the surface with one of: grated cheese; minced fresh herbs; heated, cooked asparagus; sautéed, sliced mushrooms; sautéed, seasoned chicken livers.

Serve with CREOLE SAUCE, hot homemade CHILI SAUCE, cooked side or back bacon, or sausage.

Cover with apricot or strawberry jam; orange or tomato marmalade; sliced sweetened peaches. Fold; sprinkle the folded omelet with fruit sugar; turn onto a heated plate.

FOAMY OMELET

	4 eggs
60 ml	**water**
	seasoning
15 ml	**butter** *or* **margarine**

1. Preheat the oven to 180°
   Heat an omelet pan or heavy frying pan of suitable size; add fat, tipping the pan until the bottom and sides are well coated.
2. Separate the eggs; beat the whites until stiff but not dry.
3. Beat the yolks until thick and lemon coloured; season.
4. Fold the whites into the yolks; tip into the hot pan spreading gently to cover the pan.
5. Cook over low heat until the omelet has set; lift to check the amount of browning on the sides and bottom, increasing or reducing the heat as needed.
6. When the omelet is a golden brown on the bottom place the pan in oven until the top of the omelet will spring back when pressed with the finger and the omelet is slightly puffed (5-10 min), at 180°C

7. Remove the pan from the oven; make a crease a little off centre toward the handle; fold the smaller part over the larger; tip onto a heated serving plate so that the larger half is now on top; hold in place for a moment. *Serves 2-3.*

Variations

See FRENCH OMELET for suggestions.
For instructions, see TO SEPARATE AN EGG, TO BEAT EGG WHITE, TO FOLD EGG WHITE.

EGG FOO YONG

	4 eggs
125-250 ml	**cooked bean sprouts**
125-250 ml	**cooked chopped chicken,** *or* **roast pork,** *or* **ham,** *or* **shrimp**
	3 thinly sliced green onions
	4 thinly sliced mushrooms
	1 thinly sliced celery stalk
15 ml	**soy sauce**
	pepper
	oil

1. Beat the eggs; combine with other ingredients.
2. Heat oil in a frying pan; drop the mixture from a spoon; check the first small patty for flavour and colour, adjusting the heat so that the patties will be brown on the edges and set throughout. Add oil as needed to the pan.
3. Keep patties warm on a serving plate until all are fried. Serve with CHINESE SAUCE or CHINESE PLUM SAUCE. *Yield:* 10 patties.

This mixture made in very small patties and served on sliced, toasted French roll, is a popular hors d'oeuvre. It may be baked in well-greased, tiny muffin pans; overcooking will toughen patties.

An omelet garnished with processed cheese.

Quiche is a delicious egg and cheese pie flavoured with onion and bacon.

Salmon steaks attractively arranged on a platter.

Prepared shellfish served in shells.

Soufflés

With a little care, a soufflé, which is basically a flavoured thick sauce made light with beaten egg white, is not as temperamental as is often suggested.

Expensive food such as seafood can go a long way in a soufflé; leftover food gains new elegance when incorporated into this dish.

The recipes that follow will produce delicious lunch or supper dishes that require only the accompaniment of a green salad and bread sticks to make a hearty, nutritional meal. Recipes for sweet soufflés are given in Chapter 16, Desserts.

Basic Recipe
CHEESE SOUFFLÉ

250 ml	THICK WHITE SAUCE
250 ml	shredded sharp Cheddar cheese
	seasoning
	4 egg yolks
	4-5 egg whites

1. Preheat oven to 190°C
2. Prepare the baking dish and a pan of water for oven-poaching. The ideal soufflé dish has straight sides and a flat bottom. Use individual dishes or a casserole which holds 1.5 *l*

   To increase the capacity of the dish, a collar may be added by tying on a double strip of foil or brown paper so that it extends above the rim. Use an ungreased dish, or grease and sprinkle with fine crumbs or a mixture of crumbs and grated hard cheese.

3. Prepare the cheese; reserve a spoonful for the top of the soufflé.
4. Prepare THICK WHITE SAUCE; season with salt, pepper, celery salt, a little grated onion, a pinch of dry mustard. (Sauce may be prepared ahead of time and reheated in a double boiler without stirring.)
5. Add the cheese and stir until cheese melts; cool slightly.
6. Separate the eggs; beat the yolks lightly and stir the warm sauce into them.
7. With a clean beater, beat the whites until stiff but not dry (see TO BEAT EGG WHITE); stir one spoonful into the sauce; fold the remainder into the sauce.

(An extra egg white increases the volume considerably.)

8. Pour into the prepared dish; sprinkle the reserved cheese on top; oven-poach 20-25 min for individual dishes, 40-50 min for a large soufflé. To determine whether the soufflé is cooked, test 5 min before the suggested time by moving the dish slightly. If the top seems firm, press it gently with the finger; if the crust springs back, turn off the heat but do not remove the dish until ready to serve it.
9. Place the dish on a serving plate; gently remove the collar. Serve at once, dividing a large soufflé into portions with two forks. *Serves 4-5.*

Variations
Replace the milk in the sauce with cream.

Replace the White Sauce with TOMATO SAUCE or VELOUTÉ SAUCE of thick consistency.

Add to the cheese any of the following:
   ground, salted peanuts, 50 ml
   1 sliced and sautéed small leek and 2 peeled and chopped ripe tomatoes
   3 cooked and crumbled slices of bacon and 1 small chopped onion sautéed in bacon fat.

Replace 1/3 of the cheese with chopped cooked asparagus, spinach, *or* broccoli.

Replace Cheddar cheese with any of the following:
   a mixture of Gruyère and hard cheese, grated.
   ground cooked ham and a little well-drained pickle.
   finely chopped, sautéed chicken livers and mushrooms.
   finely chopped cooked chicken, turkey, *or* duck; flavour with curry or drained CRANBERRY RELISH.
   chopped cooked shrimp, lobster, crabmeat, *or* fillet of sole; or drained canned salmon; flavour with lemon juice; fennel gives an elusive flavour of licorice.

Quick Trick—Replace the sauce with undiluted condensed soup (mushroom, tomato, chicken, or cheese) to form the base for any of the variations. Do not add salt.

Recipes, tables, etc. that appear in small capital letters, e.g., PARSLEY BUTTER, CANADA'S FOOD GUIDE, are listed in the index. Consult the index for the number of the page on which the item appears.

A soufflé. General Foods

TOMATO AND BACON SOUFFLÉ

50 ml	minute tapioca
200 ml	seasoned tomato juice
200 ml	shredded sharp Cheddar cheese
	3 slices crisp bacon, crumbled
	4 eggs, separated

1. Combine tapioca and tomato juice in a saucepan; leave 5 min
2. Stir over medium heat until the mixture boils; remove from heat; stir in the cheese and bacon, cool to lukewarm.
3. Follow the basic recipe for CHEESE SOUFFLÉ, beginning at step 6. *Serves 3-4.*

CHEESE AND CRUMB SOUFFLÉ

250 ml	milk
250 ml	dry bread crumbs
250 ml	shredded sharp cheese
15 ml	melted butter *or* margarine
	3 eggs, separated

Combine milk and crumbs; leave until crumbs are soft; add cheese and butter; season; follow the basic recipe for CHEESE SOUFFLÉ, beginning at step 6.

Use whole wheat crumbs for extra flavour and nutrition.

To Use Leftover Eggs

Hard-cooked—Chop for egg filling for sandwiches; slice to garnish salads or canapés, or add to potato salad; sieve to make topping or garnish for creamed mixtures or appetizers; devil for creamed eggs or variations.

If the eggs are not quite hard-cooked, place in boiling water and simmer until the yolks are firm.

Raw Yolks—Use in BAKED CUSTARD, CUSTARD SAUCE, SCRAMBLED EGGS, OMELET, FRENCH TOAST; add to mashed potato or meat patties; add to breading for chops; add to WHITE SAUCE or VELOUTÉ SAUCE to give colour and richness; make GOLD CAKE, POUND CAKE, BUTTER ICING; use in EGGNOGS or milk beverages. (Egg yolks alone do not make attractive scrambled eggs.)

Raw White—Use for MERINGUES; SEVEN-MINUTE FROSTING or BOILED FROSTING; MARSHMALLOW SAUCE; DIVINITY FUDGE; fruit whips, gelatine sponges, SHERBETS; ANGEL CAKE, WHITE CAKE.

Cheese

There is a variety of cheese, domestic and imported, for every purpose and taste. Cheese is made from cow's and goat's milk, from skimmed milk, whole milk, cream and "double cream." Cheese is made in Canada and also comes to us from many European countries. Canadian Cheddar, first made at Ingersoll, Ontario, Oka made by the Trappist monks at Oka, Quebec, and Ermite made by the Benedictine fathers at St. Benoît, Quebec, are as popular outside Canada as within.

Cheese is served as an appetizer, and with or in soup, entrée, salad, or dessert. With a crusty roll or biscuit, cheese is served after the entrée and before dessert, or after the dessert with coffee. Cheese provides the nutrients of milk in a concentrated form. Combinations of cheese and pasta, rice, or cereals serve as meat substitutes. With fruit and biscuits, cheese provides many of the nutrients of a meal.

The butter fat content of cheese ranges widely; plain cottage cheese, skimmed milk and processed cheeses may be eaten even by those on a restricted fat diet. Cheese may be left in its initial form as simple curds or the curds may be pressed and ripened.

Recipes, tables, etc. that appear in small capital letters, e.g., PARSLEY BUTTER, CANADA'S FOOD GUIDE, are listed in the index. Consult the index for the number of the page on which the item appears.

Ripened Cheese

The curd is salted, pressed and aged. Containing the nutrients of the milk solids, these cheeses are excellent sources of protein, calcium and riboflavin. The whole-milk cheeses provide vitamin A and a fat content of 20-30%; skim milk cheese contains 6% fat.

MILD CHEESES

New or Medium Cheddar
White to deep orange, this cheese is somewhat rubbery and mild, becoming more tender and crumbly and developing more flavour as it ages.
Our most popular and versatile cheese is medium Cheddar.

Farmer's Cheese (Colby)
A fine-textured, very mild cheese of bright orange colour.

Brick
A creamy white, soft cheese with fine holes. It is pressed into brick shape rather than the wheel characteristic of Cheddar.

Swiss
A light-coloured cheese, easily recognized by its large holes, or eyes.

Edam
Gouda
The rind of these two cheeses is dyed bright red. Edam has a flattened ball shape. Inside, both are pale yellow and mild in flavour.
Partly skimmed milk cheeses.

Mozzarella
An Italian-type cheese often sold in slices but more economical to buy in the piece, this has a stringy texture when heated and a mild, slightly acid flavour.
This is the "pizza cheese," also part of French onion soup and lasagna.

Gruyère
Small triangular packages of mild white cheese made from partly skimmed milk. It may also be purchased in bricks.
The triangles are convenient for lunches; this cheese has excellent keeping quality.

Tomme de Savoie
A dramatic-looking cheese, creamy in texture, coated with black grape seeds.
A cheese that will add interest to a cheese tray.

Fromage aux Noix
A mild, creamy cheese with a layer and coating of whole nuts. A less expensive type has chopped nuts mixed throughout.
An excellent accompaniment to fresh fruit.

Boursault
A French cheese which does not travel well. Watch for a fresh Boursault made in Quebec.
Soft creamy cheese, high in butterfat.

Bel Paese
A white, semi-soft Italian cheese.
Good in sandwiches.

Oka
A semi-soft, creamy cheese made in Quebec by Trappist monks.

Port du Salut
This famous French cheese, made by Trappists, belongs to the same family as Oka, but differs subtly in flavour and texture.

Ripened Cheese

Havarti	A smooth, buttery Danish cheese.	
Brie **Camembert**	These cheeses soften as they ripen; when fully ripe, they are runny at room temperature.	
BLUE CHEESES **Roquefort** **Danish** **Stilton**	A blue mould is grown in these cheeses under carefully controlled conditions, to give a marbled effect. They vary from soft to crumbly and have a sharp taste.	Use blue cheese in dips and spreads, and as a dessert cheese.
Bleu de Bresse **Ermite**	These are Quebec cheeses available in small amounts.	
Gorgonzola	An Italian, semi-hard, nippy cheese.	
SEMI-HARD, SHARP-FLAVOURED CHEESES **Old Cheddar**	Aged at least 1 year.	Nippy in flavour
Cheshire	A crumbly, English cheese.	
Caerphilly	A white Welsh cheese, rather sour.	
HARD CHEESES **Parmesan** **Romano** **Provolone** **Caciacavallo**	Sharp in flavour, these cheeses are often purchased already grated. They keep indefinitely. Originally Italian, they are now also made in Canada.	Use as a topping on Italian dishes, supper dishes, soups, and vegetables. 250 g = 500 ml grated
Parmigiana	This is considered by many to be the best. Use it mixed with fine crumbs for Veal Parmigiana.	
PROCESSED CHEESES **Cheddar** **Swiss (Gruyère)** **Spreads**	From different factories, cheese, usually Cheddar, is ground, melted, pasteurized, blended with milk, seasonings and colour, and treated with an emulsifier to keep it pliable. Special nippy spreads may be wine cured or smoked.	Packaged in bars, slices and jars, these cheeses keep well and melt smoothly. Both whole milk and skim milk processed cheese is available; food values are similar to unprocessed cheeses. Processed cheeses do not, however, have the individual flavour of the originals.

Fresh Cheese

To make fresh cheese, milk is treated with bacteria or rennin and separated into solid (curd) and liquid (whey) components. The whey is drained off and the curd remains to make the cheese.

COTTAGE (Dutch)	Soft white curds which are very perishable. Refrigerate.	Because of its high protein and low food-energy content, it deserves a wide use in our menus.
Pot	A large curd cheese usually found in farmers' markets.	
Creamed	Has 18% cream added, which increases not only the vitamin A content, but also the fat content.	Provides 2/3 more food energy than plain cottage cheese.
Ricotta	Italian-style cottage.	Use in such Italian dishes as Lasagna and Antipasto.
CREAM (Philadelphia, American, etc.)	A smooth, perishable cheese. Plain, it has a mild flavour; it is also sold flavoured.	Contains 38% butter fat, and is five times as high in food energy as plain cottage cheese.
Gervais	An imported cream cheese made from rich cream.	Higher in fat than domestic cream cheeses.
CHEESE CURDS	Salted, unripened curds, somewhat tough in texture.	Used as a snack food.

Storing Cheese

Soft, unripened cheeses spoil easily. Buy cottage and cream cheese in small amounts and keep refrigerated. Keep processed cheese covered; to prevent its drying out, press plastic or foil firmly around the cheese.

Cheese with a strong odour should be wrapped in plastic and kept in a container away from eggs and fats.

Mould which develops on cheese is not harmful but is wasteful. To prevent it, buy cheese in small amounts; wipe the cut surface of a large piece with vinegar or cover with melted wax and wrap tightly in plastic. Store in a cool place.

Cheese which has become hard may be grated or ground. Soft cheese should not be grated until it is needed, to prevent the development of mould.

Freezing Cheese—Although freezing changes the texture of cottage cheese, makes cream cheese watery and semi-hard cheese crumbly, it is a useful method of storing surplus cheese to be used in cooking or in spreads. Cut into serving size pieces, wrap in foil and then in plastic. Strong-flavoured cheese is best stored in a tightly-covered container after wrapping. Thaw in the refrigerator and bring to room temperature before using. A piece of cheese that has begun to mould can be trimmed, shredded and frozen for casseroles.

Cooking Cheese

Because of its high protein content, cheese must be cooked at low temperature and only for a short time. To prevent curdling, cheese should be added to a sauce just before it is taken from the heat.

CHEESE TRAY

Arrange the cheese on a cheese board, large tray, or sandwich plate, choosing for a variety of tastes and diets: include a good sharp Cheddar, a blue, and a mild type, for instance. Add interest with a red Gouda or Edam or a black Tomme de Savoie.

On the cheese tray or a separate plate arrange small bunches of grapes, crisp red apples, cored, juicy pears, whole strawberries, tangerines, peaches or nectarines.

Provide warm crusty bread, thin slices of pumpernickel, scones, bran muffins, a variety of biscuits and a container of soft butter. Include a pot of honey, a jar of homemade jam, a bowl of raisins and nuts, shelled or unshelled. Provide individual plates and fruit knives and on the tray a knife, cheese slicer, scissors for the grapes.

Remove ripened cheese from the refrigerator about an hour before serving to allow the cheese to mellow in flavour. Cream and cottage cheese should be refrigerated until served.

For cheese to serve before dinner or in the evening, allow for each guest:

125 g	**cheese**

BAKED CHEESE CUBES

A good way to use one dry hamburger bun and the end of a good strong cheese. Serve with Waldorf salad.

250 ml	bread cubes
125 ml	shredded cheese
	1 egg
250 ml	milk
	seasoning
	salt, pepper, onion flakes
	dried celery leaves

1. Grease a medium-size baking dish; arrange bread cubes and cheese in layers with the bread on top.
2. Beat the egg; add milk and seasoning; pour onto the bread; let stand 20 min
3. Preheat oven to 180°C
4. Oven-poach 45 min
   Serves 2-3.

Basic Recipe
CHEESE PIE

22 cm	1 unbaked PIE SHELL
250 ml	grated Swiss or Cheddar cheese
	3 eggs
375 ml	rich milk
2 ml	salt
	pinch nutmeg
	pinch cayenne
5 ml	sugar

1. Chill unbaked medium-size pie shell for 1 h
2. Sprinkle grated cheese into the bottom of the pie shell.
3. Beat eggs, add milk, seasonings and sugar and pour over the cheese in the pie shell.
4. Preheat oven to 200°C
5. Bake in a hot oven 10 min, then reduce heat to 180°C
   Continue to cook until the custard is set. (Insert a silver knife into the custard and it should come out free of custard.) Do not overcook, as the custard will continue to thicken out of the oven.

Variation
Quiche Lorraine—Follow basic recipe for Cheese Pie, reducing the cheese to 125 ml
Crumble 6 slices of cooked bacon and add to the grated cheese. When the pie is baked, garnish with 2 additional strips of crumbled cooked bacon and with parsley.
Cheese Tarts—The basic recipe fills 18 tarts, each 5 cm
Onion Quiche—Blanch finely chopped onions 375 ml
in boiling water 1 min; drain. Toss with melted butter 30 ml
Spread over grated cheese in pie shell and top with the egg mixture.
Spinach Quiche—Spread the pie shell with Dijon mustard; chop slightly cooked spinach leaves; season with salt, nutmeg, tarragon. Substitute Roquefort for Cheddar cheese; finish as basic recipe.

When buying cheese, check carefully to see whether it is most economical to buy grated, in the piece, or in slices.

Recipes, tables, etc. that appear in small capital letters, e.g., PARSLEY BUTTER, CANADA'S FOOD GUIDE, are listed in the index. Consult the index for the number of the page on which the item appears.

WELSH RAREBIT

This recipe was originally called Welsh Rabbit. When the hunter returned empty-handed his wife served him "Welsh Rabbit."

500 ml	sharp Cheddar cheese
2 ml	dry mustard
10 ml	Worcestershire sauce
	salt, pepper, cayenne
10 ml	butter
50 ml	milk
	1 egg, beaten

1. Shred the cheese into a chafing dish or double boiler.
2. Sprinkle the seasonings over the cheese; add butter and liquid. Heat slowly.
3. When the cheese begins to melt, stir until smooth.
4. Stir a spoon of the hot mixture into the egg; blend well. Add to the cheese, stirring constantly until the egg cooks (1 min).
5. Serve at once by pouring over toast triangles in a deep plate. *Serves 4.*

CHEESE STRATAS

	12 slices bread
	12 slices processed cheese
or	
750 ml	shredded cheese
	4 eggs
675 ml	milk
5 ml	salt
	dash each of pepper, paprika and
	minced onion
	chopped parsley

1. Alternate layers of bread and cheese in a greased, shallow baking dish, making the top layer cheese; trim if necessary to fit tightly into the dish.
2. Beat the eggs; add milk; season; pour over the bread and cheese layers; refrigerate until the bread has absorbed the liquid, about 30 min
3. Preheat oven to 150°C
4. Oven-poach until the custard has set and the top is browned (45-60 min); sprinkle with chopped parsley. Serve in squares. *Serves 6-8.*

Bread cubes dipped in fondue. Holland Cheese.

CHEESE FONDUE

Serve fondue as a supper dish or in the evening with a green salad. Although fondue pots are available, a chafing dish or deep casserole over a spirit lamp is satisfactory. Since guests must be seated around the pot, 4 or at most 6 guests are enough. For a larger party set out more than one fondue pot.

500 g	Swiss cheese, diced or shredded
45 ml	flour
	1 clove garlic
250 ml	pineapple juice
250 ml	water
15 ml	lemon juice
	nutmeg, pepper *or* paprika to taste
	2 loaves crusty French bread, cubed
	so that each has a piece of crust

1. Dredge cheese lightly with flour.
2. Rub fondue pot or utensil with garlic; pour in juice and water and heat gently until air bubbles rise to the surface.
3. Add lemon juice; add cheese by handfuls, stirring constantly with a wooden spoon until cheese melts. Add spices, and stir until blended.
4. Serve bubbling hot. Guests spear bread cubes through crust with a long-handled fork, dunk and swirl in fondue.

Swiss cheese is used because it does not become stringy.

The crust which remains at the bottom of the fondue pot is called a "religieuse." Remove it with a spatula—a special treat.

11 Fish and Shellfish

Fish

An abundance of delicious fish has always been part of our Canadian heritage. Rich in high quality protein, lower in fat than most meats (much of the fat is in the form of unsaturated fatty acids), fish is appreciated by weight watchers, the budget-conscious and connoisseurs of good food. Most fresh fish fillets are included in low salt (sodium) diets; frozen *and* fresh fillets are ideal for people on bland and light diets.

With its minimal amount of waste, fish is one of the best protein buys on the market—many varieties are cheaper than meats. The significant vitamin and mineral content varies with the species. Fat fish contain a little Vitamin A and are rich in Vitamin D. All fish are rich in minerals except iron; sea fish are rich in iodine.

All varieties of fish lend themselves to the addition of sauces which add extra flavour, richness (and food energy) and sometimes, more servings. Serve fish as a main course, alone or in casserole mixtures or fish loaves, as an appetizer, or in sandwiches, salads and chowders. See index for complete listing.

Grading of fish is not compulsory; however, packaged fish bearing a maple leaf government seal have been processed under government-approved conditions.

Purchasing Fish

Fish are marketed in the following forms:

Whole (Round)—This is the form in which fish come from the water; they must be scaled or skinned, and eviscerated. Gills and fins are always removed; the head and tail may be left on if desired.

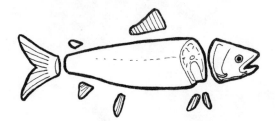

Dressed (Drawn, Eviscerated)—These fish have had the entrails and gills removed. Before cooking, remove fins and scales or skin, and head and tail if desired.

Pan-Dressed (Ready-to-Cook)—Entrails, head, gills, tail, scales, and fins have been removed and the fish is ready to cook. Very large fish are frequently cut into smaller pieces.

Steaks—These are cross sections of large, dressed fish usually cut to provide 1 serving.

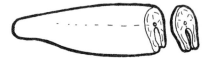

Fillets—These are the meaty sides of the fish cut lengthwise away from the backbone; they should be free of bones. Fillets are usually skinned and sold fresh or frozen.

When buying fish, choose buys that have the following characteristics:

Fresh Whole Fish—shiny, bright skin with tight scales; bright red gills; bright clear eyes; firm flesh; mild, fishy odour.

Fresh Fillets and Steaks—firm flesh; free from discolouration; if wrapped, material should be waterproof with little or no air between it and the fish.

Frozen Fish—solidly frozen; coated with a protective glaze of ice if unwrapped; flesh natural in colour; no evidence of drying, e.g. crumbled edges or white spots.

Frozen fillets packaged in sealed containers cannot be judged for quality before purchase. One must rely on brands known to the consumer or the reputation of the store.

Amount of Fish to Purchase

Whole fish—allow 2 servings per 500 g
Drawn fish—allow 2½ servings per 500 g
Fillets—allow 4 servings per 500 g

Kinds of Fish

Arctic Char	A delectable freshwater fish, harvested by Canadian Inuit, and sold only in specialty fish-markets. Its flesh is fat and creamy.	Broil or bake to bring out its superior flavour.
Bass	This is a lean freshwater game fish, available in several varieties.	Pan-fry; bake large fish.
Cod	An all-purpose saltwater fish and one of the least expensive. Varieties of cod are caught off both coasts; most are lean. Cod is available fresh, smoked, dried and salted, and frozen, usually as fillets. Most salted, dried cod is exported.	Cook by any of the conventional methods; the addition of a sauce adds richness. Combined with other ingredients in fish balls and loaves, the distinct flavour becomes milder.
Eels	These serpent-like fish come from the Atlantic and fresh water. The flesh is fat. They are marketed fresh or smoked, usually skinned, back bone removed, and cut into pieces.	Rub pieces with salt or soak in salty water for 10 min before broiling or combining with vegetables and/or other fish in soup or stew.
Flounder	This lean saltwater fish is flat in shape and mild in flavour. It is available fresh and as frozen fillets.	Prepare by any of the conventional methods.
Goldeye	A smoked delicacy with rose-coloured flesh, native to the lakes of Manitoba.	Broil or steam.
Haddock	A lean, all-purpose, saltwater fish like cod but milder in flavour and a little more expensive. When smoked it is known as finnan haddie.	Cook haddock by any of the conventional methods. Bake finnan haddie in milk or in a scalloped mixture.
Halibut	Higher in fat than haddock or cod but still considered a lean fish, halibut has a pronounced fish flavour. It is caught in salt water off the east and west coasts.	Broil or bake.
Herring	The many varieties of herring are fat fish; they may be saltwater or freshwater in origin, and are available fresh, salted (pickled herring), or salted and smoked (kippered herring). Any small, canned fish of the herring family is labelled *sardine;* some larger, imported canned herrings are called *pilchards.*	Broil kippered herring or poach in liquid. Serve pickled herring as an appetizer.
Sardines	(See herring.) Both native and imported varieties of these canned fish are available; most are packed in oil (olive oil or vegetable oil), some in mustard sauce, or tomato sauce.	Use in salads, sandwiches and appetizers.

Kinds of Fish

Mackerel
A saltwater fish from the Atlantic; available fresh, frozen and canned. The flesh is creamy, fat and similar in appearance and flavour to lighter coloured varieties of salmon (pink, Keta) but firmer in texture. Smoked fillets are also available.

Bake or broil fresh fish. Canned fish has unlimited uses; use as canned salmon. The addition of coloured vegetables such as green or red sweet peppers improves the appearance.

Perch
Lake perch are small, sweet-flavoured, bony fish. Ocean perch are large, rose-fleshed fish, usually sold as frozen fillets. Both have lean flesh.

Pan-fry fresh perch. Ocean perch fillets can be cooked by any of the conventional methods.

Pickerel
Sometimes called Walleye Pike or Doré, these fish come from freshwater lakes and rivers. The flesh is lean.

Pan-fry or bake.

Pike
This is a long, sleek fish from northern lakes and rivers; it has lean flesh and is bony. Large pike tend to be coarse-fleshed.

Pan-fry small pike; bake larger ones. If fish is very large and the flesh is coarse, cook and combine with other ingredients for fish loaf, patties, etc.

Pollock (Boston Bluefish)
This lean fish is similar in appearance, flavour and price to cod. It is usually marketed as frozen fillets, as fish sticks or in other batter-coated forms.

Cook fillets by any of the conventional methods. Use in stews and chowders, or to extend seafood in fish mixtures. Follow package directions for breaded varieties.

Salmon
A fatty saltwater fish available on both east and west coasts. This choice fish ranges in flesh colour from creamy pink to a bright coral, depending on the variety. Sockeye salmon is the reddest of Pacific salmon; Coho is not quite as bright in colour, and chum and pink are a creamy pink. The latter are less expensive and are quite adequate for use in fish loaf, mousse, etc. Salmon is available fresh, frozen, smoked and canned.

Poach, steam, or bake large fresh fish. Broil, pan-fry, or bake fish steaks. Use canned fish in salads, creamed mixtures, loaves and sandwich fillings. Use smoked salmon as an appetizer.

Smelts
Smelts are small, lean fish caught in both oceans and in the rivers which flow into them. They may be sold whole or dressed, fresh or frozen.

Pan-fry or deep fry.

Sole
This is a tender, mild-flavoured, lean fish caught off both coasts. It is sold as fresh or frozen fillets.

Poach or bake in a mild sauce.

Tomcod
These lean fish are usually caught through the ice in winter, in rivers.

Pan-fry or deep fry.

Kinds of Fish

Sturgeon	A fat fish, somewhat coarse in texture, this is the largest of our lake fish.	Cut very large fish into steaks and broil or poach; smaller fish can be poached whole. If flesh is very coarse, steam or poach and use in soup, stew, or loaves.
Trout	Lake trout and smaller species of trout (rainbow, speckled) from rivers and streams are fat and delicately flavoured, cream to coral in flesh colour. Although some are raised for market, most small trout are game fish with a limited season and take.	Bake large lake trout. Pan-fry small trout in butter or oil.
Tuna	This very large, fat fish is caught off both sea coasts; the many varieties include white-meat tuna and dark-meat tuna which is less expensive. Available fresh and as canned "solid pack," "chunks" and "flakes", the latter being less expensive and suitable for sandwiches and spreads.	Serve cold in sandwich fillings and salads; hot in creamed mixtures and casseroles.
Whitefish	This medium fat fish comes from fresh water—often caught through the ice.	Cook by any of the conventional methods; large fish are often baked with or without stuffing.

MAXIMUM STORAGE TIME FOR FISH

Type of Unit	Storage Time	Usual Temperature
Refrigerator (coldest part)	2-3 days	2°-7°C
Freezing compartment of home refrigerator	1 week	−12°--4°C
Home freezer	3 months	−18°C
Cold storage and very cold freezers	6 months	−26°C

Storage of Fish

Because fish is very perishable, it should be served as soon as possible after purchase. Proper storage is essential to maintain its quality.

Minimum storage is always preferable, from the standpoint of flavour. Fish which are classified as fat (see KINDS OF FISH) may undergo flavour changes after 2 months.

Fresh fish should be removed from wrapping material after purchase, wiped with a clean damp cloth, rewrapped in wax paper, placed in a container which can be tightly covered and refrigerated.

Fresh whole fish should always be eviscerated and rinsed before being stored as described.

Smoked fish should be handled and stored as fresh fish. The smoking process adds flavour to the fish; it does not preserve it.

Frozen fish should be purchased from a fish counter with a visible temperature indicator reading no higher than 18°C

Fish must be kept solidly frozen in airproof wrappings. Once the fish has thawed it should not be refrozen. Refrozen fish undergoes a texture change accompanied by a loss of flavour due to its inability to reabsorb the juices that have dripped out.

To maintain the delicate flavour and texture of fish while protecting it from spoilage, great care must be taken to observe proper freezer or refrigerator temperatures. Home freezing, no matter how efficient, cannot maintain temperatures low enough to store fish for extended periods.

Thawing Frozen Fish

Frozen fish which is to be rolled, stuffed, fried, broiled, or baked must be completely thawed before cooking. Leave unopened package or unwrapped fish in the refrigerator for 18-24 h; the longer period will be required to thaw a solid piece of thick fish as opposed to a mass of many small fish or fillets which require less time.

Thawing time of frozen fillets can be reduced to 1-3 h if the unopened package is placed in a dish of cold water under a slowly running cold water tap. Leaving frozen fish at room temperature for the complete thawing time or immersing it in hot water are *not* recommended methods of thawing. Both result in loss of flavour.

Precooked frozen fish fillets, fish sticks, balls, etc. should *not* be thawed before cooking.

Preparation of Fish

To Clean Fish—Using a thin, sharp knife or kitchen shears, slit the underside of the fish from the gills to the vent (the opening from the digestive tract). Remove entrails and any blood which clings to the backbone. Rinse under cold running water. To remove head, cut across base of gills, Snap the backbone by bending it over the end of the cutting board or table. Remove fins by cutting the flesh along both sides of the fins with a small knife or kitchen shears. Pull fin toward head to remove it with its base.

To Scale Fish—If fish is not to be skinned, it should be scaled preferably before cleaning when it is easier to work with. Hold fish by tail; loosen scales with knife, keeping knife close against the fish, to prevent scales from flying. Fish may be scaled under water in a large pan, so that scales will not fly about. Rinse.

Scaling a fish. Graphics Division, Environment Canada.

To Fillet Fish

1. Cut through skin and flesh along the centre back just to the backbone, from the tail to just below the head.

Filleting, step 1. Graphics Division, Environment Canada.

2. With the knife held flat along the flesh, starting at the head end, cut off the flesh on one side to the tail, easing the knife over the ribs. Remove the fillet.

3. Turn the fish over and repeat step 2 on the other side.

Filleting, step 2. Graphics Division, Environment Canada.

To Skin a Fillet, place it skin-side down on the cutting board. Hold the tail firmly with one hand and cut the skin from the flesh with quick, short strokes. Slant the knife away from the flesh to avoid cutting into it.

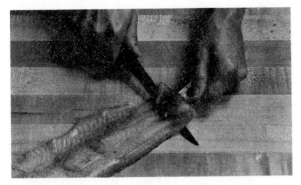

Skinning a fillet. Graphics Division, Environment Canada.

To Bone Fish

1. Hold the cleaned fish firmly with one hand, and insert the tip of the knife into the flesh, close to the backbone. Cut the flesh from the backbone and ribs, keeping knife close to the bones to avoid waste. Continue to the tail.
2. Turn fish over and repeat on the other side; loosen the backbone, and remove backbone and ribs.
3. Remove any small remaining bones with fingers or tweezers.

Boning fish, step 2. Graphics Division, Environment Canada.

General Directions for Cooking Fish

Because fish is tender and has little connective tissue, tenderizing methods of cooking are not required. Fat and liquid are often added to prevent drying and add flavour.

A short cooking period is required. Avoid overcooking; it results in loss of moisture, flavour and texture. Wherever possible, follow directions on package; these are specific to the product. Cook only until the flesh of the fish is opaque throughout and is still springy to the touch. The thickness of the fish will determine the time needed for cooking.

Pan-frying is a suitable cooking method for small and thin fish, fillets and steaks, as it prevents their drying during cooking. It is the ideal method for cooking small game fish over a campfire or at home in the kitchen. Many small fish can be pan-fried in the oven.

PAN-FRIED FISH

1. Prepare fish for cooking: whole fish should be cleaned and dressed, frozen fillets should be thawed and separated. See PREPARATION OF FISH. If desired, bones from fish steaks can be removed and the ends fastened together with toothpicks.
2. Fish can be coated or left plain. To coat, dip in (a) flour, (b) a mixture of equal parts of cornmeal and flour, (c) fine crumbs, beaten egg and crumbs, (d) BAKE-ON CRUMB COATING MIX.
3. Heat frying pan; add enough oil or melted fat to almost cover the bottom, or use more if a large amount of fish is being cooked. Heat the fat.
4. Place fish in hot fat; cook, turning once, until evenly browned on both sides. Cooking time will depend on the thickness of the fish, usually a total of 5-12 min
5. Transfer to a heated plate; garnish with parsley and serve with lemon wedges, *or* MAÎTRE D'HÔTEL SAUCE, *or* TARTAR SAUCE.

Recipes, tables, etc. that appear in small capital letters, e.g., PARSLEY BUTTER, CANADA'S FOOD GUIDE, are listed in the index. Consult the index for the number of the page on which the item appears.

DEEP-FRIED FISH

Deep frying (French frying) is a successful method of cooking thin fillets or slices of lean, fine-textured fish (free of scales and bones) and fish mixtures like fish balls. Frozen fish must be completely thawed before cooking. All must be breaded in crumbs or batter before frying.

400-500 g	fish fillets
	crumb coating *or* batter
	oil

1. Pour oil into pot to a depth of 8 cm
2. Prepare fish; cut into serving portions of even thickness.
3. Crumb or dip in batter: to crumb, dip in fine, dry crumbs, then in beaten egg and again in fine crumbs. To coat with batter, see BATTER COATING.
4. Place in a frying basket and immerse in oil at frying temperature, 185°C.
5. Fry until golden brown on both sides turning once. Serve on a heated plate with lemon wedges; garnish with parsley.

FISH BALLS

225-250 g	uncooked fish
or	
350-400 ml	cooked fish
500 ml	mashed potatoes
	1 beaten egg
15 ml	butter
	salt and pepper
	oil

1. If fish is uncooked, add only enough water to cover; simmer until tender. Drain. (If salt fish is used, freshen according to package directions before simmering).
2. Flake cooked fish and combine with mashed potatoes, beaten egg, butter and seasonings. Salted fish will not require additional salt.
3. Beat mixture until light; roll into balls. Crumb balls (see previous recipe).
4. Cook to golden brown in hot fat, according to directions in previous recipe.
5. Drain, garnish and serve with TARTAR SAUCE or CREOLE SAUCE as a main dish or an appetizer. *Yield:* 18 balls (3-4 servings).

Variations
This mixture can also be shaped into flat cakes; omit coating, and chill 15 min. Pan fry on each side until golden.

BROILED FISH

Fish fillets, steaks or split whole (thick) fish are suitable for broiling. Small fish or thin pieces of fish are better pan-fried to prevent drying.

1. Prepare fish for cooking (see PREPARATION OF FISH); sprinkle with salt and a few drops of lemon juice or vinegar and place on a wire rack or greased broiling pan.
2. If fish is very dry, as is whitefish, brush with melted butter. Preheat broiler.
3. Broil. Thin fish should be broiled on 1 side only; thicker fish may need to be turned and broiled on the second side also. Turn carefully to prevent breaking. Cooking time is 6-10 min, depending on the thickness of the fish.
4. Serve on a heated plate; garnish with lemon wedges or slices and parsley.

BARBECUED FISH

Any fish can be broiled over an outdoor fire; the fire should be less hot than for cooking steak or fowl. Spread split whole fish, small fish or fish steaks with BARBECUE SAUCE and put into a 2-sided broiler or directly onto the grill. Broil on one side; turn thick fish and broil on the other side. Cook 5-10 min on each side according to the thickness of the fish.

Variation
Fish on Skewers—Marinated cubes of thick fish can be threaded onto skewers and broiled. Turn often and baste frequently with the marinade or BARBECUE SAUCE. Cook 7-10 min

BAKED FISH

Baking is an ideal method of cooking large, thick fish with stuffing or without. Fat fish require little additional fat; lean fish may require more. Baking is also suitable for commercially breaded fish sticks and fillets; bake well under a blanket of sauce such as the many variations of WHITE SAUCE or soup sauces, to protect the fish from drying.

1. Prepare a large dressed fish or piece of fish, or thick fish steaks. See PREPARATION OF FISH.
2. Preheat oven to 230°C
3. Dressed fish can be stuffed, if desired, with PARSLEY DRESSING or a variation suitable for fish. To keep dressing from spilling out, skewer edges of stuffed fish together with small skewers or toothpicks, or sew with coarse thread or string.

4. Place on greased baking pan; sprinkle lightly with oil. A large, lean fish can be covered with a few strips of bacon or basted once with a little oil during cooking.
5. If fish is unfrozen, bake   4 min/cm of thickness. If fish is frozen when it is put in the oven, double the cooking time.
   If a sauce containing eggs, milk or cheese covers fish during baking, adjust temperature and cooking time as follows:
   Bake fish 6 min/cm at 180°C
   (The top section of a thick unstuffed fish can be lifted off and placed beside the lower section to allow the inside of the fish to cook more quickly; remove the backbone and reassemble when baked. Careful handling, perhaps with assistance, is essential if the fish is not to break.)
6. Carefully transfer cooked fish to a heated platter, remove skewers etc; serve with TARTAR SAUCE or HOLLANDAISE SAUCE and lemon wedges. Garnish with any of parsley *or* watercress and radishes *or* cherry tomatoes.

BAKED FISH FILLETS

450-500 g   fish fillets

Place in a greased pan fresh fillets, thawed fillets or partially thawed fillets which have been cut into 3 or 4 servings, and pour over them:

50 ml	**oil** *or* **melted butter** *or* FLAVOURED BUTTER
or	
125 ml	BARBECUE SAUCE *or* **herb-flavoured** FRENCH DRESSING

Season fillets which are cooked in butter or oil. Bake individual fillets about 15 min, partially thawed block about 30 min, at 230°C

PLANKED FISH

Best results are obtained if fish is fairly thick, or if steaks of large fish such as salmon or halibut are used.

1. Prepare fish for cooking. See PREPARATION OF FISH.
2. Place skin side down on fish plank.

3. Brush over with melted butter; season.
4. Place on upper rack in oven and bake 20-25 min at 180°C
   Remove from oven.
5. Prepare hot mashed potatoes; press through a large pastry tube to form a border around the fish.
6. Replace fish in oven to brown (3-4 min).
7. Garnish with watercress or parsley, and lemon.

BAKED COATED FISH FILLETS

450-500 g	**fish fillets fresh or thawed**
100 ml	**coating liquid**
125 ml	**crumbs**
50 ml	**melted butter**

Separate fillets and dip in a beaten egg combined with a little water, or in evaporated milk; then dip into a pan of fine, soft bread crumbs or crushed corn flakes. Place on a greased pan; drizzle with melted butter and bake for about 15 min at 190°C
Serve with lemon wedges and garnish with parsley.
Serves 3-4.

BAKED FISH FILLETS IN SAUCE

450-500 g   fresh or frozen fillets
375-500 ml sauce

1. Preheat oven to 200°C
2. In a greased baking dish:
   Spread thawed fillets in a single layer.
   Or place thawed fillets rolled up into turbans filled with BREAD DRESSING and fastened with toothpicks; moisten with a little water or pickle juice.
   Or place partially-thawed block or frozen fillets, cut into 3 or 4 smaller blocks of even size.
3. Cover the fillets with a sauce such as SWEET AND SOUR SAUCE, WHITE SAUCE and variations including CHEESE SAUCE, CURRY SAUCE, CREOLE SAUCE, or a CONDENSED CREAM SOUP SAUCE.
4. Topping can be added if desired: add a row of very thin unpeeled cucumber or lemon or green pepper, sprinkle with paprika. Or top with a layer of grated cheese or a layer of buttered crumbs.
5. Bake until fillets are just tender, about 15-20 min for thawed fillets, 35 min for partially thawed fish.
   If sauce or topping contains cheese, egg, or milk, cook for a longer period at 180°C

CONDENSED CREAM SOUP SAUCES

Combine 1 can of condensed cream soup (celery, mushroom, tomato, cheese or shrimp) with ¼ can of water, stock or milk.

Variations

Add any of chopped sautéed celery or green pepper, or chopped pimento. Celery soup can be flavoured with dill weed or curry powder; tomato soup with onion and thyme. Canned shrimp can be added to shrimp soup and sautéed mushrooms to mushroom soup.

FINNAN HADDIE OR SMOKED FILLETS IN MILK

1 kg	finnan haddie or smoked fillets
30 ml	butter
250 ml	milk

1. Cover fish with boiling water and simmer 10 min if fresh, 20 min if frozen. Drain.
2. Add butter and milk to fish and bake 15 min at 180°C
   Or simmer on top of the stove until fish is tender and flakes. *Serves 6.*

CISCOES AND GOLDEYES

1. Place fish in a greased pan; bake 12-15 min at 230°C
2. Remove skin; take out backbone, being careful to leave flesh unbroken.
3. Place fish on hot platter or on toast. Serve garnished with lemon and parsley. Allow 1 fish per serving.

Cooking fish in liquid includes poaching, steaming and cooking in foil (steaming). These methods are recommended for large fish like salmon and lake trout; their colour and shape are well retained for serving whole, hot or cold. However, small fish or pieces or steaks cut from large fish can also be successfully cooked in liquid. The absence of additional fat in the preparation makes these methods popular with people on low-fat diets.

STEAMED FISH

1. Choose a thick piece of fish, preferably cut from the tail end, about 1-1.5 kg
   Have it scaled and drawn.
2. Place fish on a piece of cheesecloth in the top of a steamer; cover loosely with a piece of foil; cover the steamer.
3. Steam fish until tender when tested with a fork; lift out onto flat pan. Cooking time: 20 min/kg
4. Peel off the dark skin; arrange fish on a heated platter; lift off the upper half of the fish and remove the backbone; reassemble.
5. Serve hot with a sauce, or chill and serve with MAYONNAISE.

Any of parsley, celery leaves, onion slices, stalks of tarragon, fennel, or dill may be put in the bottom of the steamer so that their aroma flavours the fish.

Cooking in Foil

Fish cooked in leakproof foil packages in a pot of boiling water, or in the oven steam in their own juices. Cooking time will depend on the thickness of the fish. Allow 4 min/cm

Fish cooked in foil in a hot oven or over a barbecue or campfire are steam-baked. Over coals, they will cook in half the time required to cook in foil in water.

Lightly grease inner side of foil to prevent sticking. Double fold seams and edges and pinch to make moisture tight.

POACHED FISH

1. Choose a large fish or piece of fish, scaled and eviscerated, or fillets.
2. Use a kettle with a cover and, if possible, a rack. A large fish should be poached in a kettle which is long enough to hold it in a horizontal position. (Special fish poachers are useful but not essential for poaching large fish). Large fish should be wrapped in cheese cloth, leaving long ends for lifting. Small fish and fillets require no special preparation.
3. Place rack in the kettle and add fish. Large fish should be lowered carefully by the cheesecloth into the pot.
4. Add poaching liquid: seasoned stock or water or COURT BOUILLON. There should be enough liquid to just cover the fish. Heat to boiling.
5. Reduce heat, cover fish and simmer until the flesh is opaque throughout and just tender when tested

with a fork. Cooking time approximately 15 min/kg

To test large fish for doneness, remove from pot, unwrap carefully and examine from the inside, near the backbone. If not quite cooked, rewrap and cook a few minutes more.

6. Remove cooked fish; unroll large fish gently onto a platter. Remove any adhering skin.

Serve fish *hot* with dill-flavoured WHITE SAUCE or EGG SAUCE. Remaining poaching liquid can be used for part of the liquid in the sauce; if necessary, boil the liquid for a few minutes to reduce its volume. 60 ml

Garnish with parsley and lemon slices.

Serve fish *cold* with MAYONNAISE or TARTAR SAUCE. Garnish with lemon slices and parsley.

COURT BOUILLON

This poaching liquid adds flavour and firmness to fish during cooking. Afterwards, it can be used with milk or milk powder to make a WHITE SAUCE to serve with the fish. If a large quantity of bouillon remains after the fish has been poached, the quantity can be reduced somewhat by boiling uncovered for a few minutes.

1.25 *l*	water
125 ml	vinegar
	fish trimmings (optional)
	2 sprigs parsley
	celery leaves
	1 onion, sliced
	2 cloves
	1 bay leaf
	1 lemon slice

Combine all ingredients in a large pot and bring to a boil. Reduce heat and simmer for 20 min. Strain. *Yield:* sufficient liquid to poach 1 large fish 1.5-3 kg Fish trimmings (heads, tails, bones) are included in authentic court bouillon, but in these days of modern marketing they are not always available. Fish markets provide fish of every variety and form—and will usually "throw in" the trimmings.

Recipes, tables, etc. that appear in small capital letters, e.g., PARSLEY BUTTER, CANADA'S FOOD GUIDE, are listed in the index. Consult the index for the number of the page on which the item appears.

Canned Fish

The many varieties of canned fish include salmon (3 types) tuna (chunk, flaked, light and dark) mackerel and chicken haddie. Chicken haddie is a mixture of several varieties of Atlantic fish: cod, hake haddock and cusk canned together to produce an inexpensive mild-flavoured product suitable for salads, sandwiches and casseroles.

Canned tuna chunks cost more than flakes; white tuna costs more than dark. Red varieties of salmon cost more than pink. Choose the variety that suits the purpose. If the fish is to be served flaked or is to be combined with other foods, the less expensive variety may be the better buy.

Canned salmon, tuna, mackerel and chicken haddie can all be used in the recipes that follow.

FISH LOAF

500 ml	cooked fish
or	
397-439 g	1 can of fish
250 ml	soft bread crumbs
50 ml	skim milk powder
	salt, pepper
3 ml	minced onion
5 ml	lemon juice
	2 eggs
125 ml	water, vegetable stock, *or* juice
15 ml	finely chopped parsley

1. Flake fish with its juices; mash bones of canned salmon.
2. Mix all ingredients together; more liquid may be added if fish is dry.
3. Turn mixture into a greased medium-size loaf pan, baking dish, or ring mould. Cover.
4. Oven-poach or steam the loaf until firm in the centre, about 30 min
5. Unmould onto a heated platter, slice and serve with any one of EGG SAUCE, CREOLE SAUCE, or CHEESE SAUCE; or serve cold with MAYONNAISE. *Serves 4-6.*

A little mayonnaise, sandwich spread, leftover WHITE SAUCE, or condensed cream soup can be combined with cooked fish to form patties. Canned mackerel and pink varieties of salmon can be used for this loaf. The addition of a little chopped green or red (sweet) pepper improves the appearance and adds to the flavour.

FISH PATTIES

Prepare mixture for FISH LOAF, substituting twice the quantity of mashed potatoes for the soft bread crumbs. Shape into flat cakes. Roll in dry bread crumbs or crushed corn flakes, or dust cakes lightly in flour. Pan-fry in a little butter or oil until golden on each side and hot throughout. Serve with TARTAR SAUCE or KETCHUP. *Serves 6.*

CASSEROLE OF FISH AND RICE

500 ml	cooked, flaked fish
75 ml	soft bread crumbs
	salt, pepper
2 ml	minced onion
30 ml	melted butter
30 ml	stock or water
15 ml	lemon juice
	1 beaten egg
625 ml	cooked rice

1. Mix the fish, crumbs and seasonings.
2. Add butter, liquid, lemon juice and egg, well beaten.
3. Grease a mould; line with rice, using about 2/3 of it.
4. Pack the centre with the fish mixture; cover with rice.
5. Cover tightly; steam or oven-poach 45 min
6. Unmould; serve with PARSLEY BUTTER or EGG SAUCE.

OLD FAVOURITE SALMON SCALLOP

397-439 g	1 tall can salmon *or* mackerel
15 ml	lemon juice
250 ml	coarsely broken soda biscuits
500 ml	seasoned medium WHITE SAUCE
250 ml	soda biscuit crumbs
15 ml	butter

1. Drain fish and save the liquid. Remove skin and break up fish into small pieces; add lemon juice.
2. Prepare WHITE SAUCE using fish juice as part of the liquid.
3. Arrange fish, broken biscuits and sauce in layers in a greased casserole, ending with sauce.
4. Top with crumbs, dot with butter and bake until sauce bubbles and crumbs are lightly browned at 180°C
   Serves 4-6.

Salmon bones are rich in calcium. The bones from canned salmon should be crushed and used with the fish.

PICKLED HERRING

	1 large salt herring
125 ml	white vinegar
30 ml	water
75 ml	sugar
30 ml	chopped onion
30 ml	mixed pickling spices

1. Clean the fish; remove the head. (See PREPARATION OF FISH.) Soak in cold water overnight in the refrigerator.
2. Bone the fish and cut into crosswise slices of 2.5 cm
   In a long shallow dish, reassemble pieces to resemble whole fish.
3. Combine the remaining ingredients and pour over the fish. Refrigerate several hours.

This Scandinavian treat may be served as an appetizer to be offered as one of the many delicacies of a smörgåsbord. Pickling replaces cooking.

BAKED COD TONGUES

This Newfoundland dish uses fresh or salted cod tongues. Canned cod tongues can be purchased at specialty food shops.

	24 cod tongues
250 ml	milk
250 ml	fine, dry bread crumbs

1. If tongues are salted, soak in water to freshen. If fresh, soak for a few minutes in milk to cover, add salt, about 15 ml
2. Drain tongues, roll in crumbs and bake in a greased baking dish for 10 min at 230°C
   Serves 4.

Other Serving Suggestions
Combine fish with a sauce such as WHITE SAUCE, CURRY SAUCE, or CHEESE SAUCE and serve on toast, over rice or noodles, or in patty shells.
Substitute for meat or fish in LEFTOVER COOKED MEAT AND FISH.

Recipes, tables, etc. that appear in small capital letters, e.g., PARSLEY BUTTER, CANADA'S FOOD GUIDE, are listed in the index. Consult the index for the number of the page on which the item appears.

Shellfish

Shellfish are nutritious, rich in high-quality protein and low in fat. Oysters and clams are rich in iron.

Shellfish spoil quickly, especially if shucked. Fresh shellfish will keep only for short periods even if refrigerated at very cold temperatures. Lobsters, crabs and shrimps can be frozen, but toughen slightly. As for any perishable food the price is affected by supply and demand as well as transportation costs. Quantities can be extended somewhat by adding other foods, including less expensive fish, without losing the shellfish flavour.

Shells of clams, oysters and mussels (mollusc family) should be tightly closed or should close on handling; shells that remain ajar indicate animal is dead; discard these. When gathering molluscs, it is important they be taken from unpolluted (sewage-free) water, especially if they are to be served raw. Scrub shells thoroughly with a hard brush before cooking or opening. Shucked oysters, mussels and clams should be plump, with clear liquor.

For each serving allow:
  in shells,   500 ml-1 l
  shucked,   100 ml

Clams—Soft and hard-shelled clams come from the Atlantic coast, and Butter, Razor and Little Neck clams from the Pacific. For convenience, purchase clams already shucked unless for serving steamed and whole or on the half shell. Canned clams are available: shucked, as clam chowder, and as clam-flavoured vegetable juice cocktail.

Oysters—Because oysters come from many different localities on both the east and west coasts, prime quality oysters are available in every season.

These delicately-flavoured shellfish are sold fresh in the shell or shucked as fresh, frozen, or canned. Fresh oysters in the shell keep several days at temperatures just barely above freezing.

To shuck oysters, pry open near hinge with an oyster knife or strong, blunt knife and sever membrane that attaches oyster to shell.

To clean, strain oysters through cheesecloth or fine sieve; save liquor or juice. Remove any traces of shell from oysters; add oysters to juice.

Mussels—These shellfish have coral-coloured flesh and long, blue-black shells. Scrub, then scrape off protruding tuft of hairs with a knife; soak in the shell in fresh water one hour so that mussels shed their sand. Found in most oceans of the world, mussels are marketed fresh, frozen and canned (shucked). Serve steamed in the shell or baked in the half shell with butter and herbs. Mussels are among the least expensive varieties of shellfish.

1 kg yields approximately 24 mussels

Scallops—Like clams and oysters, scallops are molluscs, but only the small round muscle which opens and closes the shell is eaten. It is a round, bite-sized mass of white flesh. Scallops are sold shucked, fresh and frozen. There are approximately 56 large scallops per kilogram.

For each serving allow 7 large scallops, about 120 g

SAUTÉED CLAMS OR OYSTERS

Remove tough little necks from shucked clams. Melt butter to cover the bottom of a frying pan; add shellfish and cook only until the edges curl and they are plump and hot. Season with salt, pepper, paprika and chopped parsley. Serve on buttered toast.

FRIED OYSTERS OR CLAMS

Roll shucked shellfish in salted flour, dip in slightly beaten egg and roll in fine, dry crumbs. Sauté in butter or oil until golden.

STEAMED CLAMS OR MUSSELS

Cover bottom of a large pot with water. Place the scrubbed shellfish in the pot; cover and heat only until shells steam open. Remove steamed shellfish from pot; discard any that have not opened.

Serve with bowls of hot fish stock from the kettle and bowls of melted butter for dunking the shellfish as they are removed from the shells.

At the seashore, clams are often steamed in a large pot containing sea weed and a little water. When the shells have opened, water and seaweed are discarded. Clams are removed and dipped in butter.

See also BOUILLABAISSE and ATLANTIC CHOWDER, (variations).

OYSTERS OR CLAMS ON THE HALF-SHELL

Remove one half-shell from each. Imbed the half-shells containing the seafood in crushed ice on a deep platter. Serve with freshly ground black pepper and a container of lemon juice. For oysters, include a container of COCKTAIL SAUCE. Allow 6 per person.

BAKED MUSSELS OR OYSTERS IN THE HALF-SHELL

Place half-shells containing seafood in muffin pans or imbed in rock salt to hold them level. To each shell add a spoonful of GARLIC BUTTER or HERB BUTTER. Sprinkle very lightly with fine, dry bread crumbs. Refrigerate until needed. About 2 min before serving, broil quickly until butter bubbles and crumbs are lightly browned. Serve immediately. Allow approximately 6 per serving as an appetizer; 8-10 for a main course.

SCALLOPED CLAMS OR OYSTERS

500 ml	cooked clams or raw oysters
500 ml	buttered crumbs
	salt, pepper, paprika
125 ml	chopped parsley
	1 small onion, minced
30 ml	butter
125 ml	rich milk

1. Mince clams or chop oysters and combine with ¼ of the buttered crumbs. Add seasonings, parsley and onion.
2. Place mixture in a small greased casserole dish; top with remaining crumbs and dot with butter.
3. Pour milk over all and bake for 20-25 min until bubbly and browned, at 190°C
   Serves 4.

FRICASSEED OYSTERS

30 ml	butter
	salt, pepper
	dash of cayenne
500 ml	shucked oysters
250 ml	medium WHITE SAUCE
	2 egg yolks
5 ml	lemon juice

1. Heat butter and seasoning slowly in a chafing dish or saucepan; when hot add shucked oysters. (For directions for shucking and cleaning, see OYSTERS.)
2. Cover and shake pan occasionally; oysters will be plump in 2-3 min; remove to a warm place. Save the juice.
3. Prepare WHITE SAUCE in the same pan, using liquid from oysters as part of the liquid in the sauce.
4. Beat egg yolks until thick. Blend a little of the hot sauce into yolks. Stir egg mixture into remaining sauce. Add lemon juice.
5. Reheat oysters in sauce; serve on toast, or in ramekins or shells. *Serves 4.*

BROILED OYSTERS

1. Clean oysters; dry. (For directions for cleaning, see OYSTERS.)
2. Dip in melted butter, then in very fine seasoned crumbs.
3. Broil until plump, about 3-4 min
4. Serve garnished with parsley and lemon sections, or serve with bacon or on toast with WHITE SAUCE in which oyster juice is part of the liquid.

BROILED OYSTERS DE LUXE

1. Clean oysters, drain and marinate for an hour in French dressing to which a little grated garlic and pepper have been added.
2. Drain oysters and wrap each in half a slice of bacon.
3. Broil until bacon is crisp. Serve as an appetizer or with cocktails.

OYSTER STEW

600 ml	rich milk
30 ml	fine cracker crumbs
75 ml	oyster juice
30 ml	butter
	salt, pepper
500 ml	shucked oysters
	chopped chives *or* green onions
	chopped parsley

1. Heat the milk and crumbs over low heat; add the juice from the oysters, the seasoning and the butter.

2. When the milk is hot and the butter melted, add the oysters. Cook until oysters are plump and the edges begin to curl, about 3-4 min
3. Serve at once. Sprinkle with chopped chives or green onions and parsley. *Serves 4-5.*

SAUTÉED SCALLOPS

Rinse scallops, pat dry with towel; shake in a small bag with flour until they are lightly coated. Sauté quickly in butter or oil or a combination about 7-10 min until they begin to brown. Sprinkle with chopped parsley and serve with lemon wedges. When using large scallops, cut into quarters with scissors before shaking with flour. Add 1 or 2 cloves of garlic, crushed, to the butter or oil.

POACHED SCALLOPS

Place scallops in a small saucepan with only enough liquid to cover them. For the liquid, use water and a pinch of thyme. Simmer gently about 3-4 min for large scallops, 1-2 min for small. Remove scallops and keep warm.

Thicken liquid with a little flour blended with butter. Stir, while heating slowly, to form a smooth sauce; pour sauce over scallops and serve. If desired, sprinkle with grated cheese and briefly place under the broiler; garnish with parsley.

BROILED SCALLOPS

Marinate in any fat-containing MARINADE. Broil, turning often. Serve with lemon wedges or TARTAR SAUCE.
The use of fine skewers facilitates turning if many scallops are being broiled. Other foods (mushrooms, tomatoes, green pepper, zucchini, folded strips of bacon) can be added and all served "en brochette."

FRIED SCALLOPS

Marinate scallops as for Broiled Scallops. Roll in fine crumbs; dip in beaten egg and roll again in crumbs. Fry in deep fat (see DEEP FAT FRYING) at 185°C
Serve with lemon or TARTAR SAUCE.

Recipes, tables, etc. that appear in small capital letters, e.g., PARSLEY BUTTER, CANADA'S FOOD GUIDE, are listed in the index. Consult the index for the number of the page on which the item appears.

COQUILLES ST. JACQUES

This popular supper or luncheon dish can be prepared ahead, and refrigerated or frozen until needed. For other suitable fish mixtures see SEAFOOD FILLERS FOR PASTRY SHELLS.

500 g	scallops
225 g	mushrooms
200 ml	stock
15 ml	lemon juice
50 ml	water
	½ bay leaf
	½ small onion
	salt, pepper
45 ml	butter
60 ml	flour
250 ml	stock
200 ml	milk
	2 egg yolks
125 ml	cream
	lemon juice
	fine, soft, buttered crumbs
	grated Parmesan cheese

1. Rinse scallops, slice mushrooms and combine with stock, water, lemon juice, bay leaf, onion and seasonings; simmer 4-5 min
2. Strain off stock and keep warm; set aside scallops and mushrooms.
3. In the top of a double boiler or in a heavy saucepan, melt butter, blend in flour and heat gently until mixture bubbles.
4. Remove from heat, blend in heated stock from scallops, then the milk; heat until thick and no taste of raw starch remains.
5. Combine beaten egg yolks and cream. Add a little hot sauce to the egg mixture, stirring constantly; stir egg mixture into remaining hot sauce.
6. Cook 1 min more, preferably in the top of a double boiler. If cooking over direct heat, stir to prevent burning.
7. Taste; add a few drops of lemon juice, and salt and pepper if desired.
8. Cut scallops into quarters and combine with about 2/3 of the sauce; spoon into 6 buttered scallop shells or ramekins and cover with remaining sauce.
9. Top with very fine, buttered crumbs and sprinkle with Parmesan cheese; arrange shells on a shallow pan. Refrigerate for short storage. When freezing add topping after thawing; frozen dish must be thoroughly thawed.
10. About 15 min before needed, place shells under a hot broiler and heat through until bubbly and lightly browned on top. Serve at once, garnished with a sprig of parsley. *Serves 6.*

BAKED SCALLOPS

250 ml	fine, soft bread crumbs
500 g	scallops
	salt, pepper
50 ml	milk
125 ml	melted butter
30 ml	chopped parsley

1. Choose a baking dish which will hold scallops in one layer.
2. Grease pan and spread evenly with *half* the crumbs.
3. Arrange scallops evenly over the crumbs; season.
4. Add milk slowly, using just enough to come to the top of the scallops, but not over them. Add more or less milk if necessary.
5. Spread remaining crumbs evenly over the scallops; drizzle with melted butter.
6. Bake 40-45 min at 150°C
   Sprinkle parsley on top. *Serves 4.*

Lobster and Crab

Lobster, the aristocrat of seafoods, comes from the Atlantic coastline and is available live, or cooked and frozen whole, or as canned lobster meat. During cooking, the colour of lobster turns from green to coral. Many consider lobster meat to be at its best boiled or broiled whole. Served as LOBSTER NEWBURG or LOBSTER THERMIDOR, it rates high on any menu.

Crabmeat is similar to lobster in texture and similar to it in flavour. It is creamy white in colour. Most crab is sold cooked as crabmeat. Whole crab is usually of the small, soft-shelled variety (crabs that have shed their shells and are awaiting the growth of new ones); it is available near the source of supply, cleaned and ready to cook. Some live, hard-shelled crabs are available in fish markets for boiling and serving whole. Large crabs (king crabs) from the northern Pacific coasts provide 1 or sometimes 2 servings each. Like lobsters, crabs turn red on cooking.

When purchasing live lobsters and crab, choose those which are active. Lobsters should be heavy for their bulk and have hard shells. The tail of a cooked lobster should spring back quickly after it has been stretched, indicating that it was alive just prior to cooking. Cooked lobsters and crabs should have no disagreeable odour. Live lobsters and crabs are usually killed by plunging them head first into rapidly boiling water, but it is considered more humane to bring them to the boiling point in cold fresh water, as fresh water anaesthetizes these saltwater inhabitants.

For each serving of lobster meat or crab meat allow approximately 75 g

BOILED LOBSTER

1. Fill a large kettle with water; kill lobster by either of the methods described above.
2. Simmer 20-25 min, according to size. Drain; place on back to chill.
3. When cool enough to handle, split down the front from head to tail; remove dark intestinal vein, stomach and small sac behind the head. The liver, green in colour, may be left as is or mixed with bread crumbs, salt and pepper and replaced.
4. Crack claw and arm shells, using pliers or a special tool similar to large nutcrackers.

Serve hot with melted butter to which a few drops of lemon juice have been added; or serve cold on a bed of lettuce, garnished with hard-cooked eggs, tomato slices, mayonnaise and capers.

BROILED LOBSTER

1. Place live lobster on its back, cross the large claws and hold firmly.
2. With a sharp-pointed knife, make a deep incision near the mouth to cut through the spinal cord; cut down through the body from the mouth to the end of the tail.
3. Remove the intestinal vein, liver and stomach and crack the claw shells.
4. Sprinkle with melted butter; broil 8 to 10 min on the flesh side and 6 to 8 min on the shell side.
5. Season and serve with melted butter.

LOBSTER THERMIDOR

1 kg each	2 cooked lobsters
	salt, pepper
500 ml	fish or meat stock
30 ml	chopped green onions
15 ml	minced onion
10 ml	dried tarragon
750 ml	rich medium WHITE SAUCE
5 ml	dry mustard
100 ml	grated Parmesan or Swiss cheese

1. Use broiled or boiled lobster; before broiling, split the prepared lobster lengthwise. Split boiled lobster *after* cooking.
2. Cool lobsters until meat can be carefully removed from the shells keeping the shells intact. Crack and remove meat from the claws. Season meat with salt and pepper.

3. In a saucepan, combine stock, onion and tarragon; heat quickly until the liquid is reduced in volume and is almost the consistency of paste.
4. Prepare WHITE SAUCE using cream or additional butter; combine with the stock mixture; blend in dry mustard; season to taste. Keep sauce hot.
5. Dice lobster meat, combine with sauce and pile into the lobster shells; sprinkle with grated cheese.
6. Drizzle melted butter over all; broil until bubbly and golden brown. Garnish with sprigs of parsley. *Serves 4.*

LOBSTER NEWBURG

500 ml	cooked lobster
30 ml	melted butter
575 ml	rich medium WHITE SAUCE
	salt, pepper
	1 egg yolk
5 ml	lemon juice

1. Sauté lobster for 2 or 3 min in melted butter.
2. Prepare WHITE SAUCE using light cream or additional butter; season.
3. Blend a little of the hot sauce into the beaten egg yolk, then stir egg mixture into remaining sauce. Add lemon juice.
4. Combine lobster and sauce. Season to taste and serve. *Serves 4.*

Variation
Serve in scallop shells or ramekins; add buttered crumbs and heat in a hot oven until lightly browned.

For Lobster Cocktail, see SEAFOOD COCKTAIL.

Shrimp
Coming from the Atlantic and the Pacific coasts, these small crustaceans are sold raw in the shell (green), cooked in the shell (pink) and cooked and shelled, canned, frozen and dried. Sizes range from tiny to the jumbo shrimp usually served as appetizers or as batter-dipped and fried Tempura or butterfly shrimp (split almost through and opened flat).

Shrimp are popular in hors d'oeuvres, in seafood cocktails, in salads and in sauced mixtures like curry. Most Caribbean countries have their own special dishes of shrimp, rice and tomatoes, seasoned with local spices.

Shrimp can be shelled and cleaned before or after cooking. Peel off the shell, rinse in cold water and with a sharp, pointed knife, make a shallow cut along the outside curvature of the shrimp and lift out the black intestinal vein. Remove the head.

The most common method of cooking shrimp is by poaching in the shells in seasoned water or bouillon, and serving either with GARLIC BUTTER or sauce, or cold with MAYONNAISE or COCKTAIL SAUCE. Shrimps that are shelled before cooking may be poached, sautéed, broiled, fried or cooked in sauce.

About 130 medium-size shrimp make 500 kg or 1 *ℓ*

Lobster tails, prawns, scampi and other small crustaceans are usually poached and served similarly to shrimp.

FRIED SHRIMP

1. Prepare large raw shrimp (see directions under SHRIMP). For 4 servings prepare 450-500 g Sprinkle lightly with salt; dry on towels. For butterfly shrimp slash cleaned shrimp lengthwise and open flat.
2. Dip in batter (see BATTER COATING) and fry in hot oil until brown; turn once. Fat temperature 185°C
   Drain.

Serve with small dishes of soy sauce, TARTAR SAUCE, COCKTAIL SAUCE, or lemon wedges.

SHRIMP CREOLE

450-500 g	cooked and cleaned shrimp
50 ml	butter
50 ml	green pepper, cut in strips
50 ml	celery, cut in strips
50 ml	chopped onion
	1 chopped medium-size tomato
or	
125 ml	canned tomato without juice
	¼ garlic clove, crushed
	sprinkle of basil
	pepper, salt
125 ml	vegetable stock
125 ml	tomato sauce

1. Sauté shrimp in butter for 5 min; add all remaining ingredients except liquids; sauté all for 10 min more.
2. Add remaining ingredients and cook over low heat until the vegetables are tender. Serve over hot rice. *Serves 5-6.*

This mixture can also be used for a sauce. Halve the recipe and serve over baked fish fillets.

POACHED SHRIMP

Rinse shelled or unshelled shrimp and put in a pot with water to cover. Add a few slices of lemon and onion, a few sprigs of parsley, and salt and pepper. Bring to boiling, reduce heat and simmer 3-5 min according to size, until pink and cooked through. Shrimp in shells may take up to 6 min, *no more*. Do not overcook. Serve hot as Shrimp de Jonghe (below), or in casserole mixtures, or with sauce, or serve cold with MAYONNAISE or COCKTAIL SAUCE.

SHRIMP DE JONGHE

125 ml	butter
	2 garlic cloves, crushed
	3 green onions, chopped
	salt, pepper
2 ml	tarragon
250 ml	soft bread crumbs
175-225 ml	medium-size shrimp, poached or canned
100 ml	stock *or* water
15 ml	lemon juice

1. Soften butter and combine with crushed garlic, chopped green onion (use green ends too), seasonings, and crumbs.
2. Shape mixture into a roll; chill.
3. Divide shrimp evenly among 4 individual appetizer-size sea shells or ramekins.
4. Pour liquid over shrimps, dividing it evenly; slice butter mixture and place slices on top of shrimps.
5. Bake in oven preheated to 200°C
   or place under preheated broiler and cook quickly for 3-4 min until bubbly. *Serves 4.*

SHRIMP CURRY

750 ml	shelled and cleaned shrimp
(350 g)	
45 ml	butter
50 ml	chicken stock
	1 small onion, minced
30 ml	butter
250 ml	sour cream
75 ml	flour
30 ml	curry powder
500 ml	chicken stock

1. Sauté the prepared shrimp in butter until pink; add stock and simmer for 1 minute.
2. Sauté the minced onion in the second portion of butter until soft; stir in sour cream, flour, curry powder and chicken stock.

3. Heat and stir until thick.
4. Add the shrimp and their liquid; heat over low heat until hot. Serve over hot rice. *Serves 4-6.*

Quick Curried Shrimp can be prepared from cleaned, canned shrimp combined with CURRY SAUCE or with sauce made from condensed cream of celery soup (see CONDENSED CREAM SOUP SAUCES) flavoured with curry powder.

For Shrimp Cocktail see SEAFOOD COCKTAIL. See also SEAFOOD CRÊPES.

Seafood in Shells

For inexpensive entertaining, "fish shells" provide an interesting presentation of fish or fish mixtures chosen to fit the budget. Mixtures can be prepared ahead and refrigerated or frozen until needed. Scallop, clam and cockle shells can be picked up on seashore and need only be scrubbed to become useful oven-proof baking dishes. Scallop shells are also available in houseware departments. If shells are not available, use individual ramekins, a large casserole, or Pastry Shells.

Pastry Shells—"Shells" can be made from pastry using 2 scallop shells of similar size as forms. Pat rolled pastry (see PASTRY, TO ROLL DOUGH), into a shell and place a second shell on top of it; press together lightly. Trim off excess dough; chill shells 1 h. Bake for 15-20 min at 230°C

Cool pastry in the shell before removing.

Pastry shells can be filled with hot, creamed mixtures and the edges of the pastry lightly coated with sauce to prevent browning during heating. Place filled pastry shells on a cookie sheet and heat quickly in a hot oven or under the broiler until mixture bubbles.

The addition of 1 small, beaten egg to the pastry ingredients gives extra strength.

Pastry Shells filled with fresh fruit and topped with sweetened whipped cream make an attractive dessert.

Fillings—A wide range of fish permits a wide range of costs. A small amount of expensive seafood can be combined with a larger amount of inexpensive fish without great loss of individual flavours. The addition of sautéed, chopped celery, green or red sweet pepper, pimento, or small or medium-size pasta shells, extends the mixtures as does a piped border of mashed potatoes, a base of chopped, cooked spinach (well-drained) or Frenched cooked green beans. A topping of buttered crumbs with or without grated cheese, or a sprinkling of garlic salt serves the same purpose and also adds flavour and attractiveness.

WHITE SAUCE and its many variations are suitable for combining foods; sauce made from undiluted condensed Cream of Shrimp Soup is especially good.

Top with a shrimp, a sprig of parsley, a lemon twist, a strip of pimento, a thin slice of unpeeled cucumber, or a colourful combination of any of these, to provide the finishing touch.

Any of the following may be used as filling for Seafood in Shells:
SHRIMP DE JONGHE, SHRIMP CURRY, SHRIMP CREOLE, LOBSTER NEWBURG, COQUILLES ST. JACQUES, SCALLOPED CLAMS OR OYSTERS, OLD FAVOURITE SALMON SCALLOP.

Amounts of Filling to Use
For appetizer: if shell diameter is 10 cm
use 100 ml
For main dish: if shell diameter is 13 cm
use 250 ml

CANNED TUNA FILLING

198 g each	2 cans flaked tuna
500 ml	CHEESE SAUCE
	Worcestershire sauce
	salt, pepper
284 ml	1 pkg. spinach

Combine tuna with cheese sauce; add Worcestershire sauce and seasoning to taste. Cook spinach for 1 min only, drain thoroughly and make a shallow layer in each shell, bringing it out to the edges. Divide tuna mixture among the shells, placing it in the centre. Bake until bubbly, at 230°C
Garnish with pimento strips and a sprig of parsley.
Yield: 6-8 appetizer-size portions.

Recipes, tables, etc. that appear in small capital letters, e.g., PARSLEY BUTTER, CANADA'S FOOD GUIDE, are listed in the index. Consult the index for the number of the page on which the item appears.

CANNED SALMON FILLING

454 g	1 can salmon
250 ml	chopped celery and green pepper, sautéed
500 ml	AURORA SAUCE
375 ml	buttered crumbs
125 ml	grated cheese

Remove skin from the salmon. Combine salmon, sautéed vegetables and sauce. Taste and season. Divide mixture among greased shells. Top with buttered crumbs; sprinkle with grated cheese. Bake 4-5 min until bubbly, at 190°C
Garnish with a lemon twist and a sprig of parsley.
Yield: 6-8 appetizer size portions.

SEAFOOD FILLING

454 g	fresh fillets of cod, haddock, sole, etc.
or	
396 g	canned chicken haddie
220 g	canned salmon
142 g	canned shrimp, cleaned
500-750 ml	Cream of Shrimp sauce (see CONDENSED CREAM SOUP SAUCES)

1. Poach or sauté raw fish fillets. Remove skin from salmon and use 15 ml liquid in sauce. Break fish into bite-size pieces (do not flake); divide evenly among the greased shells.
2. Discard liquid from shrimps and rinse; divide half the shrimps among the shells.
3. Spoon sauce over the fish in the shells; add remaining shrimps.
4. Bake 4-5 min, until bubbly, at 190°C
Yield: 8-10 appetizer-size shells.
For approximately 12 servings, add 1 can of lobster or crab, drained: 170 g

To Use Leftover Cooked Fish and Shellfish
1. Add mayonnaise, seasonings, serve in salads or as a spread for appetizers and sandwiches.
2. Make croquettes, fish loaf, soufflé, chowder, fish balls and patties. See recipes for LEFTOVER COOKED MEAT AND FISH.
3. Use in jellied salads, aspic, or mousse.
4. Add WHITE SAUCE, vegetables, and serve on toast, in ramekins or sea shells; or use as a filling for crêpes and pancakes.
5. Blend with other fish for SEAFOOD COCKTAIL.

12 Meat

Meat is one of the most expensive items in our diet, worthy of maximum care in purchase, storage and cooking. It is an important source of protein, phosphorus, some of the B vitamins and iron. The tender cuts are the most expensive, but cheaper cuts can be equally enjoyable when the right cooking methods are used. Grade of meat makes a difference; for example, rump roast and round steak of beef may be more or less tender, depending upon the quality of the beef as well as the method of cooking.

Meat Inspection

When meat crosses a border, inter-provincial or foreign, it must be inspected for wholesomeness by federal inspectors. Meat and meat products so inspected are stamped, tagged, or labelled with an official round purple stamp reading either "Canada Approved" or "Canada" and the registered number of the meat plant. This stamp does not indicate quality or grade but only that the food is fit for human consumption.

Grading of Meat

Grading is voluntary except in provinces that have passed grading legislation. Beef is sold by grade nearly everywhere and in some provinces consumers may buy graded lamb and veal. Pork is not sold by grade in retail stores.

Grades are based on the age of the animal, and the colour and texture of the flesh and fat. Each major cut and most retail cuts of beef are stamped with a continuous ribbonlike mark in a colour indicating grade:
Canada A—red stamp
      B—blue
      C—brown
      D—black
These marks are not always visible on the meat you buy.

There are four subdivisions of Grade A, according to the level of fat precisely measured at a specified point. Grade A1 indicates top quality meat in which the level of fat falls within the minimum range; A4 indicates the highest level of fat for A quality meat.

Grades B and C are usually leaner than grade A beef; the lean may be slightly less firm and somewhat

coarser than Canada A, and the colour of lean and fat somewhat darker. Canada C grade cuts of marginal tenderness, including round steak, sirloin tip, crossrib and rump roasts are as wholesome and nutritious as A and B grades of the same cuts, but are best cooked by moist-heat methods.

Grade D beef comes from mature cows and steers and is generally less tender than A, B and C grades.

AMOUNTS OF MEAT TO PURCHASE

For an individual serving allow approximately:
meat with some bone	200 g
boneless meat	120 g
sliced cold meat	60 g

Storing Meat

Fresh meat which is not to be frozen should be stored in the coldest part of the refrigerator just above freezing temperature. If meat has been pre-packaged for self-service, it can be stored in its package or frozen and stored in the freezer without rewrapping for no more than two weeks. See also POULTRY STORAGE. If meat is wrapped in paper when purchased, remove outer paper and rewrap loosely in waxed paper or aluminum foil, or in the inner parchment paper wrapping in which the meat was bought. Ground meats, chopped meats, and variety meats are more perishable than solid cuts.

Freezing Meat—Package meat in airtight wrappings or containers to prevent loss of moisture during freezing. Such a loss results in "freezer burn," a condition characterized by dry, stringy meat of poor flavour and colour. For large cuts, an over-wrapping of cotton stocking or other cloth protects the airtight wrapping from tears and punctures. Flavour change may result from too-long storage, particularly in pork.

To freeze meat patties, place the number of patties required for one meal on a sheet of waxed paper on a firm backing of cardboard (if many, use two sheets). Cover with waxed paper, another layer of patties and another sheet of waxed paper. Add more layers as needed; overwrap with foil or freezer wrap. Remove frozen patties by layers, returning remaining patties to freezer.

Maximum Meat Storage Time

Meat	Refrigerator 2° to 4°C	Freezer −18°C or lower
Beef (fresh)	2-4 d	6-12 months
Veal (fresh)	2-4 d	6-9 months
Pork (fresh)	2-4 d	3-6 months
Lamb (fresh)	2-4 d	6-9 months
Ground beef, veal and lamb	1-2 d	3-4 months
Ground pork	1-2 d	1-3 months
Variety meats	1-2 d	3-4 months
Luncheon meats	1 week	not recommended
Sausage, fresh pork	1 week	2 months
Sausage, dry and semi-dry (unsliced)	2-3 weeks	
Frankfurters	4-5 d	1 month
Bacon	5-7 d	1 month
Smoked ham, whole	1 week	2 months
Ham slices	3-4 d	2 months
Beef, corned	1 week	2 weeks
Leftover cooked meat	4-5 d	2-3 months

To freeze meatballs, follow basic recipe for MEAT BALLS to the end of step 3. Freeze quickly in a single layer on a cookie sheet; transfer to a plastic bag and tie. If a large quantity is being prepared, use several bags, indicating the quantity on each. Remove the required number of meat balls as needed, heat any of the liquids suggested in a saucepan or chafing dish, simmer meat balls, thawed or frozen depending on the amount of available time.

Vacuum-packaged meats including smoked and cured products and cooked, luncheon-style meats are usually purchased fresh. Freezing of these meats is not recommended. However, if it is necessary to keep these products longer than a few days they may be frozen as long as the vacuum package is not broken. Use within 4 weeks.

Some meat, poultry, fish, or their products bear the designation "Previously Frozen" or "Made from fresh and frozen parts." Complying with government regulations, this declaration indicates only that all or part of the food being sold in a thawed state was once frozen; it does not indicate lessened quality. Since repeated freezing and thawing of food results in texture and flavour changes and can increase the risk of bac-terial contamination, it is not recommended that these products be refrozen if they have been completely thawed or left in the refrigerator over 2 days.

Buying Meat for the Freezer—Careful calculation should precede the purchase of large cuts of meat for the freezer to determine if savings as well as convenience will result. Cutting a whole carcase of beef will produce 30% waste and 70% usable cuts in these proportions:

30% bones, fat
28% roasts, half of which are chuck roasts; the rest rib, rump, and sirloin tip
22% assorted steaks
20% smaller cuts for braising, stewing, or mincing

Pork, veal, and lamb will be divided in similar proportions. The majority of the cuts will be tender.

By working out the cost of individual cuts and comparing them with the current store prices for the same cuts purchased separately, one can assess the financial advantage of the investment.

Always choose top quality meat which has been prepared under sanitary conditions by a reputable dealer.

Beef Cuts

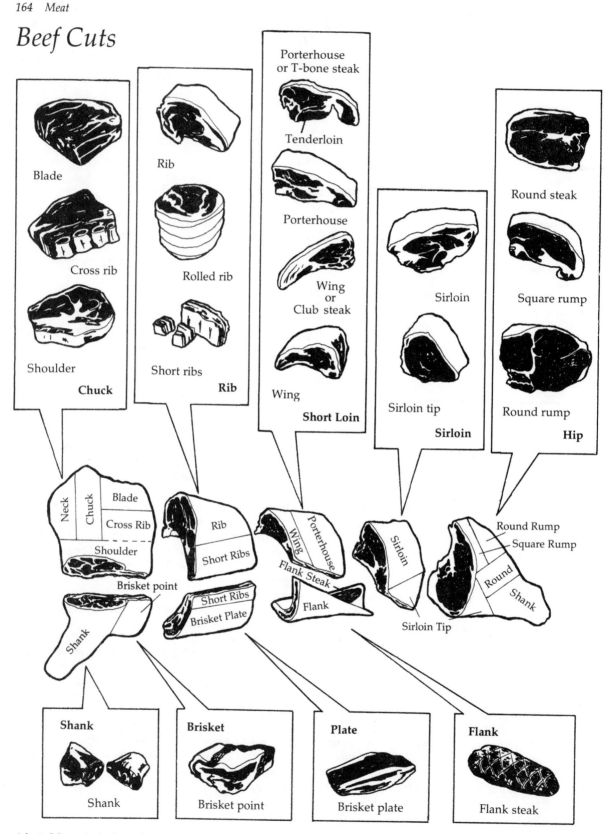

Blade

Cross rib

Shoulder

Chuck

Rib

Rolled rib

Short ribs

Rib

Porterhouse
or T-bone steak

Tenderloin

Porterhouse

Wing
or
Club steak

Wing

Short Loin

Sirloin

Sirloin tip

Sirloin

Round steak

Square rump

Round rump

Hip

Neck   Chuck   Blade

Cross Rib

Shoulder

Brisket point

Shank

Rib

Short Ribs

Short Ribs

Brisket Plate

Wing   Porterhouse

Flank Steak

Flank

Sirloin

Sirloin Tip

Round Rump

Square Rump

Round

Shank

Shank

Shank

Brisket

Brisket point

Plate

Brisket plate

Flank

Flank steak

Adapted from Agriculture Canada chart, with permission.

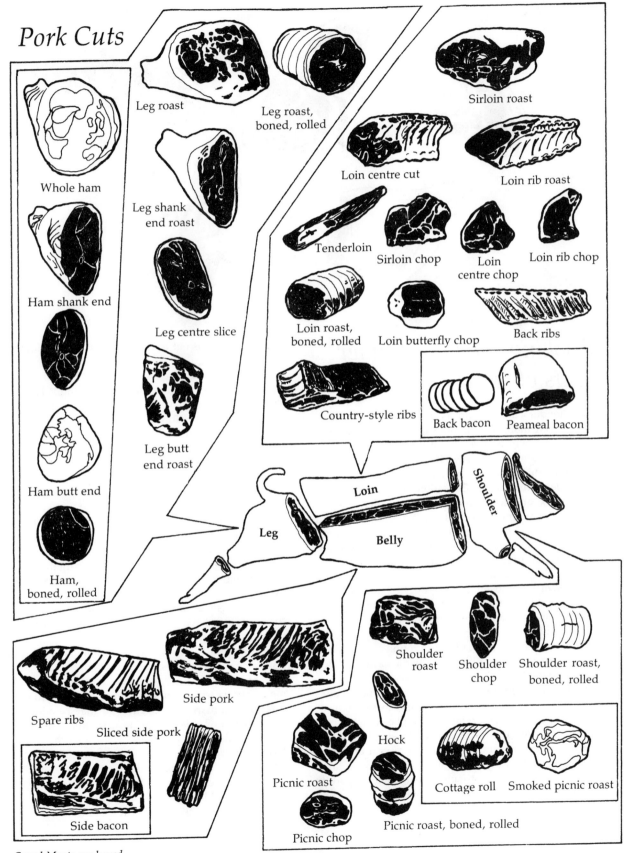

Pork Cuts

Leg roast

Leg roast, boned, rolled

Sirloin roast

Loin centre cut

Loin rib roast

Tenderloin

Sirloin chop

Loin centre chop

Loin rib chop

Loin roast, boned, rolled

Loin butterfly chop

Back ribs

Country-style ribs

Back bacon

Peameal bacon

Leg shank end roast

Leg centre slice

Leg butt end roast

Whole ham

Ham shank end

Ham butt end

Ham, boned, rolled

Leg

Loin

Shoulder

Belly

Shoulder roast

Shoulder chop

Shoulder roast, boned, rolled

Hock

Cottage roll

Smoked picnic roast

Picnic roast

Picnic chop

Picnic roast, boned, rolled

Spare ribs

Side pork

Sliced side pork

Side bacon

Cured Meats are boxed.
Adapted from Pork, *Canadian Pork Council, Ottawa, 1975*

Lamb Cuts

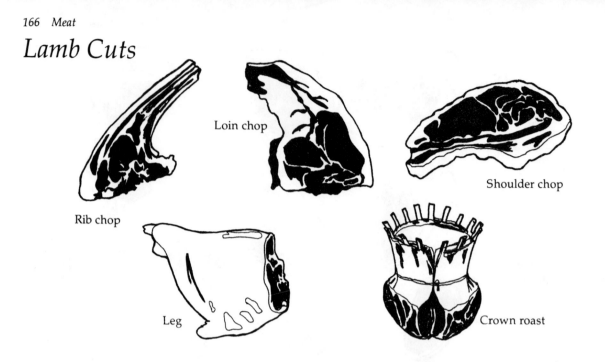

Loin chop

Shoulder chop

Rib chop

Leg

Crown roast

Cooking the Less Tender Cuts of Meat

Less tender cuts contain as much food value and often even more flavour than tender cuts since the substances which give the flavour are developed when the animal exercises. It is primarily with beef that we find differences in tenderness of the various cuts, depending on their location on the animal. All veal, pork, and lamb cuts are usually tender.

The cooking method chosen will take into account the tenderness of the cut, the amount of fat or connective tissue, and the size of the cut in order to ensure maximum flavour and tenderness.

The shoulder or chuck section of beef contains meat which has been highly exercised and is therefore not tender; this includes arm and chuck steaks and blade pot roasts which must be braised or otherwise tenderized. Other cuts suitable for braising include flank steak, short ribs, and round steak. Round steak from top quality beef, particularly the top round, may be tender enough to pan-fry.

Pot Roasting and Braising—These terms mean cooking slowly, below the boiling point, in moist heat, after browning; the former term applies to large cuts (roasts), while the latter applies to small cuts. Although they are tender, small cuts of veal and pork are usually braised; moist heat dissolves the large amount of connective tissue in veal; it allows pork to be well-cooked, as is necessary, without being dried out.

Stewing—Meat is cut into pieces and cooked slowly, submerged in liquid.

Cooking in a Large Amount of Liquid—This method, which is usually called "boiling," is misnamed since meat should always be cooked below the boiling point. It differs from braising in the amount of liquid used. Also the meat is usually not browned.

The kettle should be large enough that the meat can be completely covered with water. Simmer 2-4 h. After cooking, the meat is allowed to cool in the stock; this prevents shrinkage, makes the meat juicier and improves the flavour. The stock may be boiled to reduce the volume, flavoured and served with the meat, or it may be used for soup.

Pressure Cooking—All the moist-heat methods for tenderizing meats can be used when pressure cooking.

Grinding—All ground meat is tender because the coarse fibres have been cut through; it may be treated as a tender cut.

Pounding and Waffling—These methods also break down the connective tissue.

Use of Acid—To break down connective tissue, meat may be soaked in a flavoured oil and acid mixture called a marinade, or the acid may be added in the cooking. Tomatoes or tomato juice are commonly used for this purpose.

Use of Tenderizers—These contain enzymes that predigest the meat and so change its character. They are more successful with thin pieces of meat than with roasts. Meat may be purchased already tenderized by the packer, and bear a brand name which indicates this treatment. Usually, a shorter period of cooking is required for such meat, and cuts which are ordinarily considered marginally tender can be cooked by the methods recommended for tender meat.

Cooking the Tender Cuts of Meat

Tender cuts are usually cooked by dry heat methods, such as roasting. However, some tender cuts, especially pork and veal which need to be well cooked, are better braised to prevent them from drying out.

The following beef cuts can be depended on to produce tender meat when roasted: tenderloin, porterhouse, standing and rolled rib roasts. From red and blue brands of beef can be added short rib roasts, sirloin tip, round and rump roasts. When beef of a lesser quality is used, these latter cuts should be pot roasted.

The following cuts are suitable for broiling: tenderloin (filet mignon), porterhouse steak; T-bone, wing or club steak; round, chuck, or flank steak if marinated or tenderized. If flank steak is used it should be sliced on the bias.

Tender or tenderized steaks, chops, or smaller pieces of tender meat are usually broiled or pan-broiled. Pan-frying, sautéing, barbecuing, and stir-frying are variations of these methods.

Roasting is the process of cooking uncovered, by dry heat in an oven. If a roast has water added to it, or if it is covered during cooking so that the steam that forms is held in, the meat is being braised, not roasted. It is not wise to pay a high price for tender meat and then cook it like a less tender cut.

Roasting is the usual method for cooking large, tender cuts of meat. Very small roasts, especially if they contain bone, are not usually a good buy because of high shrinkage losses.

All meat shrinks during cooking through evaporation of juices and rendering of fat. Shrinkage can be minimized and meat will be juicier and tastier if the recommended low oven temperature for roasting without preliminary searing is used. That temperature is 160°C

Detailed methods for preparing roast beef, veal, lamb and pork are given in the recipe sections in this chapter.

INTERNAL TEMPERATURES OF MEAT

Determine the internal temperature by the use of a meat thermometer during cooking; the meat will be cooked when the specified temperature (see table) has been reached. The thermometer should be placed in the thickest part of the flesh, not touching the bone. Meat should always be thawed before inserting thermometer to prevent breakage.

	Temperature Celsius
Beef, rare	60°C
medium	70°C
well done	75°C
Veal	75°C
Lamb	80°C-85°C
Pork, fresh	80°C-85°C*
cured	70°C
Poultry, in dressing	75°C
in thigh	85°C
Turkey roll	80°C-85°C

* The lower figure in this range is currently recommended by pork institutes.

Broiling, another dry-heat method for cooking tender meat, is usually reserved for small cuts. Meat of marginal tenderness, such as round steak or flank steak, may be marinated for several hours and then broiled; meat tenderizer may render other small but less tender cuts sufficiently tender for broiling.

Meat is placed on the oven rack set at level for broiling. When meat is approximately half-cooked, it is turned and cooked on the other side. The door of an electric oven should be kept ajar during the broiling period. For details, see BROILED STEAK.

TIMETABLE FOR BROILING MEAT

2.5 cm *thick*	*Cook Each Side*
A large sirloin	10-14 min
Individual pieces	5-7 min
Meat patties	8-10 min

Pan-broiling—Tender meat is cooked quickly in a frying pan which has been lightly greased, usually with pieces of fat cut from the meat. It is browned on one side and then on the other and the heat reduced.

Pan-frying—Small tender cuts of meat which are breaded, or cuts low in fat, such as liver, are used. Meat is cooked in a thin layer of fat—just enough to cover the bottom of the pan—over moderate heat on one side and then on the other. Fat is poured off as it accumulates, or more is added as required.

Carving Meat and Poultry

Of first importance is the quality of the steel in the carving knife. A blade that will take and hold a keen edge is more important than a fancy handle.

To get the full co-operation of a carving set it must be given good care. Keep it separated from other cutlery so the knife will not be dulled or nicked. A good blade needs only occasional sharpening but it should always be steeled before using.

Electric carving knives are effective and require little maintenance.

If it is easier, stand up to carve.

Avoid changing the angle of the blade while making a slice; neat uniform slices look better and go farther.

A large roast or fowl can be carved more easily after it has stood in a warm place for 15 to 30 min in the roasting pan to absorb the juices.

Give the carver plenty of platter room and plenty of elbow room. Place glasses and dishes where they will not interfere with the carver.

When garnishing, don't be over-generous; leave space for the work to be done.

Servings cool quickly, so plates and platter *must* be heated.

Standing Rib Roast—The roast is placed on the platter with the small cut surface up and the rib side to your left.

With the guard up, insert the fork firmly between the two top ribs. From the far outside edge slice across the grain toward the ribs, to form uniform slices.

Release each slice by cutting close along the rib with the knife tip.

Rolled Roasts—The roast is placed on the platter with the larger cut surface down. With the guard of the fork up, push the fork firmly into the roast on the left side (if right-handed) toward the top.

Slice across the grain toward the fork from the far side, in uniform slices.

Remove each cord only as it is approached in making slices. Sever it with the tip of the blade, loosen it with the fork and allow it to drop to the platter.

Blade Pot Roast—Hold the pot roast firmly with the fork inserted at the left and separate a section by running the knife between two muscles, then close to the bone.

Turn the section just separated so that the grain of meat is parallel with the platter. Holding the piece with the fork, cut slices to a thickness of about 1 cm

Separate the remaining sections of the roast; note the directions of the meat fibres and carve across the grain.

Baked Whole Ham, Picnic Shoulder, or Leg of Lamb—The ham is placed on the platter with the fat or decorated side up and the shank end to the carver's right.

Insert the fork and cut several slices parallel to the length of the ham on the thin side.

A boneless, rolled roast of beef.

A T-bone steak served with braised onions.

Thin slices of roast beef rolled and served with mashed potatoes.

Turn the ham so that it rests on the surface just cut. Hold the ham firmly with the fork and cut a small wedge from the shank end.

Keep the fork in place to steady the ham and cut thin slices down to the leg bone. Release slices by cutting along bone at right angles to slices.

For more servings turn the ham back to its original position and slice at right angles to the bone.

Pork Loin Roast—It is much easier to carve a pork loin roast if the backbone is separated from the ribs before purchase. The backbone then becomes loosened during roasting.

Before the roast is brought to the table, remove the backbone by cutting between it and the rib ends.

The roast is placed on the platter so that the rib side faces you.

Insert the fork firmly in the top of the roast. Cut close against both sides of each rib. If the loin is large it is possible to cut two boneless slices between the ribs.

Roast Suckling Pig—Split pig in half by cutting through tender backbone. Separate head from body.

Separate legs from body on one side.

Cut between ribs, allowing 2 per serving, along with some meat from ham and shoulder and some skin. Repeat for other side of pig.

Chicken or Turkey—Remove all trussing equipment, such as skewers and string, in the kitchen.

Hold the drumstick firmly with fingers, pulling gently away from the body. At the same time cut through skin between leg and body.

Press leg away from body with flat side of knife. Then cut through joint joining leg to backbone and skin on the back. Separate drumstick and thigh by cutting down through the joint to the plate.

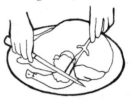

Slice drumstick and thigh meat. Chicken drumsticks and thighs are usually served without slicing.

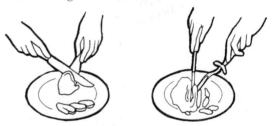

Make a deep cut into the breast to the bone, parallel to it and as close to the wing as possible.

Begin at front, starting halfway up the breast, cut thin slices of white meat down to the cut made parallel to the wing.

Remove individual servings of stuffing from an opening cut into side where leg has been removed.

For half turkey, remove wing tip and first joint, then the drumstick. Continue as above.

Beef

Basic Recipe
BRAISED BEEF

meat suitable for braising (see POT ROASTING AND BRAISING)
flour (optional)
seasonings
fat
hot liquid

1. Trim the bone and superfluous fat from the meat.
2. Dredge meat in seasoned flour if desired. If it is a small piece, pound it with a meat hammer or with the edge of a heavy plate.
3. In a heavy pan with a tight-fitting lid (an iron frying pan, Dutch oven, or electric frying pan), brown the meat in a small amount of rendered fat cut from the meat or in about 50 ml of cooking oil.
4. Season meat unless it was previously dredged in seasoned flour.
5. If necessary add a small amount of liquid; large cuts usually do not require the addition of liquid. Water, stock, or tomato juice, with or without additional flavouring, are suitable liquids. Check occasionally during the cooking; add more liquid if dry.
6. Cover tightly. A tight-fitting lid holds in the steam needed to soften the connective tissue and tenderize the meat.
7. Cook until tender on top of the stove on low heat or in the oven at 140°C
   The meat must be simmered, not boiled.
8. Make gravy from the liquid in the pan, if desired, after removing some of the excess fat. Thicken if necessary, with flour shaken with cold water in a covered jar (see GRAVY for proportions).

SWISS STEAK

1 kg	thick steak for braising
75 ml	flour
2 ml	salt
	a few grains of pepper
	fat
	1 small chopped onion
500 ml	boiling water *or* canned tomatoes

1. Prepare according to basic recipe for BRAISED BEEF, adding chopped onion to liquid ingredients.
2. Cook 2 h. *Serves 4-5.*

BEEF BIRDS

1 kg	steak for braising
	flour
	seasonings
500 ml	BREAD DRESSING
500 g	mushrooms (optional)
	fat
500 ml	liquid

1. Slice meat into servings, prepare and brown according to basic recipe.
2. If long-stemmed mushrooms are used, remove stems and chop; add to dressing. Reserve caps.
3. Divide dressing evenly, placing a scoop on each serving of meat; roll and fasten securely using string or small skewers.
4. Simmer rolled meat, covered, until tender, 1.5-2 h. Add mushrooms for last hour of cooking.
   Serves 4-6.

Variations
Substitute sticks of raw carrot and chopped onion for bread dressing. Sprinkle grated Cheddar cheese over the birds during the last half-hour of cooking, or add a tin of condensed celery, cheese, or tomato soup.

BRAISED SHORT RIBS WITH VEGETABLES

1.5 kg	short ribs
50 ml	flour
5 ml	salt
	few grains of pepper
	fat
125 ml	water
	2 small onions
	4 carrots
	4 potatoes
60 ml	diced celery

1. Cut ribs into 8 to 12 pieces; brown and drain off the fat. Follow basic recipe for BRAISED BEEF beginning at step 5.
2. Simmer 2 h; add vegetables and cook 30 min more.
3. Thicken liquid for gravy. *Serves 4.*

BRAISED FLANK STEAK WITH DRESSING

1 kg	flank steak
75 ml	cooking oil
	1 clove garlic, minced
30 ml	minced onion
30 ml	minced fresh parsley
1 *l*	day-old bread crumbs
	salt, pepper
30 ml	cooking oil
45 ml	tomato paste
750 ml	beef stock

1. Steak should be trimmed of the outer skin and the fatty ends.
2. In a heavy pan or Dutch oven, heat oil and sauté garlic and onion; add parsley and crumbs.
3. Season to taste with salt and pepper.
4. Spread stuffing on the steak and sprinkle lightly with a little stock; pat stuffing firmly onto the meat.
5. Starting at the narrow end, roll as for jelly roll and tie firmly, 2 or 3 times around and once lengthwise.
6. Heat oil and brown the meat roll on all sides; remove from pan.
7. Add tomato paste and stock to pan; blend and return steak to pan.
8. Cover and braise approximately 1.5 h or until tender. Serve sliced on a deep platter with gravy spooned on top; garnish with parsley. *Serves 8-10.*

Recipes, tables, etc. that appear in small capital letters, e.g., PARSLEY BUTTER, CANADA'S FOOD GUIDE, are listed in the index. Consult the index for the number of the page on which the item appears.

Basic Recipe
COOKING MEAT IN FOIL

Aluminum foil is particularly useful in the cooking of many of the less tender cuts, as meat can be cooked in its own steam with little or no additional liquid—thus retaining all its flavour.

Tear off a length of aluminum foil, preferably heavy-duty foil, 2.5 times the length of the meat. Centre the meat on the foil, bring up the cut edges over the meat and triple fold top and sides to make a tight, leak-proof package. Be careful not to tear or puncture the foil. If desired, use a double thickness for added strength. Place package on metal cookie or cake pan and bake at about 180°C

Cooking time will be slightly less than with other methods of braising.

Variations
Add any of CHILI SAUCE, sliced onions, mushrooms, green peppers, or ½ package dehydrated onion soup to the foil package before baking.

Basic Recipe
BEEF STEW

Beef for stewing comes from the shin or shank, neck, flank, plate or chuck; some may result from trimming other cuts. All the meat in a stew should come from the same cut so that it will cook evenly. Extra vegetables plus toppings mean more servings of stew.

0.75 kg	stewing beef
100 ml	seasoned flour
	fat
	onion
	vegetable stock *or* water
75 ml	sliced celery
	10 carrots, halved
	6 potatoes, halved
	seasonings

1. Trim the fat and coarse tissue from the meat; cut into cubes.
2. Dredge at least half the meat with flour; brown slowly in a little hot fat in a heavy kettle which has a tight-fitting lid.
3. Add remaining meat, the onion and enough liquid to completely cover meat.
4. Cover and simmer meat for 1 h; add vegetables and more liquid if necessary. Cook until vegetables are tender.

5. Thicken liquid with flour shaken in a covered jar with a little cold liquid. (see GRAVY for proportions).
6. Taste and season; serve with or without a topping.

Variations

Other combinations of vegetables can be used; add when the meat is almost cooked so that they will not be overdone.

Unbrowned Stew—Omit dredging and browning meat; place in a heavy covered pan with either of the following mixtures. Follow basic recipe directions 4 and 6; no further thickening is required.

Mixture 1

500 ml	tomato juice
150 ml	quick-cooking tapioca
15 ml	sugar
	pepper, salt, basil

Mixture 2

500 ml	water
	1 pkg. dehydrated mushroom soup

HUNGARIAN GOULASH

1 kg	stewing beef
	fat
250 ml	onions
	1 clove garlic
796 ml	1 can tomatoes
250 ml	water *or* stock
	salt, pepper
2 ml	marjoram
30 ml	paprika
	a few caraway seeds
	4 sliced potatoes
	1 green pepper
125 ml	sour cream (optional)

1. Cut meat into cubes and brown slowly in fat; sauté onions and garlic only until soft.
2. Add remaining ingredients, except sour cream, and finish as BEEF STEW, thickening if necessary.
3. Stir in sour cream and heat without boiling. Serve with dumplings. *Serves 4-6.*

Toppings for Stew

PASTRY

1. Prepare pastry using ½ recipe for PASTRY, (BASIC RECIPE).
2. Roll out pastry to a thickness of 0.5 cm to fit casserole or individual serving dishes.
3. Crimp the edges and brush with milk; score in a few places to permit steam to escape.
4. Bake pastry on top of the casserole of hot stew, supported in the centre by an inverted cup, funnel or "blackbird" for 25 min or bake pastry on a baking sheet for 15 min and serve it on top of the stew. Oven temperature 220°C

DUMPLINGS

425 ml	all-purpose flour
3 ml	salt
20 ml	baking powder
60 ml	skim milk powder
75 ml	fat
160 ml	water *or* stock

1. Mix and sift the first 4 (dry) ingredients; cut in fat until mixture is the texture of meal.
2. Stir in liquid to make a sticky dough.
3. Cut out dumplings with a large measuring spoon and place on a plate which has been sprinkled with flour.
4. Simmer the unthickened stew in a saucepan with a tight-fitting lid. Meat and vegetables should not be completely covered with liquid.
5. Drop dumplings quickly onto meat or vegetables, not into the liquid. Allow space for the dumplings to double in size.
6. Cover pan and keep stew simmering without lifting the lid for 15 min.
7. Lift out dumplings onto a plate; thicken the stew and pour it into a serving dish, arrange dumplings on top. Makes 12 dumplings.

Variations

Herb Dumplings—Add enough chopped parsley, chives, or finely chopped spinach to the mixture to give an attractive appearance.

Cheese Dumplings—Slightly reduce the amount of fat required in the recipe and add twice that quantity of grated cheese.

Whole Wheat Dumplings—Substitute whole-wheat flour for part of the all-purpose flour.

Dumplings need not be restricted to meat stews—try Cheese Dumplings with VEGETABLE STEW.

BISCUIT TOPPING

1. Make dough from DUMPLINGS recipe.
2. Roll dough and shape in any of the following ways:
   (a) Roll out dough to completely cover the casserole; score with a knife in several places.
   (b) Cut out individual biscuits in rounds or diamonds.
   (c) Cut into long strips and make a lattice.
   (d) Roll out dough into a rectangle; sprinkle with poultry spice and roll up like a jelly roll; slice.
3. Arrange shaped dough on thickened stew. Bake 20-30 min at 220°C

POTATO TOPPING

1. Prepare MASHED POTATOES from 4 boiled potatoes or from instant mashed potato; leftover mashed potato can also be used. An egg or egg yolk beaten into the mashed potatoes gives a creamy colour.
2. Spread or swirl mixture over top of casserole or make a decorative topping using a pastry bag.
3. Bake until potato begins to brown at 200°C

Recipes, tables, etc. that appear in small capital letters, e.g., PARSLEY BUTTER, CANADA'S FOOD GUIDE, are listed in the index. Consult the index for the number of the page on which the item appears.

Basic Recipe
"BOILED" BEEF

Contrary to the traditional term, meat should be simmered, not "boiled." The brisket, which can be divided into the point, which is very fat, and the leaner plate end, or left in one piece and rolled, is a boneless cut suitable for cooking by this method.

1.5-2 kg	piece of brisket
	fat
	boiling water
2 ml	salt
1 ml	pepper
250 ml	chopped celery and leaves
	1 sliced onion

1. Brown the meat slowly in a little hot fat.
2. Cover with boiling water; add seasonings and vegetables and simmer until tender, about 3 h. Drain and save liquid.
3. Serve with HORSERADISH SAUCE . *Serves 4-5.*

Variations
Old Fashioned "Boiled" Dinner—About an hour before serving, add to the pot 6 quartered potatoes, 6 small whole carrots, 6 small onions, 1 small cubed turnip and a small head of cabbage cut into wedges; cook until tender. Serve meat on a platter surrounded by the vegetables; serve stock in a pitcher with the dinner.

The liquid from boiled beef can be used for soup stock or sauces.

Beef Stew. Lawry's Foods, Inc.

Basic Recipe
POT ROAST OF BEEF

A good pot roast is flavoursome, juicy, and usually economical. Blade and arm roasts from the chuck are always pot roasted; the more tender rump and cross-rib roasts should be pot roasted if they come from old animals, while dry roasting methods can be used if the meat is of red or blue quality.

1.5-2.5 kg	**pot roast**
75 ml	**flour**
1 ml	**pepper**
	fat
125 ml	**liquid**
	vegetables

1. Wipe meat with a paper towel or clean cloth; combine the flour and seasonings and rub them into the meat.
2. Heat fat in a heavy pan (a cast-iron Dutch oven is ideal for this) and brown meat on all sides. Because much of the colour and flavour of the meat depends on the browning, this step should be done carefully.
3. Transfer meat to a rack and place in pot. If a heavy iron pot is used, it may not be necessary to add liquid; otherwise add water, vegetable stock, or tomato juice, avoiding an excess which results in a loss of flavour and colour of the meat.
4. Cover and cook over low heat on top of the stove or in the oven for about 1.5 h at 150°C
5. Add vegetables: small potatoes or large ones quartered, small whole onions or large onions quartered, small whole carrots or diced carrots, green beans or peas. As the flavour of turnip is strong, it is usually cooked separately and added at serving time.
6. Continue cooking until meat and vegetables are tender, about 1 h. Season.
7. Remove meat and vegetables to a platter. If necessary thicken the gravy with flour (see GRAVY).

Variations
Wedge several cloves into an onion and cook it with the roast.

Insert a garlic clove, cut into slivers, into gashes cut in the surface of the roast.

After browning, spread meat with prepared horseradish; add the liquid and continue at step 3, basic recipe.

Add any good meat sauce to the liquid before thickening.

During the last hour of cooking add prunes which have been soaked in an equal quantity of water for 1.5 h

SOUR BEEF (SAUERBRATEN)

	pot roast of beef
500 ml	**cider vinegar**
	2 onions, sliced
	1 small bay leaf
5 ml	**cinnamon**
5 ml	**allspice**
5 ml	**cloves**
2 ml	**salt**
2 ml	**pepper**
500 ml	**water**
500 ml	**vinegar**
	gingersnaps (optional)
	sour cream (optional)

1. Place beef in a nonmetallic bowl or crock and pour over it the cider vinegar which has been combined with the onion and spices.
2. Leave in a cool place for 2 d, turning the meat every 12 h.
3. Remove meat and drain; discard the solution.
2. Place in heavy, covered pan, add vinegar and water; cover and simmer on top of stove or bake for 3 h at 150°C
5. Thicken liquid with flour and/or add a few crushed ginger snaps; stir in sour cream. *Serves 6.*

CORNED BEEF

Rolled rib or brisket is sometimes cured in a pickling solution containing salt, spices and saltpetre, and is then called Corned Beef. Good Corned Beef should have about one quarter as much fat as lean.
1. Wipe meat, place in kettle, cover with cold water.
2. Heat to boiling point, boil 5 min, remove scum.
3. Reduce heat; cook below boiling until tender, 3 to 4 h. Serve hot or cold.

If meat is to be pressed, cool slightly in the water in which it was cooked. Place in a meat press or in a bowl or crock. Cover and weight down; leave until cold.

Vegetables may be cooked with the corned beef as in BOILED DINNER.

SPICED BEEF

4 kg	rump roast of beef
280 ml	brown sugar
280 ml	salt
30 g	saltpetre
30 ml	cloves
30 ml	mace
90 ml	allspice
30 ml	black pepper

1. Mix together sugar, salt and saltpetre and rub well into meat; let stand 24 h in a cool place.
2. Combine spices and rub into meat; let stand in a crock in a cold place and turn the meat every day for 2 weeks in the liquid which forms in the crock.
3. Place meat in a large kettle and cover with water; add liquid from crock.
4. Bring to a boil. Simmer the meat for 1 h
5. Replace meat in crock; add boiling liquid. Cover the crock with blankets to hold in the heat. Cool slowly 2-3 d. Serve cold, thinly sliced. (Take chilled meat to the butcher for slicing, paper thin, on his slicer.)

Begin the preparation of Spiced Beef in late November to have it ready for holiday buffets!

Basic Recipe
ROAST BEEF

1. Note weight of meat, wipe with a damp cloth or paper towel and place fat side up on a rack in a shallow, uncovered roasting pan. If the meat is very lean, a piece of suet should be ordered with it and placed on top, or the top of the meat should be spread with a paste of equal parts (a few spoonfuls) of dry mustard, flour and dripping or other fat.
2. Insert meat thermometer and roast meat according to directions, or according to the time and temperature indicated in the table following. (Do not use thermometer in roasts that are frozen.)
3. When roast is cooked, remove the thermometer and transfer the meat to a hot platter, leaving it in a warm place or warming oven for 10 min. This will allow time for some of the juices of the meat to be reabsorbed, facilitating carving and providing time for making the gravy.

COOKING TIMES FOR ROAST BEEF

Type of Roast	min/kg at Oven Temperature of 160°C
Standing Rib Roast (with bone)	
rare	45
medium	55
well-done	70
Rolled Rib or Loin Roast (without bone)	
rare	65
medium	70
well-done	80

To cook frozen roasts, increase cooking time to 1½ times the above.

Basic Recipe
GRAVY

These quantities will produce three servings. Any amount of gravy can be made as long as the same proportions of fat, flour and liquid are used.

30 ml	dripping (fat)
30 ml	flour
100 ml	cold liquid
250 ml	hot vegetable stock *or* water seasonings

1. Remove the roast from the pan; keep it hot in a warming oven. If there is more fat in the pan than required, pour off the surplus.
2. Blend in the corresponding amount of flour; stir until smooth.
3. Remove the pan from the stove; stir in a little cold water to make a smooth paste, then stir in the measured hot liquid.
4. Return the pan to the heat; stir until the gravy thickens. The gravy should have the consistency of cream; add more liquid if necessary.
5. Season well and add a little gravy colouring if you like. When cooked as directed, a roast should provide 1 serving of gravy for each serving of meat.

Variation of Gravy

Another method, which is useful if there is little fat, is to shake flour and cold liquid together in a small covered jar and stir mixture into the hot liquid in the pan.

YORKSHIRE PUDDING

250 ml	all-purpose flour
2 ml	salt
75 ml	skim milk powder
250 ml	water *or* vegetable stock
	3 eggs
125 ml	beef dripping

1. Sift flour with salt and milk powder. Add water or stock gradually, to prevent lumping.
2. Add eggs and beat 2 min with an egg beater. Chill 20 min; preheat oven to 220°C
3. Cover the bottom of a square cake pan or individual large muffin pans with dripping; place pans in oven until fat is sizzling hot.
4. Quickly pour in batter to a little less than half-full.
5. Place pans in oven, and immediately reset temperature to 190°C
Bake large pan approximately 50 min, muffin pans 30 min, until the pudding has risen high and become crisp. Serve with the roast and gravy.

Variation

Approximately 30-40 min before the end of baking time for the roast, lift it up onto a rack over the roasting pan and pour Yorkshire Pudding batter into the pan below. This allows the roast and the Yorkshire Pudding to be ready at the same time and the pudding to absorb the meat flavour. There cannot be gravy with this method.

BARBECUED RUMP ROAST

Order from the butcher a boned rump roast and have it larded generously with salt pork. Place the meat on a spit and cook, basting frequently with BARBECUE SAUCE. If the spit is not rotated electrically, turn it often to ensure even cooking. Place a drip pan under the meat each time it is basted; remove after each use. Cook 30 min/kg
Remove meat from the heat; let stand 5 min before slicing.

BROILED STEAK

1. Preheat broiler of oven after setting rack at broiling level.
2. While broiler is heating, wipe steak with a paper towel or damp cloth, trim off superfluous fat, slash rounded edges to prevent curling.
3. If steak is very lean, coat each side with liquid fat.
4. Broil on one side, turn and broil on the other. With an electric stove, leave oven door ajar. See table of cooking times below.
5. Season. Serve sizzling hot on a heated plate with onions, mushrooms, or PARSLEY BUTTER, or consult STEAK ACCOMPANIMENTS.

COOKING TIMES FOR BROILED STEAK

Thickness	Time
2.5 cm	15-20 minutes
3.5-4 cm	20-25 minutes
5 cm	30-35 minutes

PAN-BROILED STEAK

1. Wipe meat with a damp cloth; trim off superfluous fat. Slash rounded edges to prevent curling.
2. Melt a little fat in a heavy frying pan (extra fat cut off meat can be rendered down). Heat frying pan.
3. When the pan is very hot, put in the meat and sear on one side. Reduce heat and continue cooking about 3 to 6 min, according to the degree of cooking desired.
4. Increase heat again; turn meat and sear. Continue cooking on reduced heat until done. Season with salt and pepper. Serve sizzling hot on heated plates or platter with pan gravy, mushrooms or butter mixed with lemon juice and/or chives. Consult list of STEAK ACCOMPANIMENTS. The type of pan, and the size and thickness of steak influence the length of time required to pan-broil (pan-fry) steak. To determine if steak is cooked, cut a small gash close to the bone near the end of the cooking period and note the colour of the meat.

Rare steak: interior of steak is rose in colour.
Medium steak: interior pinkish, outer brown layer deeper than for rare.
Well-done steak: brownish-gray throughout.

COOKING TIMES FOR PAN-BROILED STEAK

Thickness		Time
2.5 cm	rare	5-7 minutes
	medium	6-8 minutes
	well-done	8-10 minutes
3.5-4 cm	Add 10 minutes to times above	
5 cm	Add 20 minutes to times above	

Steak Accompaniments

Although good steak requires little embellishment, the addition of these butters and sauces can add to the occasion: FLAVOURED BUTTERS, particularly suitable those flavoured with fresh herbs or blue cheese; MAÎTRE D'HÔTEL SAUCE.

To increase tenderness of small cuts of beef, or to add extra flavour, marinate in a favourite French dressing or in a MARINADE.

BARBECUED STEAK

4-5 cm thick   porterhouse or sirloin steak

Let steak remain at room temperature for at least an hour before cooking. Trim off excess fat, then score edges at intervals. Rub with a clove of garlic and sprinkle generously with salt and pepper. Coat with BARBECUE SAUCE using a wide brush. Place steak in a 2-sided wire broiler on the grill, or on the grill directly, and cook over a very hot fire, burned down to coals. Sear quickly on one side, about a minute, turn and sear on the other side. Continue cooking about 6-8 min longer; turn and finish cooking the other side for about the same length of time. Care must be taken to avoid overcooking. Season with salt and pepper.

Recipes, tables, etc. that appear in small capital letters, e.g., PARSLEY BUTTER, CANADA'S FOOD GUIDE, are listed in the index. Consult the index for the number of the page on which the item appears.

MARINATED BEEF

Use a porcelain or glass container slightly larger than the cut of beef which is to be marinated, or large enough to hold a single layer of small pieces of beef. Prepare or purchase sufficient marinade to reach a depth equal to half the height of the meat. Marinate meat 12-24 h in the refrigerator, using the longer time for large cuts of meat. Turn meat frequently in the marinade. See MARINADES for recipes. Broil small cuts; roast large cuts.

Broiled, marinated flank steak is known as London Broil.

BEEF STROGANOFF

500 g	beef sirloin *or* tenderized steak
15 ml	flour
30 ml	fat
250 ml	thinly sliced mushrooms
125 ml	chopped onion
	1 clove garlic, crushed
30 ml	butter *or* margarine
45 ml	flour
15 ml	ketchup *or* tomato paste
300 ml	beef stock, bouillon *or* consommé
	salt, pepper
2 ml	basil
250 ml	sour cream

1. Have beef very cold to facilitate cutting into very narrow strips; dredge in flour and brown on all sides in hot fat.
2. Add mushroom slices, chopped onion and crushed garlic and cook until golden. Remove from pan.
3. Prepare a sauce from butter or margarine, the second portion of flour, ketchup and beef stock. See SAUCES, METHODS FOR MAKING.
4. Return meat and vegetables to the pan and stir in seasonings and sour cream; heat through and serve on buttered noodles. *Serves 4.*

SPEEDY BEEF STROGANOFF

Chop and cook 1 medium onion in fat until golden; push to one side of the pan. Cut 6 minute steaks into thin strips and brown quickly in fat. Add 1 can condensed cream of mushroom soup, 0.75 can of water and an equivalent amount of sour cream. Heat through; season with Worcestershire sauce and garlic salt to taste. Serve at once over noodles or rice.

SUKIYAKI

This one-pot Japanese dish is prepared from beef and vegetables; chicken may be substituted for beef to make *tori sukiyaki*. Foods to be cooked are set out in rows in alternating colours on a tray, then cooked by the stir-fry method in a wok, chafing dish, or electric frying pan. Traditionally they are cooked over an hibachi in the presence of the partakers—or each diner may cook his or her own.

500 g	tender, boneless beef steak
60 ml	fat
125 ml	beef stock
125 ml	soy sauce
	1 bunch green onions, halved, then cut into thirds lengthwise
250 ml	celery, sliced diagonally
115 g	mushrooms, sliced
30 ml	sugar
2 ml	monosodium glutamate (optional)
225 ml	1 tin bamboo shoots (optional)
113 ml	1 tin thread noodles (optional)
	2 squares bean curd (optional)
115 ml	1 tin water chestnuts (optional)
	2 bunches watercress, shredded
	or
	1 package fresh spinach, shredded
	rice

1. Chill beef in the freezer until very firm and easy to slice; cut meat across the grain into very thin slices. Cut long slices in half.
2. On a board or tray, arrange all the foods attractively in rows.
3. Heat the fat (render fat trimmed from the steak or use cooking oil) and brown meat in it; push meat to one side of pan.
4. Combine liquid ingredients (stock and soya sauce) and add half to meat.
5. Add small amounts of onion, celery and mushrooms in separate portions; cover and cook 5 min, then push to one side of the pan.
6. Add the remaining liquid, sugar, and any of the optional ingredients; cook 3 min while tossing vegetables lightly to keep them separate.
7. Add watercress or shredded spinach; cook 3 min or until wilted.
8. Serve on hot, fluffy rice. *Serves 4.*

Bamboo shoots, thread noodles, bean curd and water chestnuts can be purchased in Oriental food shops.

Steaks from chuck, blade, flank and round can be sprinkled with meat tenderizer (follow package directions), or marinated and cooked as tender steak.

BEEF FONDUE

175-225 g	tender beef per person

1. Remove any fat or bone from meat; cut into cubes, 2 cm
2. Fill fondue pot about 1/3 full of cooking oil and bring to boiling point. Adjust heat to keep oil boiling very gently. Each person spears meat with a fondue fork and cooks the meat in the oil until it is cooked to his or her liking. It is then transferred to a plate and eaten with a regular fork.
3. Serve with a variety of sauces, hot and cold. Sour cream mixed with horseradish or blue cheese makes a tangy accompaniment. Try HOT MUSTARD SAUCE, BÉARNAISE SAUCE, or GOLDEN DIP FOR VEGETABLES. Three sauces differing in flavour, texture and temperature usually suffice for one meal.

When Beef Fondue is to be a main course at dinner, serve with it baked potatoes and a green salad.

Lamb and chicken cubes can also be prepared as Fondue. See LAMB FONDUE, CHICKEN FONDUE.

Ground Beef

Ground beef and minced beef are synonymous terms for what must be the most versatile form of beef. If the word "LEAN" appears on the label there must not be more than 17% fat; if no claim is made that the meat is lean, it may contain up to 30% fat. A label stating "Minced Round Steak" may be less meaningful than one stating "Lean Minced Beef"

Individual meat loaves are attractive. Lawry's Foods, Inc.

and the round steak may be considerably more expensive. Neck, chuck and shin beef are sources of lean beef.

Because it shrinks less, lean minced beef will usually provide more servings than will non-lean minced beef; it will also cost more.

Hot canned beans can be spooned over cooked meat patties; season with chili powder or seasoned salt; or use BARBECUE SAUCE, MUSHROOM SAUCE.

After broiling, add onion rings, chopped chives, green onions, or sliced Spanish onion.

Basic Recipe
HAMBURGER PATTIES

750 g	ground beef
2 ml	salt
	few grains of pepper
30 ml	grated onion

1. Combine meat and seasonings; avoid overmixing which toughens meat.
2. Shape into patties, rounding them with the palm of the hand or flattening them between sheets of waxed paper for serving in buns.
3. Sauté in a little hot fat or broil 5-7 min on each side.
   Makes 6 patties 1 cm thick
   Makes 12 patties 0.5 cm thick

Variations

Prepare HAMBURGER PATTIES from the preceding recipe. Broil or pan-fry and place in heated hamburger buns which have been spread with any of: plain butter or FLAVOURED BUTTER or margarine, prepared mustard, ketchup, or relish. Serve hot.

Any of the following can be served in the bun with the meat patty: sliced tomato, chopped shallots, green-pepper ring, sautéed or French-fried onion rings, sautéed mushrooms, slices of cheese (cheeseburgers).

Surprises—Roll 2 or more hamburger patties thin between sheets of waxed paper; on one patty place one of the following fillings: CHILI SAUCE thickened with grated cheese, sliced green onions, grated blue cheese blended with MAYONNAISE, or prepared mustard mixed with a little Worcestershire sauce.

Place the other patty on top and press the edges together until none of the filling shows. Cook.

After broiling plain patties on one side, turn and spread with any of KETCHUP, relish, grated or sliced cheese, and broil.

Basic Recipe
MEAT BALLS

500 g	ground beef
15 ml	finely chopped onion
125 ml	fine, soft bread crumbs
	seasonings
	½ or 1 egg
15-30 ml	flour
30-50 ml	fat
625 ml	liquid*

1. Combine the meat, vegetables, crumbs, seasonings and egg; do not add salt if dehydrated soup or other salty liquid will be used in step 4.
2. Sprinkle half of the flour lightly on a cookie pan; using both hands, shape meat into balls and roll lightly in flour, using remaining flour if necessary. Balls should have a diameter of 4 cm
3. Heat fat in a deep frying pan or electric skillet and brown balls on all sides; pour off fat.
4. Prepare one of the liquid mixtures listed below; add meat balls; cover and simmer 15-20 min
   * Suitable liquids for cooking meatballs:
   canned or dehydrated cream of mushroom, celery, tomato, or cheese soup diluted or reconstituted with water to make the required amount of liquid in the recipe

   leftover beef gravy diluted with stock or water

   tomato juice, vegetable or meat stock, or bouillon made from concentrated soup base; it may be necessary to thicken these liquids at serving time

   SWEET AND SOUR SAUCE, CURRY SAUCE, (the addition of curry powder to cream celery or mushroom soup makes a quick sauce).
5. If liquid is too thin to serve for gravy, thicken by adding a little flour shaken in a covered jar with a little cold liquid; taste and adjust seasoning if necessary. Makes about 18 meat balls.

Variations

Party Meat Balls—Prepare meat balls using double the quantities in the basic recipe. Cook browned balls in liquid made from a combination of dehydrated onion soup and cream of mushroom soup plus water. Stir in sautéed, sliced mushrooms if desired; serve from a casserole or chafing dish. Garnish with pimento and coarsely chopped parsley.

Meat Balls Romanoff—Prepare Party Meat Balls. Shortly before serving, stir in a small container of sour cream.

Porcupine Meat Balls—To the ingredients add uncooked rice, 125 ml
Form into balls. Do not brown. Dilute 1 can condensed tomato soup with an equal quantity of stock or water. Simmer balls in liquid in a covered pan or bake in a covered casserole for 50 min at 180°C.

Meat Ball Stew—Prepare vegetables for BEEF STEW and cook in beef stock for 20 min; add browned meat balls and cook until meat and vegetables are tender. Thicken gravy (see GRAVY).

Veal and Pork Meat Balls—Substitute a mixture of minced veal and pork for half of the beef in the basic recipe; cook in SWEET AND SOUR SAUCE.

Lamb Meat Balls—Substitute lamb for beef; season with a little grated orange rind and ground ginger. Serve with CURRY SAUCE or SWEET AND SOUR SAUCE.

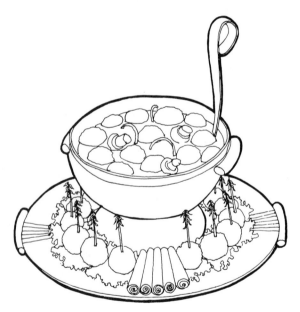

SWEDISH MEAT BALLS

30 ml	chopped onion
30 ml	bacon fat
60 ml	bread crumbs
125 ml	milk
500 g	ground beef
125 g	ground lean pork
	1 egg yolk
125 ml	cold, mashed potatoes
5 ml	salt
1 ml	pepper
	few grains each of mace, allspice, mustard and sage
5 ml	chopped parsley
30 ml	butter
250 ml	water

1. Sauté the onion in fat until golden brown.
2. Soak the crumbs in milk until soft; add the meat, onion, egg yolk, potatoes and seasoning; knead together until smooth.
3. Shape into small balls, using 2 spoons dipped in cold water.
4. Cook the meat balls in butter, shaking continually to make the balls round, until an even brown.
5. Add the water; cover and simmer 30 min. Thicken the gravy. Serve hot or cold. The water may be omitted and the meat balls served dry; in this case meat balls should be cooked for a few minutes more, after browning. Makes approximately 30-35 cocktail-size meat balls.

For a party or church supper, or for many little spontaneous supper parties during the Christmas season, prepare several pounds of meat into balls and freeze (see FREEZING MEAT). *When cooking a large quantity, cook with preheated liquid in a covered roasting pan at 180°C*
until done; transfer to serving dishes. See PARTY MEAT BALLS *for party touches.*

HAMBURGER PIE

	1 medium onion, chopped
30 ml	fat
500 g	ground beef
	salt, pepper
625 ml	cooked or canned green beans, drained
284 ml	1 tin condensed tomato soup
	5 medium potatoes, cooked
125 ml	warm milk
	1 egg, beaten
	salt, pepper

1. Brown onion in the hot fat; brown meat in the same fat; season.
2. Stir in the beans and the soup; pour into a large greased casserole.
3. Mash the potatoes; add milk, beaten egg and seasonings.
4. Arrange potatoes over meat mixture in a ring, or form into 6 mounds; bake until peaks are lightly browned, about 35 min at 180°C
   Serves 4-6.

Leftover mashed or instant mashed potatoes can be substituted for the potatoes and milk; other varieties of soup and vegetables can be used.

MEAT LOAF (BEEF LOAF)

750 g	ground beef
250 ml	bread crumbs
2 ml	salt
1 ml	pepper
	1 onion, finely chopped
2 ml	grated lemon rind
	chopped parsley
	1 beaten egg

1. Combine ingredients, mixing lightly.
2. Press into a greased loaf pan or shape into a loaf and bake on a greased pan for 1.5 h at 180°C
   For a loaf baked in a loaf pan, pour off liquid, loosen sides and bottom with spatula and turn out onto a platter.

Variations

Substitute veal or pork for 1/3 of the beef in the recipe.

Add any of: ½ chopped green pepper, 1 minced clove of garlic, 1 large grated potato *or* 3 grated carrots.

Shape mixture into 4 individual loaves and bake on a roasting pan, basting occasionally with their own juices or with tomato juice.

Substitute an equal quantity of quick-cooking rolled oats for the bread crumbs; increase the protein value and calcium by adding a few spoonfuls of skim milk powder and a little water or stock.

Serve with TOMATO SAUCE, MUSHROOM SAUCE, or any CONDENSED CREAM SOUP SAUCE.

Add a topping of mashed potatoes and/or thin slices of processed cheese to loaf; return it to the oven until cheese melts.

Meat balls with spaghetti. Lawry's Foods, Inc.

BEEF ROLL

500 g	ground beef
125 ml	chopped onion
75 ml	thinly sliced celery
75 ml	chopped green pepper
	fat
	salt, pepper
5 ml	Worcestershire sauce
	TEA BISCUIT DOUGH, 1 recipe

1. Brown the meat in a little fat; add the vegetables and sauté for 5 min. Season the mixture and cool.
2. Prepare 1 recipe of TEA BISCUIT DOUGH and roll out into a rectangle, 25 cm wide, 1 cm or less thick
3. Brush dough with melted fat and spread with the meat mixture; roll as a jelly roll and refrigerate for 15 min to facilitate slicing.
4. Slice roll into pinwheels and place pinwheels on a greased pan; bake for 30 min at 200°C
5. Serve with CHILI SAUCE, gravy, WHITE SAUCE or a CONDENSED CREAM SOUP SAUCE. *Serves 4-6.*

Variations

For the browned meat, substitute any of ground leftover roast beef or lamb moistened with gravy, or ½ can luncheon meat or 1 can tuna or salmon moistened with mayonnaise.

Recipes, tables, etc. that appear in small capital letters, e.g., PARSLEY BUTTER, CANADA'S FOOD GUIDE, are listed in the index. Consult the index for the number of the page on which the item appears.

BROWNED HASH

250 ml	minced cooked meat
500 ml	mashed potatoes
5 ml	grated onion
	salt, pepper
	1 egg
	stock, gravy *or* tomato juice
10 ml	fat
5 ml	finely chopped parsley

1. Mix meat, vegetables, seasonings and beaten egg; add enough stock to hold the mixture together.
2. Heat fat in a heavy pan; spread mixture evenly in pan.
3. Reduce heat and cook the mixture until it is evenly browned.
4. Fold as an omelet; garnish with parsley and serve with hot tomato sauce or ketchup. *Serves 2-3.*

Variations

Potato Puff—Double the quantity of ingredients required for BROWNED HASH; use canned or leftover cooked fish or cooked minced or chopped meat. Use 3 eggs and separate white from yolks. Combine all ingredients except egg whites. Beat whites and fold into mixture. Bake in a greased casserole for 40-45 min at 180°C

Shepherd's Pie—Use approximately twice the quantity of ingredients for BROWNED HASH; omit fat. Beat 1 or 2 eggs into the mashed potatoes. Add sufficient liquid to the seasoned meat to make a slightly runny mixture. Alternate layers of meat mixture with mashed potato, ending with a layer of potato. Bake at 200°C

until potatoes are browned and heated through. Garnish with a sprig of parsley. *Serves 4.*

MEAT AND VEGETABLE PIE

500-750 ml	cooked meat, diced
250 ml	cooked potato, diced
250 ml	cooked green peas, beans, carrots *or* celery
375 ml	leftover gravy
284 ml	1 can condensed cream soup
75 ml	milk
	topping

Combine meat, vegetables and liquid; heat; taste and season. Add a topping of PASTRY or BISCUIT TOPPING and bake at 200°C

until mixture is heated through and topping is cooked. *Serves 4-6.*

Basic Recipe
CROQUETTES

250 ml	very thick WHITE SAUCE, seasoned
	2 egg yolks, beaten
500 ml	chopped, ground, or flaked food*
	seasoning
	CRUMB COATING, 1 recipe

1. Blend a little of the seasoned WHITE SAUCE into the beaten egg yolks, then stir egg mixture into remaining sauce.
2. Stir the prepared food (see following list of suggested mixtures) into the sauce. Season, taste and adjust seasoning if necessary.
3. Spread mixture on a platter; cover loosely with foil or waxed paper to prevent drying. Cool.
4. Shape mixture into cones, rolls or balls; roll in crumbs, beaten egg and crumbs. Let stand 1 h.
5. Fry for 5 min in deep fat, at 190°C
   Yield: 12 medium croquettes, 4-6 servings.

*Croquette Mixtures

Turkey or Chicken—Add chicken concentrate to the sauce and include some chopped and sautéed mushrooms with the meat. Season with salt, pepper and herbs or curry powder. Serve with chicken or turkey gravy or TOMATO SAUCE and chopped parsley.

Shrimp, Lobster or Salmon—Drain canned fish; remove skin. Add any of diced and sautéed onion, mushrooms, *or* green pepper and chopped fresh tomato. Flavour with lemon juice. Serve with TARTAR SAUCE.

Ham and Cheese—Combine finely chopped cooked ham and grated old Cheddar cheese and stir into the hot sauce.

Veal, Beef or Lamb—Substitute brown meat stock or gravy for milk; season with Worcestershire sauce. Serve with TOMATO SAUCE.

For "oven-fried" croquettes, substitute BAKE-ON CRUMB COATING MIX or a commercial bake-on mix for the crumb coating and bake for 20-25 min or until golden brown, at 200°C

Serve pies at the table in individual or family-size casserole dishes with an interesting garnish. Try a topping of mashed turnip instead of potato or pastry.

STIR-FRIED MEAT AND VEGETABLES

Cut cooked chicken, pork or veal into strips and STIR FRY with a mixture of vegetables, adding meat when vegetables are nearly cooked. For additional flavour, marinate meat for 20 min (see MARINADES) before cooking.

HURRY CURRY

500 ml	diced, cooked roast lamb *or* beef
	1 large onion, chopped
	1 green pepper, chopped
75 ml	sliced celery
	1 garlic clove, crushed
45 ml	cooking oil
15 ml	curry powder
500 ml	lamb or beef gravy
or	
284 ml	1 can condensed cream soup
250 ml	stock, tomato juice, *or* water

1. Trim meat of all fat or gristle; dice or slice into strips.
2. Sauté chopped onion, green pepper, celery and garlic until soft; sprinkle curry powder over the vegetables.
3. Add gravy, omitting additional liquid if gravy is very thin, or use condensed soup diluting it with stock, juice, or water. (If gravy or soup are not available, use all stock or juice, thickened, to replace all the liquid; see THICKENING LIQUIDS.)
4. Heat meat in the liquid mixture until the meat is heated through; season and serve with hot rice. *Serves 4-6.*

Variation

For the meat, substitute fish and/or quartered hard-cooked eggs, stirring them into the hot sauce gently to prevent crumbling. Use cream soup instead of gravy.

Veal

Veal is meat from young beef animals 3 to 10 months of age. Since veal has little fat and much connective tissue, it requires long, slow cooking, Roasting, pan-frying or braising are the most suitable methods; broiling is not recommended. The flesh of veal should be a light greyish pink in colour, with a velvety texture. Fat should be firm and white. Bone should be porous and red.

The leg of veal is considered by many to be the choicest cut; loin chops are also popular. From the leg come the cutlet and the scallops, thin slices of veal which are pounded flat and used in such dishes as scaloppine of veal and Wiener Schnitzel. The shoulder of veal is more economical and is usually sold boned and rolled.

A crown roast of veal or lamb, containing an even number of ribs turned back to make a crown, can be stuffed and decorated to make a spectacular roast. It must be ordered specially, and because of the time required by the butcher for its preparation, it is expensive. Allow 2 ribs per serving.

COOKING TIMES FOR ROAST VEAL

Type of Roast	min/kg at Oven Temperature of 160°C
Leg Roast (with bone)	70
Rolled Roast (without bone)	100

When any cut of veal is roasted, a piece of fat should be placed on top to baste the meat as it cooks. Follow specific directions for ROAST BEEF.

Pot roasting is recommended for the breast of veal, which is usually stuffed, and for the heel of the round. Follow basic recipe for POT ROAST OF BEEF.

Veal Cuts for Braising and Pan-frying
To prevent small cuts of veal from drying during cooking, they should be braised (see POT ROASTING AND BRAISING) or pan-fried (see PAN-FRYING). These cuts include chops from the loin, rib, or shoulder; cutlets, which are the same cut as round steak in beef; arm and blade steaks, which are served as steaks or cutlets; and the scallops. Prepare riblets as BRAISED SHORT RIBS OF BEEF.

Recipes, tables, etc. that appear in small capital letters, e.g., PARSLEY BUTTER, CANADA'S FOOD GUIDE, are listed in the index. Consult the index for the number of the page on which the item appears.

BREADED VEAL CUTLETS

1. For cutlets buy slices from the leg, the shoulder, or the round.
2. Season pieces of veal with salt and pepper; crumb (see BREADING).
3. Brown in hot fat; reduce heat and continue cooking until tender, adding more fat if necessary.

Variations

Braised Veal Cutlet—To the browned meat add stock to half the depth of the cutlet and a dash of Worcestershire sauce. Cook below boiling point until tender, about 1 h.

Spanish Veal—Prepare as Braised Cutlet substituting for the stock CREOLE SAUCE prepared from ½ the recipe.

Smothered Veal—Prepare as Braised Cutlet substituting for the stock and Worcestershire sauce 1 can of condensed mushroom soup mixed with 0.5 can water or stock.

Devilled Veal Cutlets—Prepare as Braised Cutlet substituting a little prepared horseradish and prepared mustard for the Worcestershire sauce.

VEAL PAPRIKAS

	3 medium onions
30 ml	paprika
30 ml	fat
1 kg	arm steak *or* cutlet
500 ml	water *or* stock
45 ml	flour
250 ml	sour cream
	salt, pepper

1. Slice onions and sauté with the paprika in the fat for 10 min
2. Add meat; sauté slowly until golden brown.
3. Add stock; cover; simmer until tender, 1-1.5 h
4. Blend the flour and sour cream; when meat is almost tender stir mixture into stock slowly; heat to just below boiling point. Season to taste.
5. Serve with DUMPLINGS, noodles, or POTATO PUFFS.

SCALOPPINE OF VEAL

These slices of veal are cooked quickly, sometimes breaded, and served with lemon wedges or elegantly sauced. Allow 2 scallops per person.

750 g	veal scallops
	cooking oil
	butter (optional)

1. Purchase scallops already prepared; or place thin slices of veal cut from the leg between sheets of waxed paper and pound with a mallet or rolling pin.
2. Brush lightly with oil and brown in butter or additional oil.
3. Reduce heat and sauté gently until tender, 8-10 min, season to taste.
4. Remove to a heated platter and serve at once with lemon wedges and parsley. Fresh or broiled tomatoes complement this dish.

Variation

Scaloppine with Cheese—After cooked scallops have been transferred to a platter, melt a little butter in the pan; add an equal quantity of fine, dry bread crumbs, and of chopped parsley. Heat through and spread on meat. Sprinkle generously with grated Parmesan cheese.

VEAL CORDON BLEU

	4 veal scallops
30 ml	prepared mustard
	fines herbes
	4 thin slices cooked ham
	4 slices Swiss *or* Gruyère cheese
60 ml	seasoned flour
	1 egg, beaten
15 ml	water
60 ml	cooking oil
125 ml	bread crumbs

1. Spread scallops lightly with mustard; sprinkle each with herbs.
2. Cover scallops with a slice of ham, then a slice of cheese, trimming them if necessary to fit.
3. Roll up each, jelly-roll fashion, and secure with toothpicks.

New Zealand Spring Lamb: leg of lamb, rack of lamb, and two lamb steaks.

Meat and vegetables combine to make a tasty stew.

4. Roll in seasoned flour, dip in a mixture of beaten egg and water, then in crumbs.
5. Brown in hot oil, turning so that rolls are evenly browned on all sides; cover and cook over low heat until tender, about 20 min

Variation

Pork Cordon Bleu—Substitute for the veal, thick, butterflied pork chops. Flour and crumbs may be omitted and the *cordon bleu* browned, then pan-fried for about 35-40 min or until completely cooked.

VEAL STEW

The breast and upper shank of veal can be stewed; the neck, knuckle and lower shank can be cooked in a large quantity of water to make jelly. Follow the basic recipe for BEEF STEW; if stew of a light colour is desired, omit the dredging and browning process.

JELLIED VEAL

	1 veal shank *or* neck
3 ℓ	water
2 ml	pepper
5 ml	salt
	1 slice lemon
	1 large onion
	celery leaves *or* BOUQUET GARNI
	1 small bunch parsley
	1 bay leaf
5 ml/250 ml of liquid	gelatine
	garnishes

1. Cover the meat, including the skin and bone, with cold water; add remaining ingredients except gelatine; bring to a boil and skim.
2. Simmer about 2 h until the liquid is reduced to 1/3 the amount and the meat is tender.
3. Drain off and measure the stock, clarify if desired (see TO CLEAR SOUP STOCK), stir in the gelatine, season and chill; skim off the fat.
4. Remove skin and bones from the meat; shred or chop meat and add to chilled stock.
5. Prepare decoration (see GELATINE MOULDS—GENERAL DIRECTIONS); refrigerate jelly until set; unmould.

Variations

Chicken, or chicken and veal combined, may be jellied in the same way. Pork hocks and veal shanks make another good combination.

The meat may be left in larger pieces and placed in the mould with just enough chilled stock to begin to float the meat; place a plate with a weight on top to press the meat firmly. Chill; unmould.

Substitute seasoned salt for the seasoning; add it to the prepared stock.

OSSO BUCCO

Choose thick, meaty bones for this hearty and economical Italian dish.

	4 shank bones of veal cut into
8 cm long	pieces
	four
	salt, pepper
	oil
400 ml	water *or* stock
	1 clove, garlic, crushed
	2 onions, chopped
400 ml	chopped tomatoes (canned or fresh)
5 ml	basil
45 ml	parsley chopped

1. Roll pieces of shank in seasoned flour and heat in fat until evenly browned; cool slightly.
2. Add water or stock and bring to a boil; simmer, covered for about 20 min
3. Add garlic, onions, tomatoes and basil; cover and continue simmering until the meat is very tender, about 1.5-2 h
4. Remove the meat to a platter and simmer the liquid to thicken; taste and adjust seasoning if necessary.
5. Stir in parsley and heat through; pour over the meat. Serve with RISOTTO. *Serves 4.*

Recipes, tables, etc. that appear in small capital letters, e.g., PARSLEY BUTTER, CANADA'S FOOD GUIDE, are listed in the index. Consult the index for the number of the page on which the item appears.

Lamb

Canadian lamb is most plentiful and reasonably priced from September to December. Spring lamb refers to meat from any lamb 3 to 5 months of age, but lamb can be meat from animals up to 14 months. The colour of the lean meat in lamb varies from light to dark pink. Mutton, which is meat from animals over 14 months of age, is light to dark red. The fat is slightly pink in very young animals, becoming creamy, then finally white and brittle.

Since lamb is a young animal, all the cuts are tender and only the shank, neck and breast need long cooking. Lamb should be served either very hot or very cold on plates of the same temperature. The "fell," a thin, papery covering on the lamb carcass, is removed from steaks and chops but is usually left on the leg.

Lamb is not generally sold to consumers by grade except in the province of Saskatchewan, where it is stamped with the grades "Canada Choice," "Canada Good," "Canada Commercial," or "Canada Utility." Most Canadian lamb comes from Ontario, Alberta, Saskatchewan and Quebec; much is imported from New Zealand and Australia.

The delicate yet distinct flavour of lamb lends itself to simple treatment. More elaborate preparation produces dishes which reflect varied cultural backgrounds.

Lamb Cuts for Roasting

Cuts suitable for roasting are: leg roasts with a large proportion of meat to bone; the loin, with the backbone cut to facilitate carving; and the shoulder which is boned and rolled, or boned and stuffed, to form a cushion-like roast. A crown roast, which must be ordered specially, is expensive because of its size (a large section from the ribs or rack) and because of the time required by the butcher to shape it.

ROASTING TIMES FOR LAMB

Type of Roast	min/kg at Oven Temperature of 160°C
Leg, whole	65
Leg, half	85
Shoulder	65
Loin	55

ROAST LEG OF LAMB

1. Remove thick skin and wipe meat. Note mass.
2. Place on rack in roasting pan, season with slivers of garlic inserted in the flesh, or herbs (mint, basil), salt and pepper.
3. Roast according to preceding table.
4. Serve with BROWN SAUCE, MINT SAUCE, or CURRANT JELLY.

Variations

Rolled Leg of Lamb—Bone lamb, insert cloves of garlic or sprigs of mint, roll and tie; or provide the butcher with the garlic or mint and have him do the job; roast according to general directions.

Marinated Lamb—Marinate leg of lamb for 24 h at a cool temperature (see MARINADES), turning it often. Roast; heat marinade and serve it with meat.

GRILLED (BARBECUED) LEG OF LAMB IN FOIL

This is an ideal roast for a barbecue dinner.

Trim off all fat from a whole or half leg of lamb which has had the shank bone removed. Rub meat all over with a cut clove of garlic, then with lightly seasoned flour. Place meat in the centre of a large sheet of heavy aluminum foil and brush generously with soy sauce *or* with a mixture of bottled thick meat sauce, ketchup or chopped fresh mint. Wrap and seal meat carefully, using triple folds on all edges. Roast on the grill set at the maximum distance from the glowing coals, using the approximate times given in the ROASTING TIMES FOR LAMB table.

Slit foil and pour off the juice into a pitcher; remove meat. Let stand in a warm place for 5 min before carving. Serve with the hot juices.

Lamb Cuts for Broiling and Pan-broiling

Lamb chops (loin, rib and shoulder) can be broiled, pan-broiled or pan-fried, and baked. Loin chops contain the tenderloin. English chops are double loin chops, boned and rolled; sometimes the kidney is rolled in; these elegant cuts are expensive. Rib chops, although very tasty, contain little meat in proportion to bone. The end of the rib bone may be cleaned back and a paper frill applied to it after cooking; so attired, the chop is called a French Chop. Shoulder chops are sometimes braised, particularly if they are from older animals.

BROILED LAMB CHOPS

This is an ideal method for cooking thick chops.

2-4 cm thick   lamb chops

1. Trim chops; wipe with a damp cloth or paper towel; slash edges to prevent curling. For added flavour, marinate chops or brush with French dressing before broiling, or rub surface with a cut clove of garlic or ground ginger.
2. Broil chops approximately 6-7 min per side; if chops are very thick, increase broiling time to 9-11 min per side. Serve with large, broiled mushroom caps; garnish with watercress.

ROAST BREAST OF LAMB

This less-expensive cut can make a tasty roast if not too fat. Because it contains many bones, allow per person 500 g

2-2.5 kg	**breast of lamb**
500 ml	BREAD DRESSING
	flour
	seasoning
125 ml	**water** *or* **stock**

1. Remove bones from meat, wipe, season and cover with dressing.
2. Roll up and tie firmly; dredge with flour.
3. Place in roasting pan; add water or stock; cover and roast for 2 h, removing cover during the last half hour to brown meat, at 180°C
   Diced vegetables can be added during the last half-hour of cooking.

STUFFED LAMB CHOPS

3 cm thick	**6 lamb chops**
250 ml	BREAD DRESSING
	salt, pepper

1. Trim chops; wipe with a damp cloth or paper towel.
2. Split the lean meat to the bone to make a pocket.
3. Place dressing in pocket, press to close and fasten with toothpick; season.
4. Pan-broil or bake for approximately 1 h, turning once during cooking, at 180°C
   Serves 4-6.

Lamb Cuts for Braising and Stewing
Meat from the shank and neck should be braised, or cubed and used for stewing meat. Boned meat from the breast of lamb can make an economical pot roast if not too fat.

Shoulder lamb chops may be braised.

Riblets are stewed, after which they are sometimes glazed.

Any of these cuts can be simmered in a large quantity of water to make soup.

BRAISED LAMB CHOPS

1 kg	**6 shoulder chops**
	fat
30 ml	**flour**
	salt, pepper
15 ml	**Worcestershire sauce**
250 ml	**meat stock** *or* **milk**

1. Brown chops slowly in hot fat; remove from pan and drain off excess fat.
2. Blend flour and seasonings in the pan until brown.
3. Add Worcestershire sauce and liquid; stir until thick.
4. Simmer chops in the gravy, covered, over low heat or bake in a preheated oven for about 30 min at 180°C
   Serves 4-6.

Variation
Stir sautéed mushrooms and/or a few spoonfuls of sour cream into the gravy after the chops are cooked.

Devilled Neck Slices—Substitute an equal weight of neck slices for shoulder chops and proceed as for BRAISED LAMB CHOPS using twice the quantity of meat stock and substituting vinegar for Worcestershire sauce. Add 1 chopped onion and season with a little mustard. Simmer until tender for about 1 h. Thicken the stock for gravy (see THICKENING LIQUIDS).

Recipes, tables, etc. that appear in small capital letters, e.g., PARSLEY BUTTER, CANADA'S FOOD GUIDE, are listed in the index. Consult the index for the number of the page on which the item appears.

IRISH STEW

500-750 g	lean lamb, cubed
	salt, pepper
	12 small new potatoes, scraped
	12 small new carrots
	12 small new onions
125 ml	green peas
	1 sprig mint
15 ml	chopped parsley

1. Simmer meat in water to cover, in a pan with lid, until almost tender, about 1 h
2. Skim off any fat; add vegetables except parsley, and add more water if necessary.
3. Simmer again until potatoes are tender, about 30 min; remove the mint.
4. Thicken the stock slightly (see THICKENING LIQUIDS); sprinkle with parsley. *Serves 4-6.*

MEAT EN BROCHETTES (SHISH KABOBS)

Lamb or veal leg slices; beef tenderloin, sirloin or tenderized steak; pork (which must be well-cooked); chicken liver; and parboiled sweetbreads are suitable meats; oysters, shrimps and scallops can also be used. Meat and shrimps are usually marinated. Allow for each skewer this quantity of meat:

150 g cut in 2.5 cm cubes

Other ingredients are mushroom caps, bacon or salt pork squares, strips of bacon, tiny onions, tomatoes, cubed pineapple, olives, squares of green pepper.

1. Alternate these ingredients on firm skewers, in any desired combination with the meat; it is best to combine foods which require approximately the same cooking time.
2. Brush with melted butter or BARBECUE SAUCE if not previously marinated. Broil approximately 10 min, turning often. Serve on a bed of fluffy rice; removing the skewer carefully so that the pieces stay in the same order. For outdoor serving, the skewer may be left in.

MARINADE FOR LAMB

1 part wine vinegar *or* lemon juice
2 parts cooking oil
chopped parsley
sprinkling of marjoram *or* oregano and thyme

See also MARINADES.

LAMB FONDUE

Prepare cubes of lamb as for Brochettes; marinate several hours. Cook and serve as BEEF FONDUE using any of the sauces suggested, or RED PEPPER JELLY.

Curry powder, a blend of many exotic spices, transforms a simple mixture into an elegant dish—a curry. At home in India, curries are served "red" hot. For Western tastes, a lighter hand with the spices plus frequent tasting while seasoning is advised. Curries are served with rice and any number of accompaniments (sambals): small dishes of foods, crisp, sweet, hot and tart. Each person adds a spoonful or more of any of the sambals according to his own preference.

CURRIED LAMB

	10 small white onions
45 ml	cooking oil
	1 or 2 garlic cloves, crushed
	salt, pepper
2 ml	marjoram *or* thyme
50 ml	flour
1.5 kg	lamb, cubed
540 ml	1 can tomato juice
500 ml	celery, coarsely sliced diagonally
10 ml	curry powder
2 ml	ginger
5 ml	Worcestershire sauce
	2 green peppers
30 ml	lemon juice
10 ml	lemon rind
125 ml	raisins

1. Sauté onions in oil in a Dutch oven or heavy frying pan until lightly browned; remove from pan. Repeat using garlic.
2. Combine seasonings, herb and flour; dredge lamb cubes in the mixture.
3. Brown cubes, a few at a time in the frying pan, adding a little more oil to pan as needed.
4. Add tomato juice, celery, curry powder (adjust quantity according to preference), ginger and Worcestershire sauce.
5. Cover and cook slowly until lamb is tender, about 1-1.5 h
6. Slice green pepper into thin strips and add with browned onions and garlic to lamb.
7. Add lemon juice, rind and raisins; cover and cook until all is tender, about 25 min
8. Adjust seasoning, if necessary; serve with hot rice. *Serves 6-8.*

SAMBALS

The choice of sambals is usually influenced by the tone of the curry. Very hot curries are complemented by sambals which are mild in flavour, while a more pungent array of sambals often accompanies a milder curry. Choose 3 or more from the following, considering contrasts of flavours, colours and textures.

Mild or Sweet

banana slices sprinkled
  with lemon juice
avocado slices
  sprinkled with
  lemon juice
chopped hard-cooked
  egg
shredded coconut,
  plain or toasted
crisp, crumbled bacon
peeled, chopped
  cucumber
chopped tomato
chopped green pepper
chopped peanuts,
  almonds or cashews

raisins, plumped in
  water or fruit juice
drained Mandarin
  orange sections
drained pineapple
  cubes
sweet pepper jelly or
  relish

Hot or Sharp

chutney
preserved kumquats
hot pepper relish
chopped preserved
  ginger
sliced green onions
chili pepper seeds
  (very hot)

LAMB RIBLETS

4.5 kg	lamb riblets
	½ lemon, sliced
	1 onion, sliced
	celery leaves
375 ml	BARBECUE SAUCE

1. Cover riblets with water, add lemon, onion and celery leaves; cook until riblets are tender, about 45 min
2. Lift out riblets; save liquid for stock.
3. Broil or bake at 180°C
   for 10 min, then spread with barbecue sauce and cook 10 min more; turn and repeat on other side.
4. Continue cooking until the riblets are glazed and brown. Cut into servings; serve with rice and a green vegetable. *Serves 6-8.*

Recipes, tables, etc. that appear in small capital letters, e.g., PARSLEY BUTTER, CANADA'S FOOD GUIDE, are listed in the index. Consult the index for the number of the page on which the item appears.

MOUSSAKA

Traditionally, lamb is used in this Greek casserole, but lean ground beef or pork may be substituted. Leftover lamb, minced, can also be used.

	2 medium eggplants
	salt
	flour
	oil
250 ml	chopped onions
500 g	ground lamb
30 ml	tomato paste
75 ml	water
50 ml	chopped parsley
	salt, pepper
	cinnamon
500 ml	thin WHITE SAUCE
	2 beaten eggs
250 ml	cottage cheese
	nutmeg
125 ml	fine dry bread crumbs
125 ml	grated Parmesan cheese

1. Peel eggplants and cut into thick slices; dust with salt and let stand 15 min; drain; dust with flour.
2. Brown slices quickly in hot fat; set aside.
3. Brown onions in the same pan adding more oil if needed; lift out onions and brown meat in fat, increasing the heat if necessary.
4. Combine the tomato paste, water, parsley, seasoning and a sprinkle of cinnamon and stir into the meat.
5. Add the onions and simmer over low heat until all the liquid has been absorbed; remove from the heat.
6. Prepare WHITE SAUCE, cool slightly; beat eggs, add cottage cheese and a little nutmeg and stir into the sauce.
7. Oil a rectangular baking pan or casserole and sprinkle with crumbs; arrange alternate layers of eggplant and meat, sprinkling each layer with crumbs and Parmesan cheese.
8. Pour the cheese sauce over the top; bake until top is golden, 40-50 min, at 180°C
9. Cool for 10 min; cut in squares and serve with sour cream. *Serves 6.*

A Mixed Grill can be made up of broiled lamb chop with a mushroom cap on it, 2 or 3 small pork sausages, 1 or 2 strips of bacon and a broiled tomato slice. Sometimes a lamb kidney is included.

Pork

Pork is meat from pigs usually butchered at 5 to 7 months old. It is available fresh, cured (pickled), smoked, and canned. It is also processed (often in combination with other meats) as sausage and ready-to-serve meats.

The development, care and feeding of hogs bred especially for quality pork has produced pork high in protein content and low in fat. This meat is more nutritious and more easily digested than fat pork.

When freezing pork products, consult the chart MAXIMUM MEAT STORAGE TIME for storage times; the freezer life of pork products is less than that for other meats.

Fresh pork is tender enough that all the suitable cuts may be roasted; chops and steaks are better pan-fried or braised to prevent drying out while being thoroughly cooked.

Fresh pork should never be served unless it is well cooked. The cooked meat and its juices should not be pink.

For roasted pork, a lower internal temperature as registered on a meat thermometer when the meat is taken from the oven is now recommended. The meat will be thoroughly cooked at the lower temperatures with less shrinkage; additional cooking will produce a drier roast and greater shrinkage. Recommended internal temperatures for cooked pork are: 80-85°C

Tender cuts may be breaded to maintain moisture while they are being cooked. Ontario Pork Producers Marketing Board.

Fresh Pork Cuts for Roasting

Loin Roasts—To facilitate carving, ask the butcher to saw across rib bones, just separating them from the backbone; do not remove the backbone.

Tenderloin is very tender; little waste but expensive.

Fresh Leg can be purchased as a butt end roast, shank end roast, or middle cut roast which has least bone.

Shoulder Roasts are divided into Picnic Shoulder and the more desirable Butt; the Arm Roast, which is part of the Picnic, is less tender.

Ribs include the meaty but short back ribs; and the spare (side) ribs which are longer, less meaty, and less expensive.

ROAST LOIN OF PORK

1.5-2.5 kg   pork loin roast
seasonings

1. Preheat oven to 160°C
2. Note size of roast and determine the approximate roasting time. Roast 40 min/500 g
   If desired, insert a meat thermometer. Roast is done when thermometer registers 80-85°C
3. Place meat fat-side-up in a pan; a rack is not essential as this roast provides its own "rack."
4. Season, and roast as indicated. *Serves 4-6.*

Variations
Bake peeled onions and halved, peeled potatoes around roast during the last 45 min of cooking time.

Pineapple-glazed Roast Loin of Pork—A spectacular roast cooked outdoors on the barbecue spit or indoors in the oven.

540 ml	1 can pineapple slices
200 ml	and juice
15 ml	cornstarch
50 ml	CHILI SAUCE
or	
125 ml	puréed apricots (baby food) and sprinkle of ginger

1. Blend pineapple syrup and cornstarch; stir in CHILI SAUCE or apricots. Season apricots with a sprinkle of ginger.
2. Prepare meat for roasting or barbecuing and brush with glaze every 20 min, cooking meat according to directions in preceding recipe.
3. Just before serving, cut into but not through the top of the roast at regular intervals and place a pineapple slice in each pocket.
4. Serve from a platter decorated with parsley.

ROAST FRESH LEG OF PORK

2.5-3 kg **leg of fresh pork (with skin on)**
salt, pepper
thyme, oregano, *or* **rosemary**

1. Preheat oven to 160°C
2. Wipe pork with a damp cloth and score (slash) the skin at intervals in parallel lines, crossing the lines to make diamond shapes.
3. Rub surface with salt and pepper and desired herb; roast on a rack, about 40 min/500 g
4. Serve with apple rings, applesauce, applesauce flavoured with horseradish, pickled crabapples, or currant jelly. *Serves 4-6.*

ROAST SUCKLING PIG

4.5-5.5 kg suckling pig

Order a suckling pig; the butcher will eviscerate it and remove the eyes.
1. Preheat oven to 160°C
2. Wash pig thoroughly with salted water; rinse. Sprinkle inside with more salt and rub with half a lemon. Pack firmly with BREAD DRESSING flavoured with rosemary. Tie the legs in a forward bend position so that the roast will sit well. Prop mouth open with a ball of tightly rolled foil.
3. Place pig on racks or foil in a roasting pan; bake 3-4 h, brushing frequently with a basting sauce (use MARINADE FOR LAMB). Prick any blisters that form on the surface of the skin.
4. Remove pig to a large platter; remove strings and ball of foil. Put a red apple in mouth and encircle neck with cranberries, strung into a decorative necklace; place cranberry in each eye. Tuck parsley around the base of the pig and garnish with red pickled crabapples. *Serves 8.*

BAKED STUFFED SPARE RIBS

1.5 kg **spare ribs**
salt, pepper
50 ml **water**
½ recipe ORANGE DRESSING

1. Sprinkle the bony side of each strip of ribs with salt and pepper and broil until browned.
2. Remove from the oven and pour off any fat.
3. Mix dressing with water.
4. Lay one strip of ribs in roasting pan, browned side up, and spread the dressing and water mix-

ture over it. Cover with remaining strip, browned side down.
5. Adjust racks and reset oven to 200°C
6. Bake for 30 min; reduce temperature and continue baking until ribs are tender, about 1 h longer, at 160°C
7. To serve, cut through the 2 sections of ribs so that each serving will be a "sandwich" of ribs and dressing. *Serves 3-4.*

BAKED STUFFED TENDERLOIN

2 large, whole tenderloins
250 ml BREAD DRESSING
salt, pepper
flour
15 ml **butter** *or* **cooking oil**
or
3 bacon strips

1. Preheat oven to 160°C
2. Trim and wipe tenderloins; split lengthwise almost through, open out and flatten to about half the thickness.
3. Prepare BREAD DRESSING; sprinkle one tenderloin with salt and pepper and spread dressing over it.
4. Place other tenderloin over this; tie securely or skewer the edges.
5. Season with salt and pepper; dredge with flour.
6. Place on a rack in a baking pan; cover with strips of bacon or fat pork, or baste from time to time with hot water to which a little oil has been added.
7. Bake about 1 h; serve with red currant jelly or apple rings and garnish with parsley. *Serves 4-5.*

BAKED STUFFED PORK CHOPS

2-3 cm thick **rib chops**
BREAD DRESSING

1. Slit each chop so it may be filled with dressing; stuff dressing evenly into pocket and close with wooden toothpicks or small skewers, or by sewing with coarse thread.
2. Finish as Stuffed Tenderloin in preceding recipe.

Variations
Any of diced apple, kernel corn, and chopped celery are good additions to the dressing.

Recipes, tables, etc. that appear in small capital letters, e.g., PARSLEY BUTTER, CANADA'S FOOD GUIDE, are listed in the index. Consult the index for the number of the page on which the item appears.

BARBECUED SPARE RIBS

500 g   ribs per serving

For the many versions of barbecued spare ribs, ribs can first be parboiled (keep the liquid for meat stock) or baked to remove some of the fat which can be poured off. Cooking can be completed in the oven or on a barbecue with frequent basting with any good basting sauce.

MARINATED SPARE RIBS

2.5 kg   spare ribs
500 ml   MARINADE

1. Marinate ribs for at least an hour in marinade.
2. Grill ribs on a barbecue; bake about 1-1.5 h at 160°C

Pork Cuts for Braising and Pan-frying
Braising or pan-frying ensures thorough cooking without drying out these small cuts:
Tenderloin
Chops: Loin—choice chops; centre chops contain some tenderloin.
        Rib—more bone than loin chops, but good flavour.
        Shoulder—more economical but less tender.
        Arm and blade shoulder chops are the least tender and the cheapest.
Leg: Slices from the leg are more expensive than chops but have less waste.
Pork Hocks are best braised.

PAN-FRIED PORK TENDERLOIN

1. Trim and wipe Frenched tenderloin; dredge slices in seasoned flour.
2. Brown on both sides in an oiled frying pan; reduce heat and cook thoroughly.

Variations
Cook a slice of peeled and cored apple with each slice of meat; season with marjoram or basil.

Add a small quantity of one of the LIQUIDS FOR BRAISING PORK CHOPS.

To French tenderloin, cut each whole tenderloin into 6-8 crosswise slices; flatten slices with the flat side of a cleaver.

Basic Recipe
BRAISED PORK CHOPS

The use of a cover on the pan and/or the addition of liquid or liquid-producing foods converts a baked or pan-fried chop to a braised chop.
1. Trim off any excess fat and rub it over a hot pan; or add a little oil to the pan and heat.
2. Brown meat on both sides; reduce heat, cover and cook slowly. If necessary pour off any accumulated fat.
3. Liquid may be added to the pan to a depth equal to that of the chops. See list of suitable liquids which follows.
4. Cover and cook slowly on top of the stove or in the oven until meat is tender; thicken liquid if necessary (see THICKENING LIQUIDS) before serving.

Liquids for Braising Pork Chops

Water, vegetable or meat stock, alone or combined.

Tomato sauce, canned tomatoes or juice; diluted tomato soup, paste, or ketchup.

Mushroom soup diluted with half the quantity of water or stock.

Consommé, bouillon, or meat stock and sliced onions; during the last 10 min of cooking stir in some sour cream blended with enough flour to thicken the mixture.

Fruit juices such as pineapple, apple, or orange; juice from canned peaches or apricots diluted with water; serve with the heated fruit.

Variations
Sweet and Sour Pork Chops—Braise chops in any of the preceding liquids; add ½ recipe SWEET AND SOUR SAUCE and cook 10 min longer.
Pork Chops au Gratin—Sauté onion rings and green pepper strips with the chops. Add equal quantities of stock and tomato juice; braise in oven at 200°C
When meat is almost tender, remove cover to let liquid evaporate. Add a topping of buttered crumbs; sprinkle with grated Parmesan cheese and bake for 15 min

Baked pork chops with onion rings in sauce with pieces of raw apple. Lawry's Foods, Inc.

FRIED OR BAKED PORK CHOPS

1. Trim off any excess fat and rub it over a hot pan, or add a little oil to the pan and heat it.
2. Brown meat on both sides; reduce heat and continue cooking on top of the stove or in the oven at 180°C
   Pour off accumulated fat as necessary.
3. Pork chops are cooked when flesh and juices are no longer pink when the meat is tested with the point of a knife.

PORK STRIPS WITH VEGETABLES

500-750 g	pork blade or chops
1 cm wide	cut to strips
30 ml	oil
375 ml	stock *or* water
10 ml	soy sauce
375 ml	celery, diagonally sliced
	½ green pepper, cut into strips
	½ sweet red pepper or pimento cut into strips
125-250 ml	mushrooms, fresh or canned
125 ml	fresh or frozen peas *or* green beans
	5 water chestnuts, drained and sliced
30 ml	cornstarch
30 ml	water
	10 almonds

1. Brown meat lightly in hot fat; cover tightly and cook for 15 min
2. Heat stock; add half to the meat; simmer meat until tender.
3. Bring the raw vegetables to the boiling point in the remaining stock and cook until tender but slightly crisp, about 5 min
4. Combine meat and all the vegetables and heat; thicken the liquid with a paste made by combining the cornstarch and water, stirring constantly.
5. Add almonds and cook over low heat until mixture is thick and glossy; serve with rice or noodles. *Serves 4.*

This recipe may be stir-fried (see STIR-FRYING). Pork must be thoroughly cooked before adding vegetables; use only half the quantity of stock and add it to the pork after browning. Thicken if necessary, adjusting the amount of cornstarch accordingly.

Variations
Pork Strips with Cucumbers—Marinate pork for 30 min (see MARINADES.) Heat a garlic clove in the fat; discard clove and brown meat in the fat. Remove meat. Sauté 1 sliced onion until golden; add to meat. Peel 2 cucumbers and slice each into 7 or 8 diagonal slices; substitute for the vegetables in the preceding recipe. Add all the hot liquid to the cucumbers and proceed from step 3.

SWEET AND SOUR PORK

750 g 3 cm cubes	boneless lean pork, cubed
	2 eggs
45 ml	flour
2 ml	salt
1 ml	pepper
45 ml	oil
	3 green peppers, cut into 3 cm squares
250 ml	celery, diagonally sliced
500 ml	water
250 ml	pineapple chunks
60 ml	cornstarch
90 ml	sugar
60 ml	soy sauce
90 ml	vinegar
200 ml	pineapple juice

1. Coat pork in a mixture of beaten eggs and seasoned flour.
2. Brown meat on all sides in hot oil in a frying pan; cover and cook slowly for about 30 min, adding vegetables to the pork during the last 15 min
3. Add pineapple; cover and simmer 5 min
4. Combine cornstarch, sugar, soy sauce, vinegar and juice; cook and stir the sauce until clear, about 3 min
5. Pour sauce over the meat mixture and simmer 5 min. Serve hot over noodles or rice. *Serves 4-6.*

For a speedy sweet and sour pork, arrange slices of cold roast pork and sliced cooked or canned sweet potatoes in a shallow pan. Pour SWEET AND SOUR SAUCE over them. Broil 5-10 min

COUNTRY STYLE PORK HOCKS

Pork hocks are a meaty, inexpensive cut from the pork leg, just above the foot. They are usually stewed in liquid, with vegetables added toward the end of the cooking period. High in gelatine content, they can be substituted for veal to make jellied meat (see JELLIED VEAL).

2.5 kg	4-6 pork hocks
1 *l*	apple juice
625 ml	sliced onions
60 ml	oil
5 ml	sugar
	salt, pepper
1 *l*	diced yellow turnip *or* sauerkraut
	1 bay leaf

1. Place hocks in a single layer in a roasting pan; add juice and cover. If pan does not have a cover, use foil.
2. Braise in oven, with occasional basting, until tender, about 1.5 h at 180°C
3. Heat oil in a frying pan and sauté onions until golden; add sugar, salt and pepper; set aside.
4. Remove hocks from oven; pour off as much fat as possible. Add onions, bay leaf and turnip or sauerkraut.
5. Return to oven, covered if turnips are used, uncovered if sauerkraut is used; bake 30 min, or until tender.
6. Taste and season as desired; serve hocks and vegetables together on a heated platter. *Serves 4-6.*

Recipes Using Minced Raw Pork

Substitute pork for all or part of the beef in MEAT BALLS (BASIC RECIPE) or combine with other meats in VEAL AND PORK MEAT BALLS. Substitute pork for some of the meat in MEAT LOAF; see also HAM LOAF.

TOURTIÈRE (PORK PIE)

500 g	minced lean pork
500 g	ground veal
	2 onions chopped
	1 small clove garlic, minced
2 ml	salt
2 ml	pepper
2 ml	celery salt
5 ml	savory
1-2 ml	ground cloves
250 ml	water
125-250 ml	fine, soft bread crumbs
	PASTRY, double the recipe

1. In a large saucepan, combine all the ingredients except bread crumbs and pastry, and bring mixture to the boiling point.
2. Cook uncovered on low heat with frequent stirring for 30 min to break up the meat.
3. Add the lesser quantity of crumbs and if after 10 min most of the liquid fat has been absorbed, add no more. If necessary, add more crumbs in a similar manner; cool.
4. Fill 2 large or 8 individual pastry-lined pie pans with meat mixture; add top layer of pastry, cut to let the steam escape, and seal edges.
5. Bake until the top is a golden brown, about 30-40 min at 200°C

Makes 2 pies, diameter: 23 cm

Cured Pork

Pork may be cured (pickled), then smoked, or it may be cured and not smoked. Modern processing methods have removed the need for soaking cured pork and have reduced the cooking time needed. Much cured pork is sold already cooked.

All cured pork must be refrigerated. Because it loses flavour rapidly during freezing, storage in the freezer should be for short periods only; see MAXIMUM MEAT STORAGE TIME.

TIMETABLE FOR BAKING UNCOOKED HAM AT 160°C   325°F

Type of Ham	Mass kg	Time h
Bone in:		
Whole Ham	4	2-1/3—2-2/3
Whole Ham	6	3½
Whole Ham	8	4
Half Ham	3	2½
Picnic		
Shoulder	3	3
Boneless:		
Whole Ham	6	3½-4
Half Ham	3	2¼-2½
Cottage Roll	2	1-1/3-1½

TIMETABLE FOR BAKING PRE-COOKED HAM

Fully cooked or ready-to-serve hams have had the rind removed. To serve hot, follow the method for GLAZED BAKED HAM, reducing the cooking time slightly; see table following:

Type of Ham	min/kg at 160°C
Whole Ham, fully cooked	30
Half Ham, fully cooked	35-45
Picnic, fully cooked	50-60

Follow specific directions for cooking hams if they are provided on the label—especially for tenderized hams which may have been partially cooked.

Cuts of Cured Pork for Roasting

Whole Ham, Bone In, uncooked or cooked.
Whole or Half Ham, Boneless, uncooked or cooked
Ham sections: Shank and Butt Ends
              Centre Pieces
              Ham Steaks
Picnic Shoulder, bone in or boneless
Smoked Butt or Cottage Roll, boneless
Back Bacon

GLAZED BAKED HAM

This method is for mild, high-grade commercially cured hams which must be cooked before serving.
1. Scrub skin of the ham in cold water; place ham, fat side up, on a rack in a pan in a preheated oven, 160°C
2. Bake to the desired degree of doneness, using a meat thermometer or consult the TIMETABLE FOR BAKING UNCOOKED HAM.
3. Remove ham from oven; remove rind by loosening it with a sharp knife while pulling it gently up from the ham; pour off liquid fat.
4. If desired, the fatty surface of the ham can be scored (slashed) to form a diamond design; avoid cutting too deeply as cuts will open in the oven. Whole cloves can be centred in each diamond.
5. Spread a glazing mixture over the fatty surface, using any of the HAM GLAZES.
6. Return ham to the oven to brown and glaze, at 200°C
Garnish.

Save the hambone for making PEA SOUP or BAKED BEANS.

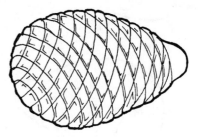

Ham Glazes

For each of the recipes that follow, blend the ingredients and apply to the fatty surface of hot, cooked ham. If desired, ham skin may be scored before applying the glaze.

ORANGE OR APRICOT GLAZE

125 ml	brown sugar
5 ml	dry mustard
5 ml	dry horseradish
	or
15 ml	prepared horseradish
75 ml	apricot jam *or* orange marmalade

JELLY GLAZE

200-250 ml	cranberry or red currant jelly
15 ml	orange juice

GINGER GLAZE

4 ml	ground ginger
5 ml	dry mustard
250 ml	brown sugar
30 ml	syrup from canned peaches or pears, *or* vinegar

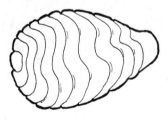

HAM GARNISHES

Garnishes can be simple—large sprigs of parsley or watercress on the platter at the base of the ham—or elaborate arrangements of fruit—pineapple slices, orange sections, peach halves, glazed apple rings accented with maraschino cherries or prunes.

MARINATED HAM

For additional flavour, a fully cooked whole or half ham may be marinated before baking; combine equal quantities of sweetened orange juice and ginger ale, and add seasonings; marinate ham in this liquid, in the refrigerator, for 18-24 h. Proceed as for GLAZED BAKED HAM following the TIMETABLE FOR BAKING PRE-COOKED HAM.

PARTY HAM

When purchasing a larged canned ham or a fully cooked boned ham, take along to the store a roll of heavy-duty aluminum foil. Ask the butcher to slice the ham on his slicing machine; tie ham firmly in its original shape and wrap in foil.

Bake following the TIMETABLE FOR BAKING PRE-COOKED HAM. During the last 30 min of baking, cover ham with orange marmalade to glaze. Remove strings and serve.

BOILED HAM

Use this method for home-cured, salty hams.
1. Cover ham with cold water; let stand overnight.
2. Drain, put in kettle, cover with fresh cold water.
3. Heat to boiling, boil 5 min, remove scum.
4. Cook below boiling point for the time indicated below.
5. If to be served cold, cool ham in water in which it was cooked; lift out; remove skin.
3 kg ham—cook 3.5 h
4.5 kg ham—cook 5 h

Uses for Leftover Cooked Ham
Chopped: in potato salad; scalloped potatoes; scrambled eggs; soufflé; ham scallop; cream corn; chef's salad; jellied salads; macaroni, baked beans.

Minced: in sandwich filling, mixed with mayonnaise; meat loaf, hash.

Bone and bits of meat can be used to make split pea soup and baked beans.

BAKED PICNIC SHOULDER

Picnic Shoulder has more fat than ham, but is less expensive. Select the leanest shoulder available.
1. Scrub surface of ham; place in a large kettle and cover with cold water.
2. Bring to a boil; simmer for 1 h; save the liquid for stock.
3. Consult the TIMETABLE FOR BAKING UNCOOKED HAM for total cooking time. Place on a rack in a pan; add a little stock and bake for remaining time at 160°C
4. During the last half hour of cooking, remove skin from the ham and finish as GLAZED BAKED HAM.

Basic Recipe
HAM ROLLS

375 ml	cooked rice
30 ml	chopped parsley
50 ml	toasted almonds
30 ml	melted butter *or* margarine
	8 thin slices cooked ham
284 ml	1 can condensed cream of chicken
	or celery soup
	½ can water

1. Preheat oven to 180°C
2. Mix rice, parsley, nuts, and melted fat; divide mixture among ham slices, placing it in the centre of each slice.
3. Roll ham slice with filling; place in a casserole with the open edge of the roll down.
4. Cover with soup and water; bake 20 min
   Serves 4.

Variations
Ham and Mushroom Rolls—Add sautéed mushrooms to the filling in the basic recipe; omit almonds.
Ham and Banana Rolls—Spread ham slices lightly with prepared mustard and substitute bananas (halved lengthwise if large) for the filling in the basic recipe. Sprinkle with grated cheese before baking.
Asparagus Ham Rolls—Substitute cooked asparagus spears for filling, using 2 or 3 spears for each roll, if they are thin. Cover with sauce, sprinkle with grated cheese, and bake.

Recipes, tables, etc. that appear in small capital letters, e.g., PARSLEY BUTTER, CANADA'S FOOD GUIDE, are listed in the index. Consult the index for the number of the page on which the item appears.

BREAKFAST BACON

1. Remove rind from bacon with scissors if rind is on; allow very cold bacon to warm before separating strips, to avoid tearing, or separate after cooking has begun.
2. Place in a cold frying pan over low heat.
3. Cook slowly; pour off the fat as it collects; turn often.
4. Drain on paper towelling; keep hot.

OVEN-COOKED BREAKFAST BACON

This is a useful method for cooking a large amount.
1. Arrange slices of bacon on a rack (a cake rack works well) in a pan; or arrange in a shallow pan and pour the fat off several times as it accumulates.
2. Bake in oven or broil to the desired degree of crispness. Oven temperature 190°C
3. Use a spatula to slip under slices to turn them.
4. Drain on paper towelling or brown paper.

FRIED BACK BACON

1. If the bacon is very lean, grease frying pan lightly.
2. Cook slowly on each side until lightly browned.

Sometimes called Canadian Style bacon, back bacon is cured and smoked. Roasted in a piece, it makes a delicious substitute for baked ham for a small family.

BACK BACON ROAST

1-1.5 kg	piece of back bacon
250 ml	fruit juice *or* stock

1. Preheat oven to 160°C
2. Place meat on a rack on a roasting pan; add liquid.
3. Cover and bake 70-80 min/kg
4. Finish as GLAZED BAKED HAM.

BOILED PEAMEAL BACON

500 g	piece of peameal bacon

Place meat in boiling water to cover; simmer until tender, 1 h or more. Serve hot or cold.

FRUITED HAM SLICE

2-4 cm thick	ham slice, ready-to-serve centre cut
3 ml	mustard
5 ml	sugar
15 ml	vinegar
125 ml	fruit juice
125 ml	orange marmalade *or* whole cranberry sauce *or* crushed pineapple *or* 4-5 slices pineapple
5 ml	ginger (optional)
30 ml	melted butter or margarine
15 ml	brown sugar (optional)

1. Place ham slice in a baking pan; slash fat edges and spread with a paste of mustard, sugar, and vinegar.
2. Add fruit juice and heat for about 40 min at 160°C
3. Spread a topping of fruit or place fruit slices on the ham; spoon the melted butter or margarine over; if pineapple is used, sprinkle with a little brown sugar.
4. Continue baking until fruit is lightly browned.

BAKED HAM SLICE WITH POTATOES AND ONIONS

Ham bought by the slice is convenient, expensive but without waste.

1 kg	thick slice of smoked ham
	6 potatoes
	flour
	2 onions
	milk

1. Preheat oven to 180°C
2. Place ham in a casserole with a cover; add a layer of potato slices and sprinkle lightly with flour.
3. Slice onions and add in a layer over the potatoes; repeat. The top layer should be potato.
4. Add milk to half fill the dish; cover and bake for 1 h, removing the cover during the last few minutes to brown the top. *Serves 4.*

Recipes, tables, etc. that appear in small capital letters, e.g., PARSLEY BUTTER, CANADA'S FOOD GUIDE, are listed in the index. Consult the index for the number of the page on which the item appears.

PINEAPPLE UPSIDE-DOWN HAM LOAF

125 ml	brown sugar
15 ml	flour
5 ml	mustard
2 ml	cloves
5 ml	nutmeg
540 ml	9 slices pineapple
1 kg	cooked, ground ham
250 ml	bread crumbs
75 ml	chopped parsley
125 ml	pineapple syrup
	2 eggs
5 ml	mustard
1 ml	cloves

1. Mix first 5 ingredients together and spread over the bottom of a square cake pan.
2. Arrange pineapple slices in rows in the pan.
3. Combine remaining ingredients and pack evenly on top of the pineapple.
4. Bake for 45 min at 180°C
   Let stand 5 min, then turn over onto a heated platter. Garnish with parsley. *Serves 6-9.*

Variety Meats

Variety meats include liver, brains, heart, kidneys, sweetbreads, tongue and tripe, and the many combinations of processed meats such as sausage. Many organ meats are excellent sources of minerals and vitamins. Since they are more perishable than other meats, they should be cooked and served soon after purchase, or frozen and stored not longer than 3 or 4 months in the freezer.

LIVER

500 g	4-5 servings of liver

A serving of pork liver meets the daily iron requirement for healthy people of all ages and stages; other varieties provide somewhat less but are still excellent sources of iron. The daily requirements of vitamin A and riboflavin are provided by one serving of liver; thiamine and niacin are also present in generous amounts.

Broil liver from calves, baby beef, lamb, chicken.
Pan-fry beef liver, pork liver.
   The tough membrane on the outer edges of the liver should be peeled off, and the liver rinsed under cold, running water. It cooks best thinly sliced.

Few foods can boast such high content of so many nutrients. If liver is seldom on the menu, try some new flavour and texture variations to increase its ratings! Liver can be ground and added to meat loaves and patties; pan-fry slowly on each side for a total of 5 min before grinding. This makes grinding much easier.

BROILED LIVER

500 g	thinly sliced liver
50 ml	cooking oil
	salt, pepper

1. Place liver on a rack over a broiling pan and brush with oil.
2. Broil until browned, approximately 3 min on each side. Cut a piece to be sure it is cooked and not pink; over-cooking gives a leathery texture.
3. Bacon and thin slices of onion brushed with oil may be broiled at the same time. *Yield:* 4 servings.

Chicken livers are especially delicious when broiled on skewers. Include them in SHISH KABOBS.

PAN-FRIED LIVER

Before cooking, liver may be coated with seasoned flour by shaking liver and flour in a paper bag. Pan-fry in sufficient hot fat to cover bottom of pan, turning liver once when brown. Reduce heat and finish cooking. Serve at once.

Variations
Liver and Onions—Sauté sliced onions in hot fat; set onions aside to keep warm while frying liver in the same fat. Serve liver with onion slices on top.
Liver and Bacon—Fry bacon in a frying pan; remove to absorbent paper in a warm place. Fry liver in bacon fat; serve with strips of bacon.

ITALIAN-STYLE LIVER

500 g	liver, cut in strips
	5 cm × 1 cm
30 ml	cornmeal
30 ml	grated Parmesan cheese
30 ml	cooking oil
	1 green pepper, sliced
	1 garlic clove, crushed
	1 onion, sliced
500 ml	2 cans tomato sauce

1. Prepare liver; combine cornmeal and cheese and roll liver in the mixture.
2. Brown liver in hot oil, add green pepper, garlic and onion, cover and simmer until tender, about 5 minutes.
3. Add tomato sauce and heat; serve over hot spaghetti or noodles. *Serves 4.*

LIVER ROLLS

500 g	beef liver, thinly sliced
250 ml	BREAD DRESSING
30 ml	fat
	salt, pepper
2 ml	oregano
284 ml	1 can condensed tomato soup
	½ can vegetable stock *or* water

1. Prepare liver and spread each slice with dressing.
2. Roll up starting at the shorter end and fasten roll with a toothpick or small skewer.
3. Brown each roll in hot fat and transfer to a casserole; add soup blended with liquid; sprinkle with salt, pepper and oregano.
4. Cover and bake until tender, about 1 h, at 180°C *Serves 4.*

CREOLE CHICKEN LIVERS

500 g	chicken livers
250 ml	thinly sliced onion
150 ml	thinly sliced celery
30 ml	cooking oil
284 ml	1 can condensed tomato soup
50 ml	chopped parsley
125 ml	water
1 ml	lemon juice

1. Cover and sauté livers, onion and celery in hot oil over low heat until tender.
2. Add remaining ingredients and heat through. Serve over rice. *Serves 5-6.*

Variations
Curried Chicken Livers—Substitute cream of celery soup for the tomato soup; add sufficient curry powder to give the desired flavour.
Chicken Livers Supreme—Substitute condensed mushroom soup for the tomato soup, and add sautéed mushrooms. Garnish with parsley and slivered almonds.
Hawaiian Chicken Livers—Sauté livers in oil; add SWEET AND SOUR SAUCE and heat through.

Kidneys

Considered a delicacy by many, kidney is an excellent source of iron. Beef kidney is also rich in riboflavin; pork kidney contains a generous amount of thiamine.

Half a beef kidney, 1 veal or pork kidney, or 2 lamb kidneys would provide 1 serving. Before cooking, wash, remove membrane and hard parts. Slice or cut kidney into pieces. Rinse thoroughly.

Veal and lamb kidneys are often left attached to chops as veal kidney chops and English lamb chops.

BEEF KIDNEY STEW

	1 beef kidney
45 ml	vinegar
50 ml	flour
5 ml	salt
3 ml	pepper
45 ml	butter
45 ml	cooking oil
	2 cloves garlic, crushed
125 ml	chopped onions
5 ml	rosemary
250 ml	water
	1 bay leaf

1. Remove membrane from the kidney and soak for 2 h in cold water and vinegar.
2. Cut into thin slices and dredge in seasoned flour.
3. Brown kidney slices in hot butter and oil (or substitute all oil); add garlic and onion; cook for 5 min and add remaining ingredients.
4. Simmer until tender, about 15 min

BROILED KIDNEY

	6 veal kidneys
	or
	12 lamb kidneys
50 ml	melted butter
	3 tomatoes
	6 large mushroom caps
	6 strips bacon
30 ml	lemon juice

1. Wash kidneys in cold water; remove skin; cut crosswise into slices.
2. Arrange on broiler pan; brush with butter.

3. Place each tomato, halved, and each mushroom cap, round side up, and the bacon on the pan; brush the tomato and mushroom with butter.
4. Broil until brown; turn; brush kidneys with butter and lemon juice; fill each mushroom cap with butter.
5. Season and broil 15 min longer.

BEEFSTEAK AND KIDNEY PIE

	1 small beef kidney
500 g	stewing beef, cubed
	1 large onion, chopped
30 ml	oil
1 ℓ	beef stock and/or water
	flour
	salt
	pepper
	½ recipe PASTRY

1. Prepare kidneys as for BEEF KIDNEY STEW;
2. Sauté onion in hot oil until golden; remove onions; add meat and brown.
3. Return onions to the pan, add stock and simmer together covered, until tender, about 1.5 h
4. Thicken stew with flour (see THICKENING LIQUIDS) taste and season.
5. Pour into a casserole and cover with a layer of pastry; bake in hot oven until pastry is golden. *Serves 4.*

Heart

Heart sizes vary with the size of the animal and the species. A baby beef heart will serve about 6, a veal heart will serve about 4 and a pork heart 2-3.

Although heart offers fewer nutrients than liver, this lean meat provides 1/3 to ½ of our daily iron requirement and a generous helping of thiamine.

STUFFED HEART

750 g	1 baby beef heart
250 ml	BREAD DRESSING
50 ml	seasoned flour
30 ml	fat *or* oil
250 ml	water *or* vegetable stock

1. Wash heart in cold water. At one side at the top is a little sac which should be split open; remove the veins and sinews; dry.

2. Prepare dressing and stuff the heart. Sew or close with skewers.
3. Dredge with seasoned flour and brown slowly in hot fat; add liquid; cover.
4. Bake at 180°C
   or simmer on a very low heat for about 2 h or until tender, or pressure cook for 45 min at maximum pressure.
5. Thicken the gravy; serve in a separate dish.
   To serve the heart, slice thinly from the pointed end, discarding the coarse top piece. *Serves 6.*

Serve sliced heart hot with gravy or cold as a nutritious addition to a cold meat plate.

BRAISED HEART

	1 baby beef heart
	or
	2 veal hearts
	1 onion
	pepper, salt
50 ml	flour
30 ml	fat *or* oil
125 ml	celery
250 ml	canned tomatoes

1. Wash the heart as in preceding recipe; steam, or simmer 30 min in water to cover. Cool.
2. Slice or dice, removing any fibres or fat; dredge with seasoned flour.
3. Brown in the hot fat; add the vegetables.
4. Cover and simmer or bake until tender, about 2 h at 180°C
   Serves 6.

Heart may also be cooked whole in a pressure cooker, for 45 min at maximum pressure.

SPICED PORK HEART

400-500 g	1 large pork heart
750 ml	water
125 ml	vinegar
	salt, pepper
	2 bay leaves
	1 onion, sliced
	1 clove garlic
15 ml	sugar

1. Wash and trim heart; place in a deep saucepan with remaining ingredients.
2. Bring to a boil; cover and simmer for 1.5-2 h; or pressure cook at maximum pressure for 35 min or until tender. Serve hot or cold.

Sweetbreads

Sweetbread is the thymus gland of young beef; veal sweetbread is the most desirable. As the animal grows, the gland disappears so that "beef sweetbread" is not truly a sweetbread but the pancreas gland, a much larger and softer organ. Sweetbreads should be used while very fresh, and before being prepared in any other way they should be parboiled by the following method.

To Parboil Sweetbreads—Soak in cold salted water 30 min; drain. Cover with boiling water to which has been added a spoonful of vinegar or lemon juice and a little salt. Simmer 20-30 min, drain and plunge into cold water. Peel off the thin membrane.

CREAMED SWEETBREADS

500 g	sweetbreads
	salt, pepper
	dash of cayenne pepper
30 ml	butter
250 ml	rich milk
30 ml	flour

1. Parboil sweetbreads; cut into thick slices.
2. From remaining ingredients prepare WHITE SAUCE; add sweetbreads.
3. Reheat; serve in Swedish timbales, patty shells, bread cases, or on toast.

Variations
Add cooked mushrooms, peas, diced chicken or ham to vary this dish.

One of the CONDENSED CREAM SOUP SAUCES can be substituted for the white sauce.

BROILED SWEETBREADS

1. Parboil sweetbreads; slice in half.
2. Brush with melted butter; sprinkle with pepper and celery salt; broil on both sides until brown.

Serve on fresh French bread.

BREADED SWEETBREADS

1. Parboil sweetbreads; dry; season.
2. Roll in fine, dry bread crumbs, in egg and in crumbs.
3. Sauté in butter; serve on toast with a green salad.

Tongue

Tongue from beef, veal, lamb, or pork may be sold fresh, pickled or smoked. After cooking, pickled and smoked tongues are red in colour; fresh tongues are grey.

"BOILED" TONGUE

1.5-2 kg	1 beef tongue
5 ml	salt
5 ml	peppercorns
	1 onion
	2 stalks celery and leaves
	water

1. Add only enough boiling water to just cover meat; add seasonings and vegetables and simmer until tender, about 3-4 h
2. Strain off the liquid and save for soup stock.
3. Remove roots of the tongue; skin. To skin, cut off the bones and gristle from the root end, slit the skin on the underside from root to tip; loosen the skin around the root end with a sharp knife and turn the tongue right side up and pull off skin.
4. Slice the tongue on a slant to produce larger slices.
5. Serve hot with mustard or horseradish, or serve cold.

Tongue can be baked, broiled, braised, or jellied after "boiling." It is a nutritious and economical addition to a platter of cold cuts.

JELLIED TONGUE

	2 small veal tongues
	1 veal knuckle or shank, split
1.25 *l*	cold water
5 ml	salt
30 ml	mixed pickling spice
	1 small onion

1. Wash tongues; soak in water; drain and add the knuckle.
2. Cover with fresh cold water; add seasonings and onion; simmer until tender, about 2 h
3. Skin the tongues (follow method in preceding recipe); curl them into a bowl so that it holds them tightly.
4. Further reduce liquid, if necessary, by boiling, so that there is a little less than half the original volume; season and pour it over the tongues in the bowl.

5. Set a plate on top to weigh them down so that tongues hold their position; cool until set.
6. Unmould. Serve with HORSERADISH SAUCE.

Shape a flower of sliced, hard-cooked egg. Make stems and leaves with watercress. Edge with sliced radishes or green peas.

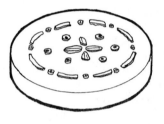

Crosswise or lengthwise slices of gherkins with slices of stuffed olives make attractive designs.

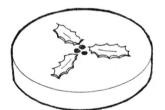

Green pepper or gherkins can be cut to resemble holly leaves; add berries of pimento.

Brains

Brains when cooked resemble sweetbreads, somewhat softer, and much less expensive. Prepare and parboil in the same way as sweetbreads or serve creamed, or combined with scalloped tomatoes. Brains have a very high cholesterol content.

Tripe

Tripe is the lining of the stomach of beef, cleaned, partly cooked and possibly pickled. The honeycomb type (from the second stomach) is superior to the plain variety (from the first stomach).

STEWED TRIPE

500 g	honeycomb tripe
500 ml	milk, tomato juice, *or* vegetable stock
250 ml	chopped onion
250 ml	chopped celery
	salt, pepper

1. Wash the tripe well; cut into strips, then into bite-size diamond shapes.
2. Add liquid and simmer for 1 h; add vegetables and seasoning and simmer for another hour until tender or pressure cook for 15 min
3. Thicken if necessary (see THICKENING LIQUIDS). *Serves 4-5.*

Chipped or Dried Beef

This smoked, thinly sliced beef is usually bought in small jars. Slices may be cut with scissors and mixed with sour cream and served over baked potato, or mixed with an unsalted WHITE SAUCE and served over toast. To lessen saltiness, pour boiling water over chipped beef in a sieve; dry.

For jellied chipped beef, dissolve the contents of 1/3 envelope of gelatine in 1 tin of hot consommé, add shredded chipped beef and chill; slice.

Recipes, tables, etc. that appear in small capital letters, e.g., PARSLEY BUTTER, CANADA'S FOOD GUIDE, are listed in the index. Consult the index for the number of the page on which the item appears.

Sausages

Sausages are on the market in great variety, both ready-to-eat and uncooked.

Ready-to-eat Sausages
Dry or "Summer" Sausages—These may be made of pork and beef. They are dried and some varieties are smoked before drying. They include salami, cervelat, pepperoni and mortedella.
Smoked Sausages—These, like the dry sausage, may be of beef or pork. They are seasoned and smoked. Common examples are the frankfurter or wiener, bologna, thuringer and kielbasa.
Cooked Specialties—These are made from a wider range of meats, and are not usually smoked. Included are liver sausage and braunschweiger.

Fresh Sausage
Fresh sausage is marketed in three forms:
Link Sausage—The meat should be rosy pink if fresh. The links may be twisted to make long or short sausages. They may be all pork or a mixture of pork and beef.
Sausage Meat—This is the same meat but it has not been put into a casing. It is sold in bulk form.
Farmer's Sausage—The meat is packed into larger casings, not linked, and sold in a coil. It may be seen more commonly at a farmers' market; purchase only if it has a good colour and odour.

To avoid the danger of trichinosis, all fresh pork products must be well cooked.

PAN-FRIED SAUSAGE

1. Place sausage links in frying pan; add a little water to a depth equal to half that of the sausages; cover and simmer for 5 min. (Do not boil, and do *not* prick the links with a fork to let juice escape.)
2. Drain off water and pan fry slowly. Continue to cook until the sausage is brown, and cooked throughout. Serve the sausage with fried apple rings or with hot chili sauce.

BAKED SAUSAGE

1. Spread a single layer of sausages in a shallow pan.
2. Cover and bake for approximately 30 min, turning to brown evenly, at 200°C

For added flavour, pour a little BARBECUE SAUCE over sausages before baking or pan-frying.

Wieners

Wieners can be cooked by several different methods: simmered in water 5-8 min, pan-fried, baked, or broiled in the oven on a lightly greased pan or on top of a casserole mixture. Slashing the surface of the wiener in diagonal lines helps to keep its shape during cooking by dry heat and adds an interesting appearance.

FILLED WIENERS

1 package wieners (10-12)
  one or more of:
  strips of cheese
  sweet pickle relish
  crushed pineapple *or* pineapple spears
  canned baked beans mixed with hot dog relish
  cole slaw
  dill pickles cut in long wedges
10-12 strips, partly-cooked, drained bacon

1. Split the wiener lengthwise not quite all the way through; add one of the materials suggested above except bacon.
2. Wrap bacon, spiral fashion around wiener.
3. Bake for 15-20 min at 200°C
   or broil until the bacon is cooked and the wiener hot. Filled wieners may also be pan-fried.
4. Serve in a hot, buttered bun. To serve on a slice of buttered bread, spread with mustard, place wiener diagonally on the bread, bring up the opposite corners and fasten with toothpicks; broil until brown.

Recipes, tables, etc. that appear in small capital letters, e.g., PARSLEY BUTTER, CANADA'S FOOD GUIDE, are listed in the index. Consult the index for the number of the page on which the item appears.

FRANKABOBS

These are really SHISH KABOBS with wieners. Cut wieners into chunks, and thread onto skewers. See recipe for SHISH KABOBS for suggestions for additions. Baste with BARBECUE SAUCE or any basting mixture. Broil, turning frequently.

BARBECUED WIENERS

Here are 3 different versions:
(a) Simmer wieners in a pan with chopped onion and BARBECUE SAUCE for 10 min or until the onions are cooked.
(b) Place wieners on grill of barbecue or on skewer. Baste with BARBECUE SAUCE. Cook and turn, basting frequently.
(c) Slit frankfurters lengthwise almost but not quite through. Open flat; brush with BARBECUE SAUCE and broil.

BARBER POLE FRANKS

500 g	wieners
	TEA BISCUIT **dough**
23 × 30 cm	**rolled into rectangle,**
2 × 30 cm	**cut into strips**
	prepared mustard

1. Prepare dough, roll out into a rectangle and spread with mustard; cut into strips.
2. Wrap each strip spiral-fashion around the wieners, pinching the dough at each end to seal it.
3. Bake 12-15 min at 220°C
   Serve with ketchup, chili sauce or mustard.

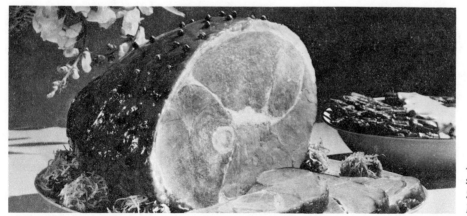

A glazed baked ham, stuck with cloves. Swift Canadian Co. Ltd.

Poultry

The poultry industry has undergone tremendous expansion in the past two decades. Advances in production, processing and storage methods provide us with a variety of poultry products the year around. Broiler chickens account for the greatest increase in production, but turkeys also are raised in vastly greater numbers; until recently turkeys were considered to be special occasion fare, but now they are eaten throughout the year.

Ninety percent of all poultry sold in Canada is eviscerated, that is, drawn and ready for cooking with minimum preparation. "Oven-ready" and "Ready-to-cook" are synonymous terms for "Eviscerated." "Dressed" poultry, by definition, has had only the blood and feathers removed.

As well as whole birds, parts of chicken and turkey such as legs and wings can be purchased; chicken breasts or completely dismembered chicken, "chicken in a basket," are also available.

Grading of Poultry

National grading regulations govern the import, export and interprovincial movement of all poultry; in many cities all poultry sold, whether shipped in from another province or processed and sold within the province, must be graded.

The Grade Mark is on a metal tag on the breast or it is printed on a transparent bag or on an insert inside the bag.

Canada Grade Special (Purple) is reserved for the commercially perfect specimens, the finest quality produced. They are not generally available in retail outlets. Grade A (Red) birds, the best quality commonly available on the retail market, are normally formed and well fatted and fleshed. Grade B (Blue) birds may have a slightly crooked breast bone; the deposition of flesh and fat may be less than that of Grade A and they may have a few more or larger tears on the skin which do not seriously detract from the appearance. Canada Grade Utility, also Blue tagged, must at least qualify for Canada Grade B but one or more parts of the bird may be missing (e.g., wing or drumstick). This can occur during processing. Canada Grade C, tagged yellow, is rarely seen on the retail market; it is usually used for canning. Large skin tears or prominent discolourations downgrade this bird.

Turkeys, ducks and geese must also bear the word "young" or "mature" on the grade panel or tag.

Storing Poultry

Fresh poultry is very perishable and should be stored in the coldest part of the refrigerator after removing the store wrappings and covering it loosely with waxed paper or foil or plastic wrap. Remove giblets from the neck or body cavity of a fresh or thawed bird and store separately, as they spoil more rapidly than the rest of the bird.

Cooked poultry should be placed in a plastic bag or wrapped in foil or plastic wrap; remove the dressing and wrap separately.

Freezing Poultry—To freeze poultry after purchase, overwrap original wrappings to prevent loss of moisture. Do not stuff birds before freezing; cooked poultry should have the stuffing removed before freezing. When freezing cooked poultry or poultry mixtures, cool quickly in the refrigerator. Remove meat from cooked whole birds and package tightly to eliminate air. Simmer the carcass for soup.

Maximum Poultry Storage Time

Meat	Refrigerator 2° to 4°C	Freezer −18°C or lower
Whole chicken and turkeys, uncooked	2-3 d	1 year
Cut-up poultry, uncooked	2-3 d	6 months
Whole geese and ducks, uncooked	2-3 d	3 months
Slices or pieces, cooked	3-4 d	1 month
Slices or pieces in broth or sauce, cooked	2-3 d	3 months
Sandwiches	2 d	1 month
Cooked mixtures	2 d	1-2 months
Fried chicken	3-4 d	3 months

Thawing Poultry—Frozen poultry should be thawed before broiling, frying, baking, or roasting. Unthawed frozen chicken will not hold a batter or coating when fried, as the formation of steam under the coating causes the batter to fall off.

For stewing or braising, complete thawing is not essential; remove giblets before braising a whole chicken.

Thaw whole bird in unopened plastic wrapping at room temperature until pliable; remove wrapping, take out giblets and neck and store them elsewhere. Wipe bird with a clean damp cloth, cover loosely with foil, plastic or waxed paper wrapping and refrigerate until completely thawed. Poultry can also be thawed in original wrapping in the refrigerator for the entire thawing period, or in cold water. A combination of these methods may be desirable to thaw a large bird; begin with refrigerator thawing for a day and finish thawing the bird in cold water or at room temperature.

APPROXIMATE TIME REQUIRED TO THAW POULTRY

	h/kg
In the refrigerator	10
Under cold water	2
At room temperature	3

Poultry may be cooked as soon as thawed or may be held in the refrigerator up to 2 d before cooking.

Preparation of Poultry

Remove any pin feathers that may remain; singe off any hairs. Wash the eviscerated bird with lukewarm, salted water. Check that the windpipe (in the neck area) and the lungs, a spongy mass in the rib area, have been removed. Rinse bird under cold water. Dry before stuffing.

Giblets should be rinsed in salted water, drained, covered with water and simmered until tender. The neck can be cooked with the giblets. Chopped cooked giblets can be added to the dressing or gravy and the liquid used for gravy or stock.

To Dress or Stuff a Bird

1. Place the fowl in a bowl, neck side up.
2. Fill the neck cavity with dressing; pull the neck skin down and over the dressing to hold it. Reverse the bird in the bowl.
3. Stuff the bird from the vent end; do not pack the dressing too tightly since overstuffing causes the dressing to become soggy when it expands. Poultry should not be stored after stuffing; do not stuff until ready to cook it.
4. Skewer the slit closed with poultry pins or small skewers; string may be laced around the skewers for extra firmness. In self-trussing turkeys (those which have the legs held in place by a band of skin) the vent opening may be too large to close; cover opening with a small piece of foil.

5. To truss the bird, use medium-size skewers to hold wings and legs close to the body, or use string. Cut a piece of string about 3 times the length of the bird and tie around the leg bones and tail so that the legs are held close to the body. Fold the wing tips back under the bird and while holding wings tightly to the body bring each end of the string back under and over the wings and under the bird. Fasten. Skewer the wings to the body if necessary to maintain shape.

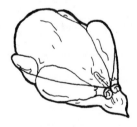

Self-trussing birds need only have the wings fastened in place.

Birds that have been stuffed should not be stored; they should be roasted immediately to prevent bacterial growth.

Cooking Methods for Poultry

Type	Description	Eviscerated mass in kg (approx.)	How to Cook
Chicken broilers and fryers (may also be labelled "chicken" only)	young birds 6-10 weeks	less than 2	broil, bake, fry or barbecue
Chicken roasters	10 weeks to 7 months, well fatted and fleshed	2 and over	roast
Chicken capons	unsexed males 5-9 months old	2.5-3.5	roast
Fowl (stewing chicken)	mature hens over 7 months old	1.4 and over	braise, stew
Cornish hens and Squabs	young, tender (allow ½-1 per serving)	0.5 0.4-0.75	roast broil
Young turkeys (turkey broilers)	15 weeks	up to 4.5	broil, roast barbecue
Young turkeys	4-8 months	over 4.5	roast
Mature turkeys	older than 8 months	over 4.5	braise
Young ducks (duckling)	less than 1 year, all dark meat; higher proportion of fat and bone than in chicken. One serves 3-4	1.8-2.7	roast
Young geese	usually under 1 year, all dark meat which is fatter than that of other birds	4-5.5	roast

Amount of Poultry to Purchase
Except where indicated otherwise in the Cooking Methods for Poultry table, and except for large turkeys (which have a greater proportion of meat to bone than do small turkeys), allow for each serving approximately 0.35-0.5 kg

Chicken

Chicken is an excellent source of high quality protein, as good as that from red meats (beef, pork, lamb). It is rich in minerals and vitamins, particularly niacin, but contains less iron than the red meats.

The skin of chicken contains fat which bastes the meat during cooking; one-third of the food energy in a serving of broiled chicken comes from the skin, which can be discarded by dieters. Much of the fat in this lean meat is unsaturated, making it suitable for low-fat, low-cholesterol diets. Tender, easily digested and mild in flavour, chicken lends itself to bland diets and simple fare; it is equally at home in its many popular variations from barbecue and take-out favourites to the gourmet's delight.

TIMETABLE FOR ROASTING CHICKEN (STUFFED) AT 160°C

	Ready-to-cook kg	Time h
Chicken	1-1.5	1½-2
	1.5-2.5	2¼-2½
Capon	2.5-3	3-4

If bird is unstuffed, roasting time will be reduced slightly.

ROAST CHICKEN

1. Prepare a roasting chicken; stuff it (for recipes, see BREAD DRESSING; for directions see TO DRESS OR STUFF A BIRD).
2. Place chicken on a rack in a roasting pan and brush with cooking oil; add no water to the pan.
3. To prevent chicken from drying during roasting, baste several times with the juices that collect in the pan. Covering the top area of the chicken with fat-soaked cheesecloth or with foil reduces the need for frequent basting.
4. Roast according to the preceding timetable. When chicken is cooked, the leg will break away at the body, the thick part of the thigh is tender when pierced with the point of a small knife, and the escaping juice should be colourless.

5. Allow the chicken to stand in a warm place 20 min after it comes out of the oven. This gives time for the juices to be absorbed; the meat sets and is easier to carve. To make gravy, see GRAVY. Remove the strings and skewers before it is taken to the table. Garnish with parsley.

A dark, crispy skin can be obtained by adding soy sauce to the pan juices for basting.

Barbecued Chicken on a Spit is prepared as Roast Chicken. A bunch of sweet herbs, tarragon, celery, green onions, etc. can be tied together and placed in the body cavity before cooking, or the chicken can be stuffed with bread dressing. Skewer or tie wings and legs in place, close to the body. Baste frequently with BARBECUE SAUCE or any of the MARINADES. Cooking times will be approximately half of those given in the TIMETABLE FOR ROASTING CHICKEN. Cornish hens can be cooked in the same manner.

BROILED CHICKEN

1. Split young chickens in half lengthwise, allowing one half for each serving.
2. Break the joints and skewer the wing and leg to the body to keep them flat and compact; season with salt and pepper.
3. Place in a broiling pan, skin side down, not on the rack; brush with melted butter or MARINADE.
4. Broil slowly; turn and brush more fat on each piece as it browns. Cook 30-50 min

CHICKEN FONDUE

Cut boned chicken breasts into bite-size pieces; cook on forks in hot oil and serve with a variety of sauces. (See BEEF FONDUE.)

Variation

Batter-dipped Chicken Fondue—Dip bite-size chicken pieces into a thin pancake batter and fry in hot oil.

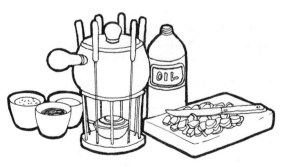

Basic Recipe
FRIED CHICKEN

1. Coat chicken pieces with one of the following, (a), (b) or (c).
   (a) *Flour*—Season flour with salt, pepper and paprika; for added flavour or texture add any of the following to the flour: rosemary, thyme, ginger, curry powder, grated orange or lemon rind, cornmeal, sesame seed or grated Parmesan cheese. Shake in a plastic or paper bag with a few pieces of chicken at a time.
   (b) *Crumbs*—First shake or dip chicken in seasoned flour, dip in beaten egg and then in crumbs (fine bread crumbs, corn-flake crumbs or sesame seeds). Oven-fried (baked) chicken can be coated with a BAKE-ON CRUMB COATING if desired, or a commercial mix, which does not require an initial flour and egg coating; because the mix contains oil, no extra fat is required during cooking.
   (c) *Batter*—Use recipe for BATTER COATING for use on either cooked or uncooked chicken; follow directions for DEEP FAT FRYING.
2. Allow coating to dry for a few minutes before frying or baking.
3. Cook by one of the following methods, (a), (b) or (c).
   (a) *Frying* (in a shallow layer of fat)—Add cooking oil to a heavy frying pan to a depth equal to ¼ that of the pan; heat until a drop of water will sizzle in it. Beginning with the meatiest pieces of chicken, cook coated pieces in fat, turning until all are evenly browned, about 15-20 min Cover tightly and cook until chicken is almost tender when tested with the point of a knife. Uncover and cook 5-10 min longer to crisp the skin and to finish cooking.
   (b) *French frying*—See DEEP FAT FRYING.
   (c) *Oven-frying*—Arrange pieces of coated chicken in a shallow greased pan and sprinkle with oil or fat. (When using a special BAKE-ON CRUMB COATING MIX or a commercial mix, do not grease pan or add fat.)
      Bake in a single layer for about 15 min, turning chicken pieces so that all are golden, at 200°C
      Reduce oven temperature to 180°C
   Cover pan and cook chicken 35-50 min or until almost tender. Uncover and finish cooking.

Variations
Maryland Style Chicken—Serve fried chicken with a WHITE SAUCE or VELOUTÉ SAUCE. (Simmer neck and giblets in water with a few onion slices and use the stock as part of the liquid in the sauce.)
Kentucky Fried Chicken—Soak 1 cut-up broiler fryer in cold, salted water to cover, 1 h or more. Drain and while still wet shake in a plastic bag with the following mixture made by thoroughly blending the seasonings in a mortar and pestle, or in a small bowl using the back of a small spoon, and combining them with the flour.

10 ml	dry chicken soup mix
10 ml	seasoned salt
1 ml	seasoned pepper
10 ml	fines herbes
10 ml	onion flakes (dried)

Prepare gravy in the pan in which the chicken was cooked, after fat has been drained off (see GRAVY). Blend the browned, baked-on juices with flour and add stock from the giblets.

GLAZED CHICKEN

1 kg	chicken legs and/or breasts
	or
	1 small chicken
60 ml	cooking oil
60 ml	concentrated frozen orange juice
60 ml	mint jelly
30 ml	lemon juice

1. Preheat oven to 180°C
2. Heat oil in a heavy frying pan and turn chicken in the oil until golden in colour; pour off any excess oil.
3. Combine remaining ingredients and pour over chicken; cut-up chicken should be in a single layer.
4. Bake uncovered until the chicken is glazed and tender, about 1 h. Baste often during cooking. *Serves 2-3.*

Variation
Substitute ginger or orange marmalade or apricot jam for the orange concentrate and mint jelly.

Recipes, tables, etc. that appear in small capital letters, e.g., PARSLEY BUTTER, CANADA'S FOOD GUIDE, are listed in the index. Consult the index for the number of the page on which the item appears.

Cutting and Boning a Chicken

It is usually more economical to cut up whole chickens at home rather than to purchase them already cut up. Chicken can be skinned and boned when the right tools and a little care are used.

Cutting-up Chicken

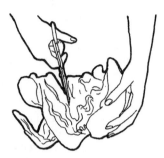

1. Place chicken breast side up. Using a sharp knife, make lengthwise slit through skin and flesh from neck to cavity. Turn bird over and repeat.

2. Using kitchen or poultry shears, cut right through rib bones; cut to one side of breast bone.

3. Turn chicken over. Cut through bones, cutting to one side of the backbone. Remove backbone.

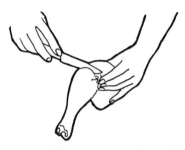

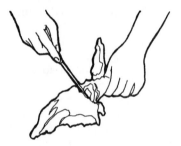

4. For quartering chicken, continue using shears. Cut across half the bird, following the natural division just below the rib cage and the breast bone.

5. Thigh may be left attached to leg for broiling; separate for frying. Bend leg joint. Cut through joint with a sharp knife, separating leg from the thigh.

6. To separate wing from the breast, bend joint. Cut through joint with a sharp knife. The chicken will now be in eight pieces and ready for frying.

Skinning and Boning Chicken Breasts
If using frozen breasts, bone while still partly frozen when bones are easily removed.

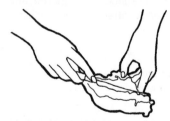

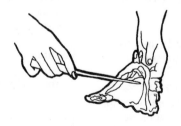

7. To bone chicken breast, use a small paring knife. Cut meat away from rib bones with quick little strokes, using the fingers to feel the way.

8. For skinned chicken breasts, use a sharp, small paring knife to start, then slip fingers between skin and flesh and peel skin.

HOW TO BROWN CHICKEN

Method I—Using Flour
For each

500 g	chicken

combine in a paper or plastic bag:

50 ml	flour
5 ml	paprika
2 ml	salt
	pepper
0.5 cm deep	cooking oil

1. Cut the chicken into serving pieces.
2. Shake the chicken, two or three pieces at a time in the bag to coat evenly with flour.
3. Pour oil to the required depth in a heavy pan and sauté chicken a few pieces at a time over medium-high heat until golden, turning it often. Finish cooking according to recipe being followed.

Method II—Without Flour
Follow directions above, omitting step 2. Brown chicken without flour and spices to give a somewhat transparent appearance or glaze to the skin. Chicken must be thoroughly dried before browning.

CHICKEN VALENCIA

	browned chicken
125 ml	orange juice
250 ml	chicken stock
	salt
5 ml	ginger
125 ml	pitted black olives
	1 sweet red pepper, cut in strips
30 ml	cornstarch
45 ml	water
	1 peeled and sliced orange

1. Combine all ingredients except cornstarch, water and orange, and cook as GLAZED CHICKEN.
2. Just before serving, combine cornstarch and water and stir into the liquid until thickened; heat orange slices quickly in the gravy.
3. Serve chicken on a heated platter over rice, with gravy and orange slices on top. Garnish with parsley.

Basic Recipe
SMOTHERED CHICKEN

This recipe is the basis for unlimited variations (see recipes which follow). To prepare ahead for a buffet supper, cook for half the recommended time, freeze or refrigerate, and finish cooking at time of serving.

	6 chicken legs or breasts
	or
1.5-2 kg	young chicken, cut up
200 ml	flour
5 ml	salt
	pepper
1 ml	ginger
	cooking oil
500 ml	light cream *or* thin WHITE SAUCE *or* cream soup
100 g	sliced mushrooms

1. Shake chicken with the dry ingredients and brown pieces in hot oil in a large, heavy pan. See Method I, HOW TO BROWN CHICKEN.
2. Pour off any fat remaining in the pan; pour the cream, WHITE SAUCE or soup over the chicken and add mushrooms.
3. Cover and bake about 1 h at 180°C
Or cook on top of the stove about 1 h, until tender. Allow approximately 1 leg or breast per serving, depending on the size. Serve with rice or noodles.

Variations
When the chicken is cooked, stir into the gravy half a small container of sour cream, or an equivalent quantity of plain yogurt. Heat through and serve.

Cook peas, sliced carrots and potatoes with the chicken in the gravy.

Chicken Paprikas—Follow recipe for VEAL PAPRIKAS, substituting chicken for veal.

Sweet and Sour Chicken—Omit flour when browning chicken and substitute SWEET AND SOUR SAUCE for the liquid ingredients of Smothered Chicken. Plump chicken wings make an economical and delicious dish when served in this way.

Recipes, tables, etc. that appear in small capital letters, e.g., PARSLEY BUTTER, CANADA'S FOOD GUIDE, are listed in the index. Consult the index for the number of the page on which the item appears.

Chicken quarters served with a spicy pilaf. Borden, Inc.

CURRIED CHICKEN

1.5-2 kg	browned young chicken, cut up
	1 crushed garlic clove
	2 chopped onions
125 ml	sliced mushrooms
500 ml	tomato or apple juice *or* chicken stock
	2 chopped green peppers
	or
	4 tart apples, peeled, cored and diced
15 ml	curry powder
	salt, pepper
2 ml	ginger
1 ml	thyme
125 ml	raisins *or* currants

1. In the pan in which the chicken was browned (see HOW TO BROWN CHICKEN) sauté the garlic, onions and mushrooms.
2. Combine remaining ingredients and simmer 5 min; pour mixture over chicken, cover and finish as SMOTHERED CHICKEN.
3. Serve over rice; garnish with toasted almond slivers and parsley.

Add a touch of drama to a buffet party by serving curried chicken with an array of SAMBALS.

CHICKEN CACCIATORE

1.5-2 kg	browned chicken
	1 onion, thinly sliced
	1 garlic clove, crushed
250 ml	water
250 ml	tomato paste
	salt, pepper
125 ml	mushrooms, sliced

1. Sauté onion and garlic in the pan in which the chicken was browned; add water, tomato paste and seasonings and blend.
2. Finish as SMOTHERED CHICKEN.
3. Add mushrooms and cook uncovered for 5 min more.

CHICKEN ALGERIAN

1.5-2 kg	browned chicken
125 ml	chicken stock
	1 garlic clove, crushed
	1 medium eggplant, peeled and chopped
250 ml	canned tomatoes *or* 2 large tomatoes, peeled and chopped
1 ml	thyme
	salt, pepper
15 ml	chopped parsley

Drain off any fat remaining in the pan after chicken is browned; add chicken stock and other ingredients; finish as SMOTHERED CHICKEN.

STIR-FRIED CHICKEN AND ALMONDS

125 ml	blanched almonds
30 ml	cooking oil
375 ml	raw, boned chicken cut into thin strips 5 cm long
125 ml	fresh *or* frozen peas
250 ml	finely sliced celery
125 ml	sliced mushrooms
	water chestnuts
	bamboo shoots
15 ml	soy sauce
125 ml	water

1. Cook almonds quickly in oil until golden; remove from pan and set aside.
2. Brown chicken and add vegetables, one variety after another at intervals, stirring constantly and adding liquid if needed.
3. If much liquid remains after the chicken and vegetables are cooked, thicken it by stirring into it a paste made by combining a little cornstarch with twice the quantity of cold water.
4. Add the almonds to the chicken mixture; serve at once. *Serves 2-3.*

See STIR-FRYING for a detailed description of the stir-fry method of cooking.

CHICKEN VERONIQUE

	6 pieces cut-up chicken
	½ lemon
	salt
175 ml	chicken stock
500 ml	seedless green grapes

1. Before browning chicken, rub pieces with half a lemon; sprinkle with salt and let dry for a few minutes.
2. Brown chicken without coating with flour. (Method II, HOW TO BROWN CHICKEN.)
3. Cook in liquid until tender, removing cover during last 15 min of cooking; just before serving, stir in grapes and heat through. Sprinkle with paprika; serve sauce separately.

Basic Recipe
STEWED CHICKEN

2-2.5 kg	chicken or fowl
	1 onion, quartered
	2 outer celery stalks and leaves
	2 slices lemon
	salt
	cold water

1. Disjoint and cut chicken into large pieces.
2. Place in large kettle with vegetables, seasonings and enough water to cover.
3. Cover and heat to boiling, then simmer until tender. Chicken will be tender in about 2 h, fowl in about 3 h
4. Lift out chicken, remove skin and bones, cut chicken into cubes or thin, flat slices. Save stock for soup, for a base in jellied chicken, or thicken for gravy.

Variation
Stewed Chicken with Vegetables—Cook cubed potatoes or potato balls, diced carrots, green peas in chicken stock. Thicken stock with flour. Add chicken; heat; season.

JELLIED CHICKEN

15 ml	gelatine
50 ml	cold water *or* chicken stock
500 ml	hot chicken stock
250 ml	stewed chicken and raw vegetables

1. Soften gelatine in cold water or stock for 5 min; dissolve in hot seasoned chicken stock. Taste and season.
2. Chill until mixture begins to set. See GELATINE MOULDS—GENERAL DIRECTIONS.
3. Moisten a mould, put in layers of jelly and chicken and if desired, add diced celery, green pepper, or sliced olives.
4. Chill until firmly set. *Serves 4-5.*

Recipes, tables, etc. that appear in small capital letters, e.g., PARSLEY BUTTER, CANADA'S FOOD GUIDE, are listed in the index. Consult the index for the number of the page on which the item appears.

CHICKEN FRICASSEE

1. Cut chicken into pieces and cook as for STEWED CHICKEN.
2. When tender drain off the stock into a deep jug; let fat rise to the top of the stock.
3. Roll the chicken in seasoned flour.
4. Spoon some fat from the top of the stock into a frying pan; heat fat and brown chicken in the pan. Remove chicken to a platter and keep it warm.
5. Add chicken stock to the drippings in the pan; if necessary thicken with a little flour shaken with cold water or stock in a covered jar.
6. Pour the gravy over the chicken; serve with hot TEA BISCUITS.

BRAISED FOWL

2-2.5 kg	chicken or fowl
500 ml	water
125 ml	uncooked rice (optional)
	2 onions, sliced (optional)

1. Rinse fowl, dry thoroughly; do not stuff or truss.
2. Brown on all sides by cooking in hot fat in a heavy pan, turning to brown evenly.
3. Place breast-side up in a deep pan; add the water.
4. Cover and cook slowly on top of the stove or bake until tender, 2-3 h, at 180°C
   Cook uncovered during the last half hour to allow the skin to become crisp.
5. Rice, rinsed and drained, and the onions may be cooked in the pan around the fowl and served with it.

INDIVIDUAL CHICKEN PIE

125 ml	diced, cooked carrots
	5 small onions, cooked
175 ml	fresh or frozen peas
125 ml	milk
175 ml	chicken gravy
	or
	½ can condensed cream of chicken soup
175 ml	cooked or canned chicken
	TEA BISCUIT dough or PASTRY dough

1. Combine all ingredients except dough; pour into 2 individual pie pans or into 1 larger one and bake for 10 min at 200°C

2. Prepare half of the recipe for TEA BISCUITS or PASTRY. Cover pan(s) with pastry rolled thin or tea biscuit dough; cut to let steam escape.
3. Bake for 25 min at 200°C

Baked TEA BISCUITS may replace unbaked toppings. Heat on top of hot mixture 15 min

---

Basic Recipe
CREAMED CHICKEN

500 ml	medium WHITE SAUCE
375 ml	cooked, diced chicken
1 ml	celery salt
	salt, pepper
	chopped parsley

1. Prepare WHITE SAUCE, substituting equal quantities of light cream and chicken stock for the milk.
2. Heat chicken in sauce, stirring frequently.
3. Season to taste.
4. Serve in patty shells, in ramekins, or on toast. Sprinkle with chopped parsley. *Serves 3-4.*

Variations

Chicken à la King

1 *l*	medium WHITE SAUCE
	2 egg yolks
2 ml	lemon juice
750 ml	diced, cooked chicken
125 ml	mushrooms, sliced and sautéed
250 ml	cooked green peas
30 ml	chopped pimento

1. Prepare WHITE SAUCE, season.
2. Beat egg yolks; stir into them a little hot sauce, then stir egg mixture into remaining sauce; stir until thick over low heat.
3. Add lemon juice and chicken and stir in other ingredients.
4. Heat and serve as Creamed Chicken. *Serves 6-8.*

The following recipes also use chicken: CHICKEN CROQUETTES, CHICKEN TETRAZZINI, BUFFET CHICKEN CASSEROLE, PAELLA.

Recipes, tables, etc. that appear in small capital letters, e.g., PARSLEY BUTTER, CANADA'S FOOD GUIDE, are listed in the index. Consult the index for the number of the page on which the item appears.

Cornish hens. Lawry's Foods, Inc.

Cornish Hens

Similar in flavour to chicken but novel in their "petiteness", these little birds make attractive party fare: No carving is required.

To roast, prepare and roast as chicken with or without stuffing; half the recipes for dressing will make sufficient stuffing for 2 birds. RICE DRESSING and Wild Rice Dressing are especially popular. If hens are unstuffed, a bunch of sweet herbs can be tied together and placed inside each during roasting. A glaze adds to the appearance and flavour; see recipes for GLAZED CHICKEN and GLAZED ROAST DUCKLING; these will make sufficient glaze for 4 Cornish hens.

Hens can also be cooked over the barbecue or on a spit with frequent basting with BARBECUE SAUCE or other basting sauces. Serve with long-grained, wild or flavoured rice, or with tiny parsley potatoes, and a green vegetable.

To broil, split hens and broil as chicken.

BRAISED CORNISH HENS À L'ORANGE

	4 Cornish hens
	salt, pepper
100 ml	**butter**
250 ml	**mushrooms**
30 ml	**green and/or red pepper cut into strips (optional)**
50 ml	**chopped onions**
50 ml	**blanched almonds, halved**
15 ml	**sugar**
500 ml	**orange juice**
2 ml	**salt**
175 ml	**chicken stock**
15 ml	**cornstarch**

1. Sprinkle insides of thawed hens with salt and pepper; tie wings and legs close to the body.
2. Heat butter in a heavy frying pan and brown hens slowly on all sides; as each hen is browned place it in a casserole dish just large enough to hold the 4 hens in a single layer.
3. Sauté mushrooms and peppers for 3 min in the butter and set aside.
4. Sauté onions and almonds for 3 min; add sugar and stir until sugar caramelizes.
5. Add juice, salt and half of the chicken stock (or chicken concentrate and water) to the pan and bring to a boil; simmer 5 min and pour over the hens.
6. Cover tightly and bake birds until tender, about 1 h; and transfer to a heated platter.
7. Combine cornstarch and remaining stock and blend in sufficient to thicken sauce; stir in mushrooms and peppers and heat through.
8. Pour over hens. *Serves 4.*

Turkey

Still a favourite for holiday meals but now available the year around, turkey is a source of high quality protein and a significant measure of iron. Canadians consume nearly 5 kg per person per year.

Turkey is sold fresh or frozen, whole or cut into parts; boneless turkey is available as frozen rolls.

Self-basting turkeys have been injected with fat deep into the flesh and do not require further basting during cooking. The label indicates the basting ingredient used; cocoanut oil is not recommended for diets low in saturated fat.

Choose birds which are roundish and broad-breasted rather than long sinewy birds. Large turkeys are a better buy than small ones (provided the meat can be used or stored), as they have a higher proportion of meat to bone.

Amounts of Turkey to Purchase
For an individual serving allow approximately:

Cut-up turkey:	drumsticks and wings	400 g
	thighs and breasts	300 g
Whole turkey:	for roasting	500 g
	for roasting and second-day snacks	750 g

The purchase of a large bird with planned leftovers may be both economical and convenient. Slice or dice leftovers and package and freeze in pre-measured amounts for use in specific recipes or sandwiches.

Turkeys which are to be stuffed must first be completely thawed. See THAWING POULTRY.

Turkey should be cooked as soon as it is stuffed, and the cooking should be a continuous process. It is not advisable to partially cook a turkey and then complete the cooking some hours later, because between the cooking periods the temperature of the bird and particularly of the dressing remains for an extended time in the "danger zone"—that range of temperatures inducive to bacterial growth and hence to food poisoning.

TIMETABLE FOR ROASTING TURKEY AT 160°C

	Eviscerated kg	Approximate Time h
Whole turkey	3.5	3¾-4½
	5.5	4¾-5½
	7.5	5¼-6
	9	5¾-6½
	11	6¼-7
Turkey halves	2	2½-3
	3.5	4-4½
	5.5	4½-5
Turkey quarters	2	3-3½
	3	3½-4
Turkey rolls	1.5	2½-3
	2	3-3½
	3	3½-4

Testing for Doneness—Begin testing turkey for doneness at the shorter time point within the range of the preceding table; stuffed and unstuffed turkeys will require the same amount of time to cook. For whole or half turkey, press thick part of drumstick; if it feels soft, the bird is done. The leg should move readily when twisted. A turkey roll will be cooked when tested with a fine skewer and found tender.

A meat thermometer can also be used; for temperatures of done turkey see INTERNAL TEMPERATURES OF MEAT.

ROAST TURKEY

1. Prepare, stuff and truss turkey as described in TO DRESS OR STUFF A BIRD. See recipes for DRESSING, POULTRY. Do not store turkey after it has been stuffed.
2. Place turkey breast side up on a rack in a roasting pan; brush with oil.
3. Cover turkey loosely with foil, leaving it open at the sides. If turkey is not of choice quality, cover the roasting pan for part of the cooking period, removing cover during the last half hour of cooking, or wrap bird completely in foil before cooking.
4. Roast according to preceding timetable; remove foil during the last hour of cooking and baste bird with drippings a few times until cooked. ("Self-Basting" or "Deep-Basted" birds do not require basting.) Serve with GRAVY and CRANBERRY SAUCE.

Variation
Roasted Half or Quarter Turkey—Tie wing and/or leg close to the body, brush skin with fat and roast skin-side up according to the timetable. When about half-cooked, shape up dressing on a piece of foil which is cut slightly smaller than the flat side of the turkey. Place turkey over the dressing and continue roasting.

To Serve Leftover Turkey
Leftover turkey can be served cold, alone or in combination with other cold meats such as ham, roast beef, jellied tongue, or other cold cuts.

It also makes delicious sandwiches and salads. Serve turkey hot in CROQUETTES, substitute it for chicken in INDIVIDUAL CHICKEN PIE, CHICKEN TETRAZZINI, BUFFET CHICKEN CASSEROLE, or other casserole dishes requiring cooked chicken. Serve it with SWEET AND SOUR SAUCE, CURRY SAUCE, VELOUTÉ SAUCE, or CHEESE SAUCE.

Freezing leftover turkey for use at a later date reduces the possibility of monotony in the use of leftovers.

Recipes, tables, etc. that appear in small capital letters, e.g., PARSLEY BUTTER, CANADA'S FOOD GUIDE, are listed in the index. Consult the index for the number of the page on which the item appears.

Roast turkey with wild rice stuffing and ghivetch.

GLAZED CHICKEN *may be varied by adding chunks of pineapple; serve with cooked polished or brown rice.*

Sausages arranged like spokes in a wheel on top of a dish of baked vegetables.

Minced meat may be served many ways.

Goose

The traditional Christmas Eve dinner of many Europeans, the goose is a large fatty bird that provides high quality protein. It is a source of B vitamins, particularly thiamine.

If stuffed, dressing should contain little or no fat; often fruit such as apple is used instead of dressing. Bread dressing flavoured with sage and onion is traditionally English; potato dressing flavoured with onion and apple is a favourite of Mennonite cooks.

When purchasing, choose a goose labelled "young"; if not graded, pick one with soft, fat yellow feet and legs covered with soft down. A red bill is a sign of age.

Amount of Goose to Purchase
For each serving allow 500-600 g

TIMETABLE FOR ROASTING GOOSE AT 160°C

Ready-to-cook kg	Time in h*
3.5-4.5	3-4
4.5-5.5	4-5

* Because variation of shape affects cooking times, allow an extra half hour in case additional time is needed.

ROAST GOOSE

1. Prepare, stuff if desired and truss goose.
2. Prick skin all over with a fork to allow fat to run out during roasting.
3. Place goose breast down on a rack in a roasting pan; sprinkle with salt; do not add water or fat.
4. Roast for 1 h, turn goose breast up and finish roasting according to timetable.
5. As bird begins to brown, cover loosely with foil; prick the skin once or twice during roasting but do not baste.
6. Pour off fat as it accumulates in the pan.
7. During the last half hour of cooking, remove foil to allow skin to become crisp; to determine when goose is cooked, test the drumstick for softness to touch and the mobility of the leg when twisted.
8. Prepare GRAVY after removing most of the fat from the pan. Serve with pickled crabapples or apple rings.

Duck

Duck has enjoyed a greater popularity in European cuisines than in Canada where its consumption is relatively low. More expensive than chicken and consisting of all dark meat and a high percentage of fat, frozen duck is available throughout the year. Like other poultry, it contributes high quality protein and B vitamins. Roast or broil, pricking skin several times during cooking to allow fat to run off. For each serving of duck allow: 500-575 g

TIMETABLE FOR ROASTING DUCK

Because duck contains more fat than chicken or turkey, it should be roasted at a higher temperature. It can be roasted at a constant moderate temperature throughout the cooking period; or it can be cooked at a high temperature for a short period to hasten the rendering of the fat, then finished at a lower temperature. If the latter method is used, turn the bird over at least once during roasting, finishing with the breast in an upright position.

Method I—Roast at constant temperature of
180°C

Method II—Roast 10 min breast side up,
10 min breast side down, at
220°C
Finish at   180°C

Total cooking time is 2.5 h for duck of approximately 2 kg

GLAZED ROAST DUCKLING

2 kg	**duckling**
	APRICOT DRESSING
	1 orange
125 ml	**water**
30 ml	**currant or apple jelly**
30 ml	**lemon juice**
125 ml	**poultry stock**

1. Rinse and dry duckling; stuff with dressing, close opening (see TO DRESS OR STUFF A BIRD). and tie legs close to the body.
2. Prick skin of duck all over with a fork; place breast down on a rack in a roasting pan; sprinkle with salt. Do not add water or fat and do not cover.

3. Follow preceding timetable for roasting duck using either method of cooking. After roasting for 45 min, turn duck breast up, prick skin again and pour off fat.
4. Continue roasting until duck has been in the oven for a total of 2 h
5. Meanwhile prepare a glazing mixture: coarsely grate orange peel and cook in water for 10 min; drain and discard water.
6. Remove and discard all white membrane from orange; chop pulp and combine with peel and remaining ingredients using stock from simmered giblets, or water and instant chicken soup base.
7. Remove duck from pan to a warm place; drain off all the fat from the pan and blend glaze mixture with meat juices.
8. Return duck to pan and baste with glaze; continue roasting, basting several times until duck is tender, about 30 min. *Serves 3-4.*

Variation

Roast Duckling with Cherries

398 ml	1 can pitted black cherries
125 ml	fruit juice *or* water
15 ml	lemon juice
15 ml	cornstarch
50 ml	water

1. Heat the juice from the cherries and substitute for the glaze in the preceding recipe, basting the duck with it frequently during the last half-hour of cooking.
2. When duck is cooked, pour off fat, remove to a platter; add fruit juice, cherries and any remaining juice to the drippings in the pan and simmer 5 min; blend or shake together cornstarch and water and blend into cherry mixture.
3. Cook, stirring until thickened. Serve sauce with duckling.

DUCKLING À l'ORANGE

2 kg	1 duckling, quartered
	salt
178 ml	1 can frozen orange juice
	concentrate
30 ml	liquid honey *or* syrup

1. Arrange duckling pieces skin-side up on a rack in a shallow pan; prick skin all over with a fork so fat can run off; sprinkle with salt.
2. Bake for approximately 2 h, draining off the accumulated fat periodically, at 180°C
3. Combine honey or syrup with an equal quantity of concentrated frozen orange juice and baste duck

with this mixture while roasting for another 30 min
4. Reconstitute the remaining orange juice concentrate with 3 times the quantity of cold water and use to make ORANGE SAUCE.
5. Serve duckling on rice, topped with Orange Sauce. Garnish with watercress or parsley. *Serves 4.*

Rabbit or Hare

Meat of the rabbit or hare is lean and rich in protein. Domestic rabbit or young wild rabbit can be substituted for chicken in many recipes.

FRICASSEE OF RABBIT OR HARE

	1 rabbit
125 ml	flour
	salt, pepper
60 ml	cooking oil
60 ml	chopped onions
250 ml	sliced mushrooms
375 ml	chicken stock, *or*
	tomato juice
2 ml	thyme, chervil, *or* basil
	sour cream *or* plain yogurt

1. Cut rabbit into pieces, dredge in seasoned flour.
2. Heat oil and sauté onions and mushrooms until golden; remove from pan.
3. Add rabbit to the pan and lightly brown it on all sides.
4. Pour the liquid over the rabbit, cover and simmer until the meat is just tender, about 1 h
5. Add the onions, mushrooms and thyme and simmer 5 min more.
6. Thicken the gravy if necessary with a little flour (see THICKENING LIQUIDS). Stir in a few spoonfuls of sour cream or yogurt if desired.
7. Taste and adjust seasoning if necessary.

RABBIT OR HARE À LA MODE (HASENPFEFFER)

Soak rabbit pieces in refrigerator for 2 d in a crock or non-metallic bowl containing vinegar and water in equal parts, to cover the rabbit, 1 sliced onion, 6 peppercorns, 1 bay leaf and a pinch of salt. Remove rabbit and prepare as Rabbit Fricassee, substituting the soaking liquid for the stock. Add sour cream or yogurt to the gravy.

Game

All game is protected in Canada and may be shot only in season. The amount which may be taken is regulated, as is the length of time it may be held in a freezer. Copies of these regulations are available from provincial Departments of Game and Fisheries.

Meat from the deer is lean, high in protein, with an extra measure of all the B vitamins. It must be hung for at least 2 weeks at above freezing temperatures; it is cooked by the same methods as veal.

If the deer was young and not run too long by the hunters, the meat will be tender but rather dry. The fat is hard, so that if venison is to be served hot it must be very hot.

If the animal is old, or if the sirloin steaks when cooked are tough, the rest of the meat should be cooked by moist heat methods.

Cuts of venison are similar to those of mutton. The best cuts for roasting are the leg, or haunch, and the saddle. Steaks and cutlets are slices from the leg and loin. Other pieces, as the flank, breast and neck, should be used in stews. The flank is sometimes included with the saddle, in which case a few pieces of celery, or celery and carrot, may be rolled in each flank, which is then skewered underneath, close to the backbone. Venison, when roasted or broiled, may be served rare.

BROILED VENISON STEAK

1. Rub steak with a cut clove of garlic and softened butter.
2. Broil quickly, unless steaks are very thick; turning them only once.
3. Season. Pour drippings over steaks and serve at once with MAÎTRE D'HÔTEL SAUCE.

VENISON PIE

1. Cut the less tender meat into small cubes; brown in hot fat.
2. Add water just to cover, salt, pepper, onion; simmer until tender; thicken (see THICKENING LIQUIDS). Cool.
3. Pour into a casserole, lined with rich pastry; put on the top crust; brush with milk.
4. Bake for 30 min at 200°C

ROAST VENISON

1. Weigh and wipe meat; place on rack in roasting pan. The meat may be larded or pieces of beef or pork fat may be laid on top of saddle.
2. Dredge meat with flour.
3. Baste every 15 min with fat from pan.
4. Roast approximately 30 min/500 g at 160°C

Other game less commonly eaten are moose, bear and buffalo. Buffalo is available only when the government reduces the size of the herds in the national park at Wainwright, Alberta. Like venison, the quality of these meats depends upon the age and condition of the animal. Bear meat, which is fat, should be treated like pork, the others like beef.

SPANISH MOOSE STEAK

1 kg	moose *or* caribou steak
50 ml	flour
	salt, pepper
30 ml	fat
	1 chopped green pepper
	1 minced garlic clove
	6 small sliced onions
250 ml	canned tomatoes
250 ml	peas (optional)

1. Dredge meat with seasoned flour; brown on both sides in hot fat; remove from the pan.
2. Sauté the pepper and garlic in the remaining fat in the pan.
3. Place the pepper and garlic on the meat; replace it in the pan; add the onions and tomatoes; simmer until tender, about 2 h
4. Shortly before the meat is cooked add the peas and more seasoning if necessary.
5. Arrange on a platter with the vegetables on top; surround with a border of potato puffs.

Recipes, tables, etc. that appear in small capital letters, e.g., PARSLEY BUTTER, CANADA'S FOOD GUIDE, are listed in the index. Consult the index for the number of the page on which the item appears.

MOOSE OR CARIBOU YUKON

1 kg	moose *or* caribou
30 ml	lemon juice
	salt
5 ml	chili powder
75 ml	flour
30 ml	fat
	water
125 ml	chopped olives *or* pimento

1. Cube the meat as for stew; sprinkle with lemon juice; stir well.
2. Season with salt and chili powder; roll in flour.
3. Heat fat and brown cubes on all sides in it; cool slightly and add water to cover.
4. Cover and simmer for about 2 h, removing the cover during the last 20 min to reduce the liquid to a rich gravy.
5. Add olives or pimento; serve with noodles or rice. *Serves 4-6.*

FROGS' LEGS

1 kg	frogs' legs
10 ml	salt
	pepper
	CRUMB COATING
10 ml	lemon juice

1. Cut legs apart at joint if large; remove feet; wipe dry and season.
2. Prepare CRUMB COATING adding lemon juice to the egg; coat legs with crumbs.
3. Fry in deep fat for 10 min (see DEEP FAT FRYING); drain. *Serves 6.*

Wild Fowl

Wild Duck—Not all varieties of wild duck are edible. Edible varieties include the mallard, red-head, canvas back, black duck and teal; they are roasted with or without stuffing. If birds are known to be young and tender, strips of bacon can be laid across the breast and the birds roasted with frequent basting. Bake until tender, 1-2 h, at 150°C

All ducks, and particularly those whose age cannot be determined, may be cooked by an alternative method: bake until brown at 200°C
then cover and cook until tender, 2-2.5 h, at 120°C

Wild Goose—The age of the goose may be determined by the size. Also, a red bill is a sign of age.

If the goose is young, cook it as wild duck, but cook it at least 2 h. Since the fat is strong, do not stuff the bird but fill the cavity with sliced apple or onion which is discarded before serving. Keep the fat drained off as it collects and baste the fowl with currant jelly blended with hot water.

Partridge—This little bird, which is almost all breast, may be cooked by broiling as chicken, or it may be roasted.

To roast, clean; do not stuff. Cover with strips of bacon and bake in oven for 40-60 min, or in an electric frying pan at 150°C

Pheasant—Stuff as chicken. Roast 1.5-2 h at 150°C

Prairie Chicken—Cook as partridge.

Currant jelly melted in hot water is a good basting sauce for wild fowl.

PARTRIDGE IN A POT

	3 partridges
30 ml	cooking oil
	1 sliced medium onion
	few celery leaves
	thyme, marjoram
15 ml	lemon juice
	1 bay leaf
	1 clove
	salt, pepper
450 ml	canned tomatoes

1. Lightly brown partridges in a deep kettle, containing oil, onion, celery leaves and a dash of thyme and marjoram.
2. Add remaining ingredients and simmer, covered for 2 h longer. Serve with rice or wild rice.

Duck, pheasant, or chicken can be substituted for partridge.

Recipes, tables, etc. that appear in small capital letters, e.g., PARSLEY BUTTER, CANADA'S FOOD GUIDE, are listed in the index. Consult the index for the number of the page on which the item appears.

Stuffing

Variety, additional flavour and more servings can result from the addition of stuffing to meat, fish, or vegetables. Different kinds of bread can be used to make the traditional bread dressing; cereals such as rice, cracked wheat and oats can be substituted to increase nutritional value (see variations following basic recipe). Spices, nuts, fruits and other ingredients can be chosen to complement the dish.

Do not stuff poultry before freezing. Stuff when completely thawed and cook immediately after stuffing. If desired, dressing can be prepared and baked separately in a casserole during the last hour of cooking; add a little stock from the simmered giblets and neck and cover bread dressing to prevent drying out; uncover during the last 10 minutes.

Basic Recipe
BREAD DRESSING

1 *l*	soft crumbs *or* cubes from day-old bread
50 ml	butter *or* margarine
125 ml	chopped celery
50 ml	chopped onion
5 ml	salt
	pepper
5 ml	sage *or* poultry seasoning, *or* savory

1. While preparing crumbs, melt the fat and sauté the celery and onion until golden.
2. Combine crumbs, salt, a little pepper and the herb; mix with the cooked vegetables and fat.
3. Pack lightly into the bird, allowing for the dressing to swell during cooking.

Makes enough dressing for a large chicken.
Prepare ½ recipe for fish or a roast; 3-4 times the recipe for a turkey.

Variations

Parsley Dressing

60 ml	minced parsley

Add parsley; omit sage. Serve with fish.

Mushroom Dressing

250 ml	chopped mushrooms

Sauté mushrooms with the celery and onions.

Oyster Dressing

250 ml	cooked oysters

Drain and chop oysters; combine with cooked celery and onions; use oyster liquid to moisten crumbs.

Apple Dressing

500 ml	apples, peeled, cored and chopped

Add chopped apples to bread.

Apricot Dressing

250 ml	tenderized, dried apricots
175 ml	seedless raisins

Chop apricots and raisins; omit onion and herbs.

Lemon Dressing

Substitute grated lemon rind for herbs. Serve with fish.

Orange Dressing

250 ml	orange sections

Add orange sections; omit onion and herbs.

Peanut Dressing

250 ml	chopped peanuts
50 ml	chicken stock

Add to mixture. If peanuts are salted, decrease salt in basic recipe.

Chestnut Dressing

175 g	chestnuts
400 ml	seasoned stock

Make a cross on the flat side of each chestnut using a paring knife; cover with boiling water and boil 5 min, a few at a time, and shell while warm. The underskin is bitter and must be removed. Freeze nuts until needed, then simmer uncovered in seasoned stock for 30 min or until tender. Drain and cool. Add to dressing.

Cracked Wheat Dressing

375 ml	cracked wheat
625 ml	chicken broth
125 ml	raisins, chopped
125 ml	nuts, chopped

Substitute cracked wheat for all the bread and sauté it with celery and onion until golden; add chicken broth and simmer covered for about 20 min. Add raisins and nuts (peanuts, walnuts, almonds, filberts, etc.).

Rolled Oats Dressing

Substitute rolled oats for part of the bread, for a pleasant and nutritious variation.

Rice Dressing

250 ml	uncooked rice
1 ℓ	chicken broth and/or orange juice

Prepare as fried rice, browning rice in butter with onions and celery; cook in chicken broth and/or orange juice; substitute for the bread. If desired, add any of chopped, pitted dried prunes, chopped apricots, or nuts.

Potato Dressing

Substitute mashed potatoes for the bread; omit sage; add any of sautéed mushrooms, chopped apple, or nuts.

A standing rib roast, glazed with spaghetti sauce and served with pasta as a change from potatoes or rice. Marinated raw vegetables make a tangy accompaniment. Lawry's Foods, Inc.

13 Vegetables

Truly beautiful are the many varieties of colourful vegetables that grace our markets. Proper storage, cooking and serving methods maintain this beauty and their high content of vitamins and minerals. Vitamin A is abundant in all yellow (orange) and green vegetables; the more vivid the colour, the greater the content of vitamin A. Carrots are very rich in vitamin A; one serving gives us three times our daily requirement!

Vitamin C is present in large amounts in many fresh vegetables including cabbage, tomatoes, and red and green sweet peppers. Broccoli not only supplies the daily requirement of vitamin A but it also supplies as much or more vitamin C per serving as an orange. It is also rich in calcium and riboflavin. Iron is present in significant amounts in green vegetables. Peas are a good source of iron and an excellent source of thiamine.

The crispness of raw vegetables provides a pleasant texture contrast with other foods, and there is little or no loss of vitamin C and folic acid which are subject to destruction by heat.

The fibre provided by vegetables, particularly beans, peas and potatoes is a valuable contribution to the diet.

Grading of Vegetables—Vegetables must be graded according to federal regulations before being shipped from one province to another or before being exported. Vegetables grown and sold within a province are usually subject to similar provincial regulations but not all provinces require the grading of the same vegetables.

Federal grade designations are Canada No. 1 and Canada No. 2, the former rating slightly higher in conformity to size, shape, cleanliness and relative freedom from blemishes, disease and injury.

Purchasing Vegetables

Buy vegetables in season; they are fresher and less expensive, and have more flavour and nutritional value. Shop in person for vegetables and choose those with the brightest colours; buy root vegetables which are firm and heavy for size in quantities in keeping with available storage space. Leafy vegetables should be crisp and should be bought in small quantities. All should be free of blemishes and soft spots.

Storing Vegetables

Vegetables should be stored in a cool place away from sunlight. To store large quantities of root vegetables over the winter months, layer the vegetables with clean sand, in boxes, beginning and ending with sand. Store in a cool place. Vermiculite may be substituted for the sand. Both sand and vermiculite retard dehydration of the vegetables by filling in air spaces while not absorbing moisture from the vegetables.

Raw vegetables do *not* freeze well. Exceptions are green pepper, celery, tomatoes, and diced onion; although they wilt on thawing, they are quite acceptable for use in cooked dishes. Other fresh vegetables to be frozen must first be blanched or parboiled for a short, timed period, then quickly plunged into cold water. Detailed information for freezing the many varieties of fresh vegetables is available in bulletins from the provincial departments of agriculture.

Most cooked vegetables freeze well. Exceptions are boiled (white) potatoes, which become mealy, and corn on the cob, which suffers a loss of flavour and texture.

Vegetable casseroles freeze well. Leftover baked potatoes can be converted to baked stuffed potatoes, foil-wrapped, and frozen for future use—or they can be prepared in advance for a special occasion.

Preparation of Vegetables

Vegetables should be thoroughly clean; if the skins are left on the vegetables they should be scrubbed with a brush. Remove only a thin layer of peeling, as most of the iron in root vegetables is found in the area just under the skin. It may be necessary to soak cauliflower and broccoli in cold, salted water for about 15 min before cooking in order to draw out any organisms that may be lodged between the flowerets. Leave vegetables in as large pieces as possible; the more exposed surfaces there are, the greater will be the loss of vitamins and minerals.

Variation of *size* and *shape* as well as texture, flavour, and colour should be considered when serving several vegetables at one time. Create a variety of shapes by choosing from the list on the next page.

Ways to Prepare Vegetables

Julienne—(vegetables cut into thin strips, sometimes referred to as *shoe-string*) Potatoes, carrots, beets, green beans.

Fingers—(vegetables cut into strips, longer and wider than Julienne) Carrots, parsnips, potatoes.

Whole—Peas, potatoes, asparagus, tiny beets, corn on the cob. Cauliflower is sometimes cooked whole and served with other vegetables from a platter.

Rounds or Slices—Beets, potatoes, tomatoes, onions.

Diced or Cubed—Turnip, potatoes, onions.

Mashed or Whipped—Potatoes, turnip, squash.

Riced—(vegetables forced through tiny holes of a ricer or food press) Cooked potatoes.

Chopped—Hash brown potatoes, onions.

Flowerets—Cauliflower, broccoli.

Shredded—Cabbage, beets (often pan-sautéed).

Wedges—Cooked cabbage, lettuce (raw).

General Directions for Cooking Vegetables

Do not overcook vegetables. Cook them until they are just tender when tested with the point of a paring knife. Season with salt, pepper and/or herbs and a little butter or margarine.

Boiling—The general rule is to cook vegetables in a small quantity of boiling water covered with a tight-fitting lid. Bring vegetable to the boil as quickly as possible, then reduce heat and boil gently until the vegetable is tender. This method of boiling ensures the maximum retention of vitamins and minerals. Leafy vegetables like spinach require only the water which clings to the leaves when washing. If vegetables such as winter cabbage have become strong in flavour through storage, increasing the amount of water used or leaving the lid off the pot for part of the cooking period will reduce the strong flavour. When cooking green vegetables, leaving the lid off the pot during the last few minutes of cooking results in a brighter green. Always start with boiling water; unless the vegetable is particularly strong in flavour, save the cooking water (vegetable stock) to dilute canned soups, to reconstitute dehydrated soups, for soup stocks, or for gravies.

Steaming—Because the water is not in direct contact with the vegetable, steaming retains more of the water-soluble vitamins than does boiling. Boiling water is placed in a pot and the vegetable is placed over it on a rack or in a separate compartment which has holes in the bottom to allow the steam to penetrate. The pot is tightly covered. This method of cooking is suitable for most vegetables. See COOKING IN FOIL.

Pressure Cooking—Follow directions given with the pressure cooker. In this method, little water is used and the cooking time is short. Therefore retention of vitamins and minerals is good. This method of cooking is suitable for all but leafy vegetables and dried peas and lentils.

Baking—Scrub vegetables with a brush. In the case of potatoes, leave skins on and prick in several places with a fork to enable steam to escape. Vegetables may be peeled and baked in large or small pieces in a covered casserole. Baking retains vitamins and minerals to a high degree and is most suited to root vegetables, squash and onions. To conserve energy, serve a baked vegetable as part of an oven-cooked meal.

Roasting—This is a variation of baking, in which vegetables are cooked in the oven around roasting meat. Sometimes vegetables are precooked in water for 10-15 min

French Frying—See DEEP FAT FRYING.

Vegetables on Skewers (on a Barbecue)—Scrub potatoes, yams, white turnips, onions, and tomatoes; leave whole and unpeeled. Thread each kind of vegetable onto its own skewer. Rotate frequently over hot coals. Cook the potatoes and yams first, approximately 60 min, then onions and turnips for about 40 min. Tomatoes will cook in 5-10 min and so should be cooked at the very last. Vegetables can be kept in a warm place without further cooking if wrapped in foil.

Cooking Frozen Vegetables—Frozen vegetables require less cooking, since the processes of blanching, freezing, and thawing tend to soften the cellulose. Follow directions given on the packages of commercially frozen vegetables. Others should be allowed to thaw slightly and then be cooked with little or no added water in a tightly covered saucepan. To ensure uniform cooking, break the melting mass apart with a fork.

Cooking Canned Vegetables—Empty canned vegetables into a saucepan and heat to boiling. Save the cooking water to dilute canned soups, or for gravy or soup stock. All *home-canned* vegetables except tomatoes must be boiled in an open saucepan 10-15 min before tasting or using.

Pan-sautéeing—Vegetables are shredded, diced, or thinly sliced and cooked in a tightly covered frying pan with a small quantity of melted butter or oil 50 ml

The fat prevents vegetables from sticking while the juices are turning into steam; the steam finishes the cooking. This method of cooking can be used effectively with most young vegetables, especially those with a high moisture content—cabbage, kale, and spinach.

Root vegetables such as carrots are cooked quickly by this method. They should be shredded coarsely. A little water must be added. See Index for specific recipes under BEETS, CABBAGE, and ASPARAGUS.

Stir-frying combines the principles of sautéeing and steaming. It is a fast method of cooking tender vegetables while retaining maximum flavour, colour, texture, and nutrients. See STIR-FRIED VEGETABLES for a description of this cooking technique.

Serving Vegetables

For variety, to dress up a vegetable, or to enhance the flavours of vegetables which have had a long winter storage, serve them with:

Herbs—such as chopped mint, chives, chervil, basil, tarragon, and parsley.

Spices—nutmeg on spinach; cinnamon on squash; caraway seeds in cabbage; celery seeds in carrots.

Lemon or Lime Juice on asparagus, broccoli, green beans, zucchini, sprinkled over the vegetable or stirred into melted butter and poured over the vegetable.

Sugar—a small spoonful added to mashed, winter turnip.

FLAVOURED BUTTERS chosen to complement the vegetable and stirred in before serving or served with a vegetable.

Crisp, Crumbled Bacon tossed with cooked green beans, carrots, or potatoes, or used as a topping for baked stuffed vegetables.

Chopped Walnuts, Slivers of Toasted Almonds or other nuts or sesame seeds, tossed with green beans, slices of zucchini, brussel sprouts.

Fine Buttered Crumbs and grated cheese tossed with cooked cauliflower, broccoli, brussel sprouts, zucchini, beans, or onions.

Small Garlic Croutons served as crumbs (see preceding variation).

Sour Cream or Yogurt on baked potatoes, cooked green or lima beans, or mixtures of sautéed or baked vegetables.

Sauces—HOLLANDAISE, CHEESE (MORNAY) SAUCE, WHITE SAUCE and variations, CURRY SAUCE.

Other Vegetables—Serve them with other cooked vegetables which complement them in flavour and colour. At time of serving heat with pearl onions, onion rings, mushrooms, kernel corn, sliced zucchini, baby carrots or potatoes, green lima beans, bean sprouts, strips of red and green sweet pepper. Combine mashed turnips with mashed carrots or mashed potatoes. Serve baked vegetables stuffed with other vegetables.

Lemon juice and herbs are friends indeed to vegetables served on low-salt, low-fat, and other restricted diets.

Recipes, tables, etc. that appear in small capital letters, e.g., PARSLEY BUTTER, CANADA'S FOOD GUIDE, are listed in the index. Consult the index for the number of the page on which the item appears.

Vegetables may be stir-fried in a wok. Ontario Ministry of Agriculture and Food.

Vegetable Cookery Chart

Kind	Preparation	Cooking Time in Min*					Amount Required for 6 Servings
		Boil	Steam	Pressure Cook	Pan-sauté (Shred)	Bake	
MILD							
Artichokes, Jerusalem	Clean and scrape. To boil add a few drops of vinegar to cooking water.	20-30	30-40	10			1 kg
French	See FRENCH ARTICHOKES.						
Asparagus	Wash, cut off tough ends; to boil, tie in bunches and stand in a deep pot with water half way up stalks (An old coffee pot works well.)	15-20	30-40	9	5-8		500 g
Beans, Wax or Green	Wash, remove stems and tips; cut into 2 or 3 pieces or slice into long, thin strips.	15-25	30-35	2-2.5	5-8		750 g
Beets, Whole	Cut off tops; wash and do not break the skin.	25-45		15-18	10	90 at 180°C	1 kg
Carrots	Wash; scrape or peel. Leave whole if small; slice or dice. Cover when baking.	15-20	20-30	2-3	5-8	35-45 at 180°C	750 kg
Celery	Clean with brush; remove leaves and cut into pieces.	20	25	2-3	5		½ bunch
Corn	Remove leaves and silk; cook in a large pot of boiling water.	8-10			10-12		12-18 cobs

Vegetable	Preparation						Amount
Eggplant	Peel just before using to avoid discolouration; dice or slice.	10-20				30 at 180°C	1 large
Endive, Belgian	Quarter or halve lengthwise. Braise by sautéeing in butter for a few minutes, then simmering in a little stock for a few minutes until just tender. Serve cold as salad.						4-6
Fennel	Trim base of bulb; discard tough outer leaves; quarter. Serve raw as a cold appetizer like radishes, or in salads. Boil (simmer); serve with sauce. Its mild licorice flavour is nice with fish.	20					3-6 bulbs with stems
Fiddleheads	If fresh, rinse. If frozen, thaw only during cooking. Cook until just tender in a small amount of water.	10-15					350-400 g
Mushrooms	Tender, fresh mushrooms need no peeling; leave whole, slice or dice. Sauté, broil, or stuff and bake.				4-5	broil 5	750 g / 750-800 ml
Parsnips	Peel or scrape; cut lengthwise or crosswise; remove cores if tough.	20-30	30-45	10			750 g
Peas	Remove from pods; rinse.	15-25	15-25	1	5		1.5 kg
Peppers, Sweet	Remove stems, seeds and membranes. Usually cut into strips or chopped, sautéed, and added to mixtures; whole peppers may be stuffed and baked.				5		
Potatoes, Irish	Wash and peel, or cook in skins.	35-40	40-50	8-10		50-60 at 200°C	1 kg
Sweet (Yams)	Scrub and cook in skins.	30-40	30-45	8		50 at 200°C	1 kg

Cooking Time in Min*

Kind	Preparation	Boil	Steam	Pressure Cook	Pan-sauté (Shred)	Bake	Amount Required for 6 Servings
Salsify	Scrub, peel, and cut into slices or cubes.	20-25					750 g
Winter Squash Hubbard	Cut into chunks, remove seeds and bake; for mashing, peel, dice, and steam.	35-45	45-50	12-15		60-90 at 180°C	1-1.5 kg
Pepper and Acorn	Cut in half; remove seeds and bake or steam cut-side down.		45			50 at 180°C	1.5 kg (3 whole)
Butternut	Slice.						
Summer Squash	Wash, do not peel; remove seeds if desired. Slice.						
Vegetable Marrow	Boil or steam.		15				1 medium marrow
Zucchini Crook-necked	Boil, stir fry, or sauté small varieties. Stuff and bake large squash.	5-10	5				1 kg
STRONG							
Broccoli	Soak in salted water 10 min, trim and cut off flowerets from main stalk; split ends of stalks.	15-20	20-30	1.5-2	5-7		1 kg
Brussel Sprouts	Remove wilted leaves; leave whole.	12-20	20-25	2			750 g
Cabbage	Remove wilted outside leaves; cut into quarters or shred.	5-15	10-20	1-1.5	5-8		1 kg

	Preparation						Quantity
Cauliflower	Remove leaves and stem; soak 10 min in salted water; divide into whole flowerets. Or leave whole.	10-20 25-30	15-30	2-3	5-7		1 kg 1 medium head
Kohlrabi	Cut off leaves; wash, pare, dice or slice.	25-30		5-6	5-8		1 kg (6 whole)
Onions	Peel onions under water; quarter or leave whole.	30-40	25-30	5-8	10-15	45-60 at 180°C	750 g
Turnips, Yellow (Rutabaga) or White	Wash, cut in slices and peel; dice.	20-30	25-35	10	5-8		1 kg
LEAFY							
Spinach Beet Tops	Remove roots, coarse stems; wash in warm water and rinse twice. Cook in water which clings to leaves—no more!	8-10	15-20		5-6		575-800 g
Swiss Chard	Remove roots, coarse stems; wash in warm water and rinse twice. Cook in water which clings to leaves—no more!	10-15	20-35	5	8-10		1 kg
Kale	Remove roots, coarse stems; wash in warm water and rinse twice. Cook in water which clings to leaves—no more!	15-25		3.5-5	5-8		1 kg

* Cooking times for vegetables which have been frozen will be somewhat less. If vegetables are commercially frozen, follow cooking directions on package.
Vegetables normally served raw as salad greens are described in the chapter on Salads.

Potatoes

Potatoes are available fresh, frozen as French fries, potato puffs, etc., dehydrated for serving as instant mashed and scalloped potatoes, and processed as potato chips. Although grown in all provinces, potatoes are produced in the greatest quantity in the Maritimes.

The most widely grown varieties are suitable for all methods of cooking. When sold, bags must show the words "Table Potatoes," the net mass or weight, grade name, and the name and address of the packer or shipper. Canada No. 1 potatoes have 3 additional categories: Canada No. 1 Large and Canada No. 1 Small, which differ from the standard in size only, and Canada No. 1 New Potatoes, a designation which is permitted before September 16 of each year for a range of young potatoes, the smallest of which would, after that date, be classified as Small.

Although potatoes are usually cheapest when bought in large quantities, buy only the quantity which can be properly stored in a cold room or other dark, well-ventilated place at 7-10°C. When stored above recommended temperatures, potatoes may sprout and shrivel; below those temperatures, potatoes develop a sweet flavour. Bringing small quantities of potatoes into room temperature for a few days before cooking results in the best flavour. Green colouring which develops on the surface of potatoes kept in the light should not be eaten but peeled off.

A versatile addition to the menu, potatoes contribute nutritionally to the diet with their high level of vitamin C, important minerals including iron and potassium, and their content of dietary fibre. Carbohydrate in the form of starch provides food energy. Served without butter or sauces, a medium potato provides no more food energy than a large apple.

BOILED NEW POTATOES

The cooking method most suited to *new* potatoes is boiling. Scrub potatoes with a brush or scrape off skins with the edge of a knife. Do not peel. Follow general directions for BOILING VEGETABLES. When new potatoes are cooked in their skins, skins can be easily pulled off with the fingers. Serve with a little butter or margarine, and chopped parsley.

For a Swedish touch, line a deep serving dish with a cloth napkin which overhangs the dish. Put in the hot, cooked potatoes and top with sprigs of fresh dill. Cover with the napkin and leave in a warm place for 10 min while the potatoes absorb the aroma. Remove dill and serve.

MASHED POTATOES

	6 medium potatoes, peeled
75 ml	hot potato stock *or* milk
30 ml	butter *or* margarine, softened
	salt, pepper

1. Peel potatoes and boil until tender. See VEGETABLE COOKERY CHART. Drain; reserve liquid.
2. Mash the potatoes. Add hot stock *or* hot milk. Beat in with butter or margarine and seasoning until light and fluffy, adding more liquid if needed. *Serves 4. Yield:* 150 ml

COLCANNON

Sometimes called Potato and Cabbage Pudding, this is a traditional Irish dish.
1. To mashed potatoes in the preceding recipe, stir in cabbage which has been cooked but is still crisp, 500 ml
2. Fry 3 slices of bacon until crisp; remove from pan and fry 1 chopped onion in the fat until golden. Pour off fat.
3. Add potato mixture to onions and heat through; transfer to a greased casserole. Top with buttered crumbs and bake until golden brown at 200°C
4. Top with crumbled bacon and serve. *Serves 4-6.*

DUCHESS POTATOES

Prepare mashed potatoes or instant mashed potatoes, *or* use leftover mashed potatoes; season. Add 1 egg or 2 yolks, well-beaten, to potatoes, 500 ml Spread potatoes in a shallow, greased baking dish, mounding them in the centre. Smooth the surface and brush with melted butter or margarine, or prepare potato rosettes by forcing mixture through a large rosette tube onto a greased baking sheet. Brown in the oven at 200°C

Variation
Potato Puffs—Beat 2 eggs yolks into potatoes; add chopped parsley and finely chopped onion to taste. Beat egg whites and fold into potato mixture. Bake in greased muffin pans until browned, at 180°C

Recipes, tables, etc. that appear in small capital letters, e.g., PARSLEY BUTTER, CANADA'S FOOD GUIDE, are listed in the index. Consult the index for the number of the page on which the item appears.

BAKED POTATOES

Choose thick, regular-shaped, mature potatoes for baking. They can be wrapped in foil before cooking for a moist potato. If time is scarce, potatoes can be parboiled 10 min while waiting for the oven to heat. The insertion of a metal skewer or the upright prongs of a potato rack hastens baking time by conducting heat into the centre of the potato.

1. Scrub and rinse potatoes; prick with a fork in several places; grease lightly if a soft shiny skin is desired.
2. Place on a rack in the oven; bake 45-60 min at 220°C
3. Cut an X in the top of each, immediately on taking from oven, to allow steam to escape. Squeeze lightly from bottom to force some of cooked potato upward.
4. Serve uncovered; add butter or margarine.
5. Garnish with parsley and/or paprika; or add a spoonful of any of the following toppings:

   Add to sour cream *or* yogurt: 125 ml
   a sprinkling of chopped chives or finely chopped green onions and/or crumbled, crisp bacon,
   or
   an equal quantity of grated Cheddar cheese (or use part blue cheese) and add chives or finely chopped green onions,
   or
   chopped fresh dill: 15 ml
   or
   dried dill: 5 ml
   or
   prepared horseradish: 10 ml

BAKED STUFFED POTATOES

	6 baked potatoes*
	salt, pepper
30 ml	butter
75-100 ml	hot milk

1. Cut a slice from the tops of the potatoes; scoop out the insides into a bowl.
2. Mash; add seasonings, butter and milk; beat until light.
3. Refill shells, heat in oven until mixture is thoroughly heated and lightly browned (about 20 min) at 200°C
   Or, cover and refrigerate or wrap and freeze filled shells and reheat when needed.

* For 6 very generous portions, cook 7 or 8 potatoes but fill only 6 shells.

Variations

For extra flavour, use any of the toppings suggested in the preceding recipe *or* stir in one or a combination of the following before placing in shells:

15 ml	finely chopped parsley, chives, *or* fresh dill
50 ml	finely chopped onion
175 ml	sour cream
250 ml	grated Cheddar cheese
125-250 ml	chopped, cooked meat (ham, veal, chicken, corned beef, or cooked sausage meat)
250 ml	CHEESE *or* CELERY SAUCE containing tuna, crab, salmon, *or* chopped cooked spinach
125 ml	TOMATO SAUCE topped with grated Mozzarella cheese and a sprinkle of oregano

FRANCONIA POTATOES

1. Choose potatoes of equal size; if large, cut into halves.
2. Wash and peel potatoes; rinse and pat dry with a towel.
3. Place in a roasting pan around meat while it is roasting.
4. Adjust oven temperature if necessary and bake potatoes 1.5 h or until tender when tested with the point of a knife, turning them occasionally in the hot fat. Oven temperature: 180°C

If potatoes are cold before cooking, less fat will be absorbed. An alternative method for preparing Franconia potatoes is to boil and drain the potatoes, and then rotate them with a fork in a small amount of dark dripping for a few minutes or until browned.

BROILER-FRIED POTATOES

1 kg	6 medium potatoes
125 ml	oil

1. Preheat broiler.
2. Prepare potatoes as in French Fried Potatoes to the end of step 2.
3. Place potatoes in broiler pan; pour oil over them and stir to coat all sides.
4. Broil 15-18 min, stirring frequently until golden brown. *Serves 4.*

SCALLOPED POTATOES

Scalloped potatoes are especially good served with meats that do not have their own gravy: ham, sausages, liver, and all cold meats. The addition of small chunks of canned salmon or ham converts scalloped potatoes into a main dish.

1.5 *l*	6 medium potatoes, thinly sliced
	1 onion, finely chopped (optional)
	salt, pepper
30 ml	flour
30 ml	butter *or* margarine
500 ml	hot milk

Method I—Using fresh milk or reconstituted skim milk:

1. Using the given quantities of ingredients as a guide only, put a layer of potatoes in a greased baking dish. Sprinkle with onion, salt, pepper and flour; dot with butter or margarine. Repeat until all the potatoes are used and the dish is about 2/3 full.
2. Pour in milk until it may be seen through the top layer.
3. Cover and bake for about 30 min; remove cover and bake for another 30-40 min or until potatoes are tender when tested with the point of a knife. Oven temperature: 160°C
   Serves 4-6.

Method II—Using skim milk powder, 175-250 ml

Whip skim milk powder into stock or water to replace the milk.

1. In a jar with a tight-fitting lid, combine stock, milk powder, flour and seasonings; shake, covered, only until thoroughly combined.
2. Pour liquid over the potato slices and chopped onion which have been layered in the casserole; dot with butter or margarine.
3. Finish as Method I, step 3.

Baking time of scalloped potatoes can be reduced by about 10-15 min by first preparing a WHITE SAUCE from the flour, fat, and milk (or milk powder and stock) and heating the sliced potatoes and chopped onion in the sauce until boiling.

Recipes, tables, etc. that appear in small capital letters, e.g., PARSLEY BUTTER, CANADA'S FOOD GUIDE, are listed in the index. Consult the index for the number of the page on which the item appears.

FRENCH FRIED POTATOES

1.5-2 kg	10 potatoes
1-1.5 kg	fat
or	
1-1.5 *l*	oil

1. Wash, peel and cut mature potatoes into fingers 1 cm × 6 cm
2. Soak in cold water 10-15 min to remove starch; drain and dry well in a towel.
3. Heat fat gradually in a deep pan until the desired temperature is reached. See DEEP FAT FRYING.
4. Place enough potatoes in a wire basket or sieve to cover the bottom and lower slowly into the fat. Fry until potatoes are crisp and golden brown, about 5-7 min at 185°C

Drain on absorbent paper. *Serves 8-10.*

POTATOES ROMANOFF

This casserole is ideal for a party buffet. For extra richness, sour cream and cheese can be increased up to twice the quantity.

125 ml	finely chopped onion
30 ml	butter
1.25 *l*	5 large potatoes, boiled, sliced
125 ml	grated Cheddar cheese
	2 eggs, beaten
250 ml	sour cream
	salt, pepper

1. Sauté onions in butter until soft.
2. Spread the cooked potatoes in a greased medium casserole (see CASSEROLES). Cover evenly with onions and half the cheese.
3. Beat together eggs, sour cream, and seasonings and pour over the potatoes; sprinkle with remaining cheese.
4. Bake until mixture is heated through and set, about 25-30 min, at 180°C

Garnish with chopped parsley. *Serves 6.*

HASH BROWN POTATOES

Dice boiled potatoes and combine with thin slices of onion. Chopped pimento or finely chopped green pepper may be added for additional flavour. Heat fat in a heavy frying pan and cook until potatoes are brown and crisp. Flatten mixture with the bottom of a lifter. Turn with 2 egg lifters and brown on the other side.

Choose from a wealth of fresh vegetables of every variety and colour to make meals nutritious and good tasting.

A hearty vegetable stew.

Grated carrot combined with pepper squash in white sauce and sprinkled with buttered crumbs before baking.

LYONNAISE POTATOES

	6 medium potatoes, boiled
125 ml	chopped onion
	salt, pepper
75 ml	oil *or* fat
30 ml	chopped parsley

1. Cut cold, boiled potatoes into thin slices about 1 cm
2. Heat fat, add potato slices and onion; fry stirring occasionally until golden; season and sprinkle with parsley. *Serves 4-6.*

POTATO PANCAKES

50 ml	flour
750 ml	grated potatoes
	(use medium grater)
	1 small onion, finely chopped
	2 eggs, lightly beaten
	salt, pepper
50 ml	melted butter *or* oil

1. Heat a heavy frying pan; add only enough oil to lightly coat the bottom and heat until a drop of water will sizzle in the pan. Reduce heat.
2. While pan is heating, combine ingredients; ladle mixture onto heated pan. For each pancake allow about 75 ml
3. Flatten the cooking mixture if necessary, using the bottom of a lifter or a glass. Cook until crisp and brown on both sides.
4. Keep cooked pancakes in a warm place until all the batter has been used; grease pan between batches. Serve as a vegetable or as pancakes with sour cream. *Yield:* 8-10 pancakes.

Kiev Latkes are potato pancakes, one of the many varieties of pancakes served during Jewish festivals. To prepare from the POTATO PANCAKES recipe, separate the eggs, folding the beaten whites into the combined ingredients containing the yolks. Fry in deep fat (see DEEP FAT FRYING). Serve with sour cream or applesauce.

BAKED SWEET POTATOES OR YAMS

Follow directions for BAKED POTATOES. Cooking time will be slightly less.

FRUITY SWEET POTATOES

	6 medium sweet potatoes
15 ml	cornstarch
75 ml	brown sugar
50 ml	sugar
50 ml	melted butter
	salt
250 ml	orange juice *or* crushed pineapple and juice
15 ml	grated orange rind

1. Boil potatoes in skins until tender, about 30 min; or use canned sweet potatoes. Drain.
2. Combine cornstarch, sugars and melted butter in a saucepan and mix until smooth; add remaining ingredients and cook, with frequent stirring until thick.
3. Peel potatoes, cut in halves or thick slices, or leave whole if not too large.
4. Arrange potatoes in a shallow, greased baking dish and pour the fruit sauce over them.
5. Cover dish and bake for about 20 min; remove cover and bake 15 min longer. Oven temperature: 180°C
   Serves 6-8.

For a speedy version using canned sweet potatoes, combine the juice and rind of 1 orange with twice the quantity of liquid from the potatoes; sweeten with a little sugar. Heat potatoes in the liquid, turning only once. Add a little butter or margarine and serve.

PAN-SAUTÉED ASPARAGUS

1 kg	asparagus
30 ml	oil
	1 garlic clove, crushed
15 ml	soya sauce

1. Wash asparagus and cut off tough ends; leaving tips whole, cut stalks into short diagonal lengths.
2. Heat oil in a saucepan, add garlic and asparagus, cover and cook over medium heat until tender but still crisp, about 5 min. Shake pan several times during cooking.
3. Stir in soya sauce, toss gently, and serve. *Serves 4-6.*

A "Vegetable Plate" of 3 or 4 contrasting vegetables, one stuffed or with a sauce such as CHEESE SAUCE or EGG SAUCE, and another served raw, adds variety to the menu while easing the budget.

FRENCH ARTICHOKES

1. Trim off most of the stem, remove outside bottom leaves and cut off any discoloured tips. This should be done just before cooking to prevent discolouration.
2. Wash thoroughly to remove all sand; stand upright in a deep saucepan and do not allow the vegetable to tip over.
3. Sprinkle with salt, and pour oil over each, about 10 ml
4. Pour in boiling water to a depth of 2-3 cm
5. Add a few onion slices and cook covered 45-60 min, adding a little more water if necessary.
6. The artichoke is cooked when a leaf can be pulled out easily and the base is soft.
7. Lift out with tongs or 2 forks, invert to drain, and cut off the base of the stem.
8. Serve with HOLLANDAISE SAUCE, MOCK HOLLANDAISE SAUCE, MAÎTRE D'HÔTEL SAUCE, melted butter, sour cream, or mayonnaise. Allow 1 artichoke per serving.

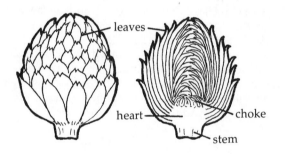

To eat, use the fingers and pick off the outer leaves, one by one, dipping the bottom fleshy end of the leaf into sauce. Pull leaf through the teeth. Discard the upper end of each leaf. Continue until the purple-tipped cone of light-coloured leaves is reached; the tips are also edible. Cut out the hairy centre growth, the choke, and discard. Eat the remaining heart with a knife and fork.

SWEET AND SOUR BEANS

500 g	**cooked green beans, drained**
125 ml	**sour cream or yogurt**
	dill weed

Serve beans with a topping of sour cream, seasoned with a sprinkle of dill weed. *Serves 4.*

GREEN BEANS NISI

Combine equal amounts of hot cooked, drained, julienne green beans and hot cooked rice. Stir in chopped pimento and toasted slivered almonds. Season to taste.

PAN-SAUTÉED BEETS

	6-8 medium beets
75 ml	**water**
15 ml	**vinegar**
5 ml	**sugar**

Peel and coarsely shred beets into a saucepan. Add other ingredients, cover and cook for 10 min or until tender, stirring twice during cooking. Add a little butter and season with salt and pepper. *Serves 4.*

HARVARD BEETS

	8-10 cooked beets (see VEGETABLE COOKERY CHART.)
125 ml	**sugar**
15 ml	**cornstarch**
	salt, pepper
50 ml	**wine vinegar**
200 ml	**water**
30 ml	**butter *or* margarine**

1. Cut cooked beets into slices or cubes, or use about 25 tiny rosebud beets.
2. Combine sugar, cornstarch, and seasonings; stir in vinegar and water to make a smooth paste.
3. Cook until thick; add beets and leave over *very* low heat or hot water for 30 min for the flavour of the sauce to penetrate.
4. Add butter or margarine and serve. *Serves 4-6.*

Orange Beets—substitute orange juice for the vinegar and reduce the sugar by one-half.

BOILED BROCCOLI

1. Soak broccoli in cold water for 10 min. If there is any sign of insects add some salt to the water and soak 5 min more. Rinse.
2. Trim off the *end* of the stem and discard. Cut through the stem and head to produce 6 or 8 sections. If the stems are long, cut a piece off each and reserve.
3. Cut into the stem end of each floweret 2 or 3 times to form a brush end which will cook in approximately the same amount of time as the floweret.
4. Stem pieces can be cut similarly at each end and if thick, cut through lengthwise. Or they can be set aside and refrigerated for serving separately at another meal. At that time, they can be peeled, cut into strips, cooked and served with or without a sauce.
5. In a pot which will hold the flowerets upright, add water to a depth of about 5 cm
6. Heat water to boiling. If stem pieces are to be cooked at this time, add them first; cover and cook for 2-3 min
7. Add remaining broccoli. Cover, bring to boiling, then cook over low-medium heat for 5 min
8. Remove cover and continue cooking until broccoli is just tender when stems are tested with the point of a knife, about 5-7 min
9. Drain; save the cooking liquid which contains vitamin C for adding to soup or gravy. Add a little butter or margarine to the broccoli and serve. If desired, serve with HOLLANDAISE SAUCE or CHEESE SAUCE . *Serves 6-8.*

The very high nutritional rating of broccoli renders it worthy of special treatment. When buying broccoli look for tender stalks with green to purplish-green, tightly closed buds which form compact clusters. Avoid yellow or brown flowers which denote age. Wrap loosely and refrigerate until needed.

Fresh broccoli stems peeled and cut into thin diagonal slices make crisp, colourful additions to Chinese food and stir-fried vegetables. To freeze, blanch for 1.5 min; cool quickly in cold water.

Recipes, tables, etc. that appear in small capital letters, e.g., PARSLEY BUTTER, CANADA'S FOOD GUIDE, are listed in the index. Consult the index for the number of the page on which the item appears.

PAN-SAUTÉED CABBAGE

1. Split a medium-size head of fresh green cabbage; remove heart; shred remainder coarsely with a sharp knife and cut shreds crosswise into short lengths.
2. Place cabbage in a heavy saucepan. Sprinkle with salt and pepper. Dribble over a little melted butter or cooking oil. Add a very small amount of water (scarcely more than enough to cover bottom of pan).
3. Cover and cook quickly over high heat. Remove cover to stir through a couple of times. Total cooking time will be 5-7 min or when cabbage has wilted (is no longer "crunchy"), is still green and has body.
4. Remove from heat and serve immediately. If desired, toss in a few caraway seeds.

Beet tops, escarole, spinach, and chard can be cooked in the same way. The stems of large leaves should be chopped and simmered while the leaves are being shredded.

RED CABBAGE AND RAISINS

1 *l*	shredded red cabbage
50 ml	raisins
	1 red apple, unpeeled, cored, thinly sliced
25 ml	lemon juice
100 ml	water
15 ml	brown sugar
	dash of ground cloves

Thoroughly combine all ingredients in a saucepan; cover and cook slowly with occasional stirring until cabbage is tender, about 10 min. Add more water if necessary. *Serves 4.*
A dash of ginger added to the stock adds zest.

CAULIFLOWER AU GRATIN

Boil a medium cauliflower whole or in flowerets until just tender. Drain thoroughly. In the bottom of a deep oven-proof serving dish pour 1/3 of the recipe for CHEESE SAUCE. Place cauliflower on top, season, and add remaining sauce. Sprinkle with a mixture of equal parts fine dry bread crumbs and grated Swiss or Mozzarella cheese—a total quantity of about 50-60 ml

About 30 min before serving, place cauliflower in the upper section of a preheated oven to heat through thoroughly and brown lightly, 190°C. *Serves 4-6* using a cauliflower with a diameter of 20 cm

GLAZED CARROTS OR PARSNIPS

	6-8 medium carrots or parsnips
	salt
30 ml	butter
125 ml	sugar
100 ml	stock

1. Peel vegetables, cut in half lengthwise. Remove core from parsnips, cook in boiling salted water for 15 min. Drain and reserve stock.
2. To the vegetables add butter, sugar, and measured stock; cook uncovered until tender and glazed, turning in the syrup until most of the water has evaporated. Sprinkle with chopped parsley or mint. *Serves 3-4.*

To prevent overcooking if vegetables are tender before water has evaporated, lift them out with a slotted spoon onto a plate. Continue cooking the liquid in the pan until the water has evaporated and a clear mixture of sugar and butter is left. Return vegetables to pan and cook a few minutes more until glazed.

Variation

Cheese-glazed Carrots—Prepare and boil carrots as in the preceding recipe. Dip each half in liquid honey or maple syrup and sprinkle with grated Cheddar cheese. Broil until the cheese melts.

CORN ON THE COB

There are two "musts" for corn on the cob. It must be freshly picked and it must not be overcooked!
1. Have a large open kettle about 2/3 filled with rapidly boiling water.
2. Husk corn, removing all the silk.
3. Drop cobs into boiling water and cover.
4. When water returns to boiling point, time the cooking from 4-8 min. At 4 min, test a kernel for tenderness with the point of a knife.
5. Drain and serve at once with butter, salt and pepper.

ROASTED CORN

Dampen the husks of the corn with water. Lay the ears on hot but well burned-down coals of a barbecue or campfire. There must be no flame. Turn frequently to prevent the husks from becoming burned through. Cook 8-10 min. Serve with butter, salt and pepper.

CORN FRITTERS

1. Prepare BATTER COATING; stir in cooked kernels, 250 ml
2. Drop from a spoon into hot fat and fry 3 minutes at 185°C
   Yield: 8-12 fritters. Serve with sausage or bacon for brunch, or as a vegetable with dinner.

CUCUMBERS IN SOUR CREAM

These are known as "Soused Cucumbers" in the Lunenburg area of Nova Scotia. Serve with hot or cold meat or fish, or on buttered bread.

	3 or 4 cucumbers
	salt
	1 onion finely sliced (optional)
250 ml	sour cream
15 ml	vinegar
50 ml	sugar
30 ml	chopped fresh dill
	pepper

1. Peel and slice cucumbers *thinly* into a bowl. Sprinkle with salt; add onion slices if desired.
2. Weigh down the cucumbers with a plate to remove their juice. Refrigerate for several hours.
3. Drain off juice. Combine remaining ingredients and pour over the cucumbers; stir to mix.

BROILED EGGPLANT

Eggplant, known also as eggfruit and aubergine, is at home in the cuisines of all Mediterranean countries.

	1 large eggplant
125 ml	butter *or* margarine, softened
2 ml	basil
2 ml	oregano
	salt, paprika
	grated Parmesan cheese

1. Wash eggplant; do not peel. Trim ends. Cut into slices 1-2 cm
2. Blend softened fat with herbs and a dash of salt and paprika; spread both sides of each slice of eggplant with the mixture.
3. Broil or pan-broil, turning once, until tender. Sprinkle with cheese just after turning.

Recipes, tables, etc. that appear in small capital letters, e.g., PARSLEY BUTTER, CANADA'S FOOD GUIDE, are listed in the index. Consult the index for the number of the page on which the item appears.

EGGPLANT WITH YOGURT SAUCE

	1 large eggplant
	1 onion, sliced
200 ml	yogurt
30 ml	chopped fresh mint
	3 garlic cloves, crushed
30 ml	oil
	salt, pepper
	paprika

1. Trim ends of unpeeled eggplant and cut into slices 1-2 cm
2. In a large heavy frying pan, heat oil; add onion slices and brown. Remove onion.
3. Brown eggplant slices on both sides, a few at a time, adding more oil as needed.
4. Return all slices to the pan; cover and cook until just tender, 5-10 min; transfer to a lightly greased ovenproof platter.
5. In a bowl, combine the remaining ingredients and pour the mixture over the eggplant; sprinkle with paprika.
6. Bake until the sauce is bubbly, 10-15 min, at 180°C
   Serve hot or cold. *Serves 3-4.*

Some eggplants contain a large amount of juice which can be bitter. To remove excess juice, slices may be sprinkled with salt before cooking, weighted down with a plate for half an hour, and drained.

EGGPLANT PARMIGIANA

	1 large eggplant
	1 egg, beaten
	crumbs
75 ml	oil
170 g	Mozzarella cheese, sliced
250 ml	TOMATO SAUCE
	basil, oregano
125 ml	grated Parmesan cheese

1. Wash eggplant; do not peel. Cut into slices 1-2 cm
2. Dip slices into crumbs, then beaten egg, then into crumbs again; pan fry in hot oil until golden. Add more oil if needed.
3. In a large shallow casserole, alternate slices of eggplant and Mozzarella cheese (cut in half) and pour TOMATO SAUCE over them.
4. Sprinkle with herbs and grated cheese. Bake until mixture is heated through and the cheese melts, at 160°C
   Serves 4-6.

BAKED STUFFED EGGPLANT

	1 large or 3 small eggplants
30 ml	oil
75 ml	finely chopped onion
250 ml	soft bread crumbs
100 ml	chopped walnuts
15 ml	chopped parsley
	1 egg, beaten
	basil
	salt and pepper
150 ml	buttered crumbs
50 ml	grated cheese (optional)

1. Cut eggplant(s) in half and cook in boiling water to cover for about 10 min. Scoop out the inside pulp of the eggplant, leaving an outer rim of about 1-2 cm
2. Heat oil in a frying pan; chop pulp and cook with the onion until vegetables are tender. Remove from heat.
3. Add crumbs, nuts, parsley and beaten egg. Add a sprinkle of basil; season with salt and pepper.
4. Fill shells with the mixture; top with crumbs and cheese, if desired. Bake until shells are tender, about 45 min at 190 °C
   Serves 4-6.

Variations
Omit nuts and egg and substitute any combination of chopped raw or cooked tomatoes, cooked kernel corn or lima beans, chopped, raw green or red sweet pepper, or slivers of cooked meat. Or combine equal quantities of MEAT SAUCE and cooked rice with the cooked pulp. Top with buttered crumbs and cheese.

SCALLOPED EGGPLANT

	1 medium eggplant
500 ml	TOMATO SAUCE
15 ml	brown sugar
250 ml	grated Cheddar *or* Parmesan cheese
125 ml	fine, dry bread crumbs

1. Peel and dice eggplant; cook in boiling salted water for 10 min; drain thoroughly and transfer to a greased casserole.
2. Prepare the sauce; add brown sugar. Pour over eggplant.
3. Combine cheese and bread crumbs; sprinkle over casserole. Bake until bubbly and brown, about 30 min at 180 °C
   Serves 6.

BAKED FENNEL PARMESAN

Fennel is a crisp, aromatic vegetable or herb, some-times called anise, which has long been enjoyed in Europe. Particularly popular when served with fish, the mildly licorice-flavoured bulb can be sliced and eaten raw as a cold appetizer (like radishes and cel-ery) or cooked as a vegetable, often sauced, or served in cream soup.

	4-6 fennel bulbs
50 ml	**butter**
250 ml	**chicken stock *or* water and soup concentrate**
	salt, pepper
125 ml	**grated Parmesan cheese**

1. Trim fennel bulbs, discarding any tough outer leaves. If bulbs are large, cut into quarters; if me-dium, cut in half.
2. Place in a saucepan, add boiling water to cover, and bring to boiling point; reduce heat and sim-mer until almost tender, 15-20 min.
3. Drain and arrange pieces cut-side down on a bak-ing dish; add chicken stock. Taste; add salt and pepper if needed.
4. Sprinkle with cheese; bake 30 min at 190°C
   Serves 6-8.

Fiddleheads are the early growth of the Ostrich Fern. They are curled, unopened shoots resembling the heads of fiddles. They are picked during this short stage of their development and cooked and served as a tender, mild-flavoured green vegetable. Although they grow extensively in many parts of North America, it is in New Brunswick that they are frozen commercially and promoted widely as a gourmet delicacy.

FRIED ONION RINGS

	6 medium onions
200 ml	**milk**
125 ml	**flour**
	salt, pepper
	fat *or* oil

Peel onions and slice into rings. Dip in milk; drain and dredge lightly with seasoned flour (or shake flour and onions together in a small disposable bag). Sauté onions in fat or fry in deep fat (see DEEP FAT FRYING). *Serves 4.*

FRIED ONIONS

	6 medium onions
50 ml	**oil *or* butter**

Peel onions; slice thinly. Heat fat in a frying pan, add onions, and sauté until golden brown, turning frequently. Season. *Serves 4.*

GLAZED ONIONS

700 ml	**small onions**
50 ml	**butter *or* margarine**
50 ml	**sugar**

1. Peel onions; parboil 15 min; drain and dry.
2. Melt butter, blend in sugar and add onions; con-tinue cooking over medium heat until onions are lightly browned, about 20 min. *Serves 4-6.*

PARTY ONIONS

	6 large white onions
100 ml	**water**
	salt
50 ml	**corn syrup**
	1 or 2 whole cloves
15 ml	**butter**
15 ml	**flour**

1. Cut peeled onions into thick slices and place in a heavy frying pan with water, salt, syrup, and cloves.
2. Cover and simmer until onions are tender, about 20 min
3. Blend butter and flour and stir into onion mixture until thick. Cook 2 min longer. Garnish with chopped parsley. *Serves 4-6.*

STUFFED ONIONS

Boil large, peeled onions in water (depth of water should be about half that of the onions) for 10 min. Lift out; remove the centres and finish as STUFFED PEP-PERS, beginning at step 3.

PEAS WITH CELERY

Simmer thinly sliced celery in water or beef stock until tender. Combine with 2 or 3 times the celery's volume of cooked fresh or frozen peas. Drain; reserve stock for other purposes or use as part of the liquid in WHITE SAUCE, and combine with vegetables.

PAN-FRIED PARSNIPS

Cut boiled parsnips into pieces. (If parsnips have hard central cores, remove them). Pan-fry in a little beef dripping or butter until brown. This is a good way to use leftover parsnips.

STUFFED PEPPERS

	4 or 5 sweet green peppers
250 ml	cooked rice
	salt, pepper
15 ml	melted butter *or* margarine
350 ml	ground, cooked meat
	(ham, veal, beef, lamb, or chicken)
1 ml	grated onion
	tomato juice
100 ml	soft, buttered crumbs

1. Select large peppers of suitable shape for stuffing; slice across the stem end, remove seeds and tongue.
2. Boil peppers in water for 10 min. Drain; reserve liquid.
3. Combine remaining ingredients except the crumbs, adding only enough tomato juice to moisten the mixture.
4. Fill peppers with the mixture; cover with buttered crumbs.
5. Stand peppers upright in a baking pan; add hot reserved liquid to a depth of about 0.5 cm
6. Bake for 30 min, adding more liquid if necessary, at 190°C

Serve stuffed peppers as an entrée or luncheon dish. Raw or cooked peppers may be refrigerated or frozen until needed.

Variations

Substitute herb-flavoured bread crumbs for the rice; add chopped nuts.

Raw ground beef can be used when browned in a little fat with chopped onion and/or green pepper.

Substitute mixed cooked vegetables (use leftovers or a packaged frozen mixture) for the meat, and seasoned bread crumbs for the rice. Moisten with 1 large fresh or canned tomato, chopped. Top each filled pepper with grated Cheddar cheese.

Substitute cream-style corn, or cooked spaghetti in tomato sauce for the filling; top each pepper with grated sharp-flavoured Cheddar cheese.

Baked pepper squash, stuffed with legumes and topped with cheese. Ontario Ministry of Agriculture and Food.

BAKED SQUASH

1. Scrub squash; cut in halves; remove seeds and stringy fibres.
2. Place cut-side down in a baking pan with a little water; cover and bake until soft, 1-1.5 h at 180°C
3. If the squash is large, scrape pulp from shell; mash, season and add a little butter or margarine. If squash is small, serve in halves, thirds, or quarters without mashing. Add butter or margarine, seasonings, and a sprinkle of brown sugar. If desired, fill with hot vegetables and return squash to oven for 10 min, at 180°C

STEAMED SQUASH

Scrub squash, cut into pieces; remove seeds and fibre. Place skin-side up in steamer. Steam until soft, about 30-40 min. Remove skin, mash, and season.

Hubbard squash are often by-passed by small families in favour of the smaller varieties of squash. However, this very flavoursome squash can be cooked, mashed, and frozen in small quantities for many future meals—at a very reasonable cost. In addition to its uses as a vegetable, cooked puréed squash can replace pumpkin in pies and puddings. Large hubbard squash have a tough skin which may be difficult to cut with a knife. The problem can be solved by placing the squash in a plastic bag and dropping it onto a concrete floor!

PUMPKIN

Prepare and cook as STEAMED SQUASH. Do not season. Scrape from shell and press through a sieve, or purée in an electric blender. For pie filling see PUMPKIN PIE. Cooked pumpkin can be beaten into instant vanilla pudding by replacing a quarter of the milk with twice the quantity of pumpkin.

STEAMED VEGETABLE MARROW

1. Cut marrow into thick slices approximately 2 cm
2. Place slices in a steamer and steam until tender, about 20-30 min
3. Lift out carefully; serve with butter or margarine, salt and pepper.

Unlike winter squash (hubbard, pepper, acorn), which can be stored for several weeks in a dry place at a moderate temperature, summer squash (zucchini, crooked-neck squash, vegetable marrow) are eaten when immature and should be kept refrigerated and eaten as soon as possible. Choose summer squash that are small, with soft rinds.

SAUTÉED ZUCCHINI

Wash and slice squash into thin crosswise or slightly diagonal slices and place in a saucepan with a little melted butter. If desired, add a little chopped onion or ½ garlic clove, crushed, for flavour. Sauté until just tender.

Variations

When zucchini is almost cooked, stir in a chopped and seeded tomato and finish cooking. Sprinkle with grated Parmesan cheese or serve with sour cream. Allow one small zucchini per person.

STUFFED ZUCCHINI

	6 zucchini, 20 cm long	8 in. long
50 ml	melted butter *or* oil	3 tbsp.
250 ml	finely chopped onion	1 cup
125 ml	medium WHITE SAUCE	½ cup
50 ml	fine dry bread crumbs	¼ cup
100 ml	grated Parmesan cheese	1/3 cup
25 ml	chopped parsley	2 tbsp.

1. Trim stem ends from zucchini and slice off the top third lengthwise.
2. Cook top and bottom sections in boiling water for 10 min. Drain. Rinse zucchini in cold water.
3. Using a small, sharp spoon, scoop out pulp, keeping bottom sections free from tears so that they may be stuffed; invert on towels to dry. Discard top sections after the pulp has been removed.
4. Melt butter in a heated saucepan, add onions and heat only until soft; add zucchini pulp and sauté for 5 min
5. Prepare WHITE SAUCE from ½ the recipe, substituting cream for part of the milk or increasing the butter to make a richer sauce; season.
6. Combine sauce, zucchini mixture, crumbs and half of the grated cheese; spoon mixture into dry zucchini shells.
7. Sprinkle tops with remaining grated cheese and drizzle with melted butter; place in a lightly greased baking dish and bake until bubbly and lightly browned, about 10 to 15 min at 230°C Sprinkle with chopped parsley.

Variation

Herb-flavoured soft bread crumbs can be substituted for the WHITE SAUCE. Omit dry crumbs and moisten mixture with a little tomato juice.

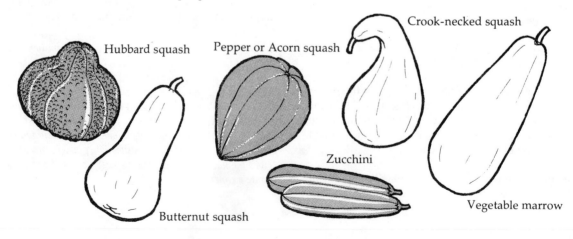

Hubbard squash

Pepper or Acorn squash

Crook-necked squash

Zucchini

Butternut squash

Vegetable marrow

BROILED TOMATOES

1. Wipe tomatoes; cut across in thick slices or halves.
2. Season with salt and pepper; brush over with butter and sprinkle with seasoned salt and fine crumbs.
3. Broil until tender, about 5 min

For added flavour, crush ½ clove of garlic in the butter, blend, and brush over tomatoes. Serve with sour cream; flavour with fresh dill and/or chives.

FRIED RED AND GREEN TOMATOES

Cut unpeeled tomatoes into thick slices. Dip *green* tomatoes in flour, salt and pepper and fry slowly in a small amount of fat until browned; turn and brown on the other side.

Dip slices of *ripe* tomatoes in beaten egg, then fine seasoned crumbs, and fry quickly on both sides until golden brown.

For extra flavour, fry tomato slices in a small amount of bacon fat after cooking and lifting out the bacon.

GHIVETCH

	2 small diced potatoes
	1 small yellow squash, thinly sliced
750 ml	turnips, cubed
500 ml	carrot coins
250 ml	fresh green beans, sliced diagonally
100 ml	celery, sliced diagonally
	½ Spanish onion, thinly sliced
	2 medium tomatoes, cored and quartered
500 ml	beef bouillon
100 ml	julienne strips green pepper
90 ml	olive oil
	2 small cloves garlic, crushed
5 ml	salt
10 ml	tarragon

1. Wash and prepare all the vegetables, cutting them into the sizes and shapes suggested.
2. Combine bouillon cube, water, oil, garlic, salt, bay leaf and tarragon in frying pan. Heat to boiling. Add drained potato, squash and turnip.
3. Cover; cook 10 min only.
4. Add carrots, green beans, celery and onion. Toss lightly. Cook another 10 min. Toss lightly.
5. Add tomatoes and green pepper. Cook 5 min only. Serve *immediately*. *Yield:* 10 to 12 servings.

RATATOUILLE

Originating in southern France, a ratatouille is a highly flavoured combination of vegetables. It can be completely cooked the day before needed, then reheated or served cold as an accompaniment to hot or cold meats. It may be served cold as an appetizer.

	2 medium onions, thinly sliced
50 ml	oil
	1 large green pepper, chopped
	1 small eggplant, peeled
	2 zucchini
	1 garlic clove, crushed
	3 tomatoes, peeled
2 ml	basil
2 ml	marjoram
	salt, pepper

1. In a large saucepan, sauté onion slices in oil until clear.
2. Add chopped green peppers and sauté 2 min more. Remove to a side dish.
3. Slice the zucchini and peeled eggplant into slices 2-3 cm
4. Cut eggplant slices into finger-length strips; sauté, stirring until brown, 2-3 min. Remove to side dish.
5. Add crushed garlic to the oil and sauté zucchini slices for about 1 min on each side.
6. Cut tomatoes in half crosswise and squeeze gently to remove seeds. Discard seeds and chop tomatoes coarsely.
7. Combine all vegetables with remaining oil, in saucepan or casserole. Cover and cook over low heat for about 45 min, with occasional stirring.
8. Add seasonings and cook 5 min longer. Serve hot or cold. *Serves 6.*

STIR-FRIED VEGETABLES

Stir-frying produces the crisp, colourful and flavoursome cooked vegetables that we associate with Chinese food. A wok or other wide but small-bottomed saucepan is used and vegetables are cooked with constant stirring by a combination of sautéeing and steaming.
1. All vegetables should be prepared before beginning the cooking. Cut vegetables into small pieces; thin diagonal slices cook most quickly.
2. Heat oil in wok or saucepan; use about 30-50 ml

3. Begin the cooking with sliced onions or other members of the onion family—leeks, scallions or garlic—which will flavour the oil and other vegetables.
4. Add any of the following vegetables in the sequence given, allowing for each serving an assortment of 250 ml

   The root vegetables—julienne carrots, turnips, kohlrabi

   The seed vegetables—peas, lima beans

   Miscellaneous vegetables—green beens, celery slices, thin slices of broccoli or cauliflower, shredded Chinese cabbage, sliced mushrooms, strips of red and green sweet pepper

   Leafy vegetables—shredded cabbage, chopped spinach, romaine, which are cooked until they are barely wilted.
5. When the cooking is completed, season with soya sauce and a little ground ginger. If garlic was not used previously, add a little garlic powder also.
6. If desired, combine cooked vegetables with a sauce made from

   15 ml cornstarch
   250 ml chicken stock

   Blend a little of the (cool) chicken stock into the cornstarch to form a paste. Stir in remaining stock. Heat until thick and clear, combine with vegetables, and serve.

SCALLOPED VEGETABLES

500 ml	cooked vegetables*
500 ml	medium WHITE SAUCE or a variation
250 ml	crumbs from crackers, appetizer biscuits, *or* crushed potato chips

1. Cut vegetables into bite-size pieces.
2. In a greased casserole, layer vegetables left whole or in pieces of suitable size with sauce (WHITE SAUCE, CHEESE SAUCE).
3. Top with crumbs and bake until mixture bubbles, about 30 min, at 180°C
   Serves 4.
* One or a combination of the following might be used: asparagus, celery, fennel, broccoli, onions, cauliflower.

Variations
Substitute cooked meat or fish, or hard-cooked eggs, for part of the vegetables. Good combinations are cauliflower and ham, tuna and mushroom, asparagus and egg, curried haddie and egg, salmon and celery.

VEGETABLE STEW

500 ml	5 or 6 medium onions, sliced
100 ml	oil
700 ml	5 medium potatoes, diced
500 ml	4-5 medium carrots
300 ml	turnips, diced
500 ml	winter squash, diced
7 ml	savory
	1 bay leaf
1 ℓ	chicken stock
300 ml	peas *or* green lima beans
500 ml	flowerets of cauliflower *or* broccoli
540 ml	1 can chick peas (optional)
	grated Cheddar or Parmesan cheese
	or DUMPLINGS

1. In a deep Dutch oven, cook sliced onions in hot oil until soft; add the peeled, diced potatoes and carrots and sauté 5 min. Remove from the pan; put in peeled diced turnips and squash and sauté 5 min.
2. Add potatoes and carrots to turnips and squash; cover and sauté for 5 min.
3. Add the seasoning and chicken stock and simmer mixture for 10 min.
4. Add the flowerets, green peas, and chick peas. Simmer mixture for 10 min or until all the vegetables are tender. Serve in soup bowls topped with grated cheese, or with dumplings cooked in the stew. *Serves 6-8.*

To Use Leftover Cooked Vegetables

1. Reheat in hot sauce, for example, CHEESE SAUCE or WHITE SAUCE.
2. Reheat in a frying pan with butter (HASH BROWN POTATOES).
3. Marinate in French dressing or serve with mayonnaise in salads.
4. Chop and add to stew, soufflé, scrambled eggs, meat pies, casseroles, and soups.
5. Purée or mash for cream soup, croquettes, toppings (DUCHESS POTATOES).

Recipes, tables, etc. that appear in small capital letters, e.g., PARSLEY BUTTER, CANADA'S FOOD GUIDE, are listed in the index. Consult the index for the number of the page on which the item appears.

Mushrooms

Mushrooms, delicate members of the fungus family, add a touch of flavour and elegance to most main dishes. Stuffed, broiled, or marinated, they are popular appetizers.

White and brown cultivated varieties are available fresh, canned, dehydrated and freeze-dried. *Although many varieties of wild mushrooms are edible, it is wise to leave them to the experts who can identify all types, poisonous as well as edible.*

Store mushrooms in the refrigerator in a ventilated container without plastic overwrap. To prepare, rinse in cold water (do not soak) and gently pat dry. Slice mushrooms lengthwise through cap and stem for the most attractive appearance. Do not peel. If caps are to be stuffed and/or served whole, save and slice stems for other purposes. Mushrooms are low in food energy (if used without butter and rich sauces). They contain significant amounts of riboflavin and niacin and a little iron and protein.

Basic Recipe
SAUTÉED MUSHROOMS

500 ml	sliced mushrooms
150 g	butter
or	
150 ml	oil
	salt, pepper

1. Wash and dry mushrooms; slice lengthwise.
2. Add fat to cover the bottom of a large saucepan. Heat and add mushrooms; sauté until tender, 5-10 min

Variations

Stewed Mushrooms

30 ml	flour
250 ml	rich milk *or* chicken stock

Sauté mushrooms 2 min only; sprinkle with flour; when blended stir in liquid. Cook over low heat until mushrooms are tender, about 10 min. Spoon over chicken, hamburger patties; or serve on toast. *Serves 4.*

Mushrooms à la Russe

5 ml	lemon juice
250-350 ml	sour cream
5 ml	paprika

Sprinkle lemon juice over sautéed mushrooms; stir in sour cream and paprika. Heat through and serve with grilled steak or hamburger patties. *Serves 6-8.*

Gourmet Mushrooms

50 ml	finely chopped onion
5 ml	brown sugar
5 ml	soya sauce
100 ml	water
5 ml	lemon juice

Sauté mushrooms until almost tender; blend ingredients and add to mushrooms. Continue cooking until mushrooms are tender. Serve with roast beef, steak, or hamburger patties. *Serves 6.*

STUFFED MUSHROOMS

	10-12 large mushrooms
125 ml	chopped cooked meat, chicken, *or* seafood
100 ml	fine, soft bread crumbs
25 ml	finely chopped walnuts (optional)
10 ml	finely chopped onion
10 ml	finely chopped parsley
	salt, pepper
100 ml	butter
250 ml	TOMATO SAUCE *or* diluted tomato paste
250 ml	fine buttered crumbs

1. Wash mushrooms; set aside the caps. Chop stems finely.
2. Mix meat, crumbs, walnuts, onions, parsley, stems, and seasonings; cook in butter 3 minutes.
3. Add about one-third of the tomato sauce to mixture, to moisten. Fill mushroom caps with the mixture; cover with buttered crumbs.
4. Place in a greased baking pan; pour remaining tomato sauce around mushrooms. Bake for 15 min at 200°C
Serves 4.

Omit step 4 and broil to serve as an appetizer or garnish.

14 Bread

Canada is a world leader in the production of wheat. Hard (spring) wheat, grown primarily in Western Canada, has a protein content of 12-14% and is an essential ingredient of yeast breads. Sown in May for harvesting in early fall, the many varieties of hard wheat are the principal wheats grown in Canada. Soft wheats, sown in the fall for harvesting the following summer, contain 8-10% protein. They are used to make pastry and cake flour.

The three basic parts of a kernel of wheat are the germ, or embryo; the endosperm; and the bran.

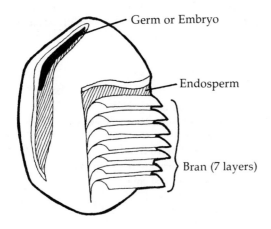
Germ or Embryo

Endosperm

Bran (7 layers)

Wheat Germ, which is rich in fat, protein, and vitamins B and E, may be added to batters and doughs of breads and quick breads or served as a topping on breakfast cereals, soups and other foods. Store in the refrigerator unless partially defatted. The defatted variety is also available in a toasted form.

Endosperm is the source of flour. Mainly carbohydrate in content, it also contains some protein, B vitamins and minerals, some of which are lost through refinement.

Bran, the outer layers of the kernel, is rich in B vitamins and dietary fibre. Bran is added to batters for muffins or other quick breads, or processed for use as breakfast cereal.

Types of Wheat Flour

White Flour is finely milled and sifted wheat flour which consists mostly of the inner, starchy portion of the grain (endosperm). White flour contains a small amount of protein but the bran and germ have been removed along with many of the vitamins and minerals, and most of the dietary fibre. In order to compensate for some of these losses, most white flour sold in Canada is enriched with B vitamins and minerals, according to government specifications; such flour is labelled "enriched."

All-Purpose Flour is a white flour composed of a blend of both hard wheat and soft wheat flours, that is, a blend of bread and pastry flour. (Bread flour, not usually available in retail outlets, is sold directly to bakeries.) All-purpose flour can be used for all types of baking. It is usually enriched.

Pastry Flour (Cake and Pastry Flour) is a white flour made from finely milled soft wheat used primarily for cake and pastry. It does not contain sufficient protein to make bread. It is very smooth and silky to the touch, and is usually enriched.

Cake Flour is a highly refined soft-wheat flour, lower in protein and finer in texture than pastry flour. This flour is best suited for cakes.

Graham Flour is white flour to which bran and other parts of the wheat kernel have been added, giving the flour a brownish colour. It is combined with white flour in the making of yeast breads and quick breads.

Whole Wheat Flour is a 95% extraction of the whole wheat kernel. It includes the bran, which gives the characteristic brown colour. Whole wheat flour is higher in protein than all-purpose flour, with which it is often combined in various proportions to produce bread, rolls, and quick breads which are lighter than those made from whole wheat flour only.

Instantized Flour is specially milled hard wheat flour which pours and blends more easily than regular flour. More expensive than regular all-purpose flour, it is useful in the thickening of sauces.

Self-rising Flour is white flour to which baking powder has been added. It is used more widely in the United States than in Canada.

Flours from Other Sources

Rye Flour, light or dark (whole grain), and **Buckwheat Flour** are other flours used in breads and quick breads to produce variety in flavour and texture.

Soy Flour is a creamy-coloured, highly nutritious flour which may be added in small amounts to other flours in the making of breads and quick breads. Although it contains about four times the quantity of protein of all-purpose flour and although the quality of soy protein is superior to that of cereal protein, it is of the non gluten-forming type and is somewhat bitter. Therefore it cannot be used alone to make yeast bread, in which gluten is required, and it should always be combined with other ingredients in order to dilute or mask its bitterness.

Rice Flour, Corn Flour and Potato Flour, like soy flour, are gluten-free. Produced in small quantities, they are used primarily in allergy diets.

Storing Flour

Buy flour in quantities which can be stored in a covered container in a cool, dry atmosphere. Whole wheat flour has a shorter shelf life than other wheat flours because it contains some of the germ; buy in small quantities unless it can be refrigerated. Because soybeans are richer in fat than are the other legumes, soy flour may be sold partially defatted. Unless it is completely defatted it should be kept refrigerated. Surplus flour may be stored in the freezer if necessary, although it is an uneconomical use of freezer space.

Flour Mixtures

The various ingredients used in flour mixtures have specific roles to play. When combined with liquid, gluten, a protein of flour, stretches to form an elastic framework around the increasing number of carbon dioxide bubbles produced by yeast or baking powder. Baking sets the framework in its expanded state. Egg protein also contributes to the structure of breads and cakes. Tenderizing ingredients, shortening and sugar, offset the effect of the structure-forming ingredients. This balance is required to produce the desired texture characteristic of yeast bread, quick breads, cakes, etc.

The *method* of combining ingredients affects the texture of the finished product. In order to develop maximum gluten formation, dough for yeast breads must be kneaded. When preparing quick breads (those which are leavened with baking powder or soda) the development of gluten is not desirable. Minimum mixing and handling are recommended for muffins and fruit loaves because of their low content of tenderizing ingredients. Pancake batters contain so much liquid that the gluten develops less readily; even so, extensive beating is not recommended. In cakes, the proportion of tenderizing ingredients is so high that excess gluten formation is less probable; however, most of the beating of cake batter must take place before the flour is added, because beating after the addition of dry ingredients results in excess loss of carbon dioxide from the baking powder—and a cake of poor volume.

Preparation of Pans for Flour Mixtures

All pans should be greased, unless the recipe states otherwise or the pans have a non-stick finish. Use oil or shortening to lightly coat surfaces including corners and crevices. Spray-on products may be used instead, but they are costly. Pans with non-stick surfaces may eventually need to be greased, as coatings wear off.

Loaf pans and cake pans should be greased and lined with a greased piece of waxed paper cut to fit the bottom; paper should extend up 2 sides of rectangular pans for easy removal of contents. Tube pans need not be lined.

Basic Ingredients for Quick Breads

Flour

In recipes in this book, *flour* refers to All-purpose Flour unless otherwise stated. (See TYPES OF FLOUR for descriptions of the various kinds of flour and their uses.) To substitute pastry flour for all-purpose flour, increase the amount of flour by one-eighth.

Fat

Vegetable Oils are used in specific recipes or in those calling for melted fat.

Margarine is a blend of hydrogenated vegetable oils mixed with emulsifiers, vitamins, colouring matter, and other ingredients. It may be used in place of butter in most recipes, but when substituting margarine for butter in baking, use solid margarine; soft margarine may not give the desired results.

Shortening may be vegetable fat or a blend of vegetable and animal fats.

Butter, an animal fat, has always been valued for the flavour it imparts. When the flavour is obscured by spices or other strong flavours, less expensive fats will give equally good results.

Lard is pork fat; it has excellent tenderizing ability.

Shortening and lard are 100% fat; since butter and margarine are not all fat, their tenderizing effect is somewhat less.

Leavening Agents

Baking Powder—Two principal types of baking powder are available today: phosphate or quick-acting, and S.A.S. or double-acting. Both give satisfactory results, but the double-acting is preferable in quick-mix recipes, where the baking powder is added at the beginning of the recipe. Unskilled cooks may find double-acting baking powder easier to use in all recipes, as the gas does not all form until the product is heated. Use either, unless a recipe states that double-acting is to be used. To substitute double-acting baking powder for quick-acting, use 2/3 the quantity.

Baking Soda is used to leaven mixtures that contain an acid ingredient such as sour milk. Depending on the proportions of the ingredients in a recipe, the soda/acid mixture may be the only leavener or baking powder may be added as well.

Yeast—See YEAST BREAD AND ROLLS.

Sugar

Sugar, like fat, has a tenderizing effect in flour mixtures.

Granulated, or White Sugar is most commonly used. **Icing** sugar is finely crushed and screened granulated sugar.

Brown Sugar may range from dark to very light, depending upon the amount of molasses it retains. To replace an equal amount of white sugar, brown sugar should be firmly packed.

Syrup—Maple or corn syrup or honey may be used to replace sugar in a recipe (see TABLE OF REPLACEMENTS). Artificial sweeteners cannot be substituted for sugar in baked mixtures (unless using recipes provided by their manufacturers).

Liquid

Milk is the most commonly used liquid in quick breads. It is not economical to use fresh milk for baking. Use skim milk powder which has been previously reconstituted, or combine it with the dry ingredients, using water to replace the liquid fresh milk. If extra richness is desired, add a little extra fat, about 5 ml fat per 250 ml of liquid

To reconstitute skim milk powder (instant variety) use: 75 ml powder to 250 ml of water

To substitute fresh or reconstituted milk for skim milk powder and water in flour mixture recipes, substitute an equal quantity of milk for water, and omit milk powder.

Sour Milk in a recipe means milk which has become sour enough to separate. Buttermilk may be used instead; or sweet milk, including powdered milk, may be substituted if it is acidified. To acidify milk (to sour it) for use in recipes calling for sour milk or buttermilk, see TO SOUR FRESH MILK.

To substitute any of these sour milks for regular (sweet) milk in a leavened product, baking soda must be substituted for all or part of the baking powder. Consult TABLE OF REPLACEMENTS.

Evaporated Milk diluted with an equal amount of water may be substituted for whole milk.

Condensed Milk, because of its high sugar content, is not successful except in specially designed recipes.

Cream tenderizes and adds richness and flavour.

Eggs

Not all flour mixtures contain eggs. When they are called for, their chief purpose is to bind ingredients together. They also help to provide structure; add nutritive value; and when beaten, hold air which acts as a leavener.

Basic Recipe
PANCAKES OR GRIDDLECAKES

500 ml	flour
50 ml	sugar
200 ml	skim milk powder
20 ml	baking powder
2 ml	salt
	1 egg
50-75 ml	oil
550 ml	water

1. Combine dry ingredients.
2. Beat egg with oil and water; combine with dry ingredients and beat with egg beater just until batter is smooth. Let stand 5 min. If batter seems too thick to pour, stir in a few spoonfuls of water.
3. Heat griddle or heavy frying pan; pan is hot enough when a few drops of water sprinkled on it will dance.

Recipes, tables, etc. that appear in small capital letters, e.g., PARSLEY BUTTER, CANADA'S FOOD GUIDE, are listed in the index. Consult the index for the number of the page on which the item appears.

4. Grease pan lightly but evenly with oil; ladle batter or pour from a jug onto the pan, allowing for each pancake about 50 ml
5. Cook over medium heat, turning once when bubbles begin to break on the surface of the pancake and a rim forms around its edge.
6. Spread cooked pancakes on a heated platter and keep warm. (Stacking pancakes results in sogginess.) *Yield:* 10-12 pancakes with a diameter of 13-15 cm

---

Serve with butter or margarine and/or any of these toppings: sour cream, hot applesauce, jam or preserves, corn syrup, maple syrup, MOCK MAPLE SYRUP, FRUIT SYRUP, HONEY BUTTER, or CINNAMON HONEY BUTTER, HARD SAUCE, or BLUEBERRY SAUCE. Syrups from canned fruit make delicious fruit syrups after boiling for a few minutes to evaporate some of the liquid.

Variations
Use whole wheat flour for half the flour in the basic recipe, to make a more nutritious pancake. (Whole wheat flour only can be used but the pancakes will be heavier and a little extra liquid will be required.)

For richer pancakes substitute sour cream for part of the liquid.

Buttermilk Pancakes—Substitute an equal amount of buttermilk or sour milk for the water; omit baking powder and milk powder and substitute baking soda, 5 ml
Blueberry Pancakes—Before cooking, carefully fold into the batter fresh or frozen blueberries, 125 ml
Cornmeal Pancakes—Substitute cornmeal for half the flour in the basic recipe.

See also recipe for PANCAKES USING A BASIC QUICK-BREAD MIX.

BUCKWHEAT PANCAKES

375 ml	buckwheat flour
125 ml	flour
175 ml	skim milk powder
15 ml	baking powder
2 ml	salt
15 ml	sugar
575 ml	water
30 ml	molasses
	1 egg
30 ml	oil *or* melted fat

Prepare according to the basic recipe for PANCAKES, combining the molasses with the liquid ingredients. *Yield:* 10-12 pancakes.

OATMEAL PANCAKES

375 ml	rolled oats
200 ml	flour
175 ml	skim milk powder
5 ml	sugar
20 ml	baking powder
	salt
	2 beaten eggs
500 ml	water

Prepare as in basic PANCAKES recipe, but before turning cook for a few minutes longer after bubbles begin to break on the surface. *Yield:* 5-6 pancakes, diameter 15 cm

THIN PANCAKES

Thinner than the pancakes in the preceding recipes, yet less delicate in texture and a little easier to handle than crêpes, these all-purpose pancakes can be served as simple pancakes or, rolled and stuffed, as crêpes.

125 ml	flour
50 ml	skim milk powder
2 ml	baking powder
1 ml	salt
	1 egg
30 ml	oil *or* melted butter
200 ml	water

1. Combine dry ingredients thoroughly.
2. In another bowl, combine egg, liquid fat and water using an egg beater and gradually stir this mixture into the dry ingredients; beat until completely smooth.
3. Heat and lightly grease a small frying pan which has a diameter of about 15 cm
4. Pour batter into the pan and rotate pan quickly to coat the entire bottom; for each pancake allow about 30 ml
5. When pancake is lightly browned on the bottom, turn and brown on the other side.
6. Serve with any of the accompaniments listed following the basic recipe for PANCAKES, or as one of the variations of CRÊPES. Or pancakes may be dusted with icing sugar and sprinkled with lemon juice, then rolled and dusted with more icing sugar. *Yield:* 10-12 pancakes.

Basic Recipe
CRÊPES

Batter for crêpes is very thin, like cream. Its texture is improved on standing, preferably overnight. An electric blender is useful for mixing the batter but is not essential. The ideal crêpe pan is small with sloping sides and made of heavy aluminum or iron.

	3 eggs
250 ml	**flour**
	sprinkle of salt
450 ml	**milk**

1. Beat eggs slightly; add flour and salt and mix thoroughly.
2. Add liquid gradually, with constant beating; let mixture stand for a minimum of 15 min to dissolve lumps and soften the starch granules.
3. Brush a small frying pan lightly with oil or add only enough oil to form a thin film on the bottom of the pan; heat.
4. When pan is hot, pour or spoon in a little batter, immediately rotating pan to cover the bottom. Use about 20 ml
5. Cook for 1 min over medium heat until the top is dry and the underside golden.
6. Loosen one edge with the blade of a knife and lift with the fingers; turn and cook for a few seconds more on the other side, then invert pan and drop out the crêpe.
7. Continue making crêpes until all the batter has been used, adding more oil to the pan as needed.
8. Serve with filling suitable for an entrée or dessert. See serving methods which follow. Makes 25-30 crêpes, diameter 12-15 cm

Crêpes may be stacked or filled and refrigerated. They freeze well. Thaw in sauce in a chafing dish while the main course is being enjoyed. Crêpes are a good party food because advance preparation is possible.

Variations
Herb Crêpes—To the basic recipe add:

15 ml	**minced fresh parsley**
15 ml	**minced fresh dill *or* chives**

Dessert Crêpes—To the basic recipe add:

15 ml	**sugar**

To Fill and Fold Crêpes
Place filling on one third of the crêpe and roll to form a cylinder beginning at the filled side, or place filling in the centre of the crêpe and fold to form an envelope or quarter circle. Place downward in a greased pan. Brush with melted butter or cover with a sauce and reheat.

For each crêpe allow about 30 ml filling
Serve 2-3 individual crêpes per person.

When serving crêpes to a group, crêpes can be spread with filling and stacked; reheat in the oven if necessary; cut into wedge-shaped servings.

Fillings for Crêpes
Serve entrée crêpes with a filling of well-seasoned WHITE SAUCE or CURRY SAUCE; to half of the sauce add finely chopped cooked chicken; to the other half add sautéed mushroom slices. Alternate fillings of chicken sauce and mushroom sauce when stacking. Or make 2 variations of CHEESE SAUCE; one with chopped or flaked cooked fish or seafood, the other with chopped cooked spinach or celery; alternate the fillings.

Other good entrée fillings are: CHICKEN À LA KING, STIR-FRIED CHICKEN, SAUTÉED MUSHROOMS, asparagus and CHEESE SAUCE, creamed spinach and strips of Swiss cheese, PASTA fillings.

Serve dessert crêpes with alternating layers of cottage or cream cheese and blueberries, sliced strawberries, or other fruit, and serve with sour cream. Other good dessert fillings are: cream cheese blended with fruit juice or FRUIT SAUCE, served with melted marmalade or preserves; canned pie fillings; bananas or spears of pineapple dipped in honey or apricot or ginger jam, served with fruit sauce, HARD SAUCE. See also CRÊPES SUZETTE.

HAM CRÊPES

	1 recipe CRÊPES
100 g	mushrooms
(250 ml)	
45 ml	butter
	salt, pepper
15 ml	flour
125 ml	sour cream
	8 thin slices of cooked ham
250 ml	seasoned WHITE SAUCE
100 ml	grated Parmesan cheese

1. Prepare crêpes according to the basic recipe.
2. Rinse, chop and sauté mushrooms in butter; season and sprinkle with flour.
3. Add sour cream; stir until mixture thickens slightly.
4. Cover each with a slice of ham and spread with a thin layer of mushroom mixture; fold edges in to form an envelope and arrange open-side down in a greased shallow baking pan.
5. Cover with sauce; sprinkle with grated cheese.
6. Bake until bubbly and lightly browned, about 20 min at 180°C
Serves 4-6.

CRÊPES SUZETTE

This is a simplified version of a classic French dessert; it features unfilled crêpes, heated in a rich orange-flavoured syrup in a chafing dish.

	1 recipe DESSERT CRÊPES
100 ml	butter, softened
100 ml	icing sugar
	juice and finely grated rind of 1 orange

1. Prepare Dessert Crêpes with a diameter about 12 cm
2. Cream remaining ingredients until smooth; melt in a chafing dish.
3. Dip crêpes in the mixture; fold into quarter circles.
4. Heat crêpes in the sauce.
Serves 4-6.

SEAFOOD CRÊPES

Using recipe for LOBSTER THERMIDOR, substitute for the whole lobster one or a mixture of cooked lobster, crabmeat, shrimp, salmon, or tuna: 750 g
Melt the grated cheese in the hot sauce. Fill the crêpes. See TO FILL AND FOLD CRÊPES. 1 recipe stuffs 12 crêpes.

Variation
Cooked spinach, drained and chopped, can be substituted for part of the seafood.

MEXICAN PANCAKES

These pancakes are unleavened and are quite unlike our traditional breakfast pancakes. Like tortillas, the staple Mexican "bread", they are best served with savoury mixtures. Although they are not true tortillas (which require a special corn flour for their preparation) they can be substituted for them in some Mexican dishes such as EGGS RANCH-STYLE. Try them rolled up with a seasoned meat mixture and baked with sauce; so served, tortillas are called enchiladas. Before rolling, cold pancakes must be softened by reheating in a lightly greased pan.

	1 egg
200 ml	flour
100 ml	cornmeal
1 ml	salt
300 ml	water

1. Beat egg in a small bowl until foamy.
2. Combine flour, cornmeal and salt and stir into the egg with a little of the water.
3. Beat until smooth, adding remainder of water gradually. Batter will be very thin.
4. Spoon out mixture onto a hot, lightly greased, heavy frying pan and quickly rotate to spread batter thinly, allowing for each pancake about 75 ml
5. Cook until edges curl and pancake is lightly browned on the bottom, about 2 min. Turn and cook 2 min more. *Yield:* 6-8 pancakes.

Recipes, tables, etc. that appear in small capital letters, e.g., PARSLEY BUTTER, CANADA'S FOOD GUIDE, are listed in the index. Consult the index for the number of the page on which the item appears.

Basic Recipe
WAFFLES

400 ml	flour
150 ml	skim milk powder
15 ml	baking powder
2 ml	salt
30 ml	sugar
	2 large *or* 3 medium eggs, separated
500 ml	water
75 ml	oil *or* melted butter

1. Heat waffle iron while combining dry ingredients.
2. Beat egg whites until stiff but not dry.
3. Beat egg yolks, water and oil until well mixed, and combine with dry ingredients. Beat until blended, about 1 min
4. Fold in beaten egg whites.
5. Pour or ladle mixture quickly into the centre section of a hot, prepared waffle iron, using about 75 ml
6. Bake without opening until batter ceases to steam and "sing." Remove to a heated plate and serve with any of the suggested toppings listed below the basic recipe for PANCAKES. *Yield:* 7-8 waffles.

Waffles freeze well, wrapped individually. Reheat in oven, bun warmer, or toaster.

Variations

Add to the batter just before folding in the egg whites *one* of the following:

	grated rind of 1 orange
or	
250 ml	chopped peeled apples
or	
200 ml	cooked dried apricots, drained and chopped

Sprinkle over the poured waffle before cooking, *one* of the following:

30 ml	fresh or frozen blueberries
or	
15 ml	shredded coconut *or* finely chopped nuts
	or
	1 strip crisp bacon, crumbled

Buttermilk Waffles—Substitute an equal quantity of buttermilk or sour milk for the water; omit milk powder and baking powder and substitute baking soda, 5 ml

Cheese Waffles—Reduce fat in basic Waffle recipe to 50 ml
With the beaten egg white fold in grated cheese, 250 ml

Cheese waffles are particularly good served topped with creamed chicken or seafood, or with fresh fruits such as strawberries or peaches, served with sour cream.

BRAN WAFFLES

These are a delicious source of bran in the diet. They absorb moisture on standing but can be made crisp again by heating in a toaster or moderate oven.

250 ml	natural wheat bran (cooking bran)
250 ml	flour
125 ml	skim milk powder
15 ml	baking powder
2 ml	salt
50 ml	brown sugar
	1 egg, beaten
125 ml	oil
300 ml	water

Combine dry ingredients; beat egg, oil and water and combine with dry ingredients. Finish according to the basic recipe for WAFFLES. *Yield:* 5 waffles.

POPOVERS

Hollow and light in texture, popovers are leavened by the rapid formation of steam. Serve at breakfast, hot from the oven; as popovers deflate on standing, make only as many as can be eaten at one meal; make an incision in each on taking from the oven. If desired, unbaked batter can be frozen in individual pans, to be thawed and baked when needed.

250 ml	flour
2 ml	salt
	2 eggs
250 ml	milk

1. Preheat oven to 220°C
2. Combine flour and salt, add eggs and milk and beat with a rotary beater until mixture is smooth.
3. Pour into 6 greased and heated custard cups or muffin pans, each with a capacity of about 150 ml
4. Bake until puffed high and golden brown, about 30 min; reduce heat and bake 15 min longer at 180°C

Serve at once with butter and/or jam. *Yield:* 6 popovers.

MUFFINS

Popular at any time as a replacement for bread, or an alternative to rich cakes and cookies, muffins can be made from a great variety of flours including nutritious whole grains and bran.

Muffin batters are low in content of tenderizing ingredients; stir only until mixed. Do not beat.

Muffins are cooked when their tops are golden brown, when their edges come away from the pan, when they feel firm when lightly touched, when batter will not stick to a fine skewer or toothpick inserted into the centre of a muffin.

Basic Recipe
MUFFINS

500 ml	flour
75 ml	skim milk powder
50 ml	sugar
1 ml	salt
20 ml	baking powder
50 ml	oil
	1 egg
250 ml	water

1. Grease muffin pans; preheat oven to 200°C
2. Thoroughly combine all the dry ingredients in a large bowl.
3. In a small bowl, beat oil, egg and water with a rotary beater; stir into dry ingredients with minimum mixing. Batter should be somewhat lumpy.
4. Fill prepared muffin pans 2/3 full; bake about 20 min
5. Cool pans on a cake rack; loosen muffins by running a small knife around the edges. Serve warm.
   Yield: 10-12 muffins, diameter 6.5 cm

Muffins taste best when served hot. Wrap in foil to reheat in the oven, or use a bun warmer or the top of a double boiler.

By measuring out dry ingredients and liquid ingredients in the evening, but not combining them until morning, muffins hot from the oven can be ready for breakfast. The oven timer can be set the night before to have oven hot when needed.

Recipes, tables, etc. that appear in small capital letters, e.g., PARSLEY BUTTER, CANADA'S FOOD GUIDE, are listed in the index. Consult the index for the number of the page on which the item appears.

Variations

Stir in raisins, currants, chopped and cooked dried apricots, nuts, or crumbled cooked bacon, about 125 ml

Buttermilk Muffins—Substitute an equal quantity of buttermilk or sour milk for the water. Omit milk powder. Use ½ the amount of baking powder required in the recipe and add baking soda: 2.5 ml

Blueberry or Raspberry Muffins—Stir in fresh or frozen berries, about 200 ml

Cheese Muffins—Add grated cheese, 125 ml and reduce shortening by 15 ml

Cornmeal Muffins—Substitute cornmeal for half of the flour and increase fat to 75 ml

Leftover cornmeal muffins are particularly good when sliced and toasted under the broiler.

Oatmeal Muffins—Substitute rolled oats for half the flour. If desired, substitute whole wheat flour for the remaining flour.

Whole Wheat Muffins—Substitute whole wheat flour for half the flour.

Raisins and currants may contain sand. If package does not indicate that fruit has been cleaned, rinse fruit several times; dry thoroughly; flour if necessary.

Muffins are a delicious accompaniment to coffee or tea. Holland Cheese Consumer Bureau.

BRAN MUFFINS

A large helping of dietary fibre is a bonus in these muffins which are delicious when served at any meal or as a snack.

250 ml	flour
500 ml	natural wheat bran (cooking bran)
75 ml	skim milk powder
15 ml	baking powder
125 ml	brown sugar
50 ml	oil
	1 egg
250 ml	water
75 ml	raisins (optional)

Prepare according to the basic recipe for MUFFINS.
Yield: 10-12 muffins, diameter 6.5 cm

APPLESAUCE MUFFINS

450 ml	flour
10 ml	baking powder
3 ml	baking soda
2 ml	salt
5 ml	cinnamon
2 ml	allspice
	sprinkle of cloves
200 ml	brown sugar
200 ml	raisins
	1 egg, beaten
75 ml	oil *or* melted fat
250 ml	sieved applesauce

Prepare according to the basic recipe for MUFFINS, adding the applesauce to the oil-egg mixture. *Yield:*
10-12 muffins, diameter 6.5 cm
or 18-20 muffins, diameter 5 cm
Make these spicy, cake-like muffins in small pans to serve with tea or coffee.

Tea biscuits. Maple Leaf Mills.

Basic Recipe
TEA BISCUITS

Tea biscuits are a versatile quick bread that can be served hot with a meal or at "tea", served warm with sweetened fruit as shortcake, or as a topping on hot meat pie. Whole wheat flour may be substituted for half the flour.

500 ml	flour
75 ml	skim milk powder
20 ml	baking powder
2 ml	salt
75-125 ml	firm shortening
150-200 ml	water

1. Preheat oven to 220°C
2. Combine dry ingredients in a mixing bowl.
3. Cut in the fat using a pastry blender or 2 knives until no lumps of fat are evident and the mixture resembles cornmeal.
4. Add the water gradually, working it in with a fork until the mixture forms a ball around the fork. Too little liquid makes a stiff dough which will crumble or crack; too much makes a sticky dough which will be difficult to handle.
5. Turn the dough out onto a floured board; knead lightly by folding the dough and pressing gently with the heel of the hand. Repeat about 6 times, turning dough slightly and picking up a little flour each time, so that it is evenly kneaded. Over-kneading toughens this dough.
6. Roll dough with a floured rolling pin or pat it flat to a thickness of 1-1.5 cm
7. Cut with a floured cookie cutter. When using a large cutter, dough should be rolled to the maximum thickness.
8. Place on an ungreased baking sheet; if a shiny surface is desired, brush tops of biscuits with milk or a mixture of milk and beaten egg yolk.
9. Bake until golden brown, about 10-15 min
   Yield: 20 biscuits, diameter about 5 cm

Time may be saved by mixing the dough a little longer in the bowl, using the maximum amount of liquid, and dropping it onto a greased baking sheet instead of kneading or rolling. These drop biscuits will have an uneven shape and rough surface but a good texture. Dough can also be rolled into a rectangle on a baking sheet, cut into squares with a sharp knife and separated before baking.

Variations

Oil can replace shortening; use the smaller quantity. Knead and roll or pat out between sheets of waxed paper.

Buttermilk Biscuits—Substitute an equal quantity of buttermilk, sour milk, or sour cream for water; omit milk powder. Use ½ the amount of baking powder and add baking soda: 2 cm

Biscuits made with buttermilk are whiter inside than those made with other milks.

Cheese Biscuits—Add to the dry ingredients grated, nippy Cheddar cheese, about 125 ml

Herb Biscuits—Add to the dry ingredients:

1 ml	dry mustard
2 ml	sage
50 ml	chopped chives

Whole Wheat Biscuits—Replace half the flour with whole wheat flour.

See also BASIC QUICK-BREAD MIX, TEA BISCUITS.

TEA BISCUIT PIZZA

	1 recipe TEA BISCUIT dough
170 ml	1 can tomato paste
125 ml	finely chopped onion
125 ml	chopped green pepper
200 ml	grated blue cheese, Cheddar *or* Mozzarella
	salt, pepper,
	oregano *or* thyme
	2 cans sardines

1. Preheat oven to 220°C
2. Knead dough into a large ball or 2 small balls; pat flat on a greased cookie sheet to form one large or 2 small circles with a thickness about 1 cm
3. Spread dough with tomato paste; sprinkle with onion, green pepper, cheese and seasonings. Arrange drained sardines or other fish or meat in an attractive pattern.
4. Bake until the edges of the pizza are a golden brown, about 15-20 min; transfer to a warm platter and serve at once. *Serves 6-8.*

Variations

Substitute for the sardines one of: anchovy fillets; crumbled corned beef; slices of Italian sausage; weiners; well-cooked, drained bulk sausage meat, bacon or hamburger.

Bambinos. Maple Leaf Mills.

Bambinos—For hot appetizers or cocktail accompaniments, use the recipe to make tiny pizzas with a diameter of 4-5 cm

Basic Recipe
SWEET TEA BISCUIT DOUGH

500 ml	flour
75 ml	skim milk powder
25 ml	baking powder
2 ml	salt
25 ml	sugar
50-75 ml	firm shortening
	1 egg
125-150 ml	water

Preheat oven to 220°C

Combine dry ingredients and cut in shortening. Beat egg with water and stir into the dry mixture. For detailed method of preparation see TEA BISCUITS (BASIC RECIPE).

Variations

For a more nutritious mixture, substitute whole wheat flour for half the flour; ¾ the quantity of oil can be substituted for the shortening; roll between sheets of waxed paper.

Currant Scones

1. To SWEET TEA BISCUIT DOUGH ingredients add cleaned raisins or currants, about 250 ml
2. Roll out dough to fit a pie plate; score top of dough in triangles and sprinkle with sugar.
3. Bake until golden brown, about 20 min at 200°C Pan capacity 750 ml

Butterscotch Muffins

1. Preheat oven to 220°C
2. Prepare a pie plate or individual muffin pans by greasing liberally with softened butter or margarine; sprinkle with brown sugar. Drizzle with corn syrup or sprinkle with water.
3. Prepare SWEET TEA BISCUIT DOUGH and roll out into a long rectangle with a width about 22 cm
4. Spread with soft butter, brown sugar, and if desired, a little cinnamon. For fruit and nut variations, add any combination of raisins, dates, canned or glazed pineapple, maraschino cherries, chopped almonds, walnuts or other nuts; well-drained, cooked apricots with grated orange rind or orange marmalade, using a total of about 250 ml
5. Roll from the long side and cut with a sharp knife into slices of 3 cm
6. Place cut side down into prepared pans and bake 15-20 min until lightly browned; on removal from oven, invert immediately on a platter allowing all the syrup to run onto muffins. *Yield:* 8 muffins, diameter 5 cm

Apple Coffee Cake

1. Prepare SWEET TEA BISCUIT DOUGH using the greater amount of liquid.
2. Spread batter in a greased cake pan; arrange 2 apples (peeled, cored and sliced) on the batter; top with one of the STREUSEL TOPPINGS. Bake 25-30 min at 190°C
   Serves 6.

Apricot Coffee Cake

1. Prepare SWEET TEA BISCUIT DOUGH using the greater amount of liquid; spread ¾ batter into a greased cake pan.
2. Spread with apricot jam almost to edges.
3. Over the remaining batter sprinkle enough flour to form a dough which is not sticky; divide into 8 pieces.
4. With well-floured hands roll each piece into the shape of a pencil.
5. Lay these criss-cross fashion over the jam; brush with milk, sprinkle with sugar; bake for 25-30 min at 190°C
   Serves 6.

Recipes, tables, etc. that appear in small capital letters, e.g., PARSLEY BUTTER, CANADA'S FOOD GUIDE, are listed in the index. Consult the index for the number of the page on which the item appears.

Apricot Swirl

1. Combine:

250 ml	apricot jam
30 ml	orange juice
5 ml	grated orange rind

2. Prepare SWEET TEA BISCUIT DOUGH using the greater amount of liquid.
3. Spread half the batter in a greased, round pan. Cover with alternating spoonfuls of the jam mixture and the remaining batter. Spiral a knife through the batter. Bake for 25 min at 190°C

Try pineapple or strawberry jam for variety.

Cranberry Nut Coffee Cake—Prepare SWEET TEA BISCUIT DOUGH using the greater amount of liquid. Add chopped walnuts. Spread in a greased cake pan. Top with CRANBERRY SAUCE, about 175 ml
When the baked coffee cake is still warm, drizzle with LEMON GLAZE or VANILLA GLAZE.

BASIC QUICK-BREAD MIX

This easily prepared mix can be stored in the refrigerator for quick preparation of pancakes, tea biscuits, shortcake and coffee cake. It is important that shortening be very finely cut; as well as causing an inferior texture in the product, too large pieces cause the mix to occupy more space, resulting in inaccurate measurement. When measuring the mix, spoon it lightly; do not pack it down.

2 ℓ	flour
400 ml	skim milk powder
10 ml	salt
75 ml	baking powder
500 ml	shortening

1. Combine dry ingredients thoroughly.
2. Cut in shortening using 2 knives or a pastry blender until the mixture resembles cornmeal. Shake to bring to surface any coarse lumps and work them out with the fingers.
3. Cover and store in the refrigerator to use as needed in the following recipes. *Yield:* about 3.5 ℓ

To substitute oil for shortening in the basic mix, use ¾ of the quantity. Mix made from oil tends to pack down more.

Pancakes

500 ml	BASIC QUICK-BREAD MIX
	2 eggs
250 ml	**water**

Beat eggs with water; stir into mix and beat with an egg beater only until batter is smooth and thin enough to pour. Finish according to basic recipe for PANCAKES. *Yield:* 6 pancakes, diameter 15 cm

Tea Biscuits

500 ml	BASIC QUICK-BREAD MIX
125 ml	**water**

Stir liquid into mix using a fork. Finish according to TEA BISCUITS (BASIC RECIPE). *Yield:* 10-12 biscuits, diameter 4 cm

Sweet Tea Biscuits or Shortcake—To tea biscuit dough made with QUICK-BREAD MIX add 1 beaten egg and sugar, 30 ml

Coffee Cake

500 ml	BASIC QUICK-BREAD MIX
50 ml	**sugar**
125 ml	**raisins**
	1 egg
125 ml	**water**

Topping

125 ml	**brown sugar**
10 ml	**cinnamon**

1. Preheat oven to 200°C
2. Combine mix, sugar and raisins; beat egg and water together and stir into dry mixture, mixing only until all is moist, but not smooth.
3. Spread batter in a greased round or square cake pan; sprinkle evenly with sugar and cinnamon. Bake about 20 min. *Serves 6.*

Orange Bread

600 ml	BASIC QUICK-BREAD MIX
175 ml	**sugar**
50 ml	**grated orange rind**
175 ml	**orange juice**
	2 eggs

1. Preheat oven to 190°C
2. Combine mix, sugar and orange rind. Beat orange juice and eggs together and combine with dry in-

gredients. Beat only enough to form a smooth batter. Bake for 50-60 min in a greased loaf pan. *Yield:* 1 loaf; pan capacity 1.25 ℓ

DOUGHNUTS

900 ml	**flour**
175 ml	**sugar**
50 ml	**skim milk powder**
20 ml	**baking powder**
1 ml	**cinnamon**
1 ml	**cloves**
	sprinkle of nutmeg
2 ml	**salt**
	2 eggs
175 ml	**water**
50 ml	**oil**

1. Combine dry ingredients; beat together eggs, water and oil.
2. Combine the liquid ingredients and dry ingredients, mixing enough to blend to a soft dough. Chill 30 min
3. Roll out dough to a thickness of approximately 1 cm
4. Cut with a doughnut cutter into rings. Heat fat to 190°C
5. Drop a few at a time into hot fat; let rise to surface and brown on the underside before turning; remove one doughnut after 3 min and break open to test adequacy of cooking time.
6. Remove with a slotted spoon or fork; drain on paper towels.
7. Shake doughnuts in a small bag containing a mixture of cinnamon and sugar, or glaze when cool. *Yield:* 30-35 doughnuts.

See also YEAST DOUGHNUTS.

Making doughnuts. Maple Leaf Mills.

Quick-bread Loaves

Like pancakes, muffins and tea biscuits, these loaves are leavened by baking powder or baking soda. Ingredients can be combined by the muffin method (liquid ingredients are combined and stirred into the dry ingredients) by the biscuit method (shortening is cut into the dry ingredients and the liquid stirred in) or by the cake method (soft fat is creamed with sugar and egg, and the dry ingredients are added alternately with the liquids). The muffin method of mixing is easiest when liquid fat is used, but the cake method gives the finest, lightest product.

Texture and flavour are improved if loaves are stored for 24 hours in a covered container before serving. They freeze well, wrapped in foil or stored in a covered container with as much air excluded as possible.

Soup cans or large fruit cans make attractive cylindrical loaves. To compare their capacity with that of standard loaf pans, measure using water.

Grease pans that do not have non-stick finish. Cut a paper liner to extend up and beyond long sides of loaf pan for easy removal of contents. Grease the paper except for the overhang.

Batter should be pushed up into the corners of the prepared loaf pans so that level of batter is higher in the corners than the centre. Baked loaf will then be level on top, without deep cracks.

Loaf is cooked when its top is golden brown, its edges come away from the pan, it is firm when lightly touched, and batter does not stick to a fine skewer or toothpick.

QUICK BROWN BREAD

This version of whole wheat bread is similar to Boston Brown Bread but it is baked in the oven rather than steamed for several hours—thus saving fuel, especially if other foods are cooked in the oven at the same time.

250 ml	flour
250 ml	whole wheat flour
2 ml	salt
5 ml	baking soda
5 ml	baking powder
300 ml	buttermilk *or* sour milk
15 ml	molasses
10 ml	oil

1. Preheat oven to 180°C
2. Combine dry ingredients; combine liquid ingredients.

3. Stir liquid ingredients into dry mixture until dough forms. Turn out onto a floured board and knead about 25 times.
4. Shape into a loaf and bake in a medium greased but unlined loaf pan for about 1 h. *Yield:* 1 loaf; pan capacity 1.25 *l*

Basic Recipe
FRUIT LOAF

400 ml	flour
75 ml	skim milk powder
10 ml	baking powder
2 ml	baking soda
125 ml	sugar
2 ml	salt
	grated rind of 1 orange
2 ml	grated lemon rind
250 ml	chopped dates *or* dried apricots
	1 egg
50 ml	oil
200 ml	water

1. Preheat oven to 180°C
2. Thoroughly combine dry ingredients, grated rinds and fruit.
3. Beat egg, oil and water with a rotary beater; stir into the dry ingredients with a minimum of mixing until combined.
4. Bake in a prepared loaf pan for about 50 min. Pan capacity 1.2 *l*

Variations
Substitute whole wheat flour for 1/3 of the flour.

Substitute any of raisins, glazed fruits, chopped nuts or shelled sunflower seeds for the dates or apricots.

DATE AND NUT LOAF

250 ml	dates
300 ml	boiling water
100 ml	shortening
350 ml	brown sugar
	1 beaten egg
5 ml	vanilla
550 ml	flour
5 ml	salt
8 ml	baking soda
100 ml	chopped nuts

1. Preheat oven to 180°C
2. Chop dates into a bowl; add boiling water, stir and leave to cool.
3. Beat shortening, sugar and egg until fluffy; add vanilla.
4. Thoroughly combine dry ingredients; add alternately with dates to the beaten mixture. Add nuts.
5. Bake in a prepared loaf pan for about 60 min. Pan capacity 1.25 ℓ

BANANA BRAN BREAD

375 ml	flour
10 ml	baking powder
2 ml	baking soda
2 ml	salt
125 ml	margarine *or* shortening
200 ml	sugar
	2 eggs
375 ml	4-5 mashed ripe bananas
15 ml	grated orange rind
250 ml	all bran cereal *or* natural wheat bran

1. Preheat oven to 180°C
2. Thoroughly combine flour, baking powder, soda and salt.
3. Cream margarine; gradually add sugar, creaming well after each addition.
4. Add eggs and beat until fluffy; beat in bananas, rind and bran and let stand 5 min
5. Stir in dry ingredients and transfer mixture to a prepared loaf pan.
6. Bake for approximately 1 hour. Pan capacity 1.25 ℓ

When bananas are marked down for quick sale, make several loaves and freeze.

LEMON BREAD

400 ml	flour
50 ml	skim milk powder
10 ml	baking powder
1 ml	salt
100 ml	butter *or* margarine
250 ml	sugar
	2 eggs
125 ml	water
15 ml	lemon juice
	grated rind of 1 lemon
50 ml	sugar
50 ml	lemon juice

1. Preheat oven to 180°C
2. Thoroughly combine flour, milk powder, baking powder and salt.
3. Cream the butter, add sugar gradually, creaming after each addition.
4. Beat in eggs until mixture is light and fluffy.
5. Combine water and small quantity of lemon juice and add to the egg mixture alternately with the dry ingredients. Add rind.
6. Pour into a prepared loaf pan and bake for about 1 h
7. Remove pan from oven; combine sugar and lemon juice and spoon evenly over the loaf. Cool loaf in the pan. Pan capacity 1.25 ℓ

Yeast Bread and Rolls

For the makers of homemade bread, the satisfactions are many—tasty, nutritious bread at economy prices, heavenly aromas, and a sense of accomplishment. Breadmaking is an acquired art which can be quickly learned.

Ingredients Used in Preparing Yeast Doughs

Flour must provide sufficient gluten to produce an elastic dough. Bread flour is best, but all-purpose flour will make an excellent bread; whole wheat flour may be used along with bread flour or all-purpose flour, but not alone. Pastry flour is unsuitable for bread-making. Because the moisture content of flour varies, the amount of flour needed will vary. For this reason, the flour requirement in a bread recipe is often expressed as a range.

Yeast used in most home baking is the dry, granular variety. The amount required varies with the length of time available for rising. Very fast results may be obtained when the amount of yeast specified in the recipe is doubled, but a slower rising allows the development of flavour.

Sugar supplies food to support the yeast activity; it furnishes material to produce carbon dioxide for leavening. Too little sugar results in a pale crust and a loaf which fails to reach its full volume.

Liquid may be water, potato water, milk, or milk and water. Potato water aids the growth of the yeast. Milk adds food value and flavour; milk sugar is not fermented by the yeast and remains to give the crust a deep colour.

Water should be boiled and cooled to lukewarm; milk should be scalded and cooled so that undesired bacteria will be destroyed. Potato water is obtained by cooking potatoes in water, mashing or ricing them, and combining them with the cooking liquid. Use 1 medium potato and 625 ml of water. Or, to that quantity of water add instant mashed potatoes: about 50 ml

Salt in yeast mixtures not only provides flavour but controls the fermentation. By retarding destruction of sugar by yeast, salt gives a deeper crust colour and a close texture to the bread. Salt-free bread is porous in texture because of the lack of salt.

Fat produces a soft, velvety crumb, an increased volume and a finer texture. In addition, it improves the keeping quality of the bread. Butter gives more colour and flavour, shortening a whiter loaf; melted fat does not give as good texture.

Steps in the Preparation of Yeast Dough

Preparing the Dough—It is essential that the temperatures of the ingredients added to the yeast be no hotter than lukewarm. Too high a temperature kills the yeast; too low a temperature means too slow rising and the development of other organisms and off-flavours. "Yeasty" bread is much more likely to be caused by too slow rising than by too much yeast. Thorough mixing at the beginning is necessary to distribute the yeast evenly and to develop the gluten. Kneading, the process of turning and working the dough with the heel of the hand, further develops the gluten and distributes the gas produced by the yeast throughout the dough. Kneading contributes to the texture.

The *straight-dough method* for making dough is used in most recipes. The mixing of ingredients takes place in one continuous operation with 2 or 3 rising periods. Contrasted to this is the *sponge method*, in which ingredients are mixed in 2 operations: the liquid and yeast are combined with a little flour to make a batter which is left to rise to form a sponge-like mixture; remaining flour is kneaded in and another rising takes place, to be followed by 2 more rising periods.

Fermentation—During fermentation the yeast is growing and using the sugar; the flavour is developing. Maintain a slightly moist atmosphere and a temperature about 27°C. A closed, warm cupboard containing a large pan of boiling water may be used; an electric dishwasher, warm and steamy after use, but turned off completely, is excellent. As the dough rises it may be punched down by pushing the fist into the dough and turning in the edges to the centre. This pushes out the large gas bubbles formed before the yeast is growing actively, and gives better texture to large loaves. This step is not necessary for rolls.

When the dough is ready for the first rising it may be put into the freezer for about 20 min to retard the fermentation. After this, the dough will keep in a refrigerator if covered with aluminum foil or waxed paper and a damp tea towel. A deep bowl is necessary to allow for expansion of dough. If it rises to the top of the bowl before it is to be used, it may be punched down once. The length of time the dough keeps will depend upon the initial temperature of the dough and the refrigerator temperature.

Shaping depends upon the product desired. When the dough has risen it should be cut into pieces, the cut edges turned under to make a smooth ball; cover with a large inverted bowl or loose plastic film and let rest 10 min before shaping.

After shaping, the dough must be allowed to stand only until it has doubled in bulk. After prolonged standing, all the sugar will have been used by the yeast, the gluten overstretched, and the volume decreased; a poor quality loaf results.

Baking—When the risen dough goes into the oven there will be a sudden expansion of the gas (known as the "spring"). For this reason space must be allowed in the pan. The bread is baked when it sounds hollow when rapped. It may be shielded with a sheet of foil if it is becoming too brown before it is cooked.

Basic Recipe
WHITE BREAD

5 ml	sugar
125 ml	warm water
10 ml	1 envelope granular yeast
500 ml	liquid
25 ml	butter
15 ml	shortening
25 ml	sugar
10 ml	salt
1.4-1.5 *l*	flour (all-purpose or bread)

1. Stir sugar into warm water; sprinkle with yeast and let stand 10 min without stirring.
2. Place the liquid (milk, water, or potato water), in a large saucepan; heat slowly until bubbles form around the edge of the pan. Cool to lukewarm.
3. Add the fat, sugar and salt and combine with the yeast mixture; stir in approximately one-third of the flour.
4. Beat with a wooden spoon to form a smooth, very elastic batter.

5. Gradually add enough remaining flour to make a soft dough which leaves the sides of the bowl; work into a ball using hands.
6. Turn out onto a floured board and knead for about 10 min or until the dough is smooth, elastic and no longer sticky.
7. Rotate dough in a lightly greased bowl to grease the surface; cover lightly with waxed paper.
8. Let rise in a warm place (24°C-30°C) until doubled in bulk, about 1-1.5 h
9. Punch down and let rise again until doubled in bulk, about 1-1.5 h
10. Punch down again and divide into 2 equal parts; roll out into a rectangle, a little narrower than the length of the pan.
11. Shape into a tight roll like a jelly roll, sealing ends with the heel of the hand. Place rolls in lightly greased bread pans, tucking ends of dough under; dough should half fill pans in depth without filling ends.
12. Cover with greased, waxed paper and let rise in a warm place for about 45 min until it is doubled in bulk, and extends above the top of the pan in the centre and touches the corners. After 35 min preheat oven to 200°C

    When the dough is pressed and a mark remains and when small bubbles begin to appear under the surface of the loaf, these are signs that the dough must be baked without delay.
13. Bake for 15 min, then reduce heat and bake for about 30 min at 190°C
14. Turn out onto a wire rack; cool. For a soft crust brush top with soft butter. Makes 2 loaves. Pan capacity 1.2 *l*

The basic recipe can be doubled to make 4 loaves using the same amount of yeast. In this case, the first rising will require about 3 h. To shorten the rising time, double the quantity of yeast.

Yeast Bread "Doneness" Test
Yeast bread is baked when its top is golden brown, it shrinks from the sides of the pan, and it sounds hollow when the crust is rapped lightly with the knuckles.

Freezing Bread
To freeze baked bread, cool and wrap tightly with freezer wrap. When only a few slices of bread will be needed at a time, the loaf may be sliced before freezing so that the entire loaf does not need to be defrosted.

Kneading (step 6 of basic recipe for White Bread).

Punching down (step 9).

Before rising in pan (step 11).

After baking.

Photos: Canadian Dairy Foods Service Bureau.

WHOLE WHEAT BREAD

Substitute whole wheat flour for half of the flour in the basic recipe for WHITE BREAD. Molasses may replace the sugar for a darker loaf.

COOL-RISE WHITE BREAD

Bread prepared by the cool-rise method can be baked any time from 2 to 24 h after refrigerating. Work area should be warm while dough is being mixed and mixing should be done quickly to prevent cooling the dough.

10 ml	sugar
125 ml	warm water
20 ml	2 envelopes granular yeast
450 ml	warm milk
30 ml	sugar
15 ml	salt
50 ml	shortening
1.4-1.5 *l*	flour

1. Prepare the dough as in WHITE BREAD (BASIC RECIPE) to the end of step 6.
2. Cover dough with plastic wrap, then a towel, and let rest for 20 min on the board. Punch down, shape and fit into the pans according to step 10 of WHITE BREAD (BASIC RECIPE).
3. Brush surface of dough with oil; cover pan loosely with greased wax paper, then plastic wrap.
4. Refrigerate pans of dough for 2-24 h. Remove from refrigerator when needed; let stand at room temperature for 10 min while preheating oven to 200°C
5. Puncture any large surface bubbles which may have formed on dough during refrigeration, using a greased toothpick.
6. Bake 30-40 min. See YEAST BREAD "DONENESS" TEST.
7. Cool on a rack. For a soft crust, brush tops of baked loaves with butter after removing from pans. *Yield:* 2 loaves; pan capacity 1.2 *l*

ENRICHED BREAD

Add the following additional ingredients to any bread recipe, allowing for every 250 ml flour

15 ml	skim milk powder
15 ml	soy flour
5 ml	wheat germ

BREAD DOUGH VARIATIONS

Vary a basic bread recipe by substituting for up to 1/3 of the flour one or a combination of: whole wheat flour, rye flour, buckwheat flour, any coarsely milled flour.

Vary bread texture by adding a few spoonfuls of one of: cracked wheat or other grains, soaked; GRANOLA, bran, coarse raw breakfast cereals, cornmeal, KASHA.

Add an attractive topping to any loaf by first brushing with egg white, then sprinkling with one of: cracked wheat, sesame seeds, caraway seeds, poppy seeds.

OATMEAL BREAD

5 ml	sugar
125 ml	warm water
10 ml	1 envelope granular yeast
750 ml	quick-cooking oats
600 ml	boiling water
50 ml	molasses
50 ml	brown sugar
15 ml	salt
50 ml	shortening
150 ml	cold water
1.5-2 *l*	flour

1. Stir sugar into warm water; sprinkle with yeast and let stand 10 min without stirring.
2. Into a large bowl, measure oats; add boiling water, molasses, brown sugar, salt and shortening and stir to combine; stir in cold water.
3. When mixture is lukewarm, stir in yeast mixture; beat in half the flour with a wooden spoon and continue beating until mixture is smooth.
4. Add enough of the remaining flour gradually to make a soft dough, working it in with a wooden spoon, then with the hands.
5. Turn out onto a floured board and knead until elastic, about 10 min
6. Rotate dough in a greased bowl to grease surface; cover and let rise in a warm place until doubled in bulk, about 1.5 h
7. Punch down; let rise again until doubled, about 45 min
8. Punch down the dough, divide into 3 equal parts. Shape into loaves, see WHITE BREAD (BASIC RECIPE), and place in 3 greased loaf pans.
9. Lightly grease tops of loaves, and let rise in a warm place until double, about 45 min. Preheat oven to 200°C
10. Bake until golden brown, about 45-60 min
    Yield: 3 loaves; pan capacity 1.2 *l*

RYE BREAD

5 ml	sugar
250 ml	warm water
10 ml	1 envelope granular yeast
250 ml	milk
25 ml	sugar
10 ml	salt
30 ml	shortening
500 ml	rye flour
750 ml-1 *l*	flour
15 ml	cornmeal

1. Prepare according to WHITE BREAD (BASIC RECIPE) to the end of step 9.
2. Grease a large cookie sheet, sprinkle lightly with cornmeal.
3. Punch down dough and divide into 2 equal pieces, shape each piece into a roll, and roll back and forth on board to make longer and thinner. Or, for a round loaf, shape dough into a ball.
4. Place loaves on prepared cookie sheet and slash the surface of each 4 or 5 times, diagonally, at intervals; brush with cold water.
5. Let rise in a warm place until doubled, about 1.25 h. Preheat oven to 220°C
6. Brush tops of loaves again with cold water; bake until lightly browned, about 30 min. Baked loaves will sound hollow when rapped with the knuckles. *Yield:* 2 loaves.

FRENCH BREAD

For a very crisp crust, use bread flour, if available, rather than all-purpose flour.

1. Use the ingredients for WHITE BREAD (BASIC RECIPE), omitting the butter, shortening, and larger portion of sugar.
2. Divide the dough into 3 equal portions and shape each into a long slightly tapered loaf about 37 × 5 cm
3. On a baking sheet, evenly sprinkle cornmeal, about 125 ml
4. Place loaves on the pan, leaving space on all sides for expansion.
5. With a very sharp knife make diagonal slashes at intervals, cutting into the surface of the dough about 1 cm
6. Combine:

100 ml	water
2 ml	salt

and brush the solution lightly over each loaf.

7. Let loaves rise until doubled in bulk, about 1 h
8. Preheat oven to 200°C
9. In the bottom of the oven place a shallow roasting pan filled with boiling water; bake bread immediately above the water for 15 min. Reduce heat to 180°C
10. Brush the loaves with the salt solution; continue baking for 10 min more, then brush loaves again.
11. Continue baking until loaves are golden and the crust is crisp (about 20 min). Cool on a rack. *Yield:* 3 loaves.

Pizza. Lawry's Foods, Inc.

ITALIAN PIZZA

5 ml	sugar
250 ml	water
10 ml	1 envelope granular yeast
5 ml	salt
50 ml	oil
750 ml	flour
162 ml	1 can tomato paste
125 ml	water
5 ml	salt
	pepper
5 ml	oregano
170 g	Mozzarella or processed cheese, thinly sliced
200 g	sliced, cooked sausages
200 ml	sliced, cooked mushrooms
75 ml	chopped green pepper
50 ml	oil
100 ml	grated Parmesan or sharp Cheddar cheese

To prepare dough:

1. Add sugar to warm water, sprinkle with yeast and let stand 10 min without stirring.
2. Stir well and combine with salt, oil and half of the flour; beat until smooth.
3. Stir in enough of the remaining flour to form a soft dough; turn out onto a lightly floured board and knead until smooth and elastic.
4. Rotate dough in a greased bowl to grease surface; cover and let rise in a warm place until doubled in bulk, about 45 min
5. Meanwhile, prepare tomato mixture by combining tomato paste, water, salt, a sprinkle of pepper, and oregano.
6. When dough is doubled in bulk, punch down and divide in half; form each half into a ball.
7. Place each ball on a greased baking sheet or pizza pan; press out with the palms of the hands into circles, leaving edges slightly higher.
8. On each circle arrange half of the sliced cheese, sausage and mushrooms; sprinkle with green pepper.
9. Spread each with half of the tomato mixture and sprinkle with half the oil and grated cheese.
10. Bake for about 25 min at 200°C
11. Serve hot, cut into wedges. *Yield:* 2 pizzas, diameter 30 cm

Although mushrooms and pepperoni are usually considered to be the extras on an "all-dressed" pizza, this famous Italian specialty may contain any combinations of: cooked shrimp; strips of ham; salami; cooked minced beef; capers; garlic; or stuffed olives.

TEA BISCUIT dough may be substituted for yeast dough in a pizza.

Basic Recipe
ROLLS

Whole wheat flour can be substituted for half of the flour in this recipe.

5 ml	sugar
125 ml	warm water
10 ml	1 envelope granular yeast
200 ml	milk
30 ml	shortening
30 ml	sugar
	1 beaten egg
5 ml	salt
750 ml	flour

1. Stir sugar into warm water; sprinkle with yeast and let stand 10 min without stirring.

2. Scald milk, then cool to lukewarm; add shortening, sugar, beaten egg, salt and yeast mixture.
3. Beat in 1/3 of the flour; knead in the remaining flour.
4. Turn out onto a lightly floured board and knead until smooth and elastic.
5. Rotate dough in a large greased bowl to grease top; cover and let rise in a warm place until doubled in bulk, about 80 min
6. Punch down; shape the dough according to any of the variations which follow.
7. Place on greased pans and let rise until doubled in bulk, about 1 h. Preheat oven to 190°C
8. Bake until lightly browned, about 15-20 min
   Yield: 12-24 rolls.

Variations

Dinner Rolls
1. Roll dough to a thickness of about 1 cm
2. With a floured cookie cutter, cut into circles and shape each over the thumb into a ball.
3. Place, with cut edges under, in greased muffin pans or side by side in a cake pan.
4. Finish beginning at step 7 of basic recipe.

Parker House Rolls
1. Roll the dough to a thickness of about 1 cm
2. With a floured cookie cutter cut dough into circles; crease each circle slightly off-centre with the back of a knife.
3. Brush the larger section with melted butter or margarine; fold the small piece over and press edges together. Arrange back to back on a buttered sheet; finish beginning at step 7 of the basic recipe.

Bow Knots
1. Roll the dough to a thickness of 1 cm
2. Cut dough into finger-length strips with a width of 1 cm
3. Roll each strip between the palms of hands and board to make a pencil-like tube; brush with melted butter or margarine.
4. Knot each strip; tuck under the loose ends and place on a greased baking sheet, leaving a space on all sides of about 2.5 cm
5. Finish beginning at step 7 of basic recipe.

"Easter Bunnies" can be made by preparing dough as Bow Knots, pulling up ends and pinching them into points for ears. When baked, ice with ICING SUGAR GLAZE and decorate with bits of peel, cherries, raisins or nuts for eyes and mouth.

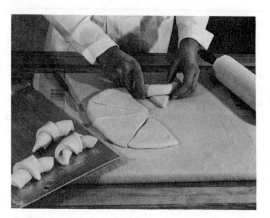

Rolling butterhorns. Maple Leaf Mills.

Butterhorns

1. Roll out dough into a circle with a diameter of 22 cm
   and a thickness of 1 cm
2. Cut circle into 12-16 wedges, roll each wedge starting at the wide end and rolling to the point.
3. Place on a greased pan with point side of roll upward; leave space between for expansion.
4. Finish according to ROLLS (BASIC RECIPE), beginning at step 7.

Crescent Rolls

Prepare as Butterhorns, bending each into a crescent. Sesame or poppy seeds may be sprinkled on lightly greased unbaked rolls.

Cutting dough for petal rolls. Maple Leaf Mills.

Petal Rolls or Fan Tans

1. Spread softened butter on dough which has been rolled to a thickness of 1 cm
2. Cut into strips with a width of 5 cm
3. Place 4 or 5 strips on top of each other and cut into squares of 5 cm
4. Stand the squares on end in greased muffin pans which have a diameter of about 5 cm
5. Finish according to ROLLS (BASIC RECIPE), beginning at step 7.

Shamrock Rolls (Cloverleaf Rolls)

1. Roll the dough to a thickness of 1 cm
2. Cut into circles with a cookie cutter, and shape each circle over the thumb to form balls.
3. Place 3 balls in each greased muffin pan; finish according to ROLLS (BASIC RECIPE), beginning at step 7.

REFRIGERATOR ROLL DOUGH

Refrigerator dough should contain sugar and salt in proportions that will extend the activity of the yeast over several days. Refrigerate only those doughs made from recipes labelled "Refrigerator Dough" or "Cool-rise," or use method outlined under FERMENTATION for checking yeast growth in the freezer.

200 ml	milk
100 ml	sugar
30 ml	salt
75 ml	shortening
10 ml	sugar
125 ml	warm water
20 ml	2 envelopes granular yeast
	1 beaten egg
1 *l*	flour

1. Scald milk; stir in the larger portion of sugar, salt and shortening; cool to lukewarm.
2. Meanwhile, stir the smaller portion of sugar into warm water; sprinkle with yeast and let stand without stirring for 10 min
3. Stir yeast into milk mixture; add beaten egg and half of the flour. Beat until smooth.
4. Stir in remaining flour to make a smooth dough; place in a greased bowl, rotate dough to grease top.
5. Cover bowl tightly with waxed paper or foil; store dough for at least 2 h or until needed (up to 3 d).
6. To use, punch down and cut off dough as needed. Shape into PARKER HOUSE, SHAMROCK, or BUTTERHORN ROLLS.
7. Let rise on greased pans until doubled in bulk; bake 15-20 min at 200°C
   Yield: 18-24 rolls.

Recipes, tables, etc. that appear in small capital letters, e.g., PARSLEY BUTTER, CANADA'S FOOD GUIDE, are listed in the index. Consult the index for the number of the page on which the item appears.

YEAST DOUGHNUTS

5 ml	sugar
125 ml	warm water
10 ml	1 envelope granular yeast
125 ml	milk
75 ml	shortening
5 ml	salt
125 ml	sugar
	2 eggs
2 ml	nutmeg
5 ml	grated lemon rind
750 ml-1 *l*	flour
	fat for frying

1. Combine the ingredients as for ROLLS (BASIC REC-IPE), using enough flour to form a soft dough.
2. Cover; let rise in a warm place until doubled in bulk.
3. Roll dough to a thickness of a little less than 1 cm
4. Cut with a doughnut cutter with a diameter of 7-8 cm
5. Place on a floured cookie sheet and let rise in a warm place until doubled in bulk, about 30-45 min
6. Heat fat to 185°C
7. Drop dough, raised-side down into hot fat; fry until brown; turn and brown on other side.
8. Drain; shake in a bag with sugar or icing sugar. *Yield:* 24 doughnuts.

See also DOUGHNUTS *for doughnuts prepared with baking powder.*

Variation
Filled Doughnuts—Cut dough into circles using a cookie cutter. Divide into 2 groups. Using egg white, brush surface near edge of one group of circles; in the centre of each, place strawberry jam, about 5 ml Top with the remaining circles, pinching edges together firmly to seal. Arrange on a floured cookie sheet; let rise in a warm place until doubled in bulk. Fry.

Recipes, tables, etc. that appear in small capital letters, e.g., PARSLEY BUTTER, CANADA'S FOOD GUIDE, are listed in the index. Consult the index for the number of the page on which the item appears.

Basic Recipe
SWEET DOUGH

Consult YEAST BREAD AND ROLLS for information concerning ingredients and basic method for preparing yeast breads. If desired, whole wheat flour can be substituted for up to one-half the quantity of flour.

10 ml	sugar
150 ml	warm water
20 ml	2 envelopes granular yeast
400 ml	milk
	rind of 1 lemon
200 ml	sugar
175 ml	shortening
7 ml	salt
	2 eggs
2 *l*	flour

1. Stir sugar into warm water; sprinkle with yeast and let stand 10 min without stirring.
2. Scald lemon rind with milk; strain; cool to lukewarm.
3. Beat together sugar, shortening, salt and eggs and add milk; stir in yeast mixture.
4. Stir in ¼ of the flour; knead in remaining flour, until dough is elastic.
5. Rotate dough in a large greased bowl to grease top; cover and let rise in a warm place until doubled in bulk; about 45-60 min
6. Punch down and divide dough into 3; shape each portion into a ball and let rest 10 min
7. Shape into buns or follow directions for the variations which follow. Let panned dough rise until doubled in bulk before baking.
8. Bake 15-20 min at 200°C

Variations
Spicy Sweet Dough—Using ingredients for SWEET DOUGH substitute for the large quantity of sugar:

250 ml	molasses

Add to the dry ingredients:

25 ml	cinnamon
5 ml	ginger
4 ml	each of cloves, cinnamon, allspice

Prepare as SWEET DOUGH (BASIC RECIPE). If a smaller quantity of spicy dough is desired, about 1/3 of the quantity of spices can be kneaded into 1/3 of the prepared Sweet Dough.

Tutti Frutti Bread

	1/3 **recipe risen** SWEET DOUGH
250 ml	**chopped glazed or dried fruits and nuts**

1. Roll dough into a rectangle 30 × 40 cm
2. Turn dough over so smooth side is down; sprinkle with a mixture of fruits and nuts.
3. Shape and finish as WHITE BREAD (BASIC RECIPE) beginning at step 11, bake in loaf pan having capacity of 1.2 *l*

Raisin Bread—Prepare as TUTTI FRUTTI BREAD using 1/3 of the recipe risen SPICY SWEET DOUGH. Add raisins, about 250 ml

Hot Cross Buns—Using SPICY SWEET DOUGH, roll out, cut and shape dough as for DINNER ROLLS. Cover and let rise until doubled in bulk. Using kitchen scissors, cut a shallow cross in top of each bun. Brush with slightly-beaten egg white and bake for about 20 min at 200°C
If desired, cuts may be filled with thin icing after buns are baked and cooled.

Individual buns can be baked in muffin pans instead of a cake pan.

CHELSEA BUNS

	1/3 **recipe risen** SWEET DOUGH
75 ml	**soft butter** *or* **margarine**
250 ml	**brown sugar**
2 ml	**cinnamon**
30 ml	**water** *or* **corn syrup**

1. Combine soft fat, sugar and cinnamon; spread 1/3 of this mixture in a square cake pan with a capacity of 1.5 *l*
   Sprinkle with water or syrup.
2. Roll dough into a rectangle 30 × 40 cm
3. Turn dough over so that smooth side is down; spread with remaining fat-sugar mixture and roll tightly starting at the long side of the rectangle.
4. With the cut edge of the roll down, slice into 12 equal pieces and place cut-side down in the prepared pan.
5. Let rise in a warm place until doubled in bulk, about 1 h. When dough is almost risen, preheat oven to 190°C
6. Bake for 30 min; while hot turn out of the pan.

Variation
Arrange chopped or halved nuts face-down on the mixture in the pan.

Sprinkle currants, raisins, or glazed fruit on dough before rolling.

Lemon Cheese Buns—Substitute the following mixture for the fat-sugar-cinnamon mixture and use for filling only:

225-250 g	**cream cheese, softened**
100 g	**currants**

Bake slices on a greased cake pan or cookie sheet. Cool and glaze buns with icing made from:

15 ml	**lemon juice**
250 ml	**icing sugar**

Swedish Tea Ring

1/3 **recipe risen** SWEET DOUGH
fruits, nuts, glaze

1. Follow directions for CHELSEA BUNS to end of step 3; spread filling almost to the edge and sprinkle with glazed fruits or nuts.
2. Join the ends of the roll and pinch together; place the ring on a greased baking sheet.
3. Using scissors, cut into the ring from the top, outer edge, but not through it (see picture) at intervals of 5 cm

Maple Leaf Mills.

4. Separate and twist each section slightly so that the spiral effect can be seen; cover loosely with waxed paper and let rise in warm place until doubled in bulk.
5. When tea ring is nearly doubled in size, preheat oven to 190°C
6. Bake ring until golden brown, about 25-30 min; when almost cool, glaze with syrup or VANILLA GLAZE and garnish with red and green cherries, and nuts.

Swedish Scroll

1. Follow the directions for SWEDISH TEA RING but do not form the roll into a ring.
2. Place the roll on a greased baking sheet; make cuts not quite to the centre from alternate sides, at intervals of about 3 cm

3. Twist each slice to alternate sides of the centre line. Cover and let rise. Finish as SWEDISH TEA RING.

Fruit Roll

1/3 **recipe risen** SWEET DOUGH
DATE FILLING
PRALINE GLAZE

1. Roll dough into a rectangle 30 × 15 cm
2. Mark the rectangle in thirds lengthwise; place on a greased baking sheet and spread the centre section with DATE FILLING.
3. Starting on one long side, cut from the edge inward to the beginning of the centre section, at intervals of 3 cm

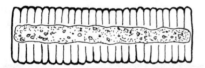

4. Repeat on the other long edge (see diagram) and bring strips alternately to the centre.

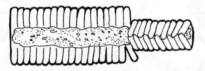

5. Let rise in a warm place until doubled in bulk; when nearly risen, preheat oven to 190°C
6. Bake 30-40 min until golden brown; while still warm brush with PRALINE GLAZE.

STOLLEN

This is traditional Austrian Christmas bread

250 ml	seedless raisins
250 ml	diced mixed candied fruit
50 ml	orange juice
150 ml	milk
125 ml	sugar
200 ml	soft butter
5 ml	salt
10 ml	1 envelope granular yeast
5 ml	sugar
100 ml	warm water
250 ml	sour cream
5 ml	vanilla
10 ml	lemon juice
	3 beaten egg yolks
1.25-1.5 ℓ	flour
100 ml	blanched almonds
30 ml	melted butter
2 ml	cinnamon
15 ml	sugar
	melted butter
	icing sugar

1. Combine raisins, candied fruit and juice; let stand at least 1 h
2. Scald milk, cool to lukewarm and stir in sugar, butter and salt; stir until the sugar is dissolved.
3. Prepare yeast as directed on the package, adding it to the sugar and warm water; combine with the sour cream, vanilla, lemon juice and egg yolk; beat thoroughly.
4. Stir in sufficient flour to make a light but not sticky dough; knead until smooth and elastic, about 10 min
5. Transfer to a greased bowl, rotate dough to grease top; cover and let rise in a warm place until doubled in bulk; punch down.
6. Drain fruit; work into dough.
7. Cut dough into two pieces; flatten each into an oval with a thickness of 2 cm
8. Brush each with melted butter, sprinkle with sugar and cinnamon. Fold over, not quite at the half-way line, so that the bottom section of dough extends beyond the top, as for an omelet.
9. Lightly roll folded dough with a rolling pin to set fold; place on greased baking sheets and let rise in a warm place until puffy, but not quite doubled. Preheat oven to 190°C
10. Bake until golden brown, about 45 min; remove from oven and brush with melted butter while loaves are warm. Brush again when cool and dust generously with icing sugar. *Yield:* 2 loaves.

JULEBROD OR JULEKAK

Although similar to many other European breads, the cardamom flavour identifies this Christmas bread as Scandinavian. Whole cardamom seeds keep better than powdered. Remove the papery cover and crush the seeds or heat with milk for breads.

10 ml	sugar
150 ml	warm water
20 ml	2 envelopes granular yeast
375 ml	whole milk *or* thin cream
15 ml	cardamom seed
or	
5 ml	ground cardamom
125 ml	sugar
5 ml	salt
250 ml	melted butter *or* oil
	2 eggs
375 ml	raisins
125 g	chopped citron peel
2 *l*	flour

1. Stir sugar into warm water; sprinkle with yeast and let stand 10 min without stirring.
2. Scald the milk with the cardamom seeds. If ground cardamom is used, add it to the flour.
3. Cool milk to lukewarm; add sugar, salt and fat.
4. Beat together 1 egg and 1 egg white (reserving one yolk to glaze the top); add beaten egg to the milk mixture.
5. Combine raisins and citron peel with a little of the flour, about 250 ml
6. Mix together milk, yeast and enough flour to make a batter; beat well, continue to add flour to make a soft dough. Add fruit and knead.
7. Transfer to a large greased bowl, rotate dough to grease top; let rise in a warm place, about 2 h, until doubled in bulk.
8. Divide dough into thirds; knead and shape each into a loaf; see WHITE BREAD (BASIC RECIPE), steps 10 and 11. Place each loaf in a greased loaf pan.
9. Combine the reserved egg yolk with about twice its volume of water and brush mixture over loaves.
10. Let rise again in a warm place; when nearly doubled in bulk preheat oven to 190°C
11. When dough has doubled in bulk, bake for about 60 min. Loaf when done will sound hollow when rapped with the knuckles. Cool on a rack. *Yield:* 3 loaves; pan capacity each 1.2 *l*

Recipes, tables, etc. that appear in small capital letters, e.g., PARSLEY BUTTER, CANADA'S FOOD GUIDE, are listed in the index. Consult the index for the number of the page on which the item appears.

BABA

5 ml	sugar
125 ml	warm water
10 ml	1 envelope granular yeast
	3 beaten eggs
50 ml	sugar
375 ml	flour
2 ml	salt
25 ml	grated lemon rind
125 ml	soft butter *or* margarine

1. Stir sugar into warm water and sprinkle with yeast; let stand 10 min without stirring.
2. When foamy, combine with beaten eggs; add sugar, 1/3 of the flour, the salt and lemon rind. Beat smooth.
3. Beat in the butter; gradually beat in remaining flour to form a smooth cake-like batter.
4. Oil a ring or turret mould or custard cups.
5. Fill half full; let rise until dough is doubled in bulk, about 1 h for large mould. Preheat oven to 200°C
6. Bake until golden brown, about 30 min
7. Turn baba out with the bottom side up; drizzle with one of the hot sauces which follow until no more sauce can be absorbed.
8. Cool; serve with whipped cream. *Yield:* 8 servings; mould capacity 1 *l*

Baba Sauce

125 ml	boiling water
200 ml	sugar
100 ml	frozen orange juice concentrate
15 ml	butter

Bring water and sugar to boiling; simmer 10 min Add juice and butter.

Variations of Sauce

Substitute apricot jam for the boiling water; omit sugar. Heat to melt and add remaining ingredients.

For a festive touch, bake individual babas in custard cups; arrange baked babas in a chafing dish, saturate with syrup, let stand several hours. Reheat in a little more syrup.

Prepare baba in a ring or tube mould and fill centre just before serving with sweetened strawberries or ice cream.

15 Fruit

Fruits not only add colour and flavour to our menus, they add important nutrients to our diets: minerals, vitamins and fibre. Nutritionists advise that 1/4 of our food money should be spent for fruits and vegetables.

Many fruits darken when they are cut because of oxidation, resulting in a loss of vitamins, especially vitamin C, and a less appetizing appearance. To prevent this, fruit should not be prepared in advance and should be stored in a cool, dark place. The ascorbic acid (vitamin C) in citrus fruits such as lemon will retard oxidation in apples, bananas, peaches, and pears; for this reason, recipes recommend sprinkling those fruits with lemon juice.

There are two basic methods of cooking fruit. To retain the shape of fruit during cooking, prepare a syrup first, then simmer the fruit in it; the sugar is absorbed and the fruit becomes translucent. (Too heavy a syrup causes fruit to become tough and wrinkled.) When you want to soften the fruit, as in making applesauce or cooking prunes, cook the fruit in water; after it is soft it may be sweetened.

Storage methods vary with the fruit. For details for freezing consult publications of provincial departments of agriculture.

Federal laws require that fresh fruit be graded for interprovincial trade or for export. Top grade is Canada No. 1 (Canada Fancy), with apples and pears having an additional higher grade, Canada Extra Fancy. Canada C (commercial or domestic), used for small fruits such as grapes, peaches, plums is equivalent to Canada No. 2. Within each province grading regulations exist, which vary from province to province.

Apples

Apples are plentiful, versatile and delicious. They are not as rich in vitamins and minerals as some fruits, but their frequent use can make a substantial contribution to our diets. The vitamin content varies with the variety and storage conditions. When the skin is eaten it provides roughage, an important factor in nutrition.

Varieties of Canadian Apples

Use for	Season	Names
Fruit Bowls	Autumn	Snow, Lobo
	Winter	Red Delicious, Russet
Cooking	Autumn	Crimson Beauty, Duchess
	Winter	Greening, Northern Spy
All purposes	Autumn	Cortland, Gravenstein, Wealthy, Jonathan, Melba, McIntosh
	Winter	Golden Delicious, McIntosh, Newton, Rome Beauty, Spartan, Northern Spy, Winesap

Which is the best apple for pies is a moot point; Spy, Greening, and McIntosh all have their advocates. The Russet apple is not a pie apple; although considered an eating apple, it may be enjoyed stewed (APPLE COMPÔTE) or baked for its special flavour.

Grading of Apples—Canada Extra Fancy and Canada Fancy Grade apples must have a certain amount of colour typical of their variety; they must be mature and well shaped, and graded according to size. Apples of these grades are appropriately served raw for table use. Canada Commercial or Canada C Grade apples are satisfactory for cooking, where shape, size and colour are not so important.

Storing Apples—Baskets of apples should be covered with perforated plastic and kept at a temperature just above freezing. Bring out a few at a time and keep them in the crisper of the refrigerator to prevent loss of moisture. Apples left uncovered in the refrigerator may flavour other foods. Apples will keep several months in a cold room stored between layers of newspapers or individually wrapped.

All fresh fruits should be well washed to remove harmful sprays and the dust and germs which they have collected.

An enticing platter of fresh fruits. Ontario Ministry of Agriculture and Food.

FRESH APPLES

Fresh apples, cored and divided into eighths, make an easy, delicious dessert. Serve with biscuits and cheese or sour cream or yogurt. Add a shaker of CIN-NAMON SUGAR, a dish of mixed nuts, peanut butter, or Halvah.

APPLESAUCE

There are two basic methods of cooking applesauce; the results differ in colour, texture and flavour—which to use is the cook's choice.

Method I—All the preparation is done before cooking. More of the apples' shape is retained and the sauce is a creamy colour.

1. Wash, quarter, core and pare the apples; put into a saucepan.
2. Add water to a depth of 2-3 cm
3. Cover pan and simmer until apples are soft. If necessary, evaporate the liquid by removing the lid and continuing to cook.
4. Add sugar to taste, allowing for each apple 15-30 ml
   Stir until sugar is dissolved.

Method II—The skins are cooked with the fruit, giving colour and flavour. Using a food mill or conical sieve, this is a faster method. The result is a smooth, pinkish applesauce.

1. Wash red apples; remove stems but do not core or pare; quarter into a saucepan.
2. Add water to a depth of 2-3 cm
3. Cover tightly, bring to boil, then simmer until apples are soft; if necessary remove lid and allow excess liquid to evaporate.
4. Press through sieve or food mill.
5. Add sugar (white or brown) to taste, for each apple approximately 15-30 ml
   Stir until sugar is dissolved.

Food mill   Conical sieve   Wooden pestle

Courtlands make a delectable pink sauce which requires very little sugar. Early green apples make a pale yellow sauce that needs the larger amount of sugar. The taste buds on our tongue, by which we perceive flavour, are affected by temperature. Applesauce that is sweetened to taste when very hot may not be sweet enough when it cools.

Add spices when apples have lost flavour at the end of the season. Cinnamon or nutmeg are popular; try coriander or fennel for applesauce to serve with pork, veal, or chicken.

Serve applesauce warm or cold with an oatmeal cookie, gingerbread, or newly baked bread.

Variations
Try these recipes in the spring when apples have less flavour:

Cider Applesauce—Substitute apple juice for water in Method I. Add grated lemon rind and a few drops of lemon juice for each apple.

Pink Applesauce—Add an amount of fresh or frozen cranberries equal to the apples at step 1 in Method II; add grated orange rind with the sugar. Or add jellied cranberry sauce, 1 part cranberry to 4 parts cooked applesauce. Taste and sweeten if necessary.

See also ORANGE APPLESAUCE TARTS.

To freeze applesauce—Cool and pack leaving a headspace.

Basic Recipe
APPLE COMPÔTE

250 ml	sugar
375 ml	water
	rind of ½ lemon
	8 apples
15 ml	lemon juice

1. Combine sugar, water and lemon rind in a broad, shallow pan; bring to a boil.
2. Wash, peel and core apples; cut into eighths; add to the syrup only enough apples to cover bottom of pan; simmer turning once until the apples are transparent; lift with a slotted spoon to serving dish.
3. Add more apples to syrup and continue until all are cooked. If the syrup becomes too thick, thin with a little boiling water. When all the apples are cooked, add lemon juice to syrup; taste; strain over the apples.

Variations

Whole Apples—Wash, peel and core apples of medium size. Cook slowly in enough syrup to cover apples at least halfway until the bottom half is soft; turn apples and cook the other half. Lift carefully into a serving dish. Add lemon juice to the syrup and pour over apples. Fill centres with red jelly, if desired, when cool.

Blushing Apples—Cook whole, red-skinned apples in syrup without peeling. When soft, remove the skin leaving the rosy apple; lift into serving dish and pour the syrup around; fill centres with red jelly.

Apple Porcupine—Chill, wash, peel and cook apples of medium size. Fill centres with jelly. Sliver blanched almonds; stick into apples. If desired, place apples under broiler to brown nuts slightly. Pour syrup around apples.

Glazed Apples—Choose red baking apples; wash; pare the top quarter, and core. Prepare syrup adding 2 cloves, 1 piece of cinnamon, 2 coriander seeds. Cook apples in syrup, turning three or four times to cook evenly.

When almost cooked, turn right-side-up in pan; fill centres with a few raisins, brown sugar and a bit of butter or margarine. Place under the broiler and baste with syrup until glazed.

Glazed Apple Rings—Prepare half the quantity of syrup; add to it vinegar in the proportion of 1 part vinegar to 4 parts syrup, or use vinegar from sweet pickles, adding 1 part sugar to 3 parts pickle juice. Arrange thick slices of cored apples in a single layer in the syrup; simmer until apples are transparent and tender, about 20-30 min. Serve with roast pork, tenderloin, chops.

Minted Apple Rings—Add a few drops of peppermint extract and, if desired, green colouring. Serve with lamb.

Curried Apple Wedges—Add to the syrup:

| 15 ml | curry powder |
| 5 ml | onion flakes |

Peel and core apples, cut into wedges. Cook according to basic recipe.

Basic Recipe
BAKED APPLES

1. Wash large cooking apples; core. Cut a strip of peel from the centre or top of the apple, or cut a shallow X into the top.
2. Place apples in a Pyrex, aluminum, or stainless steel baking dish.
3. Fill centres of apples with brown sugar, a sprinkle of cinnamon and a bit of butter.
4. Spoon brown sugar around apples; quantity for each: 30 ml
5. Pour water into dish to a depth of 2 cm
6. Bake, basting several times until tender, 30-40 min at 180°C

   Test for tenderness with a paring knife in the centre of the apple. Serve hot or cold with the syrup from the pan and/or with cream.

Variation

Soften a marshmallow on each apple before removing from the pan.

It is good economy to serve baked fruit when the oven is being used for scalloped potatoes, roast meat, cookies, etc.

APPLE BERRY COMPÔTE

This pioneer recipe combines three foods which were abundant a century and a half ago. Fresh blueberries, raspberries, and saskatoons are best. If frozen berries are used, thaw them first.

50 ml	butter *or* margarine
	4 medium apples
125 ml	maple syrup, CARAMEL SYRUP, *or*
	MOCK MAPLE SYRUP
	cinnamon
1 ℓ	berries, fresh or frozen
	lemon juice

1. Melt fat; wash, peel, core and cut apples into thick slices; sauté in fat until tender but not soft.
2. Pour syrup over apples and add a dash of cinnamon.
3. Add berries and simmer until all is cooked; some apples, such as McIntosh, will cook quickly; others such as Spies take much longer.
4. Lift fruit into serving dish with a slotted spoon.
5. Continue to cook liquid to a syrup consistency; taste and add lemon juice if syrup is too sweet; pour over the fruit. *Serves 6-8.*

Apple Fritters

1. Pare, core and slice or cube two apples; dip in orange juice; sprinkle with sugar, let stand 10-15 min; drain.
2. Drop into BATTER COATING.
3. Spoon into hot fat. Fry 3 min, drain; sprinkle with icing sugar. Frying temperature: 185°C
   Yield: 16 fritters.

Avocados

The flesh of the avocado changes from soft green to a deep cream near the large stone. The fruit must be fully ripe before the mild, nutty flavour can be perceived. At this stage the fruit will yield to slight pressure and the skin will show some black markings; it should have no soft spots; if shaken gently the stone may be heard to rattle. The pear shape and rough pebbled skin of some varieties explain the name "alligator pear" by which this fruit is sometimes known.

Unlike other fruits, the avocado has a high fat content which makes it high in food energy. It is also a good source of vitamin A, thiamine, riboflavin and vitamin C.

To use, cut with a sharp knife from top to bottom circling the large stone. Twist the two pieces apart, leaving the stone in one half if the whole fruit is not to be used at once. Dice by cutting the flesh into slices or cubes within the shell, using a large spoon to remove the pieces. Use immediately to prevent darkening.

To store cut fruit, cover with plastic wrap pressing it smoothly onto the surface to exclude the air. Fully ripe fruit which has not been cut may be refrigerated for a few days. Freezing is not successful.

To enjoy the full flavour of avocado, a little salt or lemon juice is all that need be added.

Apricots

This delicious fruit is fresh on the market only a short time. Choose plump, golden fruit and use immediately, as apricots spoil quickly. Apricots are an excellent source of vitamin A and a good source of vitamin C.

Preserve in a thin syrup or purée and freeze for use in FRUIT MIXTURES; prepare jam to use over ice cream or puddings, on hot biscuits, or with cheese.

SALZBURG FRITTERS

50 ml	almond paste
	12 fresh ripe apricots
	1 recipe BATTER COATING
250 ml	ORANGE SAUCE

1. Shape paste into 12 small balls; halve the fruit; replace the stone with a ball of almond paste, then press the two halves together firmly.
2. Dip in batter; fry 5 min in deep fat at 185°C
3. Drain, sprinkle with icing sugar; serve with ORANGE SAUCE. *Serves 4-6.*

Recipes, tables, etc. that appear in small capital letters, e.g., PARSLEY BUTTER, CANADA'S FOOD GUIDE, are listed in the index. Consult the index for the number of the page on which the item appears.

Bananas

The banana is fully ripe and best for eating when the peel is yellow, flecked with brown; for cooking choose those that are not fully ripe.

Bananas with green tips contain starch which has not yet turned to sugar. Keep at room temperature until ripe; if refrigerated they will darken without ripening. Once fully ripe they may be refrigerated; the skin will blacken but the flesh will not be altered in appearance although some flavour will be lost.

Once cut, bananas may be kept from darkening by sprinkling with lemon juice or by combining with citrus fruits and their juices.

In contrast to the avocado, the banana is practically fat-free. It is a source of minerals (especially potassium) and vitamins in an easily digested form.

FRIED BANANAS

Cut unripe bananas in half lengthwise, then into halves or quarters crosswise. Sauté until golden brown and translucent, about 10 min

Use as an accompaniment to any curried dish.

COOKED BANANAS

To serve as a vegetable:
1. Peel banana; slice lengthwise; arrange on a greased baking dish.
2. Brush with lime or lemon juice, then with melted butter; sprinkle with salt.
3. Bake about 15 min until tender at 180°C
   If desired, broil for a few minutes until brown. Serve warm with sour cream and a dusting of cinnamon; or brush with honey, sprinkle with curry powder and toasted coconut.

To serve as a dessert:
Peel banana; slice lengthwise; arrange on greased baking dish. Spread with soft butter or margarine and sprinkle with brown sugar. Pour a little liquid around the banana: pineapple juice, cranberry juice, orange juice, honey, alone or in combination. Broil or simmer until fruit is transparent (15-20 min), basting several times. Serve warm with sour cream or yogurt.

Berries

Wild berries can still be found across Canada. Renewed interest in using them reflects our appreciation of "natural" foods, as well as a willingness to spend time gathering them to save money.

The following may all be used in the same way as raspberries: bakeapples, or cloudberries, from Newfoundland and Labrador, which resemble a plump, yellow raspberry; blackberries (black raspberries, black caps, bramble berries, or thimble berries); and Boysenberries, the cross between raspberry and blackberry created in California and now grown widely in Canada.

Large, very ripe wild berries may be used for fruit pie, but because of their seediness wild berries are usually used in jam, jelly, or syrup.

Blueberries or huckleberries, and the western saskatoons keep well if cold and dry; pick out twigs and leaves, pour into cartons, and refrigerate, or freeze by spreading in a single layer on a baking sheet and packaging. These berries are a fair source of vitamin C and iron. Rinse them clean with cold water; drain. Serve raw with cream, sour cream or yogurt; sprinkle with dark brown sugar and a dash of cinnamon. Combine with sliced peaches or ice cream; serve in MERINGUE SHELLS for a special dessert. Add blueberries to muffins or pancakes. Stir into lemon jelly; into LEMON, VANILLA, or BUTTERSCOTCH PUDDING; add to other fruits in FRUIT CUP. Blueberries can also be used in FRUIT CRISP, SHORTCAKE, FRUIT ROLY POLY; COTTAGE PUDDING, and pies.

BLUEBERRY GRUNT

500 ml	blueberries
50 ml	sugar
50 ml	water
	dumplings

1. Clean berries; rinse; combine with sugar and water, cover and boil gently until there is plenty of juice to prevent the berries' sticking.
2. Prepare the dumplings from SWEET TEA BISCUIT DOUGH using half the recipe; drop onto the berries; cover tightly and do not lift the cover for 10-15 min
3. Serve hot. *Serves 4-6.*

Recipes, tables, etc. that appear in small capital letters, e.g., PARSLEY BUTTER, CANADA'S FOOD GUIDE, are listed in the index. Consult the index for the number of the page on which the item appears.

SASKATOON AND APPLE PIE

500 ml	saskatoons
	3 or 4 apples
50 ml	flour
200 ml	sugar
	cinnamon

Prepare saskatoons and apples; combine flour and sugar with a dash of cinnamon; stir through the fruit. Finish as FRUIT PIE.

Cherries

Many varieties of wild and cultivated cherries are available in late summer throughout all of Canada. Black cherries, chokecherries, and pincherries are easy to pick and prepare. Remove the stems to prevent a bitter tannin flavour. Use in jams, jellies, or syrups; bottle juice to use for gelatine salads or desserts.

Ground cherries, sometimes called ground plums or husk tomatoes, are very scarce today. Look for them on local markets in August or early September. Remove the brown papery covering; wash the waxy orange-red berry, prick once with a fork and simmer in a thin syrup until the fruit is tender. Add a little lemon juice if the fruit seems too sweet. Ground cherries make delicious tarts.

There are three common varieties of cultivated cherries. The most common is the Montmorency, the sour, red pie cherry. Consult the index for CHERRY PIE, CHERRY CONSERVE and PICKLED CHERRIES. The Napoleon cherry, creamy white with a red blush, can be used in the same recipes.

Crisp Black or Tartarian or Bing Cherries are most popular eaten fresh. Wash well and serve on a fruit salad plate or cheese tray; pit, chop, fold into cream-style cottage cheese or into yogurt; combine with other fruits in FRUIT CUP.

The recipes which follow call for canned, pitted Black Cherries; even better are fresh pitted cherries, simmered in a medium syrup until just tender.

To pit cherries, use a pitter, the curved end of a paper clip, or a clean hairpin pushed into a cork.

CHERRY COUPE

398 ml each	2 cans pitted black cherries
50 ml	red currant jelly

1. Drain cherry juice into a saucepan; add the red currant jelly and simmer until syrupy.
2. Drain liquid from the cherries into the syrup; cool.
3. Layer with ice cream in parfait glasses or spoon over ice cream in MERINGUE SHELLS. Add syrup. *Serves 8-10.*

CHERRIES JUBILEE

15 ml	cornstarch
15 ml	sugar
398 ml	1 can pitted black cherries
	3 or 4 strips of orange peel
5 ml	lemon juice
568 ml	vanilla ice cream

1. Mix cornstarch and sugar together; add liquid from canned cherries and the orange peel; stir; cook until sauce thickens; discard orange peel; add cherries and lemon juice.
2. At the table warm sauce in a chafing dish; pile ice cream balls into a shallow bowl.
3. Spoon sauce over vanilla ice cream. *Serves 6.*

Variation
Substitute red pie cherries; add red currant jelly, 50 ml

Citrus Fruits

Citrus fruits must be imported into Canada, but they are widely used because of their flavour and high vitamin C content. When native fruits are available in the summer, the need for citrus fruits is less.

Grapefruit
Choose fruit that is heavy for its size, with smooth, thin skin. The colour of the skin is not an indication of quality, but a rusty or bronze skin usually indicates juicy fruit. From April to November grapefruit is not in season and is expensive. Pink grapefruit is high in vitamin A as well as vitamin C.

GRAPEFRUIT HALVES

1. Cut fruit in half crosswise (between the stem and blossom end).
2. With a sharp paring knife or a serrated grapefruit knife cut the pulp from the membrane, in each section.
3. Run the knife around the outside edge of the pulp; do not cut into the bitter white membrane.
4. With scissors cut around the core and lift it out.
5. Sweeten if desired, with sugar, syrup, or honey. Chill.

Preparing a grapefruit half.

Preparing grapefruit sections.

BROILED GRAPEFRUIT

Prepare a grapefruit half; sprinkle with sugar— white, brown, maple—or with syrup or honey. Dot with butter; let stand 20 min. Broil until lightly browned (10 min).

GRAPEFRUIT SECTIONS

1. Place the washed fruit on a board; using a sharp knife pare the rind from the fruit, removing all white skin. This skin contains bitter oil and should be completely removed.
2. Cut out one section, by cutting along the inside of the membranes on each side of the section. Subsequent sections can be easily removed by cutting down the opposite side of the membrane already exposed and, with an upward turn of the knife along the next membrane, flicking out the next section.
3. Sweeten the sections if necessary. Serve in fruit salad; fruit cup mixtures; or in an avocado shell, alternated with avocado slices.

Oranges and Other Citrus Fruit
The navel orange, which has a tiny orange within an orange, is in season from November to May. It has no seeds, a moderate amount of juice, and firm pulp. The Valencia orange comes from California from February to November and from Florida from November to May. The Florida orange is light in colour with many seeds and a large amount of juice. Jaffa oranges from Israel and Outspan from South Africa are other varieties. Seville, the small, bitter orange which appears in February, is usually made into marmalade of special flavour.

The Temple orange is a cross between an orange and a tangerine, but closer in appearance to the orange.

Tangerines are small and easily peeled and separated into sections. The skin is bright orange, slightly pebbled, and the flesh is sweet. Mandarins are a variety of tangerine, lighter in colour and sweet in flavour with fewer seeds. The Tangelo, a cross between a tangerine and a grapefruit, has a tart-sweet flavour.

Kumquats are a small oval citrus fruit with large seeds and a bitter-sweet flavour. Calamandins are a cross between a kumquat and tangerine.

To remove the white skin from an orange, a quick method is to drop the unpeeled fruit into boiling water to cover. Leave about 2 min, remove, hold under cold water. The white membrane comes off with the skin.

Recipes, tables, etc. that appear in small capital letters, e.g., PARSLEY BUTTER, CANADA'S FOOD GUIDE, are listed in the index. Consult the index for the number of the page on which the item appears.

ORANGE SECTIONS

Follow method for GRAPEFRUIT SECTIONS. Serve sections alternated with grapefruit sections in salads; in FRUIT CUP; or with strawberries piled into sherbet dishes or orange shells.

CARAMELIZED ORANGES

	3 large oranges
100 ml	CARAMEL SYRUP
25 ml	glazed mixed fruit

1. Remove the peel from about ⅛ of one orange with a vegetable peeler; cut into fine shreds; add to the syrup.
2. Peel and section the oranges.
3. Bring syrup to a boil; pour over orange sections; add glazed fruit; chill, spooning the syrup over the sections several times to glaze. *Serves 4.*

This is an easy-to-eat version of a Spanish recipe made with whole oranges. In another version the orange is cut into thick slices, reassembled and fastened with toothpicks.

ORANGE AMBROSIA

Arrange orange slices on a serving dish; sprinkle with fresh, flaked coconut.

ORANGE APPLESAUCE TARTS

Partly fill baked tart shells (see PASTRY FOR TARTS) with thick applesauce, smoothing the surface; cover with overlapping orange sections; brush with hot APRICOT GLAZE; leave to set.

Grapes

Many varieties of Canadian grapes are on the market in September and early October, the blue Concord and the seedless Niagara and Himrod being favourites. Choose plump grapes which show no signs of shrivelling and are firmly attached; bunches should have no mouldy fruit. Pour cold water over them. Drain. Serve in small bunches, clipped from the main stem, on fruit or cheese platters.

GRAPE CHANTILLY

750 ml	seedless green grapes
50 ml	honey
5 ml	lemon juice
100 ml	orange juice
250 ml	sour cream

1. Remove the stems from washed grapes; dry. Combine grapes with honey, lemon juice and orange juice.
2. Stir in sour cream; refrigerate several hours. *Serves 4-6.*

A simpler version uses only grapes and sour cream, adding brown sugar to taste. Berries may replace grapes. Chilling time can be reduced by setting the bowl in the freezer; do not freeze.

Mangoes

This flat oval fruit is dark green with a yellow-red patch, and contains a large stone. The flesh is firm, smooth and peach-like with a flavour combining peach, pineapple and melon. Buy when slightly soft to pressure, with no really soft spots.

Wash, slit the tough skin several times from top to bottom, and pull off; or if a large amount of the fruit comes off with the skin, use a sharp paring knife.

Cube by first slitting the fruit lengthwise into the stone; then, beginning at the top, cut around the fruit in a descending spiral; remove the cubes. Serve with ice cream or add to FRUIT CUP; combine with peaches in thin syrup and process in sterilized jars (see PREPARATION OF GLASS CONTAINERS and TO FILL PRESERVING JARS); or purée and freeze, layer or swirl into slightly softened ice cream and refreeze.

In Mexico a fork is speared into the end of a peeled mango which is then eaten like a Popsicle.

Melons

Cantaloupe, the small round melon with a netted skin and sweet, salmon-coloured flesh, ripens in August. Ripe melons are fragrant and show warm colouring. Avoid those that are soft at the stem end. Cantaloupe is high in vitamin C, equal to an orange per serving, and high in vitamin A.

Watermelons ripen in time for hot August days. Buy those that sound hollow when rapped with the knuckles. Another test is to try to lift a tiny bit of the green skin with the fingernail; if it lifts easily the watermelon is ripe. Watermelon is lower than cantaloupe in vitamins C and A.

Honeydew, a pale green, smooth-skinned melon, and Spanish melon which has a dark green, ridged skin, must be ripe but not soft. Avoid those with a soft spot at the stem.

To Prepare Melons
1. Wash and chill melon.
2. Cut in half crosswise or flute if small; cut lengthwise in wedges if large.
3. Remove the seeds and stringy fibres with a spoon.

Fluting a melon.

Making a watermelon boat.

To Serve Melon—Sprinkle with salt or sugar to taste. Serve with a wedge of lemon or lime, if desired.

Fill small cantaloupe halves with blueberries, raspberries, FRUIT CUP, ice cream, or SHERBET.

See also MELON COCKTAIL.

MELON MÉLANGE

> 1 cantaloupe, halved and seeded
> 1 small honeydew, halved and seeded
> 1 large piece watermelon
> fresh blueberries *or* raspberries
> juice and grated rind of 1 lemon or lime

250 ml   thin SYRUP

1. Scoop balls out of all the melons; clean the berries; combine.
2. Add the juice and grated rind to enough syrup to cover the fruit; add fruit and refrigerate several hours.
3. Serve in glasses topped with a mint sprig, or in a watermelon boat. *Serves 6-8.*

Nectarines

A smooth-skinned, firm-fleshed fruit resembling a peach, the nectarine may be used in recipes calling for peaches, but is best eaten raw.

Peaches

The Niagara Peninsula of Ontario, the Okanagan Valley of British Columbia and the Annapolis Valley of Nova Scotia provide peaches in abundance from August to October.

Canned peaches may be substituted for fresh in the recipes which follow.

Since peaches must ripen on the tree for the best flavour, avoid those that are green and hard and buy only ripe peaches in quantities small enough for quick use.

Peaches contain a generous amount of vitamin A, some B and C, as well as iron and calcium.

To freeze, special care must be taken to minimize darkening; consult the bulletin on freezing available from your provincial department of agriculture.

To prepare peaches, remove skin using a sharp knife and pulling strips of skin from fruit. If the skin cannot be removed easily, dip the peaches into boiling water, then into cold, doing only a few at a time. Prolonged soaking of the fruit in the boiling water will result in a soft, ragged surface.

Cut Freestone peaches in half by running a sharp knife from stem to blossom end; twist apart. Cling-stone peaches will need to be sliced: cut into the stone from stem to blossom end all around the fruit and slice off.

To prevent darkening, peaches should not be prepared until serving time; unused fruit may be combined with citrus fruit or juice or brought to a boil in a thin syrup and refrigerated. Serve fresh slices in a sherbet glass, plain or with sugar, cream, sour cream or yogurt; combined with berries; in FRUIT CUP.

POACHED PEACHES

Simmer ripe peach halves in liquid (canned fruit juice) until tender. Lift the fruit out and sweeten the juice with honey or jelly; continue to boil the syrup until thick. Pour over the fruit to glaze it; serve with ice cream or custard, or top with sour cream.

BROILED PEACHES

Arrange peeled, halved peaches cut side down in a shallow baking dish. Dot with butter, sprinkle with brown sugar and broil until brown. Serve with sour cream.

Peaches sautéed or brushed with fat and broiled make appetizing garnishes for meats. The centres may be filled with currant or mint jelly.

Pears

The summer Bartlett pears are followed by the Comice, the Keiffer, the brown Bosc, the winter green D'Anjou and the little Seckel pickling pear. Pears are best picked green and ripened in a warm room. Sort daily for ripeness. Too low a temperature will result in darkening around the core. Buy firm pears and serve them at the peak of their juiciness and flavour. Pears do not freeze well.

Serve raw pears whole, with a fruit knife so they may be quartered and cored at the table. Serve them on a cheese tray, or cubed and combined with other fruits in FRUIT CUP.

Winter pears cook well. Follow the directions for POACHED PEACHES.

BAKED PEARS

Peel, halve and core firm ripe pears; place cut side up in a casserole.

Fill the centres with orange juice; dribble honey, maple syrup, corn syrup or medium SYRUP over the pears; cover. Bake until tender (20 min), basting once or twice, at 180°C

For a subtle change of flavour, simmer a piece of ginger root, dried or fresh, in the syrup.

Plums

Damsons are the dark, tart, blue-purple plums used for jam. Golden and Shiro plums are the sweet, yellow varieties which are good to eat raw. The Stanley and the Italian are the blue, more elongated prune plums often used in making jams and jellies or in fillings for coffee breads. Serve sweet plums on a cheese tray as well as in a fruit bowl. Keep cool and dry, as plums mould quickly.

Freestone plums may be easily halved and stoned before cooking. Use the clingstone type when the fruit is to be eaten raw, or strained, as in jellies.

STEWED PLUMS

Prick the skins of washed plums with a fork; steam 20-30 min or simmer in just enough water to cover until almost tender, 10-15 min. Add sugar to taste; continue to cook until sugar is dissolved.

DEEP PLUM PIE

500 g	ripe plums
50 ml	water
	1 or 2 cardamom pods
5 ml	cinnamon
125 ml	sugar (approximately)
5 ml	lemon rind
45 ml	minute tapioca

1. Preheat oven to 190°C
2. Wash plums, cut in half and pit; arrange cut side down with water in a greased, medium-sized baking dish;
3. Remove the seeds from the pods; crush; combine with the other ingredients.
4. Sprinkle over the fruit, shaking pan so that the dry ingredients sift down.
5. Cover with pastry (1/3 the PASTRY BASIC RECIPE).
6. Bake 30 min. *Serves 6.*

Pineapples

Pineapple contains significant amounts of calcium, iron, potassium, and vitamins A, C and niacin.

Uncooked pineapple contains an enzyme which digests protein. For this reason fresh pineapple or its juice will prevent gelatine mixtures from setting. Cottage cheese, sour cream, or other dairy products should not be mixed with fresh pineapple until just before serving. Cooking destroys the enzyme.

Choose short, square fruit, heavy in relation to size, with a distinct pineapple fragrance. Thump the pineapple; a dull thud is a sign of sweet, juicy fruit. The leaves should pull out easily from the crown.

Store in a warm place out of the light.

Pineapple freezes well.

Allow 1 pineapple to serve 4-6.

To Prepare a Pineapple

Wash the fruit; cut into wedges, spears, circles or cubes as described below.

Wedges—Cut the pineapple in quarters with a sharp, serrated knife and remove core; run knife along the curve of the fruit; slice from the core to the skin, leaving the wedges in position; serve with a shaker of fine sugar and a sprinkle of ginger.

Spears—Cut pineapple into eighths lengthwise; finish as wedges.

Circles—Remove a slice from the top with a sharp knife; make a diagonal cut each side of the eyes; pull off the skin; cut out any remaining eyes with a sharp paring knife or the point of a potato peeler; cut into circles; cut out the core.

Cubes—Dice the circles.

Shell—Cut the pineapple in half vertically with a sharp, serrated knife, slicing through the fronds. Cut out the flesh, leaving the shell. Slice flesh lengthwise; remove the core; dice the fruit; sweeten; combine with other fruit; refill the shell.

The skins and cores may be covered with water and simmered until tender; strain off the liquid through a fine sieve or cloth and use for fruit jelly, fruit drinks, or fruit syrup.

To Sweeten Pineapple

Add sugar or medium SYRUP and allow to stand 20-30 min.

PINEAPPLE FRITTERS

Dry sliced pineapple; leave whole or cut into wedges; drop into BATTER COATING; lift out, drain. Drop into hot fat at temperature of 185°C

Fry 3 min. Drain; sprinkle with icing sugar. Serve with LEMON SAUCE or sour cream.

FLORIDA CREAM

113 g	1 pkg. cream cheese
30 ml	icing sugar
15 ml	orange juice
50 ml	pineapple chunks

Blend together cheese, sugar and orange juice; stir in pineapple. Serve with fruit as a dip or topping.

Yield: 250 ml

Rhubarb

Choose rhubarb that is red in colour with small stalks and leaves. Remove the leaves; they are high in oxalic acid and must not be used. Remove the tough stem base; stand the stalks in a container and pour boiling water over them. (This blanching reduces the amount of sugar required.) Discard the water, cut the stalks into short pieces, measure and use in one of the recipes which follow.

To Freeze Rhubarb

Rhubarb freezes well. Pack before cooking without sugar or with sugar, 1 part to 4 parts fruit. Or cook first and pack leaving headspace.

STEWED RHUBARB (RHUBARB SAUCE)

Stir in one-quarter as much sugar as rhubarb; let stand 10 min. Cook over low heat in a covered saucepan or double boiler, or bake in a covered casserole until just tender (10 min) at 180°C
Serve with gingerbread or cookies, over cornstarch pudding or ice cream.

Variations

For added flavour, spice with dry or fresh ginger root, *or* slivered or grated orange peel.

RHUBARB-STRAWBERRY SAUCE

1 *l*	**diced rhubarb**
125 ml	**water**
250 ml	**sugar**
500 ml	**strawberries**

1. Following the direction for STEWED RHUBARB, cook until tender.
2. Add berries which have been washed, hulled and cut in half; reheat but do not boil; chill. *Serves 6.*

Strawberries

Wild strawberries are so hard to find today that they are usually eaten raw, so that their flavour can be relished "full strength."

Domestic berries should be bought in small quantities, as they spoil easily. Berries picked just after heavy rain will be sandy.

To Store Strawberries, spread them out on a large plate, removing soft or mouldy berries. Berries freeze well.

To Prepare Strawberries, wash them in a sieve under running water; drain; remove the hulls with the point of a paring knife or a strawberry huller. Sprinkle with sugar, the amount depending on the ripeness and sweetness of the fruit.

Serve plain, or with sweet or sour cream, or orange juice.

Or slice to fill the centre of avocado or melon; combine with rhubarb, pineapple, or banana.

Mash as sauce over ice cream, cornstarch pudding, custard.

Serve whole, unhulled berries with a dip of yogurt or cream cheese whipped with fresh or sour cream until fluffy, and a shaker of fruit sugar.

STRAWBERRY AND PINEAPPLE CREAM

540 ml	**1 can pineapple chunks**
500 ml	**strawberries, halved**
250 ml	**sour cream**
50 ml	CARAMEL SYRUP *or* **maple syrup**

1. Drain pineapple; combine chunks with strawberries.
2. Combine sour cream and syrup; fold into fruit; chill. To use fresh pineapple, sweeten, let stand and drain; combine just before serving.
   Serves 6-8.

STRAWBERRIES ROMANOFF

1. Slice and sweeten strawberries; add thawed frozen orange concentrate, a few drops almond flavouring; refrigerate.
2. Lift berries from the syrup into slightly softened ice cream; stir to blend; pile into serving dishes, top with whole berries; pour the syrup around.

STRAWBERRY MALMAISON

	2 oranges
500 ml	**strawberries**
125 ml	**medium** SYRUP

1. Section one orange and squeeze the juice from the other.
2. Wash strawberries; hull; cut the larger ones in half.
3. Combine berries and orange sections; place in serving dishes.
4. Combine the syrup and juice; pour over berries. *Serves 4-6.*

Recipes, tables, etc. that appear in small capital letters, e.g., PARSLEY BUTTER, CANADA'S FOOD GUIDE, are listed in the index. Consult the index for the number of the page on which the item appears.

Raspberries

More fragile than strawberries, raspberries should be gently rinsed in cool water. Drain; place in serving dishes and sprinkle with fine sugar. Serve with cream, ice cream, sour cream or yogurt.

Peaches and raspberries are a delicious combination; see PEACH BERRY PIE, PEACH MELBA.

Frozen berries make it possible to enjoy these recipes all year.

RASPBERRY MERINGUES

509 ml	ice cream
	8-10 meringue shells
500 ml	fresh raspberries
	1 pkg. frozen raspberries

Spoon ice cream into the baked shells; pile the fresh berries around. Spoon partially thawed frozen berries over the ice cream. *Serves 8-10.*

If fresh berries are plentiful, some may be mashed to replace the frozen berries.

Fruit Mixtures

Mixtures in which fresh fruits dominate bring summer into our menus. Use frozen fruits not quite thawed to give the same flavour.

Basic Recipe
FRUIT CUP

	2 grapefruit
	1 orange
	1 pear
398 ml	1 can pineapple cubes
125 ml	thin SYRUP

1. Section the citrus fruits; peel and cube the pears; add the pineapple and syrup; chill to blend the flavour.
2. Serve in a dish which enhances the appearance or in a pineapple or watermelon shell; or pile individual servings into grapefruit shells.
3. Top with sour cream, yogurt, ice cream, or LEMON SHERBET.
4. Garnish with one of mint leaves; slivered peel; toasted nuts or coconut; coloured mint or thin chocolate candies. *Serves 6.*

Variations
Sweeten with SPICED SYRUP or CARAMEL SYRUP, honey, or ginger ale.

Flavour with lemon or lime juice and grated rind; crushed cardamom seeds; staranise; ginger root; or one or two after-dinner mints.

Select other combinations of fruit (see suggestions below). With fruits such as peaches, which darken quickly, include a citrus fruit or pineapple. Do not add bananas to the basic mixture but slice them into the dish at serving time.

Suggested Combinations for Fruit Cup
Melon balls, raspberries or blueberries, pitted black cherries, seeded green grapes.

Peach slices, pear slices, quartered plums, orange sections.

Grapefruit sections, mandarin oranges, frozen strawberries.

Rhubarb sauce, sliced strawberries, orange sections, fresh pineapple wedges.

Sliced peaches, cubed mangoes, orange sections, seedless green, red, or blue grapes or quartered plums.

Sliced peaches, blueberries, apricots, preserved kumquat shreds.

When only one or two servings will be needed, freeze the mixture in small containers. Or freeze it in one tall plastic container, and cut off a slice for each serving. Return the unused fruit immediately to the freezer. Serve when just thawed.

Recipes, tables, etc. that appear in small capital letters, e.g., PARSLEY BUTTER, CANADA'S FOOD GUIDE, are listed in the index. Consult the index for the number of the page on which the item appears.

Melon balls, pieces of pear, blueberries, strawberries and slices of apple can be combined in many ways to make delicious fruit desserts.

Pear halves pressed together with ice cream and nuts are topped with Fruit Sauce.

Baked apples can be prepared in many ways.

LEMON FRUIT COCKTAIL

284 ml	1 can pineapple tidbits
284 ml	1 can mandarin orange sections
540 ml	1 can fruit cocktail
15 ml	lemon juice
125 ml	flaked coconut
114 g	1 pkg. instant lemon pudding
	2 bananas

1. Combine undrained fruits with lemon juice and coconut. Prepare pudding according to package directions.
2. Sprinkle pudding over the fruit; stir; refrigerate 2 h
3. Fold in the sliced bananas. *Serves 6-8.*

GROUND FRUIT COMBO

	1 orange
	½ lemon
	2 apples
750 ml	*fruit

* Pitted cherries, plums, peaches, grapes; cranberries, blueberries, drained canned fruit may be used alone or in combination.
1. Remove seeds and white membrane from the oranges and lemons.
2. Grind the fruits, using a coarse blade; sweeten if necessary with honey, syrup, marmalade, or sugar.
3. Refrigerate or divide into small containers and freeze.

Serve with custard or LEMON or VANILLA SAUCE. Or set with gelatine and mould for dessert or salad plate. Or combine with cottage cheese, sour cream or yogurt as a topping for gingerbread or shortcake.

Beat mayonnaise with cream cheese until smooth; fold in the fruit mixture and toasted almonds; freeze in individual moulds; serve on fruit salad plates.

Combine with cream cheese as a sandwich filling.

FRYING-PAN FRUIT

In an electric frying pan or chafing dish arrange drained fruits—peaches, plums, Bing cherries, pineapple, green grapes halved and seeded, orange sections, banana chunks—in a pattern which evenly distributes the assortment of fruits.
Add honey and fruit juice to just cover the fruit; heat.
Serve over ice cream.

BARBECUED FRUIT KEBOBS

Cut fresh, firm fruit in chunks. Thread on individual skewers; sprinkle with lemon or orange juice; chill. At serving time sprinkle with fruit, brown, or maple sugar. Broil until the sugar bubbles, turning once.

Dried Fruits

Dried fruits are low in vitamin C but high in vitamin A and in minerals, especially iron. They provide bulk; prunes have a laxative property as well. Tenderized dried fruits may be eaten without further treatment.

Basic Recipe
STEWED PRUNES

454 g	prunes
1 *l*	boiling water
	3 lemon slices
75-125 ml	sugar

1. Cover prunes with the boiling water; add lemon slices; simmer until tender (30-40 min).
2. Add sugar; allow the liquid to return to a boil; lift out the fruit and continue to simmer the syrup if a thicker liquid is desired. Pour over the fruit; serve cold. *Serves 12.*

Prunes may be soaked in water and cooked for a shorter time or refrigerated in water and eaten uncooked.
Spiced Prunes To the water in the basic recipe add ½ cinnamon stick. Use as garnish for roast pork or a salad plate.

Other dried fruits may be cooked as prunes, but will require different quantities of sugar. Apricots will need 3 times the amount indicated in the basic recipe for STEWED PRUNES.

16 Desserts

This chapter gives recipes for custards, puddings, jelly desserts and shortcakes. See also Chapter 17, Cakes; Chapter 18, Pastry; and especially Chapter 15, Fruit, which contains many suggestions for satisfying desserts that are relatively low in sugar and fat.

Desserts should be chosen to complement the earlier courses of the meal; they should not repeat either texture or flavour.

Custard

This milk-and-egg mixture is the basis for many sweet dishes, as well as being a standard item in invalid diets.

Custard should be smooth and creamy throughout, with no bubbles, lumps, or separation of ingredients. Because the main ingredients are eggs and milk, cooking temperature should be low, and overcooking must be avoided. For best results, follow carefully the instructions given here.

Tips for Making Custard
When cooking custard on the top of the stove, a "custard stir" in which the spoon is kept moving in a figure eight pattern on the bottom of the saucepan is one aid to a smooth result.

If custard is overcooked it will curdle; stove-top custard (SOFT CUSTARD) may be rescued if at the first sign of curdling you place the pan in cold water and beat with an egg beater.

Heating the milk reduces the cooking time.

Yolks alone make a more tender custard which will set at a lower temperature with less likelihood of curdling. Replace 1 egg with 2 yolks.

Whites make a stiffer custard and contribute no cholesterol. Use 2 whites to replace 1 yolk.

Reconstituted skim milk may be used or, for a rich custard, replace milk with thin cream.

Flavourings for Custard
The standard flavouring for custard is vanilla. In its place, lemon rind or thin strips of lemon peel may be heated in the milk; or add maple syrup, a tiny amount of almond flavouring, or instant coffee.

Basic Recipe
BAKED CUSTARD

	3-4 eggs
100-125 ml	sugar (white or brown)
500 ml	milk
2 ml	vanilla *or* lemon rind
	cinnamon, nutmeg, *or* mace

1. Beat eggs slightly; add sugar; stir in the milk.
2. Strain the custard mixture; add the flavouring; pour into individual custard cups or a medium CASSEROLE; sprinkle with spice.
3. Set dish in a baking pan in the oven; pour water into the pan to the level of the custard; add cold water if necessary during the baking to keep the water from boiling.
4. Test by inserting the point of a paring knife; if it comes out clean, the custard is cooked and should be immediately removed from the hot water and set in cool water to prevent curdling the custard by over-cooking. Bake individual custards 30-45 min, large custards 60 min, at 150°C
   Serves 5-6.

Custard can be cooked in the pressure cooker if covered with 2 layers of waxed paper, securely tied with a string. Use maximum pressure 3 min. Cool quickly.

Variations
Rice Custard—Reduce the eggs to 2 and add cooked rice (see RICE COOKING DIRECTIONS), 250 ml
and salt, 1 ml
   Stir custard once in the first 15 min of baking.

Caramel Custard—CARAMELIZE SUGAR and pour it into a baking dish, tilting it quickly to coat the bottom and sides; fill with the custard mixture and bake according to Baked Custard basic recipe. When cool invert and serve.

Crème Brûlée—Replace the milk in Baked Custard basic recipe with cereal cream; use the larger quantity of egg. Bake and chill the custard. At serving time set the dish in a pan of ice water; sprinkle a layer of dark brown sugar or maple sugar smoothly over the top; broil until sugar melts, watching carefully that it does not burn. Remove baking dish from water and let melted sugar harden to a glass-like covering. Crack with a spoon before serving.

Basic Recipe
SOFT CUSTARD (CUSTARD SAUCE)

This recipe uses the same ingredients as the basic recipe for Baked Custard, but combines and cooks them in a different way.

	3-4 eggs
100-125 ml	sugar (white or brown)
500 ml	milk
2 ml	vanilla *or* lemon rind
	cinnamon, nutmeg, *or* mace

1. Fill a large bowl or the sink with cold water.
2. Beat eggs just to blend whites and yolks; add sugar and milk and heat in a small, heavy saucepan or in the top of a double boiler.
3. Stir custard constantly using a figure eight motion over low heat until mixture "coats" a metal spoon, or a definite line indicates the depth to which the spoon was dipped into the custard. Test frequently to avoid overcooking; *immediately* the custard thickens, cool by setting the pan into the cold water. Taste; if there is a raw egg flavour, return the pan to the heat and stir carefully again. The custard should be the thickness of rich cream. If it begins to curdle, cool quickly and beat it smooth. Strain and add flavouring. *Serves 5-6.*

To use as a sauce over fruit, gelatine puddings, cake squares, etc., use only ½ the recipe.

Variations
Floating Island—Prepare SOFT CUSTARD using egg yolks (2 yolks replace 1 egg); strain into a serving dish; chill. Prepare soft MERINGUE from the whites. Shape the meringue into balls in a ladle and slide onto the surface of water that is steaming hot but *not*

at a bubbling boil. Cook 5 min; flip over and cook again. Lift from the water with a slotted spoon and drain on a rack; place on top of custard; dribble a little caramel or maple syrup over and garnish with glazed fruit and toasted almonds.

Trifle—Cut POUND CAKE in uniform pieces; spread each piece on one side with raspberry jam or jelly. Line an attractive bowl (bottom and sides) with half the cake; cover with rich SOFT CUSTARD then with a layer of whipped cream. Make a second layer of cake, custard and cream; garnish with fresh fruit and CHOCOLATE CURLS. Pound cake makes the best trifle but SPONGE CAKE, BUTTER CAKE, or sliced JELLY ROLL is often used.

MOCK CUSTARD SAUCE

To lessen the danger of curdling, the milk is first thickened with cornstarch. The result is a less expensive sauce, especially when skim milk powder is used.

100 ml	skim milk powder
50 ml	sugar
15 ml	cornstarch
50 ml	cold water
250 ml	boiling water
	1 egg yolk
5 ml	butter *or* margarine
	flavouring

1. Combine milk powder, sugar and cornstarch; mix to a smooth paste with the cold water; stir in the boiling water; cook with constant stirring over low heat until there is no taste of raw starch and the sauce thickens to the consistency of thin cream.
2. Beat egg yolk; add sugar and salt. Blend into it a little of the hot mixture.
3. Combine with remaining hot mixture.
4. Cook over hot water, stirring constantly until mixture thickens.
5. Remove from heat, strain; add flavouring (see FLAVOURINGS FOR CUSTARD). *Yield: 250 ml*

Recipes, tables, etc. that appear in small capital letters, e.g., PARSLEY BUTTER, CANADA'S FOOD GUIDE, are listed in the index. Consult the index for the number of the page on which the item appears.

BREAD PUDDING

Bread Puddings are custards in which bread or cake is substituted for part of the eggs.

500 ml	milk
	1 large egg *or* **1 egg plus 1 yolk**
500 ml	buttered bread, cubed or cut into strips
or	
250 ml	soft crumbs
15 ml	butter, melted
100 ml	sugar
5 ml	vanilla

Combine as BAKED CUSTARD basic recipe, adding the bread and butter to the egg-milk mixture.

Basic Recipe
CUSTARD BLANCMANGE (CORNSTARCH PUDDING)

150 ml	skim milk powder
100-125 ml	sugar
60 ml	cornstarch
100 ml	cold water
400 ml	hot water
	2 yolks *or* **1 egg**
15 ml	butter *or* margarine
5 ml	vanilla

1. Thoroughly combine the milk, sugar and cornstarch in a saucepan; blend with the cold water to a smooth paste.
2. Stir in the hot water; cook over low heat or in a double boiler stirring constantly until mixture thickens; continue to cook until there is no taste of raw starch.
3. Beat the egg well; add a small amount of the hot pudding stirring until smooth; return to the milk mixture and stir constantly until thick.
4. Remove from heat; add butter; stir and add vanilla.
5. Stir occasionally in a pan of cold water or cover to cool to prevent a skin forming.
6. Garnish with crushed berries, sliced fruit, CARAMEL SYRUP, maple syrup, or CHOCOLATE SYRUP. *Serves 4-6.*

Recipes, tables, etc. that appear in small capital letters, e.g., PARSLEY BUTTER, CANADA'S FOOD GUIDE, are listed in the index. Consult the index for the number of the page on which the item appears.

Variations
Cornstarch Soufflé—Beat 2 egg whites stiff but not dry; beat in sugar, 30 ml
Fold into pudding when it is removed from the heat.
Pineapple Soufflé—Replace cold water in the basic recipe with crushed drained pineapple; replace hot water with heated pineapple juice. Use the smaller amount of sugar. Finish as Cornstarch Soufflé.
Lemon Pudding—See LEMON PIE FILLING.
Chocolate Blancmange—Use the larger quantity of sugar; reduce cornstarch to 50 ml
Add cocoa, 50-60 ml

BUTTERSCOTCH PUDDING

50 ml	butter *or* margarine
60 ml	cornstarch
125 ml	brown sugar
150 ml	skim milk powder
400 ml	boiling water
	1 egg *or* **2 yolks**
25 ml	CARAMEL SYRUP *or* maple syrup
5 ml	vanilla

1. Melt butter in a saucepan over low heat. Blend cornstarch, sugar and milk powder; add to butter blending with a wire whip or a fork.
2. Add water, stirring constantly until thick and no flavour of raw starch remains.
3. Finish as CUSTARD BLANCMANGE.

PUDDING MIXES

These mixes can be prepared ahead of time and stored in covered containers in a cool place. Label each container.

Vanilla Pudding Mix

250 ml	cornstarch
125 ml	sugar
500 ml	skim milk powder

Chocolate Pudding Mix

200 ml	cornstarch
200 ml	cocoa
200 ml	sugar
500 ml	skim milk powder
5 ml	cinnamon

Combine all the ingredients thoroughly.

To make pudding, use mix in place of dry ingredients, as below:

300 ml	pudding mix
100 ml	cold water
400 ml	boiling water
	1 egg
15 ml	butter *or* margarine
1 ml	vanilla

Follow the method for CUSTARD BLANCMANGE (basic recipe). The mix will make three puddings, each serving 4-6.

Variations
Coffee Pudding—Add to boiling water instant coffee, 10 ml

Reconstituted skim milk may be used in any of the dessert recipes that call for milk. If extra richness is desired, add a little more fat.

CREAMY RICE PUDDING

125 ml	rice
1 ℓ	milk
	2 egg yolks
100 ml	sugar
4 ml	salt
5 ml	grated lemon rind
100 ml	raisins (optional)

1. Wash rice; cook in double boiler with milk until very soft, about 1 h
2. Beat egg yolks; add sugar, salt and lemon rind; add to rice mixture; stir and cook 5 min
3. Add raisins. Serve warm with brown sugar and cream. *Serves 4-6.*

BAVARIAN RICE

Cooked rice takes on a new look in this recipe.

250 ml	whipping cream
50 ml	sugar
5 ml	vanilla
250 ml	cooked rice, cooled
250 ml	mixed fruit and nuts*

* For variety, add any of the following, alone or in combination: crushed pineapple, sectioned oranges, slivered apricots, fresh or drained frozen

Dessert may be pudding or fruit or a combination. Borden Foods.

raspberries, marshmallows quartered, slivered blanched almonds, sliced fresh or canned peaches. Chopped crystallized ginger, grated maple sugar, or brandy may be added for flavouring.
1. Whip the cream; add sugar and vanilla; reserve a little cream for garnish.
2. Fold rice and fruit or nuts into the cream; chill. *Serves 6.*

BAKED RICE PUDDING

50 ml	rice
50 ml	sugar
1 ml	salt
500 ml	milk
15 ml	butter *or* margarine
	cinnamon *or* nutmeg
100 ml	raisins

1. Preheat oven to 150°C
2. Wash the rice. Combine all ingredients except raisins and cinnamon in a baking dish.
3. Bake 2 h; stir thoroughly after first hour of cooking; add raisins and sprinkle with cinnamon or nutmeg. Continue to bake until rice is tender, the liquid is absorbed and a golden brown crust forms. Pan capacity 1 ℓ
  Serves 4-6.

Brown rice adds fibre, minerals and vitamins; requires longer cooking.

One-half of sugar may be replaced by molasses.

Make this pudding when the oven is being used for a pot roast.

Basic Recipe
TAPIOCA CREAM

125 ml	skim milk powder
50 ml	minute tapioca
50 ml	sugar
400 ml	water
	1 egg, separated
2 ml	vanilla

1. Combine milk powder, tapioca and ½ the sugar; add water; cook over low heat stirring occasionally, until the tapioca becomes transparent and the mixture thickens (about 20 min).
2. Beat egg white until stiff but not dry; beat in the remaining sugar.
3. Beat the egg yolk; blend in some of the cooked tapioca; return mixture to remaining tapioca; stir over low heat until thick (3 min).
4. Remove from heat; fold in the meringue of step 2; reserving a little for garnish; place in serving dishes; top with remaining meringue and garnish with jam, cooked fruit, fresh berries, or peaches. *Serves 4-6.*

Variations
Coffee Tapioca Cream—Add instant coffee, 10 ml
or replace part of the milk with strong freshly brewed coffee to taste; increase the sugar if desired.
Fruit Tapioca Cream—Replace the milk with fruit juice; taste and adjust flavour by adding lemon juice or sugar. Serve with fruit garnish.

RHUBARB-STRAWBERRY TAPIOCA

250 ml	sugar
50 ml	tapioca
500 ml	water
500 ml	rhubarb, chopped
500 ml	strawberries, sliced

1. Combine sugar, tapioca and water and bring to a boil.
2. Add the rhubarb and cook until tender (5-10 min); add strawberries.
3. Remove from the heat, cover and let stand 15 min. Stir carefully; chill; serve with cream. *Serves 4-6.*

Yogurt

This cultured milk product, similar to cottage cheese in flavour but smoother in texture, is high in protein, calcium and riboflavin.

To prevent the growth of undesirable organisms, containers for making yogurt should be sterilized, and fresh milk and water should be brought to a boil and cooled before using. In the following method developed by the Canada Department of Agriculture, canned milk and skim milk powder are used; they have already been sterilized.

PLAIN YOGURT

150 ml	1 small can evaporated milk
250 ml	skim milk powder
600 ml	boiled water
25 ml	plain yogurt

1. Sterilize containers of suitable size to hold 1 *l*
2. In a clean bowl combine the milk and milk powder; stir until smooth; stir in the yogurt; add the water cooled to lukewarm, 43°C
3. Mix well with a wire whisk and pour into sterilized containers; remove foam; cover with plastic film then with lids.
4. Set the jars in a pan of lukewarm water to the level of the liquid in the jars; cover; leave undisturbed in a warm place to maintain the temperature at 43°C
   Suitable places are: on top of a frost-free refrigerator, over the pilot light of a gas stove, over the vent of an oven set at 110°C
   (It is wise the first time to check the temperature of the water constantly with a thermometer.)
5. Allow to stand without being disturbed until set (2-4 h).
6. Taste. Refrigerate or leave an hour in a warm room for it to become more acid if desired.

Refrigerated yogurt will keep 1-2 weeks; longer if the container has not been opened, so use several small containers to avoid opening before necessary.

Use a small amount of this homemade yogurt to make a new lot every 4 or 5 d. By the end of a month, yogurt will have become less acid and a new starter will be needed.

To Use Yogurt

Serve as a dessert with a sprinkle of maple sugar or brown sugar, or add fresh fruit, jam, or honey.

Flavour by stirring into yogurt one of the following. Quantities given will flavour

250 ml	plain yogurt

50 ml	sweetened applesauce

or

125 ml	mashed banana

or

125 ml	chopped, canned fruit
50 ml	and fruit syrup

or

50 ml	sliced or mashed fresh fruit
15 ml	and honey, sugar or syrup

or

15 ml	frozen orange juice concentrate, thawed
15 ml	and honey, sugar or syrup

or

15 ml	jam

Freeze yogurt in individual serving dishes; soften a few minutes before serving. Yogurt can be carried frozen in a lunch bag; it will be thawed and ready for eating in 2-3 h

Yogurt may take the place of sour cream as a topping on desserts; on pancakes or baked potato, or in gelatine desserts, flour mixtures, or mayonnaise. Yogurt has only ¼ the food energy of sour cream.

Make cream cheese from yogurt. Hang yogurt in a cloth bag to drip overnight; remove and salt contents or flavour with herbs. Serve with biscuits as a dip or spread.

1 *l*	yogurt
yields	
400 ml	cheese

YOGURT JELLY

85 g	1 pkg. pineapple jelly powder
250 ml	boiling water
100 ml	orange juice
15 ml	lemon juice
125 ml	yogurt

Prepare jelly following the directions on the package, substituting fruit juice for half the water. When partially set, beat in the yogurt.

YOGURT SAUCE

250 ml	yogurt
50 ml	SALAD DRESSING
5 ml	salt
2 ml	chives, dill or parsley

Combine the ingredients; serve with lettuce and tomatoes.

Variation

Cucumber Sauce—Peel, seed and finely chop 1 medium cucumber; stir into the Yogurt Sauce; cover and refrigerate. Serve with cold salmon, TOMATO ASPIC.

YOGURT DIP FOR FRESH FRUIT

250 ml	yogurt
50 ml	honey
15 ml	frozen orange juice concentrate

1. Combine the yogurt, honey and juice in a small bowl.
2. Place in centre of large platter and surround with fresh, unhulled strawberries, unpeeled apple slices, cantaloupe balls, pineapple wedges or other bite-sized fruit served with toothpicks.

YOGURT SHERBET

700 ml	yogurt
170 g	1 small can frozen orange juice concentrate, thawed
5 ml	vanilla
50 ml	sugar

Combine all the ingredients, mix well and place in the freezer. When partially frozen, whip until smooth; refreeze. *Yield:* 500 ml

Popsicles—Pour sherbet into paper cups; secure a stick in the centre of each and freeze until hard. Remove paper cup. Makes 12.

Batter and Dough Desserts

FRUIT FOR BATTER AND DOUGH DESSERTS

Shortcake, cobbler, roly poly pudding and cottage pudding can be made with frozen or canned fruits when fresh fruits are not available. Add a little sugar to fresh fruit. Use spice or flavouring to enhance the flavour. Thicken the juice with flour, cornstarch or tapioca. Use these fruit mixtures in the pudding recipes that follow.

1 *l*	sliced apples
125 ml	brown sugar
1 ml	cinnamon
50 ml	flour
500 ml	blueberries
125 ml	brown sugar
1 ml	cinnamon
50 ml	flour
1 *l*	pitted plums
125 ml	brown sugar
1 ml	cardamom
25 ml	cornstarch
1 *l*	sliced peaches
200 ml	white sugar
1 ml	cinnamon
50 ml	minute tapioca
500 ml	whole raspberries *or* strawberries
100 ml	white sugar
5 ml	orange *or* lemon rind
50 ml	minute tapioca
425 ml each	2 pkg. frozen fruit, thawed
100 ml	white sugar (optional)
5 ml	lemon juice
25 ml	cornstarch
1 *l*	fresh, pitted cherries
250 ml	white sugar
	few drops almond flavouring
25 ml	cornstarch
1 *l*	cut rhubarb
250 ml	brown *or* white sugar
5 ml	ginger
50 ml	minute tapioca

540 ml	1 can fruit
50 ml	white sugar (optional)
5 ml	lemon juice
25 ml	cornstarch

COTTAGE PUDDING

1. Prepare the fruit combining it with a mixture of sugar, flavouring and thickener (see FRUIT FOR BATTER AND DOUGH DESSERTS). Place in a large loaf pan, cake or pie pan, or casserole.
2. Prepare a cake batter from the recipe for ONE-EGG CAKE, white QUICK-MIX BUTTER CAKE, or GOLD CAKE. (A commercial cake mix may be used instead.)
3. Pour batter onto the fruit to a depth of 2.5 cm
4. Bake until cake is firm and fruit tender, 30-45 min at 180°C
   Serve with VANILLA SAUCE or a variation, or whipped cream. Pan capacity 2 *l*
   Serves 6-8.

Too much cake batter in proportion to the amount of fruit makes a poor product. Fill greased muffin tins with excess batter, refrigerate and bake in the last 15 min

FRUIT COBBLER (BAKED PUDDING)

1. Prepare the fruit combining it with a mixture of sugar, flavouring and thickener (see FRUIT FOR BATTER AND DOUGH DESSERTS).
2. Place the fruit mixture in a large loaf pan, cake or pie pan or casserole so that the pan is 2/3 full; dot with butter or margarine; add water to cover the bottom of the pan, approximately 100 ml
3. Cover and bake until the fruit is almost tender (20 min), at 200°C
4. Prepare recipe for SWEET TEA BISCUIT dough; drop on the filling spacing evenly, or roll to a thickness of 1 cm
5. Shape to fit the baking dish; crimp the edges so the dough will fit into the dish; brush the surface with milk and sprinkle with sugar.
6. Remove fruit from the oven; place the dough in position on the fruit and quickly return the pan to the oven; bake until the biscuit is cooked (20 min).
7. Serve warm with LEMON SAUCE, FRUIT SAUCE, sour cream or ice cream. Pan capacity 2 *l*
   Serves 6-8.

A Fruit Roly Poly can be sliced before baking. Maple Leaf Mills.

FRUIT ROLY POLY

1. Prepare the fruit, combining it with a mixture of sugar, flavouring and thickener (see FRUIT FOR BATTER AND DOUGH DESSERTS).
2. Prepare recipe for SWEET TEA BISCUIT dough; roll into a rectangle 20 × 30 cm
3. Spread with soft butter or margarine, 30 ml
4. Sprinkle with brown sugar, 125 ml
5. Spoon the prepared fruit onto the dough; from the wide side, roll like a jellyroll; seal the edges and ends.
6. Place on a greased pan; cut slits to allow steam to escape; brush with milk.
7. Bake until the centre of the roll is cooked (about 60 min) at 180°C
   Serve with VANILLA SAUCE or a variation. *Serves 6-8.*

Variations
Following step 5, cut the roll into 8 slices; place cut-side down in a greased baking dish; bake until cooked (30 min) at 180°C

Recipes, tables, etc. that appear in small capital letters, e.g., PARSLEY BUTTER, CANADA'S FOOD GUIDE, are listed in the index. Consult the index for the number of the page on which the item appears.

FRUIT CRISP

1. Preheat oven to 180°C
2. Prepare fruit, combining it with sugar and flavouring (see FRUIT FOR BATTER AND DOUGH DESSERTS); omit thickener. Place in baking dish; add water, 50 ml
3. Make a topping, using the following ingredients:

150 ml	flour
200 ml	brown sugar
100 ml	firm butter *or* margarine

   Combine flour and sugar in a bowl; cut in fat until the texture is that of coarse crumbs; sprinkle over the fruit; shake lightly.
4. Bake until topping is brown and crisp (40 min). Pan capacity 2 *l*
   Serves 6.

Variations
Add to the crumb mixture flaked coconut *or* finely chopped nuts, 125 ml

Cheese Apple Crisp—Add to the topping grated processed cheese, 250 ml
Use apple fruit mixture (see FRUIT FOR BATTER AND DOUGH DESSERTS), omitting thickener; replace cinnamon with lemon juice, 30 ml
Fruit Crumble—Add to the topping for Fruit Crisp rolled oats, 200 ml

FRUIT BETTY

50 ml	butter *or* margarine
350 ml	day-old bread, cubed
	fruit mixture*
250 ml	water

1. Preheat oven to 180°C
2. Melt the fat in a baking dish over low heat; add bread and stir until slightly browned; empty out all but 1 thin layer.
3. Measure but do not combine the fruit, sugar and flavouring (see* FRUIT FOR BATTER AND DOUGH DESSERTS).
4. Layer the fruit and bread into the casserole, ending with bread.
5. Combine the sugar and water; boil 6 min to a syrup consistency.
6. Pour the syrup over the bread; bake until fruit is tender (40 min); serve with sour cream. Pan capacity 1.5 *l*
   Serves 6.

SHORTCAKE

The SWEET TEA BISCUIT recipe makes enough for one shortcake and extra tea biscuits.

	SWEET TEA BISCUIT **dough**
	(1 recipe)
500 ml	strawberries, raspberries, *or*
	peaches, fresh or frozen
150-200 ml	sugar
	whipped cream

1. Preheat oven to 220°C
2. Prepare the dough; knead slightly to make it smooth. Roll two-thirds of the dough to a thickness of 1 cm
   Use the rest of the dough for tea biscuits.
3. Bake 15-20 min until cooked and lightly browned.
4. Cut or mash the fruit; add sugar. Save a few perfect pieces of fruit for garnish.
5. Place biscuit on a serving plate; split; spread the cut surface with butter; spoon fruit onto biscuit; cover with top crust.
6. Top with sweetened whipped cream and garnish with the reserved fruit. *Serves 4-6.*

DUTCH APPLE CAKE

	SWEET TEA BISCUIT **dough**
	(1 recipe)
	2 apples
5 ml	cinnamon
50 ml	sugar

1. Preheat oven to 200°C
2. Prepare the dough; spread in a buttered large cake pan (see CAKE PANS).
3. Wipe, quarter, core and pare apples; cut in eighths; arrange in rows, pressing sharp edges into the batter; sprinkle with cinnamon and sugar.
4. Bake until dough is cooked in the centre (25-30 min); serve with CARAMEL SAUCE. *Yield: 1.5 ℓ Serves 6-8.*

Variation
Dutch Pineapple Cake—Replace apples with 6 slices canned pineapple cut in half. Serve with FRUIT SAUCE prepared from the pineapple syrup.

STREUSEL TOPPING may replace cinnamon-sugar mix.

Baked Puddings

These puddings make their own sauce.

Basic Recipe
BUTTERSCOTCH JIFFY PUDDING

Batter

30 ml	butter *or* margarine
50 ml	sugar
2 ml	vanilla
250 ml	flour
10 ml	baking powder
100 ml	skim milk powder
150 ml	water

Sauce

200 ml	brown sugar
15 ml	butter *or* margarine
400 ml	boiling water
5 ml	vanilla *or* maple flavouring

Prepare batter:
1. Preheat oven to 190°C
2. Cream butter and sugar; add vanilla.
3. Combine flour, baking powder and milk powder; add alternately with the water to fat-sugar mixture to make a thick batter; spoon into a greased medium cake pan (see CAKE PANS).

Prepare sauce:
4. Sprinkle brown sugar over the batter; combine butter, boiling water and flavouring; pour over batter; *do not stir.*
5. Bake 45 min *Serves 6.*

Variations
Apple Jiffy Pudding—Slice one peeled apple into the bottom of the pan, or grate coarsely and add half to the batter, half to the sauce.

Fruit Jiffy Pudding—Replace sugar and water in the sauce with sweetened stewed berries and juice, 600-700 ml

Raisin Jiffy Pudding—Add raisins to batter; replace flavouring in sauce with juice and grated rind of ½ orange.

Fudge Jiffy Pudding—To the dry ingredients of the batter add:

30 ml	cocoa
50 ml	walnuts

To the sugar in the sauce add:

50 ml	cocoa

FOAMY LEMON PUDDING (SPONGE CUSTARD)

50 ml	butter *or* margarine
50 ml	flour
	2 eggs, separated
	1 lemon, grated rind and juice
125 ml	sugar
125 ml	milk

1. Melt the butter; add the flour; add lemon.
2. Add egg yolks, sugar and milk; beat well.
3. Beat the egg whites stiff but not dry; fold into the first mixture.
4. Pour into custard cups or a casserole; oven poach 30-40 min at 180°C

Serve hot or cold. *Serves 6.*

WALDORF PUDDING

	4 medium-size tart apples
125 ml	brown sugar
5 ml	cinnamon
2 ml	nutmeg
200 ml	raisins *or* dates
125 ml	walnuts (optional)
125 ml	white sugar
350 ml	flour
10 ml	baking powder
1 ml	baking soda
2 ml	salt
125 ml	salad oil
	1 egg

1. Preheat oven to 190°C
2. Peel and core apples; chop coarsely into a large bowl; mix in brown sugar, spices, raisins and walnuts.
3. Combine sugar and flour with baking powder, soda and salt; sprinkle over fruit mixture; add oil and unbeaten egg; beat for about 2 min and spread in greased small rectangular cake pan (see CAKE PANS).
4. Bake until firm (40 min); serve with VANILLA SAUCE or a variation or a slice of Cheddar cheese. *Serves 6-8.*

Steamed Puddings

Christmas Puddings may be too rich to serve with Christmas dinner but are welcome throughout the holiday season. Whole wheat flour, rye bread crumbs add flavour and food value and may take the place of flour and soft bread crumbs.

This kind of pudding must be cooked slowly enough that the suet is melted before the starch grains begin to burst; steaming is the best method. Pressure cooking is a quick and satisfactory way to steam a pudding; consult the manual for cooking times. A regular steamer may of course be used, or set the pudding in a tightly covered bowl (tie on foil or waxed paper) on sealer rings or a rack in a deep kettle which has a tight-fitting top. Add boiling water until it comes halfway up the bowl. Adjust the heat when the water boils so that it will boil gently. As necessary, add more boiling water.

To steam small puddings, spoon into 10-12 greased custard cups; cover each cup *tightly*; place on a rack in a roasting pan. Pour in boiling water to come halfway up the cups; cover the pan and oven-steam 1.5 h, at 150°C

PLUM PUDDING

1 kg	currants and raisins
250 g	blanched almonds
500 g	cut mixed fruit
250 ml	flour
5 ml	baking soda
2 ml	salt
5 ml	cinnamon
2 ml	nutmeg
1 ml	cloves
1 ml	allspice
550 ml	brown sugar, packed
1 *l*	soft bread crumbs
500 g	suet, finely chopped
125 ml	grape juice, orange juice
	8 eggs

1. Wash the currants in warm water until there is no sign of sand; spread on brown paper to dry in a warm place.
2. Combine fruit and nuts; sprinkle with ½-¾ of the flour to separate the fruit.
3. Combine remaining flour, soda, spices; add sugar, crumbs and suet; mix well; add fruit.
4. Beat the eggs; add juice; add to the dry ingredients.
5. Pour into well-greased moulds and cover; steam 3 hours. Makes 4 puddings, each 1 *l*

CARROT PUDDING

This pudding is less expensive than Plum Pudding and not as rich.

2 ml	baking soda
125 ml	flour
5 ml	salt
5 ml	cinnamon
0.5 ml	nutmeg
2 ml	allspice
200 ml	cut mixed fruit
50 ml	almonds, split
250 ml	grated carrot
250 ml	grated potato
300 ml	soft bread crumbs
500 ml	raisins and currants, combined
250 ml	brown sugar
200 ml	suet, finely chopped
30 ml	milk

1. Thoroughly combine soda, flour, salt and spices; add ingredients in order given.
2. Fill a well-greased mould not more than 2/3 full; cover with a lid or tie on heavy brown paper, greased and pleated; cover with a sheet of heavy foil.
3. Steam 3 h or pressure-cook 1.5 h at 105 kPa 105 kPa
4. Cool covered; refrigerate. *Yield*: 1.25 ℓ
   Serves 8.

To serve: steam about 1 h; unmould and cut into wedges with a sharp knife; serve with VANILLA, LEMON or CARAMEL SAUCE.

Dessert Soufflés

These light desserts provide elegance with a minimum of richness.

Basic Recipe
VANILLA SOUFFLÉ

50 ml	butter *or* margarine
50 ml	flour
1 ml	salt
125 ml	sugar
250 ml	milk
	3 egg yolks
5 ml	vanilla
	3-4 egg whites
1 ml	cream of tartar

1. Preheat oven to 180°C
2. Butter a soufflé dish and dust with sugar or ground almonds; prepare a collar (see SOUFFLÉS, GENERAL DIRECTIONS).
3. Prepare a thick WHITE SAUCE from the butter, flour, salt, sugar and milk; cool 10 min
4. Beat egg yolks until lemon-coloured; add a little of the hot sauce, blend and beat into remaining sauce; add flavouring.
5. Beat egg whites and cream of tartar until stiff but not dry; fold into the sauce.
6. Bake and serve as CHEESE SOUFFLÉ, BASIC RECIPE. *Serves 6.*

Variations

Prune Soufflé—To the sauce add thick purée of unsweetened prunes, 125 ml
and finely chopped walnuts, 50 ml

Apricot Soufflé—To the sauce add thick purée of cooked, unsweetened apricots, 125 ml
Replace vanilla with grated orange or lemon rind.

Chocolate Soufflé—add to dry ingredients cocoa, 100 ml
Reduce flour to 30 ml
Increase sugar to 150 ml
Flavour with grated orange rind; orange marmalade; or peppermint flavouring.

Cottage Cheese Soufflé—Into the thick sauce stir creamed cottage cheese, 125 ml
chopped raisins and almonds, 125 ml
grated orange and lemon rind, 5 ml

SEVEN-MINUTE PRUNE WHIP

	2 egg whites
	grated rind and juice of 1 lemon
125 ml	sugar
50 ml	prune juice
125 ml	chopped, cooked prunes

1. Combine ingredients except fruit in the top section of a double boiler.
2. Place over boiling water and beat with an egg beater until stiff enough to stand up in peaks (about 5-7 min). Remove from heat.
3. Fold in the fruit. Chill. Serve with CUSTARD SAUCE. *Serves 6.*

Gelatine Moulds—General Directions

Too little gelatine in proportion to the liquid will not set; too much results in an unpleasant rubbery texture. A very high sugar or acid concentration reduces gelatine's thickening power. For large moulds, or gelatine mixtures to be served in hot weather, reduce the liquid slightly. Boiling gives a rubbery texture. Gelatine may be beaten or egg white added to increase volume; however, firmness is reduced.

To Mould Gelatine

Rinse mould in cold water or apply light film of cooking oil. (If oil is used, gelatine mixture must be cool when it is poured into mould.) Pour prepared mixture into mould, chill and let set in refrigerator.

To Unmould

Loosen by running a sharp-tipped, thin-bladed knife around edge; dip mould in a dish of hot water; place a serving dish face down over mould; hold in place and invert quickly. Store in a cool place.

To Decorate a Mould

Meat or Salad Moulds—Lightly grease the mould; pour in a thin layer of cooled, prepared stock or liquid and gelatine, and allow it to set fairly stiff; arrange the decoration on this layer, remembering that the decoration will be reversed when the jelly is unmoulded. Spoon over it a thin layer of jelly and refrigerate it until set. Combine the meat or vegetables and remaining liquid and spoon over the jelly in the mould. Chill.

Fruit Moulds—A moulded jelly may have different fruit at each level: "floaters" that tend to stay on top during the setting process are banana slices, pear cubes, grapefruit sections, raspberries, strawberry slices, marshmallows and nuts. "Sinkers" are orange sections, peach slices, canned cherries, blueberries and seedless grapes; these tend to drop to the bottom of the mould. When the mould is inverted on the serving dish the fruit on the bottom becomes the attractive topping.

Recipes, tables, etc. that appear in small capital letters, e.g., PARSLEY BUTTER, CANADA'S FOOD GUIDE, are listed in the index. Consult the index for the number of the page on which the item appears.

Gelatine Desserts

Dessert jellies may be moulded (see general directions at left); or they may be cut into cubes and piled into dessert dishes combined with fruit or whipped cream; or they may be set in parfait glasses that are held on a slant during the setting process, placed level when set, and filled with yogurt or a jelly dessert of a contrasting colour and complementary flavour.

Basic Recipe
JELLY DESSERT

15 ml	1 envelope gelatine
50 ml	cold water
350 ml	fruit juice
	sugar *or* lemon juice (optional)

1. Sprinkle gelatine onto cold water until it absorbs the water and swells (5 min).
2. Prepare juice; use orange, apple, canned pineapple*, grapefruit juice, or a combination. Heat half the juice in a saucepan. If sweet jelly is required, dissolve sugar in the hot liquid. Add the softened gelatine; dissolve completely. Do not let mixture boil.
3. Add remaining liquid; taste and flavour; chill. When mixture drops rather than pours from a spoon, cut, drained fruit may be added as well as nuts or marshmallows.
4. Chill until firm (2-4 h). Serve with table cream, whipped cream, sour cream or CUSTARD SAUCE. *Serves 4-6.*

---

* Raw pineapple contains an enzyme which digests the protein in gelatine and prevents it setting. Only *cooked* pineapple can be used with gelatine. (Canned pineapple is cooked.)

RASPBERRY AMBROSIA

85 g	1 pkg. raspberry jelly powder
125 ml	boiling water
250 ml	canned pineapple juice
285 g	1 package frozen raspberries, thawed
125 ml	seedless green grapes
125 ml	pineapple chunks
125 ml	whipping cream
125 ml	flaked coconut

1. Dissolve jelly powder in boiling water; add pineapple juice; pour into a cake pan to a depth of 1 cm
2. Allow to set; cut into cubes.
3. At serving time layer fruit and jelly cubes into sherbet glasses or a large fruit bowl; garnish with whipped cream and coconut. *Serves 10-12.*

JELLIED APPLES

15 ml	1 envelope gelatine
250 ml	apple juice
125 ml	sugar
	strips of rind from 1 lemon
750 ml	sliced apples
	juice of 1 lemon
50 ml	glazed cut fruit

1. Sprinkle the gelatine onto ¼ of the apple juice to soften.
2. Add the sugar to remaining apple juice in a wide, shallow saucepan; simmer with strips of lemon rind 5 min
3. Peel, core and cut apples into eighths; simmer in the syrup until tender; lift out fruit; add lemon juice; measure and add water or apple juice to bring the liquid up to 400 ml
4. Dissolve softened gelatine in hot liquid; strain and chill until it begins to set; pour ¼-1/3 the amount into a mould and leave to set; to remaining jelly add apples and glazed fruit; spoon into mould; allow to set.

The cores and peelings of red-skinned apples boiled in water to cover, and strained, may be used to replace an equal amount of apple juice to give an attractive colour.

Russet apples have a different flavour, interesting in this recipe.

Recipes, tables, etc. that appear in small capital letters, e.g., PARSLEY BUTTER, CANADA'S FOOD GUIDE, are listed in the index. Consult the index for the number of the page on which the item appears.

STRAWBERRY FOAM

A foam is a gelatine mixture that is beaten when it is beginning to set. Depending upon the consistency when it is beaten, either the foam will settle to the top leaving a clear jelly layer below, or the whole jelly will be foamy, lighter in colour and doubled in volume.

85 g	1 pkg. strawberry jelly powder
125 ml	boiling water
284 g	1 pkg. frozen strawberries

Dissolve jelly powder in boiling water; add unthawed berries; stir gently to separate berries; beat 1 min; pour into dessert dishes to set.

Basic Recipe
SPONGE PUDDING (LEMON SNOW)

Sponges are gelatine desserts to which beaten egg white is added. They will triple in volume.

15 ml	1 envelope gelatine
50 ml	cold water
200 ml	boiling water
125 ml	sugar
	thin shaving of ¼ lemon rind
50 ml	lemon juice
	2 egg whites

1. Sprinkle gelatine on cold water to soften (5 min).
2. Combine boiling water, sugar and lemon rind; boil 3 min; dissolve gelatine in syrup; add lemon juice.
3. Chill, stirring frequently until syrupy. Beat egg whites until stiff; beat the gelatine mixture; beat the 2 mixtures together.
4. Pour into a moistened mould or pile lightly in sherbet dishes; chill until firm. Serve with CUSTARD SAUCE. *Serves 4-6.*

Variation
Pineapple Sponge—Use pineapple juice drained from crushed canned pineapple to replace sugar and boiling water; reduce lemon juice to 15 ml
To the beaten mixture fold in well-drained crushed pineapple, 125 ml
Grape Sponge—Use bottled grape juice to replace boiling water, sugar and lemon rind. Some grape juices need sugar; some need lemon juice. Rhubarb juice or raspberry juice may be used in this way.

APPLE SNOW

85 g	1 pkg. lemon jelly powder
125 ml	hot water
250 ml	cold water
500 ml	applesauce
	2 stiffly beaten egg whites

1. Dissolve jelly powder in hot water; add cold water; chill.
2. When jelly begins to set, beat it until foamy; beat in applesauce and egg whites.
3. Pile into dessert dishes or mould; garnish with thin slices of unpeeled apple dipped in lemon juice to prevent darkening. Serve with CUSTARD SAUCE. *Serves 6.*

Crèmes

In a crème, milk or thin cream is the liquid.

LEMON VELVET

15 ml	1 envelope gelatine
50 ml	water
250 ml	milk
125 ml	sugar
50 ml	juice and rind of 1 lemon
125 ml	whipping cream

1. Sprinkle the gelatine over the cold water; dissolve by standing the container in hot water.
2. Heat the milk and sugar to dissolve the sugar; cool to room temperature before adding the gelatine, chill until almost set.
3. Beat until foamy; add lemon juice.
4. Whip the cream; fold into gelatine mixture; spoon into serving dishes or mould (see TO MOULD GELATINE).
5. Garnish with fresh orange sections; frozen berries thawed; or FRUIT SYRUP. *Serves 6-8.*

Make sure that milk is at room temperature before adding gelatine. If gelatine is added to hot milk, the milk curdles. If curdling does occur, beat the mixture vigorously.

Variations
Brown Sugar Crème—Substitute brown for white sugar; vanilla for lemon juice; sour cream for whipping cream.
Yogurt Crème—Substitute yogurt for whipping cream.

Charlottes

Charlottes are gelatine desserts into which whipped cream has been folded; sometimes beaten egg whites are added as well. These rich desserts look elegant when moulded or served in parfait glasses or compote dishes; set in crumb crusts, these recipes create chiffon pies; set in a soufflé dish or straight-sided dish they become never-fall cold soufflés; without egg the mixture may be called a mousse.

Basic Recipe
ORANGE CHARLOTTE

15 ml	1 envelope gelatine
50 ml	cold water
50 ml	boiling water
125 ml	sugar
200 ml	orange juice
25 ml	lemon juice
	2 egg whites
250 ml	cream, whipped
	orange sections

1. Prepare first 6 ingredients as in the basic recipe for JELLY DESSERT.
2. When partly set, beat until foamy; add egg whites, beaten stiff; beat well; fold in whipped cream.
3. Turn into a mould (see TO MOULD GELATINE); chill; garnish with orange sections. *Serves 6-8.*

This mixture freezes well; remove from the freezer to the refrigerator an hour before serving.

Variations

Cherry Berry Charlotte—Replace the first 6 ingredients with:

85 g	1 envelope black cherry jelly powder
250 ml	boiling water
426 g	1 pkg. frozen raspberries

Dissolve the jelly powder in boiling water; add the partly thawed berries. Finish as Orange Charlotte beginning at step 2.

Coffee Charlotte—Replace fruit juice with cold strong coffee.

Charlotte Russe is made by lining a springform pan with split lady fingers, round side out, and filling the pan with any Charlotte or Bavarian dessert. Borden Company Ltd.

Maple Charlotte—Replace sugar and fruit juice with maple syrup, 250 ml

Chocolate Charlotte—Replace sugar and fruit juice with CHOCOLATE SYRUP, 250 ml

Replace the whipped cream with yogurt, sour cream, ice cream, whipped evaporated milk or skim milk powder. See TO WHIP.

QUICK PINEAPPLE CHARLOTTE

540 g	1 can crushed pineapple
85 g	1 pineapple jelly powder
15 ml	lemon juice
500 ml	ice cream

1. Drain crushed pineapple, measure liquid; add water to make 375 ml
   Heat part of the liquid; dissolve the jelly powder.
2. Add remaining liquid; add lemon juice; chill.
3. When partially set beat until foamy; beat in the ice cream; add drained pineapple; chill. *Serves 6-8.*

Recipes, tables, etc. that appear in small capital letters, e.g., PARSLEY BUTTER, CANADA'S FOOD GUIDE, are listed in the index. Consult the index for the number of the page on which the item appears.

Basic Recipe
SPANISH CREAM

Spanish Cream is a gelatine mixture in which the base is a custard sauce. Commercial eggnog heated may be used to replace the egg yolk, milk, sugar and vanilla.

15 ml	1 envelope gelatine
50 ml	cold water
	2 egg yolks
100 ml	skim milk powder
50 ml	sugar
350 ml	boiling water
5 ml	vanilla
	2 egg whites, beaten

1. Sprinkle the gelatine in cold water to soften (5 min).
2. Prepare CUSTARD SAUCE from the next 5 ingredients.
3. Dissolve gelatine in the sauce; chill.
4. When partly set, beat; beat in egg whites. Mould (see TO MOULD GELATINE). *Serves 4-6.*

Variations
Lemon Spanish Cream—Use filling for LEMON CHIFFON PIE.
Coffee Spanish Cream—Replace ½ of the boiling water with hot strong coffee.
Pineapple Spanish Cream—Omit skim milk powder; replace boiling water with crushed pineapple, undrained, 350 ml
Bisque Tortoni—Fold into the partly set mixture chopped almonds and flaked coconut, toasted. Spoon chopped maraschino cherries and SYRUP over each serving.
Chocolate Spanish Cream—Increase sugar to 100 ml
Add cocoa, 15 ml
Add instant coffee, 5 ml

BAVARIAN CREAM

Bavarian Cream is a Spanish Cream into which whipped cream is folded after the egg whites have been beaten in.
Strawberry Bavarian—Purée 1 package frozen strawberries, thawed. Prepare SPANISH CREAM using the purée to replace an equal amount of boiling water. Omit sugar if berries are sweetened. After the egg white is beaten in, fold in whipped cream, 250 ml

Strawberry Bavarian Surprise—Prepare a collar on a soufflé dish (see SOUFFLÉS). In the centre of the dish place a straight-sided glass to be filled with ice cubes or cold water. Pour Strawberry Bavarian around the glass in the soufflé dish; when set, remove the glass and collar and fill the space with fresh berries, crushed macaroons and almonds, or chopped fresh peaches and toasted flaked coconut.

Frozen Desserts

Frozen desserts began when the Romans served flavoured snow carried by slaves from the mountaintops. From Persia Marco Polo brought the trick of turning purées of fruit into ices by packing them in snow.

LEMON GRANITA

A granita is the simplest of ices; the least sweet, not stirred while freezing, eaten when it is the consistency of lightly packed snow.

250 ml	sugar
500 ml	hot water *or* hot clear tea
125 ml	strained fresh lemon juice
	sweetened whipped cream

Dissolve sugar in water; chill; add lemon juice; freeze without stirring until crystals have formed (4-5 h). Serve topped with cream. *Serves 4-6.*

This is a very lemony mixture; use more water and less lemon if desired.

Variation
Other fruit juices or combinations may be used.

FRUIT ICE

A water-ice is made of the same ingredients as a granita but is sweeter, is stirred to make the texture less granular and is frozen to a stiffer consistency.

2 ℓ	raspberries *or* strawberries
15 ml	lemon *or* orange juice
500 ml	sugar
1 ℓ	water

Purée fruit; add lemon juice to taste; prepare syrup by stirring the sugar and water while heating to boiling; simmer 5 min; add fruit. Freeze, stirring two or three times. *Serves 8-10.*

GRAPE JUICE FRAPPÉ

A frappé has the coarse, unstirred texture of a granita but can be sweeter and may be made with milk or may contain beaten egg white folded in.

180 g	1 can frozen grape juice
	3 cans crushed ice

Whirl the ingredients in a blender to make "slush"; refreeze or serve immediately. *Serves 4.*

Variation

Raspberry Frappé

426 g	1 pkg. frozen raspberries
250 ml	evaporated milk, thin cream *or* yogurt
125 ml	crushed ice (approximately 6 cubes)

Basic Recipe
SHERBET

Sorbets and sherbets ought to be identical, because *sorbet* is the French word for sherbet. In France, however, sorbets are made from fruit, liqueur, and wine and are only slightly sweeter than a granita. They are frozen without stirring and "sandy" in texture. Sherbets, on the other hand, contain ingredients such as gelatine, egg white or milk and are beaten during freezing to obtain a crystal small enough to be smooth to the tongue.

250 ml	medium SYRUP
25-50 ml	lemon juice
250 ml	fruit juice*
25 ml	cream, sour cream *or* yogurt
	1 egg white, beaten

1. Combine syrup, lemon juice, fruit juice and cream; whisk to combine; freeze to a firm mush (2 h) stirring once or twice.
2. Chill a bowl and beaters; beat the mixture until smooth and fluffy without melting.
3. Fold in the egg white beaten stiff but not dry; refreeze. *Serves 6-8.*
* Fruit juice may be orange, tangerine, or grapefruit. Crushed pineapple, peach, mango, or apricot purée may be used with orange juice to taste. Grape, cranberry, black currant, or raspberry juice may be used.

Variations
Blender Pineapple Sherbet—Freeze 1 can of pineapple chunks in unsweetened juice until solid. Blend to sherbet consistency. Serve immediately or refreeze. *Serves 4.*
Cranberry Sherbet—Serve this as a refreshing course after the Christmas turkey.

350 ml	cranberry jelly
	rind and juice of 1 lemon
	juice of 1 orange
	2 egg whites

1. Melt the jelly over hot water; combine with fruit juices; freeze to a mush.
2. Scrape into a cold bowl and beat quickly; fold in beaten egg whites; refreeze. *Serves 6-8.*

Water may replace the medium syrup in the basic recipe if the fruit juice has been sweetened. Too concentrated a sugar solution may not freeze at temperatures obtainable in home freezers.

FROZEN SUCKERS (POPSICLES)

These provide a nutritious snack for children if made with a minimum amount of sugar. For a smoother texture, yogurt may be added, which will add a little calcium (see YOGURT SHERBET).

500 ml	sweetened puréed fruit
250 ml	orange juice
25 ml	sugar, corn syrup *or* honey

1. Combine the ingredients; taste and sweeten if necessary.
2. Pour into individual ice-cube containers or popsicle forms and freeze until partly set. Insert sticks. Freeze solid. *Yield:* 10-12.

Ice Cream

Ice cream is one of our most popular desserts. More than one-third of the volume of commercial ice cream is comprised of solids, of which only 10% is fat. Emulsifiers and stabilizers give commercial ice cream its smoothness. The increase in volume over that of the solids used to make ice cream is known as "over-run." It occurs when the mixture is stirred in a churn-type freezer. A large over-run and a large amount of stabilizer are characteristic of less expensive ice creams.

Satisfactory ice cream desserts can be made in a home refrigerator-freezer. Follow these recipes carefully to avoid the formation of large crystals.

Flavour does not affect the taste buds as strongly when the temperature is at freezing; therefore relatively more flavouring is added to ice creams.

FRENCH ICE CREAM

	4 egg yolks
125 ml	sugar
350 ml	thin cream (10%)
5 ml	vanilla
250 ml	whipping cream

1. Prepare recipe for SOFT CUSTARD from the first four ingredients; chill.
2. Whip the cream until foamy but not stiff; fold into the chilled custard.
3. Freeze at as low temperature as can be obtained until firm (2 h).
4. Scrape into a chilled bowl; beat until fluffy without allowing the mixture to melt; pack into storage containers and return to the freezer.

Variations
Ripple Ice Cream—Stir through the ice cream when it has been beaten CHOCOLATE SYRUP, CARAMEL SYRUP, *or* FRUIT SYRUP. Do not overmix.
Peppermint Stick Ice Cream—Crush peppermint candies, 125 ml
and stir into the ice cream. The quantity will depend on the strength of the flavour in the candy and on one's personal taste.
Coffee Ice Cream—In the hot custard dissolve instant coffee, 15 ml
Chocolate Ice Cream—Reduce sugar to 50 ml
Add to the custard CHOCOLATE SYRUP, 50 ml
Fruit Ice Cream—Replace vanilla with lemon juice
Increase sugar to 150 ml
Add crushed peaches, apricots, *or* berries, 250 ml
If canned fruit is used, reduce sugar. A higher sugar content will lower the temperature at which the mixture will freeze.

Recipes, tables, etc. that appear in small capital letters, e.g., PARSLEY BUTTER, CANADA'S FOOD GUIDE, are listed in the index. Consult the index for the number of the page on which the item appears.

PEANUT BUTTER ICE MILK

This mixture qualifies as a nutritious, high-protein snack or dessert. Cut it into small squares for after-school snacks.

375 ml	milk *or* water
125 ml	skim milk powder
30 ml	flour
125 ml	sugar
	2 egg yolks
25 ml	sugar
125 ml	peanut butter
125 ml	milk
5 ml	vanilla
	2 egg whites

1. Heat larger amount of liquid to boiling. Combine milk powder, flour, and larger amount of sugar. Using a wire whisk, stir briskly while gradually adding dry ingredients to boiling liquid.
2. Cook with constant stirring over low medium heat for 5 min or cook over boiling water for 10 min
3. Beat egg yolks; stir in a little of the hot liquid and blend thoroughly. Stir egg mixture into remaining hot mixture and cook until thickened. Cool.
4. Beat egg whites until almost stiff. Sprinkle with sugar (second portion) and continue beating until mixture is stiff. Set aside.
5. In a small bowl beat peanut butter, the smaller amount of milk and vanilla using a rotary beater. Combine with cooled custard.
6. Fold in beaten egg whites and pour into a freezing tray. Freeze. Cut into squares or rectangles for dessert or snacks, or serve in parfait glasses as dessert. *Serves 6 as dessert or 18 as snacks.*

Variations
Before freezing the mixture, add GRANOLA or crunchy breakfast cereal, 250 ml

Desserts Made with Ice Cream

Refreeze these desserts after assembling them.

MARBLED ICE CREAM

Soften vanilla ice cream. Stir in frozen berries, mashed; or CHOCOLATE SAUCE with a few drops of mint flavouring; or thawed, frozen orange concentrate.

ICE CREAM MOULD

Using scoops of 2 or 3 different sherbets and ice creams, pack alternate colours into a small ring mould (see RING MOULDS). Unmould and fill centre with fresh fruit. *Serves 10-12.*

ICE CREAM SQUARES

Pat half the crumbs from a plain layer cake into an extra large square cake pan (see CAKE PANS); soften 2 bricks of butter pecan ice cream; press onto crumbs; cover with the remaining crumbs, pressing in well. Refreeze until very firm. *Serves 8-10.*

ICE CREAM BALLS

Scoop large balls of vanilla ice cream; coat with cake crumbs, toasted coconut, chopped nuts, or cereal flakes. Serve with sauce or syrup.

PEACH MELBA

Top vanilla ice cream in a dessert dish with a peach half, round-side up; pour on a thin layer of raspberry syrup.

PEAR HÉLÈNE

Press two halves of drained pears around vanilla ice cream in a dessert dish. Top with CHOCOLATE SAUCE. Garnish with nuts.

GLAMOUR LEMON SHERBET

Pile sherbet in dessert glasses; make a well in the centre; fill with frozen raspberries (thawed but still icy) or fresh pineapple shredded and sweetened.

PARFAIT

Into parfait glasses layer ice cream, WHIPPED CREAM FILLING, sherbet, fruit purée or conserve, with SYRUP or CHOCOLATE SAUCE. Avoid fruit in chunks. Cover each glass with foil and freeze.

ICE CREAM ROLL

Unroll a cooled JELLY ROLL; spread with raspberry jelly; cover with vanilla ice cream; roll; freeze. Serve slices topped with whipped cream or FRUIT SAUCE.

Variations
Chocolate Roll with PEPPERMINT STICK ICE CREAM and CHOCOLATE SAUCE.
Spice Roll with orange ice cream and peach WHIPPED CREAM FILLING.

ANGEL LAYERS

Divide an ANGEL, CHIFFON or POUND CAKE into three layers using a length of thread. Cover each layer with a different colour of slightly softened ice cream. Press together; refreeze. Frost with whipped cream; garnish with CHOCOLATE CURLS.

ANGEL SURPRISE

Cut a slice from the top of an angel cake; scoop out the cake leaving a shell on sides and bottom. Fill the hollow with ice cream; replace the top; freeze. Frost with thin BUTTER ICING or APRICOT GLAZE or WHIPPED CREAM FILLING.

DOUGHNUT DELIGHT

Split and toast baking powder DOUGHNUTS. Spread bottom halves with black currant jam; cover with a scoop of ice cream; add the top halves. Garnish with jam.

CHOCOLATE ICE CREAM PIE

Fill a chocolate CRUMB CRUST with COFFEE or PEPPERMINT STICK ICE CREAM; smooth the surface; refreeze. Garnish with whipped cream. Cut in wedges.

MERINGUE ICE CREAM PIE

Fill a MERINGUE SHELL with CHOCOLATE, MARBLED strawberry, or COFFEE ICE CREAM. Garnish and serve as Chocolate Ice Cream Pie.

Recipes, tables, etc. that appear in small capital letters, e.g., PARSLEY BUTTER, CANADA'S FOOD GUIDE, are listed in the index. Consult the index for the number of the page on which the item appears.

BAKED ALASKA

	1 round layer cake
500 ml	vanilla ice cream
500 ml	coloured ice cream
15 ml	fruit juice
	4 egg whites
1 ml	cream of tartar
1 ml	salt
125 ml	sugar

1. Choose a bowl which when inverted on the cake layer leaves a margin of cake; line the bowl with foil, pressing it smoothly into the bowl and having it extend beyond the edge.
2. Pack the vanilla ice cream into the bowl, pushing it up on the sides to leave a hollow in the centre; freeze; pack the coloured ice cream into the hollow, levelling it off on top; *freeze hard.*
3. Beat the egg whites, cream of tartar and salt until stiff but not dry in a deep bowl; add the sugar slowly, beating constantly to form a very stiff meringue. (Unless the meringue is standing up in stiff peaks and is sufficient to coat the cake and ice cream thickly, the ice cream will melt in the oven.)
4. Place the cake on a sheet of heavy white paper on a piece of corrugated paper on a cake rack or baking sheet; unmould the ice cream onto the cake; remove the foil; immediately frost the ice cream and the cake with the meringue. Freeze overnight if desired.
5. Preheat oven to 230°C
6. Sprinkle with slivered, blanched almonds or coconut; brown in oven 2-3 min. Serve at once. *Serves 8-10.*

The cake or ice cream may be spread with a thin layer of jam before it is coated with meringue.

Two bricks of ice cream may be placed side by side on a square of cake. Be sure there is a margin of cake.

Variation

Alaska Pie
1. Bake a pie crust in an oven-glass plate; cool.
2. Sprinkle with raspberries; fill with ice cream packed in firmly; sprinkle with more berries; freeze.
3. Prepare half the recipe of meringue; cover the ice cream, bringing the meringue out well to the edge of the crust; finish as Baked Alaska.

Basic Recipe
CHEESE CAKE

Crust

350 ml	graham wafer crumbs
30 ml	sugar
50 ml	melted butter

Filling

	4 eggs, separated
200 ml	sugar
250 ml	rich cream
1 ml	salt
	juice of 1 lemon
45 ml	flour
1 kg	cream cheese

1. Preheat oven to 160°C
2. Combine the crust ingredients; press most of the crumbs into the sides and bottom of a springform pan; (see CAKE PANS); chill.
3. Beat egg yolks and sugar until light and fluffy; gradually beat in the cheese; add cream, salt, and lemon juice alternately with the flour.
4. Fold in the beaten egg white.
5. Pour filling into the crumb-lined pan; sprinkle remaining crumbs on top.
6. Bake until set (45-60 min); turn off the heat; open oven door and leave the cake 1 h or until cool.
7. To serve, place the springform pan on a decorative plate; run the metal knife around the sides of the pan to loosen the cake; lift off the sides; add the topping. *Serves 10-12.*

For a smaller quantity to serve 5-6, prepare half the recipe, baking it in a deep pie plate.

Toppings for Cheese Cake
Cover chilled cake with one of the following; chill again before serving.

Sour cream topped with fresh ripe strawberries and brushed with either melted currant jelly or APRICOT GLAZE.
Yogurt, sweetened with honey and sprinkled with crushed almond roca, butter crunch candy or finely chopped pistachios, toasted filberts, or macadamia nuts.
Canned cherry or blueberry pie filling heated to spreading consistency and spooned over the cake.

Filling Variations

Refrigerated Cheese Cake

15 ml	1 envelope gelatine
125 ml	sugar
180 g	1 can frozen lemonade concentrate, thawed
350 ml	cream-style cottage cheese
540 ml	1 can fruit cocktail, drained
250 ml	whipping cream

1. Combine gelatine, sugar and lemon concentrate; heat gently until sugar and gelatine are dissolved; cool.
2. Beat cheese until smooth; stir in gelatine mixture; chill until partly set.
3. Fold in fruit and cream, whipped; spoon into crust; chill several hours. Garnish with sectioned oranges, berries or sliced peaches. *Serves 10-12.*

By substituting FRUIT CUP mixture for the canned fruit cocktail and whipped skim milk topping for the whipping cream, both sugar and fat can be reduced.

Yogurt Cheese Cake

	4 eggs, separated
150 ml	honey
200 ml	yogurt
500 ml	cottage cheese
227 g	cream cheese
1 ml	salt
	juice and rind of 1 lemon
50 ml	whole wheat flour

Preheat oven and prepare crumb-lined pan, as in steps 1 and 2 of basic recipe.

Beat egg yolks and honey until light; gradually beat in cheeses and yogurt; add salt and flour alternately with lemon juice. Fold in beaten egg white. Pour into a crumb-lined pan following the CHEESE CAKE basic recipe to finish.

Cottage cheese and yogurt replace the rich cream of the basic recipe and provide protein and calcium while maintaining a lower fat content.

INDIVIDUAL CHEESE CAKES

340 g	cream cheese
125 ml	sugar
	2 eggs
25 ml	lemon juice
10 ml	lemon *or* orange rind
	cherry pie filling
	vanilla wafers

1. Preheat oven to 150°C
2. Beat cheese with sugar until light; add eggs and beat until fluffy; beat in juice and rind.
3. Line small muffin tins with cup cake papers; in each place a vanilla wafer.
4. Fill two-thirds full of cheese mixture; bake until set (12-14 min).
5. Cool; cover each with a spoonful of cherry pie filling; return to the oven until pie filling has melted and spread; refrigerate 24 h before serving.
Yield: 32 cakes.

Basic Recipe
MERINGUES (MERINGUE SHELLS)

	4 egg whites
0.5 ml	salt
1 ml	cream of tartar
5 ml	vanilla
250 ml	sugar

1. Preheat oven to 200°C
2. Separate egg whites into a bowl; sprinkle with salt and cream of tartar; beat until foamy.
3. Add sugar and vanilla a small amount at a time, beating continuously.
4. Cover a baking sheet with lightly greased foil; spoon on the mixture making rounds with a hollow in the centre, or force the meringue through a large pastry tip.
5. Place the meringues in the oven, turn off the heat and leave without opening the door for at least two hours or overnight. If the oven is not well insulated, so that the temperature falls, bake the meringues 50-60 min at 120°C
Yield: 12 meringues, diameter 7 cm
40 meringues 2.5 cm

Store meringues in a tightly covered container.

To Use Meringues
Fill with ice cream; add a sauce or fresh or thawed frozen fruit, for an easy-to-make elegant dessert. Try COFFEE ICE CREAM, CHOCOLATE SAUCE; vanilla ice cream, sliced peaches, raspberry syrup; PEPPERMINT STICK ICE CREAM, hot fudge sauce; LEMON CUSTARD FILLING, blueberries.

MERINGUE TOWERS

Force uncooked meringue through a large rosette tip, swirling the meringue into cones in height about 5 cm
Bake and store until needed.

Push a peach half, rounded side down, into a spoonful of ice cream in a dessert glass. Set a Meringue Tower over the hollow of the peach; spoon crushed or thawed berries over the meringue leaving the peak uncovered as a garnish.

Dessert Fondue

The word *fondue* comes from the French, and means "melted." The name was given first to a dish of cheese melted in wine which originated in the French-speaking part of Switzerland.

While Chocolate Fondue is the most popular dessert fondue, the possibilities are limited only by one's imagination. Arrange cubes of POUND CAKE, FRUIT CAKE, or ANGEL CAKE, small marshmallows, banana cubes, stem-on pitted cherries, pineapple cubes drained and dried on paper, orange or tangerine sections, pieces of tenderized prunes or apricots.

Provide for each person a fondue fork for dipping, a fork for eating and a plate. Serve the fondue sauce in a fondue or chafing dish.

CHOCOLATE FONDUE SAUCE

227 g	1 pkg. cream cheese
125 ml	milk
150 ml	sugar
	2 squares unsweetened chocolate, chopped

Heat cheese and milk over low heat stirring until well blended; add sugar and chocolate. Stir constantly until mixture is smooth; pour into the fondue dish and keep warm.

EGGNOG FONDUE SAUCE

500 ml	dairy eggnog
15 ml	cornstarch
	nutmeg

1. Combine a little eggnog with the cornstarch to make a smooth paste.
2. Heat the remaining eggnog; stir in the cornstarch mixture and stir over low heat until the sauce thickens slightly and has no taste of raw starch. Pour into a heated fondue pot; add a sprinkle of nutmeg and the flavouring.

Tortes

These are desserts made from thin sheets of cake, pastry, or meringue layered with filling, usually cut in thin slices and served with whipping cream.

MOCHA BROWNIE TORTE

Make 1 recipe BROWNIES, bake in 2 round layers; put together with half the recipe for MOCHA BUTTER ICING; frost top and sides with the other half of the icing; garnish with CHOCOLATE CURLS.

ICELANDIC VINARTERTA

Make 1 recipe ROLLED COOKIE dough, shape into 6-8 large cookies and bake; spread PRUNE FILLING between the cookies, piling one on the next; cover the top and sides with BUTTER ICING; chill to set; decorate with geometric patterns of icing.

DOBOSCH TORTE

Make 1 recipe JELLY ROLL, cool, do not roll; spread CHOCOLATE BUTTER ICING with maple flavouring over the sheet of cake; cut in half lengthwise and in four crosswise; pile the eight pieces and press together; frost the sides; chill to set; cut in thin slices.

MERINGUE TORTE

Make 1 recipe MERINGUES shaped into two rounds on lightly greased brown paper on a baking sheet, with a piped rosette border around one; cool and remove paper. Place the plain circle on a serving plate; cover with sweetened puréed apricots or with apricot baby food (2 jars); place the decorated meringue on top. Fold 1 small jar of apricot baby food into whipped cream to frost sides and fill in top.

PEACH TORTE

Make 1 recipe GALETTE PASTRY rolled into 3 circles, pricked and baked; put together with FRUIT CREAM FILLING. Garnish with whipped cream and peach slices.

ALMOND TORTE

Make 1 QUICK-MIX GOLD CAKE; divide the batter between two layer cake pans; spread with MERINGUE made from 3 whites; sprinkle with cinnamon and slivered almonds. Bake. Put together meringue side up with whipped cream or other cake filling. Garnish with whipped cream and CHOCOLATE CURLS.

COOKIE STACKS

| 250 ml | WHIPPED CREAM FILLING |
| | 20 chocolate wafer cookies |

1. Use any whipped cream filling prepared for another dessert, or any CREAM PIE FILLING such as lemon, lime or cream. Spread the mixture on 1 cookie; place the next cookie on top, cover with filling and continue until you have a stack of 4 or 5. Do not cover the last cookie with filling. Coat each stack smoothly with whipped cream filling and sprinkle with finely chopped nuts or toasted coconut. Chill several hours.
2. Garnish the top with a little whipped cream and a bit of fruit. *Serves 4 or 5.*

Variations
Gingersnaps with LEMON PIE FILLING.

Vanilla wafers with COCOA WHIPPED CREAM.

17 Cake

There are times when we may prefer to make our own cakes in spite of the many mixes available; perhaps the ONE-EGG CAKE for economy, or the FRUIT CAKE which is part of our tradition. The recipes which follow contain the most nutritious and least expensive ingredients wherever possible.

There are three general types of cake:

Butter Cakes, which contain some form of fat, though not necessarily butter, are examples of drop batters.

Angel Cakes and Sponge Cakes contain no fat and are leavened by egg white, not baking powder.

Chiffon Cakes contain fat in the form of oil and baking powder, but are leavened largely by egg white.

Ingredients for Cakes

Fat should have good creaming quality; butter or margarine will give a good flavour to a plain cake; emulsified shortening is needed in a quick-mix type. To facilitate creaming, fat should be at room temperature.

Sugar—Fine sugar will dissolve more readily in the batter, thus preventing dark specks on the surface of the cake and a coarse texture.

Eggs, unless specified, are medium in size.

Liquid—If liquid milk is used in place of milk powder and water, use the quantity given for water.

Leavening Agents in butter and chiffon cakes are baking powder and/or a combination of baking soda and acid-containing ingredients (brown sugar, molasses, sour milk, raisins, cocoa). Double-acting baking powder is essential in cakes of the quick-mix type. *Other recipes, unless otherwise stated, call for regular baking powder.* Baking powder loses strength, so should be bought in small amounts and kept tightly covered.

Flour may be either pastry or all-purpose. Pastry flour gives a more tender product in the hands of an experienced cook.

Recipes, tables, etc. that appear in small capital letters, e.g., PARSLEY BUTTER, CANADA'S FOOD GUIDE, are listed in the index. Consult the index for the number of the page on which the item appears.

Methods for Making Cakes

Prepare pans for Butter Cakes by greasing lightly well into each corner; line the pan with a piece of wax paper long enough to go down one side, across and up the opposite side, narrow enough that it does not reach the corners. Do not grease pans for Angel Cakes, Sponge Cakes and Chiffon Cakes.

The batter should be deep enough to fill the pan at least halfway and no more than two-thirds of the way up the sides. Too little batter makes a cake that looks as though it hasn't risen; too much batter results in overflowing and a "fallen" cake. When filling a cake pan push the batter to the edges and corners of the pan so it is higher there than in the centre. As the cake cooks it rises higher in the centre, reaching the level of the corners.

The batter should be poured into the pan immediately the mixing is complete to avoid breaking the bubbles once they are formed; if the oven is not ready, leave the batter in the pan in a cool place. Move the pan carefully into the oven.

Place pans in the centre of the oven so that there is good circulation of hot air on all sides. The oven should not be opened from 5 min after the cake goes in until baking is almost complete.

A cake is cooked when its top is light brown, it has left the side of the pan, and it springs back when lightly pressed. Test for doneness by pricking the centre with a wooden pick or a metal skewer. No batter should stick to the toothpick or skewer. Do not move the cake until it is done.

If extra batter is being cooked in muffin pans or as cup cakes, it should be refrigerated, then placed in the oven when the large cake is cooked.

A fine, velvety texture results from thorough creaming of fat and sugar.

Larger volume may be obtained by separating the eggs and folding the beaten whites into the batter.

Beginners may find it helpful to combine the baking powder with a small amount of flour, sifting it over the batter with the last addition of flour.

Basic Recipe
BUTTER CAKE

This recipe gives the conventional method for mixing a Butter Cake. The high fat content gives the cake good keeping qualities.

150 ml	soft fat
5 ml	vanilla
250 ml	fine sugar
	2 eggs
50 ml	skim milk powder
450 ml	pastry flour
or	
400 ml	all-purpose flour
15 ml	baking powder
200 ml	water

1. Arrange oven racks so that centre of the cake will be centred in the oven. Prepare large square pan or 2 small layer pans (see CAKE PANS for sizes; see METHODS FOR MAKING CAKES for preparation method). Preheat oven to 180°C
2. Cream fat and sugar together until light and fluffy; add vanilla.
3. Add eggs one at a time, beating well after each addition until the mixture is very light.
4. Combine dry ingredients and sift.
5. Add dry ingredients alternately with liquid, about 1/3 the quantity at a time, beginning and ending with flour. After each addition stir to combine, then beat briefly. This is a drop batter and should not be stiff.
6. Pour the batter into the prepared pan.
7. Bake referring to the following cooking times. Remove and cook on a rack about 10 min; run a table knife around the pan to loosen cake, place rack on top of cake and invert; peel off the paper. Cool; reverse cake before frosting.

Cooking times: Square cake: 50 min
2 round layer cakes: 30 min

Variations

Orange Cake—Add with vanilla

30 ml	finely grated orange rind

Substitute 2 yolks for 1 egg.
Frost with orange butter icing (see FRUIT BUTTER ICING); sprinkle with grated orange rind.

Spice Cake—Add to the flour a mixture of:

5 ml	cinnamon
1 ml	cloves *or* allspice
1 ml	nutmeg *or* mace

Banana Cake

125 ml	shortening
5 ml	vanilla
250 ml	brown sugar
	2 eggs, well beaten
500 ml	pastry flour
or	
450 ml	all-purpose flour
15 ml	baking powder
2 ml	baking soda
250 ml	3 mashed ripe bananas
50 ml	milk
15 ml	orange juice and rind

Prepare as BUTTER CAKE (BASIC RECIPE), mashing bananas thoroughly and beating into butter-sugar mixture.

One-egg Cake—This is a less expensive cake ideal for COTTAGE PUDDING, UPSIDE-DOWN CAKE, and other cake desserts. Combine as BUTTER CAKE (BASIC RECIPE).

65	125 ml	soft fat
2	5 ml	vanilla
150	300 ml	sugar
		1 egg
40	75 ml	skim milk powder
225	550 ml	pastry flour
	or	
	500 ml	all-purpose flour
7	15 ml	baking powder
125	250 ml	water

Hot Water Gingerbread

125 ml	soft fat
5 ml	vanilla
125 ml	brown sugar
	2 eggs
150 ml	molasses
500 ml	all-purpose flour
10 ml	baking powder
5 ml	baking soda
5 ml	ginger
5 ml	cinnamon
2 ml	nutmeg *or* mace
250 ml	boiling water

Prepare as BUTTER CAKE (BASIC RECIPE) adding the molasses to the egg mixture.

CHOCOLATE CAKE

75 ml	shortening
400 ml	sugar
5 ml	vanilla
75 ml	hot water
125 ml	cocoa
	1 egg
250 ml	water
15 ml	vinegar
500 ml	all-purpose flour
75 ml	skim milk powder
5 ml	baking powder
5 ml	soda

1. Prepare large square pan (see CAKE PANS); preheat oven to 180°C
2. Cream sugar and shortening together; add vanilla.
3. Stir cocoa into hot water and add to mixture. Beat in egg.
4. Combine water and vinegar; combine and sift dry ingredients.
5. Add liquid ingredients and dry ingredients alternately to the shortening mixture.
6. Pour into prepared pan and bake 30-40 min

Skim milk powder, water and vinegar may be replaced with sour milk or buttermilk, 250 ml

OATMEAL CAKE

250 ml	quick-cooking rolled oats
250 ml	boiling water
75 ml	shortening
500 ml	brown sugar, lightly packed
	2 eggs
250 ml	whole wheat flour
10 ml	CAKE SPICE MIX
5 ml	baking powder
5 ml	baking soda
125 ml	chopped raisins *or* dates
50 ml	chopped walnuts

1. Prepare large square pan (see CAKE PANS); preheat oven to 180°C
2. Pour the boiling water over the rolled oats and let stand 20 min
3. Cream fat and sugar; beat in eggs one at a time; beating well after each addition.
4. Combine dry ingredients; chop the fruit and nuts; sprinkle a little of the flour mixture over them.
5. Stir the flour mixture into the sugar-egg mixture; add fruit, nuts and oatmeal; stir and beat to blend well; bake 50-60 min
6. Glaze while warm with FRUIT GLAZE, or when cool sift a thin coating of icing sugar over the top.

CARROT CAKE

Like GINGERBREAD and OATMEAL CAKE, Carrot Cake is equally good as a dessert. Top with APPLESAUCE, LEMON SAUCE, yogurt, or whipped cream.

375 ml	oil
500 ml	brown sugar
	4 eggs
500 ml	whole wheat and all-purpose flour
10 ml	baking powder
5 ml	baking soda
15 ml	spice*
2 ml	salt
750 ml	shredded carrots
250 ml	chopped walnuts and/or raisins

1. Prepare pan(s)†; preheat oven to 150°C
2. Combine oil and sugar; add the eggs one at a time beating well after each addition.
3. Mix and sift dry ingredients; combine carrots and nuts.
4. Add the two mixtures alternately to the egg mixture; stir to blend well; pour into prepared pan(s); bake 50-60 min

* Combine cinnamon, nutmeg or mace, and cloves; *or* use CAKE SPICE MIX. For a special flavour add to the carrot fresh ginger root, peeled and grated, 15 ml

† This recipe requires 1 Bundt pan or large tube pan, or 3 medium square pans, or 3 large loaf pans. (see CAKE PANS.)

BOSTON CREAM PIE

Using recipe for a BUTTER CAKE, ONE-EGG CAKE, or QUICK-MIX CAKE, bake two layers. When cool, split each cake, using toothpicks as guides and a saw-edged knife; remove the top layers; let stand 20 min. Spread each of the bottom layers with CREAM FILLING or LEMON CUSTARD. Replace the top layers; put the two cakes together with a layer of filling between. Cover the top with GLAZE or sift icing sugar through a paper lace doily to decorate.

Maple Leaf Mills.

UPSIDE-DOWN CAKE

For this cake, choose a pan of aluminum, stainless steel or Pyrex, large enough that the layer of cake batter will be shallow and the pan not more than half-full. An extra-large square cake pan (see CAKE PANS) or a large frying pan will do. Spoon extra batter into muffin pans and refrigerate to bake later.

25 50 ml	butter *or* margarine
00 150 ml	brown sugar
	fruit*
	cake batter (ONE-EGG, GINGERBREAD, or GOLD CAKE)

1. Melt fat in the pan; sprinkle sugar in evenly; arrange the fruit on the sugar. (Canned fruit must be well drained.)
2. Preheat oven to 180°C
3. Prepare the cake batter; pour over the fruit.
4. Bake 30-40 min; test; run a dinner knife around the edge, invert a serving plate over the pan and invert. Let stand a few minutes to allow the fruit to loosen; carefully lift off the pan.
5. Serve warm with whipped cream, CARAMEL SAUCE or LEMON SAUCE.

Corn syrup may be substituted for part of the sugar. The juice and rind of half a lemon may be added.

* Suggested Fruit Combinations:

Canned sliced pineapple rings, maraschino cherries; a sprinkle of cinnamon.

Cooked apricots, dry or canned, with cooked pitted prunes in a checkerboard.

Sliced peaches, cooked or raw in a pinwheel; a centre of chopped pecans, a sprinkle of lemon peel, shredded fresh ginger.

Cooked apples, quartered or sliced, and mincemeat.

Basic Recipe
QUICK-MIX BUTTER CAKE

This recipe is designed for the electric mixer. It is important to have the ingredients at room temperature.

500 ml	pastry flour
or	
450 ml	all-purpose flour
300 ml	sugar
15 ml	double-acting baking powder
100 ml	shortening
5 ml	vanilla
300 ml	milk
	1 large egg

1. Prepare large square pan (see CAKE PANS); preheat oven to 180°C
2. Mix and sift dry ingredients into a bowl; add shortening, vanilla and 2/3 of the liquid.
3. Mix with an electric mixer at medium speed for 2 min
4. Add the remaining liquid and the egg; continue beating for 2 more minutes, scraping the sides of the bowl down so that all the batter is well beaten. Do not underbeat. Bake 30-40 min

Variations
Quick-mix Gold Cake—This is a good way to use leftover egg yolks.

450 ml	pastry flour
or	
400 ml	all-purpose flour
250 ml	sugar
15 ml	double-acting baking powder
100 ml	shortening
5 ml	lemon flavouring
200 ml	milk
	3 egg yolks

Follow the method for the QUICK-MIX BUTTER CAKE basic recipe.

Recipes, tables, etc. that appear in small capital letters, e.g., PARSLEY BUTTER, CANADA'S FOOD GUIDE, are listed in the index. Consult the index for the number of the page on which the item appears.

NO-EGG CHOCOLATE CAKE

This cake may be eaten by those who are allergic to eggs or dairy products, or who are on a low-cholesterol diet.

350 ml	flour
250 ml	brown sugar
50 ml	cocoa
10 ml	baking powder
3 ml	baking soda
250 ml	warm water
15 ml	cider vinegar
5 ml	vanilla
100 ml	oil

1. Prepare a small square or small round pan (see CAKE PANS); preheat oven to 180°C
2. Combine dry ingredients; combine liquid ingredients; beat the liquid into the dry ingredients.
3. Bake 30-35 min

WHITE CAKE

A good cake for PETIT FOURS if baked in a jelly roll pan, this recipe needs only egg whites.

125 ml	shortening
2 ml	almond flavour
250 ml	sugar
350 ml	pastry flour
or	
300 ml	all-purpose flour
7 ml	baking powder
50 ml	skim milk powder
	3 egg whites
125 ml	water

1. Prepare medium tube or medium square pan (see CAKE PANS); preheat oven to 180°C
2. Cream the fat and half the sugar until light; add the flavouring.
3. Combine and sift dry ingredients.
4. Beat egg whites until stiff but not dry; beat in the remaining sugar.
5. Add the flour and water alternately to the fat-sugar mixture, folding in the egg white with the last addition.

Recipes, tables, etc. that appear in small capital letters, e.g., PARSLEY BUTTER, CANADA'S FOOD GUIDE, are listed in the index. Consult the index for the number of the page on which the item appears.

Angel, Sponge or Chiffon Cake served with bananas or berries and sauce and ice cream is a favourite dessert—though a rich one. General Foods.

ANGEL CAKE

250 ml	sifted pastry flour *or* cake flour
300 ml	fine sugar, sifted
250 ml	8-10 egg whites
1 ml	salt
5 ml	cream of tartar
5 ml	vanilla
2 ml	almond extract

1. Use an ungreased extra large tube pan (see CAKE PANS); preheat oven to 190°C
2. Mix flour and 1/3 of the sugar; sift.
3. Beat egg white (at room temperature) and salt until foamy; sift in the cream of tartar and continue beating until whites will stand up in peaks. Sprinkle the remaining sugar over the egg whites a little at a time; beating after each addition; beat in the flavouring.
4. Sift about one-quarter of the flour over egg mixture folding lightly; add remaining flour in three portions, folding lightly after each addition.
5. Turn mixture into pan; cut through batter with a knife; level it; bake until cake is firm to touch and lightly browned (35-40 min).
6. Invert cake pan over a funnel or other support. When cool, run a knife around the edge and ease out the cake. GLAZE if desired.

SPONGE CAKE

This is the true Sponge Cake in which egg is the only leavener. A tube pan is preferable to allow the heat to penetrate into the centre of the cake; the large amount of air folded into the batter acts as an insulator. If a tube pan is unavailable, a loaf pan is more successful than a square.

Pans for sponge, angel and chiffon cakes are not greased. As the batter rises it clings to the pan, attaining greater volume.

	4 eggs, separated
0.5 ml	salt
150 ml	fine sugar
15 ml	lemon juice
	grated rind of ½ lemon
200 ml	sifted cake flour *or* pastry flour

1. Use a medium tube or large loaf pan, ungreased (see CAKE PANS); preheat oven to 180°C
2. Beat egg whites with salt until foamy; gradually beat in half the sugar, beating until a stiff meringue is formed.
3. Beat yolks with remaining sugar, beating until foamy and lemon-coloured.
4. Add lemon juice and rind to yolk mixture and fold all into egg-white mixture.
5. Sift in about one-quarter of the flour; fold in; add remaining flour in three portions, folding each gently to combine.
6. Spoon into pan; cut through the batter gently to break any large air bubbles.
7. Bake about 40 min until cake springs back when pressed lightly.
8. Invert over a funnel or other support until cool; loosen the cake and ease out.

ORANGE CHIFFON CAKE

This cake combines features of both Butter and Sponge cakes.

250 ml	7 or 8 egg whites
1 ml	cream of tartar
550 ml	sifted pastry flour *or* cake flour
350 ml	sugar
15 ml	baking powder
5 ml	salt
125 ml	oil
	5 unbeaten egg yolks
200 ml	juice and grated rind of 2 oranges and water to make

1. Use extra large tube or large springform pan, ungreased (see CAKE PANS); preheat oven to 165°C
2. In a large bowl beat egg whites and cream of tartar until *very* stiff.
3. Sift together the flour, sugar, baking powder and salt into a mixing bowl.
4. Make a "well" in the dry ingredients, and add oil, egg yolks, orange juice and rind in that order.
5. Beat with a wooden spoon until perfectly smooth.
6. Pour egg yolk mixture gradually over entire surface of beaten egg whites and gently fold until just blended; bake 60 min
7. Invert over a funnel or other support to cool; loosen and ease out the cake.

POUND CAKE

The traditional flavour of this cake is that of butter; if margarine is used, extra flavourings should be added.

250 ml	butter *or* margarine
5 ml	mace
5 ml	vanilla
1 ml	lemon rind
400 ml	sugar
	5 eggs
500 ml	pastry flour *or* cake flour

1. Grease and flour 2 small loaf pans or a Bundt pan or extra large tube pan (see CAKE PANS); preheat oven to 150°C
2. Beat the butter and flavouring until very light (4 min).
3. Add sugar slowly, beating constantly until fluffy (3 min).
4. Add four of the eggs, one at a time, beating after each addition (1 min).
5. Sift in the flour, adding a quarter of the amount at a time, stirring and beating after each addition; beat in remaining egg.
6. Bake 30 min; increase heat to 180°C
   Continue to bake until firm, 25 min for loaf pans, 45 min for Bundt or tube pan.

BUNDT CAKE

Bake BUTTER CAKE, POUND CAKE, or CARROT CAKE in a Bundt Pan. Glaze if desired (see GLAZE).

Basic Recipe
JELLY ROLL

	4 large eggs, separated
1 ml	salt
200 ml	fine sugar
2 ml	lemon flavouring
200 ml	sifted pastry flour *or* cake flour
4 ml	baking powder
	icing sugar

1. Grease and line jelly roll pan (see CAKE PANS); preheat oven to 200°C
2. Beat egg whites and salt until foamy; beat in one-quarter of the sugar gradually, beating well after each addition; continue to beat until stiff peaks form.
3. Beat yolks until thick and lemon-coloured with remaining sugar; add flavouring; fold into beaten whites.
4. Mix flour and baking powder and sift over the egg mixture in three portions, folding gently to combine after each addition.
5. Turn into the prepared pan (see METHODS FOR MAKING CAKES) and bake 10-12 min, until the top springs back when pressed.
6. Turn onto a tea towel liberally dusted with icing sugar; remove paper; with a sharp knife trim off any crusty edges; roll cake from the short side (see illustration); cool on a rack.
7. Unroll; fill with LEMON BUTTER, WHIPPED CREAM FILLING, FRUIT CREAM FILLING, or ice cream; reroll and let stand, seam edge down.
8. Glaze (see GLAZE) or sift icing sugar over roll.

Variations
Spice Roll—To the flour add CAKE SPICE MIX; substitute brown sugar for white.
Chocolate Roll—Substitute vanilla for lemon flavouring and replace half the flour with cocoa.

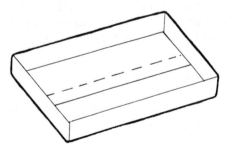

Grease the pan and line bottom with two overlapping strips of waxed paper, lightly greased.

Spread the batter evenly in the pan.

After baking, turn out onto sugared towel and peel off the paper.

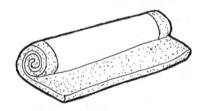

After trimming off edges with a long sharp knife, roll towel and cake loosely together; cool on a cake rack.

Unroll, spread with filling, and roll again, using the towel as an aid.
Photos: Maple Leaf Mills.

PETIT FOURS FOR 100

	3 cake recipes: POUND, WHITE, GOLD, SPONGE, or CHIFFON CAKE
1 kg each	2 pkg. icing sugar
30 ml each	3 jellies of different colours
5 ml	lemon juice
	decorations
	(see DECORATED CAKE)

I Prepare the cakes:

1. Preheat oven to 180°C
2. Bake each cake in a greased and lined jelly roll pan; cool.
3. Turn out; remove the paper; cut into strips; width: 3 cm
4. Arrange in widely spaced rows on cake racks.

II Prepare jelly glaze:

For a variety of colours, use grape or black currant jelly for one cake, red currant or raspberry for one and for the third, apple jelly with a little yellow colour, or mint jelly.

1. Melt jelly over hot water; stir in icing sugar to a *thin* pouring consistency. (Thin if necessary with a few drops of hot water). Makes approximately 500 ml
2. Pour quickly and evenly over the cake allowing the icing to coat the surface.

III Prepare Petit Four Glaze:

100 ml	hot milk
2 *l*	icing sugar
5 ml	lemon juice

1. Sift the icing sugar into the hot milk to a pouring consistency; add lemon juice.
2. Pour the glaze over the cakes moving evenly along the rows. Thin if necessary over hot water.

IV Decorate:

Before the glaze is firmly set, add decorations. See DECORATED CAKE.

CUP CAKES

Cup cakes may be made from the BUTTER CAKE, SPONGE CAKE, or CHIFFON CAKE batters.

1. For well-shaped cup cakes, grease and flour only the bottoms of the muffin pans to keep the batter from running over the pans; have the batter slightly thicker than for cake.
2. Paper liners in ungreased muffin pans save dishwashing. Peel off when the cakes are cool.
3. Never fill the cups more than half full.
4. When many cup cakes are being made, fit one paper inside another and space well apart on a baking sheet.

The BUTTER CAKE (BASIC RECIPE) will fill 24 medium paper cups or 50 small paper cups.

Lemon Cup Cakes—With a paring knife remove a cone from the top centre of the cake; fill the hollow with LEMON FILLING. Replace the cone, pressing gently so the filling comes out around the edge. Sift icing sugar thinly over the surface.

Butterfly Cup Cakes—With a paring knife, remove a cone from the top centre of the cake. Fill hollow with whipped cream or SNOWY LEMON FROSTING. Cut cake cone in half; press into filling to look like butterfly wings.

Jelly-cream Cup Cakes—Spread cup cake with whipped cream; dot centre top with a dollop of red jelly. Or spread top of cup cake with jelly; then spread sides with whipped cream or SEVEN-MINUTE FROSTING. Or spread cup cake with jelly; then coat sides with shredded coconut; let stand a few minutes.

Lacy Cocoa Cup Cakes—Cut small cardboard pattern of star, tree, etc. Place on top of cup cake; sift chocolate-milk powder over top; carefully lift off pattern.

Shamrock Cup Cakes—Snip green gumdrops to form petals and stem of shamrock. Place on top of frosted cup cake.

Coconut Cup Cakes—Make BOILED FROSTING. Frost top and sides of cakes; then sprinkle generously with flaked coconut. Tint pink for Valentine Cup Cakes.

Clown Cup Cakes—Frost top of cup cake with coloured BUTTER ICING. Make eyes, nose and mouth from snipped candied cherries. Turn cup cake on side; add colourful hat made of a conical paper cup.

Recipes, tables, etc. that appear in small capital letters, e.g., PARSLEY BUTTER, CANADA'S FOOD GUIDE, are listed in the index. Consult the index for the number of the page on which the item appears.

Fruit Cakes

DARK FRUIT CAKE

500 g	seedless raisins
500 g	seeded raisins
1 kg	currants
500 g	mixed peel, chopped
250 g	glazed red and green cherries
750 g	dates, chopped
250 g	blanched almonds, walnuts,
	or pecans
700 ml	all-purpose flour
500 ml	butter
500 ml	sugar
	8 eggs
2 ml	baking soda
	½ lemon, juice and rind
125 ml	grape or pineapple juice
10 ml	cinnamon
10 ml	cloves
10 ml	nutmeg

Spices may be varied according to taste.

Quantities of fruits and nuts need not be precise but the total quantity should not be less. Purchase the units nearest the specified amount. Currants may be replaced by raisins; dates by citron peel and cherries.

To this recipe may be added any or all of the following:

125 ml	molasses
30 g	melted chocolate
125 ml	apple *or* grape jelly
60 g	glazed pineapple

1. Prepare fruit by washing seedless raisins and currants in several waters; dry thoroughly on paper in a warm place; cut cherries in half; split almonds but leave other nuts whole.
2. Mix fruit, nuts and peel with enough of the flour so that each piece is separate and coated with flour.
3. Prepare the pans. Set them on a sheet of corrugated paper on a baking sheet; check to see that they will fit into the oven without touching. Line with three thicknesses of newspaper or heavy brown paper and a top layer of aluminum foil.
4. Preheat oven to 140°C
5. Cream butter, add sugar gradually, beating after each addition. This requires a very large mixing bowl; a plastic dish pan is a good size.
6. Beat eggs well and add to butter mixture. The mixture will appear curdled.
7. Sift remaining flour with spices and soda; add alternately with fruit juice to the butter mixture.
8. Stir in fruit and mix until all ingredients are thoroughly blended; fill prepared cake pans ¾ full. This cake rises very little during baking.
9. Place pans in oven, not touching. See baking times below. The cake is cooked if when pressed firmly the finger does not leave an impression and the cake no longer "sings."
10. Cool cake thoroughly on a rack, wrap in foil and store in a cool place for at least a month. Do not stack.
11. Glaze or frost a few days before using.

Yield: Cooked cake 4.5-5 kg

Baking Times

	h	Cooked Cake
Medium square pan	3-4	3 kg
Bundt or extra large tube pan	5-6	3.5 kg

LIGHT FRUIT CAKE 1

500 g	golden seeded raisins
120-150 g	citron peel
300 g	orange and lemon peel *or* mixed peel
250 g	glazed pineapple
250 g	glazed red and green cherries
250 ml	desiccated coconut
125-250 g	blanched, split almonds
700 ml	all-purpose flour
5 ml	baking powder
2 ml	mace or nutmeg
250 ml	butter
250 ml	sugar
	3 eggs
125 ml	warm water
5 ml	almond extract

Prepare as DARK FRUIT CAKE.
Yield: 2.5 ℓ

Cheese Tea Biscuits. Swirls are made using biscuit dough and rolling it out as for a jelly roll. Sprinkle with grated cheese, roll up pressing the edge tightly, slice and bake.

A raisin and nut loaf.

Strawberries in a meringue ring.

Trifle may be made using soft custard and sliced jelly roll.

A light fruit cake. Robin Hood Flour Mills.

LIGHT FRUIT CAKE 2

More cake but less fruit.

1 kg	golden seeded raisins
500 g	red and green glazed cherries
250 g	red and green glazed pineapple
500 g	almonds, blanched
5 ml	lemon *or* almond extract
1.25 *l*	all-purpose flour
5 ml	baking powder
2 ml	nutmeg
	1 orange (juice and rind)
500 g	butter and shortening
500 ml	sugar
	10 eggs

Prepare as DARK FRUIT CAKE.
Yield: 5 *l*

BRAZIL NUT CAKE

750 ml	whole brazil nuts
250 ml	glazed red cherries
250 ml	glazed green cherries
360 g	dates
	3 eggs
200 ml	all-purpose flour
200 ml	sugar
2 ml	baking powder
5 ml	vanilla

1. Line a large loaf pan (see CAKE PANS) with greased brown paper; preheat oven to 150°C
2. Combine nuts and fruit, uncut. Add the well-beaten eggs.
3. Mix and sift dry ingredients; combine the two mixtures. Add vanilla.
4. Bake 2 h. Have a pan of water in the oven on the rack below the cake.
5. Cool, wrap in foil; do not cut for several weeks.

FRUIT CAKE GLAZE

Used to hold candied fruits in place on top of a fruit cake.

250 ml	sugar
125 ml	water
125 ml	corn syrup

1. Mix and cook ingredients in a saucepan until mixture forms a soft ball when a little is dropped into cold water.
2. Cool slightly; spread on cake when it comes out of the oven.
3. While moist, arrange garnish of candied fruits and nuts; brush with the glaze.

FROSTING FOR FRUIT CAKE

Brush the cake with egg white beaten with a little water and allow to dry to prevent the icing from being darkened by the cake.

Use ORNAMENTAL FROSTING, or for a softer frosting which will cut easily use a rich BUTTER ICING.

If almond paste is to be used, roll it to the desired thickness on a board sprinkled with icing sugar; fit to the surface of the cake; allow to dry slightly before frosting.

LEFTOVER CAKE

Cake or cake crumbs may be used in many easy recipes.

Angel Dessert—Combine broken pieces of CHOCOLATE or ANGEL FOOD CAKE with marshmallow pieces, cubes of pineapple, chopped nuts, maraschino cherries and whipped cream. Chill for 1 h
See also TRIFLE.

Cake Pudding—Heat squares of cake in a double boiler or wrapped in foil in the oven. Serve white cake with coffee ice cream or hot LEMON SAUCE; gingerbread with LEMON SAUCE or APPLESAUCE; spread chocolate slices with cream cheese, spoon over them canned cherry pie filling.

Chocolate Tidbits—Press fruit cake crumbs into small balls; dip in CHOCOLATE or VANILLA GLAZE; roll in finely chopped nuts.

Chocolate Fondue—Arrange cubes of cake, marshmallows, fresh or canned fruit. Guests spear the food with fondue forks and dip into hot CHOCOLATE SAUCE. Twice the recipe serves 6.

Banana Sandwich—Place whipped cream or ice cream and sliced bananas between 2 cake slices; top with butterscotch sauce.

Tea Toasties—Spread cake slices with butter or margarine; sprinkle with CINNAMON SUGAR; broil till bubbly and brown.

French Toast Dessert—Dip cake slices in FRENCH TOAST mixture; sauté in butter or margarine; serve with jelly, maple syrup, or sprinkling of icing sugar.

English Crumb Mould—Grease a casserole; fill with alternate layers of cake crumbs and applesauce or stewed fruit. Press down; chill. Unmould. Serve with hot LEMON SAUCE.

Frozen Cake Balls—Roll balls of ice cream in cake crumbs. Top with chocolate, butterscotch, or FRUIT SAUCE.

Freezing Cakes

Butter Cake batter may be frozen, although a better product results when the cake is first baked then cooled and frozen. Unbaked batter should not be kept more than one week. Thaw 1.5 h at room temperature; pour into the pan and bake.

Frozen baked cake will dry out quickly after thawing, so should be wrapped and frozen in an amount suitable for one meal. Wrap as soon as cool; freeze; protect in a heavy carton or metal container. Unfrosted cake will keep 2 to 3 months; frosted 1 to 2 months.

Angel Cake is tenderized by freezing but may show a little shrinkage. Fruit cake shows less tendency to crumble after freezing.

Use butter or fudge-type icings on cake that is to be frozen; egg-white icings do not freeze well. Uncooked frostings not only freeze more successfully but are easier to handle than cooked frostings. Frost the cake, freeze it unwrapped until firm (2-3 h), then wrap, refreeze and protect. Fillings do not freeze successfully.

Defrost cake in the wrapper at room temperature (about 3 h for a large cake, 1 h for layer cake, 30 min for cup cakes, 20 min for an individual portion).

Freezing Fruit Cake
Christmas cake may be frozen after the ripening period. To make it easy to remove a few slices for quick defrosting, slice part of the cake and reassemble with wax paper between the slices before wrapping and freezing. Wrap tightly in heavy foil, place in a covered container, filling unused spaces with crumpled paper to exclude air.

Fillings for Cakes

These fillings are for layer cakes, jelly rolls, cream puffs, tortes, or coffee cakes. See also CREAM PIE FILLING and LEMON PIE FILLING. Spread generously on cooled cake layer and allow filling to become firm before icing. Cakes baked in deep pans may be split into layers and spread with filling.

LEMON BUTTER

This is a traditional English recipe, also called Lemon Cheese and Lemon Curd. It is a delicious filling for small tarts, layer cake, or cream puffs; it keeps well if refrigerated. Fold MAYONNAISE into it for fruit salad dressing; spread dressing on lengthwise sliced bananas and sprinkle with nuts, for a fruit salad.

	5 egg yolks
125 ml	sugar
	grated rind and juice of 2 large lemons
50 ml	butter *or* margarine

1. In the top of a double boiler combine egg yolks, sugar and lemon; stir over boiling water adding the butter a little at a time; stir until thick and of a creamy consistency. Taste to be sure the egg is cooked.
2. Pour into a sterilized jar; cover with a circle of wax paper and a lid; refrigerate. *Yield:* 375 ml

Bottled lemon juice is less expensive than fresh but will not give the same fresh flavour.

SPICED FRUIT FILLING

340 g	1 pkg. dried fruit mix
250 ml	cranberry juice
250 ml	water
250 ml	sugar
2 ml	cinnamon and allspice
50 ml	walnuts, chopped

1. Combine fruit and liquid; simmer until tender (30 min).
2. Strain off the liquid, reserving it; chop fruit; combine all ingredients except nuts; stir over low heat until thick; add nuts. *Yield:* 500 ml

PRUNE FILLING

340 g	1 pkg. prunes
250 ml	water
50 ml	sugar
2 ml	cardamom seeds, crushed

1. Add water to the prunes; let stand to soften; add cardamom; simmer until very tender (10-12 min).
2. Drain off and reserve the liquid; pit and purée the prunes.
3. Add liquid, sugar; stir over low heat until sugar is dissolved and mixture is thick. *Yield:* 400 ml

DATE FILLING

This filling keeps well in the refrigerator and may be used between cookies or as a sandwich filling as well as between cake layers.

250 ml	pitted dates, chopped finely
125 ml	water
50 ml	sugar
5 ml	lemon juice

Cut dates into small pieces. Add water; cook over low heat about 10 min until mixture is quite thick, stirring often to prevent scorching; add sugar; cool. Add flavouring.

Variations
Use grated rind and juice of 1 orange to replace an equal amount of the water; add the juice to the cooked fruit.

Add chopped walnuts to the cooked mixture.

CREAM FILLING FOR CAKE

Prepare one-half the CREAM PIE FILLING recipe using one egg. Fold into the cooled filling any combinations of the following: whipped cream; chopped nuts (walnuts, pecans, toasted almonds); fruit (finely cut dates, well-drained crushed pineapple, or chopped cherries).

Recipes, tables, etc. that appear in small capital letters, e.g., PARSLEY BUTTER, CANADA'S FOOD GUIDE, are listed in the index. Consult the index for the number of the page on which the item appears.

LEMON CUSTARD FILLING

Use this filling for BOSTON CREAM PIE and ANGEL DESSERT. This recipe will fill and top one layer cake or angel cake.

15 ml	1 envelope gelatine
50 ml	cold water
	6 eggs, separated
200 ml	3 large lemons, juice and rind
250 ml	sugar

1. Sprinkle gelatine into cold water to soften (about 5 min).
2. Beat egg yolks, lemon juice and rind and half the sugar; stir over hot water until mixture coats a metal spoon; remove from heat; add gelatine and stir until dissolved; cool.
3. When custard mixture is syrupy (partially set), in a separate bowl beat the whites until stiff but not dry; beat in remaining sugar a little at a time. Beat into custard mixture.
4. Use filling before it is completely set.

Basic Recipe
FRUIT CREAM FILLING

10 ml	½ envelope gelatine
125 ml	cold water
250 ml	undrained, crushed canned pineapple
30 ml	undiluted frozen orange juice
or	
15 ml	lemon juice
250 ml	whipping cream

1. Sprinkle gelatine into cold water; dissolve over low heat; stir into fruit; add juice; chill until mixture begins to set.
2. Whip the cream; fold in; chill until almost set before using.

Use to fill JELLYROLL, tiny MERINGUES, CREAM PUFFS, or ANGEL CAKE.

Variations
Peppermint Cream Filling—Soften crushed peppermint stick candy in hot milk, 125 ml
Cool; use to replace pineapple and orange juice.
Apricot Cream Filling—Substitute sweetened apricot purée for pineapple.
Strawberry Cream Filling—Substitute thawed and drained frozen berries or sliced sweetened fresh berries for the pineapple.

MARSHMALLOW FILLING

200 ml	sugar
50 ml	water
50 ml	light corn syrup
	16 marshmallows, quartered
	2 egg whites, stiffly beaten

1. Cook sugar, water and corn syrup together in a saucepan until it spins a long thread when dropped from a spoon.
2. Remove from heat immediately; drop in marshmallows; press them into the syrup but do not stir.
3. Pour gradually over stiffly beaten egg whites, beating constantly until cool.

Filling will keep several weeks in a covered jar in the refrigerator. Thin if necessary with a few drops of hot water.

WHIPPED CREAM

250 ml	whipping cream
15-50 ml	icing sugar
1 ml	vanilla

Whip cream until fluffy; slowly beat in sugar and flavouring. Beat only until cream is stiff. (Beating after this point will cause the cream to separate.)

Variations

Cocoa Whipped Cream—Add cocoa, 50 ml
Combine all ingredients; refrigerate several hours; beat until thick.
Chocolate Fleck Whipped Cream—Melt semi-sweet chocolate over hot water; cool to room temperature so that it will fleck as it is folded into whipped cream.
Ginger Cream—Add drained preserved ginger, shredded, 15 ml
Angel Whipped Cream—Add quartered marshmallows, blanched toasted almonds, drained chopped maraschino cherries.

Layer any of these mixtures with ice cream in parfait glasses; top with chocolate syrup or maple syrup; cover and freeze until serving time.

To use as decoration, squeeze through a pastry tube onto waxed paper on a baking sheet, making rosettes. Freeze uncovered; store in a plastic bag.

Frostings, Icings and Glazes

The frosting is the crowning glory for a cake—and a new frosting can give a new look to the family's favourite cake. Always consider the length of time the cake must stand before serving when choosing the type of frosting to be used.

Icing sugar alone can be used to decorate a baked cake—especially sponge cakes. For a dainty design, place a paper doily on cake and sift icing sugar over it lightly. Remove doily carefully and its pattern will be traced on the cake.

Basic Recipe
BUTTER ICING

50-75 ml	butter *or* margarine
500 ml	icing sugar
50 ml	milk
	flavouring*

* Use vanilla or almond with fruit, maple with chocolate.
1. Cream the butter with flavouring; beat in an equal amount of sugar and half the liquid.
2. Add remaining sugar and liquid alternately, to make it thick enough to spread.
3. Add flavouring or colouring; beat well.
4. Cover with a damp tea towel if not to be used immediately. *Yield:* enough to cover top and sides of a square cake. For a layer cake, use twice the recipe.

Variations

For a less sweet icing, substitute fruit juice for milk; replace one-third of the sugar with skim milk powder, blending it with the fruit juice.
Fruit Butter Icing—Replace milk with thawed frozen orange concentrate, fresh orange, lemon or lime juice, drained, crushed pineapple; mashed fresh or frozen raspberries, strawberries, or peaches; mashed banana.
Coffee Butter Icing—Add instant coffee, 5 ml
Chocolate Butter Icing—Sift with the icing sugar cocoa, 50 ml

Mocha Icing—A combination of Coffee and Chocolate Icing, but use only ½ the amount of cocoa.
Peanut Butter Icing—Replace one-third of the butter with peanut butter.

Basic Recipe
BROILED FROSTING (PRALINE GLAZE)

50 ml	softened butter *or* margarine
125 ml	brown sugar
50 ml	sour cream *or* rich milk
50 ml	chopped nuts
200 ml	coconut

1. Cream butter, add sugar and cream. Spread over top of baked cake.
2. Sprinkle coconut and nuts over the cake.
3. Broil 3-5 min. Watch carefully to prevent burning.

Variations
Lemon Coconut Frosting—Omit nuts and add lemon rind, 5 ml
Honey Coconut Frosting—Replace cream and nuts by honey, 75 ml
Peanut Frosting—Use chopped salted peanuts; replace coconut with peanut butter, 50 ml
Marshmallow Frosting—Replace coconut with miniature marshmallows.
Orange Marshmallow Frosting—Cover the warm cake with orange marmalade; arrange miniature marshmallows on top; broil until they begin to soften and brown.
Marble Frosting—Cover the surface with chocolate peppermints; as they melt spread with swirling motions; cool.

Broiled Apricot Frosting

250 ml	apricot jam
15 ml	lemon juice
250 ml	coconut
250 ml	miniature marshmallows

Combine the ingredients; spread evenly on hot cake; broil until golden brown; cool.

Recipes, tables, etc. that appear in small capital letters, e.g., PARSLEY BUTTER, CANADA'S FOOD GUIDE, are listed in the index. Consult the index for the number of the page on which the item appears.

Basic Recipe
SEVEN-MINUTE FROSTING

This is a stiff, glossy cake frosting made by cooking egg white and sugar while beating constantly until it forms stiff peaks. By hand, this beating takes about 7 min, hence its name. Using an electric beater cuts down on both time and effort. The presence of corn syrup, brown sugar, or acid (lemon juice or cream of tartar) is necessary to prevent the formation of large crystals, which results in sugary icing. Cakes iced with Seven-Minute Frosting should be used on the day on which they are iced, as the icing becomes dry and sugary on standing.

375 ml	sugar
	2 egg whites
30 ml	corn syrup
or	
1 ml	cream of tartar
125 ml	cold water
	flavouring (vanilla, almond, peppermint, etc.)

1. Combine all together in top of double boiler; let stand until sugar is partly dissolved. Beat with a rotary beater until well mixed.
2. Place over boiling water and beat until mixture forms peaks which hold their shape (4-7 min). Stir from bottom and sides with a rubber spatula.
3. Remove from heat; set the top of the double boiler in cool water, and continue to beat until the icing is cool enough to spread.
4. Spread quickly with as few strokes as possible. This amount will cover sides and top of a layer cake, or 24 small cupcakes; ½ the recipe will frost the top only.

Variations
Snowy Lemon Frosting—Replace corn syrup with lemon juice, 50 ml
Garnish with grated rind.
Mountain Frosting (Sea Foam)—Replace white sugar with brown; reduce corn syrup by one-half.
Candy Cane Frosting—To the finished frosting add crushed candy cane; garnish with a few larger pieces.
Coconut Frosting—Tint icing delicate pink or green, sprinkle flaked coconut over the frosting while soft, or leave icing white and tint coconut.

Basic Recipe
BOILED FROSTING

This fluffy white frosting is similar to SEVEN-MINUTE FROSTING but has much better keeping quality. It is worth a little practice to make it with confidence.

250 ml	white sugar
1 ml	cream of tartar
or	
15 ml	corn syrup
100 ml	boiling water
	1 egg white
	flavouring

1. Stir sugar, cream of tartar or syrup, and water in a medium saucepan over low heat until sugar is dissolved; cover briefly to allow steam to wash down any crystals.
2. Boil gently without stirring until syrup forms a long thread (see COLD WATER TEST FOR SYRUP).
3. When the syrup is almost ready, beat egg white until foamy; pour in syrup in a pencil-like stream, beating with an egg beater until the mixture begins to thicken; continue to beat with a wooden spoon until cool and of spreading consistency. A few drops of boiling water may be added if the icing is too stiff.

Yield: This recipe will frost the top of one cake; twice the quantity makes filling and frosting for a layer cake, or frosting for the top and sides of a square, or frosting for 50 small cup cakes.

Variations
Chocolate Ripple—Melt 2 squares of unsweetened chocolate with butter, 5 ml
Using a spoon, drip the chocolate around top edge of cake and let chocolate run down sides. Or swirl chocolate over the frosting with a broad spatula.
Marshmallow—Make Boiled Frosting; cut 8 marshmallows in pieces; add to syrup just before beating it into white of egg.
Pineapple—Replace water with pineapple juice. Fold into the cooked icing well drained, crushed pineapple, cherries, coconut and almonds.
Lady Baltimore—Use rum flavouring; add chopped pecans, raisins and figs to the finished icing.

Recipes, tables, etc. that appear in small capital letters, e.g., PARSLEY BUTTER, CANADA'S FOOD GUIDE, are listed in the index. Consult the index for the number of the page on which the item appears.

ORNAMENTAL FROSTING

This is the traditional wedding cake icing. It keeps well and holds its shape, but becomes very hard.

	3 egg whites
500 g	icing sugar
15 ml	lemon juice

1. Put unbeaten whites into a large bowl; sift in icing sugar; beat vigorously with a wooden spoon.
2. Add lemon juice; beat until stiff; test by cutting through the icing with a knife; if stiff enough, it will hold its shape. More liquid may be required.

Turn one half upside down and match long edges. Frost and decorate.
Photos: Maple Leaf Mills.

CHOCOLATE FUDGE FROSTING

500 ml	sugar
250 ml	water
	2 squares unsweetened chocolate
30 ml	corn syrup
30 ml	butter *or* margarine
5 ml	vanilla

1. Stir sugar, water, chocolate, corn syrup over low heat until sugar dissolves; boil slowly to soft ball stage. (see COLD WATER TEST FOR SYRUP).
2. Remove from heat; add butter and cool to lukewarm.
3. Add vanilla and beat until icing is of spreading consistency. If icing becomes too stiff, add a little boiling water.

Yield: This recipe will fill and frost 1 layer cake or frost top and sides of 1 square.

CARAMEL FUDGE ICING

375 ml	brown sugar
125 ml	milk
45 ml	butter *or* margarine
2 ml	vanilla

Combine sugar and milk; stir over low heat until sugar dissolves; finish as Chocolate Fudge Frosting.

Glazes

Glaze, a thin, sweet, often transparent coating, gives a finish to cakes, doughnuts, CREAM PUFFS, FRUIT TARTS, without being too sweet. See also CHOCOLATE GLAZE and CARAMEL GLAZE for CREAM PUFFS.

VANILLA GLAZE

10 ml	milk
10 ml	butter *or* margarine
125 ml	icing sugar
1 ml	vanilla

1. Heat milk and butter in a bowl over hot water; sift the sugar; add to the liquid stirring to a creamy consistency; add vanilla.

2. Spread over the top of the cake allowing the glaze to drip down the side of but not off the cake. (Glaze that is too thin will soak into the cake or run off. To thicken, cool or add a little more icing sugar.)

Yield: This recipe will glaze a large cake.

Variation
Fruit Glaze—Substitute for the milk, fruit juice: orange, lemon, pineapple or cherry juice or a combination; add grated rind, marmalade, jelly, or finely chopped fruit, 25 ml

LEMON GLAZE

This glaze is especially good on loaf cakes and fruit breads.

	juice and rind of 1 lemon
125 ml	sugar

Combine lemon and sugar; spread on the cake. The cake may be returned to the oven for 10-15 min or placed under broiler until bubbly. Holes poked with a wooden toothpick will increase the absorption of the glaze by the cake, doughnuts, etc.

APRICOT GLAZE

This glaze may be refrigerated and used on ice cream, fruit tarts, cornstarch or tapioca puddings, or baked custard.

125 ml	puréed apricots
125 ml	undiluted frozen orange juice, thawed
250 ml	sugar

1. Combine and stir over low heat to blend; simmer 5 min
2. Cool; pour slowly over cake, spreading with a knife.

Yield: This recipe will glaze 2 square cakes or a large ANGEL CAKE.

Variations
Omit sugar and substitute apricot jam for puréed apricots.

A jar of baby food apricots substituted for puréed apricots is convenient but has a less intense flavour.

Tips for Icing Cakes

1. A cake should be cold before icing. Turn right side up.
2. Ice cake on a rack or cake plate; protect cake plate with 4 strips of paper placed so that they overlap; when paper is pulled out after cake has been iced, the cake plate will be free of icing.

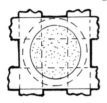

3. Heating the knife in hot water from time to time while icing the cake helps to keep icing soft for spreading.
4. Spread with quick, broad strokes. Overworking causes a rough, dull surface.

Decorated Cakes

A plastic or canvas bag and an assortment of decorating tips are necessary for professional work; when several colours are needed in small amounts or to add a little glamour, paper tubes are easily made.

Prepare a recipe of BASIC BUTTER ICING, being sure the sugar is sifted and that nothing is added that would block the tube. The icing must be firm enough to hold its shape. Divide the icing into small bowls and add colouring. More interesting effects will be obtained if the colour is not evenly blended.

Colouring, like flavouring, needs to be used with care. To the basic icing add food colouring a drop at a time. The colour will appear slightly darker in the bowl; too much colour is unattractive. Try a little green food colouring with peppermint; cherry juice or red colouring with fruit; raw egg or yellow colour for a rich creamy colour.

Trim with Coconut—Coconut may be used plain, either shredded or flaked, toasted by stirring with a fork over low heat, coloured by shaking 5 ml of water to which food colour has been added with coconut in a jar, flavoured by shaking with frozen fruit juice, undiluted.

Trim with Candies—Cinnamon hearts, crushed candy canes, sliced gum drops moulded into petals, life savers, chocolate bits.

Trim with Nuts—Whole, chopped or slivered nuts, plain or toasted, are always attractive. Brazil nuts dropped into boiling water for a few minutes may be shaved with a potato peeler into loose curls.

Trim with Fruit—Glazed or maraschino cherries, both red and green, are useful for flowers and leaves. Bits of pineapple, peel, slivered dates or apricots add colour. Angelica, on sale at Christmas, makes realistic leaves.

To Make Paper Tubes

Use a square of good white writing paper or for larger tubes tracing paper, parchment paper, freezer paper or butcher's wax paper. Divide the square into 2 triangles.

Place triangle with the point to the right and the long edge directly ahead. Place the first finger of the left hand at the centre of the long edge. Pick up point A and roll it over the finger, bringing A to C. Holding A and C firmly between thumb and first finger, lift the tube from the table and roll B over the roll to meet A and C. Slide A, B, and C back and forth until the point D is closed. Fasten the 3 points together by rolling the top of the tube forward inside the cone.

Clip the point of the cone straight off for writing, from the point up each side for a leaf, and across in points for a star.

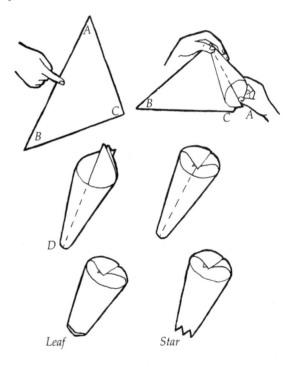

Leaf   Star

To use the tube, place a teaspoon of icing well down in the tube. Roll the folded points over the top of the cone toward the point, exerting pressure with the right hand and guiding the tip with the fingers of the left. Keep the point *close* to the surface of the cake and move the tube *slowly*. Turn the cake rather than trying to move the tube too far.

18 Pastry and Cookies

Pastry

The varieties of pastry reflect many cuisines and cultures. There is the flaky pastry of Canada and United States, the Strudel of central Europe, Germany's Kuchen, the Galette pastry which is shorter, sweeter and richer than the pastry characteristic of England and France.

Pastry Ingredients

Flour—In the basic recipe all-purpose or pastry flour can be used (see TYPES OF WHEAT FLOUR).

Fat—Lard or shortening is best for pastry. If a special method of mixing is followed, oil may be used. More fat is required to tenderize all-purpose than pastry flour; more fat is required when butter is used than when the fat is lard or shortening. Fat should be cold.

Liquids—Liquid may be water, milk, or fruit juice. Flour is moister at one time than another because of storage conditions and so the amount of liquid which is needed will vary. Add a little liquid at a time; a more tender pastry will result than if the liquid is added all at once. Too much liquid will make the pastry tough.

Deep Apple Pie (see page 328 for recipe). Maple Leaf Mills.

Basic Recipe
PASTRY

500 ml	flour (all-purpose or pastry)
5 ml	salt
150 ml	fat (for pastry flour)
or	
200 ml	fat (for all-purpose flour)
50-100 ml	very cold water

1. Sift flour and salt into a bowl; add cold fat; cut into the flour with a pastry blender or two knives until when the bowl is shaken, no pieces of fat larger than a pea appear. Cutting the fat too finely or creaming it into the flour will give a cookie-type crust known as short pastry. Flaky pastry requires small lumps of cold fat to trap layers of air.

   Beginners may find it helpful to cut half the fat into the flour until it is the size of peas, then add the remaining fat and cut it to the same size.

2. Measure the water. Sprinkle it over the flour. A shaker to hold the water will distribute it more evenly. Mix the flour up from the bottom of the bowl with a fork. As some of the mixture appears to stick together, push it to one side and sprinkle the dry flour with water. Too much moisture makes tough pastry; too little makes the dough difficult to roll out. Experience helps in determining the right amount.

3. When the flour appears damp, press it together into a ball; break the ball open; if it crumbles apart more water is required; shape all the dough into a ball but do not knead it.

4. Wrap and chill the dough until needed. (After several hours of storage, it will be necessary to allow the dough to soften a little before it can be rolled.) Divide it into two pieces, the large piece for the bottom crust, the smaller for the top.

5. Roll chilled dough on a lightly floured board, between two pieces of waxed paper or on a pastry cloth. A clean, heavy linen tea towel makes a good substitute for a pastry cloth. Let one end hang over the front end of the work surface so that it may be held in position. Rub a little flour into the cloth. A rolling-pin stocking holds flour and keeps the pin from sticking. More important than any piece of equipment is lightness of touch.

A fluted edge (top) and a decorated edge made with tiny hearts. Maple Leaf Mills.

If the dough becomes warm it will be much harder to handle.

Roll the dough from the centre out to the edge in each direction if a circle of dough is desired; roll it all in the same direction for a rectangle. Pinch together any cracks that form at the edge.

At the end of each stroke the pin should be lifted to be sure the dough is not sticking. After each 3 or 4 strokes, slide the pastry on the board to pick up a little more flour, and run a floured hand over the pin. If the dough will not move freely, loosen it carefully with the side of a knife and sprinkle a little more flour on the board.

Roll the dough to a thickness of 0.5 cm The diameter should be that of the bottom of the pan plus the depth.

6. Transfer the dough to the pie pan. Either fold it in 4, lift it into the centre of the pan and then unfold, or roll it loosely around the rolling pin and unroll it onto the pie pan. Do not stretch it but fit in lightly; trim with a knife held at an angle so that pan edge is not exposed as pastry shrinks away from edge when cooked. Overstretching the dough when rolling or fitting it into the pan will result in pastry which shrinks too much; another cause of excess shrinkage is too high a proportion of fat. Patch a tear by dampening the crust and pressing a small piece of pastry over it.

For a single crust pie shell, shape the edge by pressing with a fork. For fancy edges trim with pastry beyond the rim with scissors leaving an overhang of 1 cm

Turn under to make a double edge. Flute or decorate (see illustration above).

For a pie shell to be used for a cooked filling, prick the crust with the tines of a fork so that air between the dough and pan may escape to prevent bubbling. Do not prick if filling is to be baked with the dough.

For a double crust pie, place the bottom crust in position; add the filling, cooled if cooked.

7. Roll the top crust to the diameter of the pan including the edge. Fold it and cut a pattern in it with a fork or a sharp knife. The cuts should never be so long that the pastry tears in transferring it from board to pie. (See also Lattice Top, below.)

8. Dampen the edge of the bottom crust with cold water; fit on the top crust; with the palm of the hand, press top and bottom crust together along the edge. If there is a poor seal between top and bottom crust, if cuts are not made in the top crust to allow steam to escape, if tears in the bottom crust are not mended, the pie will stick to the pan.

9. Trim and edge; brush with milk or egg wash. A sprinkle of sugar gives an attractive sparkle.

10. Bake until just beginning to colour.
    Bake a pie shell 10-12 min at 220°C
    Bake a double crust pie 35-40 min at 190°C

Yield: pastry for 1 medium double crust pie or 2 small pie shells (see PIE PLATES).

Lattice Top—Roll the smaller part of the ball of pastry to a rectangle. Cut in strips with a sharp knife or a pastry wheel. On waxed paper placed on a baking sheet, mark a circle the size of the pie. Weave together crosswise and lengthwise strips of pastry as in the illustration. Press very lightly with a rolling pin to set the lattice; place in the freezer a few minutes; dampen the edge of the bottom crust with cold water, slide lattice into position and pat down the strips. Trim and edge.

Maple Leaf Mills.

Spiral Lattice—Fasten long strips together by dampening and pressing together. Begin in the centre of the pie, twisting and spiralling to the outside.

Variations
Flavoured Pastry—Substitute orange or pineapple juice for the water in pastry to be used for fruit pie.

Add meat extract, Worcestershire sauce, tomato juice to the water for pastry to be used for meat pie.

For cream pies add to flour instant coffee, 15 ml

Nut Pastry—Add finely ground nuts or sesame seeds to flour.

Cheese Pastry—For apple pie add to the flour grated Cheddar cheese, 100-125 ml

For cream pies and tarts, cream with the fat cottage cheese, 250 ml
Chill 3 hours.

To Freeze Pastry and Pies
Pastry and most pies can be frozen baked or unbaked. Cream Pies and Chiffon Pies do not freeze well. There are advantages to freezing before baking; the pastry will be flakier and the baking time will not be greatly increased. If frozen after baking a pie will require a 2 h period of thawing at room temperature or 30 min in an oven at 190°C

To prepare pastry for many pies or tarts and to save space, cut circles of pastry to fit bottom and sides of the baking dish, then freeze flat with foil between. To use, defrost 10 min; press into pie plate or tart tin.

When freezing a double-crust pie, unbaked, to retain moisture in the filling and prevent tearing of the top, do not cut a pattern in the top crust until pie is removed from the freezer.

GALETTE PASTRY

	1 egg yolk
15 ml	cold water
30 ml	lemon juice
250 ml	flour
2 ml	salt
15 ml	sugar
100 ml	fat

1. Beat together the egg yolk, cold water and lemon juice.
2. Finish as basic recipe for PASTRY.

REFRIGERATOR PASTRY

	1 egg
15 ml	vinegar *or* lemon juice
	water
1.35 *l*	flour
7 ml	salt
5 ml	baking powder
500 ml	lard

1. Break egg into a liquid measure; beat with a fork; add vinegar or lemon juice and enough cold water to bring the liquid to 175 ml
2. Combine dry ingredients; cut in fat; finish as PASTRY (BASIC RECIPE).
3. Pack into a container, cover tightly and refrigerate until needed. *Yield:* 3 double crusts or 6 shells, diameter 22 cm

Crumb Crusts

These easy-to-make crusts add sweetness and flavour. They are particularly suited to cream and chiffon pies.

Basic Recipe
GRAHAM WAFER CRUST

350 ml	graham wafer crumbs (about 18 wafers)
50 ml	fine sugar
2 ml	cinnamon
50 ml	melted butter *or* margarine

1. Preheat oven to 180°C
2. Crush wafers; grease a large pie plate (see PIE PLATES).
3. Mix the crumbs, sugar and cinnamon; add melted butter. Mix well.
4. Press mixture firmly into the pie plate to a thickness of 0.5 cm
5. Bake until lightly browned (8-10 min); cool.
6. Fill. Let stand before serving. Suggested fillings are: CHIFFON PIE fillings, CANNED FRUIT PIE fillings; LEMON PIE FILLING; CREAM PIE FILLING. Add the hot filling; cover with MERINGUE if desired and bake until golden.
7. Just before serving, wrap a hot wet towel under the bottom and around the sides of the pie plate. Hold towel against plate for a few minutes. This will loosen crust so that each piece of pie slips out easily.

Cream pie in a graham wafer crust. General Foods.

Variations of Graham Wafer Crust
Substitute chocolate wafers or gingersnaps (20 large, 30 small) or vanilla wafers (30) for the graham wafers; omit sugar.
Cereal Crusts—Substitute cornflakes or rice cereal, crushed, 350 ml
Increase sugar to 75 ml

ROLLED OAT CRUST

250 ml	quick-cooking rolled oats
50 ml	brown sugar
150 ml	finely chopped walnuts
100 ml	melted butter *or* margarine

Toast rolled oats in a large shallow pan in the oven (10 minutes) at 180°C
Combine and finish as GRAHAM WAFER CRUST (BASIC RECIPE).

COCONUT CRUST

30 ml	soft butter *or* margarine
350 ml	shredded coconut

1. Preheat oven to 180°C
2. Spread pan with the butter; sprinkle coconut in evenly and pat into the butter.
3. Bake until crisp and golden brown (10-12 min).

Recipes, tables, etc. that appear in small capital letters, e.g., PARSLEY BUTTER, CANADA'S FOOD GUIDE, are listed in the index. Consult the index for the number of the page on which the item appears.

Pies

These recipes are designed for a large pie plate (see PIE PLATES).
Packaged pudding and pie mix may be used instead of homemade filling.
A full pie is desirable. When a meringue topping is used the meringue should touch the pastry to prevent it shrinking away from the rim.
A full fruit pie may overflow and drip into the oven where the syrup will burn. Place a sheet of foil or a pan on the rack below the pie. A soggy crust may result from placing the pie directly on the foil.
Filling left too long in the crust before baking can cause a soggy undercrust; too low a baking temperature will have the same result.

Basic Recipe
CREAM PIE FILLING

The combination of flour and cornstarch gives a good texture. To replace the flour with cornstarch, use half the quantity.

150 ml	dried skim milk
50 ml	flour
25 ml	cornstarch
100-125 ml	sugar
100 ml	cold milk *or* water
400 ml	boiling water
	1 egg *or* 2 yolks
25 ml	butter *or* margarine
5 ml	vanilla

1. Combine milk powder, flour, cornstarch, sugar; add cold liquid; stir until smooth; stir in the hot water; cook until thick, stirring constantly; continue cooking until there is no taste of raw starch.
2. Beat egg yolks and into them stir a small quantity of the hot mixture. Blend thoroughly and return to the hot mixture; stir until thick.
3. Remove from heat, add butter; cool, stirring occasionally; add vanilla. Pour into a baked PIE SHELL or CRUMB CRUST; spread with meringue (page 325) or cool and cover with whipped cream, GLAZE, or a layer of puréed fruit.

Variations
Banana Cream Pie—Slice 2 to 3 bananas onto the baked crust and over the filling before the meringue is added.

Chocolate Cream Pie—Reduce the flour to 25 ml
Use the larger quantity of sugar. Add cocoa, 75 ml
Chocolate Chip Pie—Stir into warm cream filling 2
squares of semi-sweet chocolate cut in small pieces or
coarsely grated.
Coconut Cream Pie—To warm cream filling add
moist, shredded coconut, 125-250 ml
Reserve a little to sprinkle over meringue before
browning.
Pineapple Cream Pie—Fold into cool cream filling
well-drained crushed pineapple, 125 ml
Butterscotch Cream Pie—Substitute brown for white
sugar using the smaller quantity; add caramel, maple
syrup, or maple flavouring.
Strawberry Cream Pie—Melt currant jelly, 250 ml
Brush it on the inside of a baked pie crust; spoon in
cream filling. Arrange washed, hulled strawberries
over the filling; spoon jelly over the berries to glaze;
chill.
Raspberry Cream Pie—Substitute raspberries for the
strawberries in the preceding pie.

Spoon meringue onto cooled pie filling. Maple Leaf Mills.

*Then swirl meringue to touch the crust all around. Maple
Leaf Mills.*

Basic Recipe
MERINGUE (SOFT MERINGUE)

	2 egg whites
	salt
50 ml	sugar

1. Preheat oven to 180°C
2. Add a sprinkling of salt to the egg whites; beat
   until stiff but not dry.
3. Add sugar slowly and continue beating until very
   stiff.
4. Swirl onto the pie filling being sure the meringue touches the pastry; bake until golden
   brown (15-20 min).

If using an electric beater, add the sugar to unbeaten
egg white; beat until the mixture stands in peaks.

To use only 1 egg white, pile the meringue around
the edge of the pie leaving the centre uncovered.

Too much sugar makes a gummy meringue on
which beads of syrup appear.

Variation
To make a meringue of fine texture, melt 3-4 marshmallows over hot water; beat into the meringue.

LEMON MERINGUE PIE

Lemon Pie Filling

200-250 ml	sugar
50 ml	flour
50 ml	cornstarch
5-10 ml	grated lemon rind
500 ml	boiling water
	2-3 egg yolks
15 ml	butter
60-75 ml	lemon juice

Follow the directions for CREAM PIE FILLING, basic recipe, adding the lemon juice with the butter, the rind
with the sugar.

Bottled lemon juice may replace the fresh when
lemons are expensive; add grated orange rind if available.

For a transparent filling omit flour and increase
cornstarch to 100 ml
Lime Pie—Replace lemon juice and rind with fresh or
bottled lime juice and rind 50 ml

LEMON SPONGE PIE

	1 unbaked PASTRY shell, 25 cm
25 ml	butter
250 ml	sugar
45 ml	cornstarch
	2 eggs, separated
250 ml	milk
	1 large lemon (juice and rind)

1. Bake pastry shell 5 min at 200°C
2. Cream the butter; combine ½ of the sugar with cornstarch and blend into butter.
3. Add the egg yolks one at a time, beating after each addition until light and fluffy. Wash the beater.
4. Beat egg whites stiff but not dry; add the remaining sugar, beating it in a little at a time.
5. Stir the milk, lemon juice and rind into the butter mixture; fold in stiffly beaten egg whites.
6. Pour into the partly baked shell. Bake 35 min at 180°C

GRASSHOPPER PIE

Prepare 1 CRUMB CRUST from chocolate wafers, reserving a few crumbs to garnish; place in a large pie plate (see PIE PLATES); chill.

	25 marshmallows
200 ml	thin cream
2 ml	green crème de menthe syrup
250 ml	whipping cream

1. Combine marshmallows and thin cream; heat over low heat stirring until smooth; cool; fold in the flavouring and whipped cream.
2. Pour into the chilled crust; sprinkle on the reserved crumbs. Freeze until firm.

Chiffon Pies

LEMON CHIFFON PIE

	1 envelope gelatine
15 ml	
50 ml	cold water
	4 eggs, separated
250 ml	sugar
125 ml	lemon juice
	grated rind of 1 lemon
	1 baked PASTRY SHELL, CRUMB CRUST
	or MERINGUE SHELL, 22 cm

1. Sprinkle gelatine into cold water to soften.
2. Prepare a SOFT CUSTARD from the egg yolks, half the sugar and lemon juice and rind.
3. Add softened gelatine and stir until thoroughly dissolved; chill.
4. When mixture begins to set, beat egg whites until stiff but not dry; gradually beat in remaining sugar.
5. Beat the lemon mixture; fold the two mixtures together.
6. Pour into the pie crust and chill until set. *Serves 6.*

Black Bottom Pie—Prepare the SPANISH CREAM recipe. Divide into two portions after the gelatine is added. To one portion add chocolate bits, 100 ml

Stir until chocolate is melted and smooth; chill; pour into the baked shell and allow this layer to set.

To the second portion add maple or almond flavouring to taste. Chill; when almost set fold in the egg whites. Spoon over the chocolate mixture; chill. Garnish with whipped cream and CHOCOLATE CURLS.

Recipes, tables, etc. that appear in small capital letters, e.g., PARSLEY BUTTER, CANADA'S FOOD GUIDE, are listed in the index. Consult the index for the number of the page on which the item appears.

Black Bottom Pie, General Foods.

Fruit Pies

Basic Method

1. Preheat oven to 220°C
2. Prepare the fruit (see FRUIT PIE FILLINGS); peel, core and slice apples or peaches; pick over raspberries and blueberries; wash strawberries, remove stems and slice; wash and pit cherries; wash rhubarb and cut into short pieces.
3. Measure the thickener; minute tapioca gives a clear, slightly thickened juice; it may be replaced by flour (which is better for both apple and rhubarb) or by cornstarch.
4. Measure the sugar; part brown sugar adds flavour in apple, rhubarb or blueberry pie. Combine with thickener, salt and spice; mix with fruit.
5. Arrange fruit in an unbaked, unpricked pastry shell (see PASTRY), heaping fruit up a little in the centre; dot with butter; sprinkle flavouring over the fruit.
6. Finish with lattice top or top crust. Bake in preheated oven for 15 min; then reduce heat to 180°C Continue to bake until fruit is tender and crust is lightly browned. (about 35 min).

Fruit Pie Fillings

These fillings are cooked with the pastry, which must not be pricked. Crumb crusts are not suitable for these fillings.

Apple Pie

1.5 ℓ	7-8 apples
200 ml	sugar
40 ml	flour
15 ml	butter *or* margarine
2 ml	cinnamon

Berry Pie

1 ℓ	raspberries *or* strawberries
200 ml	sugar
50 ml	tapioca
15 ml	butter *or* margarine
5 ml	lemon juice

Blueberry Pie

750 ml	blueberries
250 ml	sugar
30 ml	cornstarch
15 ml	butter *or* margarine
2 ml	cinnamon

Cherry Pie

750 ml	pitted cherries
250-375 ml	sugar
50 ml	tapioca
15 ml	butter *or* margarine
1 ml	almond flavouring

Rhubarb Pie

1 ℓ	rhubarb
250-375 ml	sugar
75 ml	flour
15 ml	butter *or* margarine
5 ml	orange rind

Peach Pie

1 ℓ	8-9 peaches
200 ml	sugar
40 ml	tapioca
15 ml	butter *or* margarine
15 ml	lemon juice

To replace flour with tapioca use ¾ the quantity.
flour with cornstarch use ½ the quantity.
tapioca with cornstarch use 3/5 the quantity.

When preparing fruit pies for the freezer use tapioca and increase the amount by one-quarter.

Variations
Frozen Fruit Pie

1. Substitute 2 packages of frozen fruit, each 450 g
2. Thaw the fruit; drain and measure the juice.
3. Measure cornstarch, allowing

30 ml	cornstarch
per	
250 ml	juice

Add enough of the cold juice to make a smooth paste; heat the remaining juice; stir in the cornstarch paste; stir until mixture thickens.
4. Add fruit, butter and flavouring; taste and sweeten if desired; cool; pour into unbaked pie shell.
5. Finish as Fruit Pie, step 6.

Canned Fruit Pie—Follow the recipe for Frozen Fruit Pie using 2 cans of fruit, each 540 ml

Apple Cheese Pie—Use CHEESE PASTRY or cover the apples with processed cheese before adding the top crust. Use tart apples.

DEEP APPLE PIE

This one-crust pie is an easy recipe for beginners, and it also provides less food energy than most pies.
1. Preheat oven to 200°C
2. Wipe, quarter, core, pare and dice 7-8 tart apples into a buttered large casserole (see CASSEROLES); the dish should be very full.
3. For each apple measure
   flour, 5 ml
   sugar, 30 ml
   Stir carefully through the apples.
4. Dot over with small pieces of butter; if apples are not juicy, add water, for each apple 10 ml
5. Roll pastry (½ basic recipe for PASTRY) to fit the dish; make a design in the pastry; place over the apples; crimp the edge.
6. Bake 40 min. *Serves 6.*

APPLE STREUSEL PIE

1. Preheat oven to 220°C
2. Prepare the apple FRUIT PIE FILLING, reducing the sugar to 125 ml
3. Pile into an unbaked PASTRY crust.
4. Prepare STREUSEL TOPPING; sprinkle over apples and shake down through the fruit.
5. Bake in preheated oven 20 min; reduce temperature to 190°C
   Bake until apples are tender and topping is lightly browned. (40-50 min).

APPLESAUCE PIE

	1 unbaked, unpricked PASTRY shell
100 ml	flour
30 ml	sugar
2 ml	cinnamon
540 ml	1 can sweetened applesauce

1. Preheat oven to 200°C
2. Mix together flour, sugar and cinnamon. stir into applesauce; turn into pastry-lined pan. Do not prick.
3. Cover with STREUSEL TOPPING; bake 30 min

Recipes, tables, etc. that appear in small capital letters, e.g., PARSLEY BUTTER, CANADA'S FOOD GUIDE, are listed in the index. Consult the index for the number of the page on which the item appears.

UPSIDE-DOWN APPLE TART

1 kg	7-8 apples
100 ml	sugar
50 ml	butter *or* margarine
	1 lemon, juice and rind

1. Preheat oven to 190°C
2. Two deep Pyrex pie plates of the same size are most suitable for this recipe; an alternative is one pie plate and an oven-proof serving plate.
3. Peel, core and slice apples; toss in a bowl with a spoonful of sugar.
4. Coat the bottom and sides of one pie plate with butter; melt the remaining butter.
5. Sprinkle half the sugar into the buttered pie plate; arrange 1/3 of the apples over the sugar, placing the first few carefully in a pinwheel pattern; sprinkle on 1/3 of the melted butter.
6. Add two more layers of apple and melted butter; sprinkle the remaining sugar on top.
7. Roll the pastry to fit the pie plate; cut slits to let steam escape; place on top of the apples inside the edge of the bowl.
8. Bake until apples are tender and the syrup that forms is a caramel colour (45-60 min). Cover loosely with foil if necessary to prevent over-browning the pastry.
9. Invert onto the second pie plate; let stand briefly before removing the first pie plate; sprinkle the top with icing or fruit sugar.
10. Glaze under the broiler. *Serves 5-6.*

OPEN-FACE PEACH PIE

This is a Mennonite recipe from Kitchener, Ontario.

22 cm	1 unbaked PASTRY shell, unpricked
	1 recipe STREUSEL TOPPING
500 g	6-8 fresh peaches, peeled
50 ml	water
30 ml	lemon juice
0.5 ml	almond flavouring

1. Preheat oven to 190°C
2. Sprinkle ½ the STREUSEL TOPPING in a pastry-lined pan.
3. Halve or slice the peaches and arrange in an attractive pattern, cut-side down.
4. Combine the liquids; pour over the pie.
5. Cover with the rest of the STREUSEL TOPPING.
6. Bake until the crumbs are golden brown (40 to 50 min).

Cherry and rhubarb pies may be made plain or fancy: with lattice top crust (top left) and cherry cut-out design (bottom).

Peaches on the tree.

Dessert Crêpes rolled around a peach filling and topped with sliced peaches in Fruit Sauce.

SOUR CREAM PIE

Another popular recipe from the Kitchener region.

	1 unbaked PASTRY shell, unpricked, 22 cm
750 ml	tart apples, peeled and chopped
or	
600 ml	cherries, pitted
or	
600 ml	berries, cleaned
or	12-14 peach halves
250 ml	sugar
50 ml	flour
250 ml	sour cream
30 ml	CINNAMON SUGAR

1. Preheat oven to 220°C
2. Arrange fruit in a pastry-lined pan.
3. Combine the flour with the sugar.
4. Add sour cream and beat smooth; pour over the fruit.
5. Sprinkle the CINNAMON SUGAR mix over the filling.
6. Bake in preheated oven 15 min; reduce heat to 180°C
   Bake 35 min until fruit is tender.

PEACH BERRY PIE

	1 baked PASTRY shell, 22 cm
227 g	1 pkg. cream cheese
50 ml	sugar
15 ml	milk
2 ml	vanilla
200 ml	sugar
30 ml	cornstarch
350 ml	strawberries
30 ml	lemon juice
540 ml	1 can peaches, drained

1. Beat cheese, sugar, salt, milk and vanilla together; spread into the baked pastry shell, bringing the mixture up well around the sides.
2. Combine sugar and cornstarch, mixing until there are no lumps; add half the berries, crushed; stir over medium heat until clear and there is no taste of raw starch; add lemon juice and remaining berries cut in half.
3. Spoon about ½ of the mixture over the cheese; press the peaches, cut side up, into the cheese; spoon the rest of the strawberry mixture on top. Chill.

RAISIN PIE

	1 unbaked PASTRY shell, unpricked, 22 cm
	1 unbaked LATTICE TOP
500 ml	seedless raisins
500 ml	boiling water
250 ml	brown sugar
40 ml	cornstarch
50 ml	cold water
15 ml	grated orange rind
125 ml	orange juice

1. Preheat oven to 200°C
2. Wash raisins; add to water; simmer 10 min
3. Caramelize sugar (see TO CARAMELIZE SUGAR); add liquid from raisins; simmer until syrupy.
4. Combine cornstarch, orange rind and cold water stirring until smooth; add to the syrup; cook until the mixture thickens and clears; add raisins.
5. Remove from heat; add orange juice; cool; pour into unpricked shell; finish with LATTICE TOP. Bake 30 min

Variation
Raisin Squares—Substitute the grated rind and juice of 1 lemon for the orange. Cook the raisins in water with the lemon rind; combine sugar with cornstarch, increased to 50 ml
Blend with the cold water; add to the raisins; cook, stirring until mixture is thick and transparent; add lemon juice; cool.

Prepare one recipe of PASTRY and divide into two balls, one slightly larger. Choose a large square or large rectangular pan (see CAKE PANS). Roll the larger ball of dough to fit the pan and go up the sides 1 cm
Roll the second ball to just fit the pan; mark lightly in squares of 5 cm
Prick each square with the tines of a fork.

Pour cooled filling into pastry-lined pan; cover with the second piece. Bake until brown (35-40 min) at 200°C

Remove from oven and sprinkle with sugar; cut along the markings; serve hot or cold. *Yield:* 24-25 squares.

FRUIT TART

Bake PASTRY shell in a shallow rectangular pan at 190°C
Arrange canned, drained fruit in rows—peaches, green plums, apricots, pitted prunes, pears, Bing cherries, pineapple chunks. Glaze with fruit jelly or FRUIT SYRUP; bake until fruit is hot. Serve with sour cream, whipped cream, or yogurt.

PRUNE PIE

	1 unbaked PASTRY shell, unpricked
	1 unbaked LATTICE TOP
250 g	prunes (cooked)
125 ml	sugar
25 ml	tapioca
15 ml	lemon juice
100 ml	prune juice
10 ml	butter

1. Preheat oven to 200°C
2. Remove prune stones, cut prunes in pieces; add sugar, tapioca, lemon juice and prune juice. Reduce sugar if prunes have been sweetened.
3. Pour mixture into unpricked shell in a large pie plate (see PIE PLATES); dot with butter.
4. Cover with LATTICE TOP. Bake 30-35 min

Apricot Pie—Use recipe for Prune Pie; substitute cooked dried apricots for prunes. Increase sugar to 250 ml

Add blanched almonds to the fruit, or combine prunes and apricots.

MINCEMEAT PIE

	1 unbaked PASTRY shell, unpricked
750 ml	MINCEMEAT

Spoon mincemeat into unpricked shell in a large pie plate (see PIE PLATES); cover with plain or lattice crust (see LATTICE TOP). Bake for 30 min at 200°C

Serve very hot, plain or with HARD SAUCE.

Orange Mincemeat Pie—Section 3 oranges and arrange the pieces over the mincemeat under the top crust. While the pie is warm, brush with orange FRUIT GLAZE.

GRAPE PIE

	1 unbaked PASTRY shell, unpricked, 22 cm
1 ℓ	concord grapes
250 ml	sugar
50 ml	flour
10 ml	lemon juice
125 ml	oat STREUSEL TOPPING

1. Preheat oven to 220°C
2. Wash grapes; pinch off and reserve skins.
3. Bring pulp to a boil and simmer until the seeds float; sieve.
4. Combine skins, pulp, and remaining ingredients; place in the crust in a large pie plate (see PIE PLATES); cover with topping.
5. Bake 20 min in preheated oven; reduce the temperature to 190°C
   and continue to bake 15-20 min

SCANDINAVIAN FRUIT PIE

	1 unbaked PASTRY shell, unpricked
	1 unbaked LATTICE TOP
150 ml	sugar
50 ml	cornstarch
200 ml	orange juice
100 ml	prune juice
30 ml	lemon juice
200 ml	thick applesauce
125 ml	currants, washed and dried
10 ml	grated orange rind
250 ml	cut-up cooked, pitted prunes
15 ml	butter *or* margarine

1. Preheat oven to 220°C
2. Combine sugar and cornstarch in a saucepan; stir in the orange and prune juices; cook, stirring constantly until thick.
3. Remove from heat, add the remaining ingredients; set aside to cool.
4. Pour into unpricked shell; in a large pie plate (see PIE PLATES); finish with LATTICE TOP. Bake in preheated oven for 20 min; reduce temperature to 190°C
   Bake until nicely browned (30 to 40 min). Serve warm.

A rhubarb pie with a decorative cut in the top crust.
Maple Leaf Mills.

Custard Pies

The high egg content of these pies demands a lower cooking temperature. To determine when filling is cooked, slide in the point of a paring knife; if it comes out free of custard, custard is cooked. An unbaked PASTRY shell is required.

CUSTARD PIE

	1 unbaked PASTRY shell, unpricked
	2 eggs
50 ml	sugar
350 ml	hot milk
5 ml	vanilla
	few gratings nutmeg

1. Preheat oven to 230°C
2. Beat eggs slightly; add sugar.
3. Add milk slowly; strain; cool; add flavouring.
4. Place the unpricked shell in a large pie plate (see PIE PLATES) on lowest rack of preheated oven; pour in the custard.
5. Reduce temperature to 160°C
   Bake until custard is firm, 35-40 min

PUMPKIN PIE

	1 unbaked PASTRY shell, unpricked
400 ml	cooked or canned pumpkin
200 ml	brown sugar
2 ml	salt
2 ml	ground ginger
5 ml	cinnamon
1 ml	nutmeg and/or cloves
	2 eggs
300 ml	milk
200 ml	light cream *or* evaporated milk

1. Preheat oven to 200°C
2. Combine pumpkin, sugar, salt and spices.
3. Beat eggs slightly; add milk and cream and strain into pumpkin mixture.
4. Pour into chilled, unpricked shell in a large pie plate (see PIE PLATES) on the lowest rack of the preheated oven; bake 10 min; reduce temperature to 160°C
   Bake until the custard is set (30 min)
5. Garnish with pecan halves; accompany with bowls of whipped cream, candied orange rind, crystallized ginger, coarsely ground maple sugar.

Variations

Substitute sour cream for the evaporated milk, or replace an equal amount of milk with juice and finely grated rind of 1 orange.

The pumpkin filling may be oven-poached in custard cups and served with whipped cream.

Tarts

The basic recipe for PASTRY makes 18 dessert tarts, 24 tea size, or 36 hors d'oeuvres.

To Cut Pastry for Tart Forms—With a piece of string measure the outside of one tart form from the top down across the bottom and up to the top again. Using that measure find a cookie cutter, jar or saucer that has the same or slightly larger diameter and use it to cut the rolled pastry; or make a cardboard circle pattern and cut around it with a paring knife or pastry wheel. Or, shape the dough into a long roll; slice; press evenly into tart tins. Or, for tiny shallow tarts to be used for hors d'oeuvres, roll pastry the size of the whole pan. Place it on the pan and push into each small cup with the fingers. Roll the pin over the pan to cut through the pastry.

1. Prepare the pastry; cut the correct size and fit into the tart tins. If the filling is to be cooked in the tart, do not prick the pastry, but make an attractive edge. For unfilled pastry, prick well with a fork or place a few white beans in each shell until it is baked, to prevent bubbling.
2. Fill the tarts; for fruit tarts, set small circles of pastry on top of the filling to keep it from drying in the oven. Brush the circles with milk.
3. Bake unfilled shells 8-10 min at 220°C
   Bake filled tarts 20 min at 200°C
   Cool in the pan.

Variation

Cut thin slices from chocolate or plain refrigerated cookie roll. Line side of tart pan with overlapping slices; press one into the bottom; press firmly together.

Recipes, tables, etc. that appear in small capital letters, e.g., PARSLEY BUTTER, CANADA'S FOOD GUIDE, are listed in the index. Consult the index for the number of the page on which the item appears.

GLAZED CREAM TARTS

12 medium-size baked tart shells from FLAVOURED PASTRY
1 recipe CREAM PIE FILLING

1. Half-fill the tart shells with cooled filling.
2. On top of each arrange a design of fruit, using these suggestions:

   Half an apricot rounded-side up.

   1 small slice of pineapple cut in half. Stand one half up; divide the other half and place at right angles to the first piece.

   A circle of banana slices overlapping, with a cherry in the centre.

   A layer of perfect blueberries, raspberries or halved strawberries.

   A pinwheel of peach slices, or peach slices alternated with orange segments.

   An overlapping circle of green or red grapes, halved.

3. Cover with glaze (see below).

Glaze for Cream Tarts

50 ml	sugar
15 ml	cornstarch
200 ml	syrup from canned fruit

1. Combine sugar, cornstarch and enough syrup to make a thin paste; heat remaining syrup.
2. Pour the paste into the hot syrup, stirring until mixture boils; cool glaze slightly; spoon over decorated tart; let set.

MAPLE SYRUP TARTS

	8 large or 18-24 small unbaked tart shells from basic recipe for PASTRY
	1 large egg
200 ml	**maple syrup**
125 ml	**chopped pecans**

1. Preheat oven to 200°C
2. Beat egg with a fork; beat in syrup; pour into unpricked shells; sprinkle with nuts.
3. Bake 20 min

GLAZED RASPBERRY TARTS

	6 baked PASTRY **tart shells**
1 *l*	**fresh raspberries**
50 ml	**sugar**
10 ml	**½ envelope gelatine**
30 ml	**cold water**

1. Pick over the berries, filling the shells with the best.
2. Simmer remaining berries with water to prevent scorching; sieve; add sugar.
3. Measure; make up with water or fruit juice to 250 ml
4. Soften gelatine in cold water; dissolve in hot liquid; chill; when syrupy, spoon over the berries; chill until firm.

GLAZED STRAWBERRY TARTS

	6 large baked PASTRY **tart shells**
85 g	**1 pkg. cream cheese**
50 ml	**sugar**
15 ml	**cream**
15 ml	**orange juice**
2 ml	**grated orange rind**
500 ml	**fresh strawberries**
	strawberry glaze (below)

1. Beat cheese, sugar, cream, orange juice and rind until smooth. Spoon into the tart shells.
2. Wash and hull strawberries; dry on paper towels.
3. Fill tart shells with the whole berries, tips up.
4. Prepare glaze (below) spoon over strawberries; chill well.

Strawberry Glaze

125 ml	strawberries
125 ml	water
50 ml	sugar
15 ml	cornstarch

1. Crush strawberries in saucepan; add water and simmer 2 minutes; sieve strawberries.
2. Combine sugar and cornstarch; stir in sieved strawberries.
3. Cook, stirring constantly, until thickened and transparent; remove from heat; cool and spoon over berries.

Red currant or apple jelly, melted and cooled until syrupy, may be substituted.

BUTTER TARTS

	12 large unbaked PASTRY shells
250 ml	currants *or* seedless raisins
	1 egg
50 ml	butter *or* margarine
250 ml	sugar
30 ml	lemon juice *or* canned milk
2 ml	vanilla

1. Preheat oven to 190°C
2. Wash currants or raisins; soften if necessary in a sieve over boiling water; dry on paper towels.
3. Beat egg; beat in butter and sugar; add fruit and flavouring.
4. Spoon mixture into unpricked tart shells; bake 10-12 min

For a more syrupy tart, replace part of the sugar with an equal amount of corn syrup: 50 ml

HOLIDAY TARTS

	24 medium-size unbaked tart shells
	of GALETTE PASTRY *or* SHORTBREAD II
	egg white
250 ml	brown sugar
5 ml	vanilla
50 ml	chopped nuts
400 ml	chopped mixed fruit (candied pineapple, cherries, raisins, dates)
125 ml	jam (raspberry, apricot *or* black currant)
	candied cherries

1. Preheat oven to 190°C
2. Beat egg white until just stiff; gradually add brown sugar and beat after each addition.
3. Beat in vanilla; stir in nuts and fruits.
4. Spoon a small amount of jam into each tart shell; add filling and top with a cherry.
5. Bake 15-20 min until light brown.

Recipes, tables, etc. that appear in small capital letters, e.g., PARSLEY BUTTER, CANADA'S FOOD GUIDE, are listed in the index. Consult the index for the number of the page on which the item appears.

Cookies

Cookies are popular with everyone. Those with a crisp texture provide a pleasing contrast to a soft dessert. By using whole wheat flour or bran in cookies, you can add nourishment and fibre to the menu.

Basic Recipe
DROP COOKIES

150 ml	fat (butter, margarine, *or* shortening and butter combined)
200 ml	sugar (white and/or brown)
	1 egg
2-5 ml	flavouring (vanilla, almond, maple)
300 ml	flour
5 ml	baking powder

1. Preheat oven to 180°C
2. Remove the fat from the refrigerator to soften before beginning the cookies. Cream the fat.
3. Add the sugar and cream it with the fat to a fluffy mixture. (Brown sugar gives a butterscotch flavour but a slightly less crisp texture. If brown sugar is used, replace the baking powder with ½ the quantity of baking soda.)
4. Break egg into a bowl and beat with a fork or whisk before beating into the fat-sugar mixture.
5. Add flavouring.
6. Combine flour and baking powder; stir into the first mixture until dough is soft but not sticky when tested with the knuckles. Overmixing makes a tough cookie; too much flour produces a dry, tasteless product.
7. Bake one test cookie. If the dough flattens completely, more flour is needed.
8. Shape the dough (see TO SHAPE COOKIE DOUGH, page 334.)
9. Bake until edges begin to brown (10-12 min). See TO BAKE COOKIES , page 334.
10. Cool on a rack; store in tightly covered containers. *Yield:* 48, diameter 5 cm

---

Variations

Replace white flour with an equal quantity of whole wheat flour.

Replace part of the sugar with an equal quantity of ANISE SUGAR or VANILLA SUGAR.

To Shape Cookie Dough, use one of the following methods:

a) Drop the cookies by pushing the dough from a spoon onto the cookie sheet. (Staggering the rows of cookies will give them more room to spread.)

b) For a more uniform shape, roll the dough into small balls. Flatten with the tines of a fork, a potato masher, a knife dipped in cold water, or the lightly greased bottom of a glass tumbler.

c) Mould the dough with a pastry bag or cookie press.

d) Roll the dough into small balls, roll in sugar or VANILLA SUGAR; or dip into egg white, beaten slightly with a little cold water, then into cereal flakes, nuts, sesame seeds, or coconut.

e) Press dough into a thin sheet in a greased jelly roll pan; when the pan is removed from the oven sprinkle with chocolate chips, spread evenly as soon as they soften, and if desired sprinkle with slivered or finely chopped nuts; cool and cut into bars, squares or diamonds.

f) Shape the dough into a roll or bar adding as little extra flour as possible, or pack the dough into frozen juice cans from which both ends have been removed; wrap tightly. To use, remove, slice thinly as many cookies as you want to bake, rewrap and refrigerate. Covered tightly and refrigerated, dough will keep 3-4 weeks.

Photos: Maple Leaf Mills.

To Bake Cookies

For drop cookies, pans do not need greasing. Dark pans will brown the cookies more rapidly; they may be lined with aluminum foil.

The use of 3 cookie sheets will speed up baking. Place the first pan in the oven as soon as it is full. Prepare the second pan. Move the first one up in the oven and place the second one on the lower rack. Prepare the third pan. By this time the first pan can come out, the second one move up, and the third go in the bottom rack. In this way the cookies brown evenly. Baking sheets should be washed before more cookies are added.

Cookies are done when they can be moved freely on the pan and are an attractive colour. Lift cookies onto a cake rack to cool. They will become crisp as soon as they cool and if left on the sheet will break when they are being removed. If this happens return the pan to the oven for a few minutes to soften the cookies.

Cereal Cookies—Add to the basic recipe:

250 ml	all bran, corn flakes, rice flakes, Rice Crispies, and/or puffed wheat
100 ml	GRANOLA *or* toasted wheat germ

Nut Cookies—Add to the basic recipe:

100 ml	walnuts, almonds, filberts, *or* pecans
150 ml	toasted sesame seeds *or* sunflower seeds

Coffee Cookies—Add to the basic recipe:

10 ml	instant coffee
25 ml	orange *or* lemon rind

Peanut Butter Cookies—Add to the basic recipe:

50 ml	brown sugar
150 ml	peanut butter

Combine the peanut butter with the fat; add chopped salted peanuts if desired.

Toll House (Chocolate Chip) Cookies—Add to the basic recipe:

250 ml	chocolate chips
125 ml	coarsely chopped walnuts

Chocolate Pecan Cookies—Add to the basic recipe:

	4 squares semi-sweet chocolate, coarsely chopped
125 ml	pecans

The small bits of chocolate give these cookies an appearance quite different from that of Toll House Cookies.

French Cookies—Use almond flavouring, and add to the basic recipe:

125 ml	finely chopped glazed fruit
125 ml	blanched or toasted almonds, slivered

Shape the dough into a bar or roll; refrigerate; slice thinly to bake.

Golden Glow Cookies—Use white sugar, and add to the basic recipe:

150 ml	flaked coconut
15 ml	grated orange rind
125 ml	grated carrot (pack gently to measure)

Fennel Seed Cookies—Add to the flour in the basic recipe:

5 ml	crushed fennel seed

Coriander Cookies—Add to the flour in the basic recipe:

15 ml	ground coriander

Anise Cookies—Add to the flour in the basic recipe:

7 ml	crushed anise seed

Cardamom Cookies—Add to the flour in the basic recipe:

5 ml	ground cardamom

Caraway Seed Cookies—Add to the flour in the basic recipe:

25 ml	caraway seeds
5 ml	grated lemon rind

Spice Cookies—Reduce amount of sugar; use:

125 ml	brown sugar

Add to the egg mixture:

125 ml	molasses

Add to the flour:

3 ml	baking soda
3 ml	cinnamon
3 ml	nutmeg
3 ml	ginger

The spices given above may be replaced by:

5 ml	instant coffee
5 ml	cinnamon
5 ml	ginger
5 ml	crushed anise seed

or

3 ml	cinnamon
3 ml	allspice

or the equivalent amount of GINGERBREAD SPICE MIX or CAKE SPICE MIX.

Hermits—To the Spice Cookies mixture add:

500 ml	raisins, dates *or* glazed fruit
250 ml	walnuts *or* pecans

To have a variety of cookies oven-fresh for a small family, prepare the basic recipe but before adding the flour divide the fat-sugar mixture into three bowls. To each add the ingredients for a different variation, using 1/3 the quantities given above. Divide the combined dry ingredients among the bowls, adding less to the bowl to which cereals will be added, a little more to the Peanut Butter variation. Cover each bowl tightly and refrigerate, or shape and freeze (see TO FREEZE COOKIE DOUGH). Bake a few cookies whenever the oven is being used.

COOKIE MIX

Another method of having a variety of fresh cookies is to prepare a mix.

500 ml	fat
700 ml	sugar
1.5 ℓ	flour
15 ml	baking powder

Combine dry ingredients; cut in the fat to the consistency of fine meal; store in a covered container in the refrigerator. *Yield:* 2.5 ℓ
Use this mix as follows:

500 ml	mix
	1 egg
50 ml	oil
5 ml	vanilla

Beat the egg, beat in the oil and vanilla; add to the mixture the ingredients for any of the variations of DROP COOKIES except peanut butter which is added to the egg-oil mixture. Combine the two mixtures; finish as DROP COOKIES. *Yield:* 50-60 cookies.

Oatmeal Cookies

The nutty flavour of oatmeal cookies made them popular long before the nutritive value of the cereal was recognized.

OATMEAL CRINKLES

250 ml	butter *or* shortening
250 ml	brown sugar
5 ml	vanilla
50 ml	warm water
250 ml	rolled oats
450 ml	flour
2 ml	baking soda

1. Preheat oven to 190°C
2. Cream fat; add sugar and cream mixture until fluffy; add vanilla.
3. Combine oats, flour and baking soda; add to fat-sugar mixture alternately with water.
4. Flatten balls of dough onto a cookie sheet so that the pan almost shows through the dough. Bake 8-10 min. Cool on racks. *Yield:* 60-70.

These cookies may be put together with DATE FILLING at serving time.

OATMEAL CRISPS

250 ml	butter *or* shortening
300 ml	brown sugar
	1 egg
5 ml	vanilla
	or
1 ml	almond extract
400 ml	rolled oats
250 ml	coconut
250 ml	flour
2 ml	baking soda
3 ml	baking powder

1. Preheat oven to 190°C
2. Cream fat; add sugar and cream until fluffy.
3. Break egg into a bowl and beat with a fork or whisk before beating into fat-sugar mixture.
4. Add flavouring.
5. Combine dry ingredients; stir into first mixture until dough is soft but not sticky.
6. Shape and bake 10-12 min, until edges begin to brown. Cool on racks.

Variation
Press Oatmeal Crisps dough flat with a fork. Sprinkle with chopped walnuts or candied cherries.

LEMON SUGAR COOKIES

	2 eggs
150 ml	oil
10 ml	lemon juice
250 ml	sugar
500 ml	flour
10 ml	baking powder
10 ml	grated lemon rind
50 ml	sugar
2 ml	nutmeg *or* mace

1. Preheat oven to 190°C
2. Beat eggs; beat in oil, lemon juice and larger amount of sugar.
3. Combine flour, baking powder and lemon rind.
4. Combine the egg and flour mixtures; drop onto a greased baking sheet.
5. Combine the smaller amount of sugar and spice; lightly oil the bottom of a water glass and dip into the sugar-spice mixture before pressing each cookie flat.
6. Bake until edges begin to brown (8-10 min). *Yield:* 30-40.

LUNCH-BOX SPICE COOKIES

200 ml	oil
250 ml	sugar
50 ml	molasses
	1 egg
5 ml	ginger
10 ml	cinnamon
5 ml	cloves
2 ml	salt
10 ml	baking soda
500 ml	whole wheat flour

1. Preheat oven to 180°C
2. Beat oil with sugar, molasses and egg.
3. Combine spices, salt, soda and flour; stir into first mixture until dough is soft but not sticky.
4. Chill 1 h, roll into balls, diameter 2.5 ml
5. Bake balls (unflattened) on cookie sheet 10-12 min, until edges start to brown. Cool on racks. *Yield:* 40-50.

RAISIN OAT COOKIES

125 ml	margarine
125 ml	peanut butter
250 ml	brown sugar
	1 egg
200 ml	whole wheat flour
50 ml	wheat germ
125 ml	skim milk powder
5 ml	baking powder
250 ml	rolled oats
125 ml	raisins
50 ml	toasted sesame seed

1. Preheat oven to 190°C
2. Cream together margarine and peanut butter; add sugar and cream until fluffy.
3. Break egg into a bowl and beat with fork or whisk before beating into fat-sugar mixture.
4. Combine dry ingredients; add raisins; add to mixture until dough is soft but not sticky.
5. Shape as flat cookies; sprinkle sesame seed on the cookies.
6. Bake 10-12 min, until edges begin to brown. Cool on racks. *Yield:* 30-40.

Recipes, tables, etc. that appear in small capital letters, e.g., PARSLEY BUTTER, CANADA'S FOOD GUIDE, are listed in the index. Consult the index for the number of the page on which the item appears.

Basic Recipe
ROLLED COOKIES

200 ml	fat
150 ml	sugar
	1 egg
5 ml	vanilla
600 ml	flour
3 ml	baking powder

1. Preheat oven to 180°C
2. Beat together fat, sugar, egg and vanilla.
3. Thoroughly combine dry ingredients.
4. Stir 1/3 of the flour mixture into the fat mixture; add fruit or nuts as desired while the dough is soft; add remaining flour mixture until the dough is soft but not sticky; chill.
5. Roll 1/3 of the dough at a time on a lightly floured board; cut into shapes with cookie cutters dipped in flour, or use a decorated cookie stamp or rolling pin, then cut. Over-rolling will toughen the dough; cut as many cookies as possible from the first rolling. Collect remnants, press together and reroll lightly, using as little flour on the board as possible.
6. Bake on a greased cookie sheet until lightly browned around the edges (10-15 min).
7. Cool on racks, store in a tightly covered container. *Yield:* 50-60.

Variations
Valentine Cookies—Roll cookie dough thin. Cut, using 3 sizes of heart-shaped cutters or cardboard patterns, and bake. Ice the small hearts with pink icing and decorate with an arrow; place each decorated heart on top of a medium-size cookie with a spot of icing to hold it, then fasten both on top of a large one. Using a pastry tube, pipe a scroll or ruffled edge of pink icing around the small and medium hearts.

Touchdown Cookies—Bend an empty frozen orange juice or soup can into a football shape; cut cookies with it. Bake. Decorate with frosting to resemble lacings on a football.

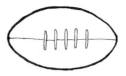

Platter Patters—Cut cookies into circles with a diameter of 12 cm
Bake; cover cookies almost to the edge with melted semi-sweet chocolate. In the centre of each place a circle of heavy white paper with the name of a popular song written on it.

Berliner Kranz Cookies—Cut cookies with a doughnut cutter; brush with beaten egg white; after baking decorate to resemble Christmas wreaths with green sugar and cinnamon candies.

Cherry Bells—Cut rolled cookies into rounds. In the centre place a spoonful of almond paste or DATE FILLING. Shape into a bell by folding each side into the centre on a slant. Place half a cherry for a clapper. Bake.

ROLLED OATMEAL COOKIES

250 ml	butter *or* margarine
250 ml	brown sugar
	1 egg
5 ml	vanilla
500 ml	rolled oats
500 ml	flour
2 ml	baking soda
10 ml	baking powder
125 ml	buttermilk

1. Preheat oven to 180°C
2. Beat together fat, sugar, egg and vanilla.
3. Thoroughly combine dry ingredients.
4. Add dry ingredients alternately with buttermilk to the first mixture.
5. Roll dough on a lightly floured board; cut; bake on a greased cookie sheet 10-12 min until edges start to brown. Cool on racks. *Yield:* 50-60.

Variations

Oatmeal Date Cookies—Before serving, put together pairs of baked and cooled cookies with DATE FILLING.

Oatmeal Pinwheels—Roll dough into 2 rectangles; spread each with DATE FILLING or strawberry jam. Roll each from the long side, sealing the edge. Refrigerate; when firm, slice thinly. Bake.

Oatmeal Squares—Roll dough on waxed paper into 2 rectangles, keeping the edges even and the 2 rectangles the same size; turn 1 onto a greased cookie pan and cover with DATE FILLING. Flip the other sheet of dough on top; press the edges together. Bake 25 min; cut into bars while warm.

Carrot Cookies—Add grated carrots, gently packed, 250 ml
Add toasted sesame seeds, 125 ml

GINGER COOKIES

250 ml	fat
125 ml	brown sugar
125 ml	molasses
25 ml	vinegar
2 ml	lemon flavouring
600 ml	flour
5 ml	baking soda
15 ml	ginger
5 ml	cinnamon

1. Preheat oven to 200°C
2. Cream fat; add sugar and cream until fluffy; add molasses, vinegar and lemon flavouring, mix well.
3. Combine thoroughly the dry ingredients; add 1/3 at a time to the first mixture; mix until dough is soft but not sticky.
4. Roll dough thinly; sprinkle generously with sugar and cut into squares with a knife, into circles with a cookie cutter; or shape into rolls, wrap and chill overnight, and slice. Bake until light brown (8-10 min). *Yield:* 40-50.

OATMEAL CHEESE CRISPS

200 ml	butter
100 ml	grated old Cheddar cheese
250 ml	flour
250 ml	rolled oats
7 ml	baking powder

1. Preheat oven to 190°C
2. Cream fat and cheese together.
3. Grind oats in a blender to the texture of whole wheat flour; combine with flour and baking powder.
4. Combine the two mixtures to form a soft dough; chill.
5. Roll into a thin sheet; cut with floured cutters; bake until edges begin to brown. *Yield:* 20-25 cookies.

Basic Recipe
SHORTBREAD

Butter is the fat that must be used in shortbread; both flavour and texture depend on it. When baked, shortbread should be cream-coloured, not brown.

250 ml	**butter**
100 ml	**sugar (fruit, icing or brown)**
500 ml	**flour**
50 ml	**cornstarch**

1. Preheat oven to 160°C
2. Cream the butter; add the sugar gradually, creaming until fluffy.
3. Combine cornstarch and flour; add a little at a time until a stiff dough is formed; turn onto a floured board, kneading it until the dough cracks around the edges.
4. Chill the dough; roll using as little flour on the board as possible to a thickness of 1 cm
   Cut into fancy shapes (see below).
5. Bake 15 to 20 min without letting shortbread colour.

Shortbread Shapes

a) Spring Hats: cut into two sizes of small rounds; place a small on a larger round; bake until edges start to brown. Cool on a rack. Decorate each to look like a hat with ribbons and flowers of BUTTER ICING.

b) Crescents: shape into 2 pencil-like rolls; cut into finger-length pieces and bend into crescents. Bake, dip the ends into melted semi-sweet chocolate, then into finely chopped nuts.

c) Pecan Surprises: wrap small pieces of rolled dough around a pecan; bake. While hot, dip several times into a bowl of VANILLA SUGAR or icing sugar.

d) Swedish Cakes: Roll the dough into small balls; dip the top of each into egg white beaten with a little water, then into finely chopped nuts. Press down the centre with the end of a wooden spoon. Bake 5 min. Remove the pan and quickly press in the centre of the cookie again. Return to the oven and continue baking. While warm, fill with red jelly.

Instead of cutting shortbread dough into small shapes, pat the dough into 2 small pie plates; crimp the edges, mark in wedges; bake 10 min; reduce heat to 150°C
Continue to bake until delicately coloured, about 30 min. Cool in the pie plate.

Variations

Nut Shortbread—Add finely ground almonds or filberts, 125 ml
Bake 15-20 minutes at 160°C

Oatmeal Shortbread—Omit the cornstarch, replace ¼-⅓ of the flour with rolled oats blended or ground to the consistency of whole wheat. Bake 15-20 min at 160°C

Chocolate Pinwheels—Divide the dough into 2 equal parts. Colour one half with 2 squares of unsweetened chocolate, melted. Chill. Roll each portion of dough separately on waxed paper into a rectangle; invert the chocolate dough onto the plain dough and pull off the paper; press layers together. Roll tightly from the long side; wrap in wax paper and chill; slice before baking 15-20 min at 160°C

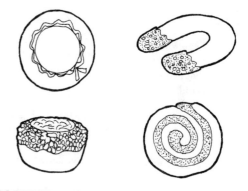

SHORTBREAD II

This is slightly less rich shortbread.

200 ml	butter
125 ml	sugar
	1 egg yolk
5 ml	vanilla
500 ml	flour

Follow directions for SHORTBREAD (BASIC RECIPE) but add the egg yolk and vanilla to the butter and sugar.

LEMON THINS

250 ml	butter
200 ml	brown sugar
15 ml	lemon juice
450 ml	flour
	CINNAMON SUGAR

1. Follow the basic recipe for SHORTBREAD to mix. Shape into small balls and press with a fork to a thickness of 1 cm
2. Sprinkle with the CINNAMON SUGAR; bake 10 min
   Yield: 36 pieces.

Basic Recipe
CARAMEL SQUARES

The many varieties of this popular cookie are prepared in two stages—a shortbread-type base and a meringue topping.

Base

125 ml	butter *or* margarine
250 ml	brown sugar
	2 egg yolks
5 ml	vanilla
400 ml	flour
5 ml	baking powder

Topping

	2 egg whites
125 ml	brown sugar
125 ml	chopped walnuts
5 ml	vanilla

1. Grease a medium rectangular or large square cake pan (see CAKE PANS); preheat oven to 180°C
2. Cream the fat; add sugar, egg yolks and vanilla; beat well.
3. Combine flour and baking powder; work into the fat mixture.
4. Pat the soft dough into the pan, working it partway up the sides.
5. Bake until lightly browned at the edges (20-25 min); remove and reduce the temperature to 160°C
6. Prepare the topping: beat the egg whites until stiff but not dry; add vanilla; beat in the sugar gradually; fold in the nuts.
7. Spread the topping on the base and return to the oven; bake until light brown and firm to the touch (25-30 min); cool in the pan; cut into squares or bars. *Yield:* 25-30 pieces.

Variations

Raspberry Squares—Spread raspberry jam on the cooled base; add topping.
Chocolate Squares—Sprinkle chocolate chips onto the cooked base and spread as they soften.
Lemon Squares—Spread LEMON BUTTER on the base; replace nuts in the topping with coconut.
Apricot Bars—Spread cooked, dried apricots, drained and chopped, onto the base; replace walnuts with almonds.

Hawaiian Bars—In the topping replace walnuts with almonds and/or coconut, vanilla, or rum flavouring; add well-drained crushed pineapple, 100 ml

Dream Cake

Base

125 ml	butter *or* margarine
50 ml	brown sugar
300 ml	flour

Topping

	2 eggs
250 ml	brown sugar
50 ml	flour
5 ml	baking powder
5 ml	vanilla
500 ml	cherries, walnuts and coconut

Beat eggs; beat in sugar; add flour and baking powder sifted together; add vanilla and fruit.

Icing

250 ml	FRUIT BUTTER ICING **(lemon)**

Prepare according to the basic recipe for CARAMEL SQUARES; frost when cool.

DIGESTIVE BISCUITS

	1 egg yolk
125 ml	oil
100 ml	water
200 ml	rolled oats
200 ml	whole wheat flour
15 ml	brown sugar
5 ml	baking powder
5 ml	salt

1. Preheat oven to 160°C
2. Beat egg, oil and water.
3. Grind the oats (or use a blender) to consistency of whole wheat flour.
4. Combine flours, sugar and baking powder; mix well.
5. Add the liquid to the dry ingredients and stir to a soft dough; chill.
6. Thickly flour the board with whole wheat flour and roll half the dough to a *thin* sheet; prick all over with a fork; cut in squares. Repeat for the second half of the dough.
7. Bake on greased baking sheets until golden brown and crisp (25-30 min). *Yield:* 36.

Serve with cheese, honey, jelly, or peanut butter.

Variation

Add toasted sesame seeds, 100 ml

Basic Recipe
MACAROONS

	2 egg whites
	sprinkle of salt
0.5 ml	cream of tartar *or* vinegar
125 ml	icing or fine sugar
2 ml	flavouring
250 ml	packaged coconut

1. Preheat oven to 120°C
2. Beat egg whites until frothy; sprinkle with salt and cream of tartar; beat until the egg stands in peaks.
3. Add sugar and flavouring a little at a time and continue beating until mixture is smooth and shiny.
4. Fold in the coconut; spoon onto a foil-lined baking sheet.
5. Bake until firm but not brown (30-40 min); pull off the foil; cool on a rack; store in a tightly covered container in a dry place. *Yield:* 20-24.

Variations

Replace some or all of the coconut with finely chopped glazed fruit or cherries; or crushed cornflakes, wheat or rice flakes; or finely sliced filberts, ground walnuts, almonds or peanuts.

Replace the white with brown sugar; add CAKE SPICE-MIX or cinnamon, 5 ml
Add chocolate chips, 100 ml
Marguerites—Spread Macaroon mixture on chocolate, ginger, graham or vanilla wafers; brown in oven at 150°C

CHINESE CHEWS

	2 eggs
150 ml	sugar
5 ml	vanilla
150 ml	flour
5 ml	baking powder
100 ml	chopped dates
100 ml	raisins
100 ml	chopped walnuts

1. Grease a medium square cake pan (see CAKE PANS); preheat oven to 180°C
2. Beat eggs until foamy; add sugar; beat well; add flavouring.

3. Combine dry ingredients; add with fruit and nuts to egg mixture; beat.
4. Spread in prepared pan; bake until golden brown and firm; cut while warm; roll in fruit sugar or icing sugar. *Yield:* 25 squares.

Variation
Fruit Balls—Cut warm Chinese Chews into 50 squares. Grease hands lightly and roll each while warm into a ball. When cool, ice with thin BUTTER ICING and roll in shaved Brazil nuts or filberts.

FLORENTINES

These are a Viennese specialty.

400 ml	fruit*
50 ml	thinly sliced almonds *or* filberts
125 ml	flour
50 ml	butter
50 ml	sugar
15 ml	corn syrup *or* honey
5 ml	lemon juice
170 g	6 squares semi-sweet chocolate

* Use sultana raisins or mixed glazed fruit, glazed cherries, glazed apricots, glazed kumquats, or glazed pineapple.

1. Preheat oven to 180°C
2. Finely chop fruit; combine with nuts and flour and toss lightly to mix.
3. Melt butter over low heat; stir in sugar, corn syrup and lemon juice; add fruit and nuts and mix well.
4. Drop the mixture onto a well-greased baking sheet, allowing for each cookie 15 ml
5. Flatten with a knife or glass dipped in cold water.
6. Bake until golden brown and crisp on the edges (8-10 min); remove pan from oven and place on a rack until cookies can be lifted off with an egg lifter. Cool top-side down.
7. Melt the chocolate; spread on cookies; cool and store with waxed paper between layers in a covered container in a cool place. *Yield:* 24.

Recipes, tables, etc. that appear in small capital letters, e.g., PARSLEY BUTTER, CANADA'S FOOD GUIDE, are listed in the index. Consult the index for the number of the page on which the item appears.

BROWNIES

250 ml	brown sugar
	2 eggs, beaten
100 ml	oil *or* melted butter
5 ml	vanilla
100 ml	flour
100 ml	cocoa
2 ml	baking powder
100 ml	coarsely chopped walnuts

1. Grease a medium square cake pan (see CAKE PANS); preheat oven to 180°C
2. Beat together sugar, eggs and vanilla; add oil.
3. Combine flour, cocoa and baking powder; stir into the first mixture; add the nuts.
4. Bake 20 min or until Brownies are firm around the edges but soft and fudge-like at the centre. Cool before cutting. *Yield:* 25 squares.

Carob powder may be substituted for cocoa in Brownies; use half the quantity. This product of the locust or tamarind tree has a chocolate flavour but no fat or stimulant, and it may be used by those allergic to chocolate.

OATMEAL SQUARES (MATRIMONIAL CAKE, DATE SQUARES)

250 ml	flour
250 ml	rolled oats
200 ml	brown sugar
125 ml	butter *or* margarine
	DATE FILLING

1. Grease a medium square cake pan (see CAKE PANS); preheat oven to 180°C
2. Combine dry ingredients; cut in the fat to the consistency of coarse crumbs, using finger tips or a pastry cutter.
3. Lightly press one-half the mixture into the prepared pan.
4. Spread with filling; sprinkle on the remaining crumbs, pressing gently to make a smooth surface.
5. Bake until lightly browned (30-35 min). Increase the temperature for a few minutes if necessary to brown the crumbs.
6. Cut in squares while hot, but allow the mixture to cool in the pan. *Yield:* 25 squares.

Recipes, tables, etc. that appear in small capital letters, e.g., PARSLEY BUTTER, CANADA'S FOOD GUIDE, are listed in the index. Consult the index for the number of the page on which the item appears.

Variations
Use MINCEMEAT to replace DATE FILLING.
Fruit Crumb Drops—Drop a spoonful of filling into the oatmeal mixture in a bowl, and coat thickly. Pat gently to smooth surface; shake off loose crumbs; bake until lightly browned (30-35 min)

To Store Baked Cookies
Cookies which contain fruit must not be stored with cookies which should remain crisp. Store fruit cookies in a tightly covered container with a slice of bread or apple. Store crisp cookies in a tightly covered container; when the oven is being used reheat a few for oven-fresh cookies.
To Freeze Baked Cookies—Baked cookies freeze well. Wrap bar cookies uncut; package drop or rolled cookies in a tightly sealed container; defrost at room temperature 10-15 min, or on a baking sheet in the oven, 3-5 min at 180°C
To Freeze Cookie Dough, shape by dropping onto a baking sheet. Cover with plastic film and freeze; remove the frozen cookies, package in heavy plastic or a sealed container. Defrost on a baking sheet at room temperature before baking.

Unbaked Cookies

PEANUT BUTTER CRISPS

50 ml	sugar
100 ml	peanut butter
100 ml	corn syrup
400 ml	cornflakes
200 ml	Rice Crispies *or* coconut

1. Combine the first 3 ingredients in the top of a double boiler, heat until sugar is dissolved; add the cereals; remove from heat.
2. Drop from a spoon onto waxed paper, keeping the pan over the boiling water. *Yield:* 35-45.

COLETTES

	6 squares semi-sweet chocolate
30 ml	butter
	peppermint flavouring (optional)

1. Heat the chocolate and butter in the top of a double boiler, over hot but not boiling water, until al-

most melted; add if desired a few drops of peppermint flavouring; remove from the heat, and stir until smooth.

2. Spoon out the chocolate to coat the inside of small paper cups. If the chocolate is too warm, it will run down into the bottom of the cup, instead of coating the sides. Make sure there is a firm edge by adding an extra layer, if necessary, around the top.

3. Chill on a baking sheet or in muffin pans in the refrigerator; before serving peel off the paper.

4. Fill with PEPPERMINT CREAM FILLING or with any WHIPPED CREAM FILLING or with ice cream. *Yield:* 24 small; 8 large.

Serve the larger of these fragile, fluted chocolate cups as a dessert, the smaller ones on a cookie tray.

PEANUT BUTTER BALLS

250 ml	icing sugar
250 ml	peanut butter
15 ml	butter *or* margarine
250 ml	Rice Crispies
100 ml	icing sugar
30 ml	skim milk powder
5 ml	vanilla
30 ml	water
250 ml	crushed peanuts

1. Mix first 7 ingredients; shape into balls.
2. Roll balls in smaller amount of icing sugar, then in crushed peanuts. *Yield:* 30-40.

FRYING-PAN COOKIES

15 ml	oil
	2 eggs
250 ml	brown sugar
400 ml	chopped dates
100 ml	glazed fruit
100 ml	pecans *or* walnuts, chopped
400 ml	Rice Crispies
150 ml	coconut

1. Measure oil into a heavy frying pan.
2. Beat the eggs; add sugar and dates; add to the oil and cook slowly, stirring often to prevent burning, until mixture is smooth and brown (20 min).
3. Add the other ingredients; cool slightly; roll into balls between lightly greased hands; drop into additional cereal or coconut to coat. *Yield:* 60-70.

RUM BALLS

30 ml	instant coffee
100 ml	boiling water
50 ml	oil
25 ml	corn syrup
5 ml	rum flavouring
100 ml	cocoa
250 ml	icing sugar
100 ml	skim milk powder
250-350 ml	crumbs (vanilla wafer, graham wafer, or dry chocolate cake)
100 ml	nuts, finely chopped

1. Dissolve the coffee in the water; add liquid ingredients and mix well.
2. Combine dry ingredients; add to the liquid and stir together.
3. Shape into balls; roll in any of chocolate shot, instant chocolate mix, toasted sesame seeds, *or* chopped nuts; refrigerate in a tightly covered container for several days to mellow; remove from the refrigerator to soften before serving. *Yield:* 35-40.

Rum Balls provide a good way to use stale cake crumbs or crumbs from broken cookies. If fresh, moist crumbs are used, the mixture may be sticky; add extra crumbs and chill before shaping.

Cookies with milk make a satisfying snack. Canadian Dairy Foods Service Bureau.

Basic Recipe
CREAM PUFF PASTRY
CHOUX PASTE (PÂTÉ A CHOUX)

250 ml	boiling water
125 ml	butter *or* margarine
1 ml	salt
250 ml	flour
	4 eggs

1. Preheat oven to 220°C
2. Measure the water into a small saucepan; add butter and salt; heat to boiling.
3. Remove from heat and add flour all at once.
4. Stir over medium heat until mixture leaves the sides of the pan and gathers around the spoon (1 min); do not overcook.
5. Cool slightly; add unbeaten eggs, one at a time, stirring until smooth after each egg is added; beat until mixture is glossy; chill until it is stiff enough to hold its shape.
6. Shape the dough onto an ungreased baking sheet using two spoons or a pastry bag. Use amounts the size of a golf ball for large puffs, the size of a walnut for small ones (bouchées), or for éclairs use strips 2.5 × 1.5 cm
   Leave between them a space double the width of each puff to allow for considerable expansion.
7. Bake until puffs have doubled in size and are beginning to brown (5-10 min for small, 15 min for medium, 20 min for large). Do not open the door during the first half of cooking time. Reduce the temperature to 180°C
   Bake until crisp and light brown.
8. Turn off heat; cut a slit in each puff and return to the oven for 10 min. Remove one puff and slice off the top; if it is crisp, with only a few threads of moisture inside, remove puffs from oven; cool slightly and glaze (see CARAMEL GLAZE and CHOCOLATE GLAZE, below).
9. Slice off the tops and scrape off any moist dough; or, for small puffs, slit to allow steam to escape.

Fill large puffs with ice cream; serve with CHOCOLATE, CARAMEL or CHERRY SAUCE.
Fill medium puffs with whipped cream, CREAM PIE FILLING, or LEMON CUSTARD FILLING.
Fill small puffs with savoury CHEESE SPREADS, chicken, fish and seafood.

Recipes, tables, etc. that appear in small capital letters, e.g., PARSLEY BUTTER, CANADA'S FOOD GUIDE, are listed in the index. Consult the index for the number of the page on which the item appears.

Caramel Glaze

200 ml	sugar
125 ml	dark corn syrup
50 ml	butter
200 ml	evaporated milk *or* thin cream
2 ml	vanilla

1. Combine and stir all ingredients except vanilla over high heat until mixture comes to a boil; continue to boil without stirring to the soft ball stage (see COLD WATER TEST FOR SYRUP); cool and add vanilla.
2. Spoon over puff or dip the top into the glaze.
This amount will glaze 12 large or 48 small puffs.

Chocolate Glaze

200 ml	icing sugar
100 ml	cocoa
50 ml	butter *or* margarine
50 ml	hot milk

1. Combine sugar and cocoa. Add butter to milk, stirring until dissolved.
2. Stir liquid gradually into combined sugar and cocoa.
Using a spoon, pour the warm glaze over the cooled puffs or dip each puff into the glaze.

Croquembouche—Prepare 1 recipe small CREAM PUFFS, 1 recipe CREAM PIE FILLING, 1 recipe CARAMEL SYRUP, 1 recipe CHOCOLATE GLAZE.
   To assemble, pipe the filling into the puffs; dip them in the syrup and build in a pyramid, the first circle having 14-16 puffs, the next row 10-11, the third row 5-6, and the fourth layer completing the pyramid. Pour the CHOCOLATE GLAZE over and sprinkle with toasted split almonds, or dribble on the remaining CARAMEL SYRUP and pass CHOCOLATE or FRUIT SAUCE. To serve, separate 2-3 puffs onto a plate using a fork and spoon.

To Freeze Cream Puffs
Cream puffs freeze well at three stages:
a) After the batter is shaped on the baking sheet they may be frozen, then removed from the sheet and stored in plastic bags. Bake the frozen puffs as usual, allowing an extra 10-15 min. Freezing seems to improve the volume of the baked puff.
b) After the puffs are baked and cooled they may be frozen. To use, allow the puff to thaw at room temperature about 30 min
c) Small cooked puffs may be filled with APPETIZER mixtures before freezing. Defrost at serving time by baking for 15 min at 200°C

Fruit and cheese make elegant desserts.

It is well worth while to preserve fresh fruit, like these ripe raspberries, for year-round enjoyment.

Preparing sweet cherries for freezing.

19 Candy

Candy rates low in nutritional value because of its high sugar content; sticky candies, which adhere to the teeth, are the worst offenders! However, for those times when tradition or impulse requires the fun of making home-made candies—and of eating them—these recipes are offered.

The use of a thermometer removes the guesswork from candy-making but if one is not available the cold water test which follows will indicate the approximate saturation of the syrup. The temperature rises slowly below 110°C

Above that the rise is rapid and it is necessary to watch carefully.

When instructed to "cool to lukewarm," cool to 43°C

Cold Water Test for Syrup

Fill a bowl with cold water and allow a few drops of hot syrup to drip off the spoon into the water. Note the appearance of the syrup as it hits the water; it may disperse quickly or it may settle as a ball in the bottom of the bowl or it may form threads. If a ball forms which can be lifted out, press it gently with the thumb to determine its consistency. Compare the results with the table below.

Stage	Characteristics	°C	Stage	Characteristics	°C
Thread	When dropped from a fork, mixture spins a fine thread in the air. When it hits the water it disperses and coats the bottom of bowl.	110-113	**Soft Crack**	Mixture forms threads like spun glass when it hits the water; threads will break when pressed.	132-143
Soft Ball	Mixture forms a soft ball in water; when pressed, the ball gradually softens and disappears.	113-116	**Hard Crack**	Mixture is very brittle both in the air and in water.	149-154
Firm Ball	Mixture forms a firm ball in water, which when pressed will flatten but not disappear.	119-121	**Clear liquid**	Sugar becomes lumpy, then melts to a clear liquid.	165
			Brown liquid	Melted liquid sugar turns reddish-brown.	170
Hard Ball	Mixture forms a hard ball in water which will hold its shape when pressed.	121-128	**Burnt sugar**	Dark brown, no longer transparent.	177

Homemade candy can be as smooth and professional looking as that produced in our finest candy shops. Choose a clear dry day; or if candy must be made in a humid atmosphere raise the cooking temperature 1°C

Better than any test is experience. Using the same saucepan on the same source of heat, the cook will recognize the moment when the candy is ready to be taken from the heat, beaten, and poured.

Crystalline Candies (Fudges and Fondants)

These candies are made up of tiny crystals; the finer or smaller the crystals, the smoother the fudge.

Large crystals, which give a coarse grainy texture, are avoided by a) adding fat in the form of butter, margarine, or cream, and protein in the form of milk, which will prevent small crystals collecting into larger ones; b) adding acid in the form of brown sugar, vinegar, cream of tartar, or lemon juice, which changes the large crystals of brown and white sugar into a form of sugar (invert) which has small crystals.

To prevent the crystals settling out of the syrup:
a) Stir until the sugar is dissolved, without splashing the sides.
b) Do not stir after boiling has begun.
c) Remove any undissolved crystals by covering the pan until steam collects to wash down the sides and by washing off the spoon used to stir the mixture.
d) Cool the syrup to lukewarm before beating it.
e) Do not alter the temperature suddenly by cooling the syrup in cold water or snow; a pan of cool water replaced as it becomes warm may be used.

The property that one crystal has of attracting other crystals is known as "seeding".

Use a saucepan of suitable size. If pan is too large the candy will cook too quickly; if too small, the syrup will boil over.

When transferring the candy from saucepan to greased pan, pour evenly; do not spread with a knife or spoon as this will destroy the gloss that is characteristic of fine fudge.

Recipes, tables, etc. that appear in small capital letters, e.g., PARSLEY BUTTER, CANADA'S FOOD GUIDE, are listed in the index. Consult the index for the number of the page on which the item appears.

Basic Recipe
OPERA FUDGE

use larger pot

500 ml	sugar
175 ml	cream
250 ml	milk
50 ml	corn syrup
30 ml	butter
5 ml	vanilla

1. Lightly grease a medium pie plate (see PIE PLATES).
2. Combine all ingredients except flavouring in a heavy saucepan, capacity 2 ℓ
3. Stir mixture over low heat until sugar is dissolved; cover for a minute to allow steam to wash down any sugar around the sides of the saucepan.
4. Boil gently without stirring, about 15 min, to the soft ball stage (see COLD WATER TEST FOR SYRUP). At intervals, scrape a spoon gently along bottom of pan to be sure candy is not sticking; if it is, lower the heat a bit.
5. Cool pan on a rack until lukewarm. To shorten the time, set pan in cool but not cold water.
6. Beat with a wooden spoon until the candy begins to lose its gloss; add vanilla and continue to beat until the candy thickens; immediately pour evenly over the greased pan.
7. Mark into squares; cool; store in a tightly covered container.

Variations
Nut Fudge—Just before fudge is ready to pour, add coarsely chopped walnuts, toasted almonds, or pecans.
Ginger Fudge—Add chopped preserved ginger just before fudge is ready to pour. If the ginger has been sugared, soak it in milk to remove the crystals and use the milk in the recipe.
Pralines—When the fudge is ready to pour, place it over hot water and drop by spoonfuls onto clusters of nuts arranged on a buttered sheet.
Walnut Logs—As soon as candy has set, cut it into four strips. Shape each into a log. Cover with a thin coating of caramel (see VANILLA CARAMELS); roll in chopped walnuts. Slice when cold.
Peanut Butter Fudge—Reduce corn syrup to half the amount in the basic recipe and add an equal amount of peanut butter to the lukewarm candy; beat until creamy.

Maple Cream

250 ml	sugar
250 ml	brown sugar
10 ml	flour
15 ml	butter *or* margarine
125 ml	milk
2 ml	vanilla

Follow the basic recipe for OPERA FUDGE.

Pineapple Fudge

500 ml	sugar
250 ml	brown sugar
125 ml	evaporated milk
540 ml	1 can crushed pineapple
30 ml	butter *or* margarine
10 ml	vanilla
125 ml	walnuts

1. Combine the sugars, milk and drained pineapple.
2. Cook following the basic method for OPERA FUDGE to soft ball stage (see COLD WATER TEST FOR SYRUP); remove from heat; add butter and vanilla; finish as OPERA FUDGE. Press a piece of walnut on each square.

Chocolate Fudge

125 ml	cocoa
500 ml	sugar
50 ml	skim milk powder
200 ml	water
50 ml	butter *or* margarine
5 ml	vanilla

1. Grease a medium pie plate (see PIE PLATES).
2. Combine dry ingredients in a heavy saucepan; add water slowly, stirring to avoid lumps; continue to stir over medium heat until mixture boils.
3. Boil without stirring approximately 15 min to soft ball stage (see COLD WATER TEST FOR SYRUP).
4. Remove saucepan from heat; add butter and vanilla; finish as basic recipe for OPERA FUDGE, starting at step 5.

Variations
Replace vanilla with one of: grated orange rind; instant coffee; or 2 drops peppermint extract.

Add chopped nuts, GRANOLA, miniature marshmallows, or coconut.

CARAMEL FUDGE

So delicious it is sinful! This is not a recipe for beginners.

750 ml	sugar
250 ml	thin cream
0.5 ml	baking soda
60 ml	butter *or* margarine
2 ml	vanilla
125 ml	pecans

1. Grease two medium pie plates (see PIE PLATES).
2. Measure 1/3 of the sugar into a small heavy pan and the remaining sugar with the cream into another saucepan.
3. Heat both at the same time over low heat, stirring the small amount of sugar constantly until it is a light-coloured caramel syrup; give the second sugar mixture an occasional stir until it comes to a boil.
4. Add the caramel syrup slowly to the boiling mixture, stirring vigorously to prevent curdling; continue to cook without stirring to the firm ball stage (see COLD WATER TEST FOR SYRUP).
5. Remove from stove, mix in soda, add butter, cool to lukewarm; add vanilla.
6. Beat until mixture is thick and heavy and shines like satin; add nuts and pour into prepared pans.

This recipe is very good with toasted almonds in place of pecans; add a grating of orange rind with the vanilla for a subtle flavour.

Fudge cut in squares and decorated with nuts and candied fruit.

DIVINITY FUDGE

This is a good recipe for beginners. If it does not set it may be thickened by adding icing sugar or by continuing to beat over boiling water; if it begins to set while still very hot a few drops of boiling water may be added. Because this candy absorbs moisture it does not keep well. It should not be combined with other candies in a package.

375 ml	sugar
75 ml	corn syrup
100 ml	boiling water
	1 egg white
2 ml	vanilla

1. Grease two small square cake pans (see CAKE PANS).
2. Combine sugar, corn syrup and water in a shallow saucepan; stir over medium heat until sugar is dissolved.
3. Continue to boil without stirring to the firm ball stage; (see COLD WATER TEST FOR SYRUP); remove from heat.
4. Beat egg white stiff but not dry; gradually beat in half the syrup; let stand.
5. Return the rest of the syrup to the heat and boil to the soft crack stage (see COLD WATER TEST FOR SYRUP).
6. Beat a little at a time into the first mixture; continue to beat until the mixture holds its shape and loses its gloss. If it becomes too thick for the egg beater use a wooden spoon.
7. Add vanilla; pour into prepared pans.

Variations
Sea Foam—Use brown sugar; reduce corn syrup to 50 ml
Add chopped nuts, candied fruits, maraschino cherries (well drained).

Drop from a spoon onto a foil-covered baking sheet to make bonbons; place the bowl over hot water to keep the mixture soft.

Fondants

Fondants, like fudges, are crystalline candies and should be handled as little as possible during the cooking and cooling period. They are used as fillings for chocolates and dried fruits. Reread the rules for CRYSTALLINE CANDIES before attempting to make fondant. A candy thermometer is essential.

BUTTER FONDANT

500 ml	sugar
0.5 ml	cream of tartar
175 ml	milk
30 ml	butter

1. Combine sugar, cream of tartar and milk in a saucepan over gentle heat.
2. Stir until sugar is dissolved; then boil, not too briskly, to the soft ball stage, 113°C
   Add butter when syrup is almost at this temperature.
3. Remove from heat; let stand a few minutes, then pour carefully onto a warm buttered platter.
4. Let stand until almost cold; stir with a flexible metal knife working from every side to the centre until it becomes opaque and white.
5. Lightly grease hands, gather up before mixture stiffens, knead until very smooth; put into a bowl, cover closely; let stand several hours. (If the mixture crumbles knead small amounts at a time, adding more crumbs until all is smooth.)
6. As the fondant ripens it softens. Before using, knead it to a smooth consistency; divide; add colour and flavour as desired to each portion. Shape into centres for dipping or for bonbons; into rolls; or form around bits of candied fruits, nuts, grapes, or stuffed dates, prunes, figs.

Variation

Chocolate Fondant
1. Make BUTTER FONDANT omitting half the butter; pour on buttered platter.
2. Cover syrup, while hot, with 2 squares of grated unsweetened chocolate.
3. Finish as BUTTER FONDANT.

Non-crystalline Candies (Taffy, Caramels, Brittles)

In the fudge-type candy, the aim is to have small crystals; in the taffy-type enough interfering material is added that no crystals should form.

The syrup for this type of candy and the finished taffy, caramel and brittle are very hot. A board should be used to protect table or counter tops, and care should be taken to avoid burning the hands. When hot taffy is poured onto thin metal pans, the metal may quickly expand causing syrup to splatter.

Basic Recipe
TAFFY

250 ml	light corn syrup
125 ml	sugar
15 ml	vinegar
15 ml	butter *or* margarine
5 ml	vanilla

1. Grease lightly a small square cake pan (see CAKE PANS).
2. Combine syrup, sugar and vinegar in a heavy saucepan; stir until the sugar is dissolved over medium heat.
3. Add butter; boil without stirring to the soft crack stage (see COLD WATER TEST FOR SYRUP).
4. Add flavouring; pour gently into the pan; cool.
5. Mark squares before the taffy is hard; when hard turn onto a board and break apart by tapping the underside with a knife handle.

Variations

Pulled Taffy—As soon as taffy is cool enough to handle, butter hands lightly and stretch the taffy between them, folding it without twisting. Work in a cool room, pulling and folding until the taffy is creamy white; twist into a rope, cut in small pieces with a heavy knife or scissors, wrap each piece in a waxed paper square.

Molasses Taffy—Substitute molasses for part of the corn syrup. (Blackstrap molasses will give a stronger molasses flavour.)

Taffy Apple—Wash and dry red apples; pierce each with a wooden skewer. Prepare basic recipe for TAFFY, substituting 8 drops oil of cinnamon for vanilla. Set the taffy over hot water to keep it from hardening; hold the apple by the skewer and plunge into the syrup; remove quickly and hold over the pan to drip, twirling to spread the syrup evenly. Cool on a cake rack; store in a dry cool place.

More flavouring is necessary in hard candies than in soft. Buy it in small quantities in a drug store. Try 4 drops of anise for a licorice flavour, 8 drops of oil of cinnamon, 12 drops of spearmint to replace the vanilla.

Recipes, tables, etc. that appear in small capital letters, e.g., PARSLEY BUTTER, CANADA'S FOOD GUIDE, are listed in the index. Consult the index for the number of the page on which the item appears.

POPCORN BALLS

1. Make TAFFY basic recipe, boiling the syrup to hard ball stage (see COLD WATER TEST FOR SYRUP); cool slightly.
2. Place in a large, lightly greased bowl popped corn, 2 *l*
3. Sprinkle cinnamon over the corn. (See TO POP CORN.)
4. Slowly pour the taffy over the corn, stirring it up from the bottom of the bowl with a fork. One person should both pour and stir to avoid getting a hand under the stream of hot syrup.
5. When the taffy is cool enough to handle, grease hands lightly and working quickly, lift the mixture out with a spoon, dropping it onto the hands and shaping it into a ball with as little pressure as possible. At this stage an assistant is useful.
6. Wrap each ball in plastic and store in a cool dry place. *Yield:* 36 balls.

Variations

Popcorn Cats—Put a small ball on top of a larger one, sticking them together with a little syrup. Cross three cellophane straws for whiskers, add a Life-Saver for a nose and gumdrops for eyes. Bend a straw for ears.

Popcorn Clowns—Instead of the straws for the Popcorn Cat add a gay paper hat made from a conical paper cup.

Krunch—Substitute flaked cereals, mixed nuts and softened raisins for an equal quantity of popped corn in the Popcorn Ball recipe. Press into a greased jelly roll pan; into paper cones or jelly moulds; or into loaf pans to slice when cold.

TO POP CORN

125 ml	unpopped corn
yields	
3 *l*	popped corn

Heat enough oil to just cover the bottom of a large saucepan. When a kernel dances in the oil add the corn quickly; cover the pan with a tight-fitting lid and shake gently, holding the pan just off the heat. Do not lift lid until all the popping has ceased. Keep unused corn in a tightly covered jar. Rinsing the corn with water just before popping it may improve corn that has been kept too long.

CARAMEL CRUNCH

250 ml	popping corn
1 *l*	cereal flakes
250 ml	mixed nuts
250 ml	butter *or* margarine
500 ml	brown sugar, packed
125 ml	corn syrup and/or molasses
2 ml	baking soda
5 ml	vanilla

1. Pop the corn (see TO POP CORN) and combine with cereals and nuts in a deep, lightly greased bowl.
2. Melt the fat, stir in sugar and corn syrup in a heavy saucepan; bring to a boil stirring constantly. Boil without stirring for 5 min; remove from heat; sift in soda; add vanilla. Pour over corn mixture slowly, mixing well.
3. Turn into a roasting pan and bake 1 h at 150°C stirring every 15 min
4. Cool, break apart and store in a tightly covered container.

SPONGE TAFFY

3 cups 750 ml	brown sugar
3/4 c 175 ml	corn syrup
175 ml	water
1 tbsp 15 ml	baking soda

1. Measure sugar, syrup and water into a saucepan.
2. Bring to a boil, stirring until sugar dissolves; boil stirring occasionally about 15 min until mixture reaches soft crack stage (see COLD WATER TEST FOR SYRUP).
3. While syrup is boiling, butter the bottom of two small square cake pans (see CAKE PANS); place in the refrigerator to chill.
4. Remove syrup; sift the baking soda through a sieve evenly over the top and stir once to completely combine the soda.
5. Pour syrup while effervescing into the chilled pan; let stand undisturbed at room temperature until cold.
6. Loosen the sides, invert the pan and turn out; cut in large squares. Wrap in waxed paper.

Variations
Peanut Sponge (Brittle)—When the mixture reaches the soft crack stage stir in chopped salted peanuts, 500 ml
Continue to cook to hard crack stage (see COLD WATER TEST FOR SYRUP); sift the soda over the syrup; pour onto a buttered baking sheet or jelly roll pan.

Chocolate Almond Sponge—Replace peanuts with toasted almonds; split most of the almonds reserving enough to chop finely for the top. Melt 1 package of chocolate chips over hot water; dribble over the sponge when it is set but still warm; spread evenly; sprinkle on the chopped nuts; cool; break into pieces by tapping underside with a hammer.

Basic Recipe
VANILLA CARAMELS

500 ml	sugar
250 ml	light corn syrup
375 ml	evaporated milk
250 ml	milk
50 ml	butter *or* margarine
10 ml	vanilla

1. Cook all ingredients except vanilla in a broad saucepan, stirring constantly to the firm ball stage (see COLD WATER TEST FOR SYRUP).
2. Remove from heat, add vanilla and pour into a buttered small rectangular cake pan (see CAKE PANS).
3. When cold turn onto a board and cut into squares with a heavy knife. Wrap in waxed paper.

Variations
Chocolate Caramels—Combine with the sugar, cocoa, 125 ml
Nut Caramels—Add to the cooked syrup split almonds or Brazil nuts cut into thick slices.

From one recipe of caramels several of the following variations may be made.
Filled Caramels—Pour the cooked caramel into two small square cake pans (see CAKE PANS) to make thinner layers. When cold, turn out of the pans, put together with a layer of FONDANT. Cut into squares with a heavy knife.
Pecan Roll—Shape BUTTER FONDANT or FUDGE into a roll. Chop walnuts or pecans coarsely and spread on a lightly buttered pan; set the roll on the nuts. Pour a thin coating of cooled caramel over the roll. Roll it onto the nuts, add enough caramel to completely cover the centre and roll again in the nuts. Slice when cold.
Turtles—On a lightly buttered jelly roll pan arrange pecans in groups of five to represent a turtle's four legs and head. Add caramel so the nuts are held together but not quite covered; cool; melt semi-sweet chocolate over hot water; spoon over the caramel.

Caramallows—Cool the caramel to lukewarm, 43°C

Place over hot water to keep it at that temperature. Skewer a large marshmallow and dip quickly in and ~~~~ ramel; drain and drop onto a lightly but- ~~~~ f aluminum foil. When cool cut through ~~~~ ssors. The caramel should be warm ~~~~ ke a thin coating but not hot enough to ~~~~ hmallow.

~~~~ ramels may be melted with a spoonful ~~~~ a small double boiler for any of these

~~~~ make Candy

~~~~ xtures require little or no cooking ~~~~ oung candy-makers.

~~~~ ISTMAS TREES

~~~~ tradition. Cut popcorn cones to ~~~~ d arrange around a mirror as a ~~~~ rround with evergreen twigs in ~~~~ animals are set.

400 ml	sifted icing sugar
	1 unbeaten egg white
1 ml	vinegar
	8 ice cream cones
1.5 ℓ	popped corn (see TO POP CORN)
	decorations

1. Combine sugar, egg and vinegar and beat until icing is smooth; add sugar to spreading consistency.
2. Cover cones with icing and roll in the loose popcorn.
3. When dry, decorate with bits of cherries, sugar-coated almonds, cinnamon drops stuck on with icing.

CHOCOLATE DROPS

170 g	semi-sweet chocolate
30 g	unsweetened chocolate
50 ml	corn syrup
15 ml	water
500 ml	flaked cereal

1. Combine and melt first four ingredients together over hot water; remove from heat.

2. With a fork stir in the cereal.
3. Drop from a spoon onto waxed paper on a cookie sheet; chill.

Variations

Replace the cereal with any one of the following: salted peanuts; broken nuts; candied mixture for FRUIT BALLS; raisins, washed and dried; finely cut, pitted dates; dried apricots or prunes; marshmallows cut in pieces or miniature marshmallows.

Chocolate Bark—Follow directions for CHOCOLATE DROPS; stir in chopped nuts; pour onto waxed paper on a baking sheet; spread with spatula, refrigerate until firm; break into irregular pieces.

COCONUT SQUARES

5 ml	butter
50 ml	cold mashed potato*
0.5 ml	salt
400-500 ml	icing sugar
	flavouring
250 ml	flaked coconut
	2 squares semi-sweet chocolate

* The potato must be dry, with no butter or milk added to it. A baked potato is a good choice.

1. Cream the butter; add mashed potato, salt and sugar; cream well together, adding more sugar if necessary to obtain a thick, smooth product; flavour; add coconut; taste and add more flavouring if necessary.
2. Line a loaf pan with foil or waxed paper; pack the mixture into the pan, pressing firmly. Let stand to dry the surface.
3. Melt chocolate over hot water; cover the surface of the candy; cool until chocolate is set; cut into squares.

CHOCOMALLOWS

125 ml	chocolate bits
50 ml	milk
50 ml	icing sugar
	16 marshmallows
500 ml	flaked or desiccated coconut
or	
125 ml	finely chopped nuts

1. In top of a small double boiler (or a small bowl) over hot water, melt chocolate; stir in milk; remove from heat; blend in icing sugar.
2. Dip marshmallows; roll in coconut or nuts.

GRANOLA

600 ml	rolled oats, wheat flakes and bran flakes
150 ml	sesame seed
50 ml	sunflower seed
200 ml	coconut, flaked or shredded
200 ml	nuts, chopped
150 ml	wheat germ
50 ml	skim milk powder
100 ml	water
200 ml	honey, molasses and maple syrup
100 ml	oil
5 ml	vanilla

1. Combine the dry ingredients.
2. Combine liquids and heat until thin; stir to blend well.
3. Dribble liquids over the dry mixture, stirring with a slotted spoon; spread in shallow pans to a depth of 1 cm
4. Bake until golden brown (1.5-2 h) at 110°C
5. Cool; store in tightly covered containers. *Yield: 2 ℓ*

Serve with dried or fresh fruit as a snack; with milk as a breakfast cereal; or sprinkle on cream pudding or ice cream as a dessert topping. Use with melted, semi-sweet chocolate as a crumb crust (add just enough chocolate to hold the crumbs together) or in cookie dough to replace nuts, coconut.

STUFFED DATES OR PRUNES

Use pitted whole dates or large pitted prunes. Stuff with FONDANT, uncooked CHOCOLATE FUDGE, nuts, peanut butter, Halvah, almond paste, or marshmallows. Shake in a bag containing fruit sugar or icing sugar or roll in flaked coconut.

Variations
Sugar may be flavoured with ground cinnamon or cardamom or with a vanilla bean.

Coconut may be coloured and flavoured with undiluted frozen orange concentrate.

CANDIED ORANGE OR GRAPEFRUIT RIND

	2 oranges
	or
	1 grapefruit
250 ml	sugar
125 ml	water

1. Save the rinds of fruit with thick skins; cover with water, bring to a boil and simmer ten minutes; rinse with cold water, scrape off and discard the white; with scissors cut the peel into thin strips.
2. Cover with water, bring to a boil, simmer 10-15 min; drain and rinse.
3. Repeat.
4. Cover with water and simmer until rind is tender (10-15 min). Save the water drained from the rind; measure the required amount and return it with the sugar to the saucepan.
5. Simmer until peel is transparent (15-20 min) or until the syrup will spin a thread (see COLD WATER TEST FOR SYRUP).
6. Lift out the rind with a fork or drain in a sieve; when almost dry sprinkle with sugar; leave several hours to dry and again coat with sugar. Store in a tightly covered container. *Yield: 250 ml*

Variations
For a chewier texture, add to the sugar corn syrup, 30 ml

Dry the drained rind without sugar; dip in semi-sweet chocolate melted over warm water; drop on a rack to cool.

Thin any syrup that remains with the water drained from the rind and bring it to a boil; bottle in a sterilized bottle and use it to sweeten fruit mixtures, drinks, or desserts such as APPLE COMPÔTE or STEWED RHUBARB.

Recipes, tables, etc. that appear in small capital letters, e.g., PARSLEY BUTTER, CANADA'S FOOD GUIDE, are listed in the index. Consult the index for the number of the page on which the item appears.

20 Food Preservation

Nicholas Appert is regarded as the father of the canning industry because he won the prize offered by Napoleon for a more palatable method of preserving food than salting. However, it was some time before the price of containers was low enough to make canning a popular method of preserving. In the beginning glass was used; the first patent on a tin can was taken out in the U.S.A. in 1825. Since that day preservation techniques have progressed rapidly.

Interest in home preserving is growing with the renewed interest in small gardens and the need to find ways to add variety when the food budget is limited. New varieties of fruits and vegetables require new methods; the provincial departments of agriculture offer constantly revised bulletins.

Pickles

Pickles are easy to make. Vary the vegetables, spices and vinegar to suit your taste. Precision is impossible because of the variation in the basic items.

Utensils for making pickles should be aluminum, glass, earthenware or plastic. (Copper, iron and tin may darken the pickle.) A heavy kettle for cooking pickles will prevent sticking.

Vegetables—Use slightly under-ripe vegetables for crispness.

Vinegar—All Canadian vinegar has a minimum acid content but above this minimum there may be a great variation in acidity. Also, it weakens with age. For this reason, taste the finished pickle and add sugar as necessary. Cider vinegar will usually be strong and will darken the pickle; it has a distinct, fruity flavour. Malt vinegar is dark in colour and strong in flavour.

Spices—Whole spice leaves the liquid clear and enables you to control the strength of the spice flavours. Tie whole spices loosely in cheesecloth or other loosely woven cotton and suspend in the pickle with a long string for easy removal. Spices become bitter when overcooked. Only fresh spices will give good flavour. Old spice will give a dusty flavour to the pickle. Buy small quantities and store in a dark, cool place.

To substitute ground for whole spices use approximately one third the quantity. Spice oils, which may be purchased at a drug store, give clarity and sharpness of flavour but may leave a bitter underflavour.

Salt—Pickling salt is preferable because it does not contain additives, such as iodine which darkens the pickle, or chemicals used to keep salt free-running, which cause cloudiness.

Preparation of Glass Containers

Wash the jars and lids and rinse well. Discard those with nicks or cracks. Place the jars upright on a rack in a kettle. Fill kettle with cold water which comes above the top of the tallest jar; bring to a boil and boil 5 min. Or fill with hot water and boil for 20 min. Boil at the same time a funnel, tongs, a cup, a silver knife, a pie plate, two forks.

Boil lids for 5 min. Dip rubber rings in boiling water just before using.

To Fill Preserving Jars

Lift one jar from the boiling water with tongs, and put it on the pie plate; drop the rubber rings (if used) into the boiling water. Fill the jar with the pickle kept simmering on the heat.

From this point on, there are two different methods that may be followed. If the recipe calls for processing the jars, follow Method 2. If not, Method 1 may be used.

Method 1—Work out air bubbles with the sterilized knife; add a little extra liquid to fill the jar; wipe the top with a clean cloth or paper. Add the rubber ring, pulling it into place with the two forks; screw on the top tightly. Repeat until all jars are full. Wash jars in warm water; label; store in a cool, dark place.

Method 2—Fill the jar leaving an air space; work out the bubbles; seal the jar following the directions which accompanied it. Place on a rack in boiling water which covers the jar to a depth of 2.5 cm Return water to boiling and boil gently the required time. Remove the jar to a board or cloth; tighten the top if it was not previously tightened; cool out of drafts with space between each jar. Wash, label and store in a cool, dark place.

Basic Recipe
VEGETABLE RELISH

> 1 medium cabbage
> 8 sweet peppers, red and green
> 8 medium carrots
> 4 medium onions
> pickling salt

Sauce

1 *l*	mild white vinegar
500 ml	sugar
15 ml	celery seed
15 ml	mustard seed

1. Prepare each vegetable: wash; remove core from cabbage; remove seeds and centre of peppers; scrape carrots; peel and quarter onions.
2. Grind the vegetables using a coarse blade; measure into a Pyrex or plastic bowl.
3. Sprinkle salt over each layer of vegetable in the following proportions:

1 *l*	**vegetable**
50 ml	**pickling salt**

4. Stir the salt through, cover and refrigerate several hours.
5. Drain off the liquid; rinse with cold water until the water does not taste too salty.
6. Empty into a jelly bag and allow to drip several hours; measure.
7. Prepare the vinegar sauce by combining the ingredients and bringing to a boil; add to the vegetable allowing one part sauce to two parts vegetable.
8. Bring to a boil stirring frequently; simmer until the vegetables have a transparent look (5 min). They should be tender but still crisp. Taste and add salt or sugar as desired.
9. Ladle into sterile jars (see PREPARATION OF GLASS CONTAINERS and TO FILL PRESERVING JARS).
10. Store in a cool, dark place. *Yield:* 4.5 *l*

Variations

For the small family several varieties of relish may be made in smaller quantities from this basic recipe by varying the vegetable combination and the vinegar sauce; the sauce will keep well and may be made in a larger quantity.

Ripe Cucumber Relish—Peel, quarter and remove seeds from 2 large ripe cucumbers; wash 1 sweet red pepper; peel 2 onions. Chop.

Measure the vinegar and sugar for 1/3 the basic sauce; add turmeric, 5 ml

or omit mustard seed and add mild prepared mustard, 50 ml

Finish as basic recipe. *Yield:* 1 *l*

Sweet Pepper and Watermelon Relish—Prepare:

650 ml	pared watermelon rind
750 ml	sweet peppers, red & green
350 ml	onion

Measure the vinegar and sugar for ½ the basic sauce; replace the spices with mixed pickling spice, 15 ml Increase sugar if desired. Finish as basic recipe. *Yield:* 1 *l*

Zucchini Relish—Wash and slice 2 medium unpeeled zucchini, peel and quarter 1 large onion, clean and chop 1 large stalk of celery.

Measure the vinegar and sugar for ½ the basic sauce recipe; replace the spices with 1 small piece ginger root and 1 stick cinnamon. Follow basic recipe. *Yield:* 500 ml

Pepper Relish—Prepare 12 sweet red peppers, 12 sweet green peppers, 12 large onions.

Prepare half the sauce recipe substituting cider vinegar and omitting the mustard seed. Follow the basic recipe. *Yield:* 2 *l*

BREAD AND BUTTER PICKLES

Recipes for Bread and Butter Pickles vary in sugar content from 1 part sugar to 2 parts vinegar all the way to 2 parts sugar to 1 part vinegar. Nutritionally the lower proportion of sugar is preferable.

1 *l*	dill cucumbers, sliced*
500 ml	large silverskin onions
50 ml	pickling salt
125 ml	sugar
250 ml	vinegar
2 ml	turmeric
2 ml	mustard seed
2 ml	celery seed
5 ml	mixed pickling spice

1. Scrub the fresh cucumbers; slice wafer-thin into a plastic, pottery or glass bowl.

2. Add the onions peeled and cut into slices the same thickness as the cucumber.

3. Dissolve the salt in boiling water; cool; pour over the vegetables; refrigerate overnight; drain; rinse vegetables and empty into a saucepan.

4. Combine sugar, vinegar and spices; bring to a boil; let stand overnight. Taste and add sugar or water if necessary; bring to a boil; strain over the vegetables.

5. Heat to just below the boiling point; lift the vegetable into sterilized jars; pour the syrup in to fill the jars to overflowing; seal; leave one month. *Yield: 1 ℓ*

* Dill cucumbers are cucumbers whose length is 7-15 cm

and whose diameter is no greater than 4 cm

Variation

Pack salted, drained tiny gherkins and tiny onions in the jars; cover with boiling tarragon vinegar; let stand overnight. Drain off vinegar, add to it salt and sugar to taste; bring it to a boil; cool to lukewarm. Pour over the vegetables to overflowing; seal.

TOMMY'S RELISH

No cooking is needed for this relish, which keeps well.

3 kg	ripe tomatoes
500 g	1 large bunch celery
500 g	4 large onions
125 ml	pickling salt
500 ml	vinegar
500 ml	sugar
85 g	mustard seed
	2 sweet red peppers.

1. Peel and chop tomatoes; cut celery finely; grind the onions; stir in salt; drain all overnight in a jelly bag.

2. Grind the peppers; add with the other ingredients to the drained vegetables; stir well together; bottle in small sterilized glasses; seal (see PREPARATION OF GLASS CONTAINERS and TO FILL PRESERVING JARS). *Yield: 1 ℓ*

Make Tommy's Relish and Chili Sauce at the same time since they need the same ingredients. Use the liquid that drains from Tommy's Relish to provide the salt in Chili Sauce.

Recipes, tables, etc. that appear in small capital letters, e.g., PARSLEY BUTTER, CANADA'S FOOD GUIDE, are listed in the index. Consult the index for the number of the page on which the item appears.

Basic Recipe
CHILI SAUCE

2 kg	ripe tomatoes
	2 large onions
	4 sweet peppers
250 ml	vinegar
150 ml	sugar
15 ml	salt
15 ml	whole cloves
30 ml	stick cinnamon
15 ml	whole allspice
5 ml	grated nutmeg *or* mace
	1 small piece of whole ginger root
	4-6 peppercorns
	1 chili pepper

1. Choose ripe, red tomatoes; wash, peel and squeeze to remove some juice and seeds (reserve the liquid for aspic or soup). Discard any green, which gives a bitter flavour. Place drained tomatoes in a large preserving kettle.

2. Remove seeds and tongues from the peppers; chop. Peel and chop the onions. Add both to the tomatoes.

3. Add vinegar, sugar and salt; cook slowly 2 h stirring frequently.

4. At the end of the first hour add the spices tied loosely in a cotton bag; continue to cook until the sauce is thick; taste adding salt or vinegar if desired.

5. Seal in sterile jars (see PREPARATION OF GLASS CONTAINERS and TO FILL PRESERVING JARS). *Yield: 1.5-2 ℓ*

Variations

Dark Chili Sauce—Use brown sugar and cider vinegar.

Celery Sauce—Add a large bunch of finely chopped celery.

Fruit Chili Sauce—Add 3 ripe pears, quartered, cored, pared and chopped; 5 ripe peaches, scalded, peeled and cubed; omit the chili pepper.

Tomato Ketchup—Simmer vegetables until soft; purée; add sugar, vinegar and salt and simmer about 30 min; add the spice bag and continue to cook until the desired flavour and consistency is reached.

PLUM KETCHUP

Catsup is a Malayan word for "taste"; ketchup is a more popular spelling today.

2 kg	plums
500 ml	vinegar
5 ml	salt
1 kg	sugar
15 ml	ground cinnamon
5 ml	ground cloves
5 ml	pepper

1. Wash plums; prick or cut the skin; add vinegar and cook until soft (20 min); sieve.
2. Add other ingredients and simmer until thick (30 min) stirring frequently.
3. Pour into sterilized jars; seal (see PREPARATION OF GLASS CONTAINERS and TO FILL PRESERVING JARS). *Yield:* 1 ℓ

Variations

Cranberry Ketchup—Substitute one-half the quantity of cranberries for the plums; simmer 10 min; sieve; finish as Plum Ketchup.

Chinese Plum Sauce—Use yellow Plums: add 1 box yellow raisins, 1 dried chili pepper, 1 piece ginger root, 4 large onions. Simmer until soft; sieve; add vinegar, salt and sugar. For the spices in Plum Ketchup substitute equal amounts of ground mustard, turmeric, nutmeg and allspice; finish as Plum Ketchup.

Preserving kettles. Modern pressurized containers like that on the right give more controlled results, when used as the manufacturer recommends. Ontario Ministry of Agriculture and Food.

EASY DILL PICKLES

Fresh crisp vegetables will remain crisp after processing according to these directions, *without* the use of the special treatments often recommended, such as a grape leaf in each jar, etc. Cloudiness in these pickles, caused by yeasts, may be ignored. If jars show bubbles or leaks during storage the jars should be opened and the liquid drained off. Make a new amount of pickling solution; pour boiling over the cucumber; process 15 min in a boiling water bath (see TO FILL PRESERVING JARS, Method 2).

Wine vinegar may be used for its fine flavour, but it may need greater dilution.

2 kg	small, fresh dill cucumbers
	fresh dill
	mixed pickling spice
	7 small hot peppers
	7 garlic cloves

Pickling Solution

125 ml	vinegar
15 ml	pickling salt
125 ml	water

1. Wash the cucumbers thoroughly, scrubbing gently; cover with cold water and refrigerate overnight; drain and dry.
2. Sterilize jars which have tight-fitting tops and which will allow a head space above the cucumbers (see PREPARATION OF GLASS CONTAINERS). In each jar put a bunch of fresh dill, a sprinkle of mixed pickling spice including one small hot red pepper, and 1 clove of garlic, peeled. Put in cucumbers.
3. Combine pickling solution ingredients; bring to a boil.
4. Pour the hot solution over the cucumbers to overflowing; seal (see TO FILL PRESERVING JARS); leave 6 weeks. *Yield:* 7 jars, each 500 ml

Variations

Dill Tomatoes—Use hard, green cherry tomatoes with no blush of colour or small firm green tomatoes. Wash, remove stem and blossom and peel thinly. Pack into sterilized jars to which pickling spice, garlic and dill have been added. A small piece of horseradish, a few slivers of green pepper may be added. Fill the jars with hot pickling solution; seal.

Pickled Cherries—Choose large sour red or Montmorency cherries; wash but do not remove the stems; pick over and remove any blemished fruit. Let cherries stand in ice water to cover for 30-40 min; drain and pack into sterilized jars. Prepare the pickling solution reducing the salt to 10 ml

In each jar place a few cloves, a small piece of stick cinnamon; fill to overflowing with cold pickling solution; seal; store in a cool place away from any light to protect the colour.

UNCOOKED GHERKINS

Small crisp gherkins are essential for these easy pickles.

1 kg	small fresh gherkins
50 ml	pickling salt
	boiling water
500 ml	vinegar
30 ml	mixed pickling spice
	1 piece ginger root (broken)
	1 stick cinnamon
250 ml	sugar
	6-8 cloves

1. Wash and scrub gherkins; place in a clean pottery, glass or plastic bowl.
2. Mix the salt well through the gherkins; add boiling water to cover; cool; refrigerate overnight.
3. Empty gherkins into a sieve; rinse well with cold water; rinse and dry the bowl.
4. Return gherkins to the bowl; add the vinegar and the spices tied loosely in a bag.
5. Measure the sugar; stir one large spoonful into the vinegar; cover the gherkins and leave in a cold place.
6. Each morning add a spoonful of sugar to the vinegar, stir well; remove the spice bag when the flavour is strong enough. Continue to add sugar each day until all is used or until the vinegar is of desired sweetness.
7. Pack into sterilized jars (see PREPARATION OF GLASS CONTAINERS); bring vinegar to a boil and pour into the jars to overflowing; seal (see TO FILL PRESERVING JARS). *Yield:* 3 jars, each 250 ml

---

Recipes, tables, etc. that appear in small capital letters, e.g., PARSLEY BUTTER, CANADA'S FOOD GUIDE, are listed in the index. Consult the index for the number of the page on which the item appears.

PICKLED ONIONS

500 g	small silverskin onions
	boiling water
50 ml	pickling salt
500 ml	vinegar
125 ml	sugar
	½ stick cinnamon
	chili pepper
	bay leaf

1. Pour boiling water over the onions and let stand a few minutes to soften the skins; drain, rinse with cold water and peel.
2. Cut a cross in each onion and place in a glass, pottery or plastic bowl; sprinkle with salt; add boiling water to cover; cool.
3. Cover the bowl and refrigerate overnight; drain and rinse.
4. Combine vinegar, sugar and spices; bring to a boil; add the onions and return to a boil; remove from heat.
5. Spoon the onions into sterilized jars (see PREPARATION OF GLASS CONTAINERS); divide the spices among them; return the vinegar to a boil; fill the jars to overflowing; seal; let stand at least 2 weeks. *Yield:* 5 jars each containing 200 ml

Sweet Pickled Onions—Increase the sugar to 250 ml

or use PICKLING SYRUP.

PICKLED MUSHROOMS

2 ℓ	mushrooms
	3 medium onions
	1 clove garlic
750 ml	wine vinegar
250 ml	water
125 ml	sugar
5 ml	salt
15 ml	fresh basil and tarragon, chopped

1. Wash mushrooms, removing stems (reserve stems for use in other recipes).
2. Slice onions, peel garlic.
3. Combine vinegar, water, sugar, salt and herbs; bring to a boil; add mushrooms, return to a boil; boil 3 min; add onion and garlic; boil 3 min. Discard the garlic.
4. Spoon the mushrooms and onions into sterilized jars (see PREPARATION OF GLASS CONTAINERS); bring the vinegar to a boil; pour over the mushrooms pressing them down gently to pack the jars; fill to overflowing; seal (see TO FILL PRESERVING JARS). *Yield:* 1.25 ℓ

Sweet Vinegar Pickles

A sweet vinegar syrup may be used to pickle a few jars of fruit to use as an attractive garnish for meats.

Basic Recipe
PICKLING SYRUP

This recipe makes enough syrup to pickle

3-4 kg	fruit
1.5 *l*	sugar
1 *l*	vinegar
250 ml	water
	3 sticks cinnamon
15 ml	whole cloves
5 ml	whole allspice
5 ml	mace *or* nutmeg
	1 small piece ginger root
	1 slice lemon

Combine sugar, vinegar and water; bring to a boil; add the spices tied loosely in cheesecloth; simmer 5 min

PICKLED FRUIT

1. Prepare PICKLING SYRUP.
2. Prepare the fruit.*
3. Add the fruit to the syrup; simmer until glazed.
4. Discard spice bag; spoon fruit into sterilized jars (see PREPARATION OF GLASS CONTAINERS).
5. Boil the syrup to a honey-like consistency or dilute with boiling water if the syrup has become too thick. Fill jars to overflowing with boiling syrup; work out any air bubbles; seal (see TO FILL PRESERVING JARS). Store in a cool dark place for a month. *Yield: 1.5 l*

*Fruits

Sweet Apples—Quarter, peel and core Tolman Sweets or Russets; cook a few at a time in syrup to cover until just tender but not soft; lift carefully into a sterilized jar. Continue until all the apples are cooked, adding water if necessary to the syrup; bring syrup to a boil and pour over the fruit. Seal.

Crabapples—Choose firm fruit, uniform in size. Cut out blossom end and prick the skin with a fork.
Pears—Choose small Seckel or winter pears; remove the blossom end; prick the skins; cover with boiling water; simmer until tender; pack into prepared jars and fill with hot syrup. Peel larger, firm pears, cut in half and core; simmer the pieces in hot syrup to cover until tender.
Peaches—Peel; cut in half and remove the pits, or leave small fruit whole; simmer in hot syrup to cover until tender.
Lemon Slices—Cut washed lemons into thick slices; simmer in water to cover until tender (20 min); add to syrup and simmer until glazed (10 min).
Orange Slices—Cover unpeeled oranges with water in a shallow saucepan; simmer 1 h; drain, slice, stick 2 or 3 cloves in each piece; simmer slices in a single layer in syrup for 15 min
Prunes—Soak prunes in water until plump; add hot syrup; simmer until glazed.

WATERMELON RIND PICKLE

8 kg	1 watermelon
50 ml	salt
4 *l*	ice water
	1 recipe of PICKLING SYRUP

1. Select a young, tender melon; cut in half or quarters and remove the fruit; cover the rind with boiling water; boil 5 min; drain and cool; pare off dark green skin and pink pulp.
2. Cut the rind into fancy shapes with small cookie cutters or cocktail tidbit cutters or into strips then diamonds, cubes or triangles.
3. Sprinkle with salt; cover with ice water; refrigerate 8 h. Drain, rinse in several cold waters and cover with fresh water; bring to a boil and simmer until tender (15-20 min); drain.
4. Prepare the PICKLING SYRUP; add the rind; simmer until rind is transparent when a piece is lifted out of the syrup (15 min); remove the spice bag; cover and leave the fruit in the syrup several hours or overnight.
5. Drain off the syrup; bring to a boil and return to the fruit. Let stand several hours again.
6. Drain off the syrup; bring to a boil; adjust to the original thickness by adding boiling water if necessary; add rind to syrup, return to a boil; lift into sterilized jars (see PREPARATION OF GLASS CONTAINERS); fill to overflowing; seal (see TO FILL PRESERVING JARS). *Yield: 4 l*

Recipes, tables, etc. that appear in small capital letters, e.g., PARSLEY BUTTER, CANADA'S FOOD GUIDE, are listed in the index. Consult the index for the number of the page on which the item appears.

Mustard Pickles

Basic Recipe
MUSTARD DRESSING

250 ml	brown sugar
125 ml	flour
50 ml	mustard
10 ml	turmeric
250 ml	water
1 ℓ	vinegar
15 ml	celery seed
5 ml	whole cloves
5 ml	mixed pickling spice

1. Combine dry ingredients; add water; mix to a smooth paste.
2. Heat vinegar with spices; simmer until the desired flavour is obtained; strain; discard spices.
3. Stir vinegar into the mustard paste; return to heat; stir until mixture just comes to a boil.

Variation
Quick Mustard Dressing—For the mustard, turmeric and spices substitute 1 jar of prepared mustard, 180 ml

PICKLING BRINE

50 ml	pickling salt
1 ℓ	water

Combine; stir to dissolve the salt.

MUSTARD PICKLES

2-2.5 ℓ	*prepared vegetables
	1 recipe PICKLING BRINE
	1 recipe MUSTARD DRESSING

1. Prepare the vegetables; combine in a pottery or plastic bowl:

   *1 cauliflower: break into small flowerets.

   24 small gherkins: whole or cut in 2-3 pieces; scrub.

   4 small green tomatoes: wash; cut in eighths.

1 small zucchini: wash; quarter lengthwise, cut in pieces.

peeled silverskin onions: 500 ml (250 g)
Boil 5 minutes in water to cover; drain.

1 medium size green cucumber: quarter lengthwise; remove seeds; cut into small cubes. (Pare if skin is tough or blemished.)

1 sweet red pepper: seed; cut into small squares or diamonds.

2. Combine salt and water; pour over the vegetables; weight down with a plate to keep vegetables under the solution; refrigerate overnight.
3. Drain the vegetables; rinse with cold water; drain well.
4. Add to hot MUSTARD DRESSING; stir until mixture boils again; do not overcook.
5. Pack the vegetables into sterilized jars (see PREPARATION OF GLASS CONTAINERS); fill to overflowing with the mustard dressing; seal (see TO FILL PRESERVING JARS). Leave one month. *Yield:* 3 ℓ

CHOPPED MUSTARD PICKLE

1 ℓ	cucumbers, peeled, seeded
500 ml	onions, chopped
	1 green and 1 red sweet pepper, seeded and chopped
	1 cauliflower, chopped
	6 stalks celery, diced
	1 recipe PICKLING BRINE
	1 recipe MUSTARD DRESSING

1. Prepare the vegetables, approximately 3 ℓ
2. Prepare hot PICKLING BRINE; pour over the chopped vegetables; let stand overnight, weighted to keep vegetables under the brine.
3. Rinse; drain well; cover with MUSTARD DRESSING; heat and stir until mixture comes to a boil. Bottle in sterilized jars, filled to overflowing (see PREPARATION OF GLASS CONTAINERS and TO FILL PRESERVING JARS). *Yield:* 3 ℓ

Unused MUSTARD DRESSING makes a good sauce on a hot vegetable such as broccoli, green or wax beans, cauliflower, or on ham or meat loaf.

CHILI RELISH

2 kg	ripe tomatoes
	20 sweet red and green peppers, seeded and chopped
	5 medium onions, chopped
125 ml	pickling salt
	1 hot red pepper, seeded and chopped
	1 recipe MUSTARD DRESSING

1. Peel the tomatoes; squeeze to remove juice and seeds (save juice for aspic or soup); chop the tomatoes.
2. Combine with sweet peppers and onions; add salt and refrigerate overnight.
3. Drain well; add hot pepper and dressing; stir over moderate heat until mixture boils.
4. Simmer until thick (10-20 min), stirring frequently.
5. Bottle in sterilized jars; seal (see PREPARATION OF GLASS CONTAINERS and TO FILL PRESERVING JARS). *Yield: 3-4 ℓ*

MUSTARD BEANS

1 kg	small, tender wax beans
	1 recipe MUSTARD DRESSING

1. Wash beans, remove tips and cut if necessary.
2. Cook in boiling salted water until just tender; drain.
3. Add to the hot MUSTARD DRESSING; cook 5 min, stirring.
4. Bottle in sterilized jars; fill to overflowing; seal (see PREPARATION OF GLASS CONTAINERS and TO FILL PRESERVING JARS). *Yield: 2.5 ℓ*

SAUERKRAUT

This traditional method of preserving cabbage depends on a natural process: the lactic acid bacteria on the cabbage decompose the natural sugar of the cabbage forming lactic acid and gas (carbon dioxide). These bacteria prevent the growth of other types which would cause spoilage. When the frothing ceases the acid has reached the maximum concentration and the bacteria will cease to grow. By keeping the liquid overflowing and thus removing the scum, the source of food for yeasts that feed upon the acid and cause spoilage is removed.

Green cabbage has more vitamins; white heads make a more attractively coloured product. Sauerkraut retains some vitamin C throughout the fermentation. One-third to one-half of the vitamin is lost during processing and a further loss occurs if the sauerkraut is cooked.

4 kg	5-10 cabbages
125 ml	pickling salt

1. Choose firm heads of cabbage. Trim off the outer leaves and any blemishes; wash, drain, quarter and core. Measure salt.
2. Shred finely into a bowl, sprinkling each layer with salt and tossing lightly together; leave until moisture begins to collect.
3. Almost fill a crock or plastic tub, packing with *firm,* even pressure to eliminate all air pockets, covering each layer with salt; repeat until all the cabbage and salt are used. Take care not to bruise the cabbage and thus discolour it.
4. Push a clean wooden stick (the handle of a wooden spoon) into the centre to make a well which will allow the gas to escape.
5. Cover the cabbage with trimmed and washed outer leaves, then with a piece of clean sheeting somewhat larger than the crock. Tuck cloth inside crock so no cabbage is exposed to the air.
6. Weight* to ensure that the cabbage will remain under the liquid, and let stand in a light place at a temperature of 20-24°C
7. Each day remove the cloth; wash the weight; rinse and replace using a clean cloth. Wash and boil the cloth removed, and use it next day.
8. When fermentation is finished (3-6 weeks) the sauerkraut is ready to use; remove the cabbage to a preserving kettle and heat to simmering. Do not boil. Pack hot into jars; cover with hot juice. Process according to Method 2, TO FILL PRESERVING JARS, 15 min for each small jar; 20 min for each large jar. *Yield: 4-5 ℓ*

Variations
Layer with the cabbage:

1 ℓ	cranberries
30 ml	caraway seed

* The traditional weight was a heavy plate or round oak board which fitted the crock loosely and was held down with a stone. To this stone was attributed special qualities in producing good sauerkraut and it was carefully cared for between seasons. The modern substitute for both cover and weight is a plastic bag (of double thickness for safety) containing enough water so the bag will rest firmly on the cabbage, sealing it from the air and forcing the liquid up to form a layer above the cabbage and over the cloth.

MINCEMEAT

500 g	ground beef
250 g	chopped suet
500 ml	currants
500 ml	raisins
1.5 ℓ	6-7 grated apples
500 ml	brown sugar
150 ml	molasses
5 ml	salt
5-10 ml	mace *or* nutmeg
5-10 ml	cinnamon
5-10 ml	cloves
500 g	glazed mixed fruit
200 ml	cider vinegar *or* boiled sweet cider
30 ml	brandy extract

1. Combine all ingredients except extract; cover and simmer, stirring often, for 2 h. Add more cider if additional liquid is needed.
2. Stir in extract, pack in sterilized jars; seal (see PRE-PARATION OF GLASS CONTAINERS and TO FILL PRE-SERVING JARS).
3. Age at least 1 month. *Yield: 6.25ℓ*

Quick Recipe—Experiment with the many commercial mincemeats available to find a likeable flavour. Add small amounts of fruit juice, maple syrup and extract as desired.

MOCK MINCEMEAT

400 ml	apples
250 ml	cranberries
250 ml	seeded raisins
250 ml	currants
125 ml	sweet cider *or* cider vinegar
200 ml	melted butter *or* oil
400 ml	brown sugar
400 ml	grape juice *or* jelly
10 ml	cinnamon
10 ml	cloves, mace, allspice, combined

1. Pare and core the apples; chop; wash and chop cranberries; wash and dry raisins and currants.
2. Combine all ingredients; cook, stirring occasionally, 30-40 min
3. Pack in sterilized jars; seal (see PREPARATION OF GLASS CONTAINERS and TO FILL PRESERVING JARS). *Yield: 1.5-2 ℓ*

Chopped green tomatoes may replace half the apple; use those that have turned white just before ripening.

Chutneys

Chutneys are popular as an accompaniment to Chinese and Indian dishes. They should be a rich brown colour, thick and clear, with bits of transparent fruit throughout.

Basic Recipe
PEACH CHUTNEY

500 ml	cider vinegar
250 ml	dark brown sugar
125 ml	lime juice
10 ml	salt
	10 cardamom pods
15 ml	mustard seed
	2 hot red chilis
	1 piece fresh ginger root
1 ℓ	ripe peaches
125 ml	sultana raisins
250 ml	sweet red and green pepper
50 ml	blanched almonds

1. Combine vinegar, sugar, lime juice and salt in a heavy saucepan.
2. Remove the seeds from the cardamom pods; crush with the mustard seed and chilis; peel and slice the ginger root.
3. Peel and slice the peaches; mince the peppers and chop the almonds.
4. Combine all the ingredients; bring to a boil; simmer until fruit is tender (20 min); empty into a colander over a bowl and drain; taste liquid; add vinegar or sugar as desired.
5. Return liquid to saucepan and boil over high heat for 10 min; return fruit to the syrup; simmer stirring frequently to the desired consistency.
6. Spoon the solids into sterilized jars (see PREPARATION OF GLASS CONTAINERS); fill to overflowing with the syrup; seal (see TO FILL PRESERVING JARS). *Yield: 1.5 ℓ*

Variations
Replace peaches with plums, pears, canteloupe, green tomatoes, rhubarb, apricots, mangoes, alone or in combination. Replace the lime juice with lemon and orange juice. Replace the cardamom with stick cinnamon, whole allspice, whole cloves, coriander seeds tied loosely in cheesecloth.

Recipes, tables, etc. that appear in small capital letters, e.g., PARSLEY BUTTER, CANADA'S FOOD GUIDE, are listed in the index. Consult the index for the number of the page on which the item appears.

Jelly, Jam, Marmalade and Conserves

Small quantities made frequently with these recipes keep their fresh flavour. They make ideal gifts and have a use beyond the breakfast table; with biscuits and cheese for dessert or a party; with fresh muffins or scones for afternoon or morning coffee; as filling for small tarts; as garnish for salads and desserts.

The high sugar content of jellies, jams and marmalades prevents the growth of yeasts and bacteria and retards the growth of moulds.

Success in the making of jellies and jams depends to a great extent upon the proper selection of fruit. Include both ripe fruit for flavour and slightly underripe fruit, which is strong in pectin and aids in the setting of jelly.

Currants, grapes, lemons, sour and bitter oranges, crabapples, tart apples and cranberries are the fruits that are richest in pectin. For these fruits the addition of sugar is all that is needed to cause the juice to jell. If commercial pectin is added to fruit, more sugar will be required and more jelly will result. Since the flavour will be diluted it is not recommended for those fruits which have sufficient pectin.

Jars of jam or jelly make welcome gifts. General Foods.

Preparation of the Fruit

Wash large fruits such as apples, cut in pieces, add water just to cover; bring to a boil, reduce the heat and simmer until the fruit is soft (20 min). Do not remove the peel or the core, as their pectin content is high.

Stems must be removed from small fruits such as grapes, berries and currants, because the tannin they contain will give a bitterness to the juice. Add only enough water to prevent these fruits from scorching; once the fruit begins to cook it may be mashed to release the juice. Cook until the seeds begin to float, at a low temperature to retain the fresh flavour.

TO MAKE JELLY

Extraction of Fruit Juice

1. When the fruit is very soft (see Preparation of the Fruit, above), pour it into a jelly bag which has been rinsed in boiling water.
2. Drip several hours; for the first extraction of juice do not squeeze the bag. The utensil in which the juice is collected may be aluminum, earthenware or plastic; it should not be copper, iron or tin, which may darken the juice. Measure and refrigerate the juice.
3. Empty the pulp into the kettle, cover with water, bring to a boil, stirring to prevent scorching, and empty again into the jelly bag. If the second extraction gives a good JELLY TEST it is possible to make a third extraction pressing the pulp and adding spice or herbs to improve flavour.

Finish each extraction separately. The first will have the best colour and flavour.

Preparation of a Jelly Bag

Use a cotton pillow case washed and kept for this purpose, or stitch a bag from a double thickness of cheesecloth or from factory cotton. Wash before using to remove any sizing or bleach. For small amounts of jelly a cloth may be supported in a sieve over a bowl; for large amounts detach the handle of a mop; support the pole between two chairs and tie the bag onto the pole; place a large bowl on the floor on newspapers.

Test for Pectin

In a custard cup mix 1 spoonful of hot fruit juice with an equal amount of rubbing alcohol; allow it to stand a few minutes. A thick clot of jelly indicates a large amount of pectin; a stringy gel indicates a fair amount; several small particles show that juice should be boiled another 10 min to concentrate it. Retest and if the result is the same use commercial pectin. DO NOT TASTE THE JELLY; RUBBING ALCOHOL IS POISONOUS.

Preparation of Jelly

1. Measure the juice into a broad saucepan with a capacity at least three times the quantity of juice.
2. Measure the sugar:
   If the TEST FOR PECTIN showed high pectin content, use an amount of sugar equal to the amount of juice.
   If the TEST FOR PECTIN showed fair pectin content, use an amount of sugar equal to ¾ the amount of juice.
   If the TEST FOR PECTIN showed a weak result, use an amount of sugar equal to 2/3 the amount of juice.
3. Prepare the glasses (see PREPARATION OF GLASS CONTAINERS). Use standard jelly glasses or small glasses with straight sides. The volume of jelly produced will be approximately 10 per cent greater than the volume of juice.
4. Boil the juice over high heat to a full rolling boil; add the sugar; stir until dissolved; continue to boil rapidly until the jelly forms. Rapid cooking gives brighter colour and flavour.

Jelly Tests

Sheet Test—The syrup has reached a thickness which prevents it falling from a spoon in a steady stream. It slides or "sheets" from the spoon forming a lip along the edge of a cold spoon.

Refrigerator Test—A small amount of syrup placed on a saucer in the refrigerator will form wrinkles if pushed with the finger.

Temperature Test—Jelly forms at approximately 104°C

5. Skim the foam with a spoon and pour the jelly into hot sterilized glasses leaving a small space at the top; dampen the corner of a clean cloth in hot water and wipe the inside of the rim of the glass.
6. Seal with wax: Melt chopped paraffin wax in a container set in a pan of boiling water. Pour a thin layer onto the hot jelly; cover the glass and cool. Add a second thin layer to fill any spaces caused by shrinkage, rotating the glasses gently to ensure that all are sealed. A tea pot or a juice can squeezed to form a spout makes a good container; cover with a plastic bag to store.
   No jelly test is exact. Before adding the second layer of wax check the consistency. Slightly thin rather than too stiff jellies are preferable. Jelly which has not set will sometimes do so if left in the sun for a few days. Or it may be reboiled or may be used as FRUIT SYRUP.
7. Cover the glass with a metal cover, foil or plastic film.
8. Wash, label, store in a cool, dry, dark place.

GRAPE JELLY

3 kg	blue grapes
250 ml	water
2 kg	sugar

1. Choose grapes which are not overripe; wash; pull from the stems.
2. Simmer with water; mash; continue to cook, stirring occasionally until the seeds float (10 min).
3. Empty the grapes into a jelly bag (see PREPARATION OF A JELLY BAG) let drip; refrigerate several hours. *Yield:* 1.5 ℓ clear juice
4. Measure out the juice, being careful not to disturb the sediment (grape juice contains tartaric acid, which in large amounts will cause acid crystals to form in the jelly); bring to a boil; TEST FOR PECTIN.
5. Measure the sugar; add to the juice.
6. Boil over high heat until the jelly forms (see JELLY TESTS).
7. Remove from heat; skim; pour into hot, sterilized glasses; seal (see PREPARATION OF JELLY). *Yield:* 6-7 glasses, each containing 180 ml
8. Prepare a second extraction by reboiling the pulp from the jelly bag with water to cover; press through a sieve; measure; allow sugar equal to 2/3 the quantity of sieved pulp. Finish according to the general directions (see TO MAKE JELLY) or prepare Spiced Grape Jelly (below). *Yield:* 1 ℓ juice

Spiced Grape Jelly—To the pulp from the first extraction add:

250 ml	water
250 ml	vinegar
50 ml	spices (whole cloves, stick cinnamon, whole allspice)

Simmer 10 min; sieve; measure the liquid; measure sugar allowing 2/3 the quantity; finish according to the general method (see TO MAKE JELLY).

Green Grape Jelly—Canadian green grapes make a delicious jelly. Follow the directions for GRAPE JELLY.

Grape and Grapefruit Jelly—Use equal amounts of fresh, strained grapefruit juice with grape juice, either blue or green. Combine the two juices; measure and finish as GRAPE JELLY.

Recipes, tables, etc. that appear in small capital letters, e.g., PARSLEY BUTTER, CANADA'S FOOD GUIDE, are listed in the index. Consult the index for the number of the page on which the item appears.

APPLE JELLY

3-4 kg	tart cooking apples
2 ℓ	water
1.5 ℓ	sugar

1. Wash apples well to remove any spray; remove stems.
2. Cut into quarters; add the water; simmer, stirring occasionally to prevent sticking until apples are very soft (10-15 min); empty into jelly bag; finish according to general directions (see TO MAKE JELLY). This amount will make enough juice for several variations.

Yield: 2 ℓ   clear juice
    8-10 glasses, each containing 180 ml

Variations
Herb Jelly—To each glass of jelly add:

5 ml	fresh, chopped herbs*
or	
1 ml	crushed, dried herbs*
	or
	1 small fresh geranium leaf

* Basil, mint, fennel or thyme.
Serve with meat or cheese and biscuits.
Cider Jelly—Substitute cider for water in Apple Jelly.
Crabapple Jelly—Bright red crabapples make a jelly of good colour and a sharper flavour than apples; follow the general method.

CURRANT JELLY

Currants, either red or black, make excellent jelly if not overripe. Follow the general method (see TO MAKE JELLY); taste the dripped juice and add a little lemon juice if it is not as acid as tart apple juice.

WILD BERRY JELLIES

Although wild berries are still to be found, they are less abundant and accessible today than they were in our grandparents' day. Hence their juice is often combined with apple juice to make jelly.

Chokecherries, pincherries and black elderberry must have stems removed because the tannin they contain gives a bitter flavour. Wash the berries, remove the stems; add enough water to cover the bottom of the saucepan containing the berries; heat to boiling, mash, strain. Combine the juice with half the amount of apple or crabapple juice, TEST FOR PEC-TIN and prepare following the general method (see TO MAKE JELLY).

Rose Hip Jelly—The red fruit which appears after the wild roses have fallen makes a jelly very high in vitamin C. Pick after the first frost. Chop the washed fruit; finish according to the general method (see TO MAKE JELLY), adding the strained juice to apple, crabapple or red currant juice.

Sumac Jelly—Collect the Staghorn sumac heads in the late summer when they are velvety. Strip the berries away from the stem allowing the wind to blow away last year's dried fluff. Add water to half cover; simmer, stirring often until the colour of the water is bright (15 min). Drip in a close-textured jelly bag; combine with an equal amount of apple juice; finish according to the general method (see TO MAKE JELLY). Serve with game, meat, or cheese.

Saskatoon Jelly—The search for this berry, resembling a red blueberry, was once the reason for all-day outings on the Prairies. Like the blueberries in the Eastern provinces, these berries are eaten raw, made into pies, or into jam. To make jelly the juice must be combined with a high pectin juice or commercial pectin.

Wild Raspberry Jelly is a delectable, sweet, dark red jelly which is a perfect accompaniment to cheese and biscuits, muffins, or hot tea biscuits. Rinse the berries gently in a sieve to remove dust; place in a saucepan with enough water to cover the bottom of the pan. Mash; simmer, stirring to prevent scorching until the seeds begin to float (15 min). Strain off the first juice for a clear jelly adding 2/3-3/4 the quantity of sugar; finish according to the general directions (see TO MAKE JELLY).

A second extraction may be made, pressing the pulp through the sieve or squeezing in a bag. This will give a less clear juice to combine with apple juice or to use with commercial pectin.

A third extraction from the pulp combined with half the amount of water and a few fresh berries to add colour and flavour may be used for FRUIT SYRUP.

High Bush Cranberry Jelly—These berries have an unpleasant odour but make a good, bright, red-orange jelly to serve with game. Pull the berries from the stems, wash and mash; finish according to the general directions (see TO MAKE JELLY).

Wild Strawberry Preserves—These berries are too small and scarce to lose any by dripping or puréeing. Remove any stems, measure the berries into a saucepan; add enough water to cover the bottom of the dish; bring rapidly to a boil; add sugar allowing 1 part to three parts of fruit; simmer until the sugar is dissolved; taste and add more sugar if desired; bring to a full rolling boil; bottle in sterilized glasses (see PREPARATION OF GLASS CONTAINERS) to use in the same way as wild raspberry syrup or as a thick preserve with toast, tea biscuits, muffins, or pancakes.

Jam

BLACK CURRANT JAM

500 ml	currants
250 ml	water
500 ml	sugar

1. Clip off the stem and blossom end of the berries; wash; measure into a saucepan.
2. Add boiling water; bring to a boil and cook until berries are tender (20 min).
3. Add sugar; boil until the juice tests for jelly (8 min—see JELLY TESTS). Finish according to the general method (see TO MAKE JELLY). *Yield:* 6 glasses, each containing 180 ml

SASKATOON OR BLUEBERRY JAM

500 ml	berries
250 ml	apple, chopped
50 ml	water
750 ml	sugar
5 ml	lemon rind
5 ml	lemon juice

1. Wash and drain berries; pare, core and chop the apple; add the water.
2. Bring to a boil; cook until almost tender; add sugar and lemon rind; bring to a boil; add lemon juice; stir frequently until thick (20 min); pour into sterilized glasses; seal (see TO MAKE JELLY). *Yield:* 3 glasses, each containing 180 ml

RASPBERRY SASKATOON JAM

A good combination, giving flavour to the saskatoons and a less seedy jam than when raspberries only are used.

1 *l*	raspberries
1 *l*	saskatoons
1.75 *l*	sugar
	½ bottle pectin

1. Wash and remove stems from both lots of berries; crush them together; add sugar.
2. Heat gently until the sugar is dissolved; bring to a rapid boil; boil 1 min stirring constantly.
3. Remove from heat; add pectin; stir to mix well.
4. Skim, pour into sterilized glasses, seal with wax (see TO MAKE JELLY).

Blueberries may be substituted for saskatoons.

Raspberry and Red Currant Jam

400 ml	red currants, stemmed
200 ml	water
2 *l*	raspberries
900 ml	sugar

Boil currants and water until mushy (10 min); drip. Combine juice and raspberries and boil 10 min; add sugar; finish according to general directions (see TO MAKE JELLY).

Three-fruit Jam—To the previous recipe add pitted, coarsely chopped red cherries, 1 *l*
Combine the fruits with the water; simmer until cherries soften; measure; add, ¾ the quantity of sugar; boil until thick (20-30 min); finish according to the general directions (see TO MAKE JELLY).

STRAWBERRY JAM

1 *l*	strawberries (prepared)
1 *l*	sugar
	juice of 1 lemon
or	
15 ml	wine vinegar

1. Wash berries in a sieve; drain; hull.
2. Slice berries; layer with the sugar into a saucepan; stir over low heat until sugar dissolves; bring to a boil; boil gently without stirring for 10 min; add lemon juice; empty into a glass or plastic bowl; let stand overnight.
3. Return to the saucepan, bring to a boil and boil slowly 10 min; skim; pour into sterilized glasses; seal with wax (see TO MAKE JELLY). *Yield:* 4-5 glasses, each containing 180 ml

TOMATO GINGER JAM

1.25 *l*	ripe tomatoes, peeled and chopped
	2 lemons
	1 onion
625 ml	brown sugar
5 ml	paprika
5 ml	ground ginger
1 ml	black pepper
1 ml	turmeric

Chop tomatoes; grind lemon and onion (or chop finely); cook over moderate heat until thick (30 min) stirring frequently; add sugar and spices; simmer, stirring frequently until jam is thick and clear (20 min). Pour into sterilized glasses and seal (see TO MAKE JELLY). *Yield:* 5 glasses, each containing 180 ml

RED PEPPER AND ORANGE JAM

	25 sweet red peppers
	2 large oranges
500 ml	**vinegar**
1 ℓ	**sugar**
10 ml	**salt**

1. Wash peppers, remove seeds and tongue; grind and drain.
2. Wash oranges; grind the whole orange including the rind.
3. Combine with drained peppers and other ingredients; simmer until sugar is dissolved; boil rapidly, stirring frequently until jam is thick and clear (25 min).
4. Pour into sterilized glasses; seal (see TO MAKE JELLY). *Yield:* 8 glasses, each containing 180 ml

RED PEPPER JELLY

500 ml	**8 sweet red peppers**
	1 small hot red pepper
250 ml	**cider vinegar**
500 ml	**apple juice**
1 ml	**salt**
	1 pkg. Certo
1.375 ℓ	**sugar**
	juice of 1 lemon

1. Wash peppers, remove tongue, seeds and stems; grind or chop finely; measure pulp and juice.
2. Place peppers, vinegar, apple juice, salt and Certo in a kettle; heat rapidly to boiling; stirring constantly; add sugar; bring to a full rolling boil.
3. Remove from heat; add lemon; skim and stir occasionally for 3 min
4. Pour into hot sterilized glasses, cover with melted wax (see TO MAKE JELLY). Let stand 2 weeks before using. *Yield:* 6-7 glasses, each containing 180 ml

---

Recipes, tables, etc. that appear in small capital letters, e.g., PARSLEY BUTTER, CANADA'S FOOD GUIDE, are listed in the index. Consult the index for the number of the page on which the item appears.

Marmalade

In this form of jelly there are thin slices of fruit, usually but not always citrus fruit.

ORANGE MARMALADE

4 thin-skinned oranges
1 large lemon
water (3 times measured pulp and rind)
sugar (¾ quantity of cooked fruit)

Method 1
1. Wash fruit; squeeze juice; cover and refrigerate. Tie pips in a small cotton bag.
2. Cut rinds in quarters; add water to cover; boil 10 min; cool.
3. Lift out rinds; pull off pulp and grind or chop it.
4. Cut rinds in *thin* slivers; add to pulp; measure.
5. To the water in which the rinds were cooked add water to make a total quantity equal to three times the measured fruit; add the pulp and pips. Allow the fruit to stand in a cool place (not refrigerated) several hours, to extract the pectin, soften the rind, and reduce the cooking time.
6. Boil uncovered until rind is soft (30-45 min); remove pips; add the refrigerated juice; measure; return to a boil.
8. Measure sugar allowing a quantity equal to ¾ the measured fruit.
9. Add sugar to fruit; boil rapidly with frequent stirring until jelly forms, about 30 min (see JELLY TESTS).
10. Remove from heat; skim and stir; bottle (see TO MAKE JELLY). *Yield:* 1.25-1.5 ℓ

Method 2
This method will give a clear jelly with few shreds of rind. The yield is less.
1. Remove peel with a sharp vegetable peeler; sliver with a sharp knife; tie loosely in cheesecloth.
2. Cut fruit and squeeze juice; strain to remove pips; tie pips in a small cotton bag and place in a preserving kettle; refrigerate juice.
3. Grind rinds using a coarse blade; *measure;* add to pips; add an amount of water equal to 3 times the total of rind and pulp, about 1.5 ℓ
4. Boil gently, uncovered, until rinds are very soft, about 1 h

5. Remove peel from the bag and add to refrigerated juice; pour fruit into a jelly bag; allow to drip several hours; measure.
6. Combine measured peel, refrigerated juice and strained juice; measure sugar, a quantity equal to ¾ the combined total of fruit.
7. Boil, stirring frequently until jelly forms (30 min). See JELLY TESTS. Remove from heat; skim and stir; pour into sterilized glasses; seal with wax.
Yield: 1-1.25 *ℓ*

Variations
Bitter Orange Marmalade—4 Seville oranges, 2 sweet oranges, 1 lemon
Yield: 5-6 glasses, each containing 180 ml
Citrus Marmalade—1 orange, 1 grapefruit, 1 lemon
Yield: 6-7 glasses, each containing 180 ml
Kumquat Marmalade—24 kumquats, 2 oranges
Yield: 5-6 glasses, each containing 180 ml
Lime Marmalade—6 limes, 3 lemons
Yield: 4-5 glasses, each containing 180 ml
Pineapple Marmalade—1 fresh pineapple, shredded; 3 lemons
Yield: 5-6 glasses, each containing 180 ml

GREEN TOMATO MARMALADE

	12 medium green tomatoes
	1 small lemon
125 ml	**tart apples, chopped**
250 ml	**sugar**
5 ml	**mixed pickling spice**
15 ml	**stick cinnamon and whole cloves**

Squeeze the juice of the lemon; slice rind thinly.

Combine tomatoes, lemon rind, apples and sugar; bring to a full rolling boil; boil, stirring frequently 20 min; add lemon juice and spices tied in a bag; continue to cook, stirring until jelly forms (20 min). See JELLY TESTS. Pour into sterilized glasses; seal with wax (see TO MAKE JELLY). *Yield:* 5 glasses, each containing 180 ml

Conserves

A conserve is a mixture of fruit to which nuts are often added. The consistency is similar to that of jam.

RHUBARB CONSERVE

1 *ℓ*	rhubarb
	1 lemon
	1 orange
250 ml	water
750 ml	sugar
250 ml	raisins
125 ml	walnuts

1. Wash rhubarb and cut into pieces.
2. Squeeze lemon and orange and save juice; grind rind.
3. Simmer rind in the water until tender (20 min).
4. Add juice, rhubarb and sugar, stir until sugar is dissolved.
5. Continue to boil rapidly, stirring constantly until thick (15 min).
6. Add raisins, washed if necessary, and nuts and bring to a boil again. Boil 5 min
7. Pour into sterilized glasses; seal with wax (see TO MAKE JELLY). *Yield:* 5 glasses, each containing 180 ml

Variations
Rhubarb and Pineapple Conserve—Replace raisins and walnuts with shredded fresh pineapple or drained crushed pineapple, 500 ml
Ginger Rhubarb Conserve—Add grated fresh ginger root, 5 ml

STRAWBERRY AND PINEAPPLE CONSERVE

500 ml	strawberries
250 ml	canned crushed pineapple, drained
750 ml	sugar

1. Wash and hull strawberries; crush.
2. Add pineapple and sugar.
3. Cook slowly until thick.
4. Pour into sterilized glasses; seal with wax (see TO MAKE JELLY). *Yield:* 4 glasses, each containing 180 ml

CRANBERRY CONSERVE

250 ml	CRANBERRY SAUCE
125 ml	crushed pineapple
50 ml	sultana raisins
15 ml	grated orange rind
50 ml	walnuts, chopped

1. Combine all ingredients except walnuts; simmer until thick, stirring occasionally (15 min). Add walnuts. Pour into sterilized glasses; seal with wax (see TO MAKE JELLY). *Yield:* 3 glasses, each containing 180 ml

Serve this conserve with ham, chicken or turkey, or combine with cream cheese to make a filling for chicken club sandwiches.

CHERRY CONSERVE

1 kg	sour cherries
	1 large orange
	1 lemon
1 *l*	sugar
250 ml	sultana raisins
250 ml	almonds, blanched

1. Wash and pit cherries; chop.
2. Squeeze juice from orange; add to the cherries; scrape off the white from the orange rind; slice rind into thin slivers and add to cherries.
3. Squeeze the juice from the lemon; add with sugar to the cherries.
4. Simmer until sugar is dissolved; boil rapidly, stirring frequently until thick (30 min).
5. Add raisins and nuts; return to a boil; remove from heat; skim and stir; pour into sterilized glasses; seal with wax (see TO MAKE JELLY). *Yield:* 8 glasses, each containing 180 ml

PRESERVED KUMQUATS

1 kg	ripe kumquats
5 ml	baking soda
1 *l*	cold water
750 ml	sugar
500 ml	water

1. Cut a cross in the stem end of each kumquat; dissolve soda in water; add kumquats and let soak 10 min
2. Drain; cover with fresh water; drain; repeat twice.
3. Cover with water, bring to a boil, simmer until fruit is just tender; drain.

4. Prepare a medium syrup by bringing the sugar and water to a boil; drop kumquats into syrup; cover and leave overnight.
5. Bring fruit to a boil; transfer kumquats to sterilized jars; boil syrup until thick; pour over kumquats to fill the jars to overflowing; seal (see TO MAKE JELLY). *Yield:* 5 glasses, each containing 180 ml

Use Preserved Kumquats on fruit salad plates; as garnish for ham, pork or duck; in fruit drinks; in FRUIT CUP; on a relish tray.

PEACH OR APRICOT PRESERVE

1.5 *l*	12 peaches or 20-30 apricots
	sugar
15 ml	lemon juice

1. Peel, chop and measure the fruit; measure the sugar allowing ¾ the quantity of fruit; combine and let stand 2 h
2. Simmer until transparent (15-20 min); lift the fruit into sterilized jars (see PREPARATION OF GLASS CONTAINERS).
3. Continue to boil the syrup until thick; add lemon juice; pour over fruit to overflowing; seal (see TO MAKE JELLY). *Yield:* 6 glasses, each containing 180 ml

Peach Cantaloupe Conserve—Add the diced pulp of a ripe cantaloupe. The clear, bright colour makes this an attractive sauce for ice cream, custard or cheese cake as well as an accompaniment to cheese and biscuits.

GROUND PEACH CONSERVE

	3 thin-skinned oranges
	1 lemon
	12 peaches
1.5 *l*	sugar

1. Wash oranges and lemon; squeeze juice; cover and refrigerate. Discard the white skin from the lemon; quarter and grind the rinds.
2. Wash peaches but do not peel; pit, quarter and grind; combine the two mixtures; let stand overnight.
3. Add the juice; bring to a boil and simmer until tender (30 min).
4. Add sugar; boil rapidly until jelly forms (20 min); pour into sterilized glasses; seal (see TO MAKE JELLY). *Yield:* 8 glasses, each containing 180 ml

Freezing

The principle involved in freezing fruits, vegetables and meat is to retard the action of enzymes found naturally in food. Many vegetables must be blanched before freezing; otherwise the enzymes continue to ripen the food, causing softening and discolouration. Some fruits must be treated with ascorbic acid to prevent colour change. New methods for food preservation are developed as new varieties of fruits and vegetables are developed. Recipes and information are available from the Information Division, Home Economics Branch of your Provincial Department of Agriculture.

The freezer space of the home refrigerator may be used to save time, energy and money by allowing advance preparation of dishes, enabling you to take advantage of sales, and providing storage for leftovers.

Tips for Freezing
Throughout this book you will find specific directions for preparing various foods for freezing; see index under FREEZING. Here are a few more tips:

Fresh Herbs—Mint, parsley, basil: rinse, dry on a cloth, chop; freeze in small plastic envelopes.

Tomatoes—Blanch, peel and freeze whole for cooking; to save space, purée.

Cherry Tomatoes—Freeze whole; slice when thawed, and use as a garnish.

Peppers—Remove the tongue from red or green sweet peppers; freeze in large pieces or dice for casserole cooking. Peel with a sharp vegetable peeler, if desired.

Leeks—Buy in autumn when they are less expensive; slice the white, rinse thoroughly; package in small containers. Blend the tops with a little water in a blender; freeze in ice cubes for addition to soup.

Mushrooms—For longer storage, blanch in boiling water 3-4 min or sauté whole or sliced. To use in a few days, package whole in a plastic bag.

Fruit—Freeze in season for use in fruit mixtures later.

Black Cherries—Wash, leaving stem on; dry on cloth; package in plastic container shaking gently to fill the container.

Fruit Purée—Freeze to have on hand for cake fillings, sherbets, glaze. fruit cup.

Fruit Juice—Juice to be used for jelly-making may be frozen and processed later.

Fruit Rind—Freeze lemon or orange rinds left after the juice has been squeezed; grind; freeze; break up with a hammer and store in a small container. If the rinds have a thick white membrane, pull off as much as possible and discard before grinding.

Sauces—Freeze special sauces that take time to prepare or that call for ingredients not usually at hand. Sauces thickened with starch or flour do not freeze well, but ROUX may be frozen for quick sauce-making.

Meats—Slice meat loaf, salmon loaf, roast fowl or roast meat; a layer of plastic between each serving will allow individual slices to be removed for sandwiches or one or two servings without thawing a whole package. Freeze chicken livers until enough accumulate to sauté and purée for chicken paté.

Flour Mixtures—Freeze crêpes for appetizers or dessert; cream puffs, shaped but unbaked; flat circles of unbaked pastry (package separately) for bottom crust, top crust or tarts; waffles and french toast to reheat in a toaster or microwave oven; quick-breads and fruit cake, sliced and packaged with foil dividers so that a few slices can be removed; unbaked cookie dough shaped in bars; baked cookies in tightly covered containers. (Heat frozen baked cookies a few minutes before serving.)

Package meal-size amounts and date them before putting them in the freezer. Ontario Ministry of Agriculture and Food.

Baby Foods

Homemade baby foods, made from foods cooked for the family, can be significantly more economical than the commercial product. Salt, sugar and other ingredients of commercial baby foods may be avoided in the homemade product; such additions develop preferences which may lead to obesity in the older child.

A blender is not essential, but it does encourage the preparation of baby food at home.

The necessity of scrupulous cleanliness in preparing baby foods cannot be over-emphasized. The prepared food may be poured into small sterilized jars (see PREPARATION OF GLASS CONTAINERS) and refrigerated for up to two days.

To freeze, pour the prepared food into individual ice-cube containers which have been washed in soapy water, rinsed and dropped into boiling water. Cover the filled cube with waxed paper and chill in the refrigerator. Freeze. Transfer to plastic freezer bags, keeping each variety separate. Close the bag tightly and label with the product and date. To use, place a cube in a small covered jar; stand in a pan of hot water until the food is thawed and lukewarm.

VEGETABLE BABY FOOD

125 ml	cooked vegetables*
25 ml	vegetable stock

Purée the vegetable or chop finely, depending on the age of the child. Combine with the liquid.

MEAT-VEGETABLE BABY FOOD

125 ml	cubed, cooked meat†
125 ml	cooked vegetable*
50-100 ml	boiled milk *or* vegetable stock

Blend the meat and vegetable with enough liquid to obtain the desired consistency.

* Popular vegetables are carrots, green beans, beets, spinach, peas, sweet potatoes and squash. To mix a new vegetable with a well-liked one may encourage acceptance.
† Veal, beef, liver, chicken or fish fillets.

FRUIT PUDDING

125 ml	cooked fruit††
	2 egg yolks
125 ml	milk
250 ml	fruit syrup and water
15 ml	cornstarch

Purée the fruit and egg yolks; add the other ingredients, the proportion of syrup to water depending on the sugar content. (If fruit is cooked without sugar all juice may be used; if canned fruit with 45% sugar syrup is used, at least ¾ of the liquid should be water.) Stir over low heat until the mixture bubbles and thickens. Cool. *Yield:* 375 ml

†† Pears, peaches apricots, prunes, apples.

Index